Contributions of Behavior Analysis to Reading and Writing Comprehension

Alessandra Rocha de Albuquerque
Raquel Maria de Melo
Editors

Contributions of Behavior Analysis to Reading and Writing Comprehension

Springer

CULTURA ACADÊMICA Editora

OFICINA UNIVERSITÁRIA

Editors
Alessandra Rocha de Albuquerque
Universidade Católica de Brasília
Brasília, Brazil

Raquel Maria de Melo
Universidade de Brasília
Brasília, Brazil

ISBN 978-3-031-40867-0 ISBN 978-3-031-40868-7 (eBook)
https://doi.org/10.1007/978-3-031-40868-7

Jointly published with Oficina Universitária/Cultura Acadêmica, Brazil

The translation was done with the help of an artificial intelligence machine translation tool. A subsequent human revision was done primarily in terms of content.

Translation from the Portuguese language edition: "Contribuições da análise do comportamento para a compreensão da leitura e escrita " by Alessandra Rocha de Albuquerque and Raquel Maria de Melo, © Faculdade de Filosofia e Ciências, Unesp, Marília 2021. Published by Oficina Universitária/Cultura Acadêmica. All Rights Reserved.

This Springer imprint is published by the registered company Springer Nature Switzerland AG
The registered company address is: Gewerbestrasse 11, 6330 Cham, Switzerland

Paper in this product is recyclable.

Preface

Behavior analysis, since its origin, is dedicated to the study of learning processes. This approach has a strong tradition in Brazil, which is considered a hub for training behavior analysts and for the production of knowledge in its philosophical, scientific, and applied aspects. Part of this production is related to reading and writing repertoires, with different populations and teaching programs, and presents robust data regarding the teaching and learning processes of these repertoires.

This book, originally published in Portuguese (Albuquerque & Melo, 2021[1]; Melo & Albuquerque, 2021[2]), represents an effort to synthesize part of that production that makes up a research line spanning more than three decades and with dozens of researchers involved. It reflects our desire for accessible material to be used with our undergraduate and graduate students in psychology, but that can also be used by students and professionals from other areas. The English version of the book gives visibility and access to a wider audience to an important line of research developed in Brazil, originally based on the equivalence paradigm. We hope that this work will provide subsidies for further research and point to ways of making evidence-based decisions in the context of teaching reading and writing.

The book brings together 31 collaborators among researchers and graduate students, linked to 11 institutions of higher education and research: Catholic University of Brasília (UCB); Federal University of ABC (UFABC); Federal University of Pará (UFPA); Federal University of Recôncavo Baiano (UFRB); Federal University of São Carlos (UFSCar); Paulista University (UNIP); São Paulo State University Júlio Mesquita Filho (UNESP), Bauru and Marília campuses; State University of Londrina (UEL); University of Brasília (UnB); and University of São Paulo (USP).

[1] Albuquerque, A. R. & Melo, R. M. (2021). Contribuições da análise do comportamento para a compreensão da leitura e escrita: Aspectos históricos, conceituais e procedimentos de ensino (volume 1). Marília/São Paulo, Oficina Universitária/Cultura Acadêmica.

[2] Melo, R. M. & Albuquerque, A. R. (2021). Contribuições da análise do comportamento para a compreensão da leitura e escrita: investigações empíricas e diálogos com outras áreas de conhecimento (volume 2). Marília/São Paulo, Oficina Universitária/Cultura Acadêmica.

Most of the collaborators are also members of the National Institute of Science and Technology on Behavior, Cognition, and Learning (INCT-ECCE).[3]

In Part I, the chapters focus on conceptual and historical aspects of the area. Chapter 1 is the reprint of a theoretical article by Júlio César de Rose (de Rose, 2005) which systematizes the understanding of reading and writing repertoires as a network of relations between stimuli and between stimuli and responses, based on the concept of stimulus equivalence. In Chap. 2, Alessandra Rocha de Albuquerque, Raquel Maria de Melo, and Izabela Casseb Saveedra-Dias map out research on the theme (in the form of masters' theses, doctoral dissertations, and articles) by Brazilian behavior analysts, contributing to an understanding of the state of the art in the area, explaining the profusion of research already conducted as well as gaps that point to paths for future research. In Chap. 3, Verônica Bender Haydu and Silvia Regina de Souza describe the scientific production of laboratories at the State University of Londrina, focused on the development of technologies for teaching reading and writing.

In Part II, the focus is on the description of teaching modules that make up the *Learning to Read and Write in Small Steps* (ALEPP) teaching program, which has been widely used in research in the area. This teaching program consists of three main modules (Modules 1, 2, and 3), which are presented in Chaps. 4 and 5. In Chap. 4, Raquel Melo Golfeto and Lidia Maria Marson Postalli detail the planning for teaching Portuguese words with orthographic irregularities or difficulties (e.g., digraphs, *x* with a z sound) in Module 2 of ALEPP from its first version (on paper sheets organized in folder catalogs) to the current computerized and *online* version. In Chap. 5, Elenice Seixas Hanna, João Vianney Barrozo Costa Severo, Camila Domeniconi, Júlio César de Rose, and Deisy das Graças de Souza describe the last developed and computerized teaching module of ALEPP, Module 3, which aims at teaching reading fluency and comprehension in children's books. The last two chapters of this section present two new teaching modules in development. In Chap. 6, Ana Claudia Moreira Almeida-Verdu, Anderson Jonas das Neves, Lidia Maria Marson Postalli, and Deisy das Graças de Souza present the need for the development of a sentence teaching module as well as features that should be considered when structuring it. Finally, in Chap. 7, Raquel Maria de Melo, Alessandra Rocha de Albuquerque, Lidia Maria Marson Postalli, and Deisy das Graças de Souza discuss the behavior analytical understanding of prerequisites for reading and writing. The chapter also presents the structure of a prerequisite teaching module (Preparatory Module) that is being tested and will integrate the ALEPP curriculum. The description of ALEPP's Module 1 (for teaching regular words), published in the original version of the book (in Portuguese), has been omitted from this volume since it is already available in English (de Souza et al., 2009[4]).

[3] https://inctecce.com.br/en/

[4] de Souza, D. G., de Rose, J. C., Faleiros, T. C., Bortoloti, R., Hanna, E. S., & McIlvane, W. J. (2009). Teaching generative reading via recombination of minimal textual units: A legacy of Verbal Behavior to children in Brazil. *The International Journal of Psychology and Psychological Therapy, 9*(1), 19–44.

Part III presents empirical research with different populations (e.g., children with intellectual and hearing disabilities). In Chap. 8, Lidia Maria Marson Postalli, Maria Clara de Freitas, and Priscila Benitez describe studies using ALEPP with people with intellectual disabilities. The authors also discuss important adaptations made to the teaching procedure in order to make it more compatible with the specific needs of this public. Chapter 9, authored by Ana Claudia Moreira Almeida-Verdu, Fernando Del Mando Lucchesi, and Leandra Tabanez Nascimento Silva, discusses research on reading, based on the equivalence paradigm, carried out with hearing-impaired individuals who have received a cochlear implant. In Chap. 10, Luana Zeolla Inhauser, Maria Martha Costa Hübner, and Valeria Mendes Tavitian focus on generalized, or recombinative, reading and present research with adults which investigate basic processes that favor the emergence of this repertoire. Chapter 11, by Alessandra Rocha de Albuquerque and Raquel Maria de Melo, reviews studies with illiterate adults and the experience of an Adult Reading Unit that operated in Brasília. In Chap. 12, Camila Domeniconi, Solange Cordeiro Calcagno, Olívia Misae Kato, Priscila Benitez, and Elenice Seixas Hanna present an important intervention, with the use of different ALEPP modules, carried out with public school students who achieved low scores on *Prova Brasil* in three regions of the country with positive results. The first replications using ALEPP with different populations (de Rose et al., 1996[5]; Melchiori et al., 2000[6]), published in the Portuguese version of this book, were also omitted from this volume, as they are already available in English in two seminal articles published on the *Journal of Applied Behavior Analysis* – JABA.

Part IV presents contributions from other areas of knowledge – speech therapy, linguistics, and education – to the understanding of reading and writing and possible dialogs between them and behavior analysis. In Chap. 13, Célia Maria Giacheti, Nathani Cristina da Silva, and Tâmara de Andrade Lindau addressed the specific disorders of reading and writing, the differential diagnosis of these disorders, and the importance of multidisciplinary action in these cases. In Chap. 14, Djenane Brasil da Conceição describes the conceptions of reading and teaching methods proposed by Bloomfield and Skinner and performs a comparative synthesis between both. In the last chapter, Chap. 15, Denise Bachega and João dos Santos Carmo present convergences of behavior analysis with Paulo Freire's proposal.

Brasília, Brazil

Alessandra Rocha de Albuquerque
Raquel Maria de Melo

[5] de Rose, J. C., de Souza, D. G., & Hanna, E. S. (1996). Teaching reading and spelling: Exclusion and stimulus equivalence. *Journal of Applied Behavior Analysis, 29*, 451–469.

[6] Melchiori, L. E., de Souza, D. G., & de Rose, J. C. (2000). Reading, equivalence, and recombination of units: A replication with students with different learning histories. *Journal of Applied Behavior Analysis 33*(1), 97–100.

Contents

Part I
Conceptual and Historical Aspects

Chapter 1
Behavioral Analysis of Learning to Read and Write

Julio Cesar de Rose

1.1 Introduction

I thank the organizers of this book for the opportunity to re-present the article of my authorship, published in 2005, on behavioral analysis of reading and writing. Some information about the production of this text may help the reader to contextualize this material and assess its possible usefulness and limitations, so long after it was published.

In the penultimate decade of the last century, I participated in the development, with my colleague Deisy de Souza, of a program to teach rudimentary reading and spelling skills to primary school students who were failing to learn this repertoire. I had just returned from a postdoctoral fellowship at a research center on what at that time was still called *mental retardation*. During the 2 years I spent there I was impressed with the sophistication of teaching procedures based on behavior analysis that were capable of establishing complex repertoires in individuals with intellectual disabilities. I was also impressed by the number of students in our elementary school who, even without intellectual disability, could not learn to read. These reflections led Deisy and I (and, later, also other contributors to this book) to try to apply knowledge from Behavior Analysis to promote literacy among underperforming students. Our efforts led to the construction of the Learning to Read and Write in Small Steps® (*Aprendendo a Ler e Escrever em Pequenos Passos* [ALEPP])

Text originally published in Revista Brasileira de Análise do Comportamento – REBAC (Brazilian Journal of Behavior Analysis – REBAC). Published with the permission of REBAC. de Rose, J. C. (2005). Análise comportamental da aprendizagem de leitura e escrita. *Revista Brasileira de Análise do Comportamento*, *1* (1), 29–50.

J. C. de Rose (✉)
Universidade Federal de São Carlos, São Carlos, SP, Brazil

A. R. de Albuquerque, R. M. de Melo (eds.), *Contributions of Behavior Analysis to Reading and Writing Comprehension*, https://doi.org/10.1007/978-3-031-40868-7_1

program, which has been successful in this proposal, as can be seen in some chapters of this book.

At the end of the 1980s or beginning of the 1990s (my memory betrays me on this point as on so many others), the late Professor Carolina Bori, who was aware of my recent work in the field of literacy, asked me to collaborate in a book that would bring together contributions from various theoretical perspectives in the field of literacy. The book would include chapters on linguistics, sociolinguistics, the Piagetian perspective, and, among other perspectives that I do not remember now, Behavior Analysis. I managed to complete and deliver my chapter on time and waited for the publication of the book, which never took place, I believe due to funding difficulties.

My chapter remained in a drawer for some years, and only came to be published in the following millennium, in 2005, not as a book chapter, but as an article, in the first issue of the Brazilian Journal of Behavior Analysis (*Revista Brasileira de Análise do Comportamento* [REBAC]). Again, despite my unreliable memory, I remember that my friend Deisy de Souza had a role in the chapter's resurrection (in the form of an article), just as she had an important role in the creation of REBAC, she who participated in the creation of so many important things for Brazilian Behavior Analysis and psychology.

When I wrote the chapter, in the 1990s, I attempted an in-depth study of the entire contribution of Behavior Analysis to the field of literacy. The article, which came to be published about 10 years later, contained little revision and updating. Although published in 2005, the article does not cite any references from the new millennium and cites only three references from the 1990s. The remaining references are older.

Therefore, the text systematizes the contribution of behavior analysis to literacy until around 1990. Three decades of intense research have passed, and during this period, there has been valuable research not only from Behavior Analysis, but also from linguistics and mainstream psychology, among other disciplines. This is a caveat that needs to be given to the reader of this chapter. Behavior Analysis is a science and, as such, it is in constant progress, making new discoveries, incorporating new knowledge, and revising knowledge taken as established. Being a science, it must also consider the contributions of other disciplines, all the *facts* that are known about the subject matter, which, as Skinner observed, in a scientific endeavor should override *desires*.

Since it has been some time since I have been active in research involving reading/writing, which continues to be so well conducted by other colleagues at the National Institute of Science and Technology on Behavior, Cognition and Teaching (*Instituto Nacional de Ciência e Tecnologia sobre Comportamento, Cognição e Ensino* [INCT-ECCE]), I am not up to date with recent advances in this area. My impression is that the material presented in this text (which was originally an unpublished chapter, then became an article, and now, for historical reasons, becomes a chapter published in this book) remains valid and has not been belied by later advances. However, the material would benefit, in my view, from updating, which I am no longer able to do, after I stopped working in the field. I have only glimpses of some content that would need to be added to update the material. I believe that if I were to write the chapter today, I would include some material on dyslexia (in the past millennium we did not take the issue of dyslexia much into account, but research on the subject has evolved a lot) and on phonological awareness (Chap. 8 of the book, which deals with prerequisites, addresses the phenomenon of phonological awareness), which is not directly mentioned in the chapter. I also think it would be interesting to expand the approach to reading/writing as a network of relations, also addressing other relations besides equivalence.

I leave this task, however, to the researchers who remain active in the field. Behavior Analysis is very important for understanding the behaviors involved in reading and writing and for promoting its teaching, but it is increasingly important that behavior analysts open themselves to the contribution of other disciplines, in addition to considering the most recent research in Behavior Analysis itself.

1.2 Reinforcement Contingencies

The behavioral perspective addressed in this article, known as behavior analysis, is based on a rejection of stimulus-response psychology, also known as S-R. In the S-R conception of traditional behaviorism, behavior is defined in terms of the form or topography of action, i.e., movements of the individual, considered as reaction (response) to environmental stimuli.

In Behavior Analysis, the term behavior does not refer to the topography of action, but to the relations between the individual's activity and environment. From these relations, Behavior Analysis distinguishes two categories of behavior.

Respondent behavior encompasses reflex reactions to specific stimuli. In operant behavior, on the other hand, the consequences of the response are of fundamental importance. The response is seen not as a reaction to a stimulus, but as a unit of behavior that operates on the environment, modifying it. These consequences of the response, in turn, modify subsequent behavior, altering the probability that similar responses will occur again. In approaching, from a Behavior Analysis perspective, the behaviors of reading and writing, it is important to consider what these behaviors have in common with any other forms of behavior, and what they have peculiar. We can take as a starting point Skinner's attempt to perform a systematic analysis of human behavior, and especially of language, based on the concepts of operant and respondent behavior (Skinner, 1953, 1957). Language was treated there as a form of operant behavior, which Skinner calls verbal behavior. Reading and writing are considered as specific types of verbal behavior, which maintain characteristic relations with the environment. To understand reading and writing we need, therefore, to address some general properties of operant behavior.

Operant behavior is shaped and differentiated through the individual's history of interactions with the environment. In the course of this history, the organism changes, partly due to maturation and other biological processes, but also largely due to relations with the environment. The fabric of these relationships in an individual's history, combined with the genetic endowment and other organic factors, determines present behavior. Behavior is thus multidetermined (cf. Skinner, 1953, 1957): each conduct is influenced by the interaction between many organic and environmental determinants.

An analysis of the relationship between behavior and environment should consider three aspects: (1) the environment preceding the behavior (discriminative stimuli), (2) the response itself, and (3) the consequences of the response. Some consequences make the repetition of similar responses more likely. These are called reinforcing consequences, or simply reinforcers. Discriminative stimuli, on the other hand, precede the response but, contrary to what the S-R formula stipulates, do not elicit its occurrence. Their role is to establish the occasion in which a response will have certain effects or consequences.

The relations between discriminative stimuli, responses and consequences are called reinforcement contingencies (Skinner, 1969). Although the three terms of the contingency relation are interrelated, we can, for didactic purposes, analyze any unit of operant behavior based on two types of relations: the relations between response and reinforcement, and between discriminative stimulus and response.

We can say that the relations between response and reinforcement are responsible for the probability of occurrence of the response, that is, the individual's inclination to engage in some type of activity. The relation between response and reinforcement is, therefore, related to what, in everyday language, we describe as motivation, interest or liking.

The relationship between response and discriminative stimulus is, as Sidman (1986a) notes, the basis of what the individual knows about his environment. All academic repertoires are based on refined relations between discriminative stimuli and responses, whether verbal or non-verbal. This relationship between discriminative stimulus and response is called stimulus control, or discrimination. Abandoning the jargon of Behavioral Analysis, we can consider discriminative stimuli to be, roughly speaking, the cues on which the individual relies in the performance of a given activity (including verbal activities).

1.3 Behavior Analysis and the Teaching of Reading and Writing

It is more convenient to analyze reading and writing not as unitary behaviors, but as repertoires involving a set of distinct behaviors. The goal of a behavioral analysis is the identification of the components of these repertoires, and a description of their characteristic relationships.

Relationships can often be learned without the need for formal teaching and, as we will see below, it is possible in many cases to plan instruction so that new relationships emerge without the need for direct teaching. Even considering informal learning and emergent learning as possible and desirable outcomes, the educational applications of Behavior Analysis are essentially based on explicit instruction of behaviors deemed necessary, based on an analysis of the relations that comprise the repertoire to be taught.

Here, behavior analysis differs from other approaches that emphasize maturation or cognitive development as preconditions for learning. Behavior analysts admit that there may be prerequisites necessary for much learning, and one of the important fields for research is precisely the identification of prerequisites for learning specific repertoires. In educational practice, however, prerequisites are often assumed without adequate scientific basis, and, even worse, there is a tendency to consider that the acquisition of these prerequisites depends solely on maturation. The classic study by Schneider (1974), confirmed by numerous subsequent studies, revealed the distortion resulting from this conception. Children who appear to lack the prerequisites for certain learning skills are considered immature and, for this reason, do not receive any instruction and are relegated to the back of the class or to the rows of the underperformers. Some may eventually "mature" by the following year (i.e., learn the relevant behaviors in their out-of-school experience), but many end up permanently segregated in special schools or institutions for disabled individuals.

The Behavior Analysis perspective leads to the consideration that, in principle, any individual is capable of learning, even those with limitations or disabilities. No diagnosis or label adequately describes a person's abilities or difficulties. Individuals of normal intelligence, and even those considered geniuses, may have serious deficiencies in specific areas, and those considered retarded may have great potential in some areas. It is the teacher's responsibility, based on analysis of the repertoires to be taught, to identify the students' abilities and the behaviors they do not master, and to teach these behaviors, constantly evaluating the results of their teaching procedures. Any failures should be attributed to inadequate procedures and not to intrinsic characteristics of the student or their environment.

It is possible that the difficulties presented by a particular student are, in fact, due to a lack of important prerequisites. In this case, instead of waiting for the student to mature, or to reach the appropriate stage of cognitive development, it is important to identify the prerequisites and teach them directly. "Maturation" involves the acquisition of the behaviors that are precursors to learning a new repertoire. This acquisition is, as we have seen, multidetermined: internal aspects may play an important role, but teaching procedures may also play a key role. Research in behavior analysis has repeatedly shown that the limits set by organic conditions can be extended through appropriate instructional procedures.

In the case of reading and writing it is also necessary to consider that rigorous studies have questioned the status of many of the supposed prerequisites. Gibson and Levin (1975), reviewing studies on this issue, show that several skills traditionally considered prerequisites are unrelated to successful learning. Other skills may, if acquired previously, facilitate learning to read and write, but the relationship is not always linear and unidirectional. For example, the ability to distinguish the constituent sounds of words may facilitate literacy; however, if the child has not had the opportunity to develop this skill in his or her preschool experience, he or she may acquire it concomitantly with the teaching of reading and. Learning to read and write may also facilitate learning to discriminate the constituent sounds of words.

For these reasons we will treat the components of reading and writing repertoires as independent relations to each other. However, as we shall see later, there are common elements between the various components such that they can become integrated and form a network of relationships.

1.4 Behavior Analysis and the Teaching of Reading and Writing

The components of reading and writing repertoires basically comprise stimulus control relations. Consider, for example, the reading of a text aloud. The reader emits a sequence of verbal responses that correspond to a text. To learn this, a child does not need to learn new responses: she already speaks her mother tongue fluently. Reading requires new control relations, between these verbal responses and a special category of discriminative stimulus that we call text. Skinner introduced the term textual behavior to designate the control relationship of text over verbal responses.

Textual behavior presumably continues to occur at a sub-vocal level in silent reading. Responses continue to be emitted on such a small scale that they no longer affect an external listener, although they continue to have effects on the reader himself.

Skinner notes that textual behavior is not the same thing as reading. It is possible to precisely emit the sequence of verbal responses corresponding to a text without understanding this text. The person doing this is emitting textual behavior, but is not reading, since reading also involves understanding the text. However, the stimulus-control relationship between text and verbal responses is a necessary, though not sufficient, condition for comprehension.

The discriminative stimuli for textual behavior are visual or tactile (Braille) and the responses are verbal (usually vocal or sub-vocal, but can also be gestural, as when a deaf person reads a text by responding in sign language). Thus, discriminative stimuli and responses (actually, the stimuli produced by the response), have important differences in their physical constitution; they involve different dimensional systems (cf. Skinner, 1957). There is, in addition, a correspondence between the discriminative stimulus and the product of the response. This correspondence involves a point-to-point relationship between stimulus units and response units. These units depend on the nature of the text: in ideographic writing, for example, each ideogram corresponds to a spoken word, whereas in alphabetic writing, there is a correspondence between letters (or combinations of letters) and the sounds (phonemes) that make up the words.

To understand how textual stimuli gain control over vocal behavior it is necessary to address some generic questions regarding stimulus control relations.

Stimulus control and cognition – Stimulus control relations cannot be determined from stimulus and response observation alone. The relationship is necessarily inferred from patterns of responses in the face of variations in stimulus aspects.

This can be illustrated from an experiment by Stoddard (1968). The subjects were 37 children aged 4–12 years old. The experimenter presented to the children an arrangement of eight lines inclined at 45 degrees, one of them inclined to the right and the others to the left. The choice of the different line, defined as correct, was reinforced. The children learned the task without the need for verbal instructions. Although they all responded similarly in the presence of the same stimuli, two simple tests showed that the relations learned could be quite different. In the first test, the slope of the lines was reversed: one was slanted to the left, and the others slanted to the right. In this test, 25 children continued to choose the different line, indicating that their choices were being made based on uniqueness (*oddity*). The remaining 12 children chose one of the lines inclined to the right, indicating that their previous choices were not based on uniqueness, but on the direction of the line.

This interpretation was confirmed in the second test, in which the experimenter removed the relational cue: only two lines were presented, one inclined to the right and the other inclined to the left. Children who, in the previous test, chose based on the direction of the line, continued to choose the line inclined to the right. Those who chose based on the singularity, on the other hand, had difficulties in this test and presented numerous incorrect answers.

These results show that the similarity in performance was only apparent. We could say that the discriminative stimulus for 25 children was the uniqueness of the line, and for the others the discriminative stimulus was the specific orientation of the line. Even this statement, however, is not accurate. Further testing might reveal that children who responded based on uniqueness, for example, might be responding under control of different aspects of the relationship between the lines.

No stimulus is, therefore, a unitary entity. Stoddard's experiment (1968) shows that even people who respond similarly in the presence of identical stimuli can have their responses controlled by different aspects of these stimuli.[1]

An analysis of stimulus control therefore involves determining the aspects or components of the stimuli that exert control over responding (both verbal and non-verbal). Aspects of stimuli that do not exert control over any of a person's responses are as it were non-existent for that person; in other words, for some aspect of the stimulus to be "known," the person must learn to respond in some way to that aspect.

One of the contributions of Behavioral Analysis has been to show how stimulus control is modified through the history of reinforcing contingencies. We could consider, metaphorically, that contingencies endow people with special "glasses" that lead them to see certain aspects of stimuli more saliently, and to ignore other aspects. In Stoddard's (1968) experiment, for example, the 25 children who responded under control of stimulus uniqueness were generally the oldest. This is not only due to the

[1]This relationship of control by an aspect or component of a complex stimulus is also called attention.

age of the child, but to the greater experience an older child has with contingencies involving relational aspects of the environment. Children who had probably been more exposed to contingencies involving relational characteristics of stimuli were able to make a more complex discrimination based on a relational aspect: the uniqueness of a figure compared to others. These same children, however, failed to pay attention to the orientation of the isolated lines, and, as noted by Stoddard, the verbalizations of some of them indicated that, in the absence of a uniqueness clue, lines pointing in opposite directions appeared identical to them.

Therefore, as noted by Skinner (1953, 1969), our knowledge of the world and of ourselves is a product of the contingencies established by the verbal community. Cultures in general, and social groups in particular, can establish contingencies that lead their members to make contact with different aspects of the stimuli of their external and internal environment.

The child's knowledge of writing – Probably one of the reasons why the educational situation is problematic is the inevitable difference in the past history of teachers and learners. The teacher has already been subjected to a previous history that has established control by the dimensions of the stimuli that the verbal community considers relevant. Students, whose past history is very different, will almost inevitably view stimuli differently. The aspects of the stimuli to which the teacher responds may not even exist for the students.

Thus, a printed page is certainly not the same object for a child beginning to learn how to read and for their teacher. The child has not yet been equipped with the "glasses" established by the reinforcement contingencies that lead to notice, on the printed page, those aspects of textual stimuli that culture has established as relevant.

This is supported by studies showing that children who have not yet learned to read may ignore relevant aspects of textual stimuli and respond preferentially to other aspects. It is possible that this depends in part on maturational factors, but there is a large body of data also suggesting an important role for reinforcement contingencies in determining these aspects of the stimuli to which children respond.

The classic study by Gibson et al. (1962), shows that younger children do not distinguish the spatial orientation of figures. For example, the letters "u" and "n", and the letters "p", "q", "b" and "d", have basically the same shape in different spatial orientations. Gibson and colleagues suggest that this difficulty of children is a result of learning. The child's entire prior history leads them to disregard this dimension because it is irrelevant to object discrimination. For example, the 4-year-old child who is asked to pick up a particular object is likely to pick it up regardless of its spatial orientation. The child's out-of-school environment includes contingencies in which spatial orientation is an irrelevant aspect of the stimuli, teaching the child that an object remains the same whatever its spatial orientation. These contingencies equip the child with "glasses" that emphasize the object's shape and are insensitive to its spatial orientation.

After a certain age, children start learning to discriminate letters. This introduces new contingencies, conflicting with the previous ones: spatial orientation becomes a relevant aspect for the discrimination of these new objects, and eventually this aspect acquires control over the child's response. The study by Gibson et al. shows that confusion between figures in different spatial orientations gradually decreases with child age, but the authors do not attribute the result to age, but to new discriminative learning. These new contingencies modify the "glasses", making them now sensitive to spatial orientation.

Studies conducted from a psychogenetic approach have also brought important clarifications about the child's knowledge about writing. For example, Ferreiro and Teberosky (1986) investigated the characteristics that an object must have for children to consider it as writing. Each child received cards with various texts and was asked to indicate those that were "good for reading" and those that were "not good for reading". The authors observed two primary criteria for children to consider something "good for reading": a minimum number of characters (between 3 and 4) and a variety of characters. In other words, the response to identify something as writing seems to be under control of at least two aspects of the stimuli: the number and variety of characters.

A more controversial point, however, is the explanation for the origin and generality of these notions. Ferreiro and Teberosky (1986) consider these notions as spontaneous constructions of the child, claiming that they could not be socially transmitted, since adults read words with one or two characters. It is likely, in fact, that these notions are not deliberately taught by adults, but this does not mean that they are spontaneous. The child's informal contact with graphic material existing in its environment establishes contingencies for discriminative learning.

This possibility is consistent with results of Lavine (1977), who investigated aspects such as quantity and variety of characters, linearity of their arrangement, and the type of characters employed. The results also indicate that quantity and variety of characters are aspects that influence children's response of classifying a graphic stimulus as "writing". Gibson and Levin (1975) interpret these results as a case of "pure perceptual learning" arising from children's contact with graphic material. This probably occurs because variety and minimal character number are features present in the samples of written material that children casually encounter in their daily lives. The few language words that are spelled with only one or two characters rarely occur in isolation in these samples: the child will probably never see an older person reading a text containing only one letter. If these notions are indeed learned through the child's contact with written material, they should not occur, or should be formed more slowly, in environments where writing is sparsely present. Gibson and Levin (1975) cite, in support of this hypothesis, results obtained by Lavine (1977) in a rural village in Mexico: children in this village showed much less knowledge about writing, cultural environment being at least as significant a variable as age.

Researchers with a psychogenetic orientation have shown that children's notions about writing gradually change, in what seems to constitute a predetermined sequence of phases (cf. Ferreiro & Teberosky, 1986). The apparent generality of this sequence could support the conclusion that these phases basically reflect an internal process of cognitive development. It should be noted, however, that the sequence of phases is usually inferred from a cross-sectional analysis of large samples of children. Longitudinal studies following the development of individual children tend to show many deviations or even idiosyncratic sequences, especially when children from different social and cultural backgrounds are considered. This suggests that the contingencies established by the child's social environment play an important role in the evolution of his or her notions about writing.

Stimulus control displacement in learning to read – Whatever the relative weight of internal factors (maturation and development) and external factors (social contingencies), it is important to know children's, and illiterate people's in general, notion of writing. The aspects of the textual stimulus that control a reader's responses may not even exist for an illiterate person, and the illiterate person's response may be controlled by aspects that a reader disregards.

This means that learning to read is not merely the establishment of stimulus control relations, but the modification of existing relations. The appropriate technical term in Behavior Analysis would be *stimulus control shift*.

For highly motivated students, this shift can occur even without any formal instruction, or with little directive instruction. Goldiamond and Dyrud (1966) cite an illustrative example of a deaf child who learned to read at age 4 and without any formal instruction. The father used to read daily to the child (through sign language) and had endeavored to teach the child a wide repertoire of verbal production and comprehension (through signs). These conditions, coupled with the child's interest in stories (an extremely powerful reinforcer, as we shall see later), were sufficient for learning. Similarly, children coming from environments where reading is valued and frequent can learn most of the skills necessary to read even before entering school, as a cumulative result of their own experiences of contact with textual stimuli and information transmitted by their elders. Unfortunately, most children do not have access to these experiences in their out-of-school environment and need more systematic instruction.

For this reason, the school must provide contingencies that equip children with sensitive "glasses" to the relevant aspects of textual stimuli. Research in behavior analysis has already enabled us to identify the conditions necessary for an aspect or dimension of stimulus to acquire control over response. For this, it is necessary that the person has experience discriminating between stimuli that differ in this dimension, with immediate *feedback* for correct responses.

In many cases, the opportunity to respond to stimuli varying in the critical dimensions, along with immediate *feedback*, is sufficient for learning. A study by Tawney (1972) is a good example, as it dealt with critical dimensions for discriminating textual stimuli. Tawney taught preschool children to distinguish between arbitrary letter-like figures that differed on dimensions critical for letter discrimination. Children subjected to this procedure improved in their discrimination of real letters. On the other hand, subjects who learned to distinguish between figures that differed in irrelevant dimensions (such as size, line thickness, etc.), showed no significant progress in letter discrimination.

These considerations suggest that an important point in promoting reading learning is to identify the relevant aspects of textual stimuli, especially those that are less likely to exert control over the response of children in the early literacy phase. We can then plan situations that teach discriminations based on these aspects of the stimuli.

These discriminations need not directly involve textual stimuli, as indicated by Tawney's (1972) results. What is important is that the child has opportunities to make discriminations based on critical aspects of textual stimuli. These opportunities for discrimination do not occur only in formal teaching situations. Many games and play provide the child with opportunities to make distinctions based on graphic or sound aspects that are critical for the acquisition of textual behavior and may constitute valuable pedagogical resources.

1.5 Minimum Units of Textual Stimulus Control

When a Brazilian college student first encounters the unfamiliar word "zeitgeist" in a Portuguese text, they may pronounce, probably clumsily, something like "zei…ti…jei…jeist…zeitijeist". This printed word does not function as a discriminative stimulus; however, the letters or sets of letters in the word constitute discriminative stimuli that exert control over vocal responses (overt or covert), each consisting of a phoneme or groups of phonemes. After having encountered this word in various texts and having heard the teacher explain its meaning, the student may read the whole word, pronouncing without hesitation something like "zait-gaist". This suggests that now the whole word functions as a response unit, under global control of the written word.

The units of operant behavior are dynamic and can change – differentiate themselves – as a result of interactions between behavior and environment. Molecular (smaller) units can chain together, integrating into molar (global) units; molar units can, in turn, be fractionated into more molecular units. Textual behavior, like any operant behavior, also undergoes modifications of this kind. Many people who learn to read under the control of molecular units such as syllables or graphemes, learn to string them together by integrating them into molar units such as words or groups of words. On the other hand, people who learn to read under control of molar units, such as whole words, eventually learn to fraction them into molecular units, whose recombination allows the reading of new words. Fluent reading involves a combination of molar units (words or groups of words) and molecular units (syllables or graphemes/phonemes).

As reading behavior develops, other aspects of the text come to control dimensions of textual behavior: punctuation marks come to control pauses and variations in intonation. Intonation can also be controlled by signals such as italics, quotation marks, etc. In addition, as one learns to be a listener to one's own textual behavior, reading also comes partially under the control of antecedent textual responses. These intraverbal relations (cf. Skinner, 1957) allow the reader to "anticipate" the sequence of a text using only part of the textual cues.

Thus, any unit used as a starting point for teaching reading will present some advantages and some difficulties when compared to others. The syllable, for example, seems to be a "natural" unit in the Portuguese language. If the student learns a small set of units (the syllabic "families") they may become able to read a large set of words. However, as will be discussed below, children seem to hear words as a whole, having difficulty distinguishing their component sounds. In addition, the student needs to learn to string these units together when they appear in words and sentences.

A more molar unit, such as the word, allows one to start from units that are already part of the child's verbal repertoire, that is, words that have meaning for him/her. However, if the child does not acquire control over molecular units, he/she will only be able to read the set of words that has been directly taught. To read new words the child will need to learn molecular units, which can be recombined into a wide variety of words.

The alphabetic system enables the development of a repertoire of minimal units (Skinner, 1957) that can be recombined when reading new words. These minimal units can be taught directly, and then chained together to form more molar units. Alternatively, the more molar units can be taught, and the student can abstract the minimal units as his experience with molar units broadens. These two approaches can, of course, be combined.

The formation and sequencing of this repertoire of minimal units requires the learner to learn to respond under control of specific characters and their relative arrangement. Many children who can discriminate single letters may have difficulty discriminating their relative arrangement, confusing for example sequences such as 'os' and 'so'. Gibson and Levin (1975) also attribute this difficulty to the fact that relative position is not a critical aspect of the discriminations that children learn in their preschool experience.

Furthermore, to read a text, the student must learn to chain the units in a defined spatial sequence. In our writing this sequence is from left to right and from top to bottom.[2] This means that gaze responses should also be under control of the spatial aspects of the text. In texts in book or notebook form, each page turn should be a discriminative stimulus for a gaze movement response to the upper left corner of the text. Gaze responses should follow left to right to the end of the line; this should act as a discriminative stimulus to move gaze to the left edge of the next line. The reader of this chapter may find such a detailed description of this chain of responses trivial, but it is by no means "natural," and needs to be learned by the child. Many children may have opportunities to learn and practice this kind of sequence at home, even before they enter school, through toys, books with silent stories, demonstration and instruction by adults or older children, etc. However, some children, especially those from environments where writing is not abundant, may enter school without having learned this sequence. They may have serious difficulties if the teacher does not schedule activities that allow them to learn and practice these behaviors.

The chaining of molar units also requires the child to learn to distinguish the component sounds of words. This is one of the major obstacles to learning the repertoire of minimal units required for reading. For the child the semantic aspects are

[2] There are exceptional cases of texts that do not follow this spatial arrangement. Violation of the conventional order usually has an artistic or decorative function.

more salient than the phonological aspects (e.g., Gibson & Levin, 1975; Rozin, 1978). This means that the component sounds of words are aspects of vocal stimuli that do not control the child's response. As we noted earlier, this means that these aspects virtually do not exist for the child. The English-speaking child, for example hears the word "cat" as a whole; the sounds /k/, /e/ and /t/ do not exist for them. So, the child has difficulty fractionating the molar unit into the three component sounds and also to string these sounds together to form the word. Similarly, it is likely that the spoken word "*gato*" functions as a molar unit for the Portuguese-speaking child. The fractionation of this molar unit into the syllables "ga" and "to", and the combination of these syllables to form the word may, due to the phonological characteristics of the Portuguese language, be more "natural" than the fractionation and recombination of sounds in English. Even so, the child must acquire new behavioral units, involving control by the phonological aspects of vocal stimuli.

We have previously noted that the necessary condition for a stimulus dimension to acquire control over responding is discriminative learning involving variations in this dimension. Acquisition of control for dimensions such as relative position or component sounds requires that children be exposed to activities involving discrimination of position or sounds with response feedback. In addition to more formal activities, there are many games that involve this type of discrimination and can be excellent teaching opportunities. These experiences may occur in many children's preschool or family history, so that by the time they enter school, these dimensions already exert some degree of control over their response and they can more easily acquire the repertoire of minimal units of textual behavior. Children who have not had this experience are not necessarily 'immature', 'retarded', 'dyslexic', etc.; most of them can readily acquire the necessary repertoire provided the relevant learning experiences are catered for.

1.6 Textual Behavior and Reading

If textual behavior has been learned well, word fragments, whole words, or groups of words, constitute discriminative stimuli that exert control over a sequence of (often covert) vocal responses that follow fluently. The individual emits a chain of verbal responses that correspond to the text. The individual may do this, however without understanding the text. For comprehension to occur, the chain must involve other responses. Basically, the child must learn to listen to their own textual behavior. To do so, it is important that the child has a developed repertoire of verbal behavior and listening comprehension, in order to act effectively as a listener of his own text. A child who already has enough practice in listening to stories, for example, should find it easier to listen to themself reading stories and detect in their own textual behavior excerpts that "do not make sense", such as words that do not exist in the child's repertoire, incomprehensible sentences, contradictions, etc. When detecting passages that do not make sense, the child should learn to, as does the experienced reader, interrupt the chain of textual behavior, and return to the previous point, producing a new textual response.

The absence of any component of the repertoire may result in defective learning. For example, children who have not learned the sequence of gaze movements may read words backwards or in an order that does not match the text. Many children may need to learn to listen to their own textual behavior in order to develop comprehension and to self-correct for excerpts that do not make sense.

Informal observations we have made in the classroom suggest that these important features of the reading repertoire are often overlooked by teachers. Contributing to this is the fact that reading is not identified as a distinct skill from writing. There seems to be an overemphasis on training children to spell-correct writing. Meanwhile, reading seems to be neglected, resulting in very few opportunities for children to learn and practice these components of the reading repertoire.

1.7 Writing

Writing is also a form of verbal behavior, functionally similar to speaking behavior: "The speaker creates an auditory pattern which is reinforced when it affects the listener as an auditory stimulus. A response which creates a visual stimulus having a similar effect is also verbal according to our definition" (Skinner, 1957, p. 69).

The visual stimuli Skinner refers to are texts. Their production requires a chain of motor responses capable of producing visible marks. There are different modalities of writing, which require different motor skills: cursive writing, handwriting, typing, Braille writing, shorthand, etc. To be able to write in any of these modalities, a person needs to learn the specific motor responses, and learn how to chain them together. In alphabetic writing, the units must be sequenced to correspond to a sequence of sound units. The production of this sequence of units is what is called *spelling*. Text writing also requires composing and editing responses (cf. Skinner, 1957) which result in an ordering of words and punctuation marks.

We can distinguish, therefore, at least three components of writing behavior: motor responses, spelling, and composition/editing. Motor responses – One of the most emphasized components of writing in Brazil seems to be the training of motor responses. The development of the motor chain of cursive writing may be important to give greater agility and intelligibility to handwriting, but it is not essential.[3] A person unable to learn the motor responses of cursive writing may write very well if he or she learns to spell and compose, using alternative motor responses. A person able to point to letters can write using a keyboard. People with severe physical disabilities have even written important works in this way. Motor difficulties do not necessarily mean a lack of maturity or readiness to learn the other components of

[3] The author had the opportunity to meet, for example, several foreign scientists who could not have passed the first grades in Brazilian schools, because they only knew how to write by hand in capital letters.

reading and writing. Unfortunately, some children's difficulty in acquiring motor responses often leads teachers to unfounded negative expectations about their overall potential, resulting in "self-fulfilling prophecies," often supported by inappropriate use of psychological assessment procedures. The resulting low achievement can lead to labels such as "special student", "learning disorder" and "mild mental handicap" and to segregation of the student in special classes or institutions (Carvalho, 1984; Ferreira, 1989; Rodrigues, 1984; Schneider, 1974).

Many of these children could, despite motor difficulty, show marked progress in reading and could also learn forms of writing that do not require such elaborate motor coordination, or learn cursive writing through a teaching program such as that developed by Skinner and Krakower (1968). In the initial stages of this program, the student would perform a stroke on letters that were fully drawn on paper. As the student progressed, the letter became dashed and the dashed line was gradually removed, from the end to the beginning of the letter.

The material was presented on chemically treated paper, so that when the stroke produced by the student departed from the correct form, its color became different. This provided immediate differential feedback for the correct stroke, helping to establish the appropriate motor responses. Training the motor chains corresponding to writing each letter of the alphabet provides the individual with a repertoire of minimal units that can be chained together to write words and texts. Different motor units constitute repertoires of equivalent minimal units: writing in capital letters, typing, shorthand, Braille writing, etc.

Writing involves the production of a sequence of these minimal units, under the control of different types of antecedent stimuli. Writing may therefore involve different stimulus control relations. These relations involve the correspondence between motor units and visual or auditory stimuli. Skinner (1957) uses the generic term transcription repertoires for all these relations.

Copying a text – Copying a text seems to be one of the most frequently used activities in Brazilian schools to teach students to write. In fact, copying a text makes it possible to train the motor responses involved in writing, but it does not necessarily have an effect on the other components of writing. Copying a text involves a relationship between textual stimuli and motor responses, such that the product of these motor responses is a reproduction of the textual stimuli. This reproduction may involve a formal correspondence, when the units of the copy are the same as those of the text, or it may involve a functional correspondence between the units of the text and the units of the copy (e.g., handwritten copy of a text in print; typewritten copy of a text in Braille).

Although it is an important skill, copying a text is only one of the transcription repertoires to be learned by the child. Another transcription repertoire is taking dictation. In this case, the relationship to be established is between a vocal discriminative stimulus (or gesture in the case of deaf persons) and a written response. The minimal units that make copying a text possible are formally the same as those that make taking dictation possible; however, in copying a text these units must be under the control of visual stimuli, formally or functionally similar to those produced by the response, while in taking dictation these units must be under the control of auditory stimuli that bear no resemblance to the product of the response.

Due to these differences, there is no guarantee that the acquisition of the skill of copying a text will result in progress in taking dictation skills, just as there is no guarantee that it will result in progress in reading. The practice of copying a text may enable motor learning of the minimal units corresponding to letters, but for the person to learn to take dictation these units must be related to different discriminative stimuli, auditory.

Taking dictation and spelling – The response emitted in the activities of copying a text and taking dictation is similar. This is probably the reason why copying a text is so widely used as a didactic resource in teaching writing. The control relations are, however, different.

In copying a text, spelling is relatively trivial, provided the person has learned the correspondence between the unit type of the original text and the type to be used in the copy. In taking dictation, however, spelling involves a correspondence between auditory stimuli and the production of a sequence of letters.

Control relations are, in this case, the reverse of textual behavior. In textual behavior, graphic stimuli control vocal responses; in taking dictation, vocal stimuli control responses that produce graphic stimuli. The control relations in both repertoires are, in fact, more complex. In Portuguese, the correspondence between graphemes and phonemes is only approximate. This approximation is even smaller in English, where virtually any sound can be represented by different combinations of graphemes, and any grapheme or combination of graphemes can represent different sounds. For this reason, both reading and spelling require additional control by intraverbal cues provided by the context in which the word occurs. For example, when the sound sequence [sell] is dictated, control over the response to spell the first letter should be exerted by the initial phoneme /s/ in combination with the context. The student should learn to write 'sell' when the context concerns exchanging goods, and 'cell' when the context concerns prisons or monasteries.

The symmetrical relationship between reading and spelling repertoires is probably one of the reasons why many researchers and educators consider writing and reading as a unitary ability. However, the integration between reading and writing is not inevitable, especially when the individual is still acquiring these repertoires. For example, Lee and Pegler (1982) showed that learning to read a set of words does not necessarily result in progress in spelling the same words. However, as repertoires are acquired, integration between them may also develop, as we will see below.

Transcription of one's own dictation and written verbal behavior: writing as expression – "Writing" comprises various abilities, characterized by different relations. All these skills have their importance. It is important to know how to copy a text, just as it is important to know how to take dictation, but most educators consider it even more important that a person learns to write in order to "express his/her own ideas and thoughts".

Expressing oneself through writing requires a "transfer" of spoken verbal behavior to written verbal behavior. As Skinner notes,

> It is quite possible that a child who has learned to write only in the sense of copying other writing will be unable to make this transfer, or that the child who has learned to write from dictation must also learn to 'transcribe his own dictation'. A child may very well learn to write, yet it may never 'occur to him' to leave a note for someone whom he cannot wait... Traditionally it would be said that the child must learn to use writing as well as learn to write (Skinner, 1957, pp. 192–193).

The emphasis on the form of behavior at the expense of relationships, which is widespread in education, is certainly one of the reasons for the frequent failure of school practices. In the case of literacy, this leads to an over-emphasis on copying texts and taking dictation at the expense of reading and expressive writing. This emphasis on form stems in part from the fact that it is easier to stick to the immediately observable than to analyze behavior by seeking to identify its functional relationships.

Copying a text, taking dictation and expressing oneself through writing are three different types of behavior, which can easily be confused because in all three cases the response is topographically similar and the product of the response is also similar. For example, when a teacher evaluates a written assignment that a student has done at home, it is important to distinguish whether the student has copied the work, merely transcribed what was dictated to him by someone else or worked out the work from his own ideas. The movements the student makes in these three cases are topographically similar, and so is the work produced; but the relations of control are different. In the first case, control is exercised primarily by a text, which the student reproduces. In the second case, control is exercised by someone else's verbalization, which the student transcribes. In the third case, the student does not reproduce oral or written verbalizations, but composes his/her own verbalization. The student can compose "dictating to himself" and transcribe this "self-dictation", or they can compose "directly on paper", without the mediation of a covert speech.

1.8 Reading and Writing as a Network of Relationships

The analysis developed so far provides a rough description of the basic behaviors involved in reading and writing in terms of stimulus control relations. The description is not complete, in that it focuses on only a few basic components of these repertoires. On the other hand, we cannot claim that our knowledge about these issues is complete: the framework outlined here can be refined or revised based on the results of new research.

An important point of this analysis is that it identifies repertoire components that must be learned in order for reading and writing to develop. These components consist of relationships which are, in principle, independent. It is also important to note that the learning of some of these relations in isolation does not ensure learning of the others. Learning textual behavior does not necessarily result in progress in spelling (cf. Lee & Pegler, 1982). Similarly, learning to copy a text does not ensure that the learner will also master dictation or reading, and learning to dictate does not necessarily result in expressive writing.

However, the need to explicitly teach each relation seems contradictory to the high degree of transfer between relations that we observe in the repertoire of experienced readers. It is necessary to consider the possibility that integration and transfer between the various relations occurs at some point during learning. Behavior analysis has made much progress in this direction, building on the studies of Sidman and colleagues (e.g., Mackay & Sidman, 1984; Sidman, 1971, 1986a, b; Sidman & Cresson, 1973; Sidman & Tailby, 1982).

From these studies one can conceive of reading and writing repertoires as a network of relations (de Rose et al., 1992, 1996; Stromer et al., 1992). These relations are at first independent, but may integrate as some of them are learned. When this integration occurs, new relations, not explicitly taught, may emerge: the teaching of some relations results in transfer to new relations, with little or no explicit teaching of these new relations.

A network of relations may comprise both relations between stimuli and responses and relations between stimuli. Inter-stimulus relations may give rise to stimulus classes, such as the one represented in Fig. 1.1, inside rectangle I: this class includes dictated words, pictures and printed words. A necessary condition for the formation of a stimulus class is that the learner learns a set of relations between

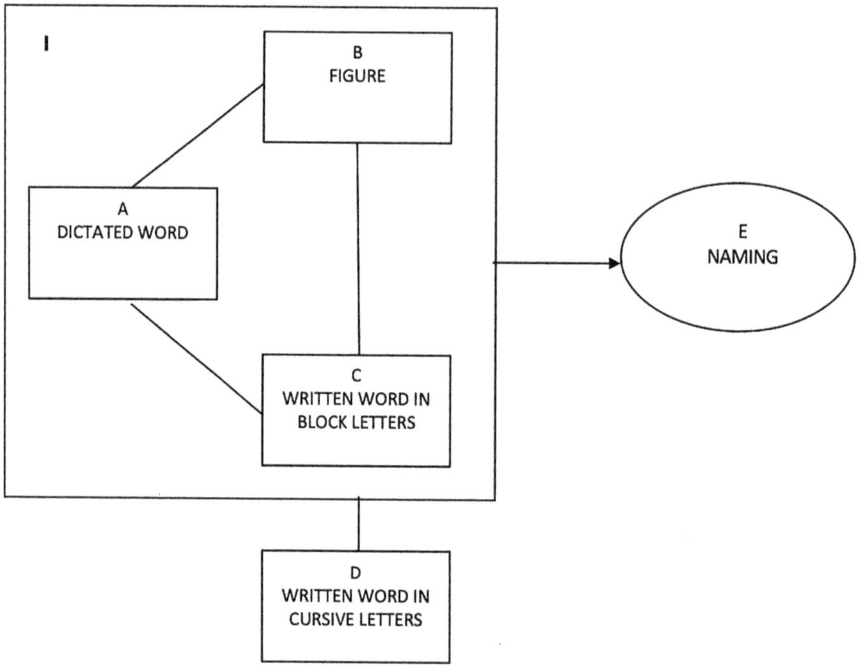

Fig. 1.1 Schematic diagram of a stimulus class that exerts control over the naming response. The diagram shows the incorporation of a new member to the class

stimuli, such that each stimulus in the class to be formed is related to at least one other stimulus in this class. For example, Sidman (1971) investigated class formation involving dictated words, pictures, and written words in a severely intellectually disabled individual. He employed twenty classes, each involving a dictated word, along with the corresponding picture and printed word. The participant had already learned the relationship between the twenty dictated words and the pictures: he was able to point to the picture when the experimenter dictated the word. Sidman then taught the relationship between the twenty dictated words and the printed words. Due to the participant's intellectual limitations, a rather long and refined procedure was necessary, at the end of which he learned to, faced with a set of printed words, choose the one that corresponded to the dictated word. After this learning, the other relations between stimuli emerged: the participant was able, without any additional teaching, to choose each of the printed words when the corresponding picture was presented, and to choose each of the pictures when the corresponding printed word was presented. The fact that these relations emerged indicates that the participant formed stimulus classes involving each written word together with the corresponding pictures and dictated words. If one of these stimuli already exerts control over a response, the new members of the class also acquire control over this response. For the participant in Sidman's study, the pictures already exerted control over the naming response. After stimulus class formation, the printed words also exerted control over the naming response, so that the participant was able to name all twenty printed words. Naming printed words is textual behavior, albeit rudimentary.

In Sidman's (1971) study, the stimulus class included only lower case words. Literate people form classes with much larger numbers of members. Larger classes can be formed gradually by adding new members to an already formed class. Figure 1.1 shows schematically the addition to the class of a new member, D (words written in cursive letters). Six new relations are formed: the three relations between D and each of the members already in the class, and the three symmetric relations between each of the members of the class and the new member D.[4] The studies show that it is not necessary to explicitly teach all these relations. Often teaching just one of them is sufficient for the new member to be added to the class, so that whichever relation is chosen, the others can emerge (e.g., Sidman & Tailby, 1982; Lazar et al., 1984).

Another possibility for adding a new member to a stimulus class is to teach the relationship between this new stimulus and one of the responses controlled by the class. Thus, the stimulus class depicted in Fig. 1.2 controls the naming response. To add a new member to the class, for example "words written on telegraph signs" (F), we could teach the relationship between F and any of the stimuli already in the class. Alternatively, we could teach the relationship between F and the response of

[4] One such relationship is difficult to assess in practice. It would involve the choice between words dictated conditional on the presentation of the word in lower case. It is not possible to dictate several words simultaneously for the subject to choose one of them. Words could be dictated sequentially, but choice could be impaired by difficulty remembering the words.

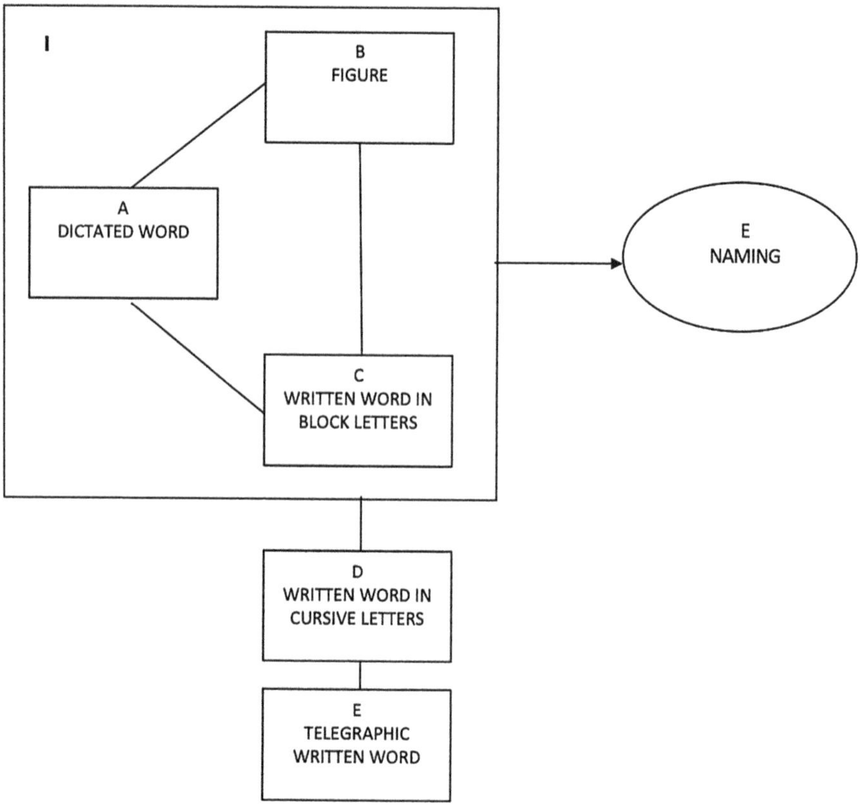

Fig. 1.2 Schematic diagram of adding a new member to a stimulus class by teaching the relationship of this member to a response already under control of the stimulus class

reading. If the individual is taught to read words written on telegraph signs, it is possible that all the relations between stimuli F and the other stimuli in the class would emerge with little or no further teaching. This conclusion is an extrapolation based on the study by Mackay and Sidman (1984), which shows that classes can expand from the teaching of relations between stimuli and responses.

Networks of relations may also include classes of responses. These classes comprise different responses that are controlled by the same stimulus. In this case, if a new stimulus gains control over one of these responses, control of this stimulus over all the other responses in the class may emerge with little or no additional teaching. For example, a literate person might be capable of different types of spelling responses: they may spell orally (by saying the names of the letters), or through various types of writing (cursive, handwriting, typing, etc.). Suppose this person learns to transcribe "self-dictated" words. Even if only one type of response is used during learning, for example cursive writing, it is quite likely that there will be transfer to all the other responses in the class: the individual will be able to type their self-dictation, even if there has been no direct learning of this relationship.

We can consider, therefore, that the network of relations involves classes of stimuli that exert control over classes of responses. Stimulus classes can receive the addition of new members, and when this happens, new relations between stimuli emerge. In this case, relations between the new member and all the responses controlled by the class will also emerge. Response classes can also expand with the addition of new members. The new response also comes under the control of the stimulus class that already controlled the old members of the response class.

We can therefore summarize what we already know about the network of relations underlying reading and writing repertoires through the schematic representation in Fig. 1.3. The rectangle I in this figure represents a class of stimuli, including dictated words (A), pictures (B) and written words (C).

This class is represented in a simplified way, because the classes in the repertoire of literate people are much larger. Written word, for example, is not a unitary

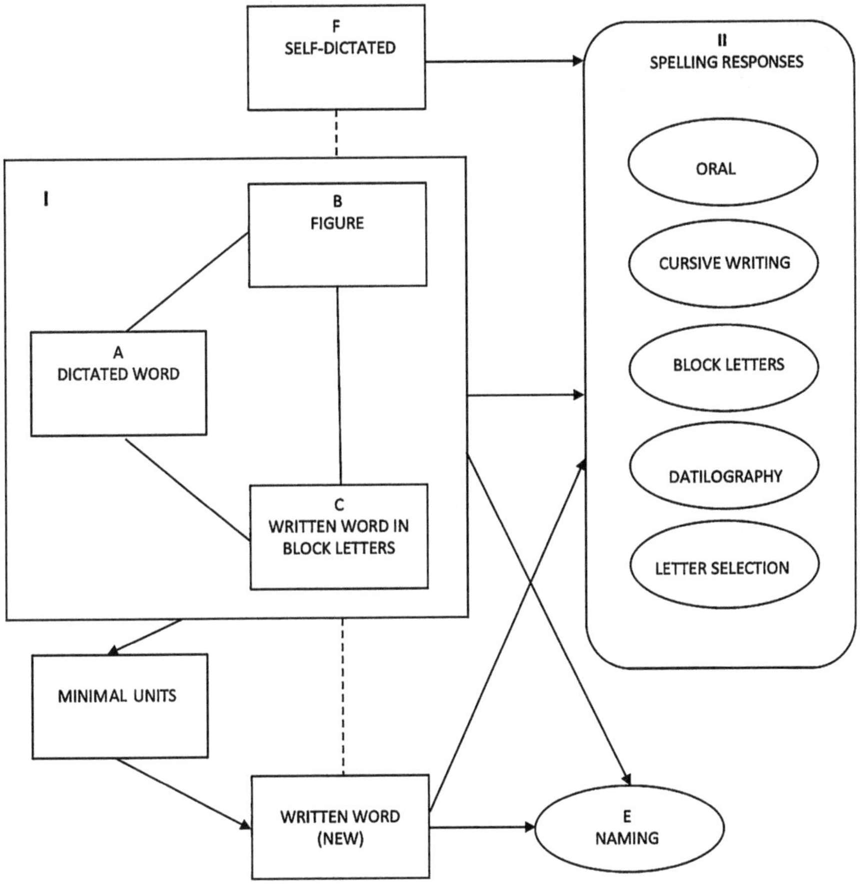

Fig. 1.3 Schematic diagram of the network of relationships components of the reading and writing repertoires

stimulus, but rather a very broad class, including words in cursive, capital and lower-case letters, and in a variety of existing types or fonts. The class involves not only pictures, but also objects, verbal descriptions of objects, etc. This class of stimuli controls the naming response. Note that naming responses, formally similar, are functionally different depending on the discriminative stimulus: if the discriminative stimulus is a dictated word, the naming response is called vocal imitation, or echoic behavior (Skinner, 1957). If the discriminative stimulus is a printed word, then the response is termed textual behavior, and if the discriminative stimulus is a figure or object, the response is termed figure or object naming. The formation of a stimulus class produces the integration of these responses, so that the existence of one of them enables the others to emerge. Thus, in Sidman's (1971) experiment, the existence of figure naming enabled, with the formation of the stimulus class, the emergence of textual behavior.

Learning to write involves the discriminative control of this class of stimuli over a class of responses, represented in rectangle II. This class includes the various modalities of spelling: a person may form words by ordering letters through cursive writing, handwriting, typing, or even by orally reciting the sequence of letters. The responses of writing and reading are controlled by the same stimulus class; this may result in a functional integration of these two repertoires. Self-dictated words are included in the network as one of the members of the stimulus class that should exert control over spelling and writing responses.

1.9 Networks of Relationships and Recombination of Units

The application of this model of networks of relations to reading and writing repertoires also has a limitation, which can be detected in Sidman's (1971) study. The participant of this study formed twenty stimulus classes, each corresponding to a word. A limited number of classes could be useful for an individual with severe disability, in that it would enable the recognition of some written words important for the individual's survival and independence. However, for reading simple texts, learning several hundred classes would be necessary.

Learning to read in English seems, at least in part, to occur in this way as students acquire an increasing vocabulary of *sight words*. However, reading development can be accelerated by unit recombination. The lower part of Fig. 1.3 complements the schematic representation of the network of relations, including the interaction with the process of acquisition and recombination of more molecular units.

Results obtained by de Rose et al. (1996) suggest an interaction between the processes of formation of networks of relations and recombination of units. The participants of this study were children with learning difficulties in reading and writing. Initial tests showed that they mastered only the most basic relations of the network in Fig. 1.3. They were able to recognize and name figures, but were not able to read or write dictated words or syllables. The experimental procedure involved, like Sidman's (1971) study, teaching relations between dictated words and written words (in lower case print). A copying performance was also taught, in which children reproduced the word using moving letters. The teaching of these two relations was sufficient for all the other relations to emerge: the children were able to read the words and relate them to figures, and showed progress in writing with movable letters and cursive writing.

In this study, the number of words taught was gradually increased. At the same time, it was verified whether the children were able to read and write new words, not directly taught. Most participants were able to read and write new words, indicating that they had learned a repertoire of minimal units for both reading and writing. The formation of this repertoire of minimal units seemed to depend, at least in part, on the number of words the children learned to read and write. This number varied from participant to participant, such that some required experience with a greater number of words than others.

Some children did not show the formation of a repertoire of minimal units with the number of words used in this study. The number of words may have been insufficient for them; if this were the case, they could possibly show the formation of this repertoire if the study were continued with the use of a larger number of words. It is also possible that some of these participants did not develop some prerequisites that the other children had already developed. Perhaps parallel exercises of discrimination of letters and letter sequences, or of discrimination of sounds that make up words would accelerate the formation of this repertoire. Motivational aspects may also be involved in these differences between children.

The study by de Rose et al. (1996) demonstrates the viability of this model based on a network of relations. This model is compatible with several features of learning complex repertoires such as reading and writing. One of these features is the origin of the repertoire in a set of distinct relations, each of which needs to be explicitly taught. However, the formation of classes of stimuli and responses enables the functional integration of repertoires, with increasing degrees of transfer to new relations: as the network of relations expands, there is a progressively greater generation of new relations.

This characteristic is consistent with what we observe in human learning. People are able to exhibit many new and appropriate behaviors that are not "trained" or "conditioned". However, this ability is not inevitable or automatic, but depends on a basic repertoire that needs to be learned, either through formal teaching or through incidental learning that occurs in the interaction of the individual with his environment, such as that provided by games or play. One of the advantages of a model based on network of relations is that it enables an analysis of the repertoire, based on which we can identify the teaching conditions to be provided for the network of relations to be formed.

The model based on a network of relations also leads us to appreciate the variety of teaching alternatives that are possible. The same network can emerge from teaching many different combinations of relations. We know that different methods of teaching reading and writing eventually result in the acquisition of this network of relations. The network allows us to identify the requirements for any method to be effective, and the alternatives that can be used when a method "fails" with a particular student. In such cases, the teacher can try alternative procedures, rather than attributing the failure to intrinsic student characteristics.

1.10 Reinforcement for Reading and Writing Behaviors

Like all operant behavior, reading and writing behaviors need to be reinforced to be learned and maintained. Once a person has learned to read and write, these behaviors can have many automatic or "natural" reinforcing consequences that ensure their maintenance and improvement. Unfortunately, as we will see below, these automatic consequences are generally not present during the learning phase of reading and writing. In the following discussion we will address only reinforcement for the behavior of reading. However, many of the issues discussed apply to the behavior of writing as well.

For those who have already become good readers, an automatic consequence of reading is hearing the textual behavior itself. Reading a story, for example, produces some of the reinforcers that occur when an individual hears a story told by someone else. As Goldiamond and Dyrud (1966) note, the legendary power of the story as a reinforcer is illustrated by the "One Thousand and One Nights" where, to gain access to the continuation of the story, the king is required to spare Scheherazade's life. Television, particularly in Brazil, analogously used to manipulate the daily behavior of its viewers, who tuned in daily to watch the continuation of a soap opera. Between the Scheherazade of legend and her electronic successor, the serial novel genre flourished, which provided reinforcement for the behavior of reading, just as the current soap opera provides reinforcement for tuning in and watching. In addition to providing access to stories, reading also provides access to the contents of letters, magazines and newspapers, movie subtitles, etc. By automatically producing access to many reinforcers, the very activity of reading can become reinforcing, strengthening the other activities to which it is consequent, according to the well-known principle of Premack (1959), which establishes that a reinforcing activity increases the probability of precurrent responses, that is, responses that produce the opportunity for the reinforcing activity. The power of reading as a reinforcing activity can be attested to by the high probability of precurrent activities: buying newspapers, magazines, or books; isolating oneself to read and repel interruptions; waiting for the postman or going to the post office to pick up mail, etc.

Even in cases in which the activity of reading is not intrinsically reinforcing, it may precede activities that give access to other reinforcers. An example of this is reading instructions: reading an instruction manual on the operation of an appliance can have as a reinforcing consequence the successful operation of the appliance. Similarly, reading a didactic text can result in a good grade on an exam or approval in a competitive examination. In our society, reading is a precursor to many everyday activities, including taking the bus, shopping, going to the movies (you have to read subtitles to follow most movies), voting, signing contracts, etc. For religious people, reading is an extremely important precurrent activity: reading books considered sacred is an obligation for the believer, a condition for acceptance into the community and worship services.

One characteristic of all of these reinforcing consequences of reading is that they are only accessible to the individual who has already become a reader. If an individual does not yet know how to read, he or she will not be able to take advantage of reading stories, the Bible, or an instruction manual. Teaching the behavior of reading requires, in most cases, more immediate reinforcers.

In addition to immediate reinforcement, learning any skill requires differential reinforcement, which provides feedback regarding the correctness of the response. This differential reinforcement strengthens responses that approach the correct pattern and enables self-correction of responses that deviate from this pattern.

In learning many skills, differential reinforcement is practically automatic. For example, when children learn to imitate vocal responses, auditory comparison of the childs vocalization with the model's vocalization provides immediate differential feedback. For children without hearing or intellectual impairment, this feedback functions as differential reinforcement, allowing the acquisition of the behavior without the need for special training.

In the early stages of learning to read, by contrast, there is no immediate differential reinforcement. Only after the child has already acquired some textual behavior can them, often with help from the teacher, use hearing their own textual behavior as differential reinforcement. From this point on, responses that "make sense" are strengthened and responses that do not make sense can be self-corrected. When a child reaches this point, reading behavior can develop with just encouragement and opportunities to exercise reading; if these opportunities exist, the very hearing and understanding of textual behavior will provide differential reinforcement to develop and improve reading. This differential reinforcement automatically produced by the reading behavior, coupled with the other reinforcers intrinsic to this behavior, develop the "taste" or "interest" in reading. In the early stages of the development of textual behavior, however, the teacher must usually supply some form of "external" differential reinforcement. It is important, however, that the teacher try to gradually decrease these external reinforcers as the student becomes sensitive to the reinforcers intrinsic to reading itself.

It is possible to conclude that many of the difficulties in learning to read are due to the absence of the reinforcement necessary to establish the initial steps of textual behavior. School literacy is done through intensive training (which may have aversive characteristics), and in a group situation in which the teacher has little possibility to follow the learning of each student and provide immediate differential reinforcement (cf. Staats & Staats, 1962). Classroom observations suggest that reinforcement is a rare occurrence. Skinner (1968) stated that students spend most of their time in school doing things to which they do not feel inclined: they do this mainly to escape punishment and avoid threats. The numerous disastrous byproducts of this practice include non-existent or failed learning, anxiety, rebellion, conformity, avoidance, and, in extreme cases, mental illness and suicide (cf. Skinner, 1968; Sidman, 1989).

Reinforcement in the classroom is problematic not only because of its scarcity: when it does occur, it may come long after the behavior and often the behaviors actually reinforced are totally inappropriate. Holt (1964) summarizes the most reinforced behaviors in a typical school, in a finding that unfortunately has not yet lost its timeliness and generality:

> a combination of bluffing, guessing, mind reading, snatching at clues, and getting answers from other people is what he is supposed to do at school; this is what school is all about (Holt, 1964, p. 146).

When it comes to reading, frequent occurrence of punishment, coupled with omission or inadequacy of reinforcement, can have a disastrous effect. If during your learning at school, reading is only an occasion for stumbling, frustration, and humiliation, it is unlikely that its reinforcing value (i.e., a taste for reading) will develop. This is what happens with a large proportion of literate people, who although they are able to name textual stimuli, with varying degrees of skill, fail to develop a good understanding of what they read, or do not develop a taste for reading.

1.11 School Contingencies That May Promote Learning to Read and Write

Based on this analysis we can draw some conclusions about the school contingencies that could promote learning to read. An important point seems to be the identification of relevant aspects of textual stimuli that normally do not exert control over the child's response. It is important to establish contingencies that involve discrimination of these aspects. These contingencies may involve systematic exercises, but informal and playful situations can be very valuable.

If the teacher is aware of the type of stimulus control to be established, they can choose playing activities that involve the relevant dimensions. For example, textual stimulus control requires control by aspects of the vocal stimuli in addition to the visual stimuli. The constituent sounds of words must gain control over the response. There are many games and playing activities that involve control by the constituent sounds of words. Playing with rhymes, for example, requires the child to discriminate word constituent sounds.

It should be borne in mind, however, that although the contingencies that promote learning are often socially established, the learning process is individual. This means that the same contingencies will have different effects for each individual, depending on the unique interaction between past history, genetic endowment, and organic conditions of each person. Thus, the same situations that promote learning for many children may be ineffective for some. Children who do not learn are not necessarily "retarded", "immature" or "dyslexic". In most cases, looking for new teaching procedures is more useful than looking for a label. For some children, variations in situations or even a little more individual attention may be enough. For students with greater difficulties, the literature on stimulus control suggests procedures that can establish the most complex forms of stimulus control by grading difficulties, that is, starting with discriminations that the student has mastered and gradually transferring control to aspects of the stimulus with which the student has difficulty. Such procedures are effective with a wide range of students, from those considered normal to those with severe degrees of learning disability (e.g., de Rose et al., 1989, 1992; Saunders & Spradlin, 1989; Sidman & Stoddard, 1966; Stoddard et al., 1986, 1987; Touchette, 1971).

Programmed instruction can be considered a way to gradually establish response and stimulus control relations. When based on an adequate analysis of the relations to be taught, it can be extremely useful in a wide variety of teaching modalities (e.g., Holland et al., 1976; Keller, 1968; Sidman & Sidman, 1965; Skinner, 1968). In our country programmed instruction has been successfully adapted for teaching reading and writing (e.g., Leite, 1980, 1982; Silveira, 1978; Teixeira, 1983a, b; Witter & Copit, 1971; Witter & Ramos, 1978). This success demonstrates the effectiveness of contingency analysis and programming in promoting the learning of reading and writing.

References

Carvalho, M. F. (1984). Da marginalização ao fracasso escolar: Estudo de uma classe de primeira série de primeiro grau. *Psicologia, 10*(1), 27–42.

de Rose, J. C., de Souza, D. G., Rossito, A. L., & de Rose, T. M. S. (1989). Aquisição de leitura após história de fracasso escolar: Equivalência de estímulos e generalização. *Psicologia: Teoria e Pesquisa, 5*, 325–346.

de Rose, J. C., de Souza, D. G., Rossito, A. L., & de Rose, T. M. S. (1992). Stimulus equivalence and generalization in reading after matching to sample by exclusion. In S. C. Hayes & L. J. Hayes (Eds.), *Understanding verbal relations* (pp. 69–82). Context Press.

de Rose, J. C., de Souza, D. G., & Hanna, E. S. (1996). Teaching reading and spelling: Exclusion and stimulus equivalence. *Journal of Applied Behavior Analysis, 29*, 451–459. https://doi.org/10.1901/jaba.1996.29-451

Ferreira, J. R. (1989). *A construção escolar da deficiência mental.* Doctoral dissertation, Universidade Estadual de Campinas. Repositório da Producão Científica e Intelectual da Unicamp. http://repositorio.unicamp.br/jspui/handle/REPOSIP/252591

Ferreiro, E., & Teberosky, A. (1986). *Psicogênese da língua escrita* (D. M. Lichtenstein, L. di Marco & M. Corso, Trad.). Artes Médicas.

Gibson, E. J., & Levin, H. (1975). *The psychology of reading*. MIT Press.

Gibson, E. J., Gibson, J. J., Pick, A. D., & Osser, H. A. (1962). A developmental study of discrimination of letter like-forms. *Journal of Comparative and Physiological Psychology, 55*, 897–906. https://doi.org/10.1037/h0043190

Goldiamond, I., & Dyrud, J. E. (1966). Reading as operant behavior. In J. Money (Ed.), *The disabled reader: Education of the dyslexic child.* John Hopkins.

Holland, J. G., Solomon, C., Doran, J., & Frezza, D. A. (1976). *The analysis of behavior in planning instruction.* Addison Wesley.

Holt, J. (1964). *How children fail.* Pitman Publishing Corporation.

Keller, F. S. (1968). Good bye, teacher. *Journal of Applied Behavior Analysis, 1*, 78–89. https://doi.org/10.1901/jaba.1968.1-79

Lavine, L. (1977). Differentiation of letter like forms in prereading children. *Developmental Psychology, 13*, 89–94. https://doi.org/10.1037/0012-1649.13.2.89
Lazar, R. M., Davis-Lang, D., & Sanchez, L. (1984). The formation of visual stimulus equivalences in children. *Journal of the Experimental Analysis of Behavior, 41*, 251–266. https://doi.org/10.1901/jeab.1984.41-251
Lee, V. L., & Pegler, A. M. (1982). Effects on spelling of training children to read. *Journal of the Experimental Analysis of Behavior, 37*, 311–322. https://doi.org/10.1901/jeab.1982.37-311
Leite, S. A. S. (1980). *O projeto de alfabetização de Mogi das Cruzes: Uma proposta para a rede de ensino público*. Unpublished doctoral dissertation. Universidade de São Paulo.
Leite, S. A. S. (1982). *Alfabetizacão: Um projeto bem-sucedido*. Edicon.
Mackay, H. A., & Sidman, M. (1984). Teaching new behavior via equivalence relations. In P. H. Brooks, R. Sperber, & C. MacCauley (Eds.), *Learning and cognition in the mentally retarded* (pp. 493–513). Lawrence Erlbaum.
Premack, D. (1959). Toward empirical behavior laws: I. Positive reinforcement. *Psychological Review, 66*, 219–233. https://doi.org/10.1037/h0040891
Rodrigues, O. M. P. R. (1984). *Caracterização das condições de implantação e funcionamento de classes especiais e caracterização das condições de avaliação de classes regulares de 1a. série de 1°. grau, para fundamentar uma proposta de intervenção*. Unpublished master's thesis. Universidade Federal de São Carlos.
Rozin, P. (1978). The acquisition of basic alphabetic principles: A structural approach. In A. C. Catania & T. A. Brigham (Eds.), *Handbook of applied behavior analysis: Social and instructional processes* (pp. 410–453). Irvington.
Saunders, K. J., & Spradlin, J. E. (1989). Conditional discrimination in mentally retarded adults: The effect of training the component simple discriminations. *Journal of the Experimental Analysis of Behavior, 52*, 1–12. https://doi.org/10.1901/jeab.1989.52-1
Schneider, D. W. (1974). Alunos excepcionais: Um estudo de caso de desvio. In G. Velho (Org.), *Desvio e divergência* (pp. 52–81). Zahar.
Sidman, M. (1971). Reading and auditory visual equivalences. *Journal of Speech and Hearing Research, 14*, 5–13. https://doi.org/10.1044/jshr.1401.05
Sidman, M. (1986a). Functional analysis of emergent verbal classes. In T. Thompson & M. D. Zeiler (Eds.), *Analysis and integration of behavioral units*. Lawrence Erlbaum.
Sidman, M. (1986b). The measurement of behavioral development. In N. A. Krasnegor, D. B. Gray, & T. Thompson (Eds.), *Advances in behavioral pharmacology, Vol 5: Developmental behavioral pharmacology* (pp. 43–52). Erlbaum.
Sidman, M. (1989). *Coercion and its fallout*. Authors Cooperative.
Sidman, M., & Cresson, O. (1973). Reading and crossmodal transfer of stimulus equivalences in severe retardation. *American Journal of Mental Deficiency, 77*, 515–523.
Sidman, R. L., & Sidman, M. (1965). *Neuroanatomy: A programmed text* (Vol. I). Little Brown.
Sidman, M., & Stoddard, L. T. (1966). Programming perception and learning for retarded children. In N. R. Ellis (Ed.), *International review of research in mental retardation* (Vol. II, pp. 151–208). Academic.
Sidman, M., & Tailby, W. (1982). Conditional discrimination vs. matching to sample: An expansion of the testing paradigm. *Journal of the Experimental Analysis of Behavior, 37*, 5–22. https://doi.org/10.1901/jeab.1982.37-5
Silveira, M. H. B. (1978). *Aquisição da leitura: Uma análise comportamental*. Unpublished doctoral dissertation. Universidade de São Paulo.
Skinner, B. F. (1953). *Science and human behavior*. Macmillan.
Skinner, B. F. (1957). *Verbal behavior*. Prentice Hall.
Skinner, B. F. (1968). *The technology of teaching*. Prentice Hall.
Skinner, B. F. (1969). *Contingencies of reinforcement: A theoretical analysis*. Prentice Hall.
Skinner, B. F., & Krakower, S. A. (1968). *Handwriting with write and see*. Lyons & Carnahan.

Staats, A. W., & Staats, C. K. (1962). Comparison of the development of speech and reading behavior with implications for research. *Child Development, 33*, 831–846. https://doi.org/10.2307/1126893

Stoddard, L. T. (1968). An observation on stimulus control in a tilt discrimination by children. *Journal of the Experimental Analysis of Behavior, 11*, 321–324. https://doi.org/10.1901/jeab.1968.11-321

Stoddard, L. T., de Rose, J. C., & McIlvane, W. J. (1986). Observações curiosas acerca do desempenho deficiente após a ocorrência de erros. *Psicologia, 12*(1), 1–18.

Stoddard, L. T., McIlvane, W. J., & de Rose, J. C. (1987). Transferência de controle de estímulo com estudantes deficientes mentais: Modelagem de estímulo, superposição e aprendizagem em uma tentativa. *Psicologia, 13*(3), 13–27.

Stromer, R., Mackay, H. A., & Stoddard, L. T. (1992). Classroom applications of stimulus equivalence technology. *Journal of Behavioral Education, 2*, 225–256. https://doi.org/10.1007/BF00948817

Tawney, J. W. (1972). Training letter discrimination in four-year old children. *Journal of Applied Behavior Analysis, 5*, 455–465. https://doi.org/10.1901/jaba.1972.5-455

Teixeira, A. M. S. (1983a). *A individualização do ensino em uma pré-escola: Relato de uma experiência*. Unpublished doctoral dissertation. Universidade de São Paulo.

Teixeira, A. M. S. (1983b). A individualização do ensino em uma pré-escola. *Psicologia, 9*(3), 53–73.

Touchette, P. (1971). Transfer of stimulus control: Measuring the moment of transfer. *Journal of the Experimental Analysis of Behavior, 15*, 347–354. https://doi.org/10.1901/jeab.1971.15-347

Witter, G. P., & Copit, M. S. (1971). *Lendo e escrevendo*. Vetor.

Witter, G. P., & Ramos, M. A. A. (1978). "Cartilha da Amazônia": Produção e teste de material de aprendizagem. *Ciência e Cultura, 30*(6), 677–685.

Chapter 2
Mapping of Brazilian Studies on Reading and Writing Based on the Equivalence Paradigm

Alessandra Rocha de Albuquerque, Raquel Maria de Melo, and Izabela Casseb Ferraz Saavedra-Dias

2.1 Introduction

As explained in Chap. 1 of this book (de Rose, 2005), reading and writing are understood in Behavior Analysis as a network of relations between stimuli (e.g., words, objects, sounds) and between stimuli and responses (e.g., copying a text, pointing, naming). According to this perspective, when faced with a sandwich, a yellow letter M, or the written word "sandwich," a child may issue the same response, saying the name of the most famous fast-food chain in the world. The understanding of reading and writing repertoires, of fundamental academic importance and in everyday life, as a network of relations and, more specifically, of interchangeable relations between the stimuli that make up this network, has as its framework a study developed by Sidman (1971) and later replicated by Sidman and Cresson (1973).

In these studies, a 17-year-old boy with severe intellectual disability (Sidman, 1971) and two children with Down Syndrome (Sidman & Cresson, 1973) learned to relate printed words to spoken words and pictures to spoken words through specific teaching procedures. From the direct teaching of these relations, other emergent behaviors (that were not directly taught) were observed: relating pictures to printed words, relating printed words to pictures, and naming printed words. It was concluded that these different stimuli (printed words, pictures, dictated words) formed equivalent classes, defined in terms of a response common to all of them.

A. R. de Albuquerque (✉) · I. C. F. Saavedra-Dias
Universidade Católica de Brasília, Brasília, DF, Brazil
e-mail: arocha@p.ucb.br

R. M. de Melo
Universidade de Brasília, Brasília, DF, Brazil

A. R. de Albuquerque, R. M. de Melo (eds.), *Contributions of Behavior Analysis to Reading and Writing Comprehension*, https://doi.org/10.1007/978-3-031-40868-7_2

Since then, the concept of stimulus equivalence was systematized (Sidman & Taylby, 1982; for an introduction on the subject see also Albuquerque & Melo, 2005) and has been used by Behavior Analysis in studies of symbolic behaviors, such as reading and writing. Brazil, the second largest center for Behavior Analysis in the world (Todorov & Hanna, 2010), also occupies a prominent place in investigations related to reading and writing from this perspective.

This chapter aims to describe the Brazilian production on learning to read and write from the perspective of behavior analysis, especially based on the paradigm of stimulus equivalence and the conditional discrimination procedure, through a literature review. To this end, the strategy initially used for the survey and selection of this production will be described. This description is important because, despite the systematized nature of this mapping, it is not intended to be exhaustive and cover the entire production in the area. In this sense, the explanation of the choices and the path followed to carry out the survey is important to justify the eventual absence of relevant studies as well as the presence of those that will be exposed here. Next, a synthesis of the doctoral dissertations, master's theses, and articles will be presented followed by final considerations.

2.2 Search for Production on Reading and Writing

The search was carried out in three sequential steps. Initially, a search for doctoral dissertations and master's theses was conducted in the *Database of Theses and Dissertations from the Coordination for the Improvement of Higher Education Personnel – Capes* (*Catálogo de Teses e Dissertações da Coordenação de Aperfeiçoamento de Pessoal de Nível Superior – Capes*). The descriptors "reading" or "writing" were used paired with the descriptor "stimulus equivalence" ("reading" AND "stimulus equivalence" and "writing" AND "stimulus equivalence"), which was limited to the following areas of knowledge: Education, Special Education, Interdisciplinary, Psychology, and Experimental Psychology.

A total of 35 doctoral dissertations and 136 master's theses were retrieved (Fig. 2.1). The titles of these 171 papers were analyzed and only those that: (1) were explicitly based on Behavior Analysis were selected; (2) addressed alphabetic reading and writing skills; (3) described empirical studies that used the stimulus equivalence framework or the conditional discrimination procedure; and (4) involved research with other language systems (e.g., Braille, Libras, and pseudo-literacy). Studies on musical reading, math and art skills, and dialogical reading were excluded, as well as those that used the perspective of Behavior Analysis, but the focus was not on reading or writing *per se* (e.g., violence in school and education in general). The sample, composed of titles that met these criteria, was reduced from 171 to 160 publications, 35 doctoral dissertations and 125 master's theses.

In the second stage of the survey, all doctoral dissertations and master's theses of the initial sample (N = 171) were accessed and the names of the supervising researchers of each study were identified (N = 33). Then, the search of their

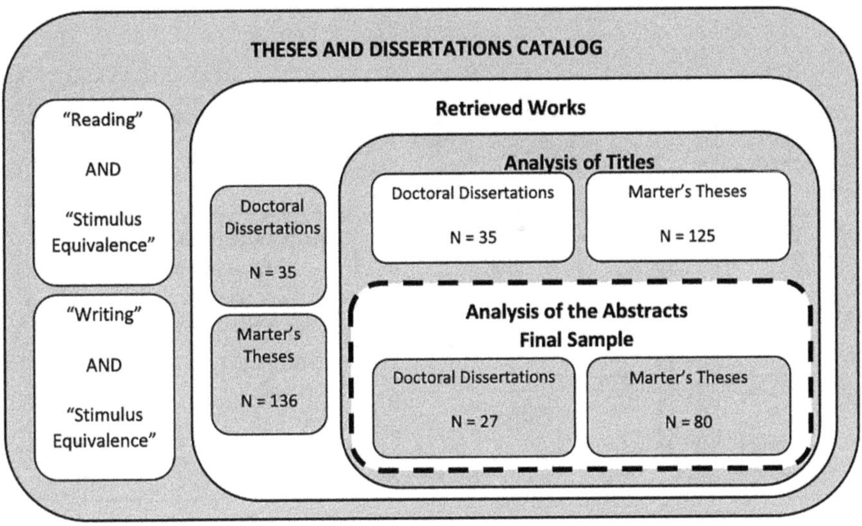

Fig. 2.1 Process of recovery and analysis of doctoral dissertations and master's theses

publications, in the form of articles, was carried out through the analysis of the curriculum of each advisor, available on the *Lattes Platform*[1] (*Plataforma Lattes*). The search was made from the articles' titles using the following descriptors in isolation: reading, writing, read, reading, write, writing, spell and spelling.

A total of 109 articles were retrieved, 85 of which were written in Portuguese and 24 in English, the latter published in both international and national journals (Fig. 2.2). The titles were analyzed and, similar to the doctoral dissertations and master's theses, those that did not meet the criteria were excluded. A total of 101 articles had their abstracts analyzed.

In the third and final step, we sought to locate in different databases, the abstracts of all doctoral dissertations (N = 35), mater's theses (N = 125) and articles (N = 101) whose titles had been pre-selected. For theses and dissertations, the search was conducted in the *Database of Theses and Dissertations from CAPES* or in institutional repositories of universities; for articles, the CAPES Journal Portal and Google Academic were used. The digital versions of four doctoral dissertations, 30 master's theses and six articles were not located. The reading and analysis of the keywords, abstracts and, if necessary, the method of the remaining titles was performed based on the same criteria previously described (items 1–4). 27 doctoral dissertations, 80 master's theses and 79 articles were selected, which will be characterized as follows.

[1] The *Lattes Platform* is a virtual system of researchers' curricula maintained by the National Council for Scientific and Technological Development (*Conselho Nacional de Desenvolvimento Científico e Tecnológico* [CNPq]). https://lattes.cnpq.br/

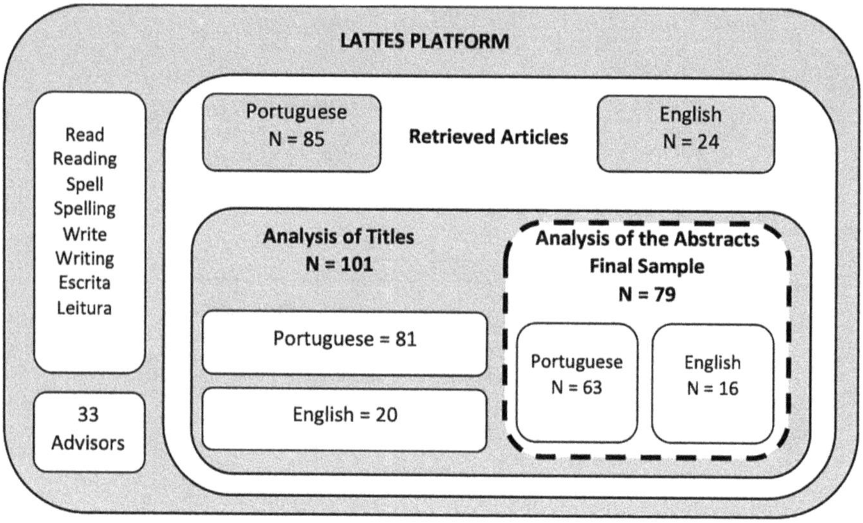

Fig. 2.2 Article retrieval and analysis process

2.3 Selected Doctoral Dissertations, Master's Theses and Articles

Figure 2.3 shows the cumulative frequency of theses and dissertations between 1996 and 2019. The first recovered master's thesis (Pereira, 1995) and doctoral dissertation (Aiello, 1995) date from 1995, but due to the unavailability of access to their respective digital files, they were not included in this review's final sample. The *Database of Theses and Dissertations from CAPES* was created only in 2002. Since its creation, information from papers in the period from 1996 to 2001 and, subsequently, papers between 1987 and 1995 were compiled in the Catalog. Despite this effort, it should be considered that files in digital format were not required by postgraduate programs until the 90s, which made them difficult to access. Once the articles were identified directly in the curriculum of the advisors, the breadth of the researched period extrapolates the theses and dissertations and comprises the years from 1989 to 2019.

The number of theses and dissertations on reading and writing, based on the equivalence paradigm, had a significant increase from 2009 (Fig. 2.3) with a regular production since then, which shows the interest of the post graduate programs in the production of knowledge related to a subject of significant social relevance. The higher number of Master's theses compared to doctoral dissertations reflects the organization of the postgraduate programs in the Brazil, with a higher number of courses and master's students compared to the doctoral ones.

The recovered theses and dissertations were produced in postgraduate programs of nine different Universities (Fig. 2.4). The Federal University of São Carlos (UFSCar) concentrates the largest amount, followed by the Federal University of

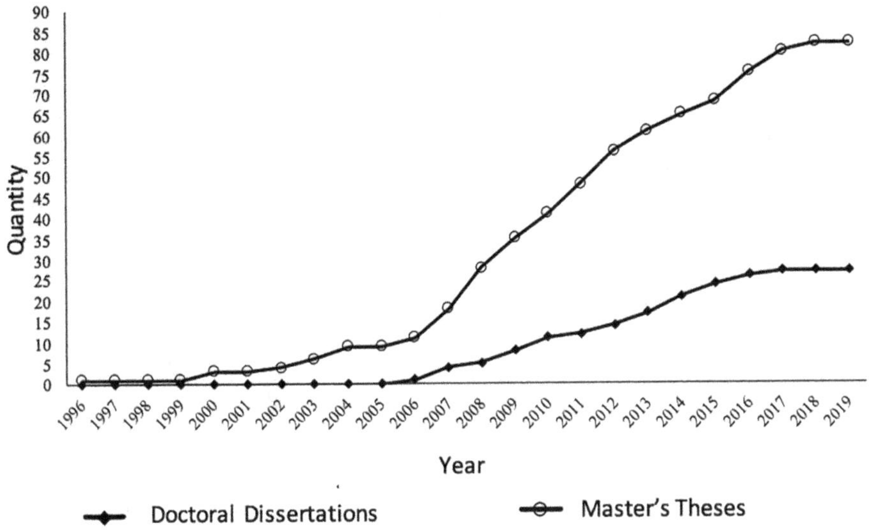

Fig. 2.3 Distribution of recovered doctoral dissertations and master's theses over the period 1995–2019

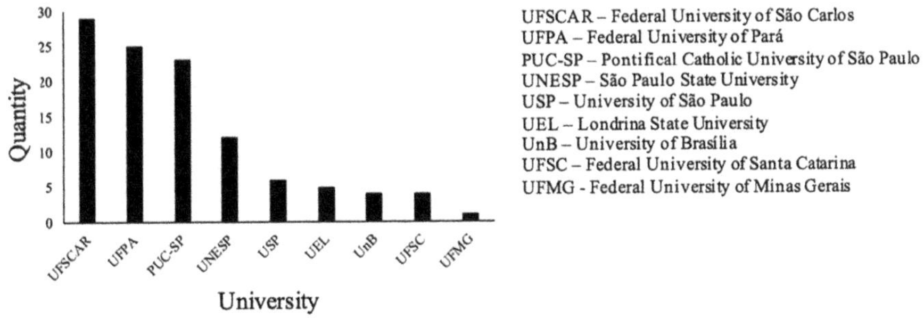

Fig. 2.4 Distribution of dissertations and theses by university

Pará (UFPA) and the Pontifical Catholic University of São Paulo (PUC-SP). UFSCar's leading role is justified by the fact that research in this area began in the Special Education program, led by UFSCar professors Deisy das Graças de Souza and Júlio César de Rose, who are also, respectively, Coordinator and Research Director of the National Institute of Science and Technology on Behavior, Cognition and Teaching (*Instituto Nacional de Ciência e Tecnologia sobre Comportamento, Cognição e Ensino* [INCT-ECCE]; https://inctecce.com.br/pt/). This Institute develops research programs at three levels: basic, translational and applied science. Each of these programs includes different research projects and subprojects, and at least three explicitly address reading and writing: (1) Recombinative generalization and symbolic repertoires; (2) Basic and remedial instruction in reading; and (3) Reading, writing and mathematics in the classroom.

Tables 2.1, 2.2 and 2.3 present, respectively, the synthesis of the selected doctoral dissertations (N = 27), master's theses (N = 82) and articles (N = 79), ordered chronologically. The following information is presented: (1) author(s) of the study; (2) information about the participants, such as age – children, teenagers and/or adults; developmental characteristics or diagnosis (e.g., typical or atypical development, specific diagnoses) and number of participants in the research (N); and (3) the teaching or assessment program used in the study. In addition, for doctoral dissertations and master's theses (Tables 2.1 and 2.2 respectively), the following are presented: (1) the Higher Education Institution (HEI) where the study was affiliated to and (2) the main textual unit used – phrases, words, syllables, letters, or texts.

Many of the characteristics reported in the theses and dissertations are repeated in the articles, since many of these are derived from those (e.g., Amorese, 2007; Amorese & Haydu, 2010; Quinteiro, 2014; Quinteiro et al., 2014; Reis, 2008; Reis et al., 2009). As for the participants, given that the investigated repertoire (reading and writing) is typically learned in the early years of education, the vast majority of studies involved children, and only a few were conducted with teenagers and/or adults. In the case of adults and teenagers, these generally presented some type of cognitive and/or physical impairment related to different diagnoses: Down Syndrome (DS), Intellectual Disability (ID), Visual Impairment (VI), Autism Spectrum Disorder (ASD), Cerebral Palsy (CP), Mental Disability (MD), Hearing Loss (HL), and Attention-Deficit Hyperactivity Disorder (ADHD). There are also studies with teenagers, adults, and college students (e.g., Hanna et al., 2008, 2011; Inhauser, 2012, described in Chap. 10; Laporte, 2014) with typical development; in this case, research aims to investigate the basic processes underlying reading and/or writing and are carried out with the use of pseudoalphabet or pseudowords. Among the studies carried out with children, there is also a predominance of participants with atypical development, with some diagnosis. Most studies were carried out with a small number of participants, between one and 23, and in only 11 studies the number was greater than 23. The predominance of single-subject designs justifies these numbers.

Most studies used computerized teaching programs, which, in general, have advantages compared to non-computerized programs in terms of planning and recording sessions, trial automation, consequences and records, minimizing errors (of procedure and record) and making sessions more flexible and dynamic. The use of the following programs/software was identified: *Reading Teaching Program* (*Programa de Ensino de Leitura* [*ProgLeit*]) in off-line version, which originated the *Learning to Read and Write in Small Steps®* (*Aprendendo a Ler e Escrever em Pequenos Passos* [ALEPP] – Rosa Filho et al., 1998); Master (*Mestre*, Goyos & Almeida, 1996), which also served as the basis for the development of *MestreLibras* (Elias et al., 2005); EQUIV (Pimentel, 1997) from which EQUIVIUM was originated (Pimentel et al., 2009); *MemoLab_LEITURA* (Carvalho et al., 2002); *Desenvolve* (Alves de Oliveira, 2004); MTS (Dube, 1991); PROLER (Assis & Santos, 2010; Assis et al., 2014); REL (Santos et al., 1997); *Scheduled Contingency* (*Contingência Programada*, Batitucci et al., 2006); EAM (Capobianco, n.d.) and

Table 2.1 Summary of selected doctoral dissertations

Author	HEI	Participants			Textual unity	Program
		Age	Features	N		
Ponciano (2006)	PUC-SP	Children Adults	In recovery Elementary school students DS VI	6	Phrase	Software: *Mestre*
Elias (2007)	UFSCar	Teenagers Adults	Deaf Experience in signaling ID	13	Word	Software: *MestreLibras*
Hayashi (2007)	UNESP	Children (C) Teacher (T)	Difficulties in reading and writing	4 (C) 3 (T)	Word	Software: *Mestre*
Zuliani (2007)	UFSCar	Children	Difficulties in reading and writing	16	Word	Software: *Mestre*
Alves (2008)	UFPA	Adults	Delayed cognitive development	4	Word	Software: REL
Bagaiolo (2009)	USP	Children Teenagers	ASD	4	Word	Software: Equiv
Carvalho (2009)	UnB	Children	Illiterate	38	Word	Software: *MemoLabLEITURA* Phonological and graphophonemic training
Sella (2009)	UFSCar	Teenagers Adults	Deaf	6	Phrase	Software: *Mestre*
Oliveira (2010a)	UFPA	Children	CP	56	Word	Software: *Desenvolve*
Oliveira (2010b)	UFSCar	Not Informed	Elementary School students ID	2	Word	Software: ALEPP (Module 1 and 2)
Silva (2010)	UFSC	Teenagers Adults	ID DS MD	8	Word	Software: *Mestre*
Machado (2011)	UFSC	Children	Preschoolers Illiterate	11	Word Syllable	Cards with pictures, syllables and words printed
de Freitas (2012)	UFSCar	Children	ID	5	Word	Prerequisite teaching software Special reading software
Oliveira (2012)	UFSCar	Teenagers Adults	University students	8	Word	Software: *MestreLibras*

(continued)

Table 2.1 (continued)

Author	HEI	Participants			Textual unity	Program
		Age	Features	N		
Reis (2013)	UFSCar	Children	Difficulty in reading and writing 1st and 2nd year students	5	Word Syllable Letter	Computerized word construction task
Souza (2013)	UFPA	Teenagers Adults	Congenital blindness Braille literate No knowledge of the Roman alphabet	3	Word Syllable Letter	Teaching procedure with Words, Syllables and Letters printed in relief (Braille and Roman alphabet)
Tripiana-Barbosa (2013)	UEL	Children Teenagers Adults	ID	6	Word Syllable	Board games
Llausas (2014)	PUC-SP	Teenagers	High school students	6	Word	Software: *MestreLibras*
Marques (2014)	UFSCar	Children	2nd, 3rd and 4th grade students	28	Word	Software: ALEPP (Module 1) ALEPP *gamified* version
Quinteiro (2014)	UFSCar	Adults	Literate Acquired VI	4	Word	Conditional discrimination with tactile stimuli (Roman and Braille)
Veiga (2014)	UFSCar	Children	Rudimentary reading repertoire	21	Word	Software: ALEPP (Module 1)
Coimbra (2015)	PUC-SP	Children	3rd and 5th year students	18		Writing assessment instrument (IAEs-I)
Garcia (2015)	UFSCar	Children	Moderate to profound hearing loss	16	Word	Software: MTS (Libras signs and Roman alphabet)
Silva (2015)	PUC-SP	Children	Preschoolers	6	Word Syllable Letter	Software: Sidman
Paixão (2016)	UFPA	Children	ASD	3	Phase Word	Software: *Proler*
Tizo (2016)	UnB	Children Teenagers	Learning disability – ID ADHD CP	20	Word	Software: ALEPP (Module 1)
Mesquita (2017)	UFPA	Children	Didn't read words or syllables, just letters	12	Word Syllable	Software: *Proler*

Table 2.2 Synthesis of the selected dissertations

Author	University	Participants			Textual unit	Program
		Type	Features	N		
Souza (1996)	UFSCar	Children	Preschoolers	12	Syllable	Software developed by Dube and McIlvanc (1989)
Rodrigues (2000)	UFSC	Children	CP	5	Word	Matching to sample Procedure
Silva (2000)	UFSCar	Children	Non-literate	7	Word	Matching to sample and exclusion procedure
Santos (2002)	UFPA	Teenagers Adults	Illiterate	6	Syllable Word	Software: *ProgLeit*
Feio (2003)	UFPA	Children	VI	4	Word	Matching to sample procedure with dictated words, objects and words written in Braille
Hayashi (2003)	UNESP	Children (C) Teacher (T)	Difficulties in reading and writing Undisciplined	4 (C) 1 (T)	Word	Software: *Mestre*
Bastos (2004)	UFPA	Children	Difficulty in reading and writing	5	Phrase Word Syllable	Conditional discrimination
Ramos (2004)	UFPA	Children	Initial grades of elementary school	8	Word	Software: *ProgLeit*
Rodrigues (2004)	UFSC	Children	Background of school failure	18	Word	Conditional discrimination with spoken and printed words
Camelo (2006)	UFPA	Children	Preschoolers	3	Word Syllable	Software: REL
Nibu (2006)	PUC-SP	Children	2nd grade students	20	Word	Software: *Mestre*
Albuquerque (2007)	UFPA	Children	Difficulty in reading	5	Phrase Word Syllable	Conditional discrimination with syllables, words and sentences, in spoken, pictorial and printed modality
Amorese (2007)	UEL	Children Teacher (T)	Early childhood education	3 (T) 32 (C)	Word	Conditional discrimination with dictated and printed word, pictures and anagram
Araújo (2007)	UFPA	Children Teenagers	Dyslexia	3	Word	Software: *Progleit*

(continued)

Table 2.2 (continued)

Author	University	Participants			Textual unit	Program
		Type	Features	N		
Barros (2007)	UFPA	Children	Preschoolers	5	Syllable	Conditional discrimination with printed and dictated syllables
Gomes (2007a)	UFSCar	Children	ASD	4	Word	Conditional discrimination with pictures, printed words and naming
Gomes (2007b)	USP	Children	Non-literate	4	Word	Software: EQUIV
Maués (2007)	UFPA	Children	Preschoolers	5	Syllable	Software for teaching conditional discriminations between syllables
Andrade (2008)	UEL	Children	Learning disabilities	5	Word	Conditional discrimination with dictated word, printed word, and word construction
Castro (2008)	UNESP	Children (C) Teacher (T)	Problems in literacy	21 (C) 3 (T)	Word	Software: *ProgLeit*
Costa (2008)	PUC-SP	Children	Indication for the make-up project	37	Word	Instrument for the assessment of reading initial repertoire (IAL-I)
de Freitas (2008)	UFSCar	Children	MD	3	Word	Software: ALEPP
Faggiani (2008)	USP	Adults	NI	12	Word Syllable	Matching-to-sample with dictated and printed words (Pseudo-Alphabet)
Fernandes (2008)	PUC-SP	Children	Diagnosis of insufficient repertoire 2nd grade students	8	Word	Software: *Mestre*
Haber (2008)	UFPA	Children	Reading difficulty	5	Phrase Word Syllable	Conditional discrimination with spoken and printed words or phrases and pictures; syllable naming
Leite (2008)	USP	Children	Preschoolers	5	Word	Software: EQUIV

(continued)

Table 2.2 (continued)

Author	University	Participants Type	Participants Features	N	Textual unit	Program
Llausas (2008)	PUC-SP	Teenagers Adults	Youngster and adult education (EJA)	5	Word	Software: *Mestre*
Reis (2008)	UFSCar	Children	Difficulty in learning to read and write 1st, 2nd and 3rd grade students	64	Word	Reading and writing teaching program developed by de Rose et al. (1989, 1996)
Barros (2009)	PUC-SP	Children Teenagers Adults	DS	4	Word	Software: *Mestre*
César (2009)	PUC-SP	Children	Elementary school students	17	Word	Software: *Mestre*
Feitosa (2009)	UFPA	Adults	Blind	3	Word	Conditional discrimination with Braille word and raised Roman alphabet word
Leitão (2009)	UFPA	Adults	Blind Readers fluent in Braille	3	Word	Conditional discrimination with Braille word and raised Roman alphabet word
Lima (2009)	UFSCar	Children	Difficulty in learning to read	13	Word	Software: ALEPP (Module 1) Recreational activity program (PAR)
Silva (2009)	PUC-SP	Children	Unsatisfactory performance Students of the 3rd grade of elementary school	40	Word	Instrument for the evaluation of reading – Initial repertoire (IAL-I) Software: *Mestre*
Souza (2009)	USP	Children	Typical development No word reading	7	Word Syllable	Software: EQUIV
Bataglini (2010)	UNESP	Children	Pre-lingual deafness CI users	9	Word	Software: MTS and exclusion
Cezar (2010)	PUC-SP	Teenagers	Diagnosis of verbal agreement repertoire (DRCVR)	20	Phrase Word	Software: *Mestre* (geography module) Diagnosis of verbal agreement repertoire (DRCVR)

(continued)

Table 2.2 (continued)

Author	University	Participants			Textual unit	Program
		Type	Features	N		
Coimbra (2010)	PUC-SP	Children	Students of the 3rd grade of Cycle I of the elementary school	15	Phrase Word Syllable	Software: *MestreLibras*
Martimiano (2010)	PUC-SP	Children	Unsatisfactory performance in literacy Students of the 4th grade of elementary school	8	Word Syllable Letter	Software: *Mestre*
Ponso (2010)	PUC-SP	Children	Background of school failure 4th grade students	8	Word	Software: *Mestre*
Vale (2010)	UFPA	Children	Difficulties in reading	6	Phrase Word Syllable	Conditional discrimination with syllables, dictated and printed words presented on cards
Aguilar (2011)	UFPA	Adults	Blind Fluent Braille readers	3	Word	Conditional discrimination with raised objects, letters and words in Braille and Roman alphabet
Anastasio-Pessan (2011)	UNESP	Children	Hearing impairment (HL) Cochlear implant (CI)	6	Word	Software: MTS
Benitez (2011)	UFSCar	Adults Family	ID	6	Word	Software: *ProgLeit* (Module 1)
Santos (2011)	PUC-SP	Adults	EJA students Background of school failure	11	Word Syllable Letter	Software: *Mestre*
Zaine (2011)	UFSCar	Children Teenagers	Developmental delay	14	Word	Simple and conditional discriminations with simple words (GEIC Software)
Zanco (2011)	PUC-SP	Adults	High school students Difficulties in reading and writing	5	Phrase Word Syllable	Software: Jclic
Guimarães (2012)	UFSCar	Adults Children	Typical development No reading repertoire	10	Word	Software: *MestreLibras* (pseudo-words)

(continued)

Table 2.2 (continued)

Author	University	Participants Type	Participants Features	N	Textual unit	Program
Inhauser (2012)	USP	Adults	University students	12	Word	Software: GEIC (pseudo-literate, phonemes)
Melo (2012)	UFPA	Adults Children	Blind	2	Word Syllable	Conditional discrimination with dictated and written syllables, naming syllables, reading text and understanding words, copying and dictating these words (Braille and raised Roman letters) and objects
Paixão (2012)	UFPA	Children	CP	3	Word Syllable	Software: PROLER
Rainatto (2012)	PUC-SP	Children	Students of the 3rd grade of elementary school Difficulty in reading and writing	5	Word Syllable Letter	Software: *Mestre* Simple and complex syllables
Santos (2012a)	PUC-SP	Children	ASD	2	Word	Software: EQUIVIUM
Santos (2012b)	PUC-SP	Teenagers Adults	ID Special school pupils	5	Word	Software: *Mestre*
Santos (2012c)	UNESP	Children	CI users or hearing aid users	20	Word Syllable Letter	Software: *ProgLeit*
Carvalho (2013)	UFSCar	Children	Asperger's syndrome	1	Word Text	Software: ALEPP (Module 2) Complementary activities
Fernandes (2013)	UnB	Children	Global developmental disorder	3	Word	Software: *Contingência Programada*
Lucchesi (2013)	UNESP	Children	Hearing impairment CI users	2	Word	Software: ALEPP (Module 1)
Pereira (2013)	UFPA	Adults	Deep AD, bilateral CI users	3	Word	Software: EAM

(continued)

Table 2.2 (continued)

Author	University	Participants			Textual unit	Program
		Type	Features	N		
Tenorio (2013)	UFSCar	Children	Difficulty in reading and writing	9	Word	Board game with choice activities with picture, dictated and printed word, picture naming, word construction (taking dictation and copying) and reading words with simple syllables.
Gomes (2014)	UFSCar	Adults Teenagers Children	ID	14	Word	Conditional discrimination similar to Module 1 of ALEPP software
Guidugli (2014)	UNESP	Children	3rd and 4th grade students Problems with externalizing behaviors	4	Word Syllable	Software: ALEPP (Module 1)
Laporte (2014)	UnB	Adults	University students	12	Phrase Word	Software: *Contingência Programada* with pseudo-phrases and pseudo-words
Neves (2014)	UNESP	Children	Prelingual HL	8	Phrase	Software: PROLER
Bandeira (2015)	UFPA	Children	Minimum repertoire of letter, syllable and word naming	7	Phrase Word	Software: PROLER
Rique (2015)	UNESP	Children	AD severe-deep CI users	3	Word	Software: MTS
Santos (2015)	UFPA	Children	Deaf	3	Word	Software: PROLER
Alvarenga (2016)	UFMG	Children	Typical development Learning disability	13	Word	Software: ALEPP (Module 1)
Bastos (2016)	PUC-SP	Children	ASD	3	Word	Software: *MestreLibras*
Donadeli (2016)	UFSCar	Children	Students of the 2nd grade of elementary school	10	Phrase Word	Conditional discrimination with dictated and printed sentence, picture
Fava-Menzori (2016)	UNESP	Children	Communication disorders and/or ID	9	Word	Software: ALEPP (Module 1)

(continued)

Table 2.2 (continued)

		Participants			Textual	
Author	University	Type	Features	N	unit	Program
Ferrão (2016)	PUC-SP	Children	Students of early childhood education	6	Word Syllable Letter	Software: *MestreLibras*
Menotti (2016)	UFSCar	Children – Parents	ASD	3	Word	Conditional discrimination with dictated and printed word, games
Rodrigues (2016)	UFSCar	Children	Students with learning difficulties	7	Word	Software: ALEPP (Module 1)
Garcia (2017)	UFSCar	Children	Less than 15% correct score on the reading and writing network (LRA) assessment	12	Word	Software: ALEPP (Module 1)
Oliveira (2017)	UFPA	Children	ASD	3	Word Syllable Letter	Exclusion and CRMTS with letters, syllables, words (dictated and printed) and pictures
Silva (2017)	UFSCar	Adults	ID	3	Word Syllable	Software: ALEPP (Module 1)
Suzuki (2017)	UEL	Children	Could not read and write words with consonants or attended early childhood education	4	Word	*AbraKedabra* game (Consonantal meeting)
Cravo (2018)	UNESP	Children	Over 5 years of hearing deprivation CI users	3	Word	Software: ALEPP (Module 2) Software: ALEPP (Module 2 adapted)
Rondon (2018)	PUC-SP	Adults	EJA students	5	Phrase	Software: Jclic

the open access Jclic, developed by Francesc Busquest (https://clic.xtec.cat/legacy/es/index.html).

The most used programs in the set of researches retrieved were ALEPP (together with *ProgLeit*) and *Mestre*, both developed at UFSCar. ALEPP is composed of three main teaching modules, Modules 1, 2 and 3, which focus, respectively, on the teaching of regular words (composed of consonant and vowel syllables), words with irregularities in the Portuguese language (e.g., digraphs, s with z sound, ç) and the reading of short texts in the form of books. These modules are described in detail in Section II of this book. Furthermore, a new module (called Preparatory Module) is

Table 2.3 Summary of selected articles

Reference	Participants			Teaching program
	Type	Features	N	
de Rose et al. (1989)	Children	Background of school failure	6	Conditional discriminations spoken-printed words (regular) and "exclusion"
Melchiori et al. (1992)	Children	Preschoolers	3	Conditional discriminations spoken-printed words and "exclusion"
de Rose et al. (1996)	Children	Non-literate	11	Conditional discriminations spoken-printed words (regular) and "exclusion" (51 words) with and without copying with construction
Medeiros et al. (1997)	Adults	Non-literate	1	Teaching spoken-printed words (regular) conditional discriminations
Maia et al. (1999)	Children	Background of school failure	10	Conditional discriminations spoken-printed words (regular) and "exclusion"
Medeiros et al. (1999)	Children	Deficit in reading and writing No background of failure	1	Conditional discriminations spoken-printed words (regular) and "exclusion"
Medeiros and Teixeira (2000)	Children	Difficulties in reading and writing	6	Conditional discriminations spoken-printed words (regular) and "exclusion"
Melchiori et al. (2000)	Children	Special education Non-literate	23	Teaching spoken-printed word and "exclusion" (51 words) conditional discriminations with and without copying with construction (de Rose et al., 1996)
Rodrigues and Medeiros (2001)	Children	CP	5	Conditional discriminations spoken-printed words
Matos et al. (2002)	Children	School age	66	Conditional discriminations spoken-printed words and pictures; oralization and copying-by-construction procedures
Medeiros and Silva (2002)	Children	In literacy process	7	Conditional discriminations spoken-printed words (regular) and "exclusion"
Saraiva and Hübner (2001)	Children	Non-literate	12	Software: EQUIV
Hanna et al. (2004)	Children	Background of failure	6	Choice with response constructed with identity delay (CRMTS)
Medeiros et al. (2004)	Children	Difficulties in reading and writing	11	Software: *Mestre*

(continued)

Table 2.3 (continued)

Reference	Participants			Teaching program
	Type	Features	N	
Péres and Carrara (2004)	Children	Difficulties in reading and writing	5	Software: *Mestre*
Bernardino Jr. et al. (2006)	Children	Difficulties in reading and writing	4	Software: ALEPP (Module 1) and phonological awareness training
Alves et al. (2007)	Teenagers Adults	Students of the Association of Parents and Friends of the Exceptional (APAE)	3	Software: REL
Medeiros et al. (2007)	Children	Absence of reading and identification of numbers	12	Software: *Mestre*
Serejo et al. (2007)	Children	Absence of reading and writing	9	Software: MTS
Souza et al. (2007)	Children	Preschoolers with typical development	18	Choose with constructed response (computerized)
Hanna et al. (2008)	Adults	University students	20	Software: MTS
Postalli et al. (2008)	Children	Background of school failure	6	Software: ALEPP
Sudo et al. (2008)	Children	Deficit in reading and writing, no background of failure	3	Games that taught different relationships: printed word-picture, printed word-manuscript, spoken word-picture, printed word-spoken word, CRMTS
de Souza et al. (2009)	Children	Low scores in reading and spelling simple words	29	Computerized program for teaching spoken word-printed words and "exclusion" (51 words) conditional discriminations with and without copying with construction (de Rose et al., 1996)
Hübner et al. (2009)	Children	Preschoolers	4	Conditional discriminations spoken words-drawings, spoken words-syllables, naming syllables
Reis et al. (2009)	Children	Difficulties in reading and writing	64	Conditional discriminations spoken-printed words and "exclusion" (de Rose et al., 1989)
Amorese and Haydu (2010)	Children	Early childhood education	32 (3 groups)	Teaching and/or assessment, with the use of paper cards, of relations: dictated or printed word-word construction, dictated word or picture-printed word, picture-printed word, printed word-picture, picture-word construction, printed word naming

(continued)

Table 2.3 (continued)

Reference	Participants			Teaching program
	Type	Features	N	
Hanna et al. (2010)	Teenagers Adults	University students	8	Software: MTS
Leite and Hübner (2009)	Children	Non-literate	5	Software: EQUIV
Lima et al. (2010)	Children	Students from 1st to 4th grade Didn't read or write	12	Recreational activity program (PAR), followed by the teaching of 6-word spoken-printed word conditional discriminations
Sampaio et al. (2010)	Children	1st grade student	9	Software: REL
Souza and Hübner (2010)	Children	Early childhood education No repertoire for reading and writing regular disyllable words	9	Games that taught different relations: printed word-picture, printed word- handwritten word, spoken word-picture, printed word-spoken word, CRMTS (Sudo et al., 2008)
Alves et al. (2011)	Teenagers Adults	Cognitive retardation	2	Software: REL
Fernandes and Moroz (2011)	Children	Difficulties in reading and writing	8	Software: *Mestre*
Hanna et al. (2011)	Teenagers Adults	University students	20	Software: MTS
Medeiros et al. (2011)	Children	Students of the 1st grade of elementary school	17	Software: *Mestre*
Nunes et al. (2012)	Children	Difficulties in reading and writing	3	Software: ALEPP
Benitez and Domeniconi (2012)	Teenagers Family	Borderline and intellectually impaired	3	Software: *ProgLeit*
Machado and Haydu (2012)	Children	Over 50% errors in word reading	17	Conditional discriminations involving spoken words, drawings and words presented on cards
Ponciano and Moroz (2012)	Children	Didn't read sentences	3	Software: *Mestre*
Santos and Almeida-Verdu (2012)	Children	Deafness No mastery of reading and libras	1	Software: MTS
Cabral et al. (2012)	Children	Unsuccessful background of learning to read and write	5	Conditional discrimination spoken-written syllables, spoken-written words exclusion (presented on Styrofoam plates)

(continued)

Table 2.3 (continued)

Reference	Participants			Teaching program
	Type	Features	N	
Souza and Assis (2013)	Teenagers	EJA/APAE students	2	Software: REL
Reis et al. (2013)	Children	Low performance in reading and spelling	4	Software: ALEPP
Neves and Almeida-Verdu (2014)	Teenagers	Cerebellar hypoplasia Impairment of oral/expressive language	1	Organized games with spoken and printed words and corresponding three-dimensional objects
Oliveira et al. (2014)	Children	CP Motor impairment Absence of fluent oral language	3	Software: PROLER
Quinteiro et al. (2014)	Adults	Acquired total visual impairment Literate Beginning braille students	4	Teaching auditory-tactile conditional discriminations (dictated or printed pseudowords in raised Roman alphabet and dictated or printed pseudowords dictated and printed in Braille)
Almeida-Verdu and Oliveira (2014)	Teenagers	Difficulties in elementary school	1	Software: *ProgLeit*
Bandini et al. (2014)	Adults	Illiterate	8	Software: ALEPP (Module 1 – Est. 1; Module 2 – Est. 2)
Zaine et al. (2014)	Children Teenagers	ID Background of difficulty in reading	14	Software: ALEPP
Anastácio-Pessan et al. (2015)	Children	HL CI	6	Software: MTS
Benitez et al. (2015)	Children	ID	16	Teaching selection relations (BB, CC, AB, AC, BC, CD) and execution (whole word, syllable, consonant and vowel reading)
Fonseca et al. (2015)	Children	Students of the 1st grade of elementary school	5	Software: PROLER
Haydu et al. (2015)	Children	7–9 years old	21	Software: PROLER
Lucchesi et al. (2015a)	Children	ID sensorineural, bilateral, deep	2	Software: ALEPP
Lucchesi et al. (2015b)	Children	Neurosensory ID, bilateral, profound with CI, 2 years old	2	Software: ALEPP
Zanco and Moroz (2015)	Teenagers	High school students	4	Conditional discriminations; Software: Jclic

(continued)

Table 2.3 (continued)

Reference	Participants			Teaching program
	Type	Features	N	
Bandeira et al. (2016)	Children	Typical development	7	Software: PROLER
Ferreira et al. (2016)	Children	Background of school failure	6	Software: *ProgLeit*
Gomes and de Souza (2016)	Children	ASD Presence of speech Non-literate Chronological age from 5 years	3	Teaching word and picture naming, picture-printed word, printed word-picture, dictated word-picture/printed word
Mesquita and Hanna (2016)	Children	Didn't read words	12	Conditional discrimination training (DMTS) with letters, syllables or words, post naming and pairing test
Silveira et al. (2016)	Children	Students of the 5th grade of elementary school Low result in Ideb	187	Reading and writing diagnosis 1 and 2, *ProgLeit* assessment
Benitez and Domeniconi (2016)	Teenagers Familuy	ID	5	Conditional discrimination training, computerized, applied by family members
Bertao and Postalli (2017)	Children	Students of the first 3 years of elementary school	6	Story books and board game
Donadeli and Domeniconi (2017)	Children	No clinical diagnosis	10	Software: ALEPP
Gomes et al. (2017a)	Children	DS ID Difficulties in oralization	2	Software: ALEPP e *ProgLeit*
Gomes et al. (2017b)	Children Teenagers Adults	Non-literate With and without ID (n = 4)	16	Software: ALEPP e *ProgLeit*
Rique et al. (2017)	Children	Severe-deep ID CI users	3	Software: MTS
Feliciano and Moroz (2018)	Teenagers	Profound deafness Communication exclusively by LIBRAS	3	Software: *MestreLibras*
Paixão and Assis (2018)	Children	ASD With repertoire of following simple instructions With a vocal repertoire of echoic behavior	3	Software: PROLER

(continued)

Table 2.3 (continued)

Reference	Participants			Teaching program
	Type	Features	N	
Cravo and Almeida-Verdu (2018)	Children	Students with a background of failure in learning to read	14	Software: ALEPP
Lucchesi et al. (2018)	Children	CI	1	Software: ALEPP
Alvarez and Almeida-Verdu (2019)	Children	Attending the resource room	9	Software: ALEPP
Menotti et al. (2019)	Children	ASD	3	*ProgLeit* (DLE) and games with printed words and pictures
Millan and Postalli (2019)	Children	ASD	2	Teaching printed picture-word conditional discriminations and picture naming
Silveira et al. (2019)	Children	Elementary School students Low performance on Prova Brasil	194	Reading and writing diagnosis 3
Suzuki and Souza (2019)	Children	Didn't read or write	1	*AbraKedabra* game and cards with pictures and words
Cravo et al. (2019)	Children	Bilateral, pre-lingual, severe and profound deafness	1	Software: ALEPP (Module 2)
Rodrigues and Postalli (2019)	Children	Low reading repertoire	3	Software: ALEPP (Module 1)

under construction with the aim of teaching prerequisites for reading and writing and is also described in Chap. 7.

The ultimate goal of the literacy process is fluent, generalized writing and reading with text comprehension, but teaching this repertoire can be based on the use of smaller units than the text. Thus, the process of teaching reading and writing involves a series of decisions, including the choice of the size of the initial textual unit to be taught. It is known that both in the natural school setting and in research situations, different textual units (syllables, letters, sentences) can be used. In the school setting, the size of the textual unit is also related to different teaching methods: phonic, syllabic and global, which use graphemes/phonemes, syllables and whole words, respectively, during the literacy process. In the set of studies presented here we observe the predominance of words as the teaching unit. The use of words is justified by the fact that most of these studies are interested in the study of reading comprehension. An additional feature of the studies with words is the predominant use of regular words with simple syllables (consonants and vowel), which is especially evident in the studies that used the ALEPP program, with Module 1 being used more frequently than the other modules.

Considering the predominant interest in reading with comprehension, the linguistic system most used in the studies is the Roman alphabet. However, studies with other systems, such as Braille (e.g., Feitosa, 2009; Leitão, 2009; Melo, 2012; Quinteiro, 2014), Libras (e.g., Elias, 2007; Garcia, 2015; Santos & Almeida-Verdu, 2012), and pseudoalphabet (e.g., Hanna et al., 2008, 2011; Inhauser, 2012; Laporte, 2014) are found.

Finally, there is a significantly larger number of studies with individual applications of teaching procedures and few studies with group applications (e.g., Amorese, 2007; Castro, 2008). Also, there is a clear predominance of investigations on reading compared to those on writing, with only two studies explicitly devoted to writing, one of them referring to the assessment of this repertoire (Coimbra, 2015) and the other to teaching (Reis, 2013). However, although the writing repertoire is not the dependent variable in most studies, this performance is often assessed and required, especially using the matching-to-sample procedure with constructed response, in the form of copying a text and taking dictation.[2] Procedures with constructed response have been used with the aim of emphasizing textual units smaller than the word to favor learning to read or, conversely, when reading is taught and secondary effects on the writing repertoire are verified (e.g., de Rose et al., 1996, 2009).

2.4 Final Considerations

This chapter presented a synthesis of some of the characteristics of the set of studies on reading and writing, based on the stimulus equivalence paradigm and the conditional discrimination procedure, developed in Brazil, based on the analysis of their abstracts. Thus, it presents the state of the art of knowledge production on the subject. In this sense, it is expected that this chapter could work as a reference material allowing people interested in the topic to easily identify studies developed with different populations, programs and teaching units and, following the references, gain access to their full versions.

The mapping of this set of studies allowed us to identify consolidated contributions in the area, as well as gaps and deficiencies. Among the contributions, a large number of studies with positive learning outcomes were conducted with populations that often have difficulties using traditional methods. Among the deficiencies in the literature, which are the starting point for raising new research problems, there is a need for more research on writing and reading with words with language irregularities as well as with textual units smaller or larger than the word. Collective, natural environment investigations have already been carried out (e.g., Amorese,

---

[2] In the *Constructed Response Matching to Sample* (CRMTS) procedure, the participant's task consists in selecting, one by one, letters, syllables or words to compose a printed or dictated word (or sentence) presented as a sample stimulus, which would characterize writing in a copy and dictation situation, respectively (Dube et al., 1991; Paixão & Assis, 2017).

2007; Castro, 2008; Reis, 2008), but similar additional investigations still have much to contribute in terms of extending the external validity of the teaching strategies being used.

As a final remark, it is also worth pointing out the limitations of the review conducted in this chapter. Bibliographic review require making decision that may include or exclude important references. In addition, the characterization of the studies was carried out primarily based on the reading of the abstracts and only when these did not provide the minimum information of interest was the method section read. Thus, details of the studies are not available in this chapter, as they are not described in their abstracts.

References

Aguilar, F. (2011). *Emergência da leitura de palavras de inglês com recombinação de onset e rime em braille e alfabeto romano em relevo para cegos.* Master's thesis, Universidade Federal do Pará. Repositório Institucional UFPA. http://repositorio.ufpa.br/jspui/bitstream/2011/10462/1/Dissertacao_EmergenciaLeituraPalavras.pdf

Aiello, A. L. R. (1995). *Efeitos de um procedimento de resposta construída sobre a rede de relações de equivalência envolvida na leitura e escrita em crianças com história de fracasso escolar.* Unpublished doctoral dissertation. Universidade de São Paulo.

Albuquerque, E. S. (2007). *Ensino de leitura de frases com compreensão a crianças de segunda série do Ensino Fundamental.* Master's thesis, Universidade Federal do Pará. Repositório Institucional UFPA. http://repositorio.ufpa.br/jspui/bitstream/2011/1907/1/Dissertacao_EnsinoLeituraFrases.pdf

Albuquerque, A. R., & Melo, R. M. (2005). Equivalência de estímulos: Conceito, implicações e possibilidades de aplicação. In J. R. Abreu-Rodrigues, & M. R. Ribeiro (Orgs.), *Análise do comportamento: Pesquisa, teoria e aplicação* (pp. 99–112). Artmed.

Almeida-Verdu, A. C. M., & Oliveira, F. M. (2014). Accuracy in dictation after improvement of reading and copying skills in a student with learning difficulties. *Estudos de Psicologia (Campinas), 31*(1), 25–34. https://doi.org/10.1590/0103-166X2014000100003

Alvarenga, O. M. B. (2016). *O efeito do treino de habilidades de consciência fonológica: sobre o aprendizado de leitura em um programa individualizado de ensino.* Master's thesis, Universidade Federal de Minas Gerais. Repositório Institucional UFMG. https://repositorio.ufmg.br/bitstream/1843/BUBD-ABYFSN/1/dissertao_2016_psicologiaolga_maria_busse_de_alvarengafichacatalogr_fica_folha_de_aprovao_pdf

Alvarez, M. F. C., & Almeida-Verdu, A. C. M. (2019). Análise dos erros dos alunos no ensino de leitura e escrita. *Revista Brasileira de Terapia Comportamental e Cognitiva, 21*(2), 186–198. https://doi.org/10.31505/rbtcc.v21i2.1205

Alves, K. R. S. (2008). *Leitura recombinativa generalizada após procedimentos de correção com fading em pessoas com atraso no desenvolvimento cognitivo.* Doctoral dissertation, Universidade Federal do Pará. Repositório Institucional UFPA. http://repositorio.ufpa.br/jspui/bitstream/2011/1791/1/Tese_LeituraRecombinativaGeneralizada.pdf

Alves de Oliveira, A. I. (2004). *Desenvolve®* [Computer Software]. Desenvolvido e registrado no INPI com o n. 07703-6.

Alves, K. R. S., Kato, O. M., Assis, G. J. A., & Maranhão, C. M. A. (2007). Leitura recombinativa em pessoas com necessidades educacionais especiais: Análise do controle parcial pelas sílabas. *Psicologia: Teoria e Pesquisa, 23*(4), 387–398. https://doi.org/10.1590/S0102-37722007000400004

Alves, K. R. S., Assis, G. J. A., Kato, O. M., & Brino, A. L. F. (2011). Leitura recombinativa após procedimentos de fading in de sílabas das palavras de ensino em pessoas com atraso no desenvolvimento cognitivo. *Acta Comportamentalia, 19*(2), 183–203.

Amorese, J. S. (2007). *Ensino de Leitura em sala de aula: contribuições do paradigma da equivalência de estímulos*. Master's thesis, Universidade Estadual de Londrina. Repositório Institucional UEL. http://www.bibliotecadigital.uel.br/document/?code=vtls000122897

Amorese, J. S., & Haydu, V. B. (2010). Ensino e aprendizagem de leitura de palavras: contribuições da análise do comportamento. *Revista Brasileira de Terapia Comportamental e Cognitiva, 12*(1–2), 197–223.

Anastácio-Pessan, F. L. (2011). *Evolução da nomeação após fortalecimento de relações auditivo-visuais em crianças com deficiência auditiva e implante coclear.* Master's thesis, Universidade Estadual Paulista Júlio Mesquita Filho – Bauru. Repositório Institucional UNESP. https://repositorio.unesp.br/bitstream/handle/11449/97500/anastaciopessan_fl_me_bauru.pdf?sequence=1&isAllowed=y

Anastácio-Pessan, F. L., Almeida-Verdu, A. C. M., Bevilacqua, M. C., & de Souza, D. G. (2015). Usando o paradigma de equivalência para aumentar a correspondência na fala de crianças com implante coclear na nomeação de figuras e na leitura. *Psicologia: Reflexão e Crítica, 28*(2), 365–377. https://doi.org/10.1590/1678-7153.201528217

Andrade, L. V. (2008). *Ensino de leitura via equivalência de estímulos: Jogos de mesa como recursos de avaliação.* Master's thesis, Universidade Estadual de Londrina. Repositório Institucional UEL. http://www.uel.br/pos/pgac/wp-content/uploads/2014/03/Ensino-de-leitura-via-equival%C3%AAnvcia-de-est%C3%ADmulos-jogos-de-mesa-como-recursos-de-avalia%C3%A7%C3%A3o.pdf

Araújo, M. W. M. (2007). *Habilidades metafonológicas e desenvolvimento de leitura e escrita recombinativas em crianças com diagnóstico de dislexia.* Master's thesis, Universidade Federal do Pará. Repositório Institucional UFPA. http://repositorio.ufpa.br/jspui/bitstream/2011/1919/1/Dissertacao_HabilidadesMetafonologicasDesenvolvimento.pdf

Assis, G. J. A., & Santos, M. B. (2010). *PROLER (sistema computadorizado de ensino de comportamentos conceituais).* Universidade Federal do Pará.

Assis, G. J. A., Fonseca, A. C. G., & Bandeira, T. M. (2014). *PROLER (sistema computadorizado de ensino de comportamentos conceituais).* Universidade Federal do Pará.

Bagaiolo, L. (2009). *Padrões de aquisição de discriminação condicional durante a emergência do controle por unidades verbais mínimas na leitura em crianças com autismo e desenvolvimento típico.* Doctoral dissertation, Universidade de São Paulo. Biblioteca Digital de Teses e Dissertações da USP. https://teses.usp.br/teses/disponiveis/47/47132/tde14092009160042/publico/leilabagaiolo.pdf

Bandeira, T. M. (2015). *Efeito do ensino por resposta construída simultânea e com atraso sobre a produção e leitura de sentenças.* Master's thesis, Universidade Federal do Pará. Repositório Institucional UFPA. http://repositorio.ufpa.br/jspui/bitstream/2011/11914/1/Dissertacao_EfeitoEnsinoResposta.pdf

Bandeira, T. M., Assis, G. J. A., & de Souza, C. B. A. (2016). Comparando o efeito dos procedimentos de pareamento ao modelo simultâneo e atrasado com resposta construída no ensino de leitura e produção de sentenças. *Perspectivas em Análise do Comportamento, 7*(2), 164–182. https://doi.org/10.18761/pac.2016.012

Bandini, C. S. M., Bandini, H. H. M., Sella, A. C., & Souza, D. G. (2014). Emergence of reading and writing in illiterate adults after matching-to-sample tasks. *Paidéia, 24*(57), 75–84. https://doi.org/10.1590/1982-43272457201410

Barros, S. N. (2007). *Ensino de discriminações de sílabas e a emergência da leitura recombinativa em crianças pré-escolares.* Master's thesis, Universidade Federal do Pará. Repositório Institucional UFPA. http://repositorio.ufpa.br/jspui/bitstream/2011/5317/1/Dissertacao_EnsinoDiscriminacoesSilabas.pdf

Barros, N. M. F. C. V. (2009). *Avaliação e ensino do repertório de leitura em indivíduos com Síndrome de Down com o uso do software educacional Mestre.* Master's thesis, Pontifícia

Universidade Católica de São Paulo. Repositório Institucional PUC-SP. https://sapientia.pucsp.br/handle/handle/16516

Bastos, E. C. M. (2004). *Ensino de leitura de frases com compreensão a alunos de 2ª série de escolas públicas de Belém.* Master's thesis, Universidade Federal do Pará. Repositório Institucional da UFPA. http://repositorio.ufpa.br/jspui/bitstream/2011/1908/5/Dissertacao_EnsinoLeituraFrases.pdf

Bastos, J. B. R. (2016). *Ensino de leitura para crianças autistas, por meio de um instrumento informatizado.* Master's thesis, Pontifícia Universidade Católica de São Paulo. Repositório Institucional PUC-SP. https://tede.pucsp.br/bitstream/handle/19340/2/J%c3%a9ssica%20Bassi%20Ramos%20Bastos.pdf

Batitucci, L. A., Batitucci, J. S. L., & Hanna, E. S. (2006). *Contingência Programada (Versão 2.0)* [Software de computador]. Instrumento não publicado.

Battaglini, M. P. (2010). *Reconhecimento de palavras, nomeação de figuras e de palavras impressas em surdos implantados pré-linguais.* Master's thesis, Universidade Estadual de São Paulo Júlio de Mesquita Filho. Repositório Institucional UNESP. https://repositorio.unesp.br/bitstream/handle/11449/86651/battaglini_mp_me_bauru.pdf?sequence=1&isAllowed=y

Benitez, P. (2011). *Aplicação de um programa informatizado de ensino de leitura e escrita por familiares de indivíduos com deficiência intelectual.* Master's thesis, Universidade Federal de São Carlos. Repositório Institucional UFSCar. https://repositorio.ufscar.br/bitstream/handle/ufscar/6017/3604.pdf?sequence=1&isAllowed=y

Benitez, P., & Domeniconi, C. (2012). Verbalizações de familiares durante aprendizagem de leitura e escrita por deficientes intelectuais. *Estudos de Psicologia (Campinas), 29*(4), 553–562. https://doi.org/10.1590/S0103-166X2012000400010

Benitez, P., & Domeniconi, C. (2016). Use of a computerized reading and writing teaching program for families of students with intellectual disabilities. *The Psychological Record, 66*, 127–138. https://doi.org/10.1007/s40732-015-0158-8

Benitez, P., Gomes, M. L. C., Schelini, P. W., & Domeniconi, C. (2015). Evidência de validade do diagnóstico da leitura e escrita (DLE) em relação ao WISC-III em deficientes intelectuais. *Boletim de Psicologia, 65*(142), 83–96.

Bernardino Júnior, J. A., Freitas, F. R., de Souza, D. G., Maranhe, E. A., & Bandini, H. H. M. (2006). Aquisição de leitura e escrita como resultado do ensino de habilidades de consciência fonológica. *Revista Brasileira de Educação Especial, 12*(3), 423–450. https://doi.org/10.1590/S1413-65382006000300009

Bertão, T. S. P., & Postalli, L. M. M. (2017). Jogo de tabuleiro: Contribuições na leitura de alunos do Ensino Fundamental. *Educere et Educare, 12*(25).

Cabral, R. P., Assis, G. J. A., & Haydu, V. B. (2012). Emergência de leitura em crianças com fracasso escolar: Efeitos do controle por exclusão. *Revista Brasileira de Terapia Comportamental e Cognitiva, 14*(3), 88–101.

Camelo, M. L. (2006). *Equivalência de estímulos com procedimentos combinados e consciência fonológica na aquisição da leitura recombinativa.* Master's thesis, Universidade Federal do Pará. Repositório Institucional UFPA. http://repositorio.ufpa.br/jspui/bitstream/2011/1653/1/Dissertacao_EquivalenciaEstimulosProcedimentos.pdf

Capobianco, D. (n.d.). *EAM (V. 4.0.04)* [Programa de computador]. Autor.

Carvalho, G. P. (2009). *Aquisição de leitura sob o paradigma da equivalência de estímulos e o comportamento precorrente auxiliar: Efeitos do treino de habilidades fonológicas.* Doctoral dissertation, Universidade de Brasília. Repositório Institucional UnB. https://repositorio.unb.br/bitstream/10482/7226/1/2009_GustavoPaivaDeCarvalho.pdf

Carvalho, B. S. S. (2013). *Programações de ensino para refinamento das habilidades de leitura e escrita de um aluno com Transtorno de Asperger.* Master's thesis, Universidade Federal de São Carlos. Repositório Institucional UFSCar. https://repositorio.ufscar.br/bitstream/handle/ufscar/3128/5017.pdf?sequence=1&isAllowed=y

Carvalho, G. P., Benayon, L., Pessoa, R., & Silva, V. (2002). *Aquisição de leitura, e equivalência de estímulos e comportamento precorrente auxiliar: Tarefas e novas medidas comportamentais realizadas em um ambiente informatizado*. Anais da XXXII Reunião Anual da Sociedade Brasileira de Psicologia, Florianópolis – SC.

Castro, A. B. D. (2008). *Ensino de leitura e escrita baseado no paradigma da equivalência: Um programa de consultoria colaborativa com o professor.* Master's thesis, Universidade Estadual de São Paulo. Repositório Institucional UNESP. https://repositorio.unesp.br/bitstream/handle/11449/97481/castro_ab_me_bauru.pdf?sequence=1&isAllowed=y

César, M. D. A. (2009). *Ensino de leitura: Uma proposta para aperfeiçoar o desempenho de alunos de 5a e 6a séries do Ensino Fundamental, com uso de software educativo.* Master's thesis, Pontifícia Universidade Católica de São Paulo. Repositório Institucional PUC-SP. https://tede.pucsp.br/bitstream/handle/16508/1/Marcelo%20de%20Abreu%20Cesar.pdf

Cézar, E. H. C. (2010). *Concordância verbal: Uma proposta de ensino de discriminações condicionais utilizando software educativo.* Master's thesis, Pontifícia Universidade Católica de São Paulo. Repositório Institucional PUC-SP. https://tede.pucsp.br/bitstream/handle/15962/1/Elisabete%20Honorio%20Custodio%20Cezar.pdf

Coimbra, C. F. S. N. (2010). *Avaliação de uma programação de ensino de leitura para alunos do Ensino Fundamental em contexto coletivo, por meio de um instrumento informatizado.* Master's thesis, Pontifícia Universidade Católica de São Paulo. Repositório Institucional PUC-SP. https://tede2.pucsp.br/handle/handle/16611

Coimbra, C. S. F. N. (2015). *Instrumento de avaliação da escrita: Repertório inicial.* Doctoral dissertation, Pontifícia Universidade Católica de São Paulo. Repositório Institucional PUC-SP. https://tede.pucsp.br/bitstream/handle/16194/1/Claudia%20Stefania%20Figueiredo%20Neves%20Coimbra.pdf

Costa, N. P. P. (2008). *Leitura: Identificação de repertório dos alunos da 2a série do Ensino Fundamental por meio de instrumento computadorizado.* Master's thesis, Pontifícia Universidade Católica de São Paulo. Repositório Institucional PUC-SP. https://sapientia.pucsp.br/bitstream/handle/16371/1/Nelia%20Paula%20Pereria%20Costa.pdf

Cravo, F. A. M. (2018). *Leitura oral e nomeação de figuras de palavras com dificuldades ortográficas por crianças com deficiência auditiva usuárias de implante coclear.* Master's thesis, Universidade Estadual Paulista Júlio Mesquita Filho – Bauru. Repositório Institucional UNESP. https://repositorio.unesp.br/bitstream/handle/11449/153311/cravo_fam_me_bauru.pdf?sequence=3&isAllowed=y

Cravo, F. A. M., & Almeida-Verdu, A. C. M. (2018). Avaliação de desempenho escolar após exposição a um programa informatizado de leitura e escrita. *Psicologia da Educação, 47*(1), 1–10. https://doi.org/10.5935/2175-3520.20180012

Cravo, F. A. M., Almeida-Verdu, A. C. M., Lucchesi, F. D. M., Silva, L. T. N., & Moret, A. L. M. (2019). Teaching a child with cochlear implant to read words with orthographic difficulties. *Trends in Psychology, 27*(4), 819–835. https://doi.org/10.9788/tp2019.4-01

de Freitas, M. C. (2008). *Programação de ensino de leitura e escrita para crianças com deficiência mental.* Master's thesis, Universidade Federal de São Carlos. Repositório Institucional UFSCar. https://repositorio.ufscar.br/bitstream/handle/ufscar/3036/2190.pdf?sequence=1&isAllowed=y

de Freitas, M. C. (2012). *Construção de um programa de ensino de pré-requisitos de leitura e escrita para pessoas com deficiência intelectual.* Doctoral dissertation, Universidade Federal de São Carlos. Repositório Institucional UFSCar. https://repositorio.ufscar.br/bitstream/handle/ufscar/5977/4730.pdf?sequence=1&isAllowed=y

de Rose, J. C. (2005). Análise comportamental da aprendizagem de leitura e escrita. *Revista Brasileira de Análise do Comportamento, 1*(1), 29–50. https://doi.org/10.18542/rebac.v1i1.676

de Rose, J. C., de Souza, D. G., Rossito, A. L., & de Rose, T. M. (1989). Aquisição de leitura após história de fracasso escolar: Equivalência de estímulos e generalização. *Psicologia: Teoria e Pesquisa, 5*(3), 325–346.

de Rose, J. C., de Souza, D. G., & Hanna, E. S. (1996). Teaching reading and spelling: Exclusion and stimulus equivalence. *Journal of Applied Behavior Analysis, 29*(4), 451–469. https://doi.org/10.1901/jaba.1996.29-451

de Souza, D. G., de Rose, J. C., Faleiros, T. C., Bortoloti, R., Hanna, E. S., & McIlvane, W. J. (2009). Teaching generative reading via recombination of minimal textual units: A legacy of verbal behavior to children in Brazil. *International Journal of Psychology and Psychological Therapy, 9*(1), 19–44.

Donadeli, J. M. (2016). *Ensino de leitura de sentenças para crianças em idade escolar.* Master's thesis, Universidade Federal de São Carlos. Repositório Institucional UFSCar. https://repositorio.ufscar.br/bitstream/handle/ufscar/7301/DissJMD.pdf?sequence=1&isAllowed=y

Donadeli, J. M., & Domeniconi, C. (2017). Ensino de leitura de sentenças para crianças em idade escolar. *Acta Comportamentalia, 25*(2), 179–195.

Dube, W. V. (1991). Computer software for stimulus control research with Macintosh computers. *Experimental Analysis of Human Behavior Bulletin, 9*, 28–30.

Dube, W. V., & McIlvane, W. J. (1989). Adapting a microcomputer for behavioral evaluation of mentally retarded individuals. In J. A. Mulick & R. F. Antonack (Eds.), *Transitions in mental retardation* (Vol. 4, pp. 104–127). Ablex.

Dube, W. V., McDonald, S. J., McIlvane, W. J., & Mackay, H. A. (1991). Constructed response matching to sample and spelling instruction. *Journal of Applied Behavior Analysis, 24*, 305–317. https://doi.org/10.1901/jaba.1991.24-305

Elias, N. C. (2007). *Procedimentos informatizados de ensino de sinais para adolescentes e adultos com surdez e/ou deficiência mental.* Doctoral dissertation, Universidade Federal de São Carlos. Repositório Institucional UFSCar. https://repositorio.ufscar.br/bitstream/handle/ufscar/2831/TeseNCE.pdf?sequence=1&isAllowed=y

Elias, N. C., Goyos, C., & Ribeiro, D. M. (2005). Desenvolvimento de um programa informatizado para ensino de Libras. In *Congresso Brasileiro de Educação Especial*, São Carlos, Anais, São Carlos, Vol. 1, p. 363.

Faggiani, R. B. (2008). *Efeitos de estímulos consequentes específicos sobre a emergência de leitura recombinativa.* Master's thesis, Universidade de São Paulo. Repositório Institucional USP. https://teses.usp.br/teses/disponiveis/47/47132/tde-12112008-075902/publico/Faggiani_me.pdf

Fava-Menzori, L. R. (2016). *Ensino de leitura e escrita em crianças com diferentes necessidades educacionais especiais por meio de um programa informatizado de ensino.* Master's thesis, Universidade Estadual Paulista Júlio Mesquita Filho – Bauru. Repositório Institucional UNESP. https://repositorio.unesp.br/bitstream/handle/11449/137817/favamenzori_lr_me_bauru.pdf?sequence=4&isAllowed=y

Feio, L. S. F. (2003). *A equivalência de estímulos e leitura recombinativa da simbologia braille em deficientes visuais: Efeito do espaçamento entre sílabas.* Master's thesis, Universidade Federal do Pará. Repositório Institucional da UFPA. http://200.239.66.43/arquivos/135000/135200/19_135286.htm

Feitosa, M. B. R. B. (2009). *Leitura recombinativa de palavras de inglês com onset e rime em braille e alfabeto romano em relevo por cegos.* Master's thesis, Universidade Federal do Pará. Repositório Institucional UFPA. http://repositorio.ufpa.br/jspui/bitstream/2011/5743/1/Dissertacao_LeituraRecombinativaPalavras.pdf

Feliciano, S. B., & Moroz, M. (2018). Ensino de escrita de orações para alunos surdos por discriminações condicionais. *Arquivos Brasileiros de Psicologia, 70*(3), 66–79.

Fernandes, M. A. P. (2008). *Leitura: Uma proposta de ensino a alunos de segunda série do Ensino Fundamental por meio de software educativo.* Master's thesis, Pontifícia Universidade Católica de São Paulo. Repositório Institucional PUC-SP. https://sapientia.pucsp.br/bitstream/handle/16369/1/Marcia%20Aparecida%20Pasqual%20Fernandes.pdf

Fernandes, A. M. A. (2013). *Avaliação de um procedimento de ensino de leitura adaptado a alunos com transtorno global do desenvolvimento.* Master's thesis, Universidade de Brasília. Repositório Institucional UnB. https://repositorio.unb.br/bitstream/10482/13655/1/2012_AnaMariaA.deAlbuquerqueFernandes.pdf

Fernandes, M. A. P., & Moroz, M. (2011). Ensino de leitura para alunos do Ensino Fundamental: Proposta com base na análise do comportamento. *Psicologia da Educação, 32*, 47–68.

Ferrão, M. F. C. (2016). *Ensino de leitura e escrita para pré-escolares com uso de software educativo.* Master's thesis, Pontifícia Universidade Católica de São Paulo. Repositório Institucional PUC-SP. https://tede2.pucsp.br/handle/handle/16225

Ferreira, L. M. S., Bandini, C. S. M., Bandini, H. H. M., & de Souza, D. G. (2016). O uso de sistema de frequência modulada no ensino de leitura para crianças com deficiência auditiva. *Acta Comportamentalia, 24*(4), 487–508.

Fonseca, A. C. G., Assis, G. J. A., & de Souza, S. R. (2015). Efeito do ensino de sentenças sobre a leitura recombinativa com compreensão: Procedimento de CRMTS. *Revista Brasileira de Terapia Comportamental e Cognitiva, 17*(3), 55–69. https://doi.org/10.31505/rbtcc.v17i3.815

Garcia, L. T. (2015). *Aprendizagem relacional em indivíduos surdos pré-linguais: Exclusão, equivalência de estímulos e superseletividade.* Doctoral dissertation, Universidade Federal de São Carlos. Repositório Institucional UFSCar. https://repositorio.ufscar.br/bitstream/handle/ufscar/7219/TeseLTG.pdf?sequence=1&isAllowed=y

Garcia, C. D. (2017). *Emergência de ditado ao longo do ensino cumulativo de discriminações condicionais entre palavras ditadas e impressas.* Master's thesis, Universidade Federal de São Carlos. Repositório Institucional UFSCar. https://repositorio.ufscar.br/bitstream/handle/ufscar/8820/DissCDPG.pdf?sequence=1&isAllowed=y

Gomes, C. G. S. (2007a). *Desempenhos emergentes e leitura funcional em crianças com transtornos do espectro autístico.* Master's thesis, Universidade Federal de São Carlos. Repositório Institucional UFSCar. https://repositorio.ufscar.br/bitstream/handle/ufscar/2975/1674.pdf?sequence=1&isAllowed=y

Gomes, R. C. (2007b). *Controle por unidades menores e Leitura recombinativa: Solicitação de comportamento textual durante aquisição de pré-requisitos.* Master's thesis, Universidade de São Paulo. Repositório Institucional USP. https://teses.usp.br/teses/disponiveis/47/47132/tde-23012008-141711/publico/Gomes_tde.pdf

Gomes, M. L. D. C. (2014). *Ensino de leitura com diferentes treinos discriminativos a aprendizes com deficiência intelectual.* Master's thesis, Universidade Federal de São Carlos. Repositório Institucional UFSCar. https://repositorio.ufscar.br/bitstream/handle/ufscar/6054/6111.pdf?sequence=1&isAllowed=y

Gomes, C. G. S., & de Souza, D. G. (2016). Ensino de sílabas simples, leitura combinatória e leitura com compreensão para aprendizes com autismo. *Revista Brasileira de Educação Especial, 22*(2), 233–252. https://doi.org/10.1590/S1413-65382216000200007

Gomes, M. L. D. C., Benitez, P., Domeniconi, C., & Almeida-Verdu, A. C. M. (2017a). Efeitos do ensino do ecoico aliado a repertórios básicos de leitura sobre a nomeação de palavras em crianças com deficiência intelectual. *Temas em Psicologia, 25*(1), 319–334. https://doi.org/10.9788/TP2017.4-18Pt

Gomes, M. L. D. C., Benitez, P., Zaine, I., & Domeniconi, C. (2017b). Ensino de leitura por diferentes treinos discriminativos para alunos com e sem deficiência intelectual. *Acta Comportamentalia, 25*(2), 157–177.

Goyos, C., & Almeida, J. C. (1996). *Mestre (Versão 1.0)* [Programa de computador]. Mestre Software.

Guidugli, P. M. (2014). *Efeitos do ensino sistemático e informatizado sobre comportamentos externalizantes concorrentes à aprendizagem de leitura e escrita.* Master's thesis, Universidade Estadual Paulista Júlio Mesquita Filho – Bauru. Repositório Institucional UNESP. https://repositorio.unesp.br/bitstream/handle/11449/115553/000807168.pdf?sequence=1&isAllowed=y

Guimarães, L. M. (2012). *Relações entre desempenho e o reforçador das relações verbais de tato e textual em contexto de equivalência de estímulo.* Master's thesis, Universidade Federal de São Carlos. Repositório Institucional UFSCar. https://repositorio.ufscar.br/bitstream/handle/ufscar/6035/4682.pdf?sequence=1&isAllowed=y

Haber, G. M. (2008). *Ensino de leitura de frases com compreensão a alunos de 1a série de escolas públicas de Belém.* Master's thesis, Universidade Federal do Pará. Repositório Institucional UFPA. http://repositorio.ufpa.br/jspui/bitstream/2011/1912/1/Dissertacao_EnsinoLeituraFrases.pdf

Hanna, E. S., de Souza, D. G., de Rose, J. C., & Fonseca, M. (2004). Effects of delayed constructed-response identity matching on spelling of dictated words. *Journal of Applied Behavior Analysis, 37*(2), 223–227. https://doi.org/10.1901/jaba.2004.37-223

Hanna, E. S., Kohlsdorf, M., Quinteiro, R. S., Fava, V. M. D., de Souza, D. G., & de Rose, J. C. (2008). Diferenças individuais na aquisição de leitura com um sistema linguístico em miniatura. *Psicologia: Teoria e Pesquisa, 24*(1), 45–57. https://doi.org/10.1590/S0102-37722008000100006

Hanna, E. S., Karino, C. A., Araújo, V. T., & Souza, D. G. (2010). Leitura recombinativa de pseudo-palavras impressas em pseudoalfabeto: Similaridade entre palavras e extensão da unidade ensinada. *Psicologia USP, 21*(2), 275–311. https://doi.org/10.1590/S0103-65642010000200005

Hanna, E. S., Kohlsdorf, M., Quinteiro, R. S., Melo, R. M. D., Souza, D. G., de Rose, J. C., & McIlvane, W. J. (2011). Recombinative reading derived from pseudoword instruction in a miniature linguistic system. *Journal of the Experimental Analysis of Behavior, 95*(1), 21–40. https://doi.org/10.1901/jeab.2011.95-21

Hayashi, E. A. P. (2003). *Dificuldades de leitura e problemas de indisciplina: Aplicação da metodologia da equivalência de estímulos e o procedimento de exclusão.* Master's thesis, Universidade Estadual Paulista Júlio Mesquita Filho – Bauru. Repositório Institucional UNESP. https://repositorio.unesp.br/handle/11449/91286

Hayashi, E. A. P. (2007). *A metodologia da equivalência de estímulos como recurso pedagógico para o professor do contraturno.* Doctoral dissertation, Universidade Estadual Paulista Júlio Mesquita Filho – Bauru. Repositório Institucional UNESP. Repositório Institucional UNESP. https://repositorio.unesp.br/bitstream/handle/11449/102269/hayashi_eap_dr_mar.pdf?sequence=1&isAllowed=y

Haydu, V. B., Zuanazzi, A. C., Assis, G. J. A., & Kato, O. M. (2015). Ensino de leitura de sentenças: Contribuições da análise do comportamento. *Psicologia: Teoria e Pesquisa, 31*(2), 145–154. https://doi.org/10.1590/0102-37722015021869145154

Hübner, M. M., Gomes, R. C., & McIlvane, W. J. (2009). Recombinative generalization in minimal verbal unit-based reading instruction for pre-reading children. *Experimental Analysis of Human Behavior Bulletin, 27*, 11–17.

Inhauser, L. Z. (2012). *Controle por unidades verbais mínimas e extensão da unidade ensinada: O efeito do treino de fonemas na emergência da leitura recombinativa.* Master's thesis, Universidade de São Paulo. Repositório Institucional USP. https://teses.usp.br/teses/disponiveis/47/47132/tde-19032013-113247/publico/inhauser_me.pdf

Laporte, F. F. (2014). *Seguimento de instruções e repertório recombinativo: Efeito da formação de classes de equivalência e do tipo de composição dos estímulos.* Master's thesis, Universidade de Brasília. Repositório Institucional UNB. https://repositorio.unb.br/bitstream/10482/16561/1/2014_F%c3%a1bioFreireLaporte.pdf

Leitão, G. M. E. (2009). *Ensino de discriminações de palavras com onset/rime e a emergência da leitura recombinativa em inglês da simbologia braille e do alfabeto romano em relevo em cegos.* Master's thesis, Universidade Federal do Pará. Repositório Institucional UFPA. http://repositorio.ufpa.br/jspui/bitstream/2011/5587/1/Dissertacao_EnsinoDiscriminacoesPalavras.pdf

Leite, M. K. S. (2008). *Controle por unidades mínimas na leitura: Análise do desempenho de pré-escolares em treinos e testes de discriminações condicionais entre palavras ditadas e impressas.* Master's thesis, Universidade de São Paulo. Repositório Institucional USP. https://teses.usp.br/teses/disponiveis/47/47132/tde-29072009-160027/publico/MARIANALEITE.pdf

Leite, M. K. S., & Hübner, M. M. C. (2009). Aquisição de leitura recombinativa após treinos e testes de discriminações condicionais entre palavras ditadas e impressas. *Psicologia: Teoria e Prática, 11*(3), 63–81.

Lima, D. C. (2009). *Programa de atividades recreativas para aprendizagem de leitura e escrita: Contextualização das palavras ensinadas.* Master's thesis, Universidade Federal de São Carlos. Repositório Institucional UFSCar. https://repositorio.ufscar.br/bitstream/handle/ufscar/3037/2499.pdf?sequence=1&isAllowed=y

Lima, D. C., de Souza, D. G., Martinez, C. M. S., & Rocca, J. Z. (2010). Atividades recreativas como suporte na ampliação de vocabulário e na aquisição de leitura para não-leitores. *Revista de Terapia Ocupacional da Universidade de São Paulo, 21*(1), 61–67. https://doi.org/10.11606/issn.2238-6149.v21i1p61-67

Llausas, R. V. (2008). *Avaliação de uma proposta de ensino de leitura e escrita para jovens e adultos utilizando software educativo.* Master's thesis, Pontifícia Universidade Católica de São Paulo. Repositório Institucional PUC-SP. https://sapientia.pucsp.br/bitstream/handle/16383/1/Rosana%20Valinas%20Llausas.pdf

Llausas, R. V. (2014). *Avaliando uma proposta de ensino de espanhol por meio de discriminações condicionais.* Doctoral dissertation, Pontifícia Universidade Católica de São Paulo. Repositório Institucional PUC-SP. https://www.sapientia.pucsp.br/bitstream/handle/16150/1/Rosana%20Valinas%20Llausas.pdf

Lucchesi, F. D. M. (2013). *Avaliação do efeito de um programa de ensino de leitura e escrita sobre a fala de crianças usuárias de implante coclear.* Master's thesis, Universidade Estadual Paulista Júlio Mesquita Filho – Bauru. Repositório Institucional UNESP. https://repositorio.unesp.br/bitstream/handle/11449/97474/lucchesi_fm_me_bauru.pdf?sequence=1&isAllowed=y

Lucchesi, F. D. M., Almeida-Verdu, A. C. M., Buffa, M. J. M. B., & Bevilacqua, M. C. (2015a). Análise dos passos de um ensino programado de leitura e escrita a crianças com deficiência auditiva e implante coclear. *Acta Comportamentalia, 23*(2), 137–151.

Lucchesi, F. D. M., Almeida-Verdu, A. C. M., Buffa, M. J. M. B., & Bevilacqua, M. C. (2015b). Efeitos de um programa de ensino de leitura sobre a inteligibilidade da fala de crianças usuárias de implante coclear. *Psicologia: Reflexão e Crítica, 28*(3), 500–510. https://doi.org/10.1590/1678-7153.201528309

Lucchesi, F. D. M., Almeida-Verdu, A. C. M., & de Souza, D. G. (2018). Reading and speech intelligibility of a child with auditory impairment and cochlear implant. *Psychology & Neuroscience, 11*(3), 306–316. https://doi.org/10.1037/pne0000139

Machado, L. M. (2011). *Características de comportamentos de interação entre participantes em um programa de ensino de ler em situação de grupo.* Doctoral dissertation, Universidade Federal de Santa Catarina. Repositório Institucional UFSC. https://repositorio.ufsc.br/bitstream/handle/123456789/95971/293085.pdf?sequence=1&isAllowed=y

Machado, L., & Haydu, V. (2012). Escolha de acordo com modelo e equivalência de estímulos: Ensino de leitura de palavras em situação coletiva. *Psicologia da Educação, 35*, 72–94.

Maia, A. C. B., Pereira, A. B., & de Souza, D. G. (1999). Aquisição de leitura e desempenho no WISC. *Psicologia: Teoria e Pesquisa, 15*(1), 17–26.

Marques, L. B. (2014). *Estudo de inserção de jogos computadorizados como recurso complementar ao ensino de leitura.* Doctoral dissertation, Universidade Federal de São Carlos. Repositório Institucional UFSCar. https://repositorio.ufscar.br/bitstream/handle/ufscar/5997/6394.pdf?sequence=1&isAllowed=y

Martimiano, T. H. T. (2010). *Avaliando uma proposta de ensino para crianças que apresentam dificuldades em leitura e escrita.* Master's thesis, Pontifícia Universidade Católica de São Paulo. Repositório Institucional PUC-SP. https://sapientia.pucsp.br/bitstream/handle/15953/1/Thais%20Helena%20Tadiotto%20Martimiano.pdf

Matos, M. A., Hübner, M. M., Serra, V. R. B. P., Basaglia, A. E., & Avanzi, A. L. (2002). Redes de relações condicionais e leitura recombinativa: Pesquisando o ensinar a ler. *Arquivos Brasileiros de Psicologia, 54*(3), 284–303.

Maués, A. S. (2007). *A recombinação de letras no ensino e emergência da leitura recombinativa generalizada em crianças da pré-escola.* Master's thesis, Universidade Federal do Pará. Repositório Institucional UFPA. http://repositorio.ufpa.br/jspui/bitstream/2011/5585/1/Dissertacao_RecombinacaoLetrasEnsino.pdf

Medeiros, J. G., & Silva, R. M. F. (2002). Efeitos de testes de leitura sobre a generalização em crianças em processo de alfabetização. *Psicologia: Reflexão e Crítica, 15*(3), 587–602. https://doi.org/10.1590/S0102-79722002000300013

Medeiros, J. G., & Teixeira, S. A. (2000). Ensino de leitura e escrita através do pareamento com o modelo e seus efeitos sobre medidas de inteligência. *Estudos de Psicologia (Natal), 5*(1), 181–214. https://doi.org/10.1590/S1413-294X2000000100009

Medeiros, J. G., Monteiro, G., & Silva, K. Z. (1997). O ensino da leitura e escrita a um sujeito adulto. *Temas em Psicologia, 1*, 65–78.

Medeiros, J. G., Antonakopoulu, A., Amorim, K., & Righetto, A. C. (1999). O uso da discriminação condicional no ensino da leitura e escrita. *Temas em Psicologia, 1*, 23–32.

Medeiros, J. G., Fernandes, A. R., Pimentel, R., & Simone, A. C. S. (2004). A função da nomeação oral sobre comportamentos emergentes de leitura e escrita ensinados por computador. *Estudos de Psicologia (Natal), 9*(2), 249–258. https://doi.org/10.1590/S1413-294X2004000200006

Medeiros, J., Santos, I., Stefani, A., & Martins, V. (2007). A emergência de leitura de frases compostas por números e palavras de ensino. *Interação em Psicologia, 11*(1). https://doi.org/10.5380/psi.v11i1.5962

Medeiros, J. G., Antunes, L., Pokreviescki, J. E. J., Bottenberg, D. G., de Amorim Ferreira, C., & Cavalhieri, K. E. (2011). Emergência de leitura de frases a partir do ensino de suas unidades constituintes. *Acta Comportamentalia, 19*(3), 317–342.

Melchiori, L. E., de Souza, D. G., & de Rose, J. C. (1992). Aprendizagem de leitura por meio de um procedimento de discriminação sem erros (exclusão): Uma replicação com pré-escolares. *Psicologia: Teoria e Pesquisa, 8*(1), 101–111.

Melchiori, L. E., de Souza, D. G., & de Rose, J. C. (2000). Reading, equivalence, and recombination of units: A replication with students with different learning histories. *Journal of Applied Behavior Analysis, 33*(1), 97–100. https://doi.org/10.1901/jaba.2000.33-97

Melo, A. S. (2012). *Emergência da leitura de palavras em braille e no alfabeto romano em relevo para cegos após ensino de discriminações de sílabas.* Master's thesis, Universidade Federal do Pará. Repositório Institucional UFPA. http://ppgtpc.propesp.ufpa.br/ARQUIVOS/dissertacoes/Andrea%20Melo%202012.pdf

Menotti, A. R. S. (2016). *Tarefas informatizadas e jogos aplicados pelos pais na aprendizagem de leitura por crianças com transtorno do espectro autista.* Master's thesis, Universidade Federal de São Carlos. Repositório Institucional UFSCar. https://repositorio.ufscar.br/bitstream/handle/ufscar/7300/DissARSM.pdf?sequence=1&isAllowed=y

Menotti, A. R. S., Domeniconi, C., & Benitez, P. (2019). Atividades aplicadas pelos pais para ensinar leitura para filhos com autismo. *Psicologia Escolar e Educacional, 23*(1), 1–9. https://doi.org/10.1590/2175-35392019015073

Mesquita, A. A. (2017). *Dois estudos em Análise do Comportamento: Emergência de leitura após diferentes tipos de ensino de sílabas e palavras e introdução ao letramento analítico-comportamental.* Doctoral dissertation, Universidade Federal do Pará. Repositório Institucional UFPA. http://repositorio.ufpa.br/jspui/bitstream/2011/10125/1/Tese_EstudosAnaliseComportamento.pdf

Mesquita, A. A., & Hanna, E. S. (2016). Ensino de relações com letras, sílabas e palavras e aprendizagem de leitura de palavras. *Acta Comportamentalia, 24*(1), 47–60.

Millan, A. E., & Postalli, L. M. M. (2019). Ensino de habilidades rudimentares de leitura para alunos com autismo. *Revista Brasileira de Educação Especial, 25*(1), 133–154. https://doi.org/10.1590/S1413-65382519000100009

Neves, A. J. (2014). *Compreensão e produção oral de sentenças em crianças com deficiência auditiva pré-lingual usuárias de implante coclear.* Master's thesis, Universidade Estadual Paulista Júlio Mesquita Filho – Bauru. Repositório Institucional UNESP. http://www.athena.biblioteca.unesp.br/exlibris/bd/cathedra/14-12-2015/000852851.pdf

Neves, A. J., & Almeida-Verdu, A. C. M. (2014). Efeitos de ensino envolvendo equivalência entre palavra ditada, palavra escrita e objeto sobre a inteligibilidade da fala em adolescentes com hipoplasia cerebelar. *Revista CEFAC, 16*(4), 1340–1350. https://doi.org/10.1590/1982-021620145413

Nibu, M. Y. (2006). *Identificação do repertório de leitura de alunos da 2ª. série do Ensino Fundamental de uma escola pública através de um programa computadorizado.* Master's thesis,

Pontifícia Universidade Católica de São Paulo. Repositório Institucional PUC-SP. https://www.sapientia.pucsp.br/bitstream/handle/16292/1/PED%20-%20Marina%20Y%20Nibu.pdf

Nunes, D. A., Takahaji, M., Benitez, P., Domeniconi, C., & Ferreira, P. R. S. (2012). Ensino informatizado de leitura em contexto de educação informal. *Revista Brasileira de Análise do Comportamento, 8*(2), 47–58. https://doi.org/10.18542/rebac.v8i2.1921

Oliveira, A. I. A. (2010a). *Integrando tecnologias para leitura de crianças com paralisia cerebral na educação inclusiva.* Doctoral dissertation, Universidade Federal do Pará. Repositório Institucional UFPA. http://repositorio.ufpa.br/jspui/bitstream/2011/10464/1/Tese_IntegrandoTecnologiasLeitura.pdf

Oliveira, G. P. (2010b). *Intervenção pedagógica individualizada para alunos com deficiência intelectual: Ensino de leitura em salas de recursos.* Doctoral dissertation, Universidade Federal de São Carlos. Repositório Institucional UFSCar. https://repositorio.ufscar.br/bitstream/handle/ufscar/2879/3644.pdf?sequence=1&isAllowed=y

Oliveira, M. A. D. (2012). *Ensino de universitários para o uso de procedimentos computadorizados de matching-to-sample no ensino de leitura.* Doctoral dissertation, Universidade Federal de São Carlos. Repositório Institucional UFSCar. https://repositorio.ufscar.br/bitstream/handle/ufscar/5969/4399.pdf?sequence=1&isAllowed=y

Oliveira, T. (2017). *Aprendizagem por exclusão: Análise de um procedimento de ensino em crianças diagnosticadas com autismo.* Master's thesis, Universidade Federal do Pará. Repositório Institucional UFPA. http://ppgtpc.propesp.ufpa.br/ARQUIVOS/dissertacoes/Thayline%20Oliveira%202017.pdf

Oliveira, A. I. A., Paixão, G. M., & Assis, G. J. A. (2014). Emergência de leitura recombinativa em crianças com paralisia cerebral. *Revista Brasileira de Terapia Comportamental e Cognitiva, 16*(3), 4–22. https://doi.org/10.31505/rbtcc.v16i3.709

Paixão, G. M. (2012). *Procedimento de ensino e teste de leitura recombinativa para crianças com paralisia cerebral.* Master's thesis, Universidade Federal do Pará. Repositório Institucional UFPA. http://repositorio.ufpa.br/jspui/bitstream/2011/10815/1/Dissertacao_ProcedimentoEnsinoTeste.pdf

Paixão, G. M. (2016). *Aplicação de um programa de ensino de leitura e construção de sentenças para crianças com autismo.* Doctoral dissertation, Universidade Federal do Pará. Repositório Institucional UFPA. http://repositorio.ufpa.br/jspui/bitstream/2011/10481/1/Tese_AplicacaoProgramaEnsino.pdf

Paixão, G., & de Assis, G. J. A. (2017). Uso do procedimento de *constructed response matching to sample*: Uma revisão da literatura. *Perspectivas em Análise do Comportamento, 8*(1), 47–60. https://doi.org/10.18761/pac.2016.038

Paixão, G. M., & de Assis, G. J. A. (2018). Efeitos do ensino via CRMTS sobre leitura e construção de sentenças para crianças com autismo. *Interação em Psicologia, 22*(1), 77–88. https://doi.org/10.5380/psi.v22i1.51327

Pereira, A. B. (1995). *Aprendizagem de leitura e escrita em aprendizes com história de fracasso escolar.* Unpublished master's thesis, Universidade Federal de São Carlos.

Pereira, F. S. (2013). *Discriminação auditivo-visual em adultos com deficiência auditiva pós-lingual e implante coclear.* Master's thesis, Universidade Federal do Pará. Repositório Institucional UFPA. http://repositorio.ufpa.br/jspui/bitstream/2011/10725/1/Dissertacao_DiscriminacaoAudioVisual.pdf

Péres, E., & Carrara, K. (2004). Dificuldades de leitura: Aplicação da metodologia da equivalência de estímulos. *Psicologia da Educação (São Paulo), 18*, 77–94.

Pimentel, E. P. (1997). *Desenvolvimento de um sistema para pesquisa em equivalência e unidades verbais menores utilizando estruturas de dados para texto e imagem.* Unpublished master's thesis. Universidade Presbiteriana Mackenzie, São Paulo.

Pimentel, E. P., Baldani, D., Piccolo, G., & Hübner, M. M. (2009). *Um ambiente para o ensino de leitura baseado na pesquisa em equivalência e controle por unidades mínimas.* Apresentação em Simpósio, Florianópolis-SC.

Ponciano, V. L. (2006). *Ensino de leitura com uso de software educativo: Novas contribuições.* Doctoral dissertation, Pontifícia Universidade Católica de São Paulo. Sistema de Publicação Eletrônica de Teses e Dissertações, PUC-SP. https://leto.pucsp.br/bitstream/handle/16277/1/VERA%20LUCIA%20DE%20OLIVEIRA%20PONCIANO.pdf

Ponciano, V. L. O., & Moroz, M. (2012). Utilizando frases como unidades de ensino de leitura: Um procedimento baseado na equivalência de estímulos. *Revista Brasileira de Terapia Comportamental e Cognitiva, 14*(1), 38–56.

Ponso, A. P. D. S. (2010). *Leitura e escrita: Uma proposta de ensino a alunos de 4a série de PIC com software educativo.* Master's thesis, Pontifícia Universidade Católica de São Paulo. Repositório Institucional PUC-SP. https://tede.pucsp.br/bitstream/handle/15948/1/Ana%20Paula%20de%20Souza%20Ponso.pdf

Postalli, L., Almeida, D., Canovas, D., & de Souza, D. (2008). Ensino de reconhecimento de palavras no contexto da leitura de histórias infantis. *Revista Brasileira de Análise do Comportamento, 4*(1). https://doi.org/10.18542/rebac.v4i1.842

Quinteiro, R. S. (2014). *Aquisição de discriminações auditivo-táteis e emergência de leitura recombinativa em braille.* Doctoral dissertation, Universidade Federal de São Carlos. Repositório Institucional UFSCar. https://repositorio.ufscar.br/bitstream/handle/ufscar/5999/6713.pdf?sequence=1&isAllowed=y

Quinteiro, R. S., Hanna, E. S., & de Souza, D. G. (2014). Emergência de leitura braille recombinativa em pessoas com deficiência visual. *Revista Brasileira de Análise do Comportamento, 10*(1), 38–52. https://doi.org/10.18542/rebac.v10i1.1541

Rainatto, R. (2012). *Leitura e escrita para alunos do 3° ano do Ensino Fundamental- avaliação de um procedimento de ensino de discriminações condicionais com uso de software.* Master's thesis, Pontifícia Universidade Católica de São Paulo. Repositório Institucional PUC-SP. https://leto.pucsp.br/bitstream/handle/16029/1/Renata%20Rainatto.pdf

Ramos, L. (2004). *Equivalência de estímulos e generalização de leitura em crianças de primeira série com dificuldades na aquisição de leitura.* Master's thesis, Universidade Federal do Pará. Repositório Institucional da UFPA. http://repositorio.ufpa.br/jspui/bitstream/2011/1918/1/Dissertacao_EquivalenciaEstimulosGeneralizacao.pdf

Reis, T. S. (2008). *Avaliação da eficácia de um programa suplementar para o ensino de leitura e escrita aplicado em ambiente escolar.* Master's thesis, Universidade Federal de São Carlos. Repositório Institucional UFSCar. https://repositorio.ufscar.br/bitstream/handle/ufscar/3021/2541.pdf?sequence=1&isAllowed=y

Reis, T. S. (2013). *Estabelecimento de escrita sob controle de ditado como base para a recombinação na leitura e na escrita.* Doctoral dissertation, Universidade Federal de São Carlos. Repositório Institucional UFSCar. https://repositorio.ufscar.br/bitstream/handle/ufscar/5983/5361.pdf?sequence=1&isAllowed=y

Reis, T. S., de Souza, D. G., & de Rose, J. C. (2009). Avaliação de um programa para o ensino de leitura e escrita. *Estudos em Avaliação Educacional, 20*(44), 425–452. https://doi.org/10.18222/eae204420092038

Reis, T. S., Postalli, L. M. M., & de Souza, D. G. (2013). Teaching spelling as a route for reading and writing. *Psychology & Neuroscience, 6*(3), 365–373. https://doi.org/10.3922/j.psns.2013.3.14

Rique, L. D. (2015). *Da leitura de palavras para textos infantis: Inteligibilidade, fluência e nomeação em crianças com implante coclear.* Master's thesis, Universidade Estadual Paulista Júlio Mesquita Filho – Bauru. Repositório Institucional UNESP. https://repositorio.unesp.br/bitstream/handle/11449/126597/000844103.pdf?sequence=1&isAllowed=y

Rique, L. D., Almeida-Verdu, A. C. M., Silva, L. T. N., Buffa, M. J. M. B., & Moret, A. D. L. M. (2017). Leitura após formação de classes de equivalência em crianças com implante coclear: Precisão e fluência em palavras e textos. *Acta Comportamentalia, 25*(3), 307–327.

Rodrigues, V. (2000). *A utilização da discriminação condicional no ensino da leitura e escrita a crianças com paralisia cerebral.* Master's thesis, Universidade Federal de Santa Catarina. Repositório Institucional UFSC. http://repositorio.ufsc.br/xmlui/handle/123456789/78231

Rodrigues, M. C. C. M. (2004). *Música e jogos num contexto coletivo de ensino usando procedimento de exclusão.* Master's thesis, Universidade Federal de Santa Catarina. Repositório Institucional UFSC. https://repositorio.ufsc.br/bitstream/handle/123456789/85974/202163.pdf?sequence=1&isAllowed=y

Rodrigues, P. N. (2016). *Efeitos da exposição combinada a programas informatizados de ensino de leitura, escrita e consciência fonológica a alunos com dificuldade de aprendizagem.* Master's thesis, Universidade Federal de São Carlos. Repositório Institucional UFSCar. https://repositorio.ufscar.br/bitstream/handle/ufscar/9060/DissPNR.pdf?sequence=1&isAllowed=y

Rodrigues, V., & Medeiros, J. G. (2001). Utilização da discriminação condicional no ensino da literatura e escrita a crianças com paralisia cerebral. *Estudos de Psicologia (Campinas), 18*(3), 55–73. https://doi.org/10.1590/S0103-166X2001000300005

Rodrigues, P. N., & Postalli, L. M. M. (2019). Phonological awareness skills improved by the teaching of reading and writing. *Psicologia Escolar e Educacional, 23*(1), 1–10. https://doi.org/10.1590/2175-35392019019961

Rondon, G. G. (2018). *Proposta informatizada de ensino para jovens e adultos.* Master's thesis, Pontifícia Universidade Católica de São Paulo. Repositório Institucional PUC-SP. https://tede.pucsp.br/bitstream/handle/21101/2/Giovanna%20Gaggini%20Rondon.pdf

Rosa Filho, A. B., de Souza, D. G., de Rose, J. C., Fonseca, M., & Hanna, E. S. (1998). *Aprendendo a ler e escrever em pequenos passos.* Research Software.

Sampaio, M. E. C., Assis, G. J. A., & Baptista, M. Q. G. (2010). Variáveis de procedimentos de ensino e de testes na construção de sentenças com compreensão. *Psicologia: Teoria e Pesquisa, 26*(1), 145–155. https://doi.org/10.1590/S0102-37722010000100017

Santos, A. C. C. (2002). *Ensino de leitura a partir de unidades mínimas a jovens e adultos.* Master's thesis, Universidade Federal do Pará. Repositório Institucional da UFPA. http://repositorio.ufpa.br/jspui/bitstream/2011/5348/1/Dissertacao_EnsinoLeituraUnidades.pdf

Santos, C. A. D. (2011). *Proposta de ensino de leitura e escrita, por meio de discriminações condicionais aplicadas com software, para jovens e adultos de um curso de EJA.* Master's thesis, Pontifícia Universidade Católica de São Paulo. Repositório Institucional PUC-SP. https://tede.pucsp.br/bitstream/handle/16008/1/Carlos%20Alberto%20Daniel%20dos%20Santos.pdf

Santos, L. C. S. (2012a). *Avaliação de um procedimento para aquisição de leitura em crianças com diagnóstico de autismo.* Master's thesis, Pontifícia Universidade Católica de São Paulo. Repositório Institucional PUC-SP. https://leto.pucsp.br/bitstream/handle/16690/1/Larissa%20Chaves%20de%20Sousa%20Santos.pdf

Santos, S. C. E. (2012b). *Ensino de leitura e escrita para aprendizes com deficiência intelectual.* Master's thesis, Pontifícia Universidade Católica de São Paulo. Repositório Institucional PUC-SP. https://leto.pucsp.br/bitstream/handle/16063/1/Sonia%20Cristina%20Esplendor%20dos%20Santos.pdf

Santos, S. L. R. (2012c). *Caracterização de desempenhos envolvidos na leitura e na escrita em crianças com deficiência auditiva.* Master's thesis, Universidade Estadual Paulista Júlio Mesquita Filho – Bauru. Repositório Institucional UNESP. https://repositorio.unesp.br/bitstream/handle/11449/97496/santos_slr_me_bauru.pdf?sequence=1&isAllowed=y

Santos, R. E. A. (2015). *Efeito do ensino de discriminação condicional de sentenças sobre a emergência de relações sintáticas para deficientes auditivos.* Master's thesis, Universidade Federal do Pará. Repositório Institucional UFPA. http://repositorio.ufpa.br/jspui/bitstream/2011/11677/1/Dissertacao_EfeitoEnsinoDiscriminacao.pdf

Santos, S. L. R., & Almeida-Verdu, A. C. M. (2012). Leitura em uma criança surda após equivalência de estímulos. *Psicologia em Revista, 18*(2), 209–226. https://doi.org/10.5752/P.1678-9563.2012v18n2p209

Santos, A. S. L., Silva, A. M. M. V., Baptista, M. Q., & Assis, G. J. A. (1997). REL 1.0: Sistema computadorizado para o ensino de discriminações simples e condicionais [Resumo]. Em Sociedade Brasileira de Psicologia (Org.), *Resumos de comunicações científicas, XXVII Reunião Anual de Psicologia* (p. 192). SBP.

Saraiva, L. Z., & Hübner, M. M. C. (2001). Uma análise comparativa de resultados em testes de vocabulário, inteligência, equivalência e generalização de leitura. *Revista Brasileira de Terapia Comportamental e Cognitiva, 3*(1), 57–68.

Sella, A. C. (2009). *Transferência de funções ordinais através de classes de estímulos equivalentes: Contribuições para a programação de ensino de adultos e crianças surdas e de crianças ouvintes.* Doctoral dissertation, Universidade Federal de São Carlos. Repositório Institucional UFSCar. https://repositorio.ufscar.br/bitstream/handle/ufscar/2852/2295.pdf?sequence=1&isAllowed=y

Serejo, P., Hanna, E. S., de Souza, D. G., & de Rose, J. C. (2007). Leitura e repertório recombinativo: Efeito da quantidade de treino e da composição dos estímulos. *Revista Brasileira de Análise do Comportamento, 3*(2), 191–215. https://doi.org/10.18542/rebac.v3i2.831

Sidman, M. (1971). Reading and auditory-visual equivalences. *Journal of Speech and Hearing Research, 14*, 4–13. https://doi.org/10.1044/jshr.1401.05

Sidman, M., & Cresson, O. (1973). Reading and crossmodal transfer of stimulus equivalences in severe retardation. *American Journal of Mental Deficiency, 77*, 515–523.

Sidman, M., & Tailby, W. (1982). Conditional discrimination vs matching-to-sample: An expansion of the testing paradigm. *Journal of the Experimental Analysis of Behavior, 37*, 5–22. https://doi.org/10.1901/jeab.1982.37-5

Silva, R. M. F. (2000). *O efeito de dois procedimentos de sondas de leitura sobre o comportamento de generalização em crianças com dificuldades de aprendizagem.* Master's thesis, Universidade Federal de Santa Catarina. Repositório Institucional UFSC. https://repositorio.ufsc.br/bitstream/handle/123456789/79277/152808.pdf?sequence=1&isAllowed=y

Silva, D. S. (2009). *Avaliação do repertório de leitura de alunos de 3a série do Ensino Fundamental: Uma análise das dificuldades apresentadas.* Master's thesis, Pontifícia Universidade Católica de São Paulo. Repositório Institucional PUC-SP. https://sapientia.pucsp.br/bitstream/handle/16523/1/Damares%20Souza%20Silva.pdf

Silva, R. M. F. (2010). *Avaliação da eficiência de um programa para ensinar palavras, números, numerais, cores, quantidades e frases compostas por estes estímulos a pessoas deficientes mentais que estão em processo de ingresso no mercado de trabalho.* Doctoral dissertation, Universidade Federal de Santa Catarina. Repositório Institucional UFSC. https://repositorio.ufsc.br/bitstream/handle/123456789/93700/288057.pdf?sequence=1&isAllowed=y

Silva, C. M. S. (2015). *O efeito do ensino de relações envolvendo sílabas e fonemas-grafemas sobre a leitura recombinativa.* Doctoral dissertation, Pontifícia Universidade Católica de São Paulo. Repositório Institucional PUC-SP. https://www.pucsp.br/sites/default/files/download/posgraduacao/programas/psicologia-experimental/camila-maria-silveira-da-silva.pdf

Silva, E. R. M. (2017). *Ensino de leitura e de escrita a adultos com deficiência intelectual matriculados na educação de jovens e adultos.* Master's thesis, Universidade Federal de São Carlos. Repositório Institucional UFSCar. https://repositorio.ufscar.br/bitstream/handle/ufscar/9700/SILVA_%c3%89rika_2018.pdf?sequence=5&isAllowed=y

Silveira, C. C., Domeniconi, C., Calcagno, S. C., Kato, O. M., & Hanna, E. S. (2016). Repertório básico de leitura e escrita em escolas brasileiras com baixa avaliação do Ensino Fundamental. *Acta Comportamentalia, 24*(4), 471–486.

Silveira, C. C., Domeniconi, C., & Hanna, E. S. (2019). Uma avaliação alternativa de compreensão de leitura para crianças. *Acta Comportamentalia, 27*(4), 423–435.

Souza, S. R. (1996). *Aquisição de habilidades básicas de escrita e leitura através de discriminação condicional em pré-escolares.* Master's thesis, Universidade Federal de São Carlos. Repositório do Núcleo Brasileiro de Dissertações e Teses. http://www.nuteses.temp.ufu.br/tde_busca/arquivo.php?codArquivo=6053&acordo=

Souza, A. C. (2009). *Efeito do ensino de palavras monossilábicas via treino de relações condicionais arbitrárias sobre o controle por unidades mínimas em leitura recombinativa.* Master's thesis, Universidade de São Paulo. Repositório Institucional USP. https://teses.usp.br/teses/disponiveis/47/47132/tde-15122009-090307/publico/DissertacaoAriene.pdf

Souza, J. A. N. (2013). *Transferência de funções discriminativas com estímulos táteis sobre a leitura em cegos*. Doctoral dissertation, Universidade Federal do Pará. Repositório Institucional UFPA. http://repositorio.ufpa.br/jspui/bitstream/2011/10482/1/Tese_TransferenciaFuncoesDiscriminativas.pdf

Souza, J. A. N., & Assis, G. J. A. (2013). Instalando pré-requisitos de leitura para dois alunos com deficiência intelectual. *Psicologia: Teoria e Prática, 15*(2), 130–143.

Souza, S. R., & Hübner, M. M. C. (2010). Efeitos de um jogo de tabuleiro educativo na aquisição de leitura e escrita. *Acta Comportamentalia, 18*(2), 215–242.

Souza, S., Goyos, C., Silvares, E. F. M., & Saunders, R. R. (2007). Emergence of printing and spelling skills from Constructed-Response Matching-to-Sample Instruction (CRMTS). *European Journal of Behavior Analysis, 8*(1), 49–64. https://doi.org/10.1080/15021149.2007.11434273

Sudo, C. H., Soares, P. G., Souza, S. R., & Haydu, V. B. (2008). Equivalência de estímulos e uso de jogos para ensinar leitura e escrita. *Revista Brasileira de Terapia Comportamental e Cognitiva, 10*(2), 223–238. https://doi.org/10.31505/rbtcc.v10i2.228

Suzuki, B. M. (2017). *Avaliação do jogo abrakedabra no ensino de palavras com dificuldades da língua*. Master's thesis, Universidade Estadual de Londrina. Repositório Institucional UEL. http://www.uel.br/pos/pgac/wp-content/uploads/2018/04/Avalia%C3%A7%C3%A3o-do-jogo-abrakedabra-no-ensino-de-palavras-com-dificuldades-da-l%C3%ADngua.pdf

Suzuki, B. M., & de Souza, S. R. (2019). Efeitos do jogo Abrakedabra sobre a leitura e a escrita de palavras com encontros consonantais. *Acta Comportamentalia, 27*(3), 351–360.

Tenório, J. P. (2013). *Programação e avaliação do ensino de leitura e escrita por meio de jogos educativos para crianças com dificuldades de aprendizagem*. Master's thesis, Universidade Federal de São Carlos. Repositório Institucional UFSCar. https://repositorio.ufscar.br/bitstream/handle/ufscar/3150/5567.pdf?sequence=1&isAllowed=y

Tizo, M. (2016). *Avaliando tecnologia de ensino de leitura e escrita informatizada e adaptada para alunos de escola pública com dificuldade de aprendizagem*. Doctoral dissertation, Universidade de Brasília. Repositório Institucional UNB. https://repositorio.unb.br/bitstream/10482/21618/1/2016_MarcileydeTizo.pdf

Todorov, J. C., & Hanna, E. S. (2010). Análise do comportamento no Brasil. *Psicologia: Teoria e Pesquisa, 26*(spe), 143–153. https://doi.org/10.1590/S0102-37722010000500013

Tripiana-Barbosa, A. (2013). *O uso de um jogo de tabuleiro educativo no ensino de leitura e escrita a deficientes intelectuais*. Doctoral dissertation, Universidade Estadual de Londrina. Repositório Institucional UEL. http://www.uel.br/pos/pgac/wp-content/uploads/2014/03/O-uso-de-um-jogo-de-tabuleiro-educativo-no-ensino-de-leitura-e-escrita-a-deficientes-intelectuais.pdf

Vale, J. B. (2010). *Emergência de leitura recombinativa de frases em crianças de escolas públicas*. Master's thesis, Universidade Federal do Pará. Repositório Institucional UFPA. http://repositorio.ufpa.br/jspui/bitstream/2011/5097/1/Dissertacao_EmergenciaLeituraRecombinativa.pdf

Veiga, D. I. (2014). *Aprendizagem e engajamento como função de consequências para o desempenho de crianças em um programa de ensino individualizado de leitura*. Doctoral dissertation, Universidade Federal de São Carlos. Repositório Institucional UFSCar. https://repositorio.ufscar.br/bitstream/handle/ufscar/5996/6382.pdf?sequence=1&isAllowed=y

Zaine, I. (2011). *Discriminações simples e reforçamento específico e diferencial no ensino de leitura a indivíduos com atraso no desenvolvimento*. Master's thesis, Universidade Federal de São Carlos. Repositório Institucional UFSCar. https://repositorio.ufscar.br/bitstream/handle/ufscar/6021/3848.pdf?sequence=1&isAllowed=y

Zaine, I., Domeniconi, C., & de Rose, J. C. (2014). Simple and conditional discrimination and specific reinforcement in teaching reading: An intervention package. *The Analysis of Verbal Behavior, 30*(2), 193–204. https://doi.org/10.1007/s40616-014-0010-2

Zanco, G. (2011). *Ensino de leitura e escrita a partir de discriminações condicionais para alunos do ensino médio*. Master's thesis, Pontifícia Universidade Católica de São Paulo. Repositório Institucional PUC-SP. https://sapientia.pucsp.br/bitstream/handle/16009/1/Giselda%20Zanco.pdf

Zanco, G., & Moroz, M. (2015). Ensino de Leitura de Orações por meio de discriminações condicionais. *Psicologia: Teoria e Pesquisa, 31*(4), 509–517. https://doi.org/10.1590/0102-37722015042363509517

Zuliani, G. (2007). *Aquisição e manutenção de comportamentos de leitura e fluência através de contingências de repetição e velocidade nos procedimentos de equivalência de estímulos.* Doctoral dissertation, Universidade Federal de São Carlos. Repositório Institucional da UFSCar. http://repositorio.ufsc.br/xmlui/handle/123456789

Chapter 3
The Stimulus Equivalence Paradigm and the Notion of Relational Networks in Teaching Reading and Writing: Contributions from Laboratories at UEL

Verônica Bender Haydu and Silvia Regina de Souza

3.1 Introduction

Reading and writing can be considered behavioral cusps as they are behaviors whose consequences go beyond the behavioral change established by contingencies. Therefore, allowing the expansion of the individual's behavioral repertoire since it exposes him/her to new learning environments (Cooper et al., 2007). Reading printed words and instructions allows the person to access, for example, different places and develop skills without the need for a contingency-shaped history. Despite the importance of reading, three out of 10 Brazilians aged 15–64 are functionally illiterate (Inaf Brasil, 2018), that is, people who have difficulty understanding and interpreting simple texts, as well as difficulty in math skills. These data indicate the relevance of studies and the development of technologies for teaching basic reading and writing repertoires.

Behavior analysis literature show (e.g., Henklain et al., 2017; Lillie & Tiger, 2018; Moroz et al., 2017) concern related to the development of teaching technologies. Behavior analysts agree with Skinner's arguments (1968) that "teaching is the arrangement of reinforcement contingencies (…) it is the act of facilitating learning" (p. 4). This chapter presents and discusses data from research carried out in two laboratories of Londrina State University, LATEC (Laboratory of Behavioral Analysis and Technology) and LADEJE (Laboratory of Development and Evaluation of Educational Games). Researchers from both laboratories have developed technologies for teaching reading and writing, including educational games based on the network of relations and the stimulus equivalence paradigm.

V. B. Haydu (✉) · S. R. de Souza
Universidade Estadual de Londrina, Londrina, PR, Brazil
e-mail: haydu@uel.br

A. R. de Albuquerque, R. M. de Melo (eds.), *Contributions of Behavior Analysis to Reading and Writing Comprehension*, https://doi.org/10.1007/978-3-031-40868-7_3

3.2 Stimulus Equivalence and the Teaching of Reading and Writing

For behavior analysts, difficulties in academic skills reflect the inadequacy of the procedures employed and, therefore, should not be attributed "to the intrinsic characteristics of the student or the environment from which they come" (as described by de Rose, 2005, p. 31; republished in Chap. 1 of this book). Considering that the teaching procedure is at the origin of academic difficulties includes assigning responsibility to those involved in the act of teaching: teachers. This way of interpreting teaching and learning is in line with what was pointed out by Skinner (1969/1975, see also Moroz & Luna, 2013) that, when teaching, teachers should identify the skills that students possess, those that they should learn, and arrange contingencies to facilitate learning.

Among the studies conducted on this topic, we highlight those that employed the principles of behavior analysis, including the notion of relational networks and the stimulus equivalence paradigm. Based on these principles, reading, and writing are verbal operants under the control of antecedent stimuli and generate consequences, like any other operant behavior, but involve mediation by a member of the verbal community (Skinner, 1957). When relations occur between verbal responses and printed texts (e.g., emission of a verbal response in the presence of a written word), this behavior is called textual behavior (Skinner, 1957). In turn, writing involves the emission of a motor response under the control of printed stimuli (copying a text) or verbal stimuli (taking dictation). Writing can also occur through the emission of a response constructed by the ordered selection of printed components (letters, syllables, or words), given the presence of a printed or verbal stimulus sample.

Among the several contributions of behavior analysts to teaching reading and writing behavioral repertoires (see reviews in Haydu & Souza, 2010; Moroz et al., 2017; Queiroz et al., 2011) is the study developed by Sidman (1971). In this study, an intellectually disabled teenager learned to select printed words in the presence of spoken words. He could choose the corresponding object or figure in the presence of the word spoken before. What was important in Sidman's study was that, at the end of the teaching stage, the teenager not only correctly paired the 20 spoken words taught with the corresponding printed word but also selected the corresponding figure/object in the presence of the printed word. Relations that had not been previously trained. This study gave rise to the paradigm proposed by Sidman and Tailby (1982) called stimulus equivalence.

The stimulus equivalence paradigm assumes that teaching at least two conditional relations between stimuli with one element in common leads to the emergence of relations not directly trained. For example, teaching the relations between the stimuli AB and BC may result in the emergence of relations between the stimuli BA and CB (symmetry relations) AA, BB, CC (reflexivity) and AC and CA (transitivity and symmetric transitivity, respectively) (Sidman & Tailby, 1982). In several studies developed by behavior analysts (cf. de Paula & Haydu, 2010; Moroz et al., 2017; Rehfeldt, 2011), reading and writing behaviors were taught based on the stimulus equivalence paradigm, similarly to what Sidman's original study demonstrated (1971). In these studies, reading and writing behaviors are understood as a network of relations (Stromer et al., 1992), including relations between stimuli and between stimuli and responses.

The *Matching-to-Sample* (MTS) procedure, as in Sidman (1971), has been used to teach conditional relations. In this procedure, a sample stimulus is presented, and an observation response produces the presentation of two or more comparison stimuli. The selection of the correct comparison stimulus (specified by the instructor/teacher or researcher) introduces a consequence with a reinforcing function. Conditional relations can also be established with the gradual addition of response elements. For example, in the presence of a printed word [e.g., MATO (BUSH)], a set of letters (H, U, B, S and/or others) is presented, and the selection, in the correct order of the letters that form the printed word (BUSH) is followed by a reinforcing consequence. According to Stromer and Mackay (1992), this procedure is called *Constructed Response Matching-to-Sample* (CRMTS).

The CRMTS was used to teach reading with comprehension and word writing, to stablish generalization of reading and to write new words formed from the component units (syllables and letters) of the words (e.g., Assis et al., 2016; Melo & Serejo, 2009; see reviews in Hübner et al., 2014; Paixão & Assis, 2017). Taking the Melo and Serejo (2009) study as an example, two children, aged between 7 and 8 years old, were submitted to the procedure that included the following steps: (a) a pre-intervention test, (b) teaching word reading with simple syllables formed by two or three syllables composed by consonants and vowels, including the copying with CRMTS, (c) teaching word reading with complex syllables, (d) teaching sentence and short texts reading. At the beginning and the end of the sessions, tasks were performed as games, which required different modalities of reading and writing responses. They also included the CRMTS assembling words from their letters and forming dictated words. The results allowed observing the development of:

> fluent reading and writing with comprehension skills evidenced by performances such as: relating dictated word to printed word and vice versa, reading teaching and recombined words formed by simple and complex syllables, and writing in handwritten dictation and dictation tasks with a constructed response (Melo & Serejo, 2009, p. 110).

3.3 Development and Evaluation of Technology for Teaching Reading and Writing: Studies Developed by LATEC Researchers

LATEC researchers conducted assessment analyses and the development of technologies for teaching reading and writing skills before the laboratory's foundation. It began when students from the *lato sensu* postgraduate course (Specialization in Behavior Analysis) became interested in the theme. On that occasion, the researchers conducted two studies. The first one, developed by Peres (1999), evaluated the effect of a teaching procedure, based on the stimulus equivalence paradigm, on the reading performance of a 12-year-old boy attending the 4th grade of elementary school who presented learning difficulties and problems with social interaction. The second study (Haydu & Tini, 2003) developed and evaluated a program for training Special Education teachers to teach reading using the Mestre® software (Goyos & Almeida, 1996). This software allows teaching relational networks based on MTS and CRMTS procedures. Haydu and Tini concluded that special education teachers could use and program activities for their students, who learned the behaviors taught.

Later, at the *stricto sensu* postgraduation level, six master's dissertations were advised in the Graduate Program in Education at UEL based on the stimulus equivalence paradigm. Four of these dissertations aimed to take the proposed technology to the classrooms, a relevant goal from a social point of view. For example, Ribeiro and Haydu (2009) developed and evaluated a teacher training course for the use of the Mestre® software, which included teaching Behavior Analysis (BA) principles and programming tasks for teaching reading to children with reading difficulties. Nine female teachers participated in the study, and the training course included the following steps: (a) teaching behavior analysis principles and the use of the Mestre® software, as well as the programming of teaching sessions; (b) pre- and post-assessment tests of 1st to 4th grade students of elementary school, who presented learning difficulties related to reading and writing; (c) execution of the teaching sessions using Mestre®; (d) evaluation of the training program. The study's results showed that the participants read 19% of the words in the pretest, and 100% in the post-test. The teachers positively evaluated the program, stating that it would be feasible to use; they even requested a copy of the CD containing the software. Two teachers prepared sessions for teaching reading to two children with partial hearing difficulties, which took place after the end of the study.

Still, regarding the dissertations developed in the Graduate Program in Education at UEL, Machado (2005, see also Machado & Haydu, 2012) conducted a study that assessed a program of teaching word reading for collective situations. Students in Early Childhood Education (aged 5–6 years old) who did not learning difficulties participated in such study. One of the researchers (the publication's first author) conducted the teaching program in three consecutive studies. The researchers prepared easy-made teaching materials (cards and letters of EVA – *Ethylene Vinyl Acetate*). Study 1 evaluated the teaching of reading nine noun words and their generalization for nine words composed of syllables of those words taught in the previous phase. The procedure consisted of: (a) an individual pretest; (b) teaching, in a collective situation, of conditional relations between dictated and printed words, and the construction of words with letters in the presence of printed words through nine steps with the addition of one word at each step; (c) individual post-test. MTS, choice by exclusion,[1] and CRMTS procedures were combined. All participants

[1] In this procedure a sample stimulus is presented (e.g., A2) and, following an observation response, two comparison stimuli are presented simultaneously (e.g., B1 and B2). One of these stimuli is known to the participant, as it has already been paired with another sample stimulus (e.g., A1 – in teaching the relation A1B1) while the other stimulus is unknown (e.g., B2). The selection of the comparison stimulus B2 by the participant, in the presence of the sample stimulus A2, occurs by exclusion of the known stimulus (Dixon, 1977).

named seven of the nine teaching words, but most participants did not correctly construct the words in the presence of pictures or dictated words. Of the 17 participants, only six read the generalization words.

In Study 2 of Machado (2005), 10 of the 17 children who participated in Study 1 were selected. He assessed the performance of the previous procedure steps but with a grouping and rearrangement of the steps' sequence. Words with common syllables were grouped into the teaching steps [e.g., LODO and DEDO (SLUDGE and FINGER); PACA and CALO (PACA and CALLUS)]. Only one of the 10 participants correctly constructed the words using the letters and was able to read the generalization words correctly. The same 10 participants from Study 2 took part in Study 3, and Machado taught six new words involving syllables shared by the teaching words from Study 2. The aim was to verify whether increasing the word reading repertoire would improve the reading of generalization words. Six of the 10 participants read the generalization words. These results demonstrated relations between words and set of letters and generalized reading; and the effectiveness of the stimulus equivalence paradigm for teaching word reading in a collective classroom context.

Based on Machado (2005), a manual for teachers entitled "How to teach your student to read with comprehension" was written (Haydu, 2008). The manual describes a teaching program based on the stimulus equivalence paradigm and the notion of relational networks – the *Program for Teaching Noun Word Reading* (*Programa de Ensino de Leitura de Palavras Substantivadas* [PELPS]). This program describes how literacy teachers can use the stimulus equivalence paradigm and educational games in group or individualized teaching situations. The manual proposes a series of activities with materials that can be easily made by teachers, using, for example, cardboard or EVA. The teaching procedure is detailed, including sequences of words the teachers can teach and adapt to different methodologies and teaching goals. The program suggests six stages, each with 13 steps (except Stage 1, which has only 11 steps). A new word is taught in each of the initial 12 steps. Step 13 assesses the reading of 9–10 generalization words. The manual includes stories the teacher can tell the students, in which the words are contextualized in the plots, as well as complementary activities, integration activities, and games (e.g., lottery with words and pictures, collective dictation, and word assembly games). The games encompass words from the teaching program, which were suggested based on a bibliographic survey of studies on stimulus equivalence and suggestions by the linguist Scliar-Cabral (2003). Table 3.1, adapted from Haydu (2008), specifies a sequence of one-step of the PELPS activities, detailed in the description in the following paragraphs.

PELPS' teaching procedure consists of establishing conditional relations between spoken and printed words, spoken words and constructing words with letters, spoken words and forming words with syllables. The words used are names of characters/objects present in stories, and the teaching goes from simple to complex words as follows:

Table 3.1 PELPS one-step activity sequence

Sequence	Procedure
Preparation	Story-telling
	Painting activity of pictures referring to the story's characters
Teaching program	Telling the story assigned to the referred step
	Teaching the relationship between spoken and printed word
	Teaching word construction with the letters in the presence of the printed word
	Reattempt to teach the relationship between the spoken and printed word
	Reattempt to teach word construction with the letters in the presence of the printed word
Evaluation procedure (perform two trials of each)	Reading the printed word
	Choosing the printed word in the presence of the picture
	Choosing the picture in the presence of the printed word
	Word construction with letters in the presence of the picture
	Word construction with letters in the presence of the spoken word
Reapplication	Reteach the relationship between spoken and printed word and reteach word construction with the letters in the presence of the printed word if the students show more than one incorrect answer in the evaluation procedures test.

Adapted from Haydu (2008)

> in Stage 1, disyllables, without word stress or digraphs; in Stage 2, disyllables and trisyllables, without word stress or digraphs; in Stage 3, monosyllables, disyllables, and trisyllables, with word stress and without digraphs; in Stage 4, monosyllables, disyllables, and trisyllables, without digraphs, with word stress, and with syllables formed with letters whose grapheme and phoneme do not correspond (e.g., "S" with "Z" sound); in Stage 5, monosyllables, disyllables, and trisyllables, with acute word stress, digraphs, and syllables formed with letters whose grapheme and phoneme do not correspond (Haydu, 2014, p. 191).

In brief, the stages of PELPS consist of teaching conditional relations, and each stage comprises the following steps, as described by Amorese and Haydu (2010, p. 202):

1. tell a story including names of the characters/objects to be taught are contextualized, and their pictures are presented;
2. show a large paper card with the current teaching printed word and ask what that word is;
3. name the word of the current step;
4. hand out cards with the teaching word from the current step and the teaching words from the previous step, and ask the students to pick up the card corresponding to the named word;
5. Distribute letters that make up the word from the current and prior steps and ask students to construct the sample word with the letters below the printed card;
6. ask the students to shuffle the letters and repeat the trial to assemble the word. At each trial, reinforce the correct answers, and when the answer is incorrect, ask if

the students are sure, allowing them to present the correct answer. If they do not get it right, show the correct answer.

After each teaching step, an individual assessment of the emergent conditional relations is suggested as follows:

1. naming the printed words,
2. testing the relationship between the printed word and the corresponding picture;
3. testing the picture choice in the presence of the printed word;
4. testing the printed word choice in the presence of the picture;
5. word construction with letters in the presence of the picture;
6. word construction with letters after the dictated word (Amorese & Haydu, 2010, pp. 202–203).

PELPS was used in the study of Amorese and Haydu (2010), which aimed to train three kindergarten teachers to apply for the teaching program in their classes with 12, 14, and 6 students. In addition to the PELPS Manual, the following research materials were used: protocols for recording categories of the teachers' behavior; a handout with the principles of behavior analysis and the stimulus equivalence paradigm (prepared by the researchers); an audio recorder and a video camera. The procedure consisted of: (a) record the teachers' behavior in the classroom before the intervention and pretest students' reading repertoire; (b) training teachers in meetings with the presentation and discussion of the teaching program; (c) implementation of the teaching program by teachers; (d) assessment of the teaching program by teachers and post-test with students. The procedure included teaching and/or tests between: dictated word and picture, dictated word and printed word, picture and printed word, naming printed word, printed word and picture, printed word and word construction with letters, picture and word construction with letters, dictated word and word construction with letters.

The results showed that in the pretest, most students did not read most of the 20 words presented in the test. In the class with 12 students, none could name the words. In the class with 14 students, three of them read 10%, 80%, and 60% of the words. In the class with six students, one named 10% of the words, and another named 5%. In the post-test, however, the students in the three classes read on average 77.91%, 90.71%, 96.26% of the teaching words, and on average 50%, 83.57%, 70% of the generalization words (formed by recombining syllables). These results allowed us to conclude that the PELPS, executed in a collective context, was adequate to teach reading with comprehension. As for the goal of training teachers, we concluded that the teaching program proposed in the Manual "How to teach your student to read with comprehension" is appropriate for preparing teachers to use the PELPS in collective teaching contexts (Amorese & Haydu, 2010).

PELPS was also used in the study of Haydu et al. (2010), which comprised nine students from a School for Youngsters and Adults. In a collective context, this study evaluated teaching reading words to youngsters and adults aged between 18 and 60. The procedures and tasks of PELPS were the same as the study developed by Amorese and Haydu (2010) but with a more significant number of steps. Haydu et al. taught conditional relations between dictated and printed words and the construction of words with letters in the presence of the printed words. Stories presented in the manual were told in 23 alternating steps. Each step involved 9–12 words, and, in the end, Haydu et al. applied a reading comprehension test. Depending on the step, they tested 10–12 generalization words. In the entire procedure, composed of five steps, they taught 63 words and tested the reading ability of 58 generalization words.

Of the nine participants who were present at the beginning of the study (Haydu et al., 2010), only six completed the procedure's five steps. All nine participants learned to relate the dictated words to the printed words and to assemble the words with letters in the presence of the printed words. Those who did not remain in the study could perform the teaching steps of the completed tasks. In the tests, participants named the printed words and assembled the words in the presence of dictated words and pictures. The errors, which happened mainly after introducing the words with language difficulties, consisted of letter position change and inversion and the inclusion of incorrect letters. In the first stages, with few language difficulties, the participants read the generalization words correctly.

The effect of playing games was highlighted in the results of the study conducted by Haydu et al. (2010). When comparing the participants' performance in the tests conducted before and after these activities, it was found that, for example, one participant had a higher percentage of correct answers in the post-test in four of the five sets of teaching words and in all five sets of generalization words. Another participant showed increased rates of correct answers in the post-test compared to the pretest in all five steps of teaching words and all five steps of generalization words following the games. Based on these results and those presented by the other participants who completed the study, the researchers affirmed that the PELPS was effective and efficient in teaching reading with comprehension to youngsters and adults. Besides this, the stages proposed in the equivalence paradigm (teaching conditional relations and testing emerging relations) can be carried out in collective classroom contexts.

The teaching of words has been privileged in the studies described so far. Still, the learning of sentence reading, also based on the stimulus equivalence paradigm, was evaluated by Haydu et al. (2015). In this study, animations (gifs representing actions) corresponding to past, present, and future sentences, spoken and printed, to which the animations should be related, were presented on a computer screen. Initially (Step 1), a pretest assessed the previous reading repertoire. Subsequently, Haydu et al. applied the following steps: training and testing of conditional relations between spoken words, printed words, and pictures (Step 2); training and testing of sentence word ordering (Step 3); the connectivity test, which assesses the possibility that the members of a sequence are related to each other, whether they are adjacent pairs or not (Step 4); and training and testing of conditional relations between spoken, written sentences, and animations (Step 5). When comparing their performance in the pretest and the post-test, participants showed an increase in the percentage of correct answers in word and sentence reading. Haydu et al. concluded that "the teaching of conditional word discriminations followed by the teaching of sentence formation through chaining and the subsequent establishment of stimulus equivalence between animations, spoken sentences, and printed sentences were efficient for establishing reading comprehension of sentences in the present, past, and future tenses" (p. 153).

The studies described in this section, as well as others developed by researchers from a variety of Brazilian research institutions (cf., Gomes et al., 2010; Haydu, 2014; Haydu & Souza, 2010; Henklain et al., 2017) and abroad (cf., Raaymakers et al., 2019; Rehfeldt, 2011), have demonstrated that the equivalence paradigm is an effective teaching technology for teaching reading and writing, as well as several other behavioral repertoires, including math skills. At LATEC, following this practice, in addition to the studies of teaching reading and writing, the researchers developed a program for teaching mathematical functions to elementary school students (Dalto & Haydu, 2015). A teaching procedure was assessed for teaching arithmetic problem-solving through representations on computer screens of scales that balanced when the correct answer was presented (Iégas & Haydu, 2015). Also, in partnership with LADEJE, Sdoukos et al. (2010) developed a game for teaching mathematical skills – DimDim[2]: Negotiating & Playing!

3.4 The Use of Educational Games for Teaching Reading and Writing: Studies Carried out by LADEJE Researchers

The Laboratory of Development and Evaluation of Educational Games (*Laboratório de Avaliação e Desenvolvimento de Jogos Educativos* - LADEJE) is linked to the Department of General Psychology and Behavior Analysis of Londrina State University. The investigations developed at LADEJE are part of the research line "Methodology and technology interventions in different contexts" of the Postgraduate Program in Behavior Analysis. At LADEJE we develop educational games based on the principles and concepts of Behavior Analysis. Its main objective is to create and assess empirically based educational technologies and evaluation methods for educational games.

In relation to games, data from a survey conducted between February and March 2018, with 2853 Brazilians from all social classes, show that 75.5% of respondents use some sort of electronic games, and 30% use board games (analog games). The Game Brazil survey also showed that 82.5% of the interviewed parents stated that their children play on some electronic game platform (Ferreira, 2018). The data from surveys such as the one conducted by Game Brazil suggest that more and more people use games as a means of their own entertainment. In the teaching context, games and gamification strategies have been employed with the purpose of

[2] *DimDim* ia a popular expression for Money in Brazilian Portuguese, similar to dough or bucks in English.

engaging learners in the tasks they perform (Huang & Soman, 2013), while teaching and/or improving academic repertoires. According to Skinner (1984):

> The fascination of video games is adequate proof. What would industrialists not give to see their workers as absorbed in their work as young people in a video arcade? What would teachers not give to see their students applying themselves with the same eagerness? (For that matter, what would any of us not give to see ourselves as much in love with our work?) But there is no mystery; it is all a matter of the scheduling of reinforcements (p. 952).

Educational games can be defined as tools that allow for the planning of teaching contingencies and keep the learner engaged in the task they perform while learning (Gris & Souza, 2016; Perkoski & Souza, 2015). The presence of natural reinforcers related to learning a skill (e.g., learning to write a new word) and the use of arbitrary reinforcers (e.g., points, scores) contribute to greater player engagement (Panosso et al., 2015). In addition to arbitrary and natural reinforcers, games usually have clear and measurable goals, repetition of responses to achieve goals, specific consequences for specific responses, a progressive increase in task complexity, and they provide constant feedback (Linehan et al., 2011). All these characteristics, which bring games closer to behavior-analytically based teaching procedures, reaffirm their potential as teaching tools (Gris et al., 2018).

Although many commercial games can be used for teaching different skills (cf., Cechin et al., 2012), game development can increase the likelihood of the game fulfilling both its educational and recreational functions because its development and assessment can be based on a learning theory without the need for adaptations. However, developing an educational game that is effective and efficient and at the same time keeps the player engaged in the task at hand is a challenge, as it involves the following steps: (a) describing the game's terminal and intermediate behavioral goals; (b) specifying the behaviors that should be taught; and (c) identifying situations in the natural environment in which the behavior should occur. It is still necessary to describe the teaching activities that allow the achievement of such goals and to establish the formal elements of the game (Souza et al., 2019). The Elemental Tetrad (Schell, 2008) has been used as a model at LADEJE to establish the formal elements of the game, i.e., the game technology, mechanics, story, and aesthetics.

Technology refers to the medium through which the game will be presented to the player (analog, digital, virtual reality, paper, or a mixture of these forms); mechanics refers to the game's rules. The story "is the sequence of events that unfolds in your game" (Schell, 2008, p. 41), and the aesthetics refers to the properties of the stimuli, such as images, sounds, shapes, and colors, and it is guided by the story (Gris et al., 2018). After elaborating on all these steps, prototypes are built and evaluated for their efficiency and effectiveness – prototype testing. The game is revised based on the feedback players give, and new prototypes are built in a process known as "iteration" or repetition (Fullerton, 2008; Salen & Zimmerman, 2012; Zimmerman, 2003).

LADEJE has developed games to teach different skills, such as: math skills [DimDim: Negociando & Brincando! (DimDim: Negotiating & Playing – developed by Sdoukos et al., 2010) and Korsan – developed by Gris & Souza, 2016]; food choices [Cestinha Mágica (Magic Basket) – developed by Panosso & Souza, 2013]; bullying [O Espião (The Spy) – developed by Perkoski & Souza, 2014 and the game Liga Escolar Nacional de Basquete sem Bullying (Bullying-Free National School Basketball League – developed by Anjos et al., 2017]; academic social skills [Space Ability: Fazendo Contato com Aliens (Space Ability: Making Contact with Aliens) – developed by Benevides & Souza, 2015]; sex education (Mazzi & Souza, 2018); and reading and writing (AbraKedabra – developed by Souza, 2007). Due to the objectives of this chapter, only the effects of AbraKedabra game on reading and writing behaviors will be presented.

AbraKedabra is an educational board game that has as its ultimate goal the teaching of reading and writing words in Portuguese. The game is based on the relational network notion and uses MTS and CRMTS procedures. Through the game, it is possible to teach Portuguese words and evaluate whether this teaching produced the learning of new words composed by recombining the syllables of previously learned words (generalization words). It was developed for children between 6 and 10 years old and should be used under the supervision of a literate adult. It can be played by up to four children simultaneously.

To enable learning to read and write words, the game was designed to teach a set of relations involving visual stimuli (printed words, printed syllables, and pictures) and auditory stimuli (words and syllables dictated and spoken by the child/player). Table 3.2 presents the relations that can be taught through the game. It is expected that teaching these relations with a set of words (teaching words) will allow recombinative reading and writing to emerge. This procedure is based on the argument made by some behavior analysts (e.g., de Rose, 2005, republished in Chap. 1 of this book; Stromer & Mackay, 1992; Stromer et al., 1992), who consider that reading and writing can be understood as behaviors comprising a relations network. The networks, in principle, are independent, but can be integrated as some behaviors are learned, leading to the emergence of relations not explicitly taught. Teaching these relations constitutes the intermediate goals of the game.

At the beginning of the game, each child gets or draws a card with a printed word (e.g., BALL). They should read the word out loud. If the child cannot read, the supervising adult should do so and ask the child to repeat the name of the word (echoic behavior). Afterward, the child who will start the game is selected by throwing the dice. This child should roll the dice and move their pawn along a track according to the number of squares shown on the dice. Then, using the printed word as a sample stimulus and the squares on the board as comparison stimuli, the player must build the word using syllable cards (Version 1 of the game) or letter blocks (Versions 2 and 3). The game ends when the printed word is built (relation between the printed word and syllable or letter set) and paired with the corresponding picture (relation between the printed word and the picture). Whoever finishes first wins the game.

Other tasks are also required (copying a text, taking dictation, spelling, reading), depending on the square in which the player's pawn stops. Due to the research results that evaluated the prototypes, the game underwent revisions. In the game first version (Version 1), the track was composed of 46 squares, of which 16

Table 3.2 Relationships taught by the game

Relationships	
Matching dictated word to printed word	Auditory-receptive reading
Matching dictated word to picture	Picture identification
Matching picture to spoken word by the child	Picture naming
Matching printed word to spoken word by the child	Textual behavior
Matching printed word to picture	Reading
Matching picture to printed word	Reading
Matching printed word to letter set	Copying a text with word construction
Matching picture to letter set	Picture recognition with word construction
Matching dictated word to letter set	Taking dictation with word construction
Matching printed word to oral spelling	Spelling
Matching printed word to handwriting	Writing
Matching dictated word to handwriting	Taking dictation
Matching picture to handwriting	Writing
Matching dictated to printed syllables	Auditory-receptive reading
Matching printed syllable to syllable spoken by the child	Textual behavior

contained syllables (*Syllable Squares*) of a syllabic family, for example, the syllabic family of D (DA, DE, DI, DO, DU); six *Bonus Squares,* in which players can take a syllable from the pile and with it construct the printed word won or drawn at the beginning of the game or new words; 10 *Picture Squares,* in which players must choose, among a set of cards with pictures, the one that corresponds to one of their words or draw a new picture and try to construct the word related to that picture; Four *Task Rooms*, in which players can choose a new word from a pile and try throughout the game, to complete that word or choose a picture from another pile and try, throughout the game, to build the name of that picture by means of rewarded syllables; *Library square,* in which the player must choose a word from the pile and read it (textual behavior); two *The Witch Who Cannot Spell*, three *The Witch Who Cannot Read and* two *The Witch Who Cannot Write* squares. On these squares, the player must read (textual behavior), write (copy a text or take dictation) and spell a drawn word correctly; a *School Transport* square. If the player's pawn falls on this square, he must take his pawn to the *Library* square and read a word drawn from the pile; and the *Start square*, from which the pawns start. For more information about the game's first version, see Souza and Hübner (2010).

Eight studies were conducted with the AbraKedabra game. This game was the first developed by LADEJE, and its development was due to a research paper published in 2007 entitled: *Emergence* of *printing and spelling skills from Constructed – Response Matching-to-Sample instruction* (CRMTS) (Souza et al., 2007). The article, composed of three experiments, originated from the doctoral thesis of the first author, a professor of the Department of Psychology and Behavior Analysis of the UEL at the time of publication.

In the first two experiments, the CRMTS procedure was used to investigate reading and writing development when teaching involved spelling syllables versus spelling familiar words. Participants in Experiment 1 were five typically developing children, aged 3–5 years, who were exposed to training procedures with familiar consonant-vowel-consonant words (e.g., CAR, PIG, TOY).[3] The words were taught by pairing printed word-letter set (AB) and spoken word-letter set (DB). Subsequently, the tests of the relations DA (spoken word – printed word) and AE (printed word – spoken word) were performed. For teaching, a computer was used. All participants learned the relations AB and DB, and the emergence of the relations DA and AE were verified. They also showed the emergence of generalized spelling and handwriting skills on post-tests. Experiment 2 replicated Experiment 1 with five additional participants, ages ranging from 3 years and 7 months to 5 years and 5 months. The procedure used in this experiment was similar to that of Experiment 1. However, syllables that did not form words known to the children (e.g., KAD, MUP, and ZOT) were employed as experimental stimuli. Again, all children learned the relations AB and DB. One child did not show the emergence of the DA relation, and two children did not show the emergence of the AE relation.

As for the handwriting, only three children correctly wrote at least one of the syllables taught. One child correctly wrote only the letters K and A that form the word KAD. The results confirm the effectiveness of the CRMTS procedure for teaching reading and writing. They, also, indicated that children could achieve better reading performance if they paired the spoken words with the corresponding pictures.

Based on the results obtained in Experiments 1 and 2, a third experiment was developed with five pairs of mothers and children, with the following objectives: (a) to verify whether parents of children considered at risk of school failure would learn to use the CRMTS procedure to teach reading and writing skills to their children, and (b) to investigate whether the procedure carried out by parents with the children would contribute to improving their children's academic performance.

After selecting the words to be taught to each child, the parents learned how to use the CRMTS procedure. Words familiar to the children with language difficulties[4] (consonantal cluster, digraph) were used as experimental stimuli (e.g., *olho* – eye; *surra* – spanking; *filho* – son; *chupeta* – pacifier). The results show that all of them learned the taught relations (AB, DB) and presented the emergence of the tested relations (DA and AE) and the correct handwriting of the trained words. The results also show that the mothers adequately carried out the procedure with their children and reaffirmed the effectiveness of the CRMTS procedure. Some mothers reported using the material developed for the study (cards with printed words and letters) to play with their children. The results of the experiments that comprised this study and the mothers' reports led to the development of the AbraKedabra game (Souza, 2007).

[3] The participants spoke English as their first language.

[4] The children participating in this study spoke Portuguese as their first language.

Initially, a prototype of the game was built and used by Sudo et al. (2008) to teach the writing of words with simple disyllables (e.g., BOLA – ball). Three children aged between 6 and 7 years old who attended elementary school and had difficulty reading these words participated. After taking dictation of 33 words, eight incorrectly written words were selected. Based on a single-subject design, seven intervention sessions were carried out in which they used: (a) a prototype of the AbraKedabra board game (Souza, 2007), (b) a memory game that allowed teaching the relationship between picture and spoken word and picture and printed word, and (c) chalkboard copying activities that allowed teaching the relationship between spoken or printed word and handwritten word. At the end of the study, the eight taught words and 10 more generalization words were dictated (post-test), and handwriting performance was evaluated. Results showed an increase in the number of correctly written words and syllables for the directly taught words and the number of correctly written generalization words for two of the three participants.

In the Sudo et al. (2008) study, instruments other than the board game were used in the intervention sessions. Considering this aspect and the fact that reading was not assessed in that study, Souza and Hübner (2010) conducted new research in which nine pre-literate children aged 5 and 6 participated. Souza and Hübner (2010) used nine disyllable words (BOLA, CAPA, FADA, VELA, MURO, TATU, JATO, GALO, and FACA [BALL, CAPE, FAIRY, CANDLE, WALL, ARMADILLO, JET, ROOSTER, and KNIFE]) as experimental stimuli for teaching. Initially, they evaluated the relations between the printed word and spoken word, spoken word and a set of syllables, spoken word and handwriting, and between picture and printed word (pretest). The intervention phase was composed of 15 sessions with the board game. Finally, the same relations tested in the pretest were again evaluated in the probe and post-test sessions. The results showed an increase in correctly written, read, and constructed teaching words and correct pairings between words and pictures. Although children showed increased correctly selected syllables, they could not accurately write the generalization words.

The less consistent performance observed for the generalization words in the studies conducted by Sudo et al. (2008) and Souza and Hübner (2010) led to a new investigation. Ximenes et al. (2011) conducted a new study to assess the number of sessions with AbraKedabra game for children to read and write both the teaching and generalization words with 100% accuracy. Two 5-year-old preschool children participated. The procedure employed was similar to that of Souza and Hübner (2010). It took 18 and 27 sessions of approximately 30 min, respectively, for Participants 1 and 2 to read, write, and compose the teaching and generalization words.

In 2014, it was questioned whether parents would learn to use the game and employ it for teaching reading and writing words with their children (Pellizzetti & Souza, 2014). Teaching parents to act as their children's teachers are engaging because it can promote the generalization of the content learned in the classroom, and parents can offer their children individualized and constant teaching. In addition, joint work with parents reduces the need for extra services at school, increases the integration between home and school, and can improve the relationship between parents and children (Souza et al., 2007).

Three mother-child dyads participated in the study. The children were 5 years old, had typical development, did not read or write, and attended Kindergarten. As for the mothers, two had completed High School, and one had completed Higher Education. Pellizzetti and Souza (2014) taught six simple disyllable words BOCA, CABO, LOBO, BOLO, BALA, LATA[5] (teaching words). They evaluated the emergent reading of eight generalization words composed by recombining the syllables of these words. In the pretest phase, they tested the relations between printed and spoken words (oral reading), between spoken words and sets of syllables (constructed response matching to sample – CRMTS), between spoken words and handwriting (taking dictation), and between pictures and printed words (matching printed words to pictures) with both the teaching and the generalization words. Next, nine sessions were conducted with the game (intervention phase). Finally, they evaluated again the relations tested initially (post-test) with all words (teaching and generalization words). Although all mothers learned the rules of the game and how to use it, the results showed an increase in the percentage of correct answers only in the pairings between printed word and picture, printed word and sets of syllables, and picture and sets of syllables. In reading and writing tasks, there were no significant changes. Gutart et al. (2016) obtained similar results in directly replicating this study.

In all previous studies, the participants were children with typical development. In 2015, however, Tripiana-Barbosa and Souza replicated the study of Souza and Hübner (2010) with six people with intellectual disabilities. An average of 13.3 intervention sessions were conducted. Tripiana-Barbosa and Souza (2015) observed an increase in the percentage of correctly read words, correctly selected syllables, correct pairings between pictures and printed words, and accurately written syllables of both teaching and generalization words. These results suggest using the AbraKedabra game to teach reading and writing to people with intellectual disabilities.

Until then, all research had been conducted using simple disyllables as experimental stimuli. Whether the game could be used for teaching Portuguese words that do not meet regular patterns of syllabic structure (CV) has been questioned. For example, words that present consonantal clusters (two consecutive consonants within the word). Interested in this issue, Suzuki and Souza (2019) employed an updated board version (Version 2) to evaluate the effects on reading and writing words with consonantal clusters. Version 2 of the game includes an internal track that allows teaching of this type of word. A 5-year-old child participated in the study. Suzuki and Souza (2019) tested the relations between picture and handwriting (CD), between picture and printed word (CB), between printed and spoken word (BA'), and between spoken word and letters (word's construction with letters – AE) with all teaching and generalization words. Then, they conducted nine sessions with the game, followed by a post-test session and a follow-up session after 1 month. The

[5] MOUTH, CAPE, WOLF, CAKE, BULLET, CAN.

post-test and follow-up sessions were similar in structure to the pretest sessions. After the intervention, there was an increase in the number of correctly read and selected words. As for the syllables with consonantal clusters, there was an increase in the number of syllables read-only for the teaching words. These results indicated the need for game readjustment and procedure modifications to assess the effects on generalization words.

Based on the results obtained with Version 2, a new version of the game was developed. Version 3 of AbraKedabra has an external track with 49 cells and an internal track with 18 cells. The outer track enables the teaching of consonant-vowel words (CV), and the inner track enables the teaching of words with consonantal cluster with the letter R (BR, CR, DR, GR, PR, TR) or consonantal digraphs (CH, LH, NH). As for the external track, there was a change only in the number of picture squares (from 10 to 8) and the *Witches Who Cannot Read and Write* squares (from 2 to 3 boxes each). This change aimed to increase the probability of the child training the spelling and writing skills. There was also the introduction of four *Shortcut squares* that allowed players to access the board's inner track. The internal track consists of six *squares with syllables* composed of consonantal meetings or digraphs, three *bonus squares*, four *shortcut squares* that allow players to access the external track, a *Wizard That Cannot Spell,* a *Wizard That Cannot Read,* and a *Wizard That Cannot Write* squares. It should be noted that in these squares, children must perform the same tasks required in the Witch squares. Three *Goblin squares* were included to bring more fun to the game since when falling in one of them, the player must draw a card from the Goblin Card Set and perform the indicated action (e.g., imitate an animal, write a word using the body).

Version 3 of the AbraKedabra Game also consists of 36 cards with words with consonantal clusters and 36 cards with corresponding pictures with a green and blue background, and 8 goblin cards with a green and blue background. Five small blocks of blank paper sheets arranged in parallel with a letter printed on each page are used to compose the words. When turning the pages, each block shows a different letter, enabling the construction of words with up to five letters. Figure 3.1 shows an image of the game and the block of letters.

Following the changes in the game, Suzuki and Souza (2022) conducted a new study, which showed that after the intervention phase, there was an increase for all participants in the number of words correctly written, picture and words perfectly matched, words correctly read (textual behavior) and letters correctly selected for both the teaching and generalization words. It is noteworthy that, besides the changes in the board, there was an increase in the number of intervention sessions (18–24 sessions).

The results obtained in the studies reported in this chapter section indicate the potential of the AbraKedabra game for teaching reading and writing. However, as games are concerned, it is necessary to consider their teaching objectives and assess how much fun they provide for the users, in this case, children. Considering this aspect, evaluations regarding usability and engagement are essential. Usability refers to the characteristics that indicate that the game's mechanics (rules, game functioning, etc.) are precise so that the player may learn them. Engagement refers

Note. PEDRA is the Portuguese word for stone.

Fig. 3.1 Board game image (Version 3) and letter block

to the player's behavior to keep playing. Game engagement and usability can be assessed through the categorized record of behaviors emitted during the games (Gris & Souza, 2016). Evaluations of the engagement and usability of the AbraKedabra game indicate that it has adequate mechanics for the population for which it is intended and enables player engagement (Suzuki & Souza, 2022).

As stated by Hübner et al. (2014), reading and writing can be learned from the combination, fragmentation, and recombination processes of units smaller than a word. It is not necessary to teach all the words in our vocabulary (Matos et al., 2002). The AbraKedabra game uses the CRMTS procedure, in which units smaller than the word (syllables and letters) are selected to compose the word used as a sample. This process can put the child under the control of smaller units than the word and contribute to the reading and writing of the taught words and other words formed by recombining syllables (recombinative reading and writing). Although teaching can happen through cards and software, and positive results are obtained with these tools, using games based on the relational network paradigm may be an exciting and fun alternative to planning teaching contingencies. As already stated by Skinner (1969/1975, pp. 223–224).

> It may seem farfetched to say that a man is reinforced when playing solitaire by the fact that he is successfully controlling his environment. The control which is shown when a game "comes out" or when the play of a single card makes that outcome more probable is far from earthshaking. Nevertheless, such consequences maintain behavior, often for hours, and they do so primarily because they occur on the variable-ratio schedule determined by the rules of the game.

3.5 Final Considerations

As mentioned, behavior analysts have made significant contributions to teaching basic repertoires such as reading and writing. These contributions are not limited to proposing principles that describe these behavioral phenomena and the processes of their acquisition and maintenance. There is a concern with the development of educational technologies, emphasizing Brazilian researchers (cf. Haydu, 2014; Haydu & Souza, 2010; Moroz et al., 2017; Queiroz et al., 2011). This production was leveraged by Sidman and Tailby (1982) formulation of the stimulus equivalence paradigm and the proposition by Stromer et al. (1992) of the network of relations for teaching reading and writing behaviors.

At Londrina State University, LATEC and LADEJE have developed technologies that enable the teaching of reading and writing based on the stimulus equivalence paradigm and the notion of relational networks, discussed in this chapter. Games are among some of the technological resources developed, which have already been part of the research developed since 2007.

The development of a teaching technology that contributes to the teaching and learning of reading and writing is considered fundamental, given the problems faced learning these behaviors (INAF Brasil, 2018). However, as stated by Skinner (1968), the reinforcement contingencies that produce changes in the behavior of organisms are hardly arranged by hand, indicating the need to develop technologies (e.g., devices, instruments, systematized programs, teaching curricula, and software).

Games are one of the ways behavior analysts can plan teaching contingencies. They can be used in teaching and retraining tasks and for testing emergent relations when developing procedures based on the stimulus equivalence paradigm for teaching reading comprehension and other academic skills such as math, music, and languages other than Portuguese. The research demonstrates its effectiveness in teaching these repertoires and engaging learners in programmed activities.

The engagement allowed by teaching technologies is an additional aspect we must consider, as they make it possible to avoid the use of aversive practices by those who teach and the counter control of those who learn (e.g., avoiding and escaping[6] from teaching situations). Thus, technologies and programs must be developed that not only target teaching but do so in ways that increase the likelihood of appropriate and timely behaviors, an issue that Skinner (1968) classifies as motivation. Research of both UEL laboratories have made efforts in this direction, and the papers described represent what has been produced over the course of more than a decade.

References

Amorese, J. S., & Haydu, V. B. (2010). Ensino e aprendizagem de leitura de palavras: Contribuições da análise do comportamento. *Revista Brasileira de Terapia Comportamental e Cognitiva, 12*(1/2), 197–223. https://doi.org/10.31505/rbtcc.v12i1/2.422

Anjos, G., Perkoski, I. R., & Souza, S. R. (2017). *Liga Escolar Nacional de basquete sem Bullying* [Jogo Educativo]. Londrina.

Assis, G. J. A., Calado, J. I. F., & Souza, S. R. (2016). Escolha de acordo com o modelo com resposta construída: Uso de reforçadores condicionais específicos. *Perspectivas em Análise do Comportamento, 7*, 36–47. https://doi.org/10.18761/pac.2015.025

Benevides, R. R., & Souza, S. R. (2015). *Space Ability: Fazendo Contato com Aliens* [Jogo Educativo]. Londrina.

Catania, A. C. (1999). *Aprendizagem: Comportamento, linguagem e cognição* (4. ed., D.G. Souza, Coord. Trad.; 4a ed.). Artmed.

Cechin, V. A., Trois, S., Silva, T. L. K., & Silva, R. P. (2012). Adaptação de jogos comerciais para a sala de aula. In *SBC – Proceedings of SBGames* (pp. 184–187). Retrieved from http://sbgames.org/sbgames2012/proceedings/papers/cultura/C_S15.pdf

Cooper, J. O., Heron, T. E., & Heward, W. L. (2007). *Applied behavior analysis*. Upple Pearson Education.

Dalto, J. O., & Haydu, V. B. (2015). Equivalência de estímulos no ensino de funções matemáticas de primeiro grau no Ensino Fundamental. *Perspectivas em Análise do Comportamento, 6*(2), 124–138. https://doi.org/10.18761/pac.2015.022

de Paula, J. B. C., & Haydu, V. B. (2010). Revisão bibliográfica de pesquisas brasileiras sobre equivalência de estímulos. *Psicologia: Teoria e Pesquisa, 26*(2), 281–294. https://doi.org/10.1590/S0102-37722010000200010

de Rose, J. C. (2005). Análise comportamental da aprendizagem de leitura e escrita. *Revista Brasileira de Análise do Comportamento, 1*(1), 29–50. https://doi.org/10.18542/rebac.v1i1.676

Dixon, L. S. (1977). The nature of control by spoken words over visual stimulus selection. *Journal of the Experimental Analysis of Behavior, 27*, 433–442. https://doi.org/10.1901/jeab.1977.27-433

Ferreira, C. (2018, maio 11). *Pesquisa Game Brasil revela o perfil dos jogadores brasileiros* [Web log post]. Retirado de https://www.torcedores.com/noticias/2018/05/pesquisa-game-brasil-2018-revela-perfil-dos-jogadores-brasileiros

[6] In an escape contingency a response terminates/interrupts an aversive stimulus that is present, and this response is negatively reinforced. For example, faced with aversive teaching conditions in the classroom, the student says he is sick, which is followed by being taken home.

In the avoidance contingency a response terminates the stimulus that anticipates the occurrence of an aversive stimulus thus avoiding or postponing the aversive stimulus, which negatively reinforces the response. For example, the student may avoid going to school on the day of a teacher's class that sets aversive teaching conditions by not attending school the student avoids that teacher's class. For more information see Skinner (1969/1975) or Catania (1999).

Fullerton, T. (2008). *Game design workshop: A playcentric approach to creating innovative games*. Taylor & Francis US.

Gomes, C. G. S., Varella, A. A. B., & de Souza, D. G. (2010). Equivalência de estímulos e autismo: Uma revisão de estudos empíricos. *Psicologia: Teoria e Pesquisa, 26*, 729–737. https://doi.org/10.1590/S0102-37722010000400017

Goyos, C., & Almeida, J. C. (1996). *Mestre* (Versão 1.0) [Programa de computador]. Mestre Software.

Gris, G., & Souza, S. R. (2016). Jogos educativos digitais e modelo de rede de relações: Desenvolvimento e avaliação do protótipo físico do jogo Korsan. *Perspectivas em Análise do Comportamento, 7*(1), 114–132. https://doi.org/10.18761/pac.2016.003

Gris, G., Perkoski, I. R., & Souza, S. R. (2018). Jogos educativos: Aspectos teóricos, aplicações e panorama da produção nacional por analistas do comportamento. In D. L. O. Vilas Boas, F. Cassas, H. L. Gusso, & P. C. M. Mayer (Orgs.), *Comportamento em foco 7: Ensino, comportamento verbal e análise conceitual* (pp. 50–67). ABPMC.

Gutart, A. K. G., Pellizzetti, G. B. F. R., & Souza, S. R. (2016). Recombinação de sílabas: Ensino de leitura e escrita por meio de um jogo de tabuleiro aplicado por mães. In S. R. Souza, V. B. Haydu, & C. E. Costa (Orgs.), *Análise do comportamento aplicada ao contexto educacional* (pp. 139–170). EDUEL.

Haydu, V. B. (2008). *Como ensinar seu aluno a ler com compreensão: Um manual para professores*. Manuscrito não publicado.

Haydu, V. B. (2014). O modelo da equivalência de estímulos na forma de jogos educativos para o ensino de leitura e escrita em contexto coletivo. In V. B. Haydu, S. A. Fornazari, & C. R. Estanislau (Orgs.), *Psicologia e Análise do Comportamento: Conceituações e aplicações à educação, organizações, saúde e clínica* (pp. 177–197). UEL.

Haydu, V. B., & Souza, S. R. (2010). Contribuições da análise do comportamento para o desenvolvimento de tecnologias de ensino. In F. N. Oliveira, P. M. Z. Alliprandini, & S. M. F. Meletti (Orgs.), *A educação em reflexão: Temáticas da formação de professores* (pp. 184–199). EDUEL.

Haydu, V. B., & Tini, J. R. (2003). Ensino de leitura e informática na educação especial: Um programa de capacitação de professores. In M. C. Marquezine, M. A. Almeida, & E. D. O. Tanaka (Orgs.), *Capacitação de professores e profissionais para a educação profissional e suas concepções sobre inclusão* (Vol. 8, pp. 47–59). EDUEL.

Haydu, V. B., da Costa, E. N. F., & Signorini, V. (2010). Ensino de leitura na educação de jovens e adultos com o modelo da equivalência de estímulos: Análise do tipo de erro como função das dificuldades da língua [Resumo]. In *Anais I Congresso de Psicologia e Análise do Comportamento: Diversidade, integração e sustentabilidade* (pp. 90–91). CPAC.

Haydu, V. B., Zuanazzi, A. C., Assis, G. J. A., & Kato, O. M. (2015). Ensino de leitura de sentenças: Contribuições da análise do comportamento. *Psicologia: Teoria e Pesquisa, 31*, 145–154. https://doi.org/10.1590/0102-37722015021869145154

Henklain, M. H. O., Carmo, J. S., & Haydu, V. B. (2017). Produção analítico- comportamental brasileira sobre comportamento matemático e de ensinar matemática: dados de 1970 a 2015. *Temas em Psicologia, 25*(3), 1453–1466. https://doi.org/10.9788/TP2017.3-24

Huang, W. H., & Soman, D. (2013). *A practitioner's guide to gamification of education*. Rotman School of Management: University of Toronto. Retrieved from http://www.rotman.utoronto.ca/-/media/files/programs-and-areas/behavioural-economics/GuideGamificationEducationDec2013.pdf

Hübner, M. M. C., Souza, A. C., & Souza, S. R. (2014). Uma revisão da contribuição brasileira no desenvolvimento de procedimentos de ensino para a leitura recombinativa. In J. C. de Rose, M. S. C. A. Gil, & D. G. de Souza (Orgs.), *Comportamento simbólico: Bases conceituais e empíricas* (pp. 373–420). Oficina Universitária.

Iégas, A. L. de F, & Haydu, V. B. (2015). Resolução de problemas aritméticos: Efeito de ensino com o modelo de uma balança virtual. *Temas em Psicologia, 23*(1), 83–96. https://doi.org/10.9788/TP2015.1-06

Inaf Brasil. (2018). *Indicadores de alfabetismo funcional. INAF Brasil 2018: Resultados preliminares*. Retrieved from http://acaoeducativa.org.br/wp-content/uploads/2018/08/Inaf2018_Relat%C3%B3rio-Resultados-Preliminares_v08Ago2018.pdf

Lillie, M. A., & Tiger, J. H. (2018). Acquisition and generative responding following print-to-braille construction response training with sighted learners. *Journal of Applied Behavior Analysis, 52*, 286–298. https://doi.org/10.1002/jaba.516

Linehan, C., Kirman, B., Lawson, S., & Chan, G. (2011). Practical, appropriate, empirically-validated guidelines for designing educational games. In *Proceedings of the 2011 annual conference on human factors in computing systems – CHI'11*. https://doi.org/10.1145/1978942.1979229

Machado, L. M. (2005). *Tecnologia da equivalência de estímulos para o ensino de leitura em sala de aula*. Unpublished master's thesis, Universidade Estadual de Londrina.

Machado, L. M., & Haydu, V. B. (2012). Escolha de acordo com modelo e equivalência de estímulos: Ensino de leitura de palavras em situação coletiva. *Psicologia da Educação, 35*, 72–94.

Matos, M. A., Hübner, M. M., Serra, V. R. B. P., & Avanzi, A. L. (2002). Rede de relações condicionais e leitura recombinativa: Pesquisando o ensinar a ler. *Arquivos Brasileiros de Psicologia, 54*(3), 285–303.

Mazzi, L. C., & Souza, S. R. (2018). *EduSex* [Jogo Educativo]. Londrina.

Melo, R. M., & Serejo, P. (2009). Equivalência de estímulos e estratégias de intervenção para crianças com dificuldade de aprendizagem. *Interação em Psicologia, 13*(1), 103–112. https://doi.org/10.5380/psi.v13i1.8723

Moroz, M., & Luna, S. V. de. (2013). Professor: O profissional do ensino! Reflexões do ponto de vista behaviorista/comportamental. *Psicologia da Educação, 36*, 115–121.

Moroz, M., Llausas, R. V., Kramm, D., & Bovolon, S. (2017). Leitura, escrita e equivalência de estímulos: Em foco procedimentos de ensino. *Psicologia da Educação, 44*, 103–111. https://doi.org/10.5935/2175-3520.20170010

Paixão, G. M., & Assis, G. J. A. (2017). Uso do procedimento de constructed response matching to sample: Uma revisão da literatura. *Perspectivas em Análise do Comportamento, 8*, 47–60. https://doi.org/10.18761/pac.2016.038

Panosso, M. G., & Souza, S. R. (2013). *Cestinha Mágica* [jogo educativo]. Londrina.

Panosso, M. G., Haydu, V. B., & Souza, S. R. (2015). Características atribuídas a jogos educativos: Uma interpretação analítico-comportamental. *Revista Brasileira de Psicologia Escolar e Educacional, 19*(2), 233–241. https://doi.org/10.1590/2175-3539/2015/0192821

Pellizzetti, G. B. D. F. R., & Souza, S. R. (2014). Controle por unidades menores que a palavra: Jogo de tabuleiro educativo aplicado por mães. *Temas em Psicologia, 22*(4), 823–837. https://doi.org/10.9788/TP2014.4-12

Peres, E. A. (1999). *Problemas de interação social e dificuldades de leitura: O paradigma da equivalência aplicado a um caso clínico*. Monografia não publicada, Universidade Estadual de Londrina.

Perkoski, I. R., & Souza, S. R. (2014). *O Espião* [jogo educativo]. Londrina.

Perkoski, I. R., & Souza, S. R. (2015). "O Espião": Uma perspectiva analítico-comportamental do desenvolvimento de jogos educativos de tabuleiro. *Perspectivas em Análise do Comportamento, 6*(2), 74–88. https://doi.org/10.18761/pac.2015.020

Queiroz, A. B. M., Martins, T. C., & Gióia, P. S. (2011). Teses e dissertações sobre leitura recombinativa disponíveis eletronicamente: Algumas características da produção brasileira. *Psicologia: Teoria e Prática, 13*, 180–193.

Raaymakers, C., Garcia, Y., Cunningham, K., Krank, L., & Nemer-Kaiser, L. (2019). A systematic review of derived verbal behavior research. *Journal of Contextual Behavioral Science, 12*, 128–148. https://doi.org/10.1016/j.jcbs.2019.02.006

Rehfeldt, R. A. (2011). Toward a technology of derived stimulus relations: An analysis of articles published in the Journal of Applied Behavior Analysis, 1992-2009. *Journal of Applied Behavior Analysis, 44*(1), 109–119. https://doi.org/10.1901/jaba.2011.44-109

Ribeiro, M. J. L., & Haydu, V. B. (2009). Dificuldades de Leitura: Capacitação de professores para a utilização de uma metodologia de ensino informatizada. In S. R. Souza, & V. B. Haydu (Orgs.), *Psicologia comportamental aplicada: Avaliação e intervenção nas áreas do esporte, clínica, saúde e educação* (pp. 113–135). EDUEL.

Salen, K., & Zimmerman, E. (2012). *Regras do jogo: Fundamentos do design de jogos*. Blucher.
Schell, J. (2008). *The art of game design: A book of lenses*. Taylor & Francis.
Scliar-Cabral, L. (2003). *Guia prático de alfabetização: Baseado em princípios do sistema alfabético do português do Brasil*. Contexto.
Sdoukos, S. S., Pellizzetti, G. B. de F. R., Ruas, T. V., Xander, P., de Souza, S. R., & Haydu, V. B. (2010, outubro). Desenvolvimento de um jogo de tabuleiro para o ensino de manejo de dinheiro com base em relações de estímulos equivalentes [Resumo]. *XI Reunião Anual da Sociedade Brasileira de Psicologia, 6*.
Sidman, M. (1971). Reading and auditory-visual equivalences. *Journal of Speech and Hearing Research, 14*, 5–13. https://doi.org/10.1044/jshr.1401.05
Sidman, M., & Tailby, W. (1982). Conditional discrimination vs. matching to sample: An expansion of the testing paradigm. *Journal of the Experimental of Behavior, 37*, 5–22. https://doi.org/10.1901/jeab.1982.37-5
Skinner, B. F. (1957). *Verbal behavior*. Applenton-Century-Crofts.
Skinner, B. F. (1968). *The technology of teaching*. Appleton-Century-Crofts.
Skinner, B. F. (1969/1975). *Contingências do reforço: Uma análise teórica* (R. Moreno, trad.). Abril Cultural.
Skinner, B. F. (1984). The shame of American education. *American Psychologist, 39*(9), 947–995.
Souza, S. R. (2007). *AbraKedabra: Construindo palavras* [jogo de tabuleiro]. Silvia Regina de Souza.
Souza, S. R., & Hübner, M. M. C. (2010). Efeitos de um jogo de tabuleiro na aquisição de leitura e escrita. *Acta Comportamentalia, 18*, 215–242.
Souza, S. R., Goyos, C., Silvares, E. F. M., & Saunders, R. (2007). Emergence of printing and spelling skills from constructed-response matching-to-sample instruction (CRMTS). *European Journal of Behavior Analysis, 8*, 49–64. https://doi.org/10.1080/15021149.2007.11434273
Souza, S. R., Perkoski, I. R., & Anjos, G. (2019). Desenvolvimento de jogos educativos para o ensino de comportamentos de prevenção contra o bullying: Procedimento de design iterativo. In A. L. Ferreira, & P. Faleiros (Orgs.), *Jogos comportamentais: Análises e atuações no contexto do dia a dia*. Imagine Publicações.
Stromer, R., & Mackay, H. A. (1992). Spelling and emergent picture-printed word relations established with delayed identity matching to complex samples. *Journal of Applied Behavior Analysis, 25*, 893–904. https://doi.org/10.1901/jaba.1992.25-893
Stromer, R., Mackay, H. A., & Stoddard, L. T. (1992). Classroom applications of stimulus equivalence technology. *Journal of Behavioral Education, 2*(3), 225–256. https://doi.org/10.1007/BF00948817
Sudo, C. H., Soares, P. G., Souza, S. R., & Haydu, V. B. (2008). Equivalência de estímulos e uso de jogos para ensinar leitura e escrita. *Revista Brasileira de Terapia Comportamental e Cognitiva, 10*(2), 223–238. https://doi.org/10.31505/rbtcc.v10i2.228
Suzuki, B. M., & Souza, S. R. (2019). Efeitos do jogo AbraKedabra sobre a leitura e a escrita de palavras com encontros consonantais. *Acta Comportamentalia, 27*(3), 351–370.
Suzuki, B. M., & Souza, S. R. (2022). Avaliação de um jogo de tabuleiro no ensino de palavras com encontros consonantais. *Acta Comportamentalia, 30*(1), 29–50.
Tripiana-Barbosa, A., & de Souza, S. R. (2015). A board game for the teaching, reading, and writing to intellectually disabled people. *Behavior Analysis: Research and Practice, 15*(1), 90–106. https://doi.org/10.1037/h0101073
Ximenes, V. S., Canato, T., & Souza, S. R. (2011). Ensino de leitura recombinativa: Efeito do número de sessões com uso de um jogo de tabuleiro [Resumo]. *Anais do XX Encontro Anual de Iniciação Científica e X Encontro de Pesquisa da UEPG*. Retrieved from http://eventos.uepg.br/eaic/anais
Zimmerman, E. (2003). Play as research: The iterative design process. In B. Laurel (Org.), *Design research: Methods and perspectives*. MIT Press. Retrieved from https://static1.squarespace.com/static/579b8aa26b8f5b8f49605c96/t/59921253cd39c3da5bd27a6f/1502745178453/Iterative_Design.pdf

Part II
Modules of the Teaching Program Learning to Read and Write in Small Steps

Chapter 4
Teaching Irregular Words Through the Teaching Program Learning to Read and Write in Small Steps

Raquel Melo Golfeto and Lidia Maria Marson Postalli

4.1 Introduction

In recent decades, school performance rates in national assessments have shown, among the various subjects, low rates in reading and reading comprehension. Despite the plans and goals established to improve educational averages, Brazil has still shown little progress in this regard. In the latest assessment of the Program for International Student Assessment (PISA), in 2018, conducted by the Organization for Economic Cooperation and Development (OECD), 50.1% of Brazilian 15-year-old students showed reading performance at level 2, considered basic, on a scale of 1–6. At this level, students are able to identify the general idea of a moderately sized text, find explicit information, and reflect on the form and purpose of the material (Brasil, 2019; OECD, 2019). In addition to these students, children in the early school years, people with disabilities, and young people in primary and secondary education have been presenting school failure and are commonly blamed for being unable to learn to read and write (Ferreiro, 2002).

The Learning to Read in Small Steps (ALEPP) teaching program is composed of several modules, some experimentally evaluated and made available for use at scale, and others in different stages of development, evaluation and revision. Deisy das Graças de Souza, Júlio C. de Rose and Elenice S. Hanna are responsible for ALEPP'S overall.

R. M. Golfeto (✉)
Universidade Federal de São Carlos, São Carlos, SP, Brazil

Aprendizagem, Ribeirão Preto, SP, Brazil
e-mail: rmgolfeto@gmail.com

L. M. M. Postalli
Universidade Federal de São Carlos, São Carlos, SP, Brazil

A. R. de Albuquerque, R. M. de Melo (eds.), *Contributions of Behavior Analysis to Reading and Writing Comprehension*, https://doi.org/10.1007/978-3-031-40868-7_4

In order to contribute to student learning, structured and systematic teaching conditions are required. One of the challenges in the scientific field has been to investigate the teaching and learning process of reading and writing skills. The purpose has been to evaluate strategies for teaching these skills so that the learner learns not only to decode the graphemes that form a printed word or correctly write the phonemes of a spoken word, but is able to understand a word or understand a sentence or text.

In Brazil, many studies have been conducted with the aim of developing teaching procedures that contribute to the acquisition of reading and writing skills with comprehension (da Paixão & de Assis, 2017; Mauad et al., 2004; Paula & Haydu, 2010). Among these studies are those that have been using the *Learning to Read and Write in Small Steps* (ALEPP) teaching program, developed in the 1980s by a group of researchers (de Rose et al., 1989, 1992, 1996; de Souza et al., 2004) and based on the principles of Behavior Analysis and the stimulus equivalence paradigm (Mackay & Sidman, 1984; Sidman & Cresson, 1973; Sidman & Tailby, 1982). From this perspective, language is understood as verbal behavior, and reading and writing are specific types of verbal behavior, subject to the same properties as operant behavior: the product of the interaction between organism and environment, subject to control relations between stimuli, between stimuli and responses, and between responses and consequences. What is characteristic of verbal behavior is that its effect on the environment will occur through the mediation of another person (de Souza & de Rose, 2006; Skinner, 1957).

The stimuli that precede a verbal response may participate in different ways in controlling these responses, which leads to different verbal operants (Skinner, 1957). Among the verbal operants, textual behavior, or reading, is characterized by the verbal response (vocal or gestural) evoked by textual stimulus; in copying a text, the written response is emitted under the control of the textual stimulus; and in taking dictation, the written response is emitted under the control of the oral stimulus. The stimulus equivalence paradigm has provided the means to study language and thus the processes by which reading and writing comprehension are acquired (Sidman, 1971, 1994, 2000; Sidman & Tailby, 1982). Relations among stimuli and between stimuli and responses can function independently (Lee & Pegler, 1982) but interrelated when the reader is proficient (for more information see Chap. 1 of this volume). When stimuli in a class (e.g., spoken word, printed word, and corresponding picture) become equivalent, the relations between them may be interrelated. When we teach the learner to relate a word he hears, e.g., *cow*[1] to the printed word COW and if the same spoken word *cow* is related to the animal **cow**, we can say that these stimuli are related by equivalence and are interchangeable if the relations between these elements attest to the mathematical properties of reflexivity (if the printed word COW is related to itself, the dictated word *cow* is related to the dictated word *cow* and the animal **cow** is related to the animal **cow**), symmetry (if *cow* is related to the animal **cow**, then **cow** is related to *cow*) and transitivity (if *cow is*

[1] *vaca* in Portuguese.

related to the animal cow and *cow* is related to the printed word COW, then **cow** is related to COW) (Albuquerque & Melo, 2005; de Souza et al., 1999; Sidman, 2000; Sidman & Tailby, 1982).

ALEPP is based on learning principles (Bori, 1974; Holland & Skinner, 1961; Keller, 1968; Skinner, 1968) and establishes the active participation of the learner as part of the learning process. During exposure to this teaching program, the learner remains continuously active and receives immediate feedback of his performance at each task. In case of error, the learner has the opportunity to redo the task, strengthening the learning process. Each teaching module is planned to the learner starts by performing tasks he is capable of doing and only then proceeds to more complex tasks. For each type of task there is an instruction that prompts a response. The learner goes through a planned sequence of steps consisting of trials so that at the end he reaches the expected performance. The module is organized in teaching steps, with a set of words to be taught, and allows the learner's performance to be continuously assessed through pre and post-tests. If the learner has met the criterion, he can start the next teaching step (de Rose et al., 1996).

The ALEPP teaching program has been showing its effectiveness in teaching basic repertoires for reading and writing skills to children with a history of school failure or at risk of school failure (de Rose et al., 1989, 1992, 1996; de Souza & de Rose, 2006; de Souza et al., 1999, 2009; Fava-Menzori et al., 2018; Hanna et al., 2004; Melchiori et al., 1992, 2000; Reis et al., 2009). It has also been shown to be a useful tool for teaching reading and writing to other populations, such as people with intellectual disabilities (Benitez & Domeniconi, 2016; de Freitas, 2012; Melchiori et al., 2000; Silva, 2018), illiterate adults (Bandini et al., 2014; Calcagno et al., 2016; Melchiori et al., 2000), and people with hearing impairment (Lucchesi et al., 2015a, b).

Currently, ALEPP consists of three teaching modules (de Souza & de Rose, 2006; de Souza et al., 2004). The first module (described in de Souza et al., 2009) aims to teach reading of regular Portuguese words, composed of two or three syllables, with simple spelling (simple syllables consonant-vowel type), such as *bolo*, *vaca*, *tatu*, *mala*, *bico* and *tubo*. Module 2 teaches reading and writing of irregular words of the Portuguese language controlled by contextual rules or composed by digraphs or consonantal meetings or by graphemes s, r, l or n (in the middle or at the end of the syllable), for example, *moça* (ç), *camiseta* (s with z sound), *placa* (with L between a consonant and a vowel), *ninho* (nh) and *banda* (with N between a consonant and a vowel). Module 3 (presented in Chap. 5 of this book) aims to assess reading comprehension of short texts from children's storybooks.

This chapter aims to describe the teaching structure of Module 2 in the initial versions and also in the current version, and to describe studies that have used this Module. To this end, it is subdivided into two main sections and concluding remarks. The first section is divided into three subsections; the first of them will present the first version of Module 2 presented in a folder-catalogue; the second will present the version planned in an offline software called ProgLeit (Rosa Filho et al., 1998) composed of two programs: one for teaching reading skills and one for writing skills; and the third subsection will present the current structure of Module 2 of the

ALEPP teaching program conducted through the GEIC platform (*Computer Individualized Teaching Manager*). The second main section will present the studies that have used Module 2 and the results obtained in its large-scale application in partnership with the city hall of a city in the state of São Paulo. Finally, the final considerations will address the main aspects addressed in the chapter.

4.2 Module 2

For beginners, relating graphemes and phonemes in reading written words, and phonemes with graphemes in writing words, often requires additional strategies to assist in the literacy process. The challenge is greater when it comes to decoding phonemes and graphemes present in Portuguese irregular words, since they are not governed by simple orthographic rules, as in the case of words with canonical or simple syllables (consonant-vowel type). For example, in Portuguese irregular words, there are cases in which phonemes may be represented by different graphemes, as in the case of the phoneme /s/ spelled by more than one grapheme in words such as *taça*, *pássaro*, and *pasto*;[2] or the opposite, cases in which the same grapheme may represent different phonemes, as in the case of X's sometimes with the sound of /z/, as in *exame*, sometimes with the sound of /ch/, in words such as *lixo*.[3]

Given the difficulties presented by the students and also the complexity of the orthographic rules of irregular words in the Portuguese language, Module 2 of ALEPP was specially designed to teach reading and writing of irregular words, with variations in grapheme-phoneme correspondences. The module is designed for learners who have mastered the contents of Module 1. The tasks are *Matching-to-Sample* (MTS) tasks between auditory and textual stimuli, according to the stimulus exclusion procedure[4] (Costa et al., 2001; Dixon, 1977; Ferrari et al., 1993) and *Constructed-Response Matching-to-Sample* (CRMTS) tasks (Dube et al., 1991; Mackay & Sidman, 1984). In Module 2, no pictures corresponding to the teaching words are used.

The composition of the Module in teaching units to work with the different irregularities of the Portuguese language (e.g., nh, lh, ge-gi among others) configures a multiple exemplar training. Teaching through multiple exemplar trainingmay contribute to the establishment of control by minimal units (Skinner, 1957). When an individual learns a large set of exemplars (words), he can gradually develop a reading repertoire controlled by minimal units: syllables or letters or target irregularities. Such units can acquire control in corresponding phonemic production, allowing

[2] In English the words mean cup, bird and pasture.

[3] In English the words mean exam and garbage.

[4] Exclusion (Dixon, 1977) is an errorless teaching procedure in which, A known word and an unknown word (to be taught) are presented as comparison stimuli when a new word is dictated in a auditory-visual matching-to-sample task. The learner can select the new word by excluding the known word.

the individual to read a variety of new words without additional training. This control by smaller units from the teaching of larger units (words) can also be observed in writing, and in with other operants (de Rose et al., 1989, 1992; de Souza et al., 2009, 2014; Hübner et al., 2009, 2014; Hübner D'Oliveira & Matos, 1993; Matos et al., 2006; Matos & Hübner-D'Oliveira, 1992; Mueller et al., 2000). If the learner reads novel words composed of recombinations of smaller units of the taught words, one can call this repertoire generalized reading or proficient reading, because the reading is under control of minimal units (de Rose et al., 1992; de Souza et al., 2014; Hübner et al., 2014).

The three versions of Module 2 will be presented below, initially applied in a folder-catalogue, later through the off-line software ProgLeit (Rosa Filho et al., 1998) and, currently, through the online software platform GEIC.

4.2.1 Initial Version of Module 2 – Folder-Catalogue

In its first version, in a folder-catalogue, Module 2 had 12 teaching units, one for each irregularity of the Portuguese language: vRc, vSc, vNc, vLc, que-qui, cRv, cLv, x with /z/ sound, ç, gue-gui, ge-gi and ch (de Rose et al., 1992). For the irregularities indicated with the letters 'v' and 'c', such as vRc, 'v' refers to the vowel and 'c' to the consonant being in this case words like *poRta*, *gaRfo*.[5] At the end of each unit, a generalization test was conducted with 25 new words with different irregularities, including the 12 directly taught and 13 untaught irregularities (ce-ci, lh, nh, soft r, rr, s with /z/ sound, ss, que-qui, ã-ão, x with /ch/ sound). The matching trials between dictated and printed words were conducted on paper sheets (in horizontal position) organized in folders. During the session, the folder was rotated 90° and placed on a support so that the spine was positioned upwards, allowing the experimenter to present the trials by turning each folder page.

Each unit was conducted in four teaching steps of four words of the same target irregularity ('nh', for example), being taught 16 words in all. Each teaching step was composed of a pre-test, a teaching step, and a post-test for taught words and also for words not taught with the same target irregularities, thus verifying the reading generalization to new words. Generalization tests with new words containing the 25 irregularities were performed between teaching units.

Traininig Step The pre-test included matching printed words to dictated words (CA) in which the auditory sample was always a baseline word (from Module 1), with one of the comparison stimuli being a baseline word (correct choice stimulus) and the other being a new word (teaching or generalization word). As soon as the printed word corresponding to the dictated word was selected, the reading of words of the target irregularity, teaching or generalization irregularity was evaluated. The trial began with the instruction "Point to" and, in sequence, the dictated word was

[5] In English the words mean door and fork.

presented, for example, "finger", simultaneously with two comparison printed words: the word finger (correct choice stimulus) and the other word with the step's target irregularity (incorrect choice stimulus), such as *roça*. After the learner made the selection response, the following instruction was presented: "And the other word, what is it?" and then the learner should read the new word. The test block consisted of 12 trials, with four trials of reading teaching words, four trials of reading generalization words, and the remaining four trials evaluated retention of the words taught in the previous step (in the first step, words with single syllables were used). In case of a pairing error, no consequence was presented, and the learner was not asked to read the other word. If the learner was 100% correct in the abilities assessed, he advanced to the pre-test of the next teaching step. If the learner scored incorrectly, he was taught the target words of this step. Table 4.1 shows the general sequence of the steps of a teaching step of Module 2 – folder-catalog.

The teaching step was composed of 14 exclusion trials and 14 novelty control trials that were presented randomly. In the exclusion trials, two printed words were presented as comparison stimuli, a baseline word (from Module 1) and a novel word (to be taught) and the auditory sample was the novel teaching word. The learner could select the novel word by excluding the known (baseline) word. In novelty control trials, the dictated word was the known/familiar word (from Module 1) and one of the comparison stimuli was a baseline word (correct choice stimulus) and the other was a novel (teaching) word. After selecting the correct word, the child was asked to read the new (unselected) word. This trial had two objectives: (1) to verify whether the learner was responding by exclusion in the trial with the new word or was just choosing a new word, which is called "control by stimulus novelty"; and (2) to teach reading the target word. Correct responses were followed by a social consequence (praise). In case of an error in the selection response, the experimenter asked "Are you sure?" and waited for a new response to be emitted by the learner. Errors in selecting the printed word that did not correspond to the dictated word prompted the question "Are you sure?" Errors in reading were followed by the presentation of the next trial. This step had no criteria for advancing to the next step.

The post-test, similar to the pre-test, consisted of the eight pairing trials between the dictated word and the printed word (AC) and the reading of the four teaching words and four generalization words. The criterion was 100% of correct responses in the post-test. In case of error, the step was repeated in the following session.

Generalization Test The generalized reading tests were performed with new words containing the 25 irregularities and occurred between teaching units. Among the words, 12 contained the taught irregularities and 13 had untaught irregularities. Ten words with single syllables taught in Module 1 were mixed with the words with irregularities. For the trials of reading irregular words, the learner's performance was consequenced with tokens, regardless of success or failure. In the trials corresponding to the reading of simple words, the correct response was followed by social reinforcement.

Table 4.1 General sequence of steps in a Module 2 teaching step – folder-catalogue

Steps	Tasks	Number of trials	Illustration of the trials	Accuracy Criteria
Pre-test	Novelty control trials: Pairing of dictated word-printed word (AC) with baseline words + Reading teaching target words (CD)	**12 trials** 12 simple words 4 teaching words and 4 generalization words and 4 baseline words	"Point *tatu*" "And the other word, what is it?" [folha tatu]	= 100%: next step ≠100%: education stage
Teaching	Exclusion trials: AC (target words) Novelty control attempts: AC (baseline words) + CD (target words)	**28 trials** 14 trials with teaching words 14 tries: simple words and 04 teaching words	"Point *molho*" [bolo molho] "Point *mala*" "And the other word, what is it?" [folha mala]	100% accuracy
Post-test	Control trials: AC (baseline words) + CD (target words)	**8 trials** 4 teaching words + 4 generalization words	"Point *bico*" "And the other word, what is it?" [bico folha]	= 100%: general post-test ≠ 100%: repeat step

Note. **The words in Portuguese were maintained in the examples presented in Tables 4.1, 4.2, 4.3 and 4.4**

4.2.2 *Progleit Offline Software Version*

The later version of Module 2, in the off-line software ProgLeit (Rosa Filho et al., 1998), consisted of two programs, one that taught reading (Reading Program) and another that taught writing in a dictation task (Dictation Program). The Module consisted of 16 teaching units, one for each irregularity: lh, ch, nh, ç, vSc, vRc, vNc,

Table 4.2 General sequence of a Module 2 teaching step – reading program

Steps	Tasks	Number of trials	Illustration of the trials	Accuracy criteria
Pre-test	Novelty control trials: pairing of dictated word-printed word (CA) with baseline words +Reading teaching target words (CD)	**8 trials:** 8 simple words 4 teaching and 4 generalization words	"Point *mala*" "And the other word, what is it?" folha mala	= 100%: next step ≠100%: education stage
Teaching	Exclusion trials: AC (target words) Novelty control trials: AC (baseline words) + CD (target words) Baseline trials: AC	**10 trials:** 4 trials with teaching words 4 trials: simple words and 04 teaching words 2 trials	"Point *molho*" molho tatu "Point *bico*" "And the other word, what is it?" palha bico "Point *bule*" gato bule	100% accuracy
Post-test	Control trials: AC (baseline words) + CD (target words)	**4 trials:** 4 simple words + 4 teaching words	"Point *vaca*" "And the other word, what is it?" vaca molho	= 100%: general post-test ≠ 100%: repeat step

Table 4.3 General sequence of a Module 2 teaching step – dictation program

Steps	Tasks	Number of trials/ words	Illustration of the trials	Accuracy criteria
Pre-test	Pairing between dictated words-printed words (AC) with baseline words	**13 trials:** 5 simple words	"Point *bule*" gato bule vaca	= 100% next step ≠ 100% education step
	Writing by composition of teaching target words (AE)	4 words of teaching and 4 generalization	"Write *folha*" fol s h c a p a d a o	
Teaching	Exclusion trials: AC (target word)	**10 trials:** 4 trials	"Point *colheita*" colheita tapete	100% accuracy
	Control trials: AC (baseline words) + AE (target words)	4 trials	"Point *aluno*". palha aluno "Write *palha*" pal s h c a p a d a o	
	AC Baseline trials	2 trials	"Point *muleta*" apito muleta	
Post-test	(baseline words)	**7 trials:** 3 tries simple words	"Point *gato*" gato bule vaca	= 100%: next step ≠ 100%: repeat step
	AE (target words)	4 teaching words	"Write *palha*" pal s h c a p a d a o	
General Post-test	AC (baseline words)	13 trials: 5 tries simple words	"Point *cow*" gato bule vaca	no criteria
	AE (target words)	4 teaching words and 4 generalization words	"Write *palha*" pal s h c a p a d a o	

Table 4.4 General sequence in a Module 2 teaching step via GEIC

Steps	Tasks	Number of trials	Illustration of the trials		Accuracy criteria
Pre-test	Dictated word-printed word (AC) pairing	**16 tries:** 4 trials teaching words and 2 with pseudowords and 2 with generalization words	"Point *palha*" palha pala	"Write *palha*" pal s h c a p a d a o	= 100% next step ≠ 100% teaching step
	Dictation by composition (AE)	8 attempts palvras teaching			
Teaching	**Multiple Difference Training**	**36 trials**	"Point *palha*" palha aluno	"Point *vaca*" vaca molho	No criteria
	Dictated word-printed word (AC) pairing	16 with teaching words and 8 baseline words			
	Dictation by composition (AE)	8 word trials at teaching	"Write *palha*" pal s h c a p a d a o	"Write the same" palha pal s h c a p a d a o	
	Copy with composition (CE)	4 word trials at Teaching			
	Critical Difference Training	12 trials 12 trials words of teaching	"Point *palha*" palha pala		
	Pairing dictated word-printed word (AC)				
	Discrimination Training Pairing dictated word-printed word (AC) Dictation by composition (AE)	12 trials 8 word trials teaching 4 word trials teaching	"Point *palha*" palha folha	"Write *palha*" pal s h c a p a d a o	
Post-test	Pairing dictated word-printed word (AC)	**16 tries:** 4 trials teaching words and 2 with pseudowords and 2 with generalization words	"Point *palha*" palha folha	"Write *palha*" pal s h c a p a d a o	100% next step ≠ 100% teaching step
	Dictation by composition (AE)	8 word trials at teaching			
Reading Test	Reading (CD)	**10 tries:** 4 trials words of teaching and 2 of generalization	"What word is this?" palha		no criteria
	Naming of pictures (BD) (Module 1)	4 figure naming trials	"What word is this?" 		

vLc, cRv, cLv, rr, r (soft), ge-gi, ce-ci, que-qui and gue-gui. For both reading and writing instructions, each unit taught 16 words with the same target irregularity and consisted of four teaching steps. Each teaching step consisted of the following steps: Pre-test, Teaching, Post-test, and General Post-test (de Souza et al., 1999).

Reading Program The Module 2 Reading Program of the ProgLeit software version (Rosa Filho et al., 1998) had a similar structure to the program conducted in folder-catalog. In this version, baseline trials with words from Module 1 were included in the teaching and the teaching units of the irregularities lh, nh, rr, r (soft) and ce-ci (and removed the teaching unit x with the /z/ sound that was only assessed).

Training Step The pre-test presented eight trials to assess the reading words which contained the target irregularity, with four words to be taught in the step and four generalization words combined with pairing trials between the dictated word and printed word, with words from Module 1. The trial began with an auditory-visual pairing task with the instruction "Point to (dictated word)" in the presence of two comparison stimuli – the printed word corresponding to the dictated word (correct choice stimulus) and the other word with the step's target irregularity (incorrect choice stimulus). After the selection response of one of the words, the following instruction was presented: "And the other word, what is it?" The learner should read the word (which would be recorded by the instructor by typing the answer using the computer keyboard). No consequences were presented for correct or incorrect responses. If the learner demonstrated mastery of the skills assessed, he was referred to the next step's teaching assessment. If the learner showed an error, he/she was taught the target words of that step. Table 4.2 presents the general sequence of a Module 2 – Reading Program teaching step.

The teaching stage consisted of four exclusion trials, four novelty control trials, and two auditory-visual pairing trials with baseline words. In the teaching trials using the exclusion procedure, two words were presented as comparison stimuli, a baseline word (from Module 1) and a novel word (to be taught), and the auditory sample was the novel word. The learner could select the new word by excluding the familiar (baseline) word. Correct responses were followed by brief computer- auditory phrase (praise); errors resulted in a correction procedure consisting of the presentation of the message "No, it isn't!" followed by a new opportunity to perform the same task.

In the novelty control trials, the learner would select the baseline word from Module 1 that corresponds to the dictated word. After the selection response, the learner was presented with the question "What about the other word?" Correct responses were rewarded with praise, and incorrect responses in the pairing task were followed by the correction procedure and in the reading task resulted in the presentation of the next trial.

In the teaching stage, pairing trials between the dictated and printed word with baseline words were also presented. These trials had the function of ensuring reinforcement density and, at the same time, strengthening or maintaining word recognition. Correct responses were followed by praise, and incorrect responses by a correction message. Exclusion, novelty control, and baseline trials were interspersed throughout the teaching phase. The required criterion was 100% of correct responses. If the learner presented an error, he/she would perform a new teaching block. After reaching the criterion in this stage, the learner went on to the post-test.

The Post-test consisted of four novelty control trials involving the selection of the printed word corresponding to the dictated baseline word and, subsequently, by reading the other target word of the taught irregularity. In case of error, the teaching step was repeated; if the performance was 100% accurate, the participant was exposed to the General Post-test, which consisted of eight reading trials: four that contained teaching words and four with words generalizing the target irregularity. No consequences were programmed for the test phase.

Generalized reading probes. Before and after teaching a target unit the reading generalization assessment was conducted with 25 irregularities, the 16 taught irregularities plus other irregularities not directly taught: ã-ão, ss, x with sound of /ch/, x with sound of /z/, s with /ç/ sound and, in the last four units, words with two irregularities taught (Rosa Filho et al., 1998). The session consisted of presenting 25 words displayed on the computer screen and the learner was asked to read each word, one by one. No differential consequences were programmed for correct and incorrect answers.

Dictation Program The Module 2 of the ProgLeit software version Dictation Program was similar to the Reading Program regarding the taught irregularities. However, the target skill was composition writing, employing the CRMTS procedure.

Training Step In the pre-test, eight trials evaluated writing through composition dictation (AE), four with words to be taught in the step and four with generalization words, and five trials were auditory-visual pairing. In these trials, the dictated word as sample stimulus and the three printed words, presented as comparison, were baseline words of the Module 1. The responses were not followed by consequences. If the learner achieved 100% of correct responses, he/she would move on to the next teaching step. If the learner did not achieve 100% of the correct responses, the training step was concluded. Table 4.3 presents the general sequence of a Module 2 Dictation Program's Teaching Step.

The teaching stage consisted of four exclusion trials; four dictated word-baseline printed word (from Module 1) pairings control trials, followed by dictated word writing by composition trials (presented as incorrect comparison stimulus in the control trials) containing the irregularity to be taught; and two trials of auditory-visual pairings between the dictated word and the baseline printed word. For all teaching trials, differential consequences for correct (praise) and incorrect (correction procedure) were programmed.

The exclusion teaching trials used two words as comparison stimuli, a baseline word and a new word (to be taught) and the auditory sample was the new word. In the control trials, pairings between the dictated word and the printed word had a baseline word from Module 1 as sample stimulus and the corresponding word (correct choice stimulus) and a teaching target word (incorrect choice stimulus) as comparison stimuli; the learner should select the printed word corresponding to the dictated word and, in the next trial, the instruction "Write (target word)" was presented, referring to the target word presented in the previous task, and the letters were displayed at the bottom of the computer screen. The learner should compose the word corresponding to the dictated word by selecting letters. Two pairing trials between dictated and printed word were also included with baseline words from Module 1, in which the sample and comparison stimuli were baseline words.

The post-test consisted of four writing by composition (AE) with the teaching words and three baseline dictated word-printed word (AC) trials. In case of 100% correct responses, the learner would take the general post-test. In case of error, the learner would perform the same teaching step again. The general post-test consisted of 13 trials, being eight composition dictation (AE) trials, four with taught words and four with generalization words, and five trials of dictated-printed baseline word pairings. The tests were conducted in extinction.

Generalized Writing Probes Before and after the teaching of a target unit, an assessment of generalized writing was conducted with 25 irregularities (the 16 taught plus nine other irregularities not directly taught). The session consisted of 25 trials in which the learner should select, in order, each of the corresponding letters to compose the word corresponding to the dictated word. No differential consequences were programmed.

4.2.3 Current Version of Module 2 – Online Application via GEIC[6]

Given the technological advance provided by the GEIC software platform, a new version of Module 2 was made available to optimize the application of the ALEPP teaching modules and the storage of the results obtained by the learners in a secure database. Thus, this new version of Module 2 teaches writing in dictation tasks, is composed of 20 units with a total of 320 words, distributed in 80 teaching sessions. The 20 units refer to the 20 irregularities selected for teaching: ç, ce-ci, lh, nh, ch, ge-gi, vRc, vSc, vNc, vLc, soft r, rr, s with sound of /z/, ss, cRv, cLv, que-qui, ã-ão, x with sound of /ch/ and gue-gui. Each unit is composed of four steps that teach four words each, all containing the same target irregularity ('ç', for example), teaching 16 words in total. Each step includes a pre-test and a post-test for taught words and also for untaught words containing the same target irregularities. Generalized writing monitoring probes are conducted before and after the teaching of each unit. Each of these steps will be described in detail below.

[6] The current version of Module 2 is available on the online *software* platform called Gerenciador de Ensino Individualizado por Computador (GEIC – http://geic.ufscar.br/site/ – Capobianco et al., 2009). GEIC enables the application of ALEPP via the internet, on a large scale, by parents, teachers and other professionals, from different contexts, with remote support (de Souza et al., 2018, 2019). The data produced at each session are stored in a database and accessed remotely by users for monitoring and research (Orlando et al., 2015).

Training Steps Each teaching step presents tasks containing the four teaching words, as well as other simple words consisting of consonant-vowel syllables taught in ALEPP's Module 1 to ensure a basis for the exclusion procedure and also for maintaining the learned repertoire.

Each step consists of a pre-test, teaching, post-test, and reading test. Teaching presents tasks organized in three distinct settings, namely, Multiple Differences Training (MDT), Critical Differences Training (CDT), and Discrimination Training (DT). For teaching the words with the target irregularity, throughout the three trainings the learner performs pairing tasks between dictated and printed word (AC relation), composition dictation (AE) and composition copy (CE). Table 4.4 presents the general sequence of a Module 2 Teaching Step via GEIC.

The first stage of the teaching step refers to the pre-test. In this stage, the words to be taught in the step, pseudo-words and generalization words are assessed by means of dictation with composition (AE) and auditory-visual pairing (AC). In this assessment (CA), the learner's task is to select, on the computer screen, a printed word before of a dictated word. In the compound dictation task, a word is dictated and a set of 14 letters is presented on the computer screen. The learner must select among these letters, in the correct sequence, those necessary to build the word corresponding to the dictated word. The pre-test consists of 16 trials, containing eight dictation with composition (AE) and eight dictated-printed word pairing (AC) trials, distributed as follows: four trials with the taught words, two trials with pseudo-words and two trials with generalization words for each task. If the learner's performance is correct in all trials, he/she is advanced to the next teaching step. Otherwise, he performs the scheduled teaching step. Correct answers are followed by sound effects that indicate correctness, and for incorrect responses there is no consequence.

The second stage refers to the teaching stage composed Multiple Difference Training (MDT) trials, Critical Difference Training (CDT) trials and Discrimination Training (DT) trials. Teaching through different training settings aims to gradually increase the discriminations required by the learner. Considering the auditory sample stimulus, the word *cup* (taça), in the first training session, the learner should discriminate between different print stimuli, for example, *taça* (correct choice stimulus) and *bico* (incorrect choice stimulus); in the second training, visual discrimination should occur between two similar stimuli, increasing the task's difficulty, for example, *taça* (correct choice stimulus) and *taca* (incorrect choice stimulus). Finally, in the last training, the learner should discriminate between words with the same target irregularity, for example, *taça* (correct choice stimulus) and *poço* (incorrect choice stimulus).

In the Multiple Differences Training, the learner performs three tasks (MTS, dictation by composition and copying a text). The first task is to select the printed word corresponding to the dictated word (AC), in which baseline and exclusion trials are interspersed. In baseline trials, the dictated word is learned in ALEPP's Module 1 (e.g., *luva, bico, bule* or *dedo*) and the corresponding printed word is the correct choice option while the incorrect choice option is a teaching word (e.g., *roça, taça maço* or *poço*). On exclusion trials, the correct printed word corresponds to the target irregularity (e.g., *roça, taça maço* or *poço*) and the incorrect choice option is a Module 1 baseline word (e.g., *luva, bico, bule* or *dedo*).

In this training trials, *Constructed-Response Matching-to-Sample* (CRMTS) interspersed with MTS trials were also included. In the CRMTS tasks, the learner writes the dictated (teaching) word by selecting in sequence the corresponding letters (taking dictation by composition – AE); and writes the word before the printed word presented as a sample at the top of the screen (copying a text by composition – CE). This stage consists of 36 trials, consisting of 24 dictated and printed word pairing (AC) trials (16 trials with teaching words of the target difficulty and eight baseline words), eight taking dictation (AE) and four copying a text (CE) with teaching words trials.

In the Critical Difference Training trials, the pairing task consists in selecting written words before dictated words presented as samples. However, the learner must select one of two words, one being the teaching word (correct alternative) that contains the language irregularity (e.g., *roça*) and another similar word with a change in the element related to the irregularity (e.g., *rossa* or *roxa*). More specifically, these can be changes such as the omission of a sign (e.g., omitting the cedilla or the tilde); omission of a consonant from the irregularity; addition of a vowel in the irregularity or transposition in the irregularity. This block is composed of 12 trials of the AC relation with the teaching words of the target irregularity.

In the Discrimination Training, the comparison stimuli differentiation refers to the presentation of other teaching words of the same difficulty as choice options in the MTS tasks. Thus, the learner's task is to select one of two written teaching words consisting of the same irregularity (e.g., *poço* and *taça*; *roça* and *maço*; *taça* and *maço*; *roça* and *poço*). In this block, the learner also performs the composition dictation (AE) task. The block is composed of 12 trials, eight of them are dictated and printed word pairing trials (AC) and four are taking dictation trials (AE). The three blocks of this teaching stage do not possess learning criteria for moving on to the next stage. Correct responses are followed by praise provided by the system, and no consequences are programmed for incorrect answers.

The third step consists of the post-test, which has the same configuration as the pre-test. In this step, it is assessed whether, after the teaching step, the learner discriminates the target printed word against the dictated word (AC) and correctly writes the words with the target irregularity (AE) referring to the teaching step. If the learner reach 100% of the AC and AE tasks correct, the learner moves on to the next step; otherwise the learner repeats the teaching steps TDM, TDC and DT once more.

Following the post-test, the reading of the taught words and generalization words is performed. In this task, a written word is presented on the computer screen and the learner should read it (CD) and then press the confirmation button at the bottom of the screen, which produces the presentation of the correct response (corresponding dictated word). It is important to note that this step was programmed to give the learner the opportunity to read the words taught, however, the emitted oral response emitted is not recorded. To ensure a minimum number of correct answers throughout the block, figure naming trials (BD) were included, in which the learner names the figure presented on the computer screen. This stage is composed of 10 trials, being six reading trials (CD), four with teaching words and two with generalization words, and four trials of figure naming (BD) used in Module 1. There is no criterion in this stage, so regardless of the performance, the learner moves on to the next step of teaching the target unit or to the Generalized Writing Assessment.

Generalized Writing Assessment This is an assessment to check the writing (taking dictation with response construction – AE) of words that were not directly taught in the teaching unit. One word from each of the 20 target irregularities make up the assessment. Each assessment presents a new list of target words. The assessment occurs before a new unit begins and after a unit is completed. Thus, throughout Module 2, 21 assessments were scheduled to assess the acquisition, maintenance, and generalization of writing and to identify the possible effects of the procedure at each unit, constituting a multiple baseline across units design (Gast & Ledford, 2014).

Each assessment is composed of 40 trials, being 20 related to word reading (CD) and 20 related to taking dictation by composition (AE). The learner has the opportunity to read the 20 words, but the responses are not registered. After reading the word, the learner hears the correct response after pressing the confirmation button on the screen. In the dictation trials, the learner has the opportunity to compose the dictated word by selecting the letters available on the computer screen. Correct responses are followed by sound effects and, in case of incorrect responses, the learner goes on to the next trial with a new word. There is no performance criterion in this stage.

4.3 Studies Conducted with Module 2

Some studies carried out with Module 2 of ALEPP will be reported below. Also described will be the results of the Alfatech Project, a partnership between INCT-ECCE (National Institute of Science and Technology on Behavior, Cognition and Teaching) and the City Hall of Santo André (SP), which allowed the large-scale application of Module 2 applied via GEIC in the years between 2017 and 2019.

The first published study on the results obtained with the application of Module 2 of ALEPP was by Rose et al. In this study, Modules 1 and 2, in the folder-catalogue version, were conducted with children in the early school years and who presented learning difficulties in reading and writing. For the emission of the responses in the CRMTS tasks, ice cream sticks with a letter on the tip were used. The four children who, at the end of Module 1, were able to accurately read most of the Portuguese language words consisting of two or three simple syllables presented in the generalized reading assessment completed Module 2. When starting Module 2, incipient word reading performances were verified in the pre-test of the first step, which increased following exposure to the exclusion procedure, reaching high performances in the teaching sessions of the following steps of the first unit. A similar trend was observed in word reading acquisition of the other steps of the same irregularity, with faster acquisition. It was also observed that as successive steps were performed, teaching words with the same irregularity, the performances in the pre-tests increased. These results indicated reading generalization, i.e., after learning to read some words containing a specific irregularity, the participant started reading new words containing the same irregularity.

In a second study, de Souza et al. (1999) evaluated the effectiveness of Modules 1 and 2 in the computerized version of the *off-line software* ProgLeit (Rosa Filho et al., 1998) where 40 typically developing students with a background of school failure participated. Initially, the children performed Module 1's consonant-vowel compound word teaching. The results showed that the participants learned to correctly relate the dictated words to the corresponding pictures and written words. Additionally, the emergence of relationships not directly taught between pictures and written words and written words and pictures and the reading of simple words (consonant-vowel type) was verified. Eight participants who completed Module 1 also performed Module 2 (reading and taking dictation program). The results showed that the eight children learned to match printed words to dictated word, reading and writing of words with Portuguese language irregularities and, therefore, showed improvement in reading and writing repertoires of words taught in both versions of the program. Regarding generalization words, four out of eight participants showed immediate generalization in word reading after teaching the first irregularity, and for the remaining four, reading and writing of generalization words occurred as they progressed in the teaching units. These results demonstrate the effectiveness of ALEPP's Modules 1 and 2 for teaching reading and writing repertoire to children with learning difficulties in these skills.

As highlighted by the authors of both studies (de Rose et al., 1992; de Souza et al., 1999), results regarding generalized reading suggest proficient reading once participants developed the minimal unit repertoire. The reading and writing performance of new words is due to the control by the minimal units (not directly taught), since it can be abstracted from the teaching of a set of larger units (whole words) containing the smaller target units (the irregularities of the language). The teaching of the smaller units from larger units (words) (Skinner, 1957) planned by teaching multiple exemplars in Module 2 may have favored generalization by: (1) teaching different words in a specific unit; and (2) continuous and frequent exposure to teaching with reading.

Given the promising results previously obtained regarding the acquisition of reading new words, Lorena (2003) investigated whether reinforcement contingencies for teaching whole-word reading would produce stimulus control by a target unit (language irregularities) using the ProgLeit *offline software* version of the Reading Program. Two studies were conducted. 11 children enrolled in the initial years of elementary school in the São Carlos public school system who had completed Module 1 participated in the study. The sessions were held at the Reading Unit of UFSCar. A multiple baseline between-unit design was used to assess reading performance before and after teaching each of the 16 target units as a measure of generalization. The general post-test was adapted for the research objectives, and was programmed to assess the reading of the taught words (excluding the generalization words) in the step and, thus, served as criteria for the participant to proceed in the Module: if 100% correct, the participant would proceed to the next step; if incorrect, the participant would repeat the step. Participants only performed the steps teaching the irregularities that did not demonstrate reading proficiency. Results showed that participants went on to read the directly taught words and many of the words assessed in the generalized reading probes. For nine out of the 11 participants, the percentage of correct responses to each generalized reading probe was above the expected percentage of correct answers, indicating that participants were reading more than expected, i.e., more than the number of words with the irregularities taught by that time. Overall, there was an increasing trend in the percentages of correct responses for nine of the 11 participants, indicating systematic increases in reading repertoire as they learned a new language irregularity. According to the author, the results showed that the participants' performances in the generalized reading probes, suggest that there was control by minimal units, since once they were taught to read a set of words with language irregularities, the participants started reading the taught words and new words made up of the same set of irregularities. Thus, the data suggest that the control by minimal units may be a functional strategy to establish generalized reading.

The second study was conducted to teach the reading of words with "x" pronounced with /z/ sound with the three participants who showed low scores of correct answers in the reading of words with this irregularity. The procedures were the same as in the previous study. In general, the three participants achieved high correct scores after the pre-test of the second teaching step, with small individual variations. The reading of a considerable number of new words after the second teaching step suggests that the teaching procedure was effective in establishing the reading repertoire under the control of smaller minimal textual units for this irregularity. The results of the reading probe, performed at the end of the teaching unit, suggest that there was immediate emergence of the reading of new words, since all three participants were successful in reading generalization words and pseudowords, confirming once again the effectiveness of the procedure.

The study conducted by Carvalho (2013) aimed to assess the effects of Module 2 of ALEPP on the reading and writing repertoire of a student diagnosed with Asperger's syndrome. He was 9 years and 11 months old and attending the 3rd year of elementary school. The sessions were held in the Reading League (UFSCar laboratory), during after school hours. The two programs that made up Module 2 in the ProgLeit off-line software version were used: Reading and Dictation Programs. In the initial assessment of reading and writing, the participant showed superior performance in reading compared to writing. Given this performance, the two programs that made up this version of Module 2 were applied alternately, allowing the participant to get in touch with the words in the Reading Program first and then in the Dictation Program. However, throughout the procedure, the participant showed mastery in reading words with language irregularities, advancing one or more teaching steps; at this time the Reading Program was suspended and the Dictation Program was continued until reaching the criterion for concomitant application of the programs. In general, the participant needed more exposure to the steps of the writing instruction than to reading instruction program. An analysis of writing performance showed that responses varied in: letter omission (e.g., when faced with the dictated word *colcha*, the participant wrote *cocha*); letter addition (e.g., when faced with the word *gincana*, the participant wrote *gicanina*); changes in the letter sequence (e.g., when faced with the dictated word *aparelho*, the participant wrote *apalhero*); mute and sound phonemic exchanges (e.g., when faced with the dictated word *farda*, the participant wrote *varda*); and even errors due to not paying attention to the correct sound of words (e.g., when faced with the dictated word *lanche*, the participant wrote *leche*). As for the probes performed between teaching units, both for reading and writing, generalization was observed in reading and writing of words not directly taught, with variation in the percentage of correct responses in the first assessments, with a more stable performance at the end.

ALEPP's Module 2 was also applied with illiterate adults. Bandini et al. (2014) assessed the effects of Module 1 (Study 1) and the Module 2 Reading Program (Study 2) of the ALEPP. Four adults participated in Study 2, three males and one female (who participated in Study 1) aged between 28 and 46 years, who were students of Youngsters and Adults Education Program, and showed initial repertoires ranging between zero and 52% accuracy in reading. The results of the generalization tests showed an increase in the percentages of correct answers in both reading and writing starting from the second test, with higher scores in reading compared to writing. The authors concluded that ALEPP can also be used to promote advances in adults' reading and writing repertoires.

The study by Calcagno et al. (2016) analyzed the errors made during the process of learning to read and write in adult participants submitted to ALEPP's Modules 1 and 2. The version of Modules 1 and 2 used in this study refers to the current version applied via GEIC. Fifteen adults underwent pre-assessment, seven started Module 1, and only two advanced to Module 2; eight started the procedure in Module 2: five did not achieve the criterion of 70% accuracy in writing in the pre-assessment, although they achieved above 70% accuracy in reading; and three achieved lower than 70% accuracy in reading and writing. No participant finished Module 2. The results showed that the categories with the highest incidence of errors in writing in the taking dictation by construction task were: letter substitution, deletion, and addition, phonemic competition between two graphemes, and substitution of complex syllables for simple syllables. Other categories with moderate incidence of errors included difficulties with nasalization, oral support when a grapheme has two possible phonemes and the participant chooses the incorrect one, and syllable exchange, omission or addition. In relation to the errors issued in the reading tasks, and dictation by construction, there was an error reduction between pre-assessment and assessments throughout teaching, being more persistent in the pre-assessment and tests throughout teaching in the dictation by construction task. The authors argue that the performance presented in the task of dictation by construction may be related to the participants' restricted experience with computerized resources. Therefore, they suggest the direct teaching of writing by composition starting in Module 1 for this population.

The study of Barbosa (2017) was conducted with eight students, aged between 6 and 10 years old, from the initial grades of elementary education in two public schools. The participants were exposed to the first 10 units of the current version of Module 2 of ALEPP, with application via GEIC. The sessions were held in the Reading League at UFSCar, during after-school hours. The results showed that four of the eight students showed systematic progress in emergent writing, one student showed gradual acquisition, and three showed little or no progress, maintaining intermediate performances. The writing assessments suggested minimal unit abstraction from word teaching (larger units), which also allowed writing new words in which the sound and textual units were recombined into new words. The author pointed out that the analyses were preliminary, but the results suggest that gains in writing occurred for most students.

The most recent results obtained with the application of ALEPP's Module 2 refer to those produced by the Alfatech Project in the city of Santo André, São Paulo (de Souza et al., 2018, 2019). The design of the Alfatech Project was conceived by the Enactus Team of the Federal University of ABC (UFABC), providing the partnership under an institutional cooperation term between INCT-ECCE, UFSCar, ENACTUS UFABC and the Municipal Secretariat of Education of Santo André (SP). The objective was to implement, in a sample of eight municipal public schools of Santo André, the ALEPP computerized teaching program through the GEIC platform. The activities were carried out in the computer room of each school, during regular class hours; students were scheduled to leave the classroom three times a week while they participated in the ALEPP activities. Modules 1 and 2 were applied, and students could progress from Module 1 to 2, or they could start directly in Module 2, depending on their results in the assessment instrument of reading and writing skills referring to each teaching Module. The results showed that between 2017 and 2019, 466 students who had insufficient learning in reading and writing attended the project. In 2018 and 2019, 434 and 91 students, respectively, from eight schools participated in the project. Ages ranged from 7 to 15 years old and more boys than girls with learning gaps were identified. In general, there was progress in both reading and writing by the students who carried out Module 1, indicating that the higher the weekly attendance to the teaching sessions, the greater the students' progress. In the year 2018, data showed progress in writing words with irregularities of the Portuguese language among the 151 students exposed to Module 2. In the year 2019, 51 students were exposed to Module 2, showing average accuracy percentage of close to 70% in reading and 50% in writing in the initial assessment and 90% in reading and 80% in writing in the final assessment. The results of the assessments performed at the beginning and end of the school years showed statistically significant differences in the reading and writing repertoires. Such results confirm those obtained in previous research, in controlled laboratory situation, showing the effectiveness of systematic, individualized and computerized teaching. It was also verified that regularity in the performance of the activities is a critical factor for learning to read and write: students who did not miss sessions showed better performance than those who did sessions only once or twice a week. The results allow recommending the application of ALEPP on a large scale, as a contribution to improving the effectiveness of teaching in the early stages of literacy.

4.4 Final Considerations

This chapter aims to historically review the development of ALEPP's Module 2 as a systematic procedure for teaching reading and writing of irregular words by presenting the teaching structure of the Module and also the results of studies conducted. As described, Module 2 has been improved over the years, currently having a teaching structure focused on writing skills and made available via GEIC. Considering the population for whom the teaching program was planned – children with a background of school failure – the results obtained in studies with Module 1 highlighted the importance of teaching writing skills of words with irregularities presented in Module 2, since at the end of Module 1, most participants show superior performances in reading compared to writing (de Rose et al., 1989, 1992, 1996; de Souza et al., 2004; Hanna et al., 2004; Melchiori et al., 2000; Reis et al., 2009).

It is noteworthy that despite the application of Module 2 with a reasonable number of participants, most of them participated in university extension activities (Federal University of São Carlos and University of Brasilia), for example, in the Reading League that receive children in after school hours. The data collected in this situation are accompanied by the instructor and researchers to guide decision making in the application of the teaching resource, however, unfortunately they were not published in scientific journals. Thus, we can verify a reduced number of published studies in which the Module 2 was object of analysis. On the other hand, from the analysis of the set of these studies gathered (Bandini et al., 2014; Barbosa, 2017; Carvalho, 2013; de Souza et al., 1999; Lorena, 2003), it is possible to verify that participants, in general, showed varied performances in writing (taking dictation by composition) both for the same participant (in different assessments) and among participants. These results are consistent with Skinner's (1957) indication that reading and writing are related but independent repertoires. However, teaching one may contribute to the development of the other, demonstrating interdependence between these operants.

One aspect that should be highlighted is the important role of the word construction task in recombinative generalization for reading and writing repertoires. The CRMTS procedure (Dube et al., 1991; Mackay, 1985) requires the construction of the response from the selection of elements (letters or syllables) that make up the word, and allows demonstration of the effectiveness in establishing discriminative control by the minimal units that make up the sample stimulus (e. g., printed or dictated word) (Dube et al., 1991; Mackay, 1985). Also favoring generalization is the planned structure of the target unit, in which teaching with multiple exemplars of the same irregularity can produce abstraction of the sound unit, i.e., make it possible to read and write new words containing the same target unit, as pointed out by Stokes and Baer (1977).

Finally, the results obtained with the application of Module 2 demonstrated its efficiency and effectiveness, and also demonstrated the importance of assessing teaching conditions, constantly seeking to review them. Given the reality of Brazilian education, the importance of investing in the development of technologies for teaching reading and writing of irregular textual units is highlighted.

References

Albuquerque, A. R., & Melo, R. M. (2005). Equivalência de Estímulos: Conceito, implicações e possibilidades de aplicação. J. Abreu-Rodrigues & M. R. Ribeiro (Orgs.), *Análise do comportamento: Pesquisa, teoria e aplicação* (pp. 245–264). Artmed.

Bandini, C. S. M., Bandini, H. H. M., Sella, A. C., & de Souza, D. G. (2014). Emergence of reading and writing in illiterate adults after matching-to-sample tasks. *Paidéia, 24*(57), 75–84. https://doi.org/10.1590/1982-43272457201410

Barbosa, T. B. (2017). *Abstração e recombinação de unidades de estímulos como base para a emergência de escrita* [Monografia não publicada]. Universidade Federal de São Carlos.

Benitez, P., & Domeniconi, C. (2016). Use of a computerized reading and writing teaching program for families of students with intellectual disabilities. *The Psychological Record, 66*, 127–138. https://doi.org/10.1007/s40732-015-0158-8

Bori, C. M. (1974). Developments in Brazil. In F. S. Keller & J. G. Sherman (Eds.), *PSI – The Keller plan handbook* (pp. 65–72). W. A. Benjamin.

Brasil. (2019). *Relatório Brasil no Pisa 2018*. Instituto Nacional de Estudos e Pesquisas. http://download.inep.gov.br/acoes_internacionais/pisa/documentos/2019/relatorio_PISA_2018_preliminar.pdf

Calcagno, S., Barros, R. S., Ferrari, I. S., & de Souza, D. G. (2016). Análise dos erros apresentados por adultos iletrados de um programa informatizado de ensino de leitura e escrita. *Acta Colombiana de Psicologia, 19*(1), 123–136. https://doi.org/10.14718/ACP.2016.19.1.7

Capobianco, D., Teixeira, C. A. C., Bela, R. E., Orlando, A. F., de Souza, D. G., & de Rose, J. C. (2009). *GEIC – Gerenciador de Ensino Individualizado por Computador* [Software de Computador]. UFSCar. http://geic.ufscar.br/site/

Carvalho, B. S. S. (2013). *Programações de ensino para refinamento das habilidades de leitura e escrita de um aluno com Transtorno de Asperger* [Dissertação de Mestrado, Universidade Federal de São Carlos]. Repositório Institucional da UFSCar. https://repositorio.ufscar.br/handle/ufscar/3128

Costa, A. R. A., McIlvane, J. W., Wilkinson, K. M., & de Souza, D. G. (2001). Emergent word-object mapping by children: Further studies using the blank comparison technique. *The Psychological Record, 51*, 343–355.

da Paixão, G., & de Assis, G. (2017). Uso do procedimento de constructed response matching to sample: Uma revisão da literatura. *Perspectivas em Análise do Comportamento, 8*(1), 47–60. https://doi.org/10.18761/pac.2016.038

de Freitas, M. C. (2012). *Construção de um programa de ensino de pré-requisitos de leitura e escrita para pessoas com deficiência intelectual* [Tese de Doutorado, Universidade Federal de São Carlos]. Repositório Institucional da UFSCar. https://repositorio.ufscar.br/handle/ufscar/5977

de Rose, J. C., de Souza, D. G., Rossito, A. L., & de Rose, T. M. S. (1989). Aquisição de leitura após história de fracasso escolar: Equivalência de estímulos e generalização. *Psicologia: Teoria e Pesquisa, 5*, 325–346.

de Rose, J. C., de Souza, D. G., Rossito, A. L., & de Rose, T. M. S. (1992). Stimulus equivalence and generalization in reading after matching to sample by exclusion. In S. C. Hayes & L. J. Hayes (Eds.), *Understanding verbal relations* (pp. 69–82). Context Press.

de Rose, J. C., de Souza, D. G., & Hanna, E. S. (1996). Teaching reading and spelling: Exclusion and stimulus equivalence. *Journal of Applied Behavior Analysis, 29*(4), 451–469. https://doi.org/10.1901/jaba.1996.29-451

de Souza, D. G., & de Rose, J. C. (2006). Desenvolvendo programas individualizados para o ensino de leitura. *Acta Comportamentalia, 14*(1), 77–114.

de Souza, D. G., de Rose, J. C., Fonseca, M. L., & Hanna, E. S. (1999). Stimulus control research and minimal units for reading. *Experimental of Human Behavior Analysis Bulletin, 17*(1), 20–23.

de Souza, D. G., de Rose, J. C. C., Hanna, E. S., Calcagno, S., & Galvão, O. F. (2004). Análise comportamental da aprendizagem de leitura e escrita e a construção de um currículo suplementar. In M. M. Hübner & M. Marinotti (Orgs.), *Análise do Comportamento para a educação: Contribuições recentes* (pp. 177–203). Esetec.

de Souza, D. G., de Rose, J. C., Faleiros, T. C., Bortoloti, R., Hanna, E. S., & McIlvane, W. J. (2009). Teaching generative reading via recombination of minimal textual units: A legacy of verbal behavior to children in Brazil. *International Journal of Psychology and Psychological Therapy, 9*(1), 19–44.

de Souza, D. G., Hanna, E. S., Albuquerque, A. R., & Hübner, M. M. C. (2014). Processos recombinativos: Algumas variáveis críticas para o desenvolvimento de leitura. In J. C. de Rose, M. S. C. A. Gil, & D. G. de Souza (Orgs.), *Comportamento simbólico: Bases conceituais e empíricas* (pp. 421–462). Oficina Universitária; Cultura Acadêmica.

de Souza, D. G., Caetano, M. S., Golfeto, R. M., Postalli, L. M. M., de Rose, J. C., Hanna, E. S., Campos Jr., R. F. C., & Rocca, J. Z. (2018). *Implementação do currículo ALEPP em escolas públicas da rede municipal de ensino de Santo André – SP*. Instituto Nacional de Ciência e Tecnologia sobre Comportamento, Cognição e Ensino. https://inctecce.com.br/images/arquivos/00-projeto-alfatech.pdf

de Souza, D. G., Caetano, M. S., Golfeto, R. M., Postalli, L. M. M., de Rose, J. C., Hanna, E. S., & Campos, R. F. C., Jr. (2019). *Implementação do currículo ALEPP em escolas públicas da rede municipal de ensino de Santo André - SP: Ano 2*. Instituto Nacional de Ciência e Tecnologia sobre Comportamento, Cognição e Ensino.

Dixon, L. S. (1977). The nature of control by spoken words over visual stimulus selection. *Journal of the Experimental Analysis of Behavior, 27*, 433–442. https://doi.org/10.1901/jeab.1977.27-433

Dube, W. V., McDonald, S. J., McIlvane, W. J., & Mackay, H. A. (1991). Constructed response matching to sample and spelling instruction. *Journal of Applied Behavior Analysis, 24*, 305–317. https://doi.org/10.1901/jaba.1991.24-305

Fava-Menzori, L. R., Lucchesi, F. M., & Almeida-Verdu, A. C. M. (2018). Ensino informatizado de leitura e escrita em uma sala de recursos. In D. L. O. Vilas Boas, F. Cassas, H. L. Gusso, & P. C. M. Mayer (Orgs.), *Comportamento em Foco 7: Ensino, comportamento verbal e análise conceitual* (p. 84–95). ABPMC.

Ferrari, C., de Rose, J. C., & McIlvane, W. J. (1993). Exclusion vs. selection training of auditory-visual conditional relations. *Journal of Experimental Child Psychology, 56*, 49–63. https://doi.org/10.1006/jecp.1993.1025

Ferreiro, E. (2002). *Passado y presente de los verbos ler y escribir* [Passado e Presente dos verbos ler e escrever]. Cortez.

Gast, D. L., & Ledford, J. R. (2014). *Single case research methodology: Applications in special education and behavioral sciences*. Routledge.

Hanna, E. S., de Souza, D. G., de Rose, J. C., & Fonseca, M. L. (2004). Effects of delayed constructed-response identity matching on spelling of dictated words. *Journal of Applied Behavior Analysis, 37*(2), 223–227. https://doi.org/10.1901/jaba.2004.37-223

Holland, J. G., & Skinner, B. F. (1961). *The analysis of behavior: A program for self-instruction*. McGraw-Hill.

Hübner, M. M. C., Gomes, R. C., & McIlvane, W. (2009). Recombinative generalization in minimal verbal unit-based reading instruction for prereading children. *Experimental Analysis of Human Behavior Bulletin, 27*, 11–17.

Hübner, M. M. C., Souza, A. C., & Souza, S. R. (2014). Uma revisão da contribuição brasileira no desenvolvimento de procedimentos de ensino para a leitura recombinativa. In J. C. de Rose, M. S. C. A. Gil, & D. G. de Souza (Orgs.), *Comportamento simbólico: Bases conceituais e empíricas* (pp. 373–420). Oficina Universitária; Cultura Acadêmica.

Hübner-D'Oliveira, M. M., & Matos, M. A. (1993). Controle discriminativo na aquisição da leitura: Efeito da repetição e variação na posição das sílabas e letras. *Temas em Psicologia, 1*, 99–108.

Keller, F. (1968). Good Bye Teacher. *Journal of Applied Behavior Analysis, 1*, 79–89. https://doi.org/10.1901/jaba.1968.1-79

Lee, V. L., & Pegler, A. M. (1982). Effects on spelling of training children to read. *Journal of the Experimental Analysis of Behavior, 37*, 311–322. https://doi.org/10.1901/jeab.1982.37-311

Lorena, A. B. (2003). *Identificação experimental de fontes de controle de estímulos por unidade textuais mínimas eleitura generalizada* [Monografia não publicada]. Universidade Federal de São Carlos.

Lucchesi, F. M., Almeida-Verdu, A. C. M., Buffa, M. J. M. B., & Bevilacqua, M. C. (2015a). Análise dos passos de um ensino programado de leitura e escrita a crianças com deficiência auditiva e implante coclear. *Acta Comportamentalia, 23*, 137–151.

Lucchesi, F. M., Almeida-Verdu, A. C. M., Buffa, M. J. M. B., & Bevilacqua, M. C. (2015b). Leitura e inteligibilidade de fala: Efeitos de ensino programado com crianças usuárias de implante coclear. *Psicologia: Reflexão e Crítica, 28*, 500–510. https://doi.org/10.1590/1678-7153.201528309

Mackay, H. A. (1985). Stimulus equivalence in rudimentary reading and spelling. *Analysis and Intervention in Developmental Disabilities, 5*, 373–387. https://doi.org/10.1016/0270-4684(85)90006-0

Mackay, H. A., & Sidman, M. (1984). Teaching new behavior via equivalence relations. In B. Sperber, C. MacCauley, & P. H. Brookes (Eds.), *Learning and cognition in the mentally retarded* (pp. 493–513). Lawrence Erlbaum.

Matos, M. A., & Hübner-D'Oliveira, M. M. (1992). Equivalence relations and reading. In S. C. Hayes & L. J. Hayes (Eds.), *Understanding verbal relations* (pp. 83–94). Context Press.

Matos, M. A., Avanzi, A. L., & McIlvane, W. J. (2006). Rudimentary reading repertoires via stimulus equivalence and recombination of minimal verbal units. *Analysis of Verbal Behavior, 22*, 3–19. https://doi.org/10.1007/BF03393023

Mauad, L. C., Guedes, M. C., & Azzi, R. G. (2004). Análise do comportamento e a habilidade de leitura: Um levantamento crítico de artigos do JABA. *Psico-USF, 9*(1), 59–69. https://doi.org/10.1590/S1413-82712004000100008

Melchiori, L. E., de Souza, D. G., & de Rose, J. C. (1992). Aprendizagem de leitura por meio de um procedimento de discriminação sem erros (exclusão): Uma replicação com pré-escolares. *Psicologia: Teoria e Pesquisa, 8*(1), 101–111.

Melchiori, L. E., de Souza, D. G., & de Rose, J. C. (2000). Reading, equivalence and recombination of units: A replication with students with different learning histories. *Journal of Applied Behavior Analysis, 33*, 97–100. https://doi.org/10.1901/jaba.2000.33-97

Mueller, M. M., Olmi, D. J., & Saunders, K. J. (2000). Recombinative generalization of within-syllable units in prereading children. *Journal of Applied Behavior Analysis, 33*, 515–531. https://doi.org/10.1901/jaba.2000.33-515

Organização para Cooperação e Desenvolvimento Econômico. (2019). *Brazil – Country Note – PISA 2018 Results*. OECD Publishing. https://www.oecd.org/pisa/publications/PISA2018_CN_BRA.pdf

Orlando, A. F., Souza, L. J. S., de Souza, D. G., Pimentel, M. G. C., Teixeira, C. A. C., de Rose, J. C., Golfeto, R. M., & Hanna, E. S. (2015). *GEIC – Gerenciador de Ensino Individualizado: Manual do Usuário: Volume 2*. Instituto Nacional de Ciência e Tecnologia sobre Comportamento, Cognição e Ensino. http://inctecce.com.br/br/producao/softwares.

Paula, J. B. C., & Haydu, V. B. (2010). Revisão bibliográfica de pesquisas brasileiras sobre equivalência de estímulos. *Psicologia: Teoria e Pesquisa, 26*(2), 281–294. https://doi.org/10.1590/S0102-37722010000200010

Reis, T. S., de Souza, D. G., & de Rose, J. C. (2009). Avaliação de um programa para o ensino de leitura e escrita. *Estudos em Avaliação Educacional, 20*(44), 425–449.

Rosa Filho, A. B., de Rose, J. C., de Souza, D. G., Hanna, E. S., & Fonseca, M. L. (1998). *Aprendendo a ler e a escrever em pequenos passos* [Software de Computador].

Sidman, M. (1971). Reading and auditory-visual equivalences. *Journal of Speech and Hearing Research, 14*, 5–13. https://doi.org/10.1044/jshr.1401.05

Sidman, M. (1994). *Equivalence relations and behavior: A research story*. Authors Cooperative.

Sidman, M. (2000). Equivalence relations and the reinforcement contingency. *Journal of the Experimental Analysis of Behavior, 74*, 127–146. https://doi.org/10.1901/jeab.2000.74-127

Sidman, M., & Cresson, O. (1973). Reading and crossmodal transfer of stimulus equivalences in severe retardation. *American Journal of Mental Deficiency, 77*(5), 515–523.

Sidman, M., & Tailby, W. (1982). Conditional discrimination vs. matching to sample: An expansion of the testing paradigm. *Journal of the Experimental Analysis of Behavior, 37*, 5–22. https://doi.org/10.1901/jeab.1982.37-5

Silva, E. R. M. (2018). *Ensino de leitura e de escrita a adultos com deficiência intelectual matriculados na Educação de Jovens e Adultos* [Dissertação de Mestrado, Universidade Federal de São Carlos]. Repositório Institucional da UFSCar. https://repositorio.ufscar.br/handle/ufscar/9700

Skinner, B. F. (1957). *The verbal Behavior*. Appleton-Century-Crofts.

Skinner, B. F. (1968). *The technology of teaching*. Meredith Corporation.

Stokes, T. F., & Baer, D. M. (1977). An implicit technology of generalization. *Journal of Applied Behavior Analysis, 10*(2), 349–367. https://doi.org/10.1901/jaba.1977.10-349

Chapter 5
Teaching to Read Storybooks

Elenice S. Hanna, João Vianney Barrozo Costa Severo, Camila Domeniconi, Julio Cesar de Rose, and Deisy das Graças de Souza

5.1 Introduction

This chapter describes a module for teaching reading comprehension of Portuguese language with short children's stories and illustrates its application with results from six elementary school students. The module is part of the complementary teaching program for literacy that generated the Learning to Read and Write in Small Steps Program® (*Aprendendo a ler e Escrever em Pequenos Passos* [ALEPP]), developed by researchers from the Federal University of São Carlos (Deisy das Graças de Souza, Julio Cesar de Rose and students) and the University of Brasília (Elenice S. Hanna and students). ALEPP currently comprises three modules that gradually build the complex skills involved in the literacy process. Module 1 (de Rose et al., 1996; de Souza & de Rose, 2006) aims to teach decoding (textual behavior, Skinner, 1957) and reading comprehension of Portuguese words consisting of two or three simple syllables (with regular consonant-vowel sequence; e.g., bolo [cake], pipa [kite], fogo [fire]) and monosyllables with vowel meetings (e.g., lua [moon], rio [river]). In Module 2 (de Rose et al., 1992; de Souza et al., 1999) Portuguese words with orthographic difficulties are introduced which present correspondences between letters and phonemes different from Module 1, such as consonantal meetings (e.g., CH, LH, R-consonant, S-consonant), digraphs (SS, RR) and graphemes representing more than one sound (more detailed description in

E. S. Hanna (✉)
Universidade de Brasília, Brasília, DF, Brazil
e-mail: elenicehanna@gmail.com

J. V. B. C. Severo
Câmara dos Deputados, Brasília, DF, Brazil

C. Domeniconi · J. C. de Rose · D. das Graças de Souza
Universidade Federal de São Carlos, São Carlos, SP, Brazil

A. R. de Albuquerque, R. M. de Melo (eds.), *Contributions of Behavior Analysis to Reading and Writing Comprehension*, https://doi.org/10.1007/978-3-031-40868-7_5

Chap. 4). Module 3, of special interest in this chapter, is designed for children who can already read words with regular sequences and some spelling difficulties, but have difficulty reading short stories and understanding them.

ALEPP was developed primarily to address students who have underperformed with the methods traditionally used to teach reading. It is not a general literacy 'method', but a tool that has been shown to be effective for a group of students who, to some extent, fail with school methods.

de Rose et al. (1996, see also de Rose et al., 1992; de Souza et al., 2009) have shown that the first Module of the program teaches relationships that make dictated words and corresponding pictures and written words equivalent (Sidman & Tailby, 1982), and develops functional reading (de Rose, 2005, republished in Chap. 1 of this book). This way of reading requires learning: (1) point-to-point correspondences between sounds (phonemes, syllables, and spoken words) and text (letters, syllables, and written words); and (2) relationships between the text (written words) and events it "represents" (pictures, objects, actions, etc.). The regularity of correspondences between sounds and text, even considering orthographic irregularities, when manipulated during the teaching of different words/syllables, allows the development of so-called generalized reading (or decoding ability), the ability to read text not directly taught based on the recombination of textual units already learned, such as syllables or correspondences between graphemes and phonemes (for example, having learned to read **bolo** [cake] and **vaca** [cow], the student may be able to read **boca** [bake] or **cola** [glue] when encountering these words for the first time). Teaching based on relationships between words and events teaches the reader, indirectly, to seek "the meaning" of texts in general, and this behavioral tendency is what can be called functional reading. When reading, the child makes relationships from the text to present or historical events (it can also be remembered, imagined and never seen events). The skills taught in ALEPP Modules 1 and 2 are therefore the basis for fluent and functional reading, which are the objectives of this literacy curriculum.

Although the reading of sentences and small texts can be taught concurrently with word reading, ALEPP only introduces the reading of larger texts (sentences, paragraphs, stories with multiple paragraphs) when the child has already acquired a good repertoire of decoding isolated words. Given the program's target audience, who have already shown learning failure, the transition from isolated words to books is made carefully, taking into account the amount of text that a reader in the early learning phase can go through without losing interest in the activity and whether their repertoire as a reader will enable them to understand the books without additional formal teaching.

This chapter also addresses issues specific to this later stage of reading, and some reflections on additional implications for decoding and comprehension follow when a story becomes the textual unit.

5.2 The Book as a Textual Unit

A book is composed of paragraphs, which in turn contain sentences, made up of words separated by spaces and graphic characters in addition to letters (full stop, exclamation mark, comma, etc.). A child who has already mastered reading words still has a lot to learn in order to read a book.

Among the new skills they need to develop to decode the story are those of identifying the beginning and end of each word, sentence, and paragraph, and what the graphic characters, that do not make up words, add in controlling the reader's behavior (short pause, breathing, change of intonation, etc.). A story often repeats some of the speech one hears in everyday life. Part of the child's difficulty when reading a story is now learning correspondences between speech without pauses, which are represented in separate words, and different pronunciations than the sound-text correspondences that have been or will be learned formally. Additionally, the relationships that give meaning to the text also increase in complexity. Some words, such as adverbs and prepositions, change meaning relations when combined with others (e.g., put in, put out; or put this on that, put this under that). The same written word can have different meanings relative to different events in different contexts (e.g., tell a lie, lie down). An excerpt of a story may not make sense until another excerpt appears, or an excerpt may change meaning when another passage is read. Contextual control is, in a text, common and new to a beginning reader. All these new learnings occur in relation to a much larger amount of textual stimuli and the increase in complexity may generate greater or lesser interest in reading.

Understanding a story or any passage of a story should ideally be an integral part of reading. However, a person may or may not understand a story when it is read aloud by another person, just as they may or may not understand the story when the person reads it themselves. Skinner (1957) emphasizes this issue by calling textual behavior the verbal operant under the dimensional control of textual stimuli, which does not necessarily imply understanding the text: we can, for example, when faced with a text in Latin, pronounce the words written in the text with reasonable accuracy, since Portuguese and Latin languages have many phonetic similarities. This does not mean, however, that we understand the text. Something similar can happen even when a person reads texts in their own language: they do not necessarily understand what they read, although they can say the words (textual behavior). The conclusion that someone has understood what they have read is often based on the control that the words or text read has over other behaviors that would not occur without the reading (Goldiamond, 1966; Skinner, 1957). When the text is an instruction manual, for example, reading increases the likelihood of behaviors that properly operate the equipment, which in turn implies "knowing what to do" with each part. This is what is called the instructional function of reading with comprehension (Layng et al., 2011; Leon et al., 2011; Sota et al., 2011). In academic situations it is common to use multiple choice questions to assess comprehension of stories, so they have also been incorporated into the module described in this chapter. Answering this type of question requires both the writer's and the reader's repertoire to be controlled by similar relations so that readers are able to identify the correct alternatives defined by the writer (Leon et al., 2011). In addition, contextual variables must be similar to those present when the text was written and read. The large possibility of variation in context implies different responses to the same stimuli. For example, a story written in the 1940s, when women's voice was not heard and they were unable to vote, may imply different responses to questions that assess the relevance of female behaviors to criticize sexism if answered today or when the text was written.

When moving beyond the dimensional control by words, aiming at reading with understanding of stories or other types of text, therefore, the complexity of the network of repertoires that is necessary to teach/learn is expanded. New dimensional controls need to be established and numerous relationships between words, sentences and paragraphs need to establish control over classes of responses other than the oral responses corresponding to texts. Building a curriculum for teaching reading comprehension that gradually presents these complexities may be instrumental, not only in teaching these repertoires, but also in maintaining student motivation for reading. The following section will describe the module of the ALEPP teaching program that introduces children's stories with the aim of increasing fluency and comprehension in reading.

5.3 Module 3 – ALEPP

The reading of children's stories has been part of the ALEPP Program since the 1990s, in versions used at UFSCar and UnB, after a first version experimentally evaluated by Miura (1992). Following Module 2, the child was encouraged to read children's storybooks with the help of an instructor. The books of *Estrelinha* collection (*Coleção Estrelinha*), by Sônia Junqueira, and others with similar levels of difficulty were used. This collection, consisting of 15 books, presents an increasing order of difficulty (1, 2 and 3 stars), with five books at each level. In Miura's study, an instructor who accompanied the completion of the tasks asked the child to read the sentences of each page, and provided a sample (saying the correct word) in case of error (i.e., as a correction procedure) or after a long pause to read a word, using the delayed cue procedure (the experimenter or instructor waits a few seconds for the occurrence of a response and provides the cue if the response does not occur during this interval; cf., Charlop et al., 1985; Halle et al., 1979; Touchette, 1971). When the student completed reading the story portion, the instructor asked a question about the passage read, without a standardized script. One or more questions and/or comments could be asked/made. The instructor was told to praise the reading, the correct answers, the attentive posture and the engagement in the task. In each session, one book was read. Oral reading, the frequency of sample presentation (correction; cue), and the frequency with which the student corrected his or her own response (self-correction) were recorded. However, except for the initial work by

Miura (1992), there were no records of the questions prepared, nor of the children's answers, which made it impossible to publish the results of these subsequent works.

In 2013, with the approval of the project "An assessment of the reading repertoire and intervention with new teaching technologies for students from schools with low levels in Prova Brasil" (Edital 049 OBEDUC – CAPES), under the general coordination of Camila Domeniconi, the authors of the present chapter developed an automated version of Module 3 to be applied on a large scale. The 3-year project would monitor children from 3rd to 5th grade in six public schools in São Carlos, Brasília, and Belém, assessing their reading repertoire and intervening with the ALEPP Program when any difficulty was identified in learning to read words and texts. More detailed information about the project is described in Chap. 12 of this book. This chapter will describe Module 3 and the analyses of student performance that can be derived from the application of the module and the data recorded.

The automation of Module 3 involved two complementary stages: the programming of the software (to manage the presentation of all the material and record the student's answers) and the teaching programming itself. To present the interactive books via computer, a book manager was developed, with functionalities designed by the research team. The manager controls the presentation of events and records information of the session and the answers that occur in the Microsoft Office PowerPoint environment, from programming in VBA (Visual Basic for Application) for Excel. The choice of an application presented offline was due to the difficulties of stable internet (when available) in public Brazilian schools, but an online version programmed in the Manager of Individualized Teaching by Computer (GEIC – http://geic.ufscar.br/site/) is being tested. Once the manager was ready and tested with a single book, the other 14 books were inserted. The team's work consisted in uploading sounds and images for each book and creating the questions, and then assembling, almost by hand, each book in the manager and testing each functionality. This task required several months of work and counted with the help of teachers and students.[1]

The teaching arrangement took into consideration the learning principles underlying the Personalized System of Instruction (PSI; Bori, 1974; Bori et al., 1965; Keller, 1968/1999; Kienen et al., 2013; Nale, 1998): starting from clearly defined goals (reading with comprehension and fluency); starting from the learner's input repertoire; choosing teaching activities and materials (if the target behavior is reading, the activities should provide opportunities for the learner to encounter texts); organizing and sequencing the teaching material in small units, with gradually increasing difficulty; providing immediate feedback; ensuring excellence in one activity before proceeding to another; and respecting the learner's learning pace.

The books and their reorganization for presentation by computer make it possible to meet the recommendations previously mentioned. Small units of text are

---

[1] Collaborators for sound recording and testing, preparation and review of questions, and testing of books: Ana Karla Fabrino, Andréa Souza, Beatriz Saar, Beatriz Scandiuzzi, Camila Vieira, Danielle Vieira, Fernanda Diaz, Gisele Coelho, Graziela Oliveira, Jorgete Altoé, Lara de Moraes, Larissa Ribeiro, Letícia Salles, Liduína Rodrigues, Marcilene Barbosa, and Paula Natalino.

interspersed with multiple-choice questions so that the student is not immediately confronted with the entire text; the questions require additional behavior to reading and are intended to promote comprehension. Each interactive book consists of 13 story portions and 15 or 16 questions. The first story screen presents the book cover illustration with the title, and author and illustrator's names, and gives credit to the programmer and designer (Fig. 5.1, Panel a). The book title, besides being presented in writing, can be heard: the corresponding sound is triggered with a click. The other screens of the story present the text corresponding to two pages of the printed book, typed at the top of the screen with the background illustration (Panel b). The words with orthographic difficulties in their sound-text correspondences (digraph, consonantal meetings, etc.) are highlighted and the auditory version can be presented, through the computer speaker, when the reader clicks on each one. To advance in the book, once the reading of the passage has been completed, the learner must click on the arrow positioned in the top right corner (panel b).

All screens with excerpts from the story are followed by questions that set the context for the student to think about what they have just read. All comprehension questions are multiple-choice: they have the statement and four alternatives, only one of which is defined as correct. This is similar to a Matching-to-Sample (MTS, Cumming & Berryman, 1965) format that teaches or tests conditional discriminations, but the sample and comparisons are more complex than those used in most research.

To develop the questions, we used some procedures based on research evidence on stimulus control and reading. The first was to vary the presentation of the

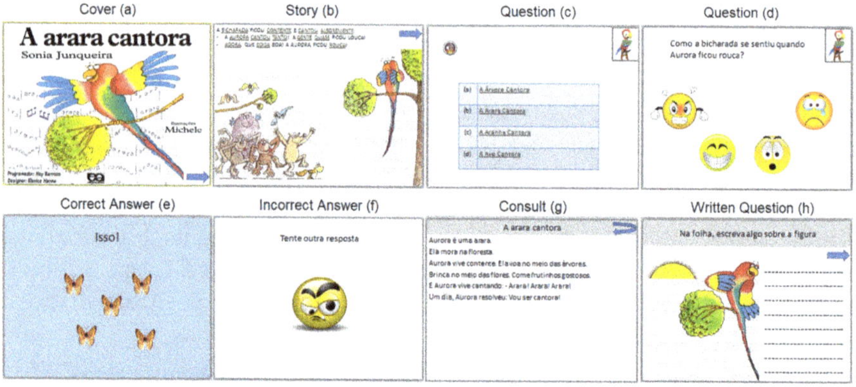

Fig. 5.1 Screenshot Samples of Interactive Book Functionalities. *Note.* (**a**) cover with information about the book; (**b**) text relating to part of the story, with words underlined that could be heard with a click; (**c**) question with auditory statement, written alternatives and query button; (**d**) question with a written statement, pictures as alternatives and a query button; (**e**) hit screen with animated gifs, written praise and musical excerpt presentation; (**f**) error screen with animated smiley face that rotates the eyes and spoken and written message to try another alternative; (**g**) query screen with the story excerpt up to a certain part of the story; and (**h**) written question to be answered using pencil and paper

statement and alternatives, which could either indicate or generate stimulus equivalence (Sidman & Tailby, 1982), or the instructional control of the text (Leon et al., 2011). The question statement can be spoken (Fig. 5.1, Panel c) or written (Panel d). The spoken statement is presented along with the response alternatives and can be heard again by clicking on the speaker button inserted above the alternatives (Panel c). The alternatives are in text (Panel c) or image (Panel d) format. To get the learner to observe various relevant aspects of the story, the statement and the alternatives, they have some semantic or formal similarity. For example, in the question presented in Panel c, which contains the question "What is the name of the book?", only the middle word changes between the alternatives. In addition, the chosen words (*árvore, arara, aranha* and *ave – tree, macaw, spider, and bird*) share some similarities in physical features (they all start with the same letter) and semantics (three of the alternatives refer to animals). In the question of Panel d, smiley faces were used, which are physically similar stimuli (circular, with mouth, eyes, and eyebrows). Due to the difficulties that children under 10 years old may have to discriminate emotions in faces (Lawrence et al., 2015), the three incorrect alternatives presented expressions opposite to the correct answer. The smiley faces appeared in at least one question of several books since it was common to report character's emotions in the stories.

To increase control for relevant aspects of the text and accuracy of comprehension, the incorrect alternatives of some questions also contained: information from other parts of the story (e.g., action occurred in a previous passage) or from other books (e.g., the name of a character from a previously read book); figures or words from the same category (e.g., adjectives used as praise or a scene containing the same object); part of the correct alternative (e.g., the title of the book missing a word); and words spelled similarly to the correct one but with a different meaning (e.g., whole and hole).

In case of error, the response to one of the three incorrect alternatives was followed by the same smiley face and circular eye movement (Fig. 5.1, Panel f), a written message, "No, try another one!", together with the same spoken message with a duration of 2 s. The repetition of the consequences for error was planned to prevent the learner from choosing wrong alternatives for novelty and stimuli more interesting to the child than those correlated to the correct alternative.

The program also included continuous and immediate reinforcement contingencies for correct responses (Fig. 5.1, Panel e). Choosing the correct alternative is followed by a 2 s sound, an animated gif, and a written praise, presented simultaneously. The three consequence modalities were varied throughout the questions to avoid satiation effect and to motivate the learner to get the question right. The sounds could be spoken praise (e.g., right, great, very good), stimuli related to successful situations (e.g., clapping, kissing, "uhuu"), or joyful pieces of music (e.g., Beat it, *Castelo Ratimbum, Lepo Lepo*). The images with movement are drawings of animals (Panel e), children playing, or funny smiley faces. The written praise mostly corresponds to the spoken praise. Following the consequences for correct answers, the next screen with excerpt from the story or another question is presented. The last comprehension question is always followed by the same 6 s excerpt from the Happy song to indicate task completion.

In all questions, there is the option to reread the part of the book presented up to that point. A click on the icon located in the upper right corner of the screen (Fig. 5.1, Panels c and d), which contains picture of a bird or a smiley face reading, gives access to the part of the story in running text format, without picture (Panel g). The learner can review the story as many times as they want and for as long as necessary, without any aversive consequences. The inclusion of the entire part of the story already read was based on the premise that answering the question correctly may depend on understanding a passage that may precede the last one presented.

After the last comprehension question, one of the illustrations from the book is presented along with the dictated and written prompt for the learner to write something about the picture. The instructor should at this point make paper, pencil, and eraser available for the learner. This discursive question was included only to assess writing and no contingency was programmed for the responses emitted by the child.

The 15 books were divided into three teaching units. Figure 5.2 compares the total number of words (left chart) and characters (right chart) for each book in the three units. These measures include words or characters from the story and questions. For all five books, Units 1 and 2 have similar or lower levels of difficulty than Unit 3, considering the number of words and characters.

Table 5.1 presents a more detailed analysis of the books, including the titles, number of questions, the word and character count of the story and questions for each book and for each unit. In Units 1 and 2 only one book has 16 questions and in Unit 3, two books. The word and character count were similar in units 1 and 2, but higher in Unit 3. Regarding questions, the amount increased across the units.

The teaching Module should be carried out under the supervision of a literate adult, who may be a parent, teacher or an instructor. Instructions for implementation can be obtained by contacting one of the authors of this chapter[2]. Importantly, there

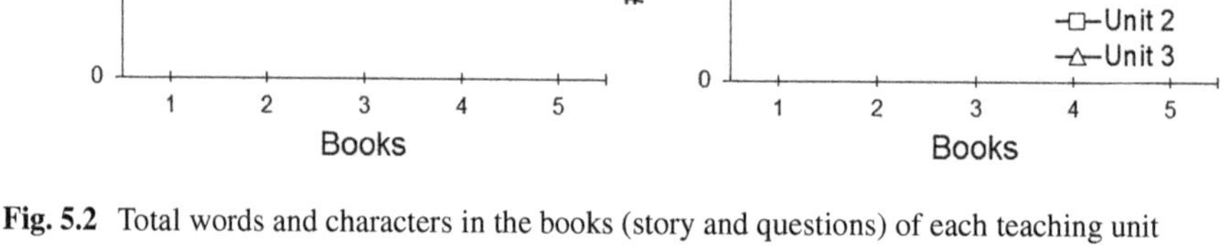

Fig. 5.2 Total words and characters in the books (story and questions) of each teaching unit

[2] Application instructions are also available at the following link: InstructionsForApplication

Table 5.1 Information about each interactive book of the teaching units

Book title	No. of questions	No. of words		No. of characters	
		Story	Questions	Story	Questions
UNIT I					
Regina e o Mágico [Regina and the Magician]	15	219	126	894	546
O caracol viajante [The traveling snail]	15	193	236	904	1126
O peru de peruca [The wig turkey]	16	246	190	973	791
A foca famosa [The famous seal]	15	247	189	999	747
O menino e o muro [The boy and the wall]	15	179	205	842	930
Total	76	1084	946	4612	4140
UNIT II					
A onça e a anta [The jaguar and the tapir]	15	153	185	603	771
O macaco medroso [The scared monkey]	15	254	191	1169	841
O sonho da vaca [The cow's dream]	15	200	236	949	1075
A arara cantora [The singing macaw]	16	203	208	980	996
O barulho fantasma [The ghost noise]	15	154	226	728	1019
Total	76	964	1046	4429	4702
UNIT III					
O peixe pixote [The pixote fish]	15	303	257	1346	1179
Um palhaço diferente [A different clown]	15	327	175	1677	813
A festa encrencada [The troubled party]	15	285	180	1367	849
O susto do piriquito [The scare of the parakeet]	16	290	248	1402	1171
O mistério da Lua [The mystery of the moon]	16	256	316	1066	1350
Total	77	1461	1176	6858	5362

is empirical evidence that the behavior of the instructor influences the degree of program effectiveness (Muniz, 2019). The first book should be carried out with the instructor next to the learner, so that all the functionalities of the teaching program are taught. Before letting the learner do it by himself, the instructor should make sure that he understands how everything works and what he should do. Information should be presented slowly as the screens appear to the child. The student should: (a) differentiate a reading screen from a question screen; (b) identify the function of the arrow that appears on the reading screens; (c) identify when and how to listen for underlined words; (d) identify the function of the reread/help button indicated by the smiley face on the question screens, and (e) choose an alternative for each question after reading/looking/listening to the statement and alternatives. The goal is that the learner can interact with the book properly, without the need for help.

To advance in the books, the learner must get all the questions (15 or 16) right on the first attempt. In case of one or more mistakes, the book must be repeated. This criterion was chosen because it is possible to get the questions right even without reading the text and the question, since the learner can try all the alternatives until the correct one is found. The requirement of getting it right in the first attempt discourages strategies that do not require reading and understanding the text and the question. It is suggested that book monitoring be done whenever the student needs the third exposure to one of the books. In this case, the instructor should: (1) verify that the complete reading of the story excerpts and the questions is being performed; (2) ask the child to point to the answer alternative he/she thinks is correct before clicking; and (3) in case of error, suggest that the child review the text again before making the final choice.

5.4 Analysis of Results Generated by Module 3 – ALEPP

This next section presents results from six children who took Module 3 – ALEPP to illustrate some possible analyses of the data that is recorded by the interactive book software. The data used in these analyses are from students from two public schools in Brasilia that participated in the OBEDUC project, described in Chap. 12. The children were selected from 4th and 5th-grade elementary school students who read words with simple syllables in consonant-vowel sequence (e.g., rato [rat]), vowel meetings (e.g., lua [moon]) and words with spelling difficulties such as digraphs (e.g., chat, parrot, share) and other consonantal meetings (e.g., lista [list], atleta [athlete]), but had difficulty in reading and understanding short texts. The Behavioral Assessment of Reading and Writing Repertoires (*Avaliação Comportamental de Leitura e Escrita* [ACoLE][3]) instruments 1 and 2 (developed by de Souza et al., 1996) and 3 (Silveira et al., 2019) were used. The results of three students from each school who had low (30% correct), medium (55% correct), and relatively high (70% correct) scores are presented below. Module 3 – ALEPP was applied by teachers from each school (who were prepared by the team for this task).

The first analysis (Fig. 5.3) refers to the number of exposures to the five books of each unit for each learner of Schools 1 and 2. This measure allows verifying how many times the students repeated the books throughout the three units. Since the number of books per unit is five, the closer to five the number of exposures the learner had, the fewer repetitions he made. Students with a score of 70 (A70) from both schools repeated the Unit 1 books less than students with scores of 55 (A55) and 30 (A30) on the initial assessment (ACoLE,[3] Silveira et al., 2019). Four of the six participants showed decreased exposures to the books from Unit 1 to 2, but there was variability in Unit 3, likely as a result of the increased complexity of the books in this unit. Students in School 2 generally required more exposures to the books than those in School 1. School 1 had a much smaller number of students than School

[3] The term ACoLE started to be used in 2020 to refer to the assessment instruments developed by the INCT-ECCE group that before were called Reading and Writing Diagnosis (*Diagnóstico de Leitura e Escrita* [DLE]) (e.g., Silveira et al., 2019) and Reading and Writing Network Assessment (*Avaliação da Rede de Leitura e Escrita* [ARLE]) (e.g., de Souza & Rocca, 2018).

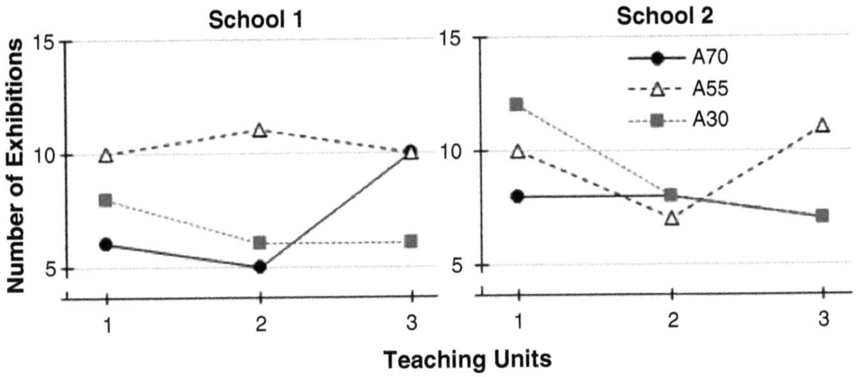

Fig. 5.3 Number of exposures to books of teaching units for each student in Schools 1 and 2

2, and so students were attended more regularly and activities with the teachers were carried out individually. This may have accelerated the students' learning. When Module 3 is done by the child at least three times a week, even if he/she needs to repeat all the books, he/she completes the program in 3 or 4 months.

To assess whether changes in reading fluency occur, a reading rate measure can be used. In the second analysis (Fig. 5.4) the number of characters in the digital book divided by the time to complete reading the story and questions on first exposure to each book was used. This is an approximate measure, as it does not take into account re-readings and repetitions of the questions that the student may have performed on the first exposure, as well as the limitation of the accuracy of recording done in minutes. In general, the reading rates of children in School 1 were higher than those in School 2. Four of the six students showed an increase in the number of characters read per minute over the course of the teaching units. One student from each school showed a small decrease.

The questions were inserted in the books to assess story comprehension and, therefore, it is important to know how the answers varied throughout the books. In each question, a correct answer allowed advancing through the story, but choosing incorrect alternatives resulted in a return to the same question until the child selected the correct alternative. Therefore, the measure of correct answers will always be 15 or 16, i.e., equal to the number of questions, but errors could vary. The error total was, for this reason, chosen as the most sensitive measure of reading comprehension. The closer to zero, the greater the accuracy of the answers to the questions. Figure 5.5 presents the total errors made in the five books of each unit.

Errors decreased from Unit 1 to 2 (except A55 at School 1), but increased again in Unit 3 (except A70 at School 2), as the complexity of the texts increased. It is interesting to note that for both schools, the number of errors in Unit 1 is correlated to the score in the initial test (30, 55 and 70, according to the participant's pseudonym). In the other units, participants with intermediate score (A55) made more errors when compared to those with lower and higher performances, which showed a substantial reduction. As only six participants were selected to illustrate the

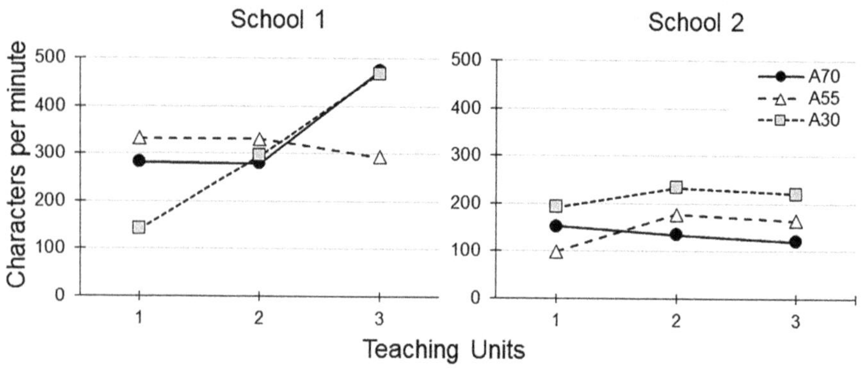

Fig. 5.4 Unit reading rate for each student in Schools 1 and 2

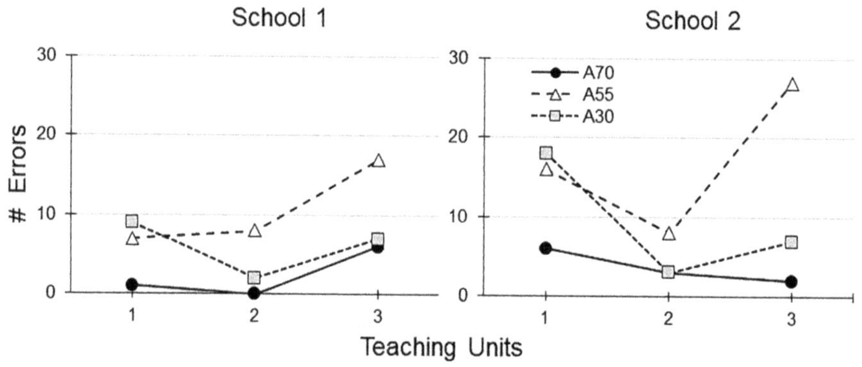

Fig. 5.5 Number of errors in each teaching unit for each student in Schools 1 and 2

analyses that can be performed with the data collected in the program, it is not possible to state whether these results represent patterns to be expected for most students.

Two other measures recorded are: (a) the consultation time (ms) of the story excerpt read up to that point; and (b) the number of consultations of the underlined words (for presenting some orthographic difficulty) on the story screens.

The button to query the written passage was available in all questions (Fig. 5.1, panels c and d) and once on the query screen (Fig. 5.1, Panel g), the learner only returned to the question screen by dragging the mouse over the top right corner of the screen. The query time was calculated from the response on the query button to the response to return to the question screen. Figure 5.6 presents the query time in each unit for each participant from the two schools in the top graphs. The two participants with higher scores on the initial assessment (A70) showed very little query time across all units and, in several books, there was no query at all. For the other participants, in general, the consultation time was longer in the first and third units.

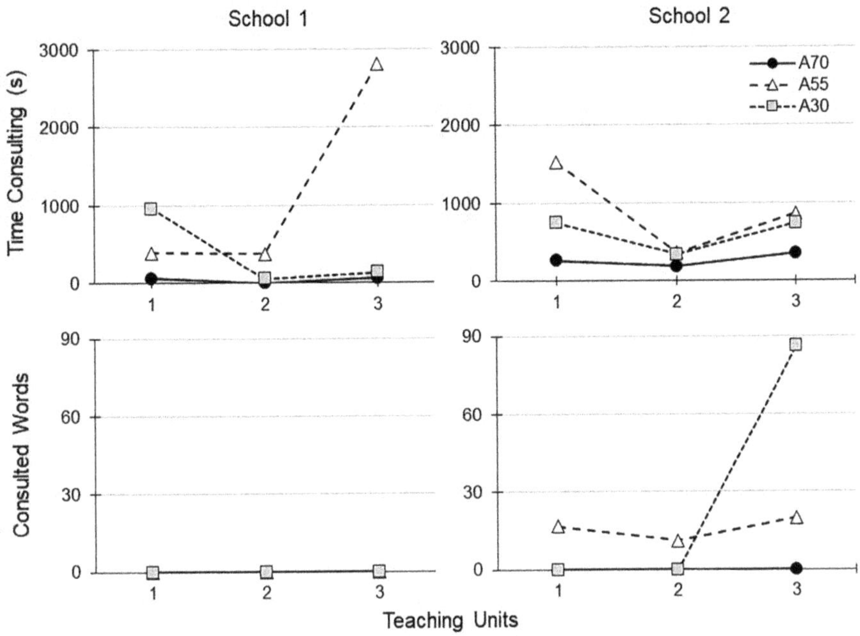

Fig. 5.6 Story consultation time and number of words consulted in the teaching units, for each student in Schools 1 and 2

Word sound consultation could occur only in the story screens (Fig. 5.1, Panel b). The total number of words consulted in each unit for each student is presented in the lower graphs of Fig. 5.6. The three participants from School 1 and A70 from School 2 did not consult any word throughout the three units, which shows that there was error in the application of the program. During training, teachers were instructed to teach all program features with demonstration. Thus, at least one word should have been consulted in the first book, which did not happen for five learners who did not consult any of the words in Unit 1.

Low access to the two query features of the program may influence its effect on learning. Rereading the text on the query screens and confirming the reading of words with spelling irregularities by producing the corresponding sound may amplify the textual and instructional control of the story. In a recent study (Muniz, 2019), it was observed that continuous training of instructors, with videorecording and feedback for their behaviors during the application of the program, reduced the number of learners' errors, increased query time, and increased reading comprehension scores.

The last analysis to be presented is not derived from data collected during the application of the teaching units but from the comprehension assessment, here called ACoLE 3. Figure 5.7 shows the scores of the versions of the test applied before and after Module 3 – of reading comprehension. This is a generalization measure of reading comprehension, since the tests are carried out in a different

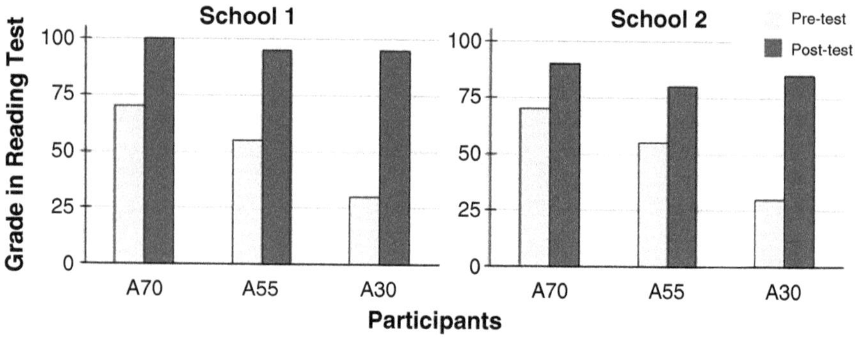

Fig. 5.7 Reading test score (ACoLE 3) before and after application of Module 3 for students in Schools 1 and 2

context (paper and pencil in the classroom) from that in which teaching is carried out (on the computer, in the computer lab). In addition, complete short texts are presented followed by some questions, totaling 20 multiple-choice questions (more details about the content of this instrument can be obtained in Silveira et al., 2019). Six learners whose results are presented in this chapter showed change in generalized reading comprehension: comparing the scores of ACoLE 3 applied before and after the completion of Module 3, an increase is observed for all learners (Fig. 5.7). Greater changes are observed for learners who started with lower scores (A30). Despite differentiated pre-test scores, all three learners in each school finished the program with similar high reading comprehension scores (greater than 75%).

The log file generated by the program includes a final tab in the Excel spreadsheet that presents the results in table and graph of each session performed, with correct answers in the first attempt, errors, total time on the help screens and total words consulted. Figure 5.8 shows the printout of A30's results from School 2. Displaying the results session by session can help the teacher or instructor to track each child's performance throughout the program. Note, for example, that A30 only began to look up words from Book 11 onwards (bottom right-hand panel).

Other analyses that can assist the teacher in making decisions about additional materials and procedures for a child with specific difficulties can still be carried out. For example, it is possible to identify whether comprehension difficulties appear in specific contexts, such as questions with the statement and alternatives presented in text, but not when the statement is dictated and the alternatives are in written format. Additionally, the difficulty may not occur when the correct answer is explicitly presented in the text, but errors occur when it is necessary to make some additional relationship or inference. One can also analyze the characteristics of the words that are queried to identify difficulties in decoding the words. This information would require molecular analysis of the data, but is important for monitoring students who need special teaching procedures.

Book	Date	Correct Answers	Incorrect Answers	Help	Words
1	20/08/2014	14	1	56217	0
1	21/08/2014	14	1	0	0
1	27/08/2014	14	1	1375	0
1	28/08/2014	15	0	5468	0
2	09/03/2014	12	5	39296	0
2	09/04/2014	14	1	33610	0
3	16/09/2014	13	5	99293	0
3	16/09/2014	16	0	81309	0
3	17/09/2014	16	0	0	0
4	23/09/2014	12	4	51841	0
4	30/09/2014	15	0	0	0
5	10/07/2014	15	0	2812	0
7	10/08/2014	15	0	0	0
6	28/10/2014	14	1	20717	0
6	28/10/2014	14	1	3562	0
6	29/10/2014	15	0	8421	0
8	29/10/2014	15	0	37856	0
9	11/04/2014	16	0	33076	0
10	11/05/2014	14	1	58947	0
10	11/05/2014	15	0	7546	0
11	25/11/2014	15	0	68978	36
12	25/11/2014	11	6	125901	47
12	26/11/2014	16	0	27513	71
13	26/11/2014	15	0	21013	119
14	27/11/2014	16	0	60872	61
15	27/11/2014	15	1	63168	22
15	12/02/2014	16	0	0	64

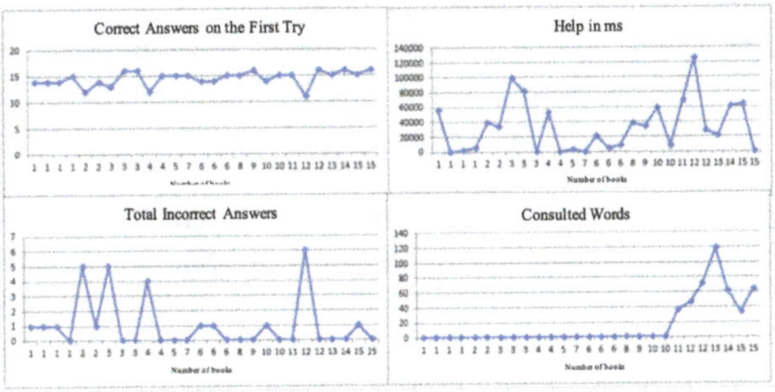

Fig. 5.8 Presentation of session-by-session results in the log file produced by Module 3 of student A30 of School 2

5.5 Final Considerations

In the present chapter some thoughts on implications for decoding and book comprehension following word learning were presented. It then described a computerized teaching procedure for reading comprehension and illustrated analyses that can be carried out to assess its effect and to track the performance of students undertaking the teaching module.

Results were presented in this chapter and in Chap. 12 that show that Module 3 increases the reading repertoire of literacy learners by reducing initial differences between children's repertoires, leading to equally improved final scores. The reduction in initial variability and improvement in reading comprehension skills observed is similar to the results obtained with the application of the other ALEPP teaching modules (e.g., de Rose et al., 1996; Tizo, 2016; de Souza et al., 1999). The procedure favored the comprehension of small texts, ideal for the initial reading phase, when children can already read isolated words and need to improve control over larger textual units. The way we programmed the instruction was initially a challenge for students with difficulty in reading comprehension of stories, but it was successful because it presented cues (e.g., picture, possibility of checking the sound of words with spelling difficulties), small parts of the story at a time, the possibility of repeating the question until the correct answer was found, which was always followed by arbitrary and immediate consequences. The measure of comprehension used was based on the answers to multiple choice questions related to the stories read. The questions and the similarity between the alternatives increased the control for several aspects of the story.

The process throughout the application of Module 3 varied between children, as initial skills and how they interacted with the material were also different between them, but learning was observed for most children who participated in Module 3 to date (Domeniconi et al., 2022; and Chap. 12).

Since this is the first computerized version of Module 3, it was already possible to identify aspects that need to be changed and improved for it to work as a research and teaching tool. It would be important to control the number of questions, at least within each unit, as well as question difficulty. Assessments already carried out indicate that negative statements and questions that require abstractions and relations not directly indicated in the text (implicit answers) generate more errors than questions whose answers are explicit in the text. It will be necessary to perform a content analysis of the questions to add gradually increasing difficulties throughout the units. Furthermore, despite the significant improvement in reading comprehension, 15 books were not enough for some children to achieve high scores (greater than 80%), suggesting the need to increase the number of books and perhaps the level of story difficulty in an additional unit.

The computerized Module 3 is a procedure that allows the large-scale teaching of a complex skill and, at the same time, the monitoring of the individualized learning process. Its modifications need to have their effectiveness evaluated, but it has already shown great potential as a complementary activity to the activities developed in the classroom by the teacher.

References

Bori, C. M. (1974). Developments in Brazil. In F. S. Keller & J. G. Sherman (Eds.), *PSI – The Keller plan handbook* (pp. 65–72). W.A. Benjamin.

Bori, C. M., Pessotti, I., & Azzi, R. (1965). Um curso moderno de psicologia. *Ciência e Cultura, 17*(2), 219.

Charlop, M. H., Schreibman, L., & Thibodeau, M. G. (1985). Increasing spontaneous verbal responding in autistic children using a time delay procedure. *Journal of Applied Behavior Analysis, 18*, 155–166. https://doi.org/10.1901/jaba.1985.18-155

Cumming, W. W., & Berryman, R. (1965). The complex discriminated operant: Studies of matching-to-sample and related problems. In D. I. Mostofsky (Ed.), *Stimulus generalization* (pp. 284–329). Stanford University Press.

de Rose, J. C. (2005). Análise comportamental da aprendizagem de leitura e escrita. *Revista Brasileira de Análise do Comportamento, 1*(1), 29–50. https://doi.org/10.18542/rebac.v1i1.676

de Rose, J. C., de Souza, D. G., Rossito, A. L., & de Rose, T. M. S. (1992). Stimulus equivalence and generalization in reading after matching to sample by exclusion. In S. C. Hayes & L. J. Hayes (Eds.), *Understanding verbal relations* (pp. 69–82). Context Press.

de Rose, J. C., de Souza, D. G., & Hanna, E. S. (1996). Teaching reading and spelling: Exclusion and stimulus equivalence. *Journal of Applied Behavior Analysis, 29*(4), 451–469. https://doi.org/10.1901/jaba.1996.29-451

de Souza, D. G., & de Rose, J. C. (2006). Desenvolvendo programas individualizados para o ensino de leitura. *Acta Comportamentalia, 14*(1), 77–98.

de Souza, V. H., & Rocca, J. Z. (2018). *Avaliação das habilidades constitutivas do repertório de leitura e escrita e suas inter-relações na aprendizagem*. Anais da X Mostra da Pós-Graduação: Direitos Humanos, trabalho coletivo e redes de pesquisa na Pós-Graduação, Universidade Federal de Mato Grosso, Cuiabá, MT. Retrieved from http://eventosacademicos.ufmt.br/index.php/mostradaposgraduacao/xmostra/paper/view/8317

de Souza, D. G., de Rose, J. C., & Hanna, E. S. (1996). *Diagnóstico de leitura e escrita: Tarefas para avaliação de repertórios rudimentares de leitura e escrita*. Instrumento de avaliação. Universidade Federal de São Carlos e Universidade de Brasília.

de Souza, D. G., de Rose, J. C., Fonseca, M. L., & Hanna, E. S. (1999). Stimulus control research and minimal units for reading. *Experimental Analysis of Human Behavior Bulletin, 17*, 20–23.

de Souza, D. G., de Rose, J. C., Faleiros, T. C., Bortoloti, R., Hanna, E. S., & McIlvane, W. J. (2009). Teaching generative reading via recombination of minimal textual units: A legacy of verbal behavior to children in Brazil. *International Journal of Psychology and Psychological Therapy, 9*(1), 19–44.

Domeniconi, C., Hanna, E. S., de Rose, J. C. C., & de Souza, D. G. (2022). *Programa individualizado de compreensão de leitura* de textos com compreensão. *Acta Comportamentalia, 30*(4), 705–724.

Goldiamond, I. (1966). Perception, language, and conceptualization rules. In B. Kleinmuntz (Ed.), *Problem solving: Research, method, and theory* (pp. 183–224). Wiley.

Halle, J. W., Baer, D. M., & Spradlin, J. E. (1979). Teacher's generalized use of delay as a stimulus control procedure to increase language use in handicapped children. *Journal of Applied Behavior Analysis, 14*, 389–409. https://doi.org/10.1901/jaba.1981.14-389

Keller, F. S. (1968/1999). Good-bye, teacher. *Journal of Applied Behavior Analysis, 1*(1), 79–89. https://doi.org/10.1901/jaba.1968.1-79

Kienen, N., Kubo, O. M., & Botomé, S. P. (2013). Ensino programado e programação de condições para o desenvolvimento de comportamentos: Alguns aspectos no desenvolvimento de um campo de atuação do psicólogo. *Acta Comportamentalia, 21*, 481–494.

Lawrence, K., Campbell, R., & Skuse, D. (2015). Age, gender, and puberty influence the development of facial emotion recognition. *Frontiers in Psychology, 6*, 1–14. https://doi.org/10.3389/fpsyg.2015.00761

Layng, T. V. J., Sota, M., & Leon, M. (2011). Thinking through text comprehension I: Foundation and guiding relations. *The Behavior Analyst Today, 12*(1), 3–11. https://doi.org/10.1037/h0100706

Leon, M., Layng, T. V. J., & Sota, M. (2011). Thinking through text comprehension III: The programing of verbal and investigative repertoires. *The Behavior Analyst Today, 12*(1), 22–33. https://doi.org/10.1037/h0100708

Miura, R. K. K. (1992). *Oportunidade de resposta seguida por modelo: Um procedimento para o desenvolvimento de leitura em alunos com dificuldades de aprendizagem.* Unpublished master's thesis. Universidade Federal de São Carlos.

Muniz, C. C. (2019). *Efeitos do treino de mães e professoras como aplicadoras de um programa de ensino de leitura de histórias infantis.* Unpublished master's thesis. Universidade de Brasília.

Nale, N. (1998). Programação de ensino no Brasil: O papel de Carolina Bori. *Psicologia USP, 9*(1), 275–301. https://doi.org/10.7804/106150

Sidman, M., & Tailby, W. (1982). Conditional discrimination vs. matching-to-sample: An expansion of the testing paradigm. *Journal of the Experimental Analysis of Behavior, 37*, 5–22. https://doi.org/10.1901/jeab.1982.37-5

Silveira, C. C., Domeniconi, C., & Hanna, E. S. (2019). Uma avaliação alternativa de compreensão de leitura para crianças. *Acta Comportamentalia, 27*(4), 423–435.

Skinner, B. F. (1957). *Verbal behavior.* Prentice Hall. https://doi.org/10.1037/11256-000

Sota, M., Leon, M., & Layng, T. V. J. (2011). Thinking through text comprehension II: Analysis of verbal and investigative repertoires. *The Behavior Analyst Today, 12*(1), 12–21. https://doi.org/10.1037/h0100707

Tizo, M. (2016). *Avaliando tecnologia de ensino de leitura e escrita informatizada e adaptada para alunos de escola pública com dificuldade de aprendizagem.* Doctoral dissertation, Universidade de Brasília. Repositório Institucional UnB. https://repositorio.unb.br/bitstream/10482/21618/1/2016_MarcileydeTizo.pdf

Touchette, P. E. (1971). Transfer of stimulus control: Measuring the moment of transfer. *Journal of the Experimental Analysis of Behavior, 15*, 347–354. https://doi.org/10.1901/jeab.1971.15

Chapter 6
Resources Needed to Expand the Program for Teaching Verbal Repertoires Toward Sentences

Ana Claudia Moreira Almeida-Verdu, Anderson Jonas das Neves, Lidia Maria Marson Postalli, and Deisy das Graças de Souza

6.1 Introduction

Language acquisition is a dynamic, multidetermined process that depends on interactions between biological and environmental/behavioral components. These interactions involve, on the one hand, the integrity of anatomical structures as well as their differentiation during development; on the other hand, they depend on a context in which there are communicative interactions (Levine et al., 2016; Lopes-Ornat & Gallo, 2004; Papalia & Olds, 2000). Language is essential for the development of complex human functions – such as planning, thinking, abstraction, memory, and communication (Levine et al., 2016) – and identifying the variables and processes related to its acquisition and complexity are tasks of scientific and social importance.

Language, or verbal behavior (the name used in this chapter), is not directly associated with a response modality or type (that is, the topography of the response may be vocal, gestural, or the product of motor action such as writing), but rather

The Learning to Read in Small Steps (ALEPP) teaching program is composed of several modules, some experimentally evaluated and made available for use at scale, and others in different stages of development, evaluation and revision; Deisy das Graças de Souza, Júlio C. de Rose and Elenice S. Hanna hold the responsibility for the overall coordination of ALEPP; and Ana Cláudia M. Almeida-Verdu, Raquel Melo Golfeto, Lídia Maria Marson Postalli and Anderson Jonas das Neves lead the team for development of the Sentence Module.

A. C. M. Almeida-Verdu (✉)
Universidade Estadual Paulista, Rio Claro, SP, Brazil
e-mail: ana.verdu@unesp.br

A. J. das Neves · L. M. M. Postalli · D. das Graças de Souza
Universidade Federal de São Carlos, São Carlos, SP, Brazil

A. R. de Albuquerque, R. M. de Melo (eds.), *Contributions of Behavior Analysis to Reading and Writing Comprehension*, https://doi.org/10.1007/978-3-031-40868-7_6

with its function, which is to modify someone's behavior. Verbal behavior will affect another person's behavior if both share the same conventions and practices of the verbal community. For example, saying "turn on the light" to an American native speaker will increase the chances that the request will be answered and that person will touch the switch to turn on the lamp in the room, while it will not produce the same reaction if the person who heard it is not an American English speaker, such as a Chinese or an Arab.

From the ontogenetic point of view, reading and writing are linguistic repertoires that will appear later in development. Typical Brazilian children begin to systematically learn these skills from the age of six, when they enter formal schooling and undergo the process called literacy (Nascimento, 2007).

The fact is that, in our reality, many children do not benefit from the education offered in the regular network. Based on this scientific and social demand, and the need to better understand the processes related to the acquisition of increasingly complex communicative and social repertoires – especially reading and writing, not just words, but sentences and texts-, this chapter will explore this topic with a view to identifying subsidies for the development of a sentence teaching module in a context that already has a teaching program developed and tested for simple and complex words (de Souza et al., 2009a) and for small texts (Bertini, 2017). To this end, it is subdivided into four main sections.

The second section will start from the already consolidated literature on programming conditions for teaching words and will propose extensions and subsidies for teaching sentences. The reader will find in this section an operational description of reading and writing and procedures for teaching them accurately and fluently. We will also use as examples some stimuli whose complexity involves words. In the following sections, extensions will be made to sentence complexity stimuli.

In the third section, a brief review of the evolution of the *Learning to Read and Write in Small Steps®* (*Aprendendo a Ler e Escrever em Pequenos Passos* [ALEPP]) teaching program Modules applied through the Computer Individualized Teaching Manager (*Gerenciador de Ensino Individualizado por Computador* [GEIC]) will be presented. The Modules are composed of different complexities (regular words, words with spelling difficulties and small texts). The need for the development of a sentence teaching module will be presented.

In the fourth section, the unit of analysis of isolated words will be expanded to sentences. Although they are built as students are exposed to teaching conditions, verbal skills (listening, speaking, reading, and writing) with sentences are repertoires whose acquisition and integration (among them) depend on the programming of special teaching conditions, requiring specific procedural arrangements. Different laboratories in Brazil and abroad have produced consolidated knowledge about conditions and procedures for teaching verbal repertoires, and the potential of the equivalence relations model for teaching word reading and writing. In this direction, the chapter will also present literature on the generative potential (semantic and syntactic) of teaching sentences, as well as teaching procedures and stimulus organization that favor this potential.

Given the possibility of expanding the teaching program and including an intermediate Module between the Modules of words and small texts – which is a Module for teaching sentences – the sentence will be presented as the unit of analysis, with a brief review of recent studies that have programmed the teaching of verbal skills with sentences and demonstrated indicators of effectiveness, efficiency and generality for different populations. Finally, we will present aspects that subsidize this proposal for the Module of sentence teaching and what characteristics this Module should have.

6.2 Reading, Writing, Comprehension and Fluency of Words

Reading can be defined as a discriminated operant behavior (i.e., under stimulus control) that is selected, maintained, and becomes more complex from reinforcing contingencies of the verbal community (Skinner, 1957). This behavioral description of reading was a major contribution to understanding the conditions under which a person reacts to printed materials (e.g., signs, billboards, text). Comprehension reading as operant behavior means that it is a behavior that produces consequences that modify the environment, and that the behavior itself is affected by these changes. Describing it based on stimulus control means that consequences select not only the behavior that produced them, but also the relationship between this behavior and the conditions that were present when it occurred. In the case of reading, teachers, parents, and people who participate in the verbal community produce many social and generalized consequences when a child begins to read-such as "Congratulations! You're reading!" – which increases the likelihood that the learner will continue to read, and selects the emission of specific sounds (phonemes) in the face of textual stimuli (graphemes).

This analysis allows for the planning of teaching conditions, based on reinforcement contingencies, for learners who did not benefit from the educational conditions proposed in the classroom. In this direction, many studies have been developed in Brazil in the last 30 years and have supported the proposal of an effective program for teaching basic reading and writing skills (e.g., de Souza & de Rose, 2006; de Souza et al., 2009b). The reader will find a synthesis of this material in Chap. 2 of this book.

In general, this chapter proposes to start from the definition of reading as a textual verbal behavior, under control of each minimal textual unit that composes it, in which the response (usually vocal) should possess arbitrary and point to point correspondence with these textual stimuli (Skinner, 1957). The reading of textual units cannot be random, but should be sequenced, because changing the order of what is read affects its meaning (e.g., STUDY and DUSTY) or makes it meaningless (e.g., DUTSY). Although reading does not necessarily depend on hearing, as in the case of deaf people who communicate in sign language and react with an agreed sign to printed words, there is an auditory domain involved. Auditory-textual relations are at the basis of our written language, because our system is alphabetic and requires that graphic signs (graphemes) correspond arbitrarily to the sounds of language (phonemes) (Godoy, 2008).

Echoic behavior, which consists of accurately repeating what others say, is also relevant. Echoic behavior is similar to textual behavior in that it also requires the ability to reproduce point by point the auditory pattern produced by another person (de Souza et al., 2009b). Reading then requires textual and auditory discrimination and the ordered vocalization of the minimal units present in each word (de Rose, 2005, republished in Chap. 1 of this volume).

But textual reading alone does not guarantee comprehension (Skinner, 1957). Reading with comprehension requires the tact, which is an operant generally defined by vocal control over a non-verbal discriminative event such as objects, pictures, scenes or events, and public or private events. This verbal skill is also known, informally, as naming. However, there are theoretical distinctions between tact and *naming*, which were detailed by Miguel (2016).

The teaching program *Learning to Read and Write in Small Steps (*ALEPP), developed by several of the authors of chapters in this book (de Rose et al., 1989, 1992), presents teaching contingencies that allow relating these different verbal operants (e.g., listening, tacting, reading); it was initially used in printed cards arranged in a tabletop folder-catalogue. Later, it was computerized and made available in a software (Rosa Filho et al., 1998) and is currently hosted in the platform of the Computer Individualized Teaching Manager (GEIC) (Capobianco et al., 2009). ALEPP presents a word teaching program and covers auditory, textual and pictorial stimuli that control, respectively, the vocal responses of echoic behavior, reading and the tact; these stimuli and responses can be related and integrated by equivalence relations (de Souza et al., 2009a). From these teaching conditions, the discriminative functions of stimuli that precisely control a vocal response can be extended to other equivalent stimuli. For example, in listeners, oral production is precisely controlled by the picture (e.g., the tact); after exposure to the teaching program, oral production emitted in the presence of the pictorial stimulus is now emitted in the presence of the printed stimulus (e.g., reading). The discriminative function of the pictorial stimulus is said to have been transferred to the printed word stimulus when the response originally emitted only in the presence of the picture is emitted in the presence of the printed word, which has no physical similarity to the picture; this process may occur after a succession of pairings between stimuli (e.g., dictated word-picture and dictated word-printed word) that have a stimulus in common, in this case, the dictated word (de Rose, 2005, republished in Chap. 1 of this book; Mackay et al., 2011).

More specifically, after teaching conditional discriminations between words and pictures and between words and pictures to hearing and non-reading children, it can be observed that vocal responses already established for pictures are also emitted before printed words. New relations that were not directly taught, such as conditional relations between printed words and pictures and vice versa, may also be observed, demonstrating that the learner understands what he or she reads. The most common procedure for teaching conditional discriminations is *matching-to-sample* (MTS), in which the selection of a comparison stimulus, from among two or more available for choice, is conditional on the stimulus presented as a sample (Sidman & Tailby, 1982; Rexroad, 1926).

For readers to be fluent, that is, to be able to read any word, known or unknown, they must have the ability of recombinative reading (de Souza et al., 2009b, 2014; Hanna et al., 2010). This skill consists of responding under control of each component of the text (letters or syllables), despite its position (Goldstein, 1983), demonstrating that the response is controlled by the word's minimal units, so that the smallest distinctive component of the word (letters or syllables) evokes differentiated vocal responses. For example, when faced with the word BOLO (cake), the learner may show well-established discriminative control and say /bo/ and /lo/ (respectively), and may also be successful in reading the word LOBO (wolf) when the units are presented in a different order. There are different ways or procedures to obtain control by minimal units and recombinative generalized reading: (a) matching between smaller dictated and printed units; (b) use of the *Constructed-Response Matching-to-Sample* (CRMTS) procedure; and (c) use of whole words with overlapping components (letters or syllables).

In the case that control for smaller units is established through (a) matching between smaller dictated and printed units (Gomes & de Souza, 2016), the left portion of Fig. 6.1 shows a task in which the learner must point to the written letter or syllable that corresponds to the dictated letter or syllable. Discriminating and abstracting the word's smaller units corresponds to what is called phonemic awareness (Capovilla & Capovilla, 2004).

In a complementary manner, it would be possible to teach the vocalization of each of the small units that make up words, i.e., scaled oralization (Matos et al., 1997). The right portion of Fig. 6.1 exemplifies this strategy, in which the educator provides the sample of which vocalization to utter in the presence of certain printed syllables or letters. After such a procedure, presumably, learners would any word, sentence or text in a language. However, this would be the case if there were no

Note. SUCO is the Portuguese word for juice. This figure was made with freepik.com

Fig. 6.1 Teaching control by smaller units than the word, established by matching between dictated syllable with the printed syllable (left portion) and by scaled oralization (right portion). (*Note*. SUCO is the Portuguese word for juice. This figure was made with freepik.com)

problematic elements involved, such as language irregularities (e.g., different sounds are emitted before the grapheme 's' at the beginning of the word and between two vowels), and intonation and prosody, which are typical speech components (de Souza et al., 2014).

The control by smaller units can also be facilitated through the (b) CRMTS procedure (de Souza et al., 2009b; Dube et al., 1991; Mackay & Sidman, 1984). This procedure is a variation of the MTS that establishes conditional relations between stimuli, which requires as a response the ordered selection of smaller units (which can be letters, syllables, and words) to construct a stimulus that is related to the sample (Calcagno et al., 1994). The construction of printed words can occur conditionally on dictated words and printed words, as in the example in Fig. 6.2. ALEPP's[1] word reading and writing teaching modules employ the CRMTS procedure to establish control by minimal units (syllables or letters) that constitute the word.

This book is full of reports of experiments demonstrating the effects of deliberately planned teaching of verbal relations, which favor the transfer of control exerted by stimuli and control by minimal units in the emergence of generalized reading (de Souza et al., 1997; Hanna et al., 2004; McIlvane, 1992). These verbal relations are organized in an *Equivalence-Based Instruction* (EBI) program (Critchifield & Fienup, 2010; Fienup et al., 2010) that aims to teach different verbal relations between stimuli and between stimuli and responses involved in reading and writing words in such a way that they can be substituted for each other (e.g., the word "ball"

Fig. 6.2 Constructed-response matching-to-sample (CRMTS) procedure. (*Note. SUCO* is the Portuguese word for juice. This figure was made with freepik.com)

[1] Currently, ALEPP is part of a project by the National Institute of Science and Technology on Behavior, Cognition and Teaching (INCT-ECCE), whose purpose is to improve the existing modules, test their application in large scale and move forward with the development of new teaching modules, among these, the sentence teaching module, whose subsidies are discussed in this chapter.

can be said in the presence of both the picture and the written word or other event associated with it). This is an operational model of semantic relations as shown at the top of Fig. 6.3. This model has supported the teaching technologies that have proven effective with different populations, such as children with a background of school failure, intellectual disabilities, autistic spectrum disorder, and hearing impaired and cochlear implant (CI) users.

The flexibility observed in the control by minimal textual units is not restricted to words and can be expanded to sentences (de Souza et al., 2009b; Skinner, 1957). According to de Souza et al. (2009b), "words within phrases, sentences, or other word sequence can function as minimal textual units" (p. 3). The control by smaller units in sentences will be discussed in detail in the third section of this chapter.

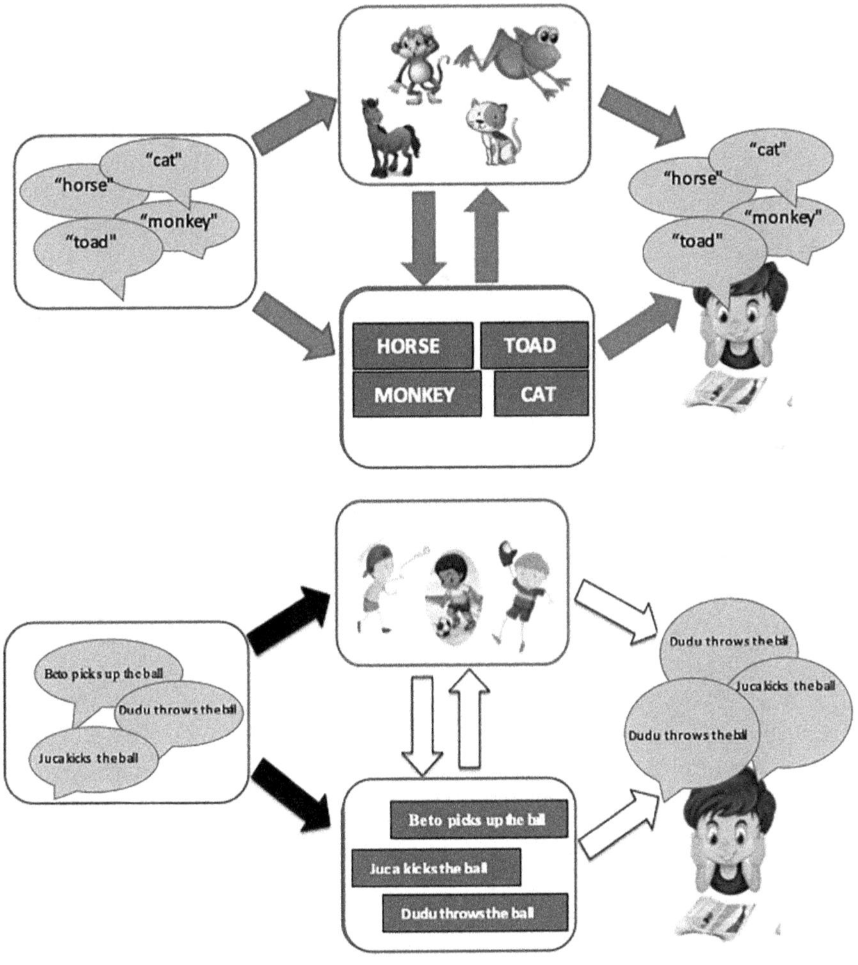

Fig. 6.3 Semantic relations that can be established via EBI, with different stimuli complexity

Table 6.1 Types of overlapping minimal units in some word exemplars and possibilities of recombination

Repeating the syllable		Redundancy		Manipulation of a phonemic unit		
(/BO/ at the beginning)	BOCA	/BO/	BOBO	/A/ or /O/	CALA	CALO
(/BO/ at the end)	SEBO	/LO/	LOLO	/C/ or /L/	COCA	LOCA

Note. BOCA (mouth), BOBO (fool), CALA (shut up), CALO (callus), SEBO (tallow), LOLO (lolo), COCA (coke), LOCA (loca)
Words that can emerge from the recombination of smaller units: LOBO, CABO, BOLA, among others

Another possibility to obtain control by smaller units, such that recombinative processes occur, is from whole words with overlapping word components, such as: BOCA and CABO, in which syllables may appear at the beginning or at the end of the word; BOBO and LOLO, with syllable redundancy; CALA and CALO or COCA and LOCA, in which almost the whole word is preserved and the phonemic unit is manipulated (de Rose et al., 1996; Hübner et al., 2009). Some words that can emerge from recombinations of these smaller units are LOBO, CABO, BOLA, among others.

Overlapping, redundant syllables or letters, and manipulation of phonemic units facilitate control by minimal units, since teaching the relationship between dictated words (e.g., "*bolo*" *(cake)*, "*boca*" *(mouth)*, "*boto*" *(boto)*, and so on) and written words (e.g., BOLO, BOCA, BOTO...) allows derivation of the relationship between the vocal verbal unit "bo" and its graphemic representation BO. The repeated occurrence of a syllable unit in multiple stimulus exemplars may favor generalization (Stokes & Baer, 1977); thus, recognition of the textual unit BO or the vocal utterance "bo" in different positions and in different words (e.g., ***BO**LA (ball)*, *RE**BO**TE (rebound)*, *NA**BO*** (*turnip*) may be observed. Table 6.1 shows the conditions that, if guaranteed, can promote recombinative processes.

6.3 An Overview of ALEPP Modules and the Proposition of a Sentence Teaching Module

The teaching program *Learning to Read and Write in Small Steps – ALEPP* (de Rose et al., 1989, 1992, 1996, 2004, 2009a, b; de Souza & de Rose, 2006), as described in Chaps. 4 and 5, was proposed with the aim of teaching the most elementary skill of recognizing words, as an important step towards the acquisition of reading with comprehension and of generalized and fluent reading. So far, the teaching program consists of three teaching modules. Modules 1 and 2 aim to teach disyllable or trisyllable words (composed of simple consonant-vowel syllables) and words composed of complex syllables (consisting of consonantal meetings, digraphs, and graphemes whose corresponding phoneme depends on context, e.g., ge-gi; ce-ci), respectively. These teaching modules have been widely used in scientific research with a variety of populations, with demonstration of their effectiveness and efficacy in teaching reading and writing repertoire, and are currently used in large-scale use (Cravo & Almeida-Verdu, 2018; de Souza et al., 2019). Module 3, with a current, computerized version, aims at comprehending short texts (as described in Chap. 5). In this module, 15 children's storybooks from the *Estrelinha* collection (*Coleção Estrelinha*), authored by Sonia Junqueira, are used (books for children who are learning to read).

As mentioned, ALEPP was designed to promote relevant reading and writing repertoires and the Modules were built based on a gradual increase in stimulus complexity (words considered simple and complex, and short texts). Over the years of application of the ALEPP teaching program, the need to plan "intermediate steps" between the modules with isolated words (especially Module 2 involving irregular and more complex words) and the module with small texts (Module 3) was identified. The proposal of teaching sentences as an intermediate module considers that the reading and writing repertoire with isolated words (already established in Modules 1 and 2) should be gradually and systematically expanded to ordered combinations of words – of two components, such as [noun]-[adjective], and of sentences of three or more components – until the learner can master the reading and writing production of short texts (expected in Module 3).

This teaching sequence – from isolated words to sentences and short texts – is supported by the operant description of verbal repertoire extension (Skinner, 1957; Sundberg, 2008) and the Personalized System of Instruction (PSI) proposal (Keller, 1968), which is close to evidence-based literacy programs (Adams et al., 1997; Whalon et al., 2009). A sentence teaching module offers the opportunity to build skills of categorizing and abstracting words (by grammatical classes or syntactic function) and ordering them according to linguistic conventions (syntactic rules). These skills, in turn, are important and required when dealing with statements and short texts, where word order affects reading comprehension and the construction of new sentences by the recombination of words occupying the same ordinal function (syntactic productivity).

In order to advance the development of teaching technology that meets the needs of learners, a series of studies are currently being conducted to evaluate the conditions necessary for teaching sentences, as a starting point for expansion of ALEPP and the insertion of a Sentence Teaching Module.

6.4 Sentence Expansion

In a country whose performance in Portuguese Language is very low in large-scale assessments in typical populations, even without considering the target audience of Special Education, investing in programs for teaching the fundamentals of reading and writing is not only of scientific interest, but also of social relevance (Silveira et al., 2016). An essential behavioral process for intervention in reading problems consists of flexibility and recombination of phonemes into syllables, syllables into words, and words into sentences (de Souza et al., 2009b). This flexibility can be the target of teaching, especially when dealing with sentences as a verbal unit, in order to identify the conditions under which learners learn to read and understand sentences, decompose them into smaller units and recombine them into new units.

This section of the chapter aims to contribute in this direction, given the need to invest in teaching programs for larger textual units, such as sentences. Based on experimental and applied studies, it is considered that semantic, syntactic features and generative potential should be deliberately planned into a teaching program (Mackay, 2013). These semantic-syntactic properties and their generative potential will be described and analyzed below.

6.4.1 Semantic Relationships

Semantic relations can be defined as comprehension, and comprehension depends on the relations between events that are established and agreed upon by a given verbal community. The equivalence relations model (Sidman, 2000; Sidman & Tailby, 1982) is a robust model to describe and operationally analyze symbolic behavior (de Rose et al., 2014) and, after more than 30 years of experimental studies, it has subsidized the construction of EBI programs to teach different types of content.

The equivalence relations model can establish relations considered semantic[2] between stimuli and between stimuli and responses (Sidman, 2000; Sidman & Tailby, 1982). Considering the types of responses, in addition to the selection responses that are typical of MTS tasks, oral production, handwriting, and constructed responding (present in CRMTS tasks) can be included (Mackay, 1985; Mackay & Sidman, 1984; Remington, 1994). In general, studies involving EBI establish relationships between content and stimuli that lack physical similarity to each other, but that share common elements (a node, at least), so that the stimuli become interchangeable with each other under certain contexts (Albright et al., 2016; Critchifield & Fienup, 2010; Fields et al., 2009; Fienup et al., 2010; Pytte & Fienup, 2012), no matter the length and complexity of the stimulus, as illustrated in the two diagrams in Fig. 6.3. The diagrams represent semantic relations, and the relations that will be taught or tested will depend on the purpose of the study and participant's baseline.

As an example, according to the diagram in the upper panel of Fig. 6.3, after teaching two conditional relations with a common node represented by black arrows (e.g., between the dictated word and the printed word, and between the dictated word and the picture, with the dictated word as a "node" between these relations), all other relations between stimuli (picture-printed word and printed word-picture) and between stimuli and responses (naming the picture and reading the printed

[2] Relationships will be considered semantic if they attest to the formal properties of equivalence, namely, reflexivity (ArA, BrB, CrC, where 'r' reads 'relates to'), symmetry (if ArB, then BrA; if ArC, then CrA), and transitivity (if ArB and ArC, then BrC and CrB) (sf. Sidman & Tailby, 1982).

word) represented by white arrows can be obtained. Similarly, semantic relations can be established with stimuli of higher complexity, such as sentences. According to the bottom panel of Fig. 6.3, once conditional relations with a common element are established (e.g., between dictated sentence and printed sentence, and between dictated sentence and scene figure), the other relations between stimuli (between printed sentence and figure of a scene, and between picture of a scene and sentence) and between stimuli and responses (naming scene pictures and reading printed sentences) can be observed.

In the scope of this book, several experiments are found that are based on EBI and teach different types of content. The main purpose when adopting an EBI is to deliberately obtain new relations that were not taught directly (derived relations that are verified in specific tests) by teaching two or more conditional relations with a node. However, a peculiar feature of sentence teaching is that, depending on the choice and arrangement between stimuli, syntactic relations can be obtained, which will be explored below.

6.4.2 *Syntactic Relationships*

Syntactic relations can be operationally described as order relations between linguistic stimuli, based on the conventions of the verbal community (Mackay, 2013). These syntactic relations are defined by ordinal properties of asymmetry, irreflexivity, transitivity and connectivity (Green et al., 1993). To exemplify these properties, consider the number sequence $1 \rightarrow 2 \rightarrow 3$, which is learned at a young age; the "→" indicates that one number "is sequential to" (or "is followed by") another. The property of irreflexivity describes that each element of the sequence cannot "come after" itself, so that $1 \rightarrow 1$, $2 \rightarrow 2$, and $3 \rightarrow 3$ are not possible sequences. When considering the sequences $1 \rightarrow 2$ or $2 \rightarrow 3$, it can be observed that the relations between these numbers are unidirectional and cannot be reversed (they exhibit the property of asymmetry), and the sequences $2 \rightarrow 1$ and $3 \rightarrow 2$ are also considered incorrect. Transitivity can be described when sequences share common elements and new sequences can be obtained; hence, if the sequence $1 \rightarrow 2$ and then $2 \rightarrow 3$ are taught, where "2" is the element in common to the two sequences, the learner will likely be able to order 1 and 3 consistently with the teaching ($1 \rightarrow 3$), without having been taught directly. Finally, the connectivity property reports to all ordinal relations in the sequence, with elements close (adjacent pairs) or far apart (non-adjacent pairs) and consistent with teaching; in this example, the relations that attest to connectivity are $1 \rightarrow 2$, $2 \rightarrow 3$, $1 \rightarrow 3$, and $1 \rightarrow 2 \rightarrow 3$.

Many experimental studies have shown that ordinal relations between stimuli are established through different teaching procedures such as chaining (Assis & Costa, 2004), superposition of adjacent stimuli (Holcomb et al., 1997; Stromer & Mackay, 1993), CRMTS (Yamamoto & Miya, 1999) and matrix teaching (Goldstein, 1983; Remington, 1994). Semantic and syntactic relations can demonstrate generative potential if some conditions are guaranteed, such as CRMTS procedures that teach the order relation directly, scaled oralization of each of the words that make up the sentence, or overlapping of common elements in the training stimuli that also puts behavior under control of the overlapping unit, organized in matrices.

Productivity or generativity refers to the ability to produce combinations (Sidman, 2009) and sequences (Mackay, 2013) that are novel with the stimuli that participated in the teaching. In the case of novel combinations involving syntactic relations, an illustration was presented in Fig. 6.3. Contextual control is a critical aspect in semantic and syntactic relations, as syntactic (order) transformations can occur as a function of stimulus or audience control (Crepaldi et al., 2018; Lazar & Kotlarchick, 1986). For example, a child may sequence the [adjective] before the [noun] and say "*green ball*" if talking to English speakers, while a different order must be constructed when interacting with Portuguese speakers as "bola verde".

Most experimental studies have described semantic and syntactic productivity separately (Assis et al., 2006; Almeida-Verdu et al., 2006; Green et al., 1993; Holcomb et al., 1997; Sampaio et al., 2010; Sidman, 1986). This book presents several studies that describe semantic productivity from the EBI. Syntactic productivity, in turn, can be identified in Study 2 of Sampaio, (Sampaio et al., 2010) in which children learned to construct three sentences ("The frog jumps fast", "A cat eats a lot" and "The bear swims poorly") through the chaining procedure: each word was presented gradually to be ordered, so that they initially selected only THE, then ordered THE and FROG (THE→FROG) when presented, until they constructed the complete sentence THE→FROG→JUMPS→FAST – and syntactic productivity was demonstrated when they all constructed new sentences, such as "THE FROG EATS FAST" and "A CAT JUMPS A LOT", by recombining words that occupied the same ordinal position.

Other studies described the establishment of semantic-syntactic relations jointly. More specifically, they established order relations between stimuli in a set (a process analogous to syntactic relations), which were transferred to new stimuli in another set after pairing by MTS (a process analogous to semantic relations) (Assis & Costa, 2004; Lazar, 1977; Stromer & Mackay, 1993). In Lazar's (1977) classic study, adults initially learned to order geometric figures in some sequences (e.g., A1 → A2 and B1 → B2). Then, conditional relations between stimuli in these sequences (e. g., A1 → A2) and new stimuli (C1 and C2) were taught by MTS; when A1 was sampled, selecting C1 was set correct and not C2, and when A2 was sampled, C2 was correct and not C1. All participants were able to correctly order the new stimuli (C1 → C2) without ever having been taught directly, which showed that the ordinal function of stimuli (in a sequence) can be extended to other stimuli by MTS. Taken together, these studies support the effect of different procedures for teaching conditional and ordinal relations on the emergence of semantic and syntactic classes.

As already mentioned in other chapters of this volume, many Brazilian researchers are engaged in studying and planning teaching conditions and have developed computerized programs for teaching verbal repertoires and manipulated the effect of related procedural variables. The goal is to teach, based on EBI, different types of verbal repertoires such as reading, writing and math conceptual repertoires.

Technological resources allow for the programming and application of teaching, and we can mention GEIC (Capobianco et al., 2009), PROLER (Assis & Santos, 2010), EQUIV (Leite & Hübner, 2010), Mestre (Goyos & Almeida, 1996) and Programmed Contingency 2.0 (Hanna et al., 2014). Equivalence-based teaching programs aim to teach relations between stimuli and between stimuli and responses by establishing stimulus control relations relevant to what is considered verbal repertoire (oral, gestural and written). ALEPP (de Rose, et al., 1989, 1992), a teaching program subdivided into modules already described here and for which a sentence teaching module is outlined, is currently hosted in the GEIC platform, enabling the application of the reading and writing teaching program in a computerized and online manner.

6.4.3 Sentences as a Teaching Unit

In the context of larger language units, such as sentences, recombinative generalization can be achieved through several teaching procedures and arrangements, such as CRMTS (described above), *matrix training* (Goldstein, 1983; Remington, 1994), and the combined use of matrix training and CRMTS (Neves et al., 2018; Silva et al., 2017; Yamamoto & Miya, 1999). A literature review in national and international journals on the use of CRMTS as a facilitator variable of reading and writing emergence, especially involving sentences, can be obtained in Paixão and Assis (2017).

Matrix learning is a strategy to organize stimuli and promote recombinative generalization. It consists in arranging the stimuli in rows and columns, in matrix format, so that the intersection of these stimuli in the matrix cells produces ordered combinations (Goldstein, 1983; Goldstein & Mousets, 1989). Some combinations of the matrix are directly taught, while the others are evaluated to verify recombinative generalization.

The definition of which combinations should be taught depends on the learner's initial repertoire (baseline) and may require more or less overlapping stimulus components. Teaching several stimuli with overlapping components promotes discriminative learning of each component, while teaching stimuli without overlapping components promotes learning of component order relations (Frampton et al., 2016). Consider a matrix composed of animal names (cat, mouse, and cow) in the columns and color names in the rows (green, pink, and blue), as presented in matrix 1 at the top of Fig. 6.4. If the learner does not know how to name animals and colors, we can plan teaching with [animal]-[color] combinations that have overlapping components, such as teaching to name "green mouse," "green cow," "pink cat," "pink cow," "blue cat," and "blue mouse" (shaded). From this teaching, naming may emerge with novel combinations such as "green cat", "pink mouse" and "blue cow" which are arranged on the diagonal of the matrix (blank). However, if the learner already names the animals and colors, we can teach it with fewer exemplars, starting with the combination of words presented on the diagonal of matrix 2: teach to name

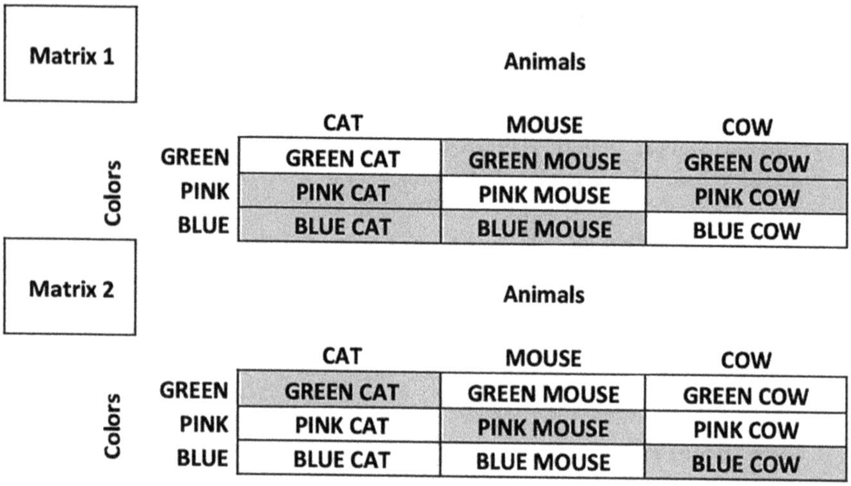

Fig. 6.4 Illustration of combining nouns and objects according to matrices, teaching some combinations and emergence of others

"green cat", "pink mouse" and "blue cow" (diagonal of the matrix with shaded cells). Then, the learner could respond appropriately when stimuli with the new combinations were presented (blank cells of matrix 2), as indicated at the bottom of Fig. 6.4. The responses to the blank cell stimuli are considered emergent because they are not taught directly, but are derived from the teaching performed with stimuli from the shaded cells.

In another example, the teacher's task is to teach preschool children with some deficit in communicative repertoires to name colored objects through [object]-[color] combinations. Using toys, such as a ball and a duck, and the colors blue and green, the teacher can design a matrix in which the object names are in the rows and the colors in the columns; the intersection of these stimuli in the matrix will produce the combinations "blue ball," "green duck," "blue duck," and "green ball". After teaching to name "blue ball" and "green duck", the teacher could check whether children would be able to name "green ball" and "blue duck" without direct teaching; if this naming occurs, children would demonstrate a generalized response to novel stimuli by recombining the components of the taught stimuli. These results were observed in studies such as Yokoyama et al. (2006) with children with autistic spectrum disorder and Merlin et al. (2019) with children with cochlear implantation.

Many complex repertoires involve responding under order control (such as telling a story, writing an essay, and solving arithmetic calculations) and show generative potential through recombination of components occupying a given ordinal position or function (Mackay, 2013). Recombinative processes involving sentences have been observed experimentally in different populations, with different amounts of terms (action-object, object-quality, subject-action-object, subject-action-article-object, and definite article-subject-action-indefinite article-object) and in distinct language repertoires, such as scenes tact (Goldstein, 1983; Golfeto & de Souza,

2015; Neves et al., 2018; Silva et al., 2017), sentence construction (Yamamoto & Miya, 1999; Neves et al., 2018; Neves, 2019; Silva et al., 2017), receptive performances, and instruction-following behavior (Axe & Sainato, 2010; Postalli et al., 2013; Striefel et al., 1976). A child who knows how to name some scenes he sees in the park – such as "Boy throws the ball," "Girl picks up the doll," and "Baby eats the fruit" – may be able to name new scenes, such as "Boy picks up the fruit" as soon as he sees a boy picking up a fruit, or "Baby throws the doll" upon seeing the baby throwing the doll on the ground; in this case, the construction of these new sentences may occur without direct teaching, through recombination of words that occupied a position in the learned sentences. The process is analogous, to some extent, to that observed in the recombination of minimal units involving words.

The sentence is a linguistic unit, usually composed of more than one word, and endowed with structure and meaning (Lacerda, 2010) and, as a unit of analysis, it must integrate semantic and syntactic relations described above, so that the meaning will be given through a specific word order; Furthermore, as the order is arbitrarily defined in each language, the sentence may also be under contextual control (Mackay, 2013); for example, a Brazilian Portuguese speaker would say "O menino pequeno", organizing the sentence in [article]-[name]-[adjective], whereas American English speakers invert the position of the [name] and the [adjective] and would speak "*The little boy*". A child who says "I saw one in the duck pond" is likely to produce strangeness in the listeners and will not produce the expected effects on the audience even though he or she has pronounced the words correctly. On the other hand, if the child says "I saw a duck in the pond", it will be quickly understood by the people around him who might reinforce his behavior of describing what he saw.

The possibility of combining teaching procedures and verifying the generative potential of semantic-syntactic relations, such as CRMTS and matrix training (which promote stimulus overlapping), may contribute to the recombinative generalization between sentences' minimal textual units. The resulting process is similar to that of words, but instead of recombination of letters and syllables, recombination occurs with words that make up sentences. If further tests show that new sentences can emerge from the recombination of elements of the trained sentences, syntactic productivity would be guaranteed (Mackay, 2013).

In summary, EBI with CRMTS procedures and stimuli organized in matrices have been effective in promoting semantic, syntactic relations and verbal generativity, with different sentence lengths (from three to five terms), for different populations (Neves, 2019; Neves et al., 2016, 2018; Silva et al., 2017). Matrix planning, combined with MTS and CRMTS tasks (in EBI), has promoted important conditions for establishing relations (taught and derived) between stimuli, strengthening a minimal unit response, and for the emergence of recombinative repertoires (receptive and expressive).

In the reported studies, the combined use of matrix training and CRMTS established relevant stimulus control so that the learner responded under the control of each smaller unit of the sentence and formed syntactic stimulus classes based on position (i.e., the class of first components or subjects, second components or verbs, and third components or objects). These relations underlie verbal sentence repertoires. Below we will report recent studies with sentences that support adding a Module for teaching sentences in the ALEPP program.

6.4.3.1 Recent Studies with Sentence Teaching

We report here some studies developed within the scope of the INCT-ECCE and by other laboratories, which adopted the equivalence relations model for teaching sentences, the organization of stimuli based on matrices, and/or the CRMTS teaching procedure. In this direction, recent studies with sentences have covered, especially, the auditory rehabilitation process in children who received a cochlear implant (CI) in the process of learning to hear or speak and regarding the cycle of reading and writing. However, the findings can be expanded to listeners by placing the focus on reading and writing, regarding the cycle of listening and speaking (Lee & Sanderson, 1987).

Golfeto and de Souza (2015) were pioneers in the investigation of sentence learning by children with CI. This study aimed to verify the effects of teaching conditional relations between dictated sentences and video and echoic scenes, on the accurate naming of scenes (taught and that recombined components of the taught scenes), in three children with CI. The stimuli were organized by matrices, in which the sentences' subjects were arranged in the rows, the verbs in the columns, and the object remained invariant; each matrix produced nine sentences, six taught and the three diagonals were tested. Teaching consisted of selecting scenes from videos conditional to the dictated sentences (AB) and orally imitating these same sentences (echoic). After teaching, all participants learned the taught relations, correctly named the six video scenes used in the teaching stage, and were able to name three video scenes referring to the diagonal sentences of the matrices.

Similarly, Merlin et al. (2019) evaluated the effects of *Multiple Exemplar Instruction* (MEI) on accurate naming of colored pictures by children with Auditory Neuropathy Spectrum Disorder (ANSD) and using CI. Matrices were arranged with nouns (e.g., doll, wolf, and house) in the rows, and colors (e.g., yellow, pink, and brown) in the columns, so as to produce nine [noun]-[adjective] combinations; the three combinations on the diagonal of the matrices ("pink doll," "brown wolf," and "yellow house" were directly taught and the other six only tested. The echoic, auditory recognition (selection of pictures conditional to the dictated sample), and picture naming tasks were presented in this sequence and for the same stimulus, and the participant's response consisted of repeating the dictated sentence, selecting the picture conditional to the dictated sentence, and naming the picture; for example, echoing "pink doll", then selecting the picture (among other available pictures) when "pink doll" was dictated, and then naming "pink doll" in the presence of the respective picture. Participants learned the relationships between dictated sentences and colored pictures, increased accurate naming of the taught pictures, and were able, without direct instruction, to name new pictures (referring to the remaining cells in the matrices) through orderly recombination of names and colors.

Neves et al. (2018) assessed whether three children with CI who were able to read would be able to demonstrate auditory comprehension of sentences, accurate naming of scene pictures (teaching), and verbal productivity of sentences, after an EBI combined with matrix training. The names (Juca, Beto and Dudu), verbs (peel, squeeze and grate) and the object (lemon, which was invariable) were organized in a matrix and produced nine sentences structured in [subject]-[verb in the simple present]-[object], such as "Juca squeezes the lemon". Participants were exposed to EBI – which included selecting pictures of scenes (by MTS, AB) and constructing printed sentences (by CRMTS, AE) conditional on the dictated sentences – with the three diagonal sentences of the matrix. All participants learned the taught relations (AB and AE), but many repetitions occurred during the teaching of the AB relation. After the EBI, all participants demonstrated comprehension of the sentences (verified in tasks of scene picture selection conditional to the written sentences, and by constructing written sentences conditional to the pictures), correctly named the three taught scene pictures (diagonal of the matrix), and named six novel scene pictures using sentences that recombined words from the taught sentences (e.g., speaking "Dudu squeezes lemon" in the presence of the respective picture).

Similar results were obtained in studies replicating Neves et al. (2018), employing EBI with five literate children with CI (Neves et al., 2019), one literate child with Down Syndrome (Neves et al., 2016); and one pre-literate child with CI, expanding the proposal to five-term sentences (such as "Malu listens to the radio") (Silva et al., 2017).

Neves (2019) contributed to this line of investigation with two studies. Studies 1 and 2 adopted EBI and matrix training similar to those of previous studies, with the same relations taught (AB and AE) and organization of stimuli in matrices (diagonal sentences were taught and the others tested). Considering that children with CI and readers presented difficulties in learning the conditional relations between dictated sentences and scene pictures (AB) (Neves et al., 2018, 2019; Silva et al., 2017), Study 1 employed errorless teaching procedures (teaching by exclusion[3] and by fading out[4]) and evaluated the effects on this relational learning. Participants learned AB relations by both procedures, however teaching by exclusion proved more effective in establishing the dictated sentence-scene picture relations and with virtually no errors. Five of the six participants formed equivalence relations (between dictated and written sentences and scene pictures), increased accurate speech in the presence of scene pictures and were able, without direct teaching, to name scene

[3] In general, instruction by exclusion involves establishing a baseline, e.g., some relations between a dictated word and a picture. Once this initial learning has been established, if totally new stimuli (i.e., dictated word and picture) are presented with known stimuli remaining present, it is highly likely that the participant will relate the new stimuli to each other on the first trial. This response, which relates new stimuli while rejecting known stimuli (because they have already been related to others in the participant's history) is called learning by exclusion (Dixon, 1977).

[4] Fading refers to a gradual change in some dimension of a stimulus, either fading in or fading out (Terrace, 1963). When fading is superimposed on the MTS procedure, arbitrary conditional discriminations can be taught with reduced occurrence of errors.

pictures (referring to the six sentences in each matrix) by recombining words from the taught sentences.

Study 2 by Neves (2019) advanced, in a translational effort, by proposing a Module for teaching sentences. The sets of sentences were defined by gradual levels of difficulty in textual decoding and speech production (called complex sentences), underwent phonological balancing and semantic evaluation, and were inspected by speech therapists. Set 1 included simple sentences (with disyllable words composed of consonant-vowel syllables, without textual decoding and pronunciation difficulties, such as "*Mila seca o bule*"); Set 2 involved complex sentences (with disyllable and trisyllable words, with decoding and production difficulty components, such as /ch/ and /lh/, like "*Dinho chuta a latinha*") and Set 3 was composed by pseudo-sentences (like "*Deva mupa a guzata*").

Study 2 of Neves (2019) aimed to evaluate the effects of EBI and matrix training, with these three 4-term [subject]-[verb]-[item]-[object] sentence sets, on sentence comprehension (i.e., equivalence relations between dictated and printed sentences, and scene pictures), accurate naming of scene pictures, and recombinative performances (receptive and expressive), involving both taught sentences and sentences that recombined words from the same and different sets. EBI in each set consisted of direct teaching of conditional relations between dictated sentences and scene pictures (AB relation) by MTS and by exclusion (which proved most effective in Study 1), and the construction of printed sentences under dictation (AE relation) by CRMTS. The derived relations of sentence construction under picture control (mute dictation, BE), sentence reading, and scene picture naming, for the taught and recombined sentences, were systematically assessed throughout the teaching of each set. All participants learned AB and AE relations, formed equivalence classes, and increased speech accuracy in scene picture naming. Throughout successive tests, receptive (such as relating scene pictures to dictated sentences) and expressive (such as naming scene pictures) recombinative performances were demonstrated, within and across sets, by all participants, which highlights the potential of the sentence teaching program module to promote verbal sentence generativity.

Studies with sentences have also been extended in second language teaching. Crepaldi et al. (2018) verified the effects of sentence EBI on verbal skills in second language (in this case, English) for three Brazilian Portuguese-speaking children. Multiple probes assessed the conditional relations between stimuli and verbal operants (echoic, picture naming, reading, and translation), in Portuguese, in English, and in Portuguese↔English. The teaching occurred by exclusion and involved conditional relations between stimuli in Portuguese and English. At first, relations were taught between dictated sentences and pictures of scenes (AB) and between dictated and written sentences (AC), in Portuguese. Then, relations were taught in English involving dictated sentences and pictures of scenes (DB) and dictated and written sentences (DE). All participants formed equivalent stimulus classes with Portuguese sentences (ABC) and increased accuracy in naming scene pictures and reading sentences. Two of the three participants learned the relations taught in English, expanded the equivalence class (ABCDE) and showed, without direct teaching, "translation" repertoire when speaking Portuguese sentences in the presence of dictated and written English sentences.

Similar results were observed in studies conducted in other laboratories. Haydu et al. (2015) verified the effects of teaching conditional discriminations and chaining on the emergence of generalized reading involving sentences with eight typical development children who had more than 50% of errors in initial sentence reading tests. The sentences were composed by five terms and organized in article, subject, verb and object (numeral + noun). The study involved teaching and testing the conditional relations between the dictated and printed words and their minimal textual units, by MTS and CRMTS. Then, 36 sentences were taught by chaining, i.e., words that composed a sentence were presented to the participants and they should organize them according to a certain order, forming the sentence; the number of words that composed a sentence was gradually increased and, in each chaining trial, the words were added one by one, until all words of the sentence were available for the participant to sequence them. The production of new sentences and the construction of new sentences composed of the same number of components as the trained sentences, but with other stimuli such as different verbal tenses, were evaluated. The final phase of the study involved the teaching and testing of conditional discriminations between spoken sentences, written sentences and animations, and a final reading post-test. The results, in general, showed that the procedure was effective in establishing reading comprehension and sentence syntactic productivity.

More recently, Paixão and Assis (2018) taught three children with Autistic Spectrum Disorder to read three-term sentences ([article]-[subject]-[verb]) composed of regular words with comprehension and in a generalized manner. Teaching was in EBI and adopted MTS and CRMTS procedures. Although participants demanded more physical cues and, at times, restricted stimulus control had to be circumvented, the results showed that levelling task difficulty from words to sentences and EBI combined with CRMTS was relevant for the establishment of generalized reading. These studies demonstrate the robustness of procedures for teaching relations between stimuli – either by pairing or by ordering – configuring what have been called semantic-syntactic relations and allowing the proposition of a teaching module.

6.5 Features of a Sentence Teaching Module

Considering the above, the reviewed national and international literature gathers theoretical and methodological subsidies for the proposal of a sentence teaching module, with the possibility of being integrated into ALEPP as an intermediate module between complex words and small texts. Besides the theoretical and methodological conditions, the results obtained so far offer sufficient scientific evidence for the proposal of a module that meets the dimension of applied research. This activity is already part of the context of the ongoing work of the INCT-ECCE. Here, we present the essential characteristics that the module must have:

1. be organized via EBI. Once the network of equivalence relations is programmed, the module will allow: (a) to assess which verbal relations the learner knows (input repertoire); (b) to define teaching plans and the verbal relations that will be directly taught; (c) to assess the effects of teaching on the learning of the relations taught; and, (d) to monitor the semantic potential, in order to observe new relations (derived relations). The application of the sentence teaching module should meet different teaching needs and consider the learner's initial repertoire as well as the preserved verbal topography and sensory modalities, in order to favor the learning of target skills for each child. Thus, children with no hearing impairment can learn to read sentences through this module from the auditory recognition and scene naming, potentially already established. Children with hearing impairment and CI, despite being reading beginners, can increase the accuracy of speech in the presence of pictures of scenes (usually weaker repertoire) after being exposed to instruction with such characteristics, because the accuracy of speech controlled by the minimum textual units is controlled by the pictures, following being related as equivalent. However, issues related to reading in hearing impaired and CI children and speech accuracy as a teaching target will be addressed in another chapter of this book.
2. incorporate procedures and stimulus arrangements that promote recombinative repertoires. Several studies that have been described have shown the potential of procedures, such as matrix training and CRMTS, to foster syntactic productivity (Neves, 2019; Neves et al., 2018, 2019; Yamamoto & Miya, 1999).
3. be programmed to teach in a cumulative manner. This cumulative learning can involve the gradual increase of complexity, from regular word sentences with irregular words to pseudo-sentences, as observed in Neves (2019). Another possibility is the gradual increase in the number of words (Haydu et al., 2015) and the variation of verb tenses, such as active and passive voice (Paixão & Assis, 2018).

6.6 Final Considerations

In summary, the results obtained with ALEPP, especially with the first two teaching modules, showed the efficiency and effectiveness of the methods employed, proving to be an adequate resource for the establishment of basic reading and writing repertoires. In this chapter, we present the importance and need to expand the teaching program, creating strategies to advance in the establishment of more complex repertoires.

Data from the 2018 PISA (Program for International Student Assessment) assessment, conducted in several countries by the OECD (Organization for Economic Cooperation and Development), showed that half of Brazilian 15-year-old students reached a basic level of learning in reading and reading comprehension. According to the assessment, the performances of Brazilian students have shown that these skills have stagnated over the last decade (Brasil, 2019; OECD, 2019).

These data indicate the need for the development of instructional resources that meet the national demand for the development of more complex reading and writing repertoires; thus, the development of a sentence teaching module may contribute to advance the establishment of existing skills between reading an isolated word and understanding a text, developing intermediate reading skills and understanding a sentence. Silveira et al. (2016) applied the assessments of the first two ALEPP Modules, aiming to map the basic reading and writing repertoires of 187 fifth grade students from schools in three different regions of the country (Belém/PA, Brasília/DF, and São Carlos/SP). The results reveal well-established (i.e., copying a text), weakly established (i.e., receptive reading) and absent (i.e., taking dictation) skills. Based on these results, the authors argue that identifying the student's initial repertoire allows directing the teaching program to the student's required level, in addition to favoring effective teaching based on individual planning and remediation of skills that were not identified.

The proposed expansion of ALEPP with the insertion of a sentence teaching module meets the proposal of building a teaching program based on the gradual and systematic increase of stimulus complexity, starting with the teaching of simple and complex isolated words, and then the teaching of sentences.

With this, the ALEPP Teaching Program extends its functionality by creating teaching procedures that can meet different demands and learning levels. Thus, the inclusion of sentence teaching as a step after complex word teaching (Module 2) can contribute to the development of more complex reading repertoires, moving on to reading and comprehension of texts (Module 3).

References

Adams, M. J., Treinman, R., & Pressley, M. (1997). Reading, writing, and literacy. In I. Sigel & A. Renninger (Eds.), *Handbook of child psychology: Child psychology in practice* (Vol. 4, pp. 275–355). John Wiley & Sons Inc.

Albright, L., Schnell, L., Reeve, K. F., & Sidener, T. M. (2016). Using stimulus equivalence-based instruction to teach graduate students in applied behavior analysis to interpret operant functions of behavior. *Journal of Behavioral Education, 25*(3), 290–309. https://doi.org/10.1007/s10864-016-9249-0

Almeida-Verdu, A. C. M., de Souza, D. G., & Lopes, J., Jr. (2006). Formação de classes ordinais após a aprendizagem de sequências independentes. *Estudos de Psicologia, 11*(1), 87–99. https://doi.org/10.1590/S1413-294X2006000100011

Assis, G. J. A., & Costa, L. C. A. (2004). Emergência de relações ordinais em crianças. *Interação em Psicologia, 8*(2), 199–216. https://doi.org/10.5380/psi.v8i2.3256

Assis, G. J. A., & Santos, M. B. (2010). *PROLER – Sistema Computadorizado para o Ensino de Comportamentos conceituais (versão 6.4)*. Universidade Federal do Pará.

Assis, G. J. A., Élleres, C. F., & Sampaio, M. E. C. (2006). Emergência de relações sintáticas em pré-escolares. *Interação em Psicologia, 10*(1), 19–29. https://doi.org/10.5380/psi.v10i1.5786

Axe, J. B., & Sainato, D. M. (2010). Matrix training of preliteracy skills with preschoolers with autism. *Journal of Applied Behavior Analysis, 43*(4), 635–652. https://doi.org/10.1901/jaba.2010.43-635

Bertini, M. T. (2017). *Desenvolvimento de compreensão de textos e fluência de leitura: avaliação de um programa informatizado* Master's thesis, Universidade Estadual de Londrina. http://www.uel.br/pos/pgac/wp-content/uploads/2018/04/Desenvolvimento-de-compreens%C3%A3o-de-textos-e-flu%C3%AAncia-de-leitura-avalia%C3%A7%C3%A3o-de-um-programa-de-ensino-informatizado.pdf.

Brasil. (2019). *Relatório Brasil no Pisa 2018*. INEP/MEC. Retrieved in http://download.inep.gov.br/acoes_internacionais/pisa/documentos/2019/relatorio_PISA_2018_preliminar.pdf

Calcagno, S., Dube, W. V., Galvão, O. F., & Sidman, M. (1994). Emergence of conditional discriminations after constructed-response matching-to-sample training. *The Psychological Record, 44*, 509–520. https://doi.org/10.1007/bf03395141

Capobianco, D., Teixeira, C., Bela, R. E., Orlando, A. F., de Souza, D. G., &, de Rose, J. C. (2009). *GEIC-LECH – Gerenciador de Ensino Individualizado por computador*. Software para pesquisa não registrado.

Capovilla, A. G. S., & Capovilla, F. C. (2004). *Alfabetização: Método fônico* (3rd ed.). Fapesp, CNPq.

Cravo, F. A. M., & Almeida-Verdu, A. C. M. (2018). Avaliação de desempenho escolar após exposição a um programa informatizado de leitura e escrita. *Psicologia da Educação, 47*, 1–10. https://doi.org/10.5935/2175-3520.20180012

Crepaldi, G. C., Neves, A. J., & de Souza, D. G. (2018, Outubro). *Usando o paradigma da equivalência de estímulos para ensinar sentenças em inglês para crianças nativas do Português Brasileiro*. Poster apresentado na 48ª Reunião Anual da Sociedade Brasileira de Psicologia. https://doi.org/10.13140/RG.2.2.21950.95041.

Critchfield, T. S., & Fienup, D. M. (2010). Using stimulus equivalence technology to teach statistical inference in a group setting. *Journal of Applied Behavior Analysis, 43*(4), 763–768. https://doi.org/10.1901/jaba.2010.43-763

de Rose, J. C. (2005). Análise comportamental da aprendizagem de leitura e escrita. *Revista Brasileira de Análise do Comportamento, 1*(1), 29–50. https://doi.org/10.18542/rebac.v1i1.676

de Rose, J. C., de Souza, D. S., Rossito, A. L., & de Rose, T. M. S. (1989). Aquisição de leitura após história de fracasso escolar: Equivalência de estímulos e generalização. *Psicologia: Teoria e Pesquisa, 5*, 325–346.

de Rose, J., de Souza, D. G., Rossito, A. L., & de Rose, T. M. S. (1992). Stimulus equivalence and generalization in reading after matching to sample by exclusion. In S. C. Hayes & L. J. Hayes (Eds.), *Understanding verbal relations* (pp. 69–82). Context Press.

de Rose, J. C., de Souza, D. G., & Hanna, E. S. (1996). Teaching reading and spelling: Exclusion and stimulus equivalence. *Journal of Applied Behavior Analysis, 29*(4), 451–469. https://doi.org/10.1901/jaba.1996.29-451

de Rose, J. C., Gil, M. S. C. A., & de Souza, D. G. (2014). *Comportamento simbólico: Bases conceituais e empíricas*. Oficina Universitária/Cultura Acadêmica.

de Souza, D. G., & de Rose, J. C. (2006). Desenvolvendo programas individualizados para o ensino de leitura. *Acta Comportamentalia, 14*(1), 77–98.

de Souza, D. G., Hanna, E. S., de Rose, J. C., Fonseca, M. L., Pereira, A. B., & Sallorenzo, I. H. (1997). Transferência de controle de estímulos de figura para texto no desenvolvimento de leitura generalizada. *Temas em Psicologia, 1*, 33–46.

de Souza, D. G., de Rose, J. C., Hanna, E. S., Calcagno, S., & Galvão, O. F. (2004). Análise comportamental da aprendizagem de leitura e escrita e a construção de um currículo suplementar. In M. M. C. Hübner & M. Marinotti (Orgs.), *Análise do comportamento para a educação: Contribuições recentes* (pp. 177–203). ESETec.

de Souza, D. G., de Rose, J. C., & Domeniconi, C. (2009a). Applying relational operants to reading and spelling. In R. A. Rehfeldt & Y. Barnes-Holmes (Eds.), *Derived relational responding: Applications for learners with autism and other developmental disabilities* (pp. 171–207). New Harbinger.

de Souza, D. G., de Rose, J. C., Faleiros, T. C., Bortoloti, R., Hanna, E. S., & McIlvane, W. J. (2009b). Teaching generative reading via recombination of minimal textual units: A legacy of verbal

behavior to children in Brazil. *International Journal of Psychology and Psychological Therapy, 9*(1), 19–44.
de Souza, D. G., Hanna, E. S., Albuquerque, A. R., & Hübner, M. M. C. (2014). Processos recombinativos: Algumas variáveis críticas para o desenvolvimento de leitura. In J. C. de Rose, M. S. C. A. Gil, & D. G. de Souza (Orgs.), Comportamento simbólico: Bases conceituais e empíricas (pp. 421–462). Oficina Universitária; Cultura Acadêmica.
de Souza, D. G. et al. (2019). *Projeto Alfatech – Implementação do Currículo ALEPP em Escolas Públicas da Rede Municipal de Ensino de Santo André – SP (2017–2018).* Recuperado em https://inctecce.com.br/images/artigo/2019/00-projeto-alfatech.pdf.
Dixon, L. S. (1977). The nature of control by spoken words over visual stimulus selection. *Journal of the Experimental Analysis of Behavior, 27*(3), 433–442. https://doi.org/10.1901/jeab.1977.27-433
Dube, W. V., McDonald, S. J., Mcllvane, W. J., & Mackay, H. A. (1991). Constructed-response matching to sample and spelling instruction. *Journal of Applied Behavior Analysis, 24*(2), 305–317. https://doi.org/10.1901/jaba.1991.24-305
Fields, L., Travis, R., Roy, D., Yadovker, E., Aguiar-Rocha, L., & Sturmey, P. (2009). Equivalence class formation: A method for teaching statistical interactions. *Journal of Applied Behavior Analysis, 42*(3), 575–593. https://doi.org/10.1901/jaba.2009.42-575
Fienup, D. M., Covey, D. P., & Critchfield, T. S. (2010). Teaching brain-behavior relations economically with stimulus equivalence technology. *Journal of Applied Behavior Analysis, 43*(1), 19–33. https://doi.org/10.1901/jaba.2010.43-19
Frampton, S. E., Wymer, S. C., Hansen, B., & Shillingsburg, M. A. (2016). The use of matrix training to promote generative language with children with autism. *Journal of Applied Behavior Analysis, 49*(4), 869–883. https://doi.org/10.1002/jaba.340
Godoy, D. (2008). Por que ensinar as relações grafema-fonema? *Revista Psicopedagogia, 25*(77), 109–119.
Goldstein, H. (1983). Recombinative generalization: Relationships between environmental conditions and the linguistic repertoires of language learners. *Analysis and Intervention in Developmental Disabilities, 3*(4), 279–293. https://doi.org/10.1016/0270-4684(83)90002-2
Goldstein, H., & Mousetis, L. (1989). Generalized language learning by children with severe mental retardation: Effects of peers' expressive modeling. *Journal of Applied Behavior Analysis, 22*(3), 245–259. https://doi.org/10.1901/jaba.1989.22-245
Golfeto, R. M., & de Souza, D. G. (2015). Sentence production after listener and echoic training by prelingual deaf children with cochlear implants. *Journal of Applied Behavior Analysis, 48*(2), 363–375. https://doi.org/10.1002/jaba.197
Gomes, C. G. S., & de Souza, D. G. (2016). Ensino de sílabas simples, leitura combinatória e leitura com compreensão para aprendizes com autismo. *Revista Brasileira de Educação Especial, 22*(2), 233–252. https://doi.org/10.1590/S1413-65382216000200007
Goyos, C., & Almeida, J. C. B. (1996). *Mestre* (Versão 1.0) [Programa de computador]. Mestre® Software.
Green, G., Stromer, R., & Mackay, H. (1993). Relational learning in stimulus sequences. *The Psychological Record, 43*, 599–616. https://doi.org/10.1007/bf03395902
Hanna, E. S., de Souza, D. G., de Rose, J. C., & Fonseca, M. L. (2004). Effects of delayed constructed response identity matching on spelling. *Journal of Applied Behavior Analysis, 37*(2), 223–227. https://doi.org/10.1901/jaba.2004.37-223
Hanna, E. S., Karino, C. A., Araújo, V. T., & de Souza, D. G. (2010). Leitura recombinativa de pseudopalavras impressas em pseudoalfabeto: Similaridade entre palavras e extensão da unidade ensinada. *Psicologia USP, 21*(2), 275–311. https://doi.org/10.1590/s0103-65642010000200005
Hanna, E. S., Batitucci, L. A. V., & Batitucci, J. S. L. (2014). Software Contingência Programada: utilidade e funcionalidades. *Revista Brasileira de Análise do Comportamento, 10*(1), 84–91. https://doi.org/10.18542/rebac.v10i1.3949

Haydu, V. B., Zuanazzi, A. C., Assis, G. J. A., & Kato, O. M. (2015). Ensino de leitura de sentenças: Contribuições da análise do comportamento. *Psicologia: Teoria e Pesquisa, 31*(2), 145–154. https://doi.org/10.1590/0102-37722015021869145154

Holcomb, W. L., Stromer, R., & Mackay, H. A. (1997). Transitivity and emergent sequence performances in young children. *Journal of Experimental Child Psychology, 65*(1), 96–124. https://doi.org/10.1006/jecp.1996.2360

Hübner, M. M. C., Gomes, R. C., & McIlvane, W. (2009). Recombinative generalization in minimal verbal unit-based reading instruction for pre-reading children. *Experimental Analysis of Human Behavior Bulletin, 27*, 11–17.

Keller, F. (1968). Good-bye, teacher.... *Journal of Applied Behavior Analysis, 1*(1), 79–89. https://doi.org/10.1901/jaba.1968.1-79

Lacerda, P. B. G. (2010). Sobre a constituição do objeto de estudos em sintaxe: Considerando alguns princípios de Saussure. *Revista Gatilho (PPGL/UFJF), 11*, 1–9.

Lazar, R. (1977). Extending sequence-class membership with matching to sample. *Journal of the Experimental Analysis of Behavior, 27*(2), 381–392. https://doi.org/10.1901/jeab.1977.27-381

Lazar, R., & Kotlarchyk, B. J. (1986). Second order control of sequence class equivalence in children. *Behavioural Processes, 13*(3), 205–215. https://doi.org/10.1016/0376-6357(86)90084-7

Lee, V. L., & Sanderson, G. M. (1987). Some contingences of spelling. *The Analysis of Verbal Behavior, 5*, 1–13. https://doi.org/10.1007/bf03392815

Leite, M. K., & Hübner, M. M. C. (2010). Aquisição de leitura recombinativa após treinos e testes de discriminações condicionais entre palavras ditadas e impressas. *Psicologia: Teoria e Prática, 11*(3), 63–81.

Levine, D., Stother-Garcia, K., Golinkhoff, R., & Hirsh-Pasek, K. (2016). Language development in the first year of life: What deaf children might be missing before cochlear implantation. *Otology & Neurotology, 37*(2), 56–62. https://doi.org/10.1097/mao.0000000000000908

Lopes-Ornat, S., & Gallo, P. (2004). Acquisition, learning or development of language: Skinner's "verbal behavior" revisited. *The Spanish Journal of Psychology, 7*(2), 161–170. https://doi.org/10.1017/S1138741600004868

Mackay, H. A. (1985). Stimulus equivalence in rudimentary reading and spelling. *Analysis and Intervention in Developmental Disabilities, 5*(4), 373–387. https://doi.org/10.1016/0270-4684(85)90006-0

Mackay, H. A. (2013). Developing syntactic repertoires: Syntheses of stimulus classes, sequences, and contextual control. *European Journal of Behavior Analysis, 14*(1), 69–85. https://doi.org/10.1080/15021149.2013.11434446

Mackay, H. A., & Sidman, M. (1984). Teaching new behavior via equivalence relations. In P. H. Brooks, R. Sperber, & C. MacCauley (Eds.), *Learning and cognition in the mentally retarded* (pp. 493–513). Erlbaum.

Mackay, H. A., Wilkinson, K. M., Farrell, C., & Serna, R. W. (2011). Evaluating merger and intersection of equivalence classes with one member in common. *Journal of the Experimental Analysis of Behavior, 96*(1), 87–105. https://doi.org/10.1901/jeab.2011.96-87

Matos, M. A., Peres, W., Hübner, M. C., & Malheiros, R. H. S. (1997). Oralização e cópia: Efeitos sobre a aquisição de leitura generalizada recombinativa. *Temas em Psicologia, 5*(1), 47–64.

McIlvane, W. J. (1992). Stimulus control analysis and nonverbal instructional methods for people with intellectual disabilities. In N. Bray (Ed.), *International review of research in mental retardation, 18* (pp. 55–109). Academic.

Merlin, A. M. B., Almeida-Verdu, A. C. M., Neves, A. J., Silva, L. T. N., & Moret, A. L. M. (2019). Ensino e integração de comportamentos de ouvinte e falante com unidades sintáticas substantivo-adjetivo em crianças com DENA e IC. *CODAS, 31*(3), e20180135. https://doi.org/10.1590/2317-1782/20182018135

Miguel, C. (2016). Common and intraverbal bidirectional naming. *The Analysis of Verbal Behavior, 32*(2), 121–138. https://doi.org/10.1007/s40616-016-0066-2

Nascimento, A. M. (2007). A infância na escola e na vida: Uma relação fundamental. In BRASIL. Ministério da Educação. Secretaria de Educação Básica. In *Ensino fundamental de nove anos: Orientações para a inclusão de crianças de seis anos de idade*. (p. 85–96). MEC.

Neves, A. J. (2019). *Avaliação de procedimentos de ensino para ampliar a produção oral de sentenças em crianças com implante coclear* Doctoral dissertation, Universidade Federal de São Carlos. Repositório institucional UFSCar. https:// repositorio.ufscar.br/bitstream/handle/ufscar/11756/Tese_Neves2019_FINAL. pdf?sequence=4&isAllowed=y.
Neves, A. J., Almeida-Verdu, A. C. M., & de Souza, D. G. (2016). *Fortalecimento de relações de leitura e nomeação oral de sentenças em criança com Síndrome de Down*. Trabalho apresentado no XXV Encontro Brasileiro de Psicologia e Medicina Comportamental.
Neves, A. J., Almeida-Verdu, A. C. M., Assis, G. J. A., Silva, L. T. N., & Moret, A. L. M. (2018). Improving oral sentence production in children with cochlear implants: Effects of equivalence-based instruction and matrix training. *Psicologia: Reflexão e Crítica, 31*(14), 1–27. https://doi.org/10.1186/s41155-018-0095-y
Neves, A. J., Almeida-Verdu, A. C. M., Silva, L. T. N., & Moret, A. L. M. (2019). Ensino baseado em equivalência e produção de sentenças em crianças com implante coclear. *Revista Brasileira de Análise do Comportamento, 15*(1), 1–14. https://doi.org/10.18542/rebac.v15i1.7918
OECD. (2019). *Brazil – Country Note – PISA 2018 Results*, PISA/OECD Publishing. Retrieved in https://www.oecd.org/pisa/publications/PISA2018_CN_BRA.pdf Acesso em 02 de março de 2020.
Paixão, G. M., & Assis, G. J. A. (2018). Efeitos do ensino via CRMTS sobre leitura e construção de sentenças para crianças com autismo. *Interação em Psicologia, 22*(1), 77–88. https://doi.org/10.5380/psi.v22i1.51327
Paixão, G., & de Assis, G. J. A. (2017). Uso do procedimento de constructed response matching to sample: Uma revisão da literatura. *Perspectivas em Análise do Comportamento, 8*(1), 47–60. https://doi.org/10.18761/pac.2016.038
Papalia, D. E., & Olds, S. W. (2000). *Desenvolvimento humano*. (D. Bueno, Trad.; (7a ed.). Artes Médicas.
Postalli, L. M. M., Nakachima, R. Y., Schmidt, A., & de Souza, D. G. (2013). Controle instrucional e classes de estímulos equivalentes que incluem verbos e ações. *Psicologia: Reflexão e Crítica, 26*(1), 136–150. https://doi.org/10.1590/s0102-79722013000100015
Pytte, C. L., & Fienup, D. M. (2012). Using equivalence-based instruction to increase efficiency in teaching neuroanatomy. *The Journal of Undergraduate Neuroscience Education, 10*(2), 125–131.
Remington, B. (1994). Augmentative and alternative communication and behavior analysis: A productive partnership? *Augmentative and Alternative Communication, 10*(1), 3–13. https://doi.org/10.1080/07434619412331276720
Rexroad, C. N. (1926). Verbalization in multiple choice reactions. *Psychological Review, 33*(6), 451–458. https://doi.org/10.1037/h0075682
Rosa Filho, A. B., de Souza, D. G., de Rose, J. C. C., Fonseca, M. L., & Hanna, E. S. (1998). *Progleit: Software para programação de atividades para o ensino de leitura*. Research Software.
Sampaio, M. E. C., Assis, G., & Baptista, M. Q. G. (2010). Variáveis de procedimentos de ensino e de testes na construção de sentenças com compreensão. *Psicologia: Teoria e Pesquisa, 26*(1), 145–155. https://doi.org/10.1590/S0102-37722010000100017
Sidman, M. (2000). Equivalence relations and the reinforcement contingency. *Journal of the Experimental Analysis of Behavior, 74*(1), 127–146. https://doi.org/10.1901/jeab.2000.74-127
Sidman, M. (2009). Equivalence relations and behavior: An introductory tutorial. *The Analysis of Verbal Behavior, 25*(1), 5–17. https://doi.org/10.1007/bf03393066
Sidman, M., & Tailby, W. (1982). Conditional discriminations vs. matching-to sample: An expansion of the testing paradigm. *Journal of the Experimental Analysis of Behavior, 37*(1), 5–22. https://doi.org/10.1901/jeab.1982.37-5
Sidman, M. (1986). Functional analysis of emergent verbal classes. In T. Thompson e M. D. Zeiler (Eds.) Analysis and integration of behavioral units (pp. 213–245). Hillsdale, NJ: Erlbaum.
Silva, R. V., Neves, A. J., & Almeida-Verdu, A. C. M. (2017). Ensino de relações de equivalência com sentenças de cinco termos e produção oral em uma criança com implante coclear. *Acta Comportamentalia, 25*(3), 289–306.

Silveira, C. C., Domeniconi, C., Calcagno, S. C., Kato, O. M., & Hanna, E. S. (2016). Repertório básico de leitura e escrita em escolas brasileiras com baixa avaliação do ensino fundamental. *Acta Comportamentalia, 24*(4), 471–486.

Skinner, B. F. (1957). *Verbal behavior*. Prentice Hall.

Stokes, T. F., & Baer, D. M. (1977). An implicity technology of generalization. *Journal of Applied Behavior Analysis, 10*(2), 349–367. https://doi.org/10.1901/jaba.1977.10-349

Striefel, S., Wetherby, B., & Karlan, G. R. (1976). Establishing generalized verb-noun instruction-following skills in retarded children. *Journal of Experimental Child Psychology, 22*(2), 247–260. https://doi.org/10.1016/0022-0965(76)90005-9

Stromer, R., & Mackay, H. A. (1993). Human sequential behavior: Relations among stimuli, class formation, and derived sequences. *The Psychological Record, 43*(1), 107–131.

Sundberg, M. L. (2008). *VB-MAPP: Verbal behavior milestones assessment and placement program*. AVB Press.

Terrace, H. S. (1963). Discrimination learning, with and without "errors". *Journal of the Experimental Analysis of Behavior, 6*(1), 1–27. https://doi.org/10.1901/jeab.1963.6-1

Whalon, K. J., Al Otaiba, S., & Delano, M. E. (2009). Evidence-based reading instruction for individuals with autism spectrum disorders. *Focus on Autism and Other Developmental Disabilities, 24*(1), 3–16. https://doi.org/10.1177/1088357608328515

Yamamoto, J., & Miya, T. (1999). Acquisition and transfer of sentence construction in autistic students: Analysis by computer-based teaching. *Research in Developmental Disabilities, 20*(5), 355–377. https://doi.org/10.1016/s0891-4222(99)00017-7

Yokoyama, K., Naoi, N., & Yamamoto, J. (2006). Teaching verbal behavior using the picture exchange communication system (PECS) with children with autistic spectrum disorder. *Japanese Journal of Special Education, 43*(6), 485–503. https://doi.org/10.6033/tokkyou.43.485

Chapter 7
Teaching Relevant Prerequisites for Learning to Read and Write and Expanding the ALEPP Teaching Program

Raquel Maria de Melo, Alessandra Rocha de Albuquerque, Lidia Maria Marson Postalli, and Deisy das Graças de Souza

7.1 Introduction

For Behavior Analysis, reading and writing are complex verbal repertoires involving several interconnected discriminative operants, although it is common to consider them as unitary behaviors (e.g., reading a sentence, writing a dictated word). Additionally, reading comprehension involves responding to a network of conditional relations between stimuli and between stimuli and responses, which include stimuli from different categories (e.g., printed text with different fonts, spoken words, pictures, objects, people, actions) and different response modalities (e.g., naming aloud, silent naming, pointing/relating). Similarly, writing involves different behaviors in the face of different modalities of stimuli or situations, such as copying in a notebook the text the teacher wrote on the board, typing the cell phone number spoken by a friend, writing on a piece of paper the shopping list dictated by someone else, writing a sentence in the presence of a picture, completing the spaces in a crossword game in the presence of clues, among others (de Rose, 2005, republished in Chap. 1 of this book; Sidman, 1971, 1994).

The analysis of reading and writing as a network of relations allows the identification of verbal performances already learned and the selection of a minimum

R. M. de Melo (✉)
Universidade de Brasília, Brasília, DF, Brazil
e-mail: rmelo@unb.br

A. R. de Albuquerque
Universidade Católica de Brasília, Brasília, DF, Brazil

L. M. M. Postalli · D. das Graças de Souza
Universidade Federal de São Carlos, São Carlos, SP, Brazil

A. R. de Albuquerque, R. M. de Melo (eds.), *Contributions of Behavior Analysis to Reading and Writing Comprehension*, https://doi.org/10.1007/978-3-031-40868-7_7

number of relations to be taught, from which new performances may emerge (e.g., Albuquerque & Melo, 2005; Sidman, 1971, 1990). This network also allows us to verify behaviors in early stages of acquisition or not yet learned, as well as basic behavioral repertoires or prerequisites that may enable learning to read and write (Hanna et al., 1999; Sidman, 1977). Among these, performances such as looking at the presented words/pictures and following instructions to locate or point to a given word/picture, often also called supportive behaviors (Iñesta, 1972/1980), may be considered to have already been learned or should be previously taught.

This chapter aims to analyze the prerequisites for reading and writing performance. The first section will characterize the basic repertoire that enables learning the set of behaviors involved in the network of relationships that characterize reading and writing based on studies of equivalence and the functional analysis of the performances involved. The traditional notion of prerequisites and readiness for literacy will also be addressed, which focuses on the repertoire immediately prior to the child's entry into the 1st year of elementary school and is often related to the sequence of child development. Another skill that has been addressed as a prerequisite for reading and writing is phonological awareness, or the "awareness that speech may be segmented and the ability to manipulate such segments" (Capovilla & Capovilla, 2000). The second section will analyze the performances required to perform the procedures involved in teaching regular words (composed of syllables formed by consonants followed by vowels) in Module 1 of the Learning to Read and Write in Small Steps teaching program (*Aprendendo a Ler e Escrever em Pequenos Passos* [ALEPP]; de Rose et al., 1996), which will allow us to identify, based on this analysis, fundamental prerequisites that favor learning with this teaching program. The third section will describe the proposal of a new teaching module, called Preparatory Module, which aims to promote the repertoires identified as prerequisites to improve the learning of regular word reading for learners exposed to Module 1. Finally, in the final considerations, a summary of the main issues addressed in the chapter will be presented.

7.2 Prerequisites for Learning to Read and Write

According to Sidman (1995), before teaching new behavior it is necessary to verify if all the prerequisites have already been learned, that is, if the learner knows how to do everything that the behavior to be learned requires. This principle is consistent with Keller's (1968/1999) and Skinner's (1968/1972) proposals for programming teaching contingencies, which emphasize the importance of planning teaching in gradual steps, in small units, and achieving accuracy in previously taught performances before moving on to teach more complex behaviors. This principle also converges with linguistic perspectives, more specifically with the Bloomfieldian proposal that points out three fundamental prerequisites for the literacy process, as explained by Conceição in Chap. 14: "being a fluent listener and speaker of the language in which one will learn to read; following visual stimuli in the left-to-right direction and identifying the letters of the alphabet as discrete units, being able to distinguish and name each of them regardless of the order in which they occur in the alphabet".

Prerequisites, therefore, can be considered as the behavioral repertoire that enables the learning of new behaviors. Regarding reading and writing, Hanna et al. (1999) state that "the teaching of prerequisites, combined with the use of methodology appropriate to the child's behavioral characteristics, is the main way to prevent failure in literacy" (p. 79). The prerequisite behaviors are specific in relation to a particular teaching program (Iñesta, 1972/1980), i.e., they constitute the initial repertoire, already learned, which is a necessary or relevant condition for new learning to occur (e.g., considering the performance of a child with typical development, to teach reading, speaking in front of printed words, it is necessary that she knows how to speak; to teach handwriting, it is necessary that she knows how to hold the pencil and make certain movements when producing strokes / shapes on paper). Additionally, there is a set of basic, non-specific behaviors that allow the learning of a wide variety of other behaviors, especially in the academic context, which are called by Iñesta (1972/1980) supportive repertoires. The supportive repertoires, not being specific for learning a new behavior, may be considered generalized repertoires. Among these, imitation, attention, following instruction and discrimination (responding differentially to stimuli of different modalities, visual, auditory, tactile, etc.) may be cited. However, in certain teaching situations, some of these supportive behaviors may also be considered prerequisite behaviors (e.g., following instruction and paying attention to stimuli may be considered both supportive and prerequisite behaviors for teaching reading and for teaching arithmetic operations).

Studies on prerequisites or readiness for literacy aim to identify which behaviors children need to develop to learn to read and write, as well as to verify the relationship between such behaviors and the greater or lesser probability of success in learning to read and write, considering that these are hierarchical and complex repertoires. In general, such studies have analyzed the child's repertoire immediately before entering the first year of elementary school. In addition to this predictive interest, there is concern in assessing and teaching such prerequisites to prevent academic failure (Hanna et al., 1999; Leite, 1988).

According to Hanna et al. (1999), the analysis of prerequisites should be considered from the assessment of the child's behavioral repertoire development. The learning process of such behaviors is prior to the onset of literacy. Thus, it is possible to identify topographic and functional similarities between behaviors that occur from birth and those observed when the formal teaching of reading and writing begins. For example, visual discrimination, exemplified by the identification of similar and different objects or pictures, as well as auditory discrimination, present in the differentiation of environmental sounds, are also necessary for later reading behavior, since they are present in the differentiation of textual stimulus elements (letters, syllables and words) and speech sound units (e.g., initial and final word sounds, rhymes). The motor control required to copy the letters of the alphabet is preceded by simpler movements, such as touching a mobile, holding an object with the hands, placing objects in containers, stacking objects, picking up pencils and scratching, and making large circular movements. Considering this perspective, Hanna et al. (1999) analyzed eight scales and/or instruments for monitoring child development and identified more primitive forms of behaviors assessed in these instruments, considered important prerequisites to reach the final behavior of reading and writing, which should be related to the following objectives: (a) reading comprehension of short texts; (b) writing words with comprehension; and (c) reporting stories or events. The selected behaviors were organized into 23 basic categories, including attention, visual discrimination, auditory discrimination, fine motor or visual-motor coordination, verbalization, sequencing, analysis and synthesis.

Tables 7.1 and 7.2 present the definition of each of the 23 categories and the identification of some behaviors involved in reading and writing. These categories were regrouped into: (a) basic repertoires and (b) complex repertoires. Basic repertoires start from birth, and comprise the following categories: attention, visual discrimination, auditory discrimination and visual-motor coordination (Table 7.1).

Complex repertoires (Table 7.2) can be subdivided into: concept use and comprehension (identifying, naming and using the word in appropriate situations involving discriminations such as shapes, position, size and direction), categorization (grouping and naming sets of stimuli with common characteristics), analysis (identifying or separating parts of a whole; may include body scheme), synthesis (identifying or constructing the whole from its component elements) and sequencing (performing a series of motor or verbal behaviors in sequence); and verbalization (pronunciation, grammar and comprehension). These categories, however, can be

Table 7.1 Categories of basic behavioral repertoires, definition and specification of their relationship to reading and writing

Category	Definition	Relationship with reading and/or writing
Attention	Gaze directed at stimuli (objects, printed material, videos, people).	Oral or written response under control of textual stimuli and speech sounds.
Visual discrimination	Identify same and different visual stimuli	Ability to differentiate and find similarities in textual stimuli; it is required in reading and writing with respect to letters, words, etc.
Auditory discrimination	Identify same and different auditory stimuli	Ability to differentiate and find similarities in speech sounds in relation to words and their parts (letters and syllables); involved in the tasks of correctly selecting words, letters and syllables, as well as selecting the letters or syllables corresponding to dictated words, letters or syllables
Fine motor or visomotor coordination	Perform from instruction, or sample, precise finger movements using an instrument (pencil, brush, logic blocks, letter cards, or keyboard, etc.)	Emission of sequences of motor responses to produce graphic symbols corresponding to printed text (letter, syllables, words) in the case of copying a text with cursive response, or when the word is dictated (handwritten dictation); selecting movable letters or typing keys corresponding to printed text or speech sounds

Note. Table adapted from Hanna et al. (1999)

Table 7.2 Categories of complex behavioral repertoires, definition and specification of their relationship to reading and writing

Category	Definition	Relationship with reading and/or writing
Laterality	Identify and use the concepts of right and left in the body and in environmental stimuli	Differentiate letters in relation to their parts, or elements positioned on the left and right sides; respond to textual stimuli (e.g., syllable, word, sentence) from the left
Space distance	Identify and use the concepts that indicate the space separating objects and people from each other (far/close, together/apart)	Identify different words based on the distance between them; produce verbal responses under control of the distance between textual stimuli. It is also related to text comprehension, other people's speech and verbal reporting (oral or written)
Space position	Identify and use concepts related to the location of objects or people in space (in/out, above/below, behind/ in front/side, between)	Related to text comprehension, other people's speech and verbal reporting (oral or written). Involves responding differentially (selecting, naming) to verbal stimuli that describe the relative position of objects, people or pictures
Direction	Identify and use the concepts to the direction of movement of objects or people (up, down, forward, backward, right, left)	Related to text comprehension, other people's speech and verbal reporting (oral or written). Involves responding differentially (selecting, naming) to verbal stimuli that describe the direction of movement of objects or people
Size	Identify and use the concepts of size, length and thickness of objects (small/large, thin/ thick, short/high, short/long)	Related to text comprehension, other people's speech and verbal reporting (oral or written). Respond differentially (select, name) to verbal stimuli that describe the size of objects or people
Quantity	Identify and use concepts indicating volume and density (full/empty, plenty/ poor, whole/half, more/less, none)	Related to text comprehension, other people's speech and verbal reporting (oral or written). Respond differentially (select, name) to verbal stimuli that describe volume and density
Form	Identify and name examples of geometric shapes	Differentiate the shapes of distinct letters printed in different formats
Color	Identify and name colors	Related to text comprehension, other people's speech and verbal reporting (oral or written). Differential response (selecting, naming) to verbal stimuli that describe color
Weight	Identify and name concepts related to weight (light/ heavy)	Related to text comprehension, other people's speech and verbal reporting (oral or written). Differential response (selecting, naming) to verbal stimuli that describe the weight of objects or people
Temperature	Identify and name concepts related to temperature (hot/ cold)	Related to understanding texts, other people's speech and verbal reporting (oral or written). Differential response (selecting, naming) to verbal stimuli that describe temperature

(continued)

Table 7.2 (continued)

Category	Definition	Relationship with reading and/or writing
Time	Identify and name concepts related to time (morning, afternoon, evening, yesterday, tomorrow)	Related to text comprehension, other people's speech and verbal reporting (oral or written)
Categorization	Grouping or naming, with the same label, objects that have some common characteristic or function	Related to text comprehension, other people's speech and verbal reporting (oral or written). It is involved in identifying regularities in speech and writing, such as accurately using plural and verb tenses
Verbalization pronunciation	Articulate spontaneously, in a dialogue situation or by imitation, the sounds of the Portuguese language	Accurate reading aloud of words and phrases in textual material
Verbalization comprehension	Show symbolic relations between names/oralizations and their referents (actions, objects, people, relations, etc.); use expressions in appropriate contexts	Involves reporting and understanding events and stories presented in textual material or reported by others
Verbalization grammar	Express oneself orally in accordance with the rules of the Portuguese language	Emission of original (oral) verbal behavior using the rules established by the verbal community
Sequencing	Produce a series of behaviors, motor or verbal, obeying the sample or instruction's sequence; reproduce behaviors according to a temporal sequence	Report orally or in writing an event or story accurately, in the sequence of events and according to the verbal units defined by the verbal community. It is also involved in the production of chained motor responses in writing (handwritten or by composition) each letter to produce words and sentences
Analysis	Identify or separate the component parts of a whole	Identification of the elements (letters, syllables or words) of the whole (word or sentence) and the production of corresponding sounds or combinations of sounds or spelling
Synthesis	Identify or construct the whole from its elements	Production of verbal response units in an integrated and sequential manner in word and sentence reading and writing. It is necessary that the set of letters or syllables be "understood" as a new stimulus (control another response), i.e., can be related to objects, people, actions or events
Body scheme	Identify and name the parts of the body	Identification of parts of a whole (analysis) and naming, which are basic skills involved in reading and writing

Note. Table adapted from Hanna et al. (1999)

combined, and the same behavior may belong to more than one (e.g., identifying parts of a picture is a behavior that involves analysis and visual discrimination). According to the authors, the proposal specifies the continuity and sequence of the development of behaviors, organized in 11 age groups from birth to 7 years, and allows monitoring the learning process of behaviors related to reading and writing and developing intervention procedures for specific behaviors in the family environment, at school or in a childcare institution.

In addition to the categories listed by Hanna et al. (1999), several studies consider phonological awareness as a prerequisite for learning to read and write (e.g., Bernardino Jr. et al., 2006; Pestun, 2005; Santos & Barrera, 2017). Phonological awareness comprises a set of skills that involves recognizing speech segments at the lexical (words) and sublexical (rhymes, alliterations, syllables, and phonemes) levels, while the term phonemic awareness is directly related to the recognition of phonemic units (Capovilla & Capovilla, 2000; Cardoso-Martins, 1995). In behavioral terms, phonological awareness corresponds to the discrimination of speech sounds or the abstraction of sound units smaller than a word (de Souza et al., 2009b; Mueller et al., 2000).

Learning phonological awareness skills is a gradual process. Children learn to identify the syllables that make up words before identifying phonemes (Adams, 1990) and the initial and final sound of words before recognizing individual phonemes (Roazzi et al., 2013; Treiman & Zukowski, 1996). In general, phonemic awareness develops during the formal literacy process, especially from learning the correspondence between graphemes (printed text) and phonemes (speech sounds). On the other hand, awareness of phonological units larger than a phoneme may be present before learning to read and write (e.g., experiences with rhymes are frequent in children's games and songs), which in this case would improve learning of such behaviors. Thus, there is an interaction between phonological awareness skills and learning to read and write (Bernardino Jr., 2006; Roazzi et al., 2013).

Longitudinal studies with Brazilian children that assessed phonological awareness skills before the beginning of literacy (or even during preschool) and subsequent performance in reading and writing at the end of the first year of elementary school showed a positive correlation between phonological awareness skills (e.g., syllabic and phonemic analysis and synthesis – decomposition and recomposition of words from syllables or phonemes; rhyme and alliteration) and oral reading and writing in taking dictation (Castro & Barrera, 2019; Pestum, 2005), and between syllabic and phonemic segmentation and fusion tasks (decomposition and recomposition) and oral reading (Roazzi et al., 2013).

However, since phonological awareness involves different behaviors, it is difficult to evaluate their individual role in the process of learning to read. Thus, the initial step in this assessment should be the clear identification and operationalization of the behaviors that define phonological awareness. Only then is it possible to assess the impact of these behaviors on the literacy process (de Freitas & Reis, 2017). In this sense, some studies have evaluated the impact of direct training of phonological awareness skills on learning to read and write (e.g., Bernardino Jr. et al., 2006; Capovilla & Capovilla, 2000; Justino & Barrera, 2012; Santos & Barrera, 2017).

Bernardino Jr. et al. (2006) assessed the effect of direct, sequential, or blended teaching of the 10 phonological awareness skills that are part of the Phonological

Table 7.3 Phonological awareness skills and tasks of the PCF

Skills	Tasks
Rhyme	Judge, among three words spoken by the evaluator, the two that end with the same sound
Alliteration	Judge, among three words, the two words that begin with the same sound
Syllable segmentation	Separate a word spoken by the evaluator into its component syllables
Syllabic synthesis	Unite the syllables spoken by the evaluator, saying the word resulting from the union
Syllabic manipulation	Add and subtract syllables from words and say which word is formed
Syllabic transposition	Invert the syllables of the word spoken by the evaluator and say the new word
Phonemic segmentation	Separate a word spoken by the evaluator into its component phonemes
Phonemic synthesis	Unite the phonemes spoken by the evaluator, saying which word results from the union
Phonemic manipulation	Add or subtract phonemes and say which word is formed
Phonemic transposition	Invert the phonemes of words and say which word is formed

Note. Table adapted from Bernardino Jr. et al. (2006)

Awareness Test (PCF; Capovilla & Capovilla, 1998), shown in Table 7.3. The teaching activities included different tasks, such as: rhyme and alliteration identification (e.g., Which two words start/end with the same sound? ***rato**, boné, **raiz** / **queijo**, moça, **beijo***),[1] syllabic manipulation (e.g., If you add "g" at the end of "le", what word is formed?), phoneme segmentation (e.g., If you remove the /s/ from the beginning of *soco*,[2] what word is formed?). Four students with learning difficulties in reading and writing demonstrated learning of these repertoires after direct teaching of phonological awareness skills. Such evidence points to the advantages of assessing, identifying, and programming teaching conditions that ensure the presence or learning prerequisites before reading and writing behaviors are directly taught.

In summary, for programming contingencies for teaching reading and writing it is important to identify the child's initial repertoire in relation to the behaviors that are necessary or relevant for the execution of the teaching tasks, as well as the supporting behaviors (e.g., paying attention, imitating, following instructions). The prerequisite behaviors for reading (speaking in the presence of printed words) and writing (in dictation situations) are learned gradually, develop from simpler behaviors (e.g., differentiate and identify similarities, decompose and recombine visual and auditory stimuli, differentiate and name objects and pictures and relationships between them, and perform behaviors in sequence), and can be improved during the

[1] The corresponding English words are: rat, cap, root / cheese, girl, kiss.

[2] The corresponding English word is punch.

formal teaching process in which grapheme (printed text) – phoneme (speech sounds) correspondences are explicitly taught. The identification of prerequisites should be made, however, in a contextualized manner, based on the clear definition of the final repertoire to be achieved, since prerequisites are specific behaviors that allow for progress in a given teaching program (Iñesta, 1972/1980). Thus, some relevant prerequisites for learning regular words using Module 1 of the ALEPP will be presented below.

7.3 Learning Simple Regular Words: Procedures Involved in Teaching and Identification of Prerequisites

Reading and writing, although interconnected, are independent and distinct repertoires. Thus, children in the early stages of literacy may copy words written by the teacher on the board but not read them, or may have learned to read a set of words but not write them in a dictation task. To understand such differences in learner performance, it is necessary to identify the stimuli that are present when the response is requested (e.g., word written on the board or dictated by the teacher) and the modality of the response (e.g., speaking aloud, handwriting, typing on a keyboard). In reading, the oral response is required in the presence of printed material, that is, there must be point-to-point correspondence between the text and the verbal response, and this performance is termed textual behavior (de Rose, 2005; Skinner, 1957). In handwriting, a sequence of motor responses must be emitted to produce the correct spelling of letters that make up each word. If the task is copying text, the printed text is available and it is sufficient to reproduce (or draw) each letter. If the task is taking dictation, the sequence of movements to produce the letters in a specific order must be emitted in the presence of the dictated sounds or words (de Rose et al., 1996; de Souza et al., 2009a).

The textual, copying and taking dictation behavior involve control relations in which a sequence of verbal responses (e.g., oral response, motor response) is emitted in the presence of specific stimuli (e.g., printed text, dictated word) according to the rules of the verbal community (Skinner, 1957). Such behaviors are basic repertoires involved in reading and writing, but for the learner to understand what he or she has read and write it is necessary to learn relations between stimuli and between stimuli and responses, i.e., it is necessary to relate the printed word with environmental events (e.g., picture, object, actions). Such relations are called arbitrary, because they are defined by each verbal community and there is no physical similarity between the related stimuli, and they also involve symbolic behavior, to the extent that the printed words are symbols for the sounds of spoken words and the stimuli to which they refer to (de Rose, 2005; Sidman, 1994).

Learning one of these repertoires (textual behavior, reading comprehension, copying or taking dictation) and not another may indicate inefficient teaching conditions or, what is the focus of this chapter, to teaching conditions that, although well planned (based on evidence), are dependent on the learners' input repertoires (supportive or prerequisites) not assessed or absent at the beginning of the teaching process. Thus, as already stated, the clear definition of target behaviors should guide the identification of necessary prerequisites, present or to be directly taught, so that the teaching objectives are achieved.

The ALEPP teaching program, described in detail in Chaps. 4 and 5, proposed for children with learning difficulties in reading and writing in the early years of elementary school, has been used with different populations (for examples of uses with different populations, see section III of this book) and is based on the premise that anyone can learn to read and write, provided that appropriate teaching conditions are planned. However, despite the positive evidence described with the use of different versions of this teaching program, studies with some populations, such as children with intellectual disabilities, have demonstrated the need to plan complementary conditions for teaching behaviors that are prerequisites to the reading and writing repertoires taught in Module 1 of this program.

Module 1 of the ALEPP (de Souza et al., 2009a) teaches relationships between dictated words/syllables and corresponding printed words/syllables (or word and syllable recognition), between dictated words and pictures, and between printed words and writing letter-by-letter construction. These relations allow verifying the occurrence of behaviors that were not directly taught, or the emergence of reading comprehension (relations between dictated words and pictures and vice versa) and textual behavior, naming printed words, and taking dictation. The use of words formed by simple syllables, with regularities in the correspondence between sound and spelling, and with repetition of letters and syllables among the 51 words taught, together with syllabic training (dictated syllable – printed syllable) and copying with construction, improve the reading of new words formed by recombining parts of the words taught (e.g., de Souza et al., 2009a; Reis et al., 2009).

Before starting the teaching program of Module 1 of the ALEPP, it is essential to assess the student's initial repertoire, which will guide the next stages of teaching. De Souza et al. (2009a) present a list of behaviors that should be assessed for including verbal relations involved in reading and the immediate prerequisites, i.e. relevant performances for learning the relations to be taught. Verbal relations include: echoic behavior (repeating a dictated word), picture naming, printed word naming (textual behavior), taking dictation with constructed response (writing a spoken word by selecting letters provided) and handwritten response, copying with constructed response (producing a written word presented from the selection of letters provided) and handwritten response. The pairing tasks involve: pairing the identity of pictures and printed words, pairing the printed word and the picture corresponding to the dictated word, pairing the printed word corresponding to the picture and the picture corresponding to the printed word, and pairing the printed word with uppercase and lowercase letters and vice-versa.

Based on the analysis of the network of verbal relations that characterize reading and writing, target behaviors of ALEPP's Module 1 (which involve pairing tasks and pairing with constructed response) and the learning difficulties observed in children with intellectual disabilities, de Freitas (2012) proposed a prerequisite teaching program for these children that should be performed before exposure to an adapted version of ALEPP's Module 1 (de Freitas, 2009; see also Chap. 8). The prerequisite teaching program was composed of tasks of: (1) visual identity discriminations between pictures and textual stimuli (letter, syllable, 3- and 4-letter words), which simultaneously taught identity discriminations between the sample and comparison stimuli and also enabled differentiation between comparison stimuli in addition to successive discriminations between sample stimuli presented on each trial; (2) auditory-visual pairings between dictated words and pictures or corresponding words that taught the receptive repertoire of selecting pictures in the presence of their respective dictated names, with the possibility of establishing control for the printed words as a whole or for their parts, and successive auditory discrimination between the dictated words presented as samples at each trial; (3) pairing with constructed responses, which involved teaching to identify the parts of the sample stimuli (letter, syllables, 3- and 4-letter words) and selecting each letter in sequence from left to right to build the sample stimulus; (4) picture naming, which involved assessing and teaching, if necessary, the oral response to pictures with Portuguese language referents, visual discrimination of the presented stimulus, and oral pronunciation of the stimulus name; and (5) pairing of a dictated word with a printed word and with a constructed response (copying), which were included to prepare participants for the two types of tasks that would be the target of the adapted version of ALEPP's Module 1. Additionally, it was suggested assessing and, if necessary, carrying out the teaching of echoic behavior, which involves reproducing oral response, sounds with point-to-point correspondence with the dictated stimulus (letter, syllable, or word). In some situations, additional teaching procedures were included and adapted to each participant's repertoire to ensure learning of the prerequisite behaviors. In Study 4 of de Freitas (2012), four participants who had been exposed to prerequisite teaching performed the adapted version of ALEPP's Module 1 proposed by de Freitas (2009). The results showed that all participants learned the behaviors trained in the adapted reading program, suggesting that the prerequisite program was effective in teaching the relevant behaviors.

The program used by de Freitas (2012) was based on the analysis of the target behaviors included in ALEPP's Module 1 and was developed based on the analysis of the participants' performances as they were exposed to the teaching procedures and the verification of the absence of supportive repertoires or prerequisites in specific children. However, the computerized prerequisite module developed by de Freitas (2012) was programmed in a computer language incompatible with more modern technological resources, which prevents replication in other studies. Additionally, the protocols of the teaching and testing sessions used by de Freitas (2012) are not available for developing a new version of the program in a more current programming language.

The studies by de Freitas (2009), Bernardino Jr. et al. (2006) and others (e.g., Justino & Barrera, 2012; Santos & Barrera, 2017) evaluated, with positive results, the effect of direct teaching of different prerequisites on learning to read and write. These studies are socially relevant and point to efficient and cost-effective paths for planning reading and writing instruction, particularly with special populations with a background of school failure. These results and the prerequisite teaching program developed by de Freitas (2012) served as the basis for the proposal of a new teaching module, called the Preparatory Module, which makes up the ALEPP, which will be described in the next section of this chapter.

7.4 Description of a Proposed Module for Teaching Prerequisites for Reading and Writing

The planning of the prerequisite Module (Preparatory Module) was based on the literature on teaching technology (Skinner, 1968/1972), the analysis of prerequisite behavior repertoires (Hanna et al., 1999) related to the target behaviors of receptive and expressive reading of simple regular words taught in ALEPP's Module 1, and the teaching of discrimination skills as a basis for the formation of the network of relations involved in reading and writing (e.g., de Freitas, 2012; Dube, 1996; Hanna et al., 1999). This Module was planned and is currently being programmed and developed; it will be applied via Computer Individualized Teaching Manager (*Gerenciador de Ensino Individualizado por Computador* [GEIC]) remote execution platform.

The Preparatory Module consists of a general pre-test, 10 teaching units and a general post-test. The number of steps per unit ranges from one (Units 2, 3 and 8) to 20 (Unit 4). Each teaching step is composed of 36 trials, except those in the fourth unit which are composed of 18 trials. The exposure to the steps that make up each unit is sequential and may be repeated if the learner does not perform correctly in all trials. After the second exposure (repetition), the learner goes on to the next teaching step even if he/she presents errors. Limiting repetitions in each session aimed to minimize possible deleterious effects of errors and repetitions. To compose the teaching units and steps, simple regular words (composed of consonant-vowels and represented by pictures from ALEPP's Module 1), letters, syllables, geometric figures (e.g., star, square, circle), and pictures/symbols (e.g., clover, lock, horseshoe) are used. In the teaching units, visual discrimination, auditory discrimination, verbalization and composition tasks are performed in order to develop basic discriminative (Table 7.1) and more complex repertoires (Table 7.2), e.g., laterality, position, direction, among others. The planning of teaching steps also includes: observation response, when necessary; longer instruction in the first trials and fading out along the following trials; and gradual insertion of comparison stimuli. Correct responses are followed by sound consequences, similar to those used in other ALEPP modules (e.g., Yeh!, Very good!, Great!), and incorrect responses result in a correction procedure (e.g., "No, it's not", followed by repetition of the sample stimulus).

7.4.1 General Pre- and Post-test

The general pre-test and the general post-test of the Preparatory Module aim to assess the effects of the prerequisite teaching program. The learner's initial performances in each of the skills to be taught will be measured before teaching (pre-test) and after completing the teaching program (post-test). The tests consist of five trials of each task of the 10 teaching units of the Module, totaling 60 trials, presented in the following order: echoic behavior, simple discrimination, figure identity matching, matching between a dictated word and a picture, picture naming, matching between a dictated word (ordinal) and a picture, matching between pictures and between letters with rotation, identity matching with a sequence of four elements, matching printed words, copying, matching between a dictated word and a printed word, matching between a dictated letter and a printed letter, and letter naming. Differential consequences for correct and incorrect answers are presented during the pre- and post-test, where correct answers are reinforced with sound effects and praise, and incorrect answers result in the presentation of the next trial.

7.4.2 Teaching Units 1 to 4

The purpose of these units is to teach visual and auditory discrimination, indicated by Hanna et al. (1999) as basic prerequisites (Table 7.1), as well as verbalization/pronunciation, categorization and laterality, considered complex prerequisites (Table 7.2). Each of the four units prioritizes one of these prerequisites, but the combined teaching of more than one prerequisite will occur, given the difficulty of isolating them.

Unit 1 targets auditory discrimination and involves the direct teaching of echoic behavior and visual discrimination by selecting the picture experimentally designated as a positive stimulus (simple discrimination). Units 2 and 3 teach visual discrimination, with increasing degrees of complexity, as well as categorization (equal/different) and laterality, respectively. Unit 4 explores the prerequisites already taught in the previous units (visual and auditory discrimination), through the selection of the picture in the presence of the dictated word, in addition to teaching picture naming.

Unit 1 This first teaching unit is composed of two tasks: simple discrimination and echoic behavior (Fig. 7.1, Unit 1), which involve, respectively, receptive (pointing) and expressive (speaking) responding. The objectives are to teach visual discrimination, establishing responding under discriminative control (the choice of the picture defined as positive/correct stimulus – S+) and to teach auditory discrimination (responding in different ways to different sounds). To achieve this goal, visual discriminations are initially taught (the choice of the picture defined as positive/correct stimulus – S+), followed by verbalization/pronunciation prompts (oral repetition of the dictated word). Thus, blocks of discrimination trials (27 trials), beginning with

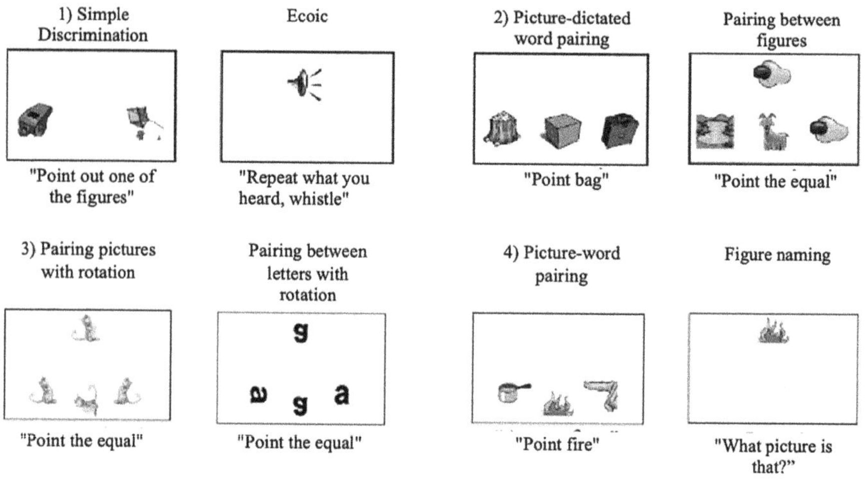

Fig. 7.1 Illustration of an attempt of each task performed in Units 1 to 4

the presentation of one picture and then two, are alternated with blocks of echoic behavior trials (nine trials) in which the names of words corresponding to the picture (S+) are presented as auditory models to be repeated by the learners. Four sets of six pictures and the respective words of the positive stimuli (S+) are used, totaling 24 pictures and 12 words. A different set of stimuli is used in each teaching step (Table 7.4).

Unit 2 In the second unit (Fig. 7.1, Unit 2) the selection of the picture corresponding to the dictated word (dictated word-picture matching) and the identity between pictures (picture matching) are taught. In the pairing between the dictated word and the picture (27 trials), when two or three pictures are presented, the picture corresponding to the dictated word should be indicated. In the pairing between pictures (nine trials) the learner should, simultaneously, discriminate equal (identity between the sample and comparison stimuli in each trial) and different (different sample stimuli between successive trials) stimuli. Thus, this unit prioritizes the direct teaching of visual discrimination and categorization and, additionally, the auditory discrimination. In each trial a different sample stimulus is presented, totaling 36 stimuli/trials. This unit is composed of one teaching step.

Unit 3 In this unit, consisting of one teaching step, the task of identity pairing between pictures and between letters with rotation is used (Fig. 7.1, Unit 3). A sample stimulus is presented at the top of the screen and three comparison stimuli at the bottom, and the incorrect comparison stimuli differ from the sample only in terms of rotation. Thus, in the trials with figures (24 trials) a figure identical to the model (correct alternative) and the same figure with different rotations from the model (incorrect alternatives) are presented as comparisons. The trials with letters (12 trials) also use this configuration, for example, if the letter "b" is the sample stimulus,

Table 7.4 Unit, skills, tasks, number of attempts per task, steps and stimuli

Unit	Skills	Tasks	No. Attempts by task	No. Steps	No. stimuli
Pre-test	All provided in the teaching units	All teaching units	5	1	–
1	Auditory discrimination Verbalization pronunciation Visual discrimination	Simple discrimination Echoic behavior	27 9	4	24
2	Visual discrimination Categorization Auditory discrimination	Dictated word and picture matching Pairing between pictures	27 9	1	36
3	Laterality Visual discrimination	Pairing between pictures with rotation Pairing between letters with rotation	24 12	1	Pictures 16 Letters 9
4	Verbalization understanding Verbalization pronunciation Visual discrimination	Dictated word-picture pairing Picture naming	12 6	20	60
5	Analysis Sequencing Visual discrimination	Pairing between sequential sample and picture of elements	36	3	12
6	Sequencing Visual discrimination	Pairing between pictures with sequential elements	36	3	27
7	Synthesis Sequencing	Identity matching between textual stimuli Copying per composition	28 8	2	3 letters, 3 syllables and 41 words with 3 (17), 4 (12), 5 (2) and 6 (10) letters
8	Understanding Visual discrimination Auditory discrimination	Matching between dictated/written word/ picture and picture or printed word Pairing between the dictated word and the printed word	24 12	1	24

(continued)

Table 7.4 (continued)

Unit	Skills	Tasks	No. Attempts by task	No. Steps	No. stimuli
9	Visual discrimination of letters Categorization of letters	Pairing between dictated/printed letter and printed letter Pairing between upper case and lowercase printed letters	24 12	7	21
10	Auditory letter discrimination Visual discrimination of letters Verbalization pronunciation of letters	Pairing between dictated letter and printed letter (upper case and lower case) Letter naming	24 12	7	21
Post-test	All provided in the teaching units	All teaching units	5	1	–

the letters "d", "p" or "q" can be the incorrect comparison stimuli. This task, of visual identity pairing between pictures and letters, aims to teach visual and laterality discrimination.

Unit 4 In this unit, the learner performs again the tasks of pairing a dictated word with a picture and of picture naming (Fig. 7.1, Unit 4). These tasks require visual discrimination of the presented stimuli, verbalization and comprehension. Twenty sets of three words and pictures from Module 1 are used, each composing a teaching step. In each teaching step, 18 trials are presented, with pairing blocks between the dictated word and picture (12 trials) alternated with picture naming blocks (six trials).

7.4.3 Teaching Units 5 and 6

The focus of these units is on teaching prerequisites sequencing skills (emphasizing 'beginning' and 'end' discrimination) through visual and auditory/visual discrimination tasks.

Unit 5 In this unit, the pairing task (36 trials) between sequential sample and elemental pictures (Fig. 7.2, Unit 5) aims to teach the prerequisites of analysis and sequencing by identifying the component elements of the sample stimulus and the position they occupy in a sequence of pictures (e.g., beginning or end). The picture sequences used are composed of two, three or four elements (geometric pictures and/or pictures/symbols with black outline and white filling), presented side by side. This unit is composed of three teaching steps that are differentiated by the dictated words presented together with the sequential sample: (1) first and last; (2) beginning and end; and (3) before and after. Therefore, the task requires visual discrimination between the elements of the picture sequence under control of the dictated word to select the corresponding picture. The instruction in the first trials will be complete, for example, "Which of the pictures is the first?", and reduced in the following trials (e.g., "first"). Between trials, it is also necessary for the learner to differentiate between the presented sample stimuli (successive discrimination).

Unit 6 In the sixth unit, the identity pairing between pictures with sequential elements is taught (36 trials), using stimuli composed of two, three or four elements (geometric figures and/or pictures/symbols) also used in the previous unit (Fig. 7.2, Unit 6). In this task, simultaneous identity discriminations between the sample and comparison stimuli and successive discriminations between the presented sample stimuli are required, focusing on the sequencing skill. The trials present comparison stimuli with elements different from the sample stimulus or in a different sequence from the sample stimulus. In a set of trials, the incorrect comparison stimuli present at least one element different from the sample stimulus. For example, in the case of a sample stimulus consisting of a heart, a clover and a horseshoe, an incorrect comparison stimulus would be a lock, a clover and a horseshoe. In another set of trials, incorrect comparison stimuli have the same elements as the sample stimulus with a change in the sequence of at least two elements. For example, in the presence of a sample stimulus composed of four elements – a heart, a horseshoe, a clover and a

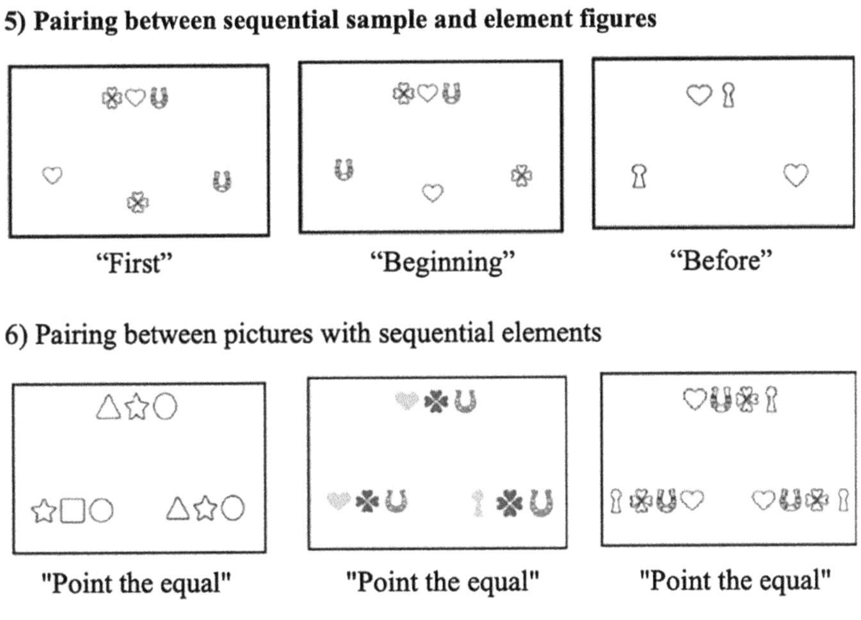

Fig. 7.2 Illustration of a trial of each task performed in Units 5 and 6

lock – a possible configuration of incorrect comparison stimulus would be a lock, a clover, a horseshoe and a heart. This unit will be composed of three teaching steps: (1) identity pairing with two and three blank elements with black outlines; (2) identity pairing with two and three colored elements; and (3) identity pairing with four blank elements with black and colored outlines.

7.4.4 Teaching Units 7 and 8

Units 7 and 8 introduce letters, syllables, and words in tasks that teach visual and auditory discrimination, sequencing, comprehension, and synthesis.

Unit 7 In this two-step unit, letters, syllables and words (three to six elements, with gradual increase in the number of elements over the trials) are used in selection and composition tasks (Fig. 7.3, Unit 7). The selection task is an identity pairing task (28 trials) between textual stimuli (letter, syllables, words with three to six letters) and requires visual discriminations between the elements that compose the textual stimuli and the sequence in which they are presented. The composition task (eight trials) requires copying a word presented as a sample. In this task, the learner must discriminate the visual elements of the sample stimulus (letter, syllables, words) and select, among a set of letters (gradually increasing over the trials), presented below the printed word, in the sequence from left to right, those necessary to compose the word identical to the sample. This task directly teaches the prerequisite of synthesis, composing a textual stimulus from its elements (letters). In both tasks, uppercase and lowercase letters are used in different trials.

Unit 8 The eighth unit focuses on teaching visual and auditory discriminations and comprehension in tasks involving printed words. Two tasks are performed in the single teaching step. In the pairing between dictated/printed word/picture and picture or word (24 trials) the learner is required to select one of the visual comparison stimuli corresponding to the sample stimulus (composed of an auditory stimulus and two visual stimuli – printed word and picture); in one set of trials the printed word will be the correct alternative (Fig. 7.3, Unit 8, a) and in another, the picture will be the correct alternative (Fig. 7.3, Unit 8, b). The second type of task of this unit is the pairing between the dictated word and the printed word (12 trials).

7.4.5 Teaching Units 9 and 10

In the last two teaching units of the Preparatory Module (Fig. 7.4) the focus is on visual and auditory discrimination and letter naming.

Unit 9 In this unit, two types of tasks are performed: (1) discrimination teaching (24 trials) between visual comparison stimuli (letters) corresponding to a sample

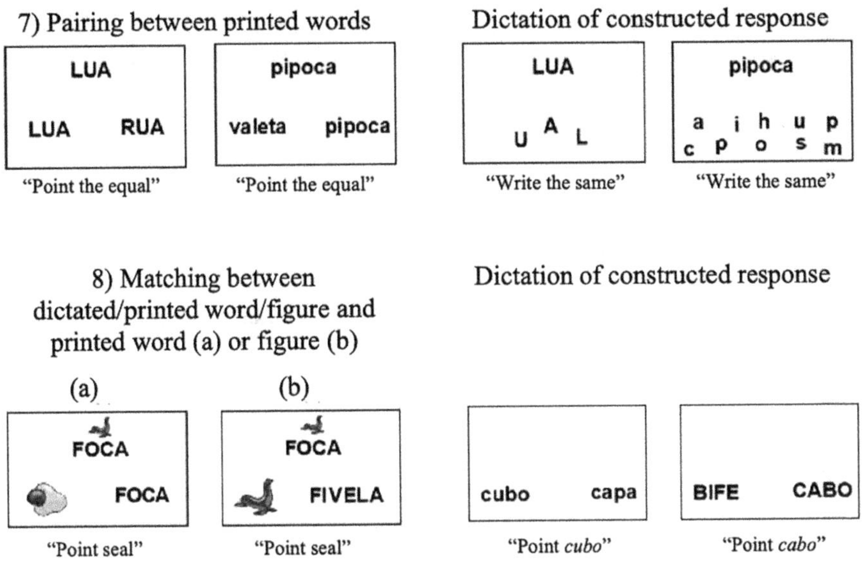

Fig. 7.3 Illustration of a trial of each task performed in Units 7 and 8
Note. The words in Portuguese were maintained in the examples: lua (moom); rua (street); pipoca (popcorn); valeta (ditch); foca (seal); fivela (buckle); cubo (cube); capa (cape); bife (steak); cabo (cable)

stimulus composed of an auditory stimulus (dictated letter) and a visual stimulus (printed letter); and (2) teaching of arbitrary relation between sample stimulus and comparison stimuli with capital and small letters (12 trials), which also involves discrimination between the simultaneously presented visual comparison stimuli. The unit is composed of seven teaching steps, each consisting of three letters of the alphabet.

Unit 10 In this last unit, pairing tasks between dictated and printed letters (24 trials) and letter naming (12 trials) are used to teach auditory and visual discrimination and letter naming, throughout seven teaching steps, using the same seven sets of three letters of the alphabet used in Unit 9.

7.5 Final Considerations

This chapter aimed to analyze the prerequisites for reading and writing performance and describe a proposed teaching module. As indicated by the literature, the prerequisite behaviors for reading and writing are learned gradually, from simpler behaviors and can be improved during formal education. As prerequisite behaviors, we highlight the abilities to differentiate and identify similarities, decompose and recombine visual and auditory stimuli, differentiate and name objects and pictures

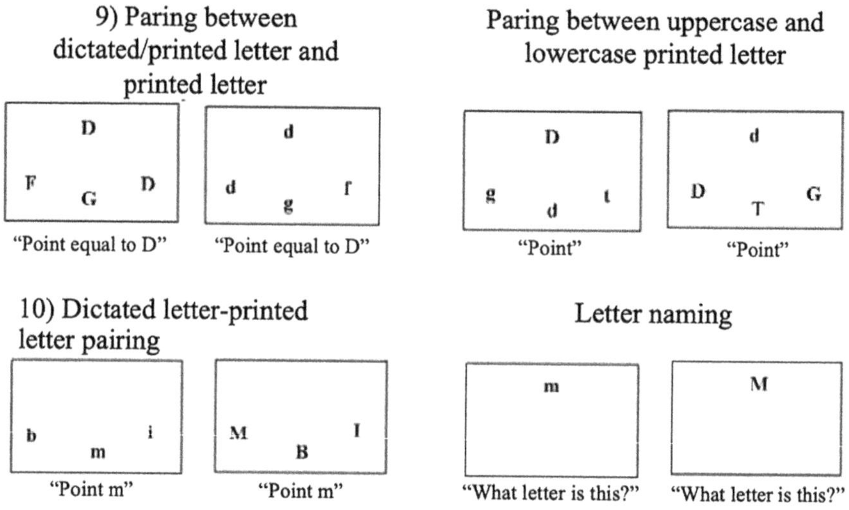

Fig. 7.4 Illustration of a trial of each task performed in Units 9 and 10

and relationships among them (e.g., position, distance), and issue behaviors in sequence. The planning of the Preparatory Module sought to create teaching conditions that gradually advance in demands, starting with simple discrimination tasks, followed by pairing to the generalized identity model, advancing to pairing to the arbitrary sample and pairing to the constructed response sample (Dube, 1996). In addition, the list of behaviors indicated by de Souza et al. (2009b) as verbal relations involved in reading, the immediate prerequisites described by Hanna et al. (1999), the notion of behavioral tree (Neves Filho, 2018; Neves Filho et al., 2019), and the findings of de Freitas (2009, 2012) guided this planning.

The notion of behavioral tree (Neves Filho, 2018; Neves Filho et al., 2019), a conceptual tool for mapping demands, planning teaching, and training prerequisites in order to promote new repertoires, is based on the premise "that by mapping a vast number of behaviors into baseline measures, it becomes possible to use components of these behaviors as pivotal units,[3] or prerequisites to be recombined toward the final target behaviors" (Neves Filho et al., 2019, p. 359). In this sense, the definition of relevant prerequisites for the achievement of final target behaviors in reading and writing should be based on the clear definition of these final behaviors, which is why the Preparatory Module was proposed based on the analysis of the repertoires taught in ALEPP'S Module 1.

In the studies conducted by de Freitas (2009, 2012), a prerequisite teaching program for participants with intellectual disabilities was proposed and implemented prior to the application of an adapted version of ALEPP'S Module 1 (de Freitas, 2009). The results obtained showed that all four participants learned reading and

[3]As described by Neves Filho et al. (2019), pivotal behavior is one that "when learned, allows other similar behaviors to occur without the need for additional specific training" (p. 355).

writing skills from the adapted program, demonstrating that the prerequisite program established the learning of relevant prerequisite behaviors. The studies by de Freitas identified, manipulated and analyzed a series of variables indicated as necessary for reading and writing repertoires, presenting promising results of the effects of teaching conditions of prerequisite behaviors.

Considering the indications in the literature, the proposal of the Preparatory Module aims to contribute to the establishment of an initial repertoire of behaviors prerequisites for teaching reading and writing. As a successive step to planning, the module is under development process in the Computer Individualized Teaching Manager (GEIC). Given the basis of its planning, presented in this chapter, exposure to this module can be expected to have positive effects on the learning of prerequisite behaviors for reading and writing, however, the validation of its effect depends on the development of future research.

References

Adams, M. J. (1990). *Beginning to read: Teaching and learning about print.* MIT Press.

Albuquerque, A. R., & Melo, R. M. (2005). Equivalência de estímulos: Conceito, implicações, implicações e possibilidade de aplicação. In J. Abreu-Rodrigues & M. R. Ribeiro (Orgs.), *Análise do Comportamento: Pesquisa, Teoria e Aplicação* (pp. 245–264). Artmed.

Bernardino Júnior, J. A., Freitas, F. R., de Souza, D. G., Maranhe, E. A., & Bandini, H. H. M. (2006). Aquisição de leitura e escrita como resultado do ensino de habilidades de consciência fonológica. *Revista Brasileira de Educação Especial, 13*(3), 423–450. https://doi.org/10.1590/S1413-65382006000300009

Capovilla, A. G. S., & Capovilla, F. C. (1998). Prova de consciência fonológica: Desenvolvimento de dez habilidades da pré-escola à segunda série. *Temas sobre Desenvolvimento, 7*(37), 14–20.

Capovilla, A. G. S., & Capovilla, F. C. (2000). Efeitos do treino de consciência fonológica em crianças com baixo nível socioeconômico. *Psicologia Reflexão e Critica, 13*, 7–24. https://doi.org/10.1590/S0102-79722000000100003

Cardoso-Martins, C. (1995). Consciência fonológica e alfabetização. *Vozes.*

Castro, D. A. S., & Barrera, S. D. (2019). The contribution of emergent literacy skills for early reading and writing achievement. *Trends in Psychology, 27*, 509–522. https://doi.org/10.9788/TP2019.2-15

de Freitas, M. C. (2009). *Programação de ensino de leitura e escrita para crianças com deficiência mental.* Unpublished master's thesis. Universidade Federal de São Carlos.

de Freitas, M. C. (2012). *Construção de um programa de ensino de pré-requisitos de leitura e escrita para pessoas com deficiência intelectual.* Doctoral dissertation, Universidade Federal de São Carlos. Repositório Institucional UFSCar. https://repositorio. ufscar.br/handle/ufscar/5977?show=full

de Freitas, M. C., & Reis, T. S. (2017). Ensaio sobre desenvolvimento humano e análise do comportamento. *Educere et Educare, 12*(25).

de Rose, J. C. (2005). Análise comportamental da aprendizagem de leitura e escrita. *Revista Brasileira de Análise do Comportamento, 1*(1), 29–50. https://doi.org/10.18542/rebac.v1i1.676

de Rose, J. C., de Souza, D. G., & Hanna, E. S. (1996). Teaching reading and spelling: Exclusion and stimulus equivalence. *Journal of Applied Behavior Analysis, 29*, 451–469. https://doi.org/10.1901/jaba.1996.29-451

de Souza, D. G., de Rose, J. C., Faleiros, T. C., Bortoloti, R., Hanna, E. S., & McIlvane, W. J. (2009a). Teaching generative reading via recombination of minimal textual units: A legacy of verbal

behavior to children in Brasil. *International Journal of Psychology and Psychological Therapy, 9*, 19–44.
de Souza, D. G., de Rose, J. C., & Domeniconi, C. (2009b). Applying relational operants to reading and spelling. In R. A. Rehfeldt & Y. Barnes-Holmes (Eds.), *Derived relational responding: Applications for learners with autism and other developmental disabilities*. New Harbinger Publications.
Dube, W. V. (1996). Teaching discrimination skills to persons with mental retardation. In C. Goyos, M. A. Almeida, & D. G. de Souza (Eds.), *Temas em Educação Especial III* (pp. 73–96). EDUFSCar.
Hanna, E. S., Melo, R. M., & Albuquerque, A. R. (1999). Desenvolvimento infantil e alfabetização. In M. G. T. Paz & A. Tamayo (Eds.), Escola, saúde e trabalho: Estudos psicológicos (pp.71–100). Editora UnB.
Iñesta, E. R. (1972/1980). *Técnicas de modificação do comportamento: Aplicação ao atraso no desenvolvimento* (D. P. P. Soares, Trad.). EPU.
Justino, M. I. S. V., & Barrera, S. D. (2012). Efeitos de uma intervenção na abordagem fônica em alunos com dificuldades de alfabetização. *Psicologia: Teoria e Pesquisa, 28*, 399–407. https://doi.org/10.1590/S0102-37722012000400009
Keller, F. S. (1968/1999). Good-bye, teacher. *Journal of Applied Behavior Analysis, 1*(1), 79–89. https://doi.org/10.1901/jaba.1968.1-79
Leite, S. A. S. (1988). *Alfabetização e fracasso escolar*. Edicon.
Mueller, M. M., Olmi, D. J., & Saunders, K. J. (2000). Recombinative generalization of within-syllabic units in prereading children. *Journal of Applied Behavior Analysis, 33*(4), 515–531. https://doi.org/10.1901/jaba.2000.33-515
Neves Filho, H. B. (2018). *Criatividade: Suas origens e produtos sob uma perspectiva comportamental*. Imagine Publicações.
Neves Filho, H. B., Leite, F. L., Araripe, N. B., & Picanço, C. R. F. (2019). Uma proposta conceitual para o estudo comportamental do desenvolvimento e criatividade individual: A árvore de comportamentos. *Revista Brasileira de Terapia Comportamental Cognitiva, 21*(3), 350–371. https://doi.org/10.31505/rbtcc.v21i3.1341
Pestum, M. S. V. (2005). Consciência fonológica no início da escolarização e o desempenho ulterior em leitura: Estudo correlacional. *Estudos de Psicologia (Natal), 10*(3), 407–412. https://doi.org/10.1590/S1413-294X2005000300009
Reis, T. S., de Souza, D. G., & de Rose, J. C. (2009). Avaliação de um programa par ao ensino de leitura e escrita. *Estudos em Avaliação Educacional, 20*, 452–450. https://doi.org/10.18222/eae204420092038
Roazzi, A., Roazzi, M. M., Justi, C. N. G., & Justi, F. R. R. (2013). A relação entre a habilidade de leitura e consciência fonológica: Um estudo longitudinal em crianças pré-escolares. *Estudos e Pesquisas em Psicologia, 13*(2), 420–446.
Santos, M. J. D., & Barrera, S. D. (2017). Impacto del entreno en habilidades de consciencia fonológica en la escritura de pre-escolares. *Psicologia Escolar e Educacional, 21*(1), 93–102. https://doi.org/10.1590/2175-3539/2017/02111080
Sidman, M. (1971). Reading and auditory-visual equivalences. *Journal of Speech and Hearing Research, 14*, 4–13. https://doi.org/10.1044/jshr.1401.05
Sidman, M. (1977). Teaching some basic prerequisites for reading. In P. Mittler (Ed.), *Research to practice in mental retardation: Education and training* (Vol. 2, pp. 353–360). University Park Press.
Sidman, M. (1990). Equivalence relations: Where do they come from? In D. E. Blackman & H. Lejeune (Eds.), *Behavior analysis in theory and practice: Contributions and controversies* (pp. 93–114). Lawrence Erlbaum Associates.
Sidman, M. (1994). *Equivalence relations and behavior: A research story*. Authours Cooperative, Publishers.
Sidman. (1995). Aprendizagem-sem-erros e sua importância para o ensino do deficiente mental. *Psicologia, 11*(3), 1–15.

Skinner, B. F. (1957). *Verbal behavior*. Appleton Century-Crofts.
Skinner, B. F. (1968/1972). *Tecnologia do ensino* (R. Azzi, Trad.). EPU.
Treiman, R., & Zukowski, A. (1996). Children's sensitivity to syllables, onsets, rimes, and phonemes. *Journal of Experimental Child Psychology, 61*, 193–215. https://doi.org/10.1006/jecp.1996.001

Part III
Studies with Different Populations

Chapter 8
Teaching Reading and Writing to People with Intellectual Disabilities and the ALEPP Teaching Program

Lidia Maria Marson Postalli, Maria Clara de Freitas, and Priscila Benitez

8.1 Introduction

Thirty years ago, a group of Brazilian researchers produced their first paper about a procedure for teaching reading and writing to children with a history of school failure (de Rose et al., 1989). The study aimed to investigate the effectiveness of the exclusion procedure in teaching generalized reading to children who presented failures and difficulties in literacy through the application of the traditional pedagogical curriculum, in the classroom context. Additionally, it aimed to construct a teaching program that would allow the acquisition of reading by children who presented difficulties in learning by conventional teaching methods and also to understand the learning processes involved in the acquisition of reading and writing repertoires. The development of this program provided the basis for structuring a complementary and supplementary alternative curriculum to teach basic reading and writing skills – Learning to Read and Write in Small Steps® (*Aprendendo a Ler e Escrever em Pequenos Passos* [ALEPP]) (de Rose et al., 1989, 1992, 1996; de Souza & de Rose, 2006; de Souza et al., 2009).

L. M. M. Postalli (✉)
Universidade Federal de São Carlos, São Carlos, SP, Brazil
e-mail: lidiapostalli@ufscar.br

M. C. de Freitas
Universidade Estadual de Londrina, Londrina, PR, Brazil

P. Benitez
Universidade Federal do ABC, Santo André, SP, Brazil

A. R. de Albuquerque, R. M. de Melo (eds.), *Contributions of Behavior Analysis to Reading and Writing Comprehension*, https://doi.org/10.1007/978-3-031-40868-7_8

The ALEPP teaching program is based on the stimulus equivalence paradigm (Sidman, 1971, 1994, 2000; Sidman & Tailby, 1982) and the principles of behavior analysis. Currently, ALEPP is composed of three individualized teaching modules, all which are computerized, and the first two available *online* (a detailed description of Modules 2 and 3 is available in Chaps. 4 and 5).

Module 1 aims at teaching regular words with simple consonant-vowel syllables (e.g., "bolo", "tatu", "selo"); Module 2 foresees teaching irregular words with difficulties in the Portuguese language, such as "x", "s" with "z" sound, "ç", "lh", "nh", among others; and Module 3 was developed with the aim of teaching reading comprehension of short texts from storybooks (de Souza & de Rose, 2006; de Souza et al., 2004).

Since then, a series of research studies have been conducted with the ALEPP teaching program replicating the results obtained in the initial studies, expanding the target population and also contributing to the improvement of teaching procedures. One of the populations for whom attempts have been made to apply and adapt the program are people with intellectual disabilities (ID), which will be the focus of this chapter.

This chapter aims to identify, describe and analyze studies that have used the ALEPP teaching modules with people with intellectual disabilities, with greater emphasis on subject and procedure variables that contributed to the learning of reading and writing by this population. The chapter will present, in the first section, data on school inclusion of students targeted for special education, the definition of intellectual disability, and the studies that have employed the ALEPP teaching program with people with intellectual disabilities. The second section will present a discussion of the findings of these studies and the possibilities of teaching reading and writing to children, youth, and adults with ID in various settings. Finally, a synthesis of the main points raised in the chapter will be presented, with recommendations for future development in the area.

8.2 ALEPP and Intellectual Disability (ID)

The investment in studies that seek to develop reading and writing teaching strategies for people with intellectual disabilities is justified mainly to ensure their social inclusion and also by the increase in the number of enrollments of the entire special education target audience (students with disabilities, global developmental disorders, and high abilities/giftedness). According to data from the K-12 Education Census published in 2019, there has been an increase in the number of enrollments in recent years of students targeted by special education: from a total of 930,683 enrollments in 2015, there are 1,250,967 in 2019 (Brasil, 2019). Assessing the quality of permanence and completion of studies is still a gap to be filled by educational indicators with this target audience. Considering the teaching and learning of basic reading and writing skills, the ALEPP teaching program can be a supplementary and complementary teaching alternative for people with ID who present difficulties in acquiring these skills.

According to the Diagnostic and Statistical Manual of Mental Disorders (DSM 5), intellectual disability is fundamentally characterized by functional limitations, both intellectual and adaptive, in the conceptual, social and practical domains, beginning in the developmental period. In intellectual functions, individuals may present limitations in functions such as reasoning, problem solving, planning, abstract thinking, judgment, academic learning, and learning by experience. Deficits in adaptive functions may compromise personal independence and social responsibility, limiting, without continued support, functioning in daily activities, such as communication, social participation, and independent living, and in multiple environments, such as home, school, workplace, and community (APA, 2014).

Taking into account the particularities of people with intellectual disabilities, it is therefore necessary to provide ongoing support and adaptations for any teaching to be successful. This is also true of ALEPP: modifications tend to be made to ALEPP applications depending on the population of interest. With regard to the population of children with ID, for example, some studies have applied the teaching modules directly (e.g., de Rose et al., 1996), others have trained different applicators (e.g., Benitez & Domeniconi, 2016), and others still have made modifications to the teaching procedures themselves (e.g., de Freitas, 2008, 2012). If, on the one hand, these changes are necessary and respect the principle of individualization of teaching, aiming at the success of teaching in each study, on the other hand, they make it difficult to compare learning data between different conditions and studies. Thus, it is necessary to systematize the recurring suggestions for changes and identify the relevant variables in these applications, both to draw conclusions about the applicability of the ALEPP teaching program with this population and to advance knowledge in the area.

To achieve the objective of this work, we searched the works of the research group that developed the ALEPP, identifying those that had as target audience people with intellectual disabilities. Initially, this search prioritized the articles and studies under the guidance of the principal researchers involved in the creation of the reading program and, subsequently, extended to the analysis and reading of the references of these works. National and international articles, book chapters, unpublished theses and dissertations available online were included, and undergraduate research works and monographs were excluded. When theses and dissertations were published in article format, the reading of the article was prioritized.

Table 8.1 describes the results obtained through the literature survey. A total of eight studies were retrieved in the period from 2000 to 2018. The participants varied in terms of age, involving from children, adolescents to adults, with and without comorbidities, enrolled in regular and special schools.

The version of the ALEPP used also varied from the presentation in paper folders, a computerized version in the ProgLeit *software* (Rose Filho et al., 1998), and the most recent online version, which is presented through the Computer Individualized Teaching Manager (*Gerenciador de Ensino Individualizado por computador* [GEIC]) platform (Orlando et al., 2016). Changes to the structure of the

Table 8.1 Overall analysis of studies employing ALEPP with individuals with ID, listed in chronological order

Studies	Participants	Purpose of the study	Version ALEPP	ALEPP Module	Application context/ applicator	Modifications in the Module?	Procedural additions?
Melchiori et al. (2000)	5 students with global developmental delay who attended a special class	Verify the applicability of the program (ALEPP) for different populations	Paper folders	1	Place not indicated/ researcher	Yes	No
Oliveira (2010)	1 DI (16 years old) and 1 DI with down syndrome (9 years old)	Improve the reading and writing skills of two students with ID who attended resource rooms	Software	1 e 2	School (resource room)/ researcher	No	No
De Freitas (2012)	9 children with ID (4 in study 1, 3 in study 2 and 5 in study 3 – but only 2 new	Build a prerequisite module to be used before a special module or module 1	Software		Special school/ researcher	Yes	Yes
De Freitas et al. (2016)	3 children with ID included in regular classrooms	Modify module 1 to create a special module	Software		School (room provided)/ researcher	Yes	Yes
Benitez and Domeniconi (2016)	5 adolescents and adults with ID	To evaluate the application of the supplementary education program (ALEPP) in a home situation, with parents as implementers	Software	1	Home/parents	No	No

Tizo (2016)	20 public school students, including 5 with ID	To evaluate the effects of module 1, applied as part of the activities of a public school to 20 students in the third and fourth grades of elementary school, who presented learning difficulties with the methods proposed by the teachers	Softwar	1 e 2	School/ researcher	Yes	Yes
Silva (2017)	DI (adults)	To evaluate the acquisition of reading and writing repertoires using module 1 of ALEPP with three adults with ID who were attending youth and Adult education	Online	1	School/ researcher	No	No
Menzori et al. (2018)	5 children, 4 with ID (of the 4, 2 had ADHD)	To verify the effect of the implementation of ALEPP in a resource room to children with different diagnoses of special needs	Online	1	School (resource room)/ researcher	No	No

procedure were also made in four studies to accommodate participants' goals and needs, such as adding different teaching tasks, providing extra cues, and adding social or tangible consequences. The applicators were mostly the researchers themselves; in only one study was the application carried out by parents or family members of the students. Below, these studies will be described, discussed, and separated into three thematic categories proposed here, which sought to consider some variables, namely: the ALEPP applicators and the place of application, the age of the participants with ID, and the degree of modification performed in the procedure. The categories were, therefore: (1) application of ALEPP with children with ID in laboratory and school situations, (2) application of ALEPP with young people and adults with ID in residential and school situations, and (3) ALEPP and ID: proposition of a Special Module.

8.3 Application of ALEPP with Children with DI in Laboratory and School Settings

The first study to employ Module 1 of the ALEPP teaching program with children with ID was by Melchiori et al. (2000), and aimed to verify the applicability of the procedure for different populations, including five students enrolled in a special education class, aged 8 to 12 years. The authors did not make explicit whether the room in which the program was applied was laboratory or school. The results showed that the children learned the relations taught and presented emergence of the relations evaluated. It was verified in this study that children enrolled in a special class performed a larger number of teaching sessions to reach the learning criterion in relation to the other participants, which meant 3.9 sessions for each unit for these children, 2.0 for students with a history of school failure, 1.5 for non-literate adults, and 1.1 for preschoolers. In view of the difficulties presented by children enrolled in special class, additional remedial procedures were used, consisting of special steps for teaching the unlearned words.

Oliveira (2010) assessed the effectiveness of Modules 1 and 2 of ALEPP to improve the reading and writing skills of two students with ID who attended elementary school resource rooms. The application was conducted by the researcher who worked as a special education teacher. The student J., with Down syndrome, 9 years and 5 months old, attended the second grade of elementary school. The participant took Module 1 of ALEPP. The student F., with ID, 16 years old, was enrolled in the fifth grade of elementary school. The participant had completed the Module 2 of ALEPP. The results showed that, in general, the ALEPP teaching programs benefited students with ID, in the sense that they presented higher percentages of correct answers in the posttest measures, compared to the pre-test.

The version of the teaching module used in the study by Oliveira (2010) was unchanged and no additional teaching procedures were included. In summary, the author considered ALEPP to be an important pedagogical resource in specialized support services because it allows for individualized intervention; however, she made important recommendations for future applications of the program with this population. For example, Oliveira (2010) indicated the repetition of tasks for skill retention, but with caution, especially if the participant is showing difficulty in the condition proposed by the teaching procedure; the reduction of the teaching session length; the adoption of more flexible reading criteria considering colloquial issues (e.g., reading 'pitu' when presented with the word '*apito*', whistle); the replacement of unfamiliar pictures by familiar ones; the gradual increase in the number of letters available to compose the word in dictation by letter composition; the use of more discriminative subsequent stimuli (consequences) for participants with special needs and a history of exposure to errors. Finally, the researcher also recommended the preparation of a manual to guide the teacher/applicator in the use of the computerized instructional resource.

Still on the use of Module 1 of ALEPP in the resource room context, the study of Menzori et al. (2018) verified the effect of the implementation of Module 1 of ALEPP in a resource room with children targeted for special education, with different diagnoses. Of the five children, aged 7–9 years old, who participated in the study, four had ID and one had an unspecified school developmental disorder. Of the four children with ID, two were also diagnosed with Attention Deficit Hyperactivity Disorder (ADHD). In this study, the authors did not introduce any changes in the program, precisely to verify its applicability to children with different repertoires and diagnoses. Thus, the criteria of accuracy in performance for changing the steps were maintained, as well as formal aspects of the program such as the presentation of stimuli in lowercase letters.

Menzori et al. (2018) observed the effectiveness of the teaching program in the development of reading and writing skills, based on data from the final performance assessments whose percentages were higher in almost all skills compared to the initial assessments. Another relevant result refers to the number of repetitions of teaching steps by participants in the initial steps and the decrease in the amount throughout the exposure to the teaching procedure. The exception was the last steps of Module 1 (in the same version employed by Silva, 2017, with 60 words), which again presented higher levels of repetitions. In this teaching unit, words with the letter z were taught. The authors suggested for future studies the investigation of the type of error made by the participant in word reading, since some participants initially did not read the words; with exposure to the procedure, they started to invert the syllables of the words until they read them in the correct way.

Considering the application of ALEPP in a school context, the thesis of Tizo (2016) assessed the effects of Module 1, applied as part of the activities of a public school to 20 students in the third and fourth grades of elementary school, who presented learning difficulties, according to their teachers. Of these 20 students, seven had clinical diagnoses, five of which had intellectual disabilities. A group design was used in this study, with repeated measures, in which all students underwent the teaching program at different times: while Experimental Group 1 (EG1) was exposed to the intervention, Experimental Group 2 (EG2) was only submitted to the initial assessment and to routine school teaching procedures. As soon as the intervention with EG1 was concluded, assessments were made again with both groups and the intervention with EG2 was initiated. At the end of the intervention with EG2, assessments were repeated with both groups. Thus, it was possible to evaluate the effect of the intervention for each group at different times, and verify the maintenance of the teaching for EG1. The overall application results showed that when the group did not receive reading instruction via ALEPP, remaining only in school, the mean increases were 35% in reading and 28% in dictation, whereas when participating in school along with ALEPP, the reading scores were close to 100% correct and dictation scores were close to 90% correct. These results were maintained in the follow-up measures of the EG1, conducted approximately 5 months after the intervention.

The experimental groups were balanced based on the mean scores of initial performance and, therefore, the performance of children with ID was not examined individually. Although Tizo (2016) also states that participants performed most or all tasks without receiving additional interventions, at some point, all participants in EG1 and six students in EG2 needed at least one of seven types of complementary procedures. The decision to add some type of aid was individual, based on functional analysis of the difficulties presented. Examples of aids include: verbal and non-verbal cues in the tasks of composition copying and selection of pictures corresponding to dictated words (in evaluations); cues, partial feedback, and additional consequences during teaching for motivational reasons, task understanding, and/or fatigue; help using the computer mouse; the creation and preliminary application of a specific instruction aiming to teach discrimination of topographically similar letters (t-f, p-q, d-b, i-j); and the use of the verbal cue "Are you sure?" signaling an error in teaching tasks, which enabled correction.

The author indicated that 19 out of 20 participants completed the ALEPP, except for one who was diagnosed with ID and epilepsy. According to Tizo (2016), the procedure was interrupted because this student showed an absence of prerequisite skills that went beyond those originally measured in the initial assessments, such as listening and understanding instructions, following rules, and remaining seated for 20 minutes. As a conclusion of the study, the Teaching Module was considered effective for different populations, without diagnostic differentiation. Thus, the clinical diagnoses of the research participants did not interfere in the learning process when exposed to Module 1, highlighting that the participants learned to read and write in a similar way to those who did not present clinical diagnoses.

8.4 Application of ALEPP with Young People and Adults with DI in Residential and School Settings

Regarding the domestic use of the ALEPP, Benitez and Domeniconi (2016) investigated the effectiveness of Module 1 applied by parents and family members at the homes of five young people and adults with intellectual disabilities. The results showed that the procedure was successful for learning and increasing the reading repertoire of participants with ID, who showed null or less than 20% correct responses in the pretest and higher percentages of correct responses in reading words directly taught (89.3%) and new words (52%) in the post-test. Regarding the analysis of the behavior of the parents or family members, the study showed evidence that parents applied the teaching tasks with the minimum programmed frequency – a condition considered as fundamental for the learning of the repertoire by their children, but the applications occurred primarily in the presence of the researcher. Another point analyzed referred to the tips given by parents or family members during the application, which were categorized as appropriate (such as praising and repeating the instruction given by the software) and inappropriate (e.g., pointing out errors in the response of students with ID or responding for them) to the teaching process (cf. Benitez & Domeniconi, 2012). The four categories of cues (adequate and inadequate) decreased throughout the student's exposure to Module 1, except for one mother who increased the number of cues between the first and fourth units, in the category 'Praise'. The data were considered as satisfactory confirming the importance of supervision in the residence. The authors discussed that the implementation of teaching practices more similar to those commonly used by formal and informal educators, in their natural settings, could favor their adherence to the procedure, even in the absence of the researcher, ensuring the continuity of task application after the end of the interventions.

The study of Silva (2017) aimed to assess the acquisition of reading and writing repertoires using Module 1 of the ALEPP with three adults with ID who attended Youth and Adult Education (AE). In this research, the teaching version of Module 1 consisting of 5 units (with 60-word teaching) was used. The application occurred through the Computer Individualized Teaching Manager (LECH-GEIC). The participants were aged between 26 and 37 years and had attended AE for more than 2 years. Only one participant attended special education; however, the other participants had previously attended special education. Data collection was conducted by the researcher in a room at the school they students attended, 3 days a week in the afternoon. The sessions were held individually, lasting approximately 20–60 minutes. The criterion for repeating the same teaching step was a maximum of five times. If the participant did not meet the criterion in the fifth repetition, he or she would move on to the next teaching step. This decision was made so as not to expose the student excessively to the same teaching step, and thus create conditions for the student to come into contact with the programmed teaching contingencies, thus preventing the program from becoming aversive for the participant. For one of the participants (P2), it was necessary to explain explicitly that syllables were parts of words and that together they could form the words he was learning in the program and others as well (e.g., the syllable "BO" was a part of "BO-LO", *cake*, but could also be part of "CA-BO", *cable*, or "BO-CA", *mouth*); when presenting pseudowords (e.g., "reveca", "rocabu", or "fuvapa"), the researcher informed the participants that the word did not exist, if they had difficulty reading fluently (joining the syllables and reading the word as a unit).

The results showed that the three adults with ID benefited from Module 1 of instruction, showing gains in reading and writing performance. In general, in the final evaluation, the two participants who completed the five teaching units showed over 80% of correct answers in reading, composition writing, and handwriting; and the third participant, who completed four of the five units and performed better than the other two participants in the initial evaluation, also had high percentages of correct answers in reading and handwritten dictation in the extensive evaluation of the program.

The results of the initial general evaluation showed that participants had prerequisite skills (e.g., identity relations and figure naming) for the acquisition of reading and writing repertoires, which enabled the completion of Module 1 and contributed to the learning of reading and writing simple words. The author pointed out that future studies should use standardized tests as an additional form of evaluation, potentially reinforcing items and topics of interest to the participants. The importance of working in partnership with teachers and parents was also highlighted, aiming to investigate ways for the generalization of this knowledge to different situations and settings and improve the social validity of using the teaching program.

8.5 ALEPP and DI: Proposition of Special Modules

Considering the applicability of teaching procedures based on stimulus equivalence, the study conducted by de Freitas et al. (2016) aimed to investigate the conditions necessary for teaching children with ID using a computer-based program (based on Module 1 of ALEPP) and adapt the conditions to make it compatible with the needs of people with intellectual disabilities. With this, the study evaluated and implemented the adaptations, modifying Module 1 of the ALEPP and building a Special Module.

To ensure that only necessary modifications were implemented while maintaining the essence of the original program, a multiple baseline design was employed across participants with moving criteria. This design required modifications to be inserted into sets of changes, with each set dependent on the results of implementing the previous set. In addition, at each new set of changes, the previous students remained, allowing the comparison of their previous performance, and new students were inserted, who started the procedure already modified.

The first set of modifications was based on the literature review about common facilitators for this population, creating a first modified program (PM1), which was applied to a child with ID (P1), and the analysis of this child's errors and difficulties was the source for a new set of changes to be implemented, resulting in the second modified program (PM2). This program was then applied to P1 and to a new child, P2, whose results were analyzed to compose a third set of modifications. The third program (PM3), resulting from these changes, was then applied to the two previous children, P1 and P2, and to another new child, P3. The final analysis of these sets of changes resulted in the final program, the Special Module.

In summary, PM1 changed only formal aspects of the ALEPP, such as changing pictures, words, sounds, consequences, and the use of capital letters. PM2 introduced more structural changes, such as the overtraining of words already learned (only one new word was inserted per step, and not three, so as to always overtrain two words from previous steps), the choice of words with critical differences between them (Birnie-Selwyn & Guerin, 1997), forcing attention to all letters of words (e.g., sample "cake" and comparisons "cake" and "lake"), and the use of block teaching, i.e., by blocks of model stimuli (Saunders & Spradlin, 1989), strengthening the relationship between model and positive comparison, which consists in initially always presenting the same stimulus class as a sample. For example, we started with a block of trials with the stimulus class "cake", so that all trials of different relations had this sample ("point cake", "write cake", etc.). After reaching the criterion of 100% correct responses with the "cake" block, we moved to a block of "dog", and only after 100% correct responses in the two block words, there was a set of trials of different abilities, but interleaving the samples (e.g., "point dog", "write cake", "point cake", "write dog", etc.). Finally, PM3 kept this structure, only decreasing the number of trials, shortening the procedure.

Results as a whole showed acquisition and maintenance of the trained repertoires, as well as emergence of untrained relations such as those between picture and printed word and vice-versa, word naming, and dictation by compounding both directly taught and new generalization words. At the end of the procedure, step repetition rates reached the minimum level of only one exposure to each teaching step for each child, and training time also reached the rates presented by other populations (e.g., de Rose et al., 1996; Melchiori et al., 2000).

To identify what would be the prerequisite skills for building a preliminary module of the ALEPP teaching program, de Freitas (2012) reviewed the network of relations used in the original version and two categories of relations were identified and selected for direct teaching. In the first category, the same learned relations were taught, but with subdivisions in the taught stimuli. That is, since ALEPP starts by teaching the entire printed word, the identity, copy, recognition and naming of printed stimuli tasks were subdivided in order to present a gradual increase in the composition of the printed stimulus, being letters, syllables and words (e.g., one-letter, two-letter, three-letter and four-letter words). The second category included directly teaching some skills that were not taught directly because they were assumed to be part of the input repertoire of the ALEPP student, such as identity between printed stimuli and between pictures, picture selection and naming (receptive and expressive), and echoic behavior.

To teach these skills, de Freitas (2012) conducted four consecutive studies. The first study examined the possibility of building a prerequisite program based on the strategies employed in the original program and concluded that it was necessary to use different strategies in the teaching trials, different from those commonly employed by ALEPP. In the following two studies, strategies such as fading in[1] the stimuli, observation responses to the model, and a new strategy created by the author called dragging-to-sample,[2] which consisted in clicking on the comparison stimulus and dragging it over the sample to record the response, were added. The choice of the different strategies was based on the pattern of errors of each participant, so that each student received personalized support procedures.

The results (de Freitas, 2012) showed the success of the prerequisite teaching program, especially with the participants in the third study, in which four out of five participants successfully reached the end of the program. The fourth study consisted of applying the ALEPP Special Module to the participants of studies 1, 2 and 3. The results indicated significant gains in the reading and writing skills of participants in Study 4, with results close to 100% of correct responses in the post-test, and maintenance of the baseline of prerequisite skills taught. In addition, two other data stand out: the low number of repetitions per step, only 1.5, as well as the absence of need to implement other support procedures for the Special Module of teaching. The author highlighted that the results together showed that the teaching programs indeed taught the necessary prerequisites for children to successfully perform the reading program (Special Module). More than that, after learning the prerequisites, the students went through the reading program without difficulties, which is itself one of the pillars of behavioral teaching programs: errorless learning (Melo et al., 2014; Sidman, 1985).

8.6 Possibilities of Teaching Reading and Writing to Children, Young People, and Adults with ID in Various Settings: Discussion on Mapped Studies

In general, the studies cited show that the use of Module 1 of ALEPP with people with ID had positive impacts on the teaching and learning process of isolated consonant-vowel words, with participants of different ages (children, adolescents, and adults), with researchers and parents/family members as implementers, and with application in different settings (school, laboratory, and home). However, additional adaptations and teaching procedures were necessary in some cases for this to occur. These modifications involved changes in the form of the stimuli presented (uppercase *versus* lowercase letters, for example), in the structure of the teaching module (with modification of tasks and insertion of hints), and even the creation of a new set of teaching steps, composing a special module (prior to Module 1, as

[1] The fading procedure, or gradual introduction of stimuli, is characterized by the gradual change in one or more physical dimensions (e.g., intensity, size, color) of, at least, one of the discriminative stimuli (Melo et al., 2014).

[2] In the dragging-to-sample procedure the student is asked to drag the comparison stimulus until it is placed over the sample stimulus.

proposed by de Freitas et al., 2016), intended to teach different relations between stimuli, considered as prerequisites, related to reading and writing.

It is essential to emphasize that the changes proposed in the previous studies are positive because they produce the learning of the behaviors of reading and writing, in addition to reducing the number of repetitions for each phase of education. This means that when planning teaching conditions, it is essential to design individualized teaching programs that respect each student's individual learning pace. As highlighted by de Rose (2005; available in Chap. 1 of this book), Behavior Analysis considers that anyone is capable of learning, even those with limitations or disabilities. According to the author, it is up to the professional who is working with the individual to identify the skills and behaviors that the student does not master, and teach these behaviors, constantly evaluating the results of teaching procedures used. The author also highlights that:

> Any failures must be attributed to inadequate procedures and not to the intrinsic characteristics of the student or the environment from which they come. It is possible that the difficulties presented by a particular student are in fact due to the lack of important prerequisites. In this case, instead of waiting for the student to mature, or to reach the appropriate stage of cognitive development, it is important to identify the prerequisites and teach them directly (p. 31).

It should also be considered that the intellectual disability, evaluated by health professionals, should be analyzed with caution, since many times the professional does not explicitly or objectively report the individual's performance. First, cases of comorbidity are very common, in which ID is accompanied or accompanies the presence of another condition that affects the child's development. In the studies exposed here, for example, there were cases of children with ID and Down syndrome, epilepsy, and ADHD. While this is part of the uniqueness of each child and supports the importance of individualizing the procedure, it is an uncontrolled variable that can impact attempts to generalize research data. In addition, an important factor refers to the beginning of the treatment, as well as its intensive workload. The earlier the child starts the intervention, the better the results.

Even when considering only diagnoses of intellectual disability, there are caveats to be made. A person assessed in an intelligence test – in this case the WISC-IV (Weschler, 2013), with an intelligence quotient equal to or below 69 (meaning intellectually disabled) may present a wide behavioral variety, in terms of performance in the teaching tasks proposed in the reading and writing teaching procedures. A student with the same intelligence quotient and diagnosis may remain sitting in a chair and perform identity matching-to-sample tasks, while another may have difficulties performing identity tasks, such as the student with ID and epilepsy who was the exception in the study of Tizo (2016). Despite different initial repertoires, both students will have the same classification "intellectual disability" (Benitez et al., 2015). Therefore, the assessment of the initial repertoire of the skill intended to be taught is essential to outline the starting point, especially in the case of complex repertoires such as reading and writing.

Another aspect considered fundamental in teaching people with ID refers to the planning of teaching conditions that minimize errors, since exposure to errors can cause deleterious effects on the learner's behavior, producing temporary or permanent behavioral arrest, in addition to the collateral emotional effects, such as decreased self-esteem and motivation of the learner (Carmo, 2003, 2012; Matos, 2001; Stoddard et al., 1986). Thus, the student with ID who begins a teaching procedure may have a history of prolonged exposure to the deleterious effects of errors, which may itself become a factor to be considered in the teaching program. It is important to emphasize that, when designing the teaching proposal, professionals should be aware of the goals they want to achieve, i.e., they should establish in detail the behaviors they want to observe in their students' repertoire (Todorov et al., 2009), considering the entry repertoire in a teaching situation (Gioia & Fonai, 2007). Thus, knowing this history and taking it into account when programming strategies is advisable for this population.

Finally, it is necessary to take into account the types of errors made by learners throughout the learning process. The traditional practice of classifying the error as "all or nothing" compromises the identification of all variables involved in the production of the error (Carmo, 2010). In an attempt to operationalize this variable, Carmo (2010) defines error as "a pattern of response that did not reach a certain criterion that allows for the teacher's approval and/or the passage to another learning stage" (p. 214). This understanding opens the perspective so that we can look at errors as data that allows the professional to analyze the contingency that produces it (Carmo, 2003). Thus, the analysis of stimulus control is essential in error situations, because any element or aspect of the stimuli may eventually exert control over the response (and this may vary from one individual to another) (de Rose, 2004). Thus, the functional analysis of response contributes to the identification of possible sources of control, enabling the change of teaching contingencies (Carmo, 2003; de Rose, 2004).

For planning appropriate and functional teaching contingencies as explained by Holland (1960),

> The behavioral engineer who prepares good teaching-machine material must be under the control of the student's responses. When the student has trouble with part of a program, the programmer must correct this. The student's answers reveal ambiguities in items; they reveal gaps in the program and erroneous assumptions as to the student's background. The answers will show when the program is progressing too rapidly, when additional prompts are necessary, or when the programmer should try new techniques. When unexpected errors are made, they indicate deficiencies not in the student but in the program (p. 284).

A concern identified recurrently in the planning of teaching procedures for reading and writing refers to the familiarity of the word, i.e., considerations about the student's preference and interest, through a contextual analysis, to select the words to be taught directly, which may promote favorable conditions for the acquisition of repertoires by the learner (de Freitas, 2008; Gomes, 2008; Millan & Postalli, 2019; Oliveira, 2010). This knowledge, again, comes from the individualization of teaching, from the learner's knowledge, i.e., his or her behavioral repertoire and preferences, to change the contingencies in favor of his or her learning and engagement. Thus, reviews and changes in the words taught (as done by de Freitas et al., 2016), as well as the introduction of procedures to familiarize students with the stimuli, such as those presented by Lima (2009), may be positive. In this study, the author worked with children who performed Module 1 of the ALEPP with parallel activities, for example, by using objects corresponding to the taught words.

Another aspect that should be highlighted for successful learning by people with intellectual disabilities, in addition to the teaching conditions to be programmed for each skill intended to be taught, refers to the collaborative work between professionals, services/institutions, governmental bodies, family, i.e., different agents who work with the person (Schmidt & de Souza, 2008). By proposing a teaching program that involves different agents in the teaching of reading and writing, through ALEPP, the psychologist (for example, as a collaborative consultant) can contribute to the mediation between these segments, with a common teaching objective (Benitez & Domeniconi, 2018).

8.7 Final Considerations

In summary, the premise of this chapter was to generate reflections, albeit embryonic, on the possibility of ensuring the teaching and learning of elementary academic repertoires of reading and writing during the learning process of people with intellectual disabilities of varying ages, involving school (regular and special) and home settings. Thus, the objective of the chapter was to identify and describe studies that employed the ALEPP teaching program with people with intellectual disabilities, aiming at the discussion of variables that favored the learning of reading and writing by this population.

The use of differentiated strategies was identified as a promoter of teaching and learning, such as session breaks (Melchiori et al., 2000), structural changes such as overtraining learned words (de Freitas et al., 2016), inserting one new word at a time (de Freitas et al., 2016), changing the application setting, and having parents as program implementers (Benitez & Domeniconi, 2016), among others.

It should also be noted that, in order to benefit from the computerized learning Module, the participant should present behaviors generally known as "readiness skills" or "basic skills" for learning, such as making eye contact, following instructions, sitting in a chair, waiting, imitating, and handling instruments such as pencils, among others (Gomes & Silveira, 2016; Maurice et al., 1996). In addition to these behaviors, others, considered prerequisites, are equally important, such as identifying and relating one stimulus to another (physical familiarity-identity recognition relationships), figure recognition (identification and naming), letter sequencing (copying), among others. Once these preliminary conditions are guaranteed and the individualization of the procedure is maintained, making changes if necessary, using the ALEPP teaching program with people with ID has shown satisfactory results in learning initial repertoires of reading and writing.

This chapter reviewed studies that applied Module 1 of ALEPP on people with ID and identified adjustments in the original procedure and the performance of additional procedures to adapt the teaching condition and favor student learning.

The results described with such procedures contribute to the planning and conduct of future applications of the ALEPP teaching modules. However, they should not be considered a final solution, since the population with ID presents distinct characteristics, which requires an individualized analysis, an analysis that is, in fact, essential in Applied Behavior Analysis.

Based on the studies presented here, it is recommended that each student with ID, regardless of whether it is a child, young person, or adult, should have their entry repertoire assessed in order to make a decision about how the teaching process will take place. If, from the initial assessment, the student shows certain elementary behaviors such as identity matching using pictures and printed words and copying printed words, we suggest following Module 1 of ALEPP. If the student has flaws in these repertoires, the use of the Special Module similar to that proposed by de Freitas (2016) is suggested. If the difficulties are even more elementary, such as in echoic behavior, identity between simple printed stimuli (single letters), and picture identity, identification, and naming, it seems necessary to implement a prerequisite Module similar to that proposed by de Freitas (2012; for a discussion of reading prerequisites see Chap. 7).

In addition, once the teaching phase has begun, data analysis of each application must be performed daily so that decisions can be made as early as possible regarding possible support procedures or simpler modifications such as the use of sessions with a smaller number of trials, implementation of additional consequences or a change in teaching criteria, for example. Thinking about a personalized and individualized teaching program requires constant analysis of the student's performance, comparing their performance with themselves, so that decision-making can create better teaching opportunities.

In conclusion, the chapter identified subject and procedural variables that contributed to learning reading and writing skills by students with ID. The studies reported in this chapter demonstrated that the ALEPP teaching program can contribute to the acquisition of reading and writing skills by people with intellectual disabilities. It is expected that the analyses presented in the studies may trigger reflections and future inclusive proposals on teaching and learning through teaching conditions that consider the individual learning pace of each student; use the principle of gradual progression to establish complex repertoires; carefully choose the antecedent teaching-learning situations; avoid errors, and continuously assess the learner's performance (Matos, 2001), ensuring appropriate teaching conditions for the target audience with intellectual disabilities.

References

American Psychiatric Association – APA. (2014). *Manual diagnóstico e estatístico de transtornos mentais – texto revisado* (5a. ed., Maria Inês Corrêa Nascimento ... et al., Trad., Aristides Volpato Cordioli ... et al., Technical review). Artes Médicas. (Original work published in 2013).

Benitez, P., & Domeniconi, C. (2012). Verbalizações de familiares durante aprendizagem de leitura e escrita por deficientes intelectuais. *Estudos de Psicologia (Campinas), 29*(4), 553–562. https://doi.org/10.1590/S0103-166X2012000400010

Benitez, P., & Domeniconi, C. (2016). Use of a computerized reading and writing teaching program for families of students with intellectual disabilities. *The Psychological Record, 1*, 01–12. https://doi.org/10.1007/s40732-015-0158-8

Benitez, P., & Domeniconi, C. (2018). Atuação do psicólogo na inclusão escolar de estudantes com autismo e deficiência intelectual. *Psicologia Escolar e Educacional, 22*(1), 163–172. https://doi.org/10.1590/2175-35392018013926

Benitez, P., Gomes, M. L. C., Domeniconi, C., & Schelini, P. W. (2015). Leitura, escrita e capacidades avaliadas pelo WISC-III: Estudo correlacional envolvendo deficientes intelectuais. *Boletim de Psicologia, 565*, 83–96.

Birnie-Selwyn, B., & Guerin, B. (1997). Teaching children to spell: Decreasing consonant cluster errors by eliminating selective stimulus control. *Journal of Applied Behavior Analysis, 30*(1), 69–91. https://doi.org/10.1901/jaba.1997.30-69

Brasil. (2019). *Censo da Educação Básica 2019 – Notas estatísticas*. Brasília: MEC, 2019. Recovered from https://www.gov.br/inep/pt-bron May 12, 2020.

Carmo, J. S. (2003). Dificuldades de aprendizagem ou dificuldades de ensino? Algumas contribuições da análise do comportamento. In M. Z. da S. Brandão, F. C. de S. Conte, F. S. Brandão, Y. K. Ingberman, C. B. de Moura, V. M. da Silva, & S. M. Oliane (Orgs.), *Sobre Comportamento e Cognição* (Vol. 16, pp. 396–401). ESETec.

Carmo, J. S. (2010). Produção de erros no ensino e na aprendizagem: Implicações para a interação professor-aluno. In M. G. N. Mizukami & A. M. M. R. Reali (Orgs.), *Aprendizagem profissional da docência: Saberes, contextos e práticas* (pp. 211–277). EdUFSCar.

Carmo, J. S. (2012). *Aprendizagem: Contribuições da Psicologia*. UAB-UFSCar.

de Freitas, M. C. D. (2008). *Programação de ensino de leitura e escrita para crianças com deficiência mental* Master's thesis, Universidade Federal de São Carlos. Repositório Institucional UFSCar. https://repositorio.ufscar.br/bitstream/handle/ufscar/3036/2190.pdf?sequence=1&isAllowed=y

de Freitas, M. C. D. (2012). *Construção de um programa de ensino de pré-requisitos de leitura e escrita para pessoas com deficiência intelectual* Doctoral dissertation, Universidade Federal de São Carlos. Repositório Institucional UFSCar. https://repositorio.ufscar.br/bitstream/handle/ufscar/5977/4730.pdf?sequence=1&isAllowed=y

de Freitas, M. C., Reis, T. S., de Rose, J. C. C., & de Souza, D. G. (2016). Delineamentos de pesquisa na escola. In S. R. Souza, Haydu, V. B., & C. E. Costa (Orgs.), *Análise do comportamento aplicada ao contexto educacional* (pp. 11–33). EDUEL.

de Rose, J. C. (2004). Além da resposta correta: Controle de estímulo e o raciocínio do aluno. In M. M. Hübner & M. Marinotti (Orgs.), *Análise do comportamento para educação: Contribuições recentes* (pp. 103–113). ESETec.

de Rose, J. C. (2005). Análise comportamental da aprendizagem de leitura e escrita. *Revista Brasileira de Análise do Comportamento, 1*(1), 29–50. https://doi.org/10.18542/rebac.v1i1.676

de Rose, J. C., de Souza, D. S., Rossito, A. L., & de Rose, T. M. S. (1989). Aquisição de leitura após história de fracasso escolar: Equivalência de estímulos e generalização. *Psicologia: Teoria e Pesquisa, 5*, 325–346.

de Rose, J., de Souza, D. G., Rossito, A. L., & de Rose, T. M. S. (1992). Stimulus equivalence and generalization in reading after matching to sample by exclusion. In S. C. Hayes & L. J. Hayes (Eds.), *Understanding verbal relations* (pp. 69–82). Context Press.

de Rose, J. C., de Souza, D. G., & Hanna, E. S. (1996). Teaching reading and spelling: Exclusion and stimulus equivalence. *Journal of Applied Behavior Analysis, 29*(4), 451–469. https://doi.org/10.1901/jaba.1996.29-451

de Souza, D. G., & de Rose, J. C. (2006). Desenvolvendo programas individualizados para o ensino de leitura. *Acta Comportamentalia, 14*(1), 77–98.

de Souza, D. G., de Rose, J. C., Hanna, E. S., Calcagno, S., & Galvão, O. F. (2004). Análise comportamental da aprendizagem de leitura e escrita e a construção de um currículo suplementar. In M. M. C. Hübner & M. Marinotti (Orgs.), *Análise do comportamento para a educação: Contribuições recentes* (pp. 177–203). ESETec.

de Souza, D. G., de Rose, J. C., Faleiros, T. C., Bortoloti, R., Hanna, E. S., & McIlvane, W. J. (2009). Teaching generative reading via recombination of minimal textual units: A legacy of verbal behavior to children in Brazil. *International Journal of Psychology and Psychological Therapy, 9*(1), 19–44.

Gioia, P. S., & Fonai, A. C. V. (2007). A preparação do professor em análise do comportamento. *Psicologia da Educação, 25*, 179–190.

Gomes, C. G. S. (2008). *Desempenhos emergentes e leitura funcional em crianças com transtornos do espectro autístico* Master's thesis, Universidade Federal de São Carlos. Repositório Institucional UFSCar. https://repositorio.ufscar.br/bitstream/handle/ufscar/2975/1674.pdf?sequence=1&isAllowed=y

Gomes, C. G. S., & Silveira, A. D. (2016). *Ensino de habilidades básicas para pessoas com autismo: Manual para intervenção comportamental intensiva* (1ª ed.). Appris.

Holland, J. G. (1960). Teaching machines: An application of principles from the laboratory. *Journal of the Experimental Analysis of Behavior, 3*(4), 275–287. https://doi.org/10.1901/jeab.1960.3-275

Lima, D. C. D. (2009). *Programa de atividades recreativas para aprendizagem de leitura e escrita: contextualização das palavras ensinadas metacontingência.* Master's thesis, Universidade Federal de São Carlos. Repositório Institucional UFSCar. https://repositorio.ufscar.br/bitstream/handle/ufscar/3037/2499.pdf?sequence=1&isAllowed=y

Matos, M. A. (2001). Análise de contingências no aprender e no ensinar. In E. S. Alencar (Ed.), *Novas contribuições da Psicologia aos processos de ensino e aprendizagem* (pp. 143–165).

Maurice, C., Green, G., & Luce, S. C. (1996). *Behavioral intervention for young children with autism: A manual for parents and professionals*. PRO-ED.

Melchiori, L. E., de Souza, D. G., & de Rose, J. C. C. (2000). Reading, equivalence, and recombination of units: A replication with students with different learning histories. *Journal of Applied Behavior Analysis, 33*(1), 97–100. https://doi.org/10.1901/jaba.2000.33-97

Melo, R. M., Hanna, E. S., & Carmo, J. S. (2014). Ensino sem erro e aprendizagem de discriminação. *Temas em Psicologia, 22*(1), 207–222. https://doi.org/10.9788/TP2014.1-16

Menzori, L. R. F., Luchesi, F. M., & Almeida-Verdu, A. C. M. (2018). Ensino informatizado de leitura e escrita em uma sala de recursos. In D. L. O. Vilas Boas, F. Cassas, H. L. Gusso, & P. C. M. Mayer (Orgs.), *Comportamento em Foco 7: Ensino, Comportamento Verbal e Análise Conceitual* (1ª ed., pp. 84–95). ABPMC.

Millan, A. L., & Postalli, L. M. M. (2019). Ensino de habilidades rudimentares de leitura para alunos com autismo. *Revista Brasileira de Educação Especial, 25*(1), 133–154. https://doi.org/10.1590/s1413-65382519000100009

Oliveira, G. P. (2010). *Intervenção pedagógica individualizada para alunos com deficiência intelectual: Ensino de leitura em sala de recursos.* Doctoral dissertation, Universidade Federal de São Carlos. Repositório Institucional UFSCar. https://repositorio. ufscar.br/bitstream/handle/ufscar/2879/3644.pdf?sequence=1

Orlando, A. F., de Souza, D. G., Souza, L. J. S., Pimentel, M. G. C., Teixeira, C. A. C., de Rose, J. C., Golfeto, R. M., Hanna, E. S., & Marques, L. B. (2016). *Manual do usuário. GEIC – Gerenciador de Ensino Individualizado por Computador* [online]. Recuperado de http://geic.ufscar.br/manual/

Rosa Filho, A. B., de Rose, J. C. C., de Souza, D. G., Fonseca, M. L., & Hanna, E. S. (1998). *Aprendendo a ler e escrever em pequenos passos.* Research Software.

Saunders, K. J., & Spradlin, J. E. (1989). Conditional discrimination in mentally retarded adults: The effect of training the component simple discriminations. *Journal of the Experimental Analysis of Behavior, 52*, 1–12. https://doi.org/10.1901/jeab.1989.52-1

Schmidt, A., & de Souza, D. G. (2008). Uma análise de metacontingências na escola inclusiva. In W. C. M. P. Silva (Org.), *Sobre comportamento e cognição* (Vol. 21, pp. 267–281). ESETec.

Sidman, M. (1971). Reading and auditory-visual equivalences. *Journal of Speech and Hearing Research, 14*, 5–13. https://doi.org/10.1044/jshr.1401.05

Sidman, M. (1985). Aprendizagem-sem-erros e sua importância para o ensino do deficiente mental. *Psicologia, 11*(3), 1–15.

Sidman, M. (1994). *Equivalence relations and behavior: A research story*. Authors Cooperative.

Sidman, M. (2000). Equivalence relations and the reinforcement contingency. *Journal of the Experimental Analysis of Behavior, 74*(1), 127–146. https://doi.org/10.1901/jeab.2000.74-127

Sidman, M., & Tailby, W. (1982). Conditional discriminations vs. matching-to sample: An expansion of the testing paradigm. *Journal of the Experimental Analysis of Behavior, 37*(1), 5–22. https://doi.org/10.1901/jeab.1982.37-5

Silva, É. R. M. D. (2017). *Ensino de leitura e de escrita a adultos com deficiência intelectual matriculados na Educação de Jovens e Adultos*. Master's thesis, Universidade Federal de São Carlos. Repositório Institucional UFSCar. https://repositorio.ufscar.br/bitstream/handle/ufscar/9700/SILVA_%c3%89rika_2018. pdf?sequence=5&isAllowed=y

Stoddard, L. T., de Rose, J. C., & McIlvane, W. J. (1986). Observações curiosas acerca do desempenho deficiente após a ocorrência de erros. *Psicologia, 12*(1), 1–18.

Tizo, M. (2016). *Avaliando tecnologia de ensino de leitura e escrita informatizada e adaptada para alunos de escola pública com dificuldade de aprendizagem*. Doctoral dissertation, Universidade de Brasília]. Repositório Institucional UnB. https://repositorio.unb.br/bitstream/10482/21618/1/2016_MarcileydeTizo.pdf

Todorov, J. C., Moreira, M. B., & Martone, R. C. (2009). Sistema personalizado de ensino, educação à distância e aprendizagem centrada no aluno. *Psicologia Teoria e Pesquisa, 25*(3), 289–296. https://doi.org/10.1590/S0102-37722009000300002

Wechsler, D. (2013). *Escala Weschsler de inteligência para crianças: Manual Técnico* (4a. ed.) – (WISC-IV). Translation of the original manual Maria de Lourdes Duprat. Casa do Psicólogo.

Chapter 9
People with Hearing Loss: Effects of Reading Instruction on Vocal Verbal Repertoire

Ana Claudia Moreira Almeida-Verdu, Fernando Del Mando Lucchesi, and Leandra Tabanez Nascimento Silva

9.1 Introduction

This chapter is divided into sections. Considering the applicability of the paradigm of equivalence relations in the development of teaching technology of verbal repertoires to different populations, specifically the hearing impaired, the second section aims to present a brief review of studies on the usual difficulties of the population with hearing loss (HL) and cochlear implant (CI) in relation to different modalities of verbal repertoires (receptive and expressive) considering the multidisciplinary literature (Speech Therapy, Psychology, Otorhinolaryngology, and Education). It also describes the characteristics of some teaching programs observed in the literature.

The third section describes the characteristics that intervention studies should have in order to incorporate evidence-based practice criteria. Additionally, it will present the recommendation by Byiers et al. (2012) in an article published in the American Speech and Hearing Association (ASHA) that single-subject designs that incorporate evidence-based practice criteria can be adopted more frequently in communication research.

The fourth section will briefly resume the paradigm of equivalence relations and will present Equivalence Based Instruction (EBI) as a methodological proposal for

---

A. C. M. Almeida-Verdu (✉)
Universidade Estadual Paulista Júlio de Mesquita Filho, Bauru, SP, Brazil
e-mail: ana.verdu@unesp.br

F. D. M. Lucchesi
Universidade Paulista, Bauru, SP, Brazil

L. T. N. Silva
Hospital de Reabilitação de Anomalias Craniofaciais, Bauru, SP, Brazil

A. R. de Albuquerque, R. M. de Melo (eds.), *Contributions of Behavior Analysis to Reading and Writing Comprehension*, https://doi.org/10.1007/978-3-031-40868-7_9

teaching different contents and, in this case, reading and other receptive and expressive verbal repertoires in hearing-impaired children.

The last section will report the results of research conducted within the scope of the National Institute of Science and Technology, Studies on Behavior, Cognition and Teaching (*Instituto Nacional de Ciência e Tecnologia, Estudos sobre Comportamento, Cognição e Ensino* [INCT-ECCE]), in the interaction between different universities (UFSCar, UNESP, and USP), which adopt Equivalence-Based Instruction and single-subject design as a technological alternative to circumvent the needs of developing verbal repertoires in hearing-impaired children who received cochlear implantation, especially expressive repertoires and speech accuracy.

9.2 Teaching Programs and the Communication Needs of People with Hearing Loss and Cochlear Implants: A Brief Review

Cochlear implants are the most recommended electronic devices for people with sensorineural, bilateral, severe-profound hearing loss. With the use of this device, and the earlier it is received, the better the chance hearing impaired children have to access spoken language and learn to speak (Geers et al., 2007; Levine et al., 2016; Svirsky, 2017). In the scope of learning linguistic repertoires, this can occur by incidental and naturalistic means or by systematic teaching. Considering that the cochlear implant device enables sound detection, but learning more complex listening skills, such as listening with comprehension and the extensions to accurate and intelligible speech, require learning to use the device, the interest lies on the optimization of cochlear implant use under naturalistic conditions and the benefits of systematic teaching in the development of verbal repertoires.

9.2.1 Literature Review

In a recent literature search in December 2018 in the PubMed database and for the purpose of this chapter, the following terms and Boolean markers were entered into the search field: speech production AND, cochlear implant AND teaching. Sixty-four articles returned; the first five occurrences were analyzed and added to the three best matches suggested by the database. All eight studies reported only research on speech skills assessment. In general, studies on listening with speech understanding and production in children with hearing loss and cochlear implantation still assess the effects of cochlear implantation on auditory recognition and speech performance and its components (Coelho et al., 2017; Cupples et al., 2018; Sarant et al., 2018; Spencer et al., 2018). In most publications, therefore, the independent variable is still device use, as also pointed out by previous literature reviews (Lucchesi & Almeida-Verdu, 2017; Neves et al., 2015).

Specifically regarding the evaluation of speech production in the population of children with pre-lingual hearing impairment (established before speech) and implants, the main difficulties are found in the expansion and maintenance of expressive vocabulary (Convertino et al., 2014; Lund, 2016), but also especially in the accuracy of the topography of oral production, with imprecision in the point-to-point correspondence of the emitted responses with those conventionalized in the verbal community (Beadle et al., 2005; Ertmer & Gofman, 2011; Uziel et al., 2007), significantly affecting the understanding of the population's speech within the community and, therefore, their social insertion. In this aspect, which will be explored in more detail in the last section of the chapter, research on the relationships between different types of tasks, which involve oral production and other language repertoires, point out that the already literate population shows higher speech accuracy in word reading activities than in picture naming tasks (Anastácio-Pessan et al., 2015; Golfeto & de Souza, 2015; Lucchesi et al., 2015).

Considering reading, that is, vocalizing in the presence of printed stimuli, as a verbal skill, in the same way, when searching for the terms reading AND cochlear implant AND teaching in PubMed, 51 results were obtained, of which the first five occurrences added to the best matches suggested by the database were analyzed. Again, all reported evaluation studies. The studies adopted the cohort method to analyze variables such as the effects of exposure to a second language (Beeres-Scheenstra et al., 2017), the relationship between the development of skills such as phonological awareness, cognitive skills, reading and working memory on literacy and spelling (Wass et al., 2018), effects of age and visual/manual speech cues on literacy (Colin et al., 2017), and which skills are predictors of reading (Harris et al., 2017). Cohort studies typically select participants of different ages and under different conditions and analyze the effects of one variable or take measures of the skills of interest. In the studies analyzed, measures of different experiences such as therapy, family stimulation, and schooling were made from standardized tests of cognitive and reading skills. Strong correlations were identified between present conditions, such as certain types of experiences (therapy, schooling), even if incidental, and the best development of cognitive and reading skills.

The literature reports that students with hearing loss usually demonstrate problems with literacy and reading comprehension, but more recently, this problem has been partially solved by using cochlear implants and improvement in spoken language (Colin et al., 2017; Gallego et al., 2016). Recent studies have verified reading comprehension in participants with hearing impairment and cochlear implantation and verified some variables that can influence it, such as early implantation (before 24 months) or late implantation (after 24 months). The results of Gallego et al. (2016) showed that children implanted early did not show statistically significant differences with their hearing peers in sentence reading comprehension tasks, in tasks such as completing sentences whose last word had been omitted or choosing a word among others with syntactic or semantic challenge. This finding is confirmed by other studies assessing skills (morphosyntactic awareness) and acquisition of other languages such as French during schooling (Beeres-Scheenstra et al., 2017) or Spanish (Lópes-Higes et al., 2015).

The effects of cochlear implantation on hearing and speech production are well known; however, there are still few studies on interventions verifying which variables in procedures are relevant to optimize use of the device compared to incidental teaching. In addition, there are still few studies whose independent variable is the teaching procedure and its effects on the dependent variables of speaker and listener, and locating them may depend on indexers, descriptors adopted and database.

In addition to the PubMed survey, a search on the CAPES Periodicals database was conducted with the same descriptor terms and Boolean markers adopted in the previous search, namely, speech production AND cochlear implant AND teaching. This search resulted in only 16 hits. However, six were interventions (Alves et al., 2016; Connor et al., 2000; Lucchesi et al., 2015; Neves et al., 2018; Pascoe et al., 2013; Rique et al., 2017b).

On the other hand, a search in the CAPES Journals website with the terms reading AND cochlear implant AND teaching returned 554 items from peer-reviewed journals. Inspection of the first 10 items revealed six teaching studies (Anastácio-Pessan et al., 2015; Lucchesi et al., 2015, 2018; Neves et al., 2018; Reichmuth et al., 2013; Smith & Wang, 2010) and four evaluation studies (Desjardin et al., 2011; Moshtaghi et al., 2017; Pascoe et al., 2013; Spencer & Tomblin, 2009). Of the six teaching studies, four were conducted in the scope of the INCT-ECCE (Anastácio-Pessan et al., 2015; Lucchesi et al., 2015, 2018; Neves et al., 2018) and associated universities such as UFSCar, Unesp, and USP, which establish interaction between Speech Therapy and Behavior Analysis in the study of verbal rehabilitation in children with cochlear implants. Intervention studies are still scarce, but are beginning to appear.

This brief result found in the search made in the CAPES Periodicals is consistent with a recent literature review (Lucchesi & Almeida-Verdu, 2017) that located and analyzed 156 articles. Of the 24 productions selected according to the proposal criteria, only 10 were experimental studies, pointing out the need to invest in teaching procedures.

9.2.2 Programs for Teaching Communicative Repertoires in People with Hearing Loss

Although the database search returned few studies on teaching the hearing impaired with cochlear implants, there is a well-established experience of intervention programs in children's language development after cochlear implantation (Moog & Stein, 2008). The main target of Moog and Stein's program is communication through spoken language. From neonatal screening and early diagnosis of hearing impairment, the Moog Center for Deaf Education, with units located in several states of the United States of America, has a curriculum focused on the care of children up to 3 years of age and their families. Some features that denote the quality of the program offered include: communicating effectively through speech and developing age-appropriate reading; supporting hearing behavior through accurate device fitting; classrooms must provide quiet listening in small classes; teachers are trained in techniques to develop spoken language in hearing-impaired children; parents are considered critical support for spoken language success and therefore programs are also family-centered in addition to the child; programs focus on training children for successful participation.

The programs of the Moog Center (Moog & Stein, 2008) have as components the development of listening skills, speaking skills, and language skills aimed at clear and precise communication, organized in a continuum of lessons for conversation, directed by teachers, and may involve different degrees of repetition, i.e., are systematized. A daily schedule of activities involves syntax, vocabulary, auditory training, conversational speaking and pre-academic skills, all interspersed. Moog and Stein report that the teaching techniques that have provided effective acceleration of spoken language in children with hearing loss (HL) are, in addition to a focus on teaching auditory skills, modeling and imitation; the child refines their speech, increasingly more precisely and by successive approximations (modeling) from the duplication of a model provided by the teacher (imitation).

Considering specifically the studies on reading assessment, the recognition of printed words, phonological awareness, language and speech production and perception of children with HL and CI and with normal hearing have been assessed skills as in the study by Ambrose et al. (2012). The performance of the groups had no statistically significant difference for recognition of printed material. This study shows that children with CI have the potential to develop age-appropriate reading skills; however, they are steps behind their hearing peers in phonological awareness.

Other studies of Speech Therapy and Special Education, however, point out that the difficulty in learning to read is frequent among implanted patients (Connor & Zwolan, 2004; Marschark et al., 2007), mainly associated with variables directly or indirectly related to sound deprivation, and that the consequences of this initial difficulty may endure even after several years of implant use (Casserly & Pisoni, 2013; Geers & Hayes, 2011).

Regarding the intervention studies recently found in the literature, few articles describe curricula/methods/teaching programs whose main – or even intermediate – objective is reading. According to Tucci et al. (2014) and to our observations from the search conducted in the present chapter, the methods for teaching reading to individuals with HL described in the scientific literature are still scarce, and the most prominent approaches can be divided into: (a) *Cued Speech* – In which the relationship between graphemes and phonemes is taught through speech with specific gestural cues; (b) *Visual Phonics* – a sign language, but different from ASL (American Sign Language); (c) *Speech Reading* – A combination of visual cues through lip-reading; (d) *Finger Spelling* – Teaching grapheme-phoneme relationships through digital alphabet, however with variations between digital alphabet and more complex signs; (e) *Iconic/Semantic Representation* – Teaching through relationships between figures, letters, and words; (f) *Morpheme* – Teaching word formation and effects on reading and generalization of the same with potential to generate new words.

This diversity of approaches, if synthesized, demonstrates the importance of the establishment of the grapheme/phoneme relationship strengthened by different types of cues (e.g., visual cues from different topographies such as sign language, orofacial reading, digital alphabet), by establishing semantic representations, and by the generative power for new words.

Among the studies that can be cited that use some of these methods, the research of Smith and Wang (2010) and Lund and Schuele (2014) stand out. Smith and Wang evaluated the teaching of reading using the *Visual Phonics* program and also a curriculum to establish phonological awareness through textual, auditory, and picture stimuli. Lund and Schuele exposed five preschool children and cochlear implant users to reading training aimed at expanding vocabulary by means of the relationship between pictures and words. These studies and methods clearly show the importance of teaching discriminative relations between visual stimuli (text or pictures) and auditory stimuli (word segment or whole word) in learning reading and writing repertoires. Still, there are few studies in which the independent variable is the teaching procedure and the dependent variable is its effects on speaking and listening skills.

In the specific case of the studies produced by a group of researchers linked to the National Institute of Science and Technology on Behavior, Cognition and Learning, in a partnership that brings together professionals from the Hospital for Rehabilitation of Craniofacial Anomalies, procedures similar to those adopted by Smith and Wang (2010) and Lund and Schuele (2014) in discriminative training between different auditory (words or segments as dictated syllables) and visual (pictures and words or segments as written syllables) stimuli were adopted and it was observed that poor speech accuracy in picture naming observed before teaching, was improved after making well-established reading skills as a prerequisite for the teaching curriculum (Almeida-Verdu, & Gomes, 2016; Anastácio-Pessan et al., 2015; Lucchesi et al., 2015, 2018; Rique et al., 2017a). More specifically, from elementary repertoires of relating textual stimuli (visual) and their sound stimuli (auditory) and teaching the relationship between these and the figures, there was improvement in speech accuracy in figure naming.

These results, together with those of international research, not only present a path to be followed in the investigation of better conditions for teaching verbal repertoires to hearing-impaired individuals, but also expand the set of data demonstrating the importance of systematic interventions, as opposed to naturalistic teaching, in the development of verbal skills (Lund, 2016). In the study developed by Lund and Schuele (2014), for example, auditory discrimination training alone, i.e., receptive repertoires, was not enough to ensure the emergence of expressive behaviors and, in the research by Lund and Douglas (2016), a group of participants learned about ten times more words per week after intervention with systematic training by multiple exemplars, when compared to the group exposed to naturalistic teaching of receptive behaviors. These results represent relevant dimensions to be considered in future studies on the establishment of receptive and expressive repertoires in people with hearing loss and cochlear implants.

9.3 Criteria for Evidence-Based Practice and Single Subject Design in Communication Research

Considering the possibilities of auditory-visual training and its extensions to the receptive and expressive repertoires, there is a general lack of teaching programs in the literature, whether computer-based or not, but which adopt scientific rigor that enables evidence-based clinical and educational use (Melo et al., 2015; Nanjundaswamy et al., 2018).

In the search for practices based on scientific evidence, many criteria have been developed to identify the best interventions (with indicators of effectiveness, efficacy, and generalizability) at the clinical or educational level. In the international scenario, Sweetow and Palmer (2005) carried out a systematic review with the objective of identifying the effectiveness of Computer Based Auditory Training Programs (CBATP's), in adults. Of the 42 articles identified, only six met strict scientific criteria with the use of the randomized clinical trial (RCT). The RCT is a scientific methodology with many participants randomly assigned to an experimental group or a control group and with statistical analysis of the data. Among the studies analyzed, many did not use a control group, the number of participants was small or the results did not present relevant statistical significance. The authors suggest that well-defined criteria should be adopted when conducting studies so that they meet the requirements of an evidence-based approach.

A more recent study conducted by Nanjundaswamy et al. (2018) aimed to examine the effectiveness of CBATP's according to scientific criteria. The review identified, in Google Scholar and PubMed search databases, 124 articles related to intervention studies in children with hearing impairment and who received some hearing aid device, either with the use of a Sound Amplification Device (ISAD) or cochlear implant (CI). After applying the inclusion criteria (participants with hearing loss with ISAD or CI, younger than 18 years old, comparison of CBATP's group to regular therapy, having at least one more measure related to expressive language, and experimental design), only five articles remained. However, only one study (Glyde et al., 2014) adopted more than one expressive language outcome measure. The results of this national and international literature review demonstrate a lack of research on computer-based auditory training and expressive language measures in people with hearing impairment and CI designed to incorporate the body of evidence in clinical and educational practice.

Considering experimental control, although randomized clinical trials have many advantages in understanding the relationship between the variables of a study, Kazdin (1982) argued that the single-subject experimental design may contribute to understanding the strength of an intervention and may be an alternative to designs with larger groups. The American Speech-Language-Hearing Association (ASHA, 2005) has incorporated evidence-based practice within its clinical practice and presented the potential strength of single subject experimental design in demonstrating the internal validity of an intervention (Byiers et al., 2012). This is a design frequently adopted by Experimental Behavior Analysis, a discipline that intersects with Audiology and Speech-Language Pathology in the study of language. In the single-subject design, the exposure of participants to independent variables (teaching conditions, procedures, stimulus sets, environments) is controlled and occurs in a stepwise manner, and systematic measurements of the dependent variable are made across participants, across procedures, and across stimulus sets (Byiers et al., 2012; Schimidt, 2009). Thus, the exposure to the independent variable occurs for all participants and each participant is always compared to themselves.

In addition, the replication of an outcome is one of the highly recommended objectives in the scientific methodology literature (Byiers et al., 2012; Munafò et al., 2017; Tawney & Gast, 1984). For interventions to be adopted according to evidence-based practice criteria, at least five (direct or systematic) replications with at least 20 participants, and conducted by three different research groups should be conducted (Byiers et al., 2012), i.e., it is through the (direct or systematic) repetition of experiments, with controlled manipulation of parameters, that the feasibility of a procedure or technique to be adopted on a larger scale is affirmed. This chapter is based on the premise that language and verbal behavior teaching programs can incorporate the criteria of scientific evidence.

9.4 Equivalence Based Instruction (EBI) as a Methodological Proposal for Teaching Verbal Repertoires

According to behavior analysis, expressive and receptive language are behaviors and can be understood and described as operants, selected and maintained by reinforcement contingencies. The operant affects the environment and is modified by it, however, the environment that the verbal behavior affects is the behavior of another person (the listener). It is the listener's behavior that provides consequences that select and maintain someone else's behavior (the speaker). Speaker and listener, with their behaviors, provide discriminative and reinforcing stimuli for each other (Skinner, 1957). Thus, verbal behavior is not merely vocal, but includes any topography that results in a verbal function (Skinner, 1957; Greer & Ross, 2008).

Elementary verbal operants can be divided into six categories, namely, tact, mand, echoic, intraverbal, transcription (copy and dictation), and textual (Skinner, 1957). These operants occur in a context composed of objects, words (spoken, written, heard), other people's behaviors and consequences mediated by the listener's behavior. Except for the mand, whose reinforcement is the object specified in the speaker's behavior, all other verbal operants are maintained by generalized reinforcement (Skinner, 1957).

The analysis and description of relations between verbal performance and environment is particularly important in programming teaching conditions for this repertoire, because the same verbal topography may have different functions depending on the stimulus control involved. The verbal behaviors of interest in this chapter are tact and transcription (copying and dictation). According to the categories of verbal behavior proposed by Skinner (1957), saying "ball" may describe a (1) *tact*, if the antecedent stimulus is the toy itself; and it may be a (2) *transcription*, handwritten or by composition, from the selection of letters, in a situation of (a) *dictation* if the antecedent is the dictated word, or (b) *copying* if the antecedent is a written word. Success in teaching verbal operants will depend on the accurate analysis of these behaviors and the arrangement of coherent teaching contingencies.

The more someone's speech corresponds point-to-point to the conventions of a verbal community, the greater the understanding of that person's verbal behavior and the more it will affect other people's behavior (Barreto & Ortiz, 2008; Ertmer, 2010). It is in this scenario that teaching procedures that establish elementary verbal repertoires with punctual accuracy (between what is heard, what is said and what is printed) has scientific and social relevance. This analysis also includes another topography of verbal behavior, such as motor-gestural, for example, although it is not the target of this study.

9.4.1 Equivalence Relations Paradigm

An especially important question in learning verbal behavior is how people learn to behave similarly in the presence of a spoken word, a written word, and the object itself, since these are very different stimuli. Equivalence is observed between objects and their names and there is an extensive and systematic body of studies on how equivalence relations can be obtained as a function of a history of reinforcement of relations between stimuli and between stimuli and responses (Sidman, 2000). The stimuli that precede and control the verbal behavior of tact (picture or object) and transcription (dictated word or textual stimulus) can be related by equivalence (as described in Chap. 1) and we know exactly how to behave in the presence of each of them; when faced with the written word "water" or a picture of a drinking fountain, we do not try to drink them, but we know that they are related to the real event as a result of a history of stimulus pairing.

In Brazil, many systematized and computerized programs based on the equivalence paradigm and incorporating scientific evidence criteria have been developed by researchers of the Experimental Analysis of Behavior. Such programs aim to establish different types of verbal repertoires, especially reading and writing, as well as other conceptual repertoires such as mathematics, such as: Learning to Read and Write in Small Steps® (*Aprendendo a Ler e Escrever em Pequenos Passos* [ALEPP]; Capobianco et al., 2009), Computerized System for Teaching Conceptual Behaviors (*Sistema Computadorizado de Ensino de Comportamentos Conceituais* [PROLER]; Assis & Santos, 2010), System for Research on Equivalence and Smaller Verbal Units using data structures for text and image – EQUIV (Pimentel, 1996), Master Computational Educational Program (Mestre®; Goyos & Almeida, 1994), Programmed Contingency 2.0 (*Contingência Programada*; Hanna et al., 2014). The purpose of most of these programs is to teach relations between stimuli and between stimuli and responses by addressing flaws in control between stimuli (e.g., between the printed word and its minimal textual units and pictures) and between stimuli and vocal responses (e.g., reading is called reading when controlled by the printed word and its minimal textual units, and naming is called naming when controlled by an image).

The study on symbolic functioning has been driven by the paradigm of equivalence relations first described by Sidman (1971, 1994, 2000). Derived relations (equivalence and other) and transfer/transformation of stimulus functions can operationally describe symbolic behavior, i.e., how we relate dissimilar stimuli (e.g., an apple pie, the picture of a pie, the set of representative graphemes that form the written word, and the set of related phonemes that make up the dictated word) and come to react to them in the same way (Cricthfield et al., 2018). Equivalence relations are the basis of many communicative and language processes.

The basic procedure involves, at least, teaching two conditional discriminations with one element in common and testing new relations between stimuli that were presented in training but were not related to each other. For example, the conditional discriminations between the dictated word and the written word ("soap" and SOAP) and between the dictated word and a figure ("soap" and the figure of a bar of soap); the dictated word is the common element. After learning these relations with a set of auditory, textual and pictorial stimuli (soap, shuttlecock, horse, hanger, etc.), we test new relations, such as between the pictorial and the printed word and vice versa, with the same set of stimuli. According to the equivalence relations paradigm, this property – the emergence of a new relation – is evidence of symbolic function. Children with hearing impairment and good symbolic functioning demonstrate comprehension of the written word SOAP not only if they can decode it and vocally produce the corresponding sounds, but also if they can identify which event (pictorial or real) it is related to.

Another relevant skill in reading, besides comprehension, is fluency, that is, decoding any words within the alphabetic system. For this it is necessary to segment the word into smaller units (syllables and letters) and recombine them in a generalized manner. As an example, after learning to read the words as **b**at and **c**all, also to read the words **c**at and **b**all, among others, composed of the same syllables as the trained words, but in a different order, should also be read. There are several procedures for teaching this skill, which we call recombinative generalization, but describing them is not the goal of this chapter. The network of relations between stimuli, stimuli and responses and their minimal units can be seen in Fig. 9.1.

The point to be highlighted here is that Stromer et al. (1992) proposed that technology derived from the stimulus equivalence paradigm could be used as supplementary instruction to literacy activities and be useful when traditional instruction fails. Currently, the term proposed to this technology is Equivalence-Based Instruction (EBI), which has been adopted by different researchers (Albright et al., 2016; Pytte & Fienup, 2012; Fields et al., 2009; Fienup et al., 2010) and for teaching different contents such as statistics for university students and neurology concepts, among others.

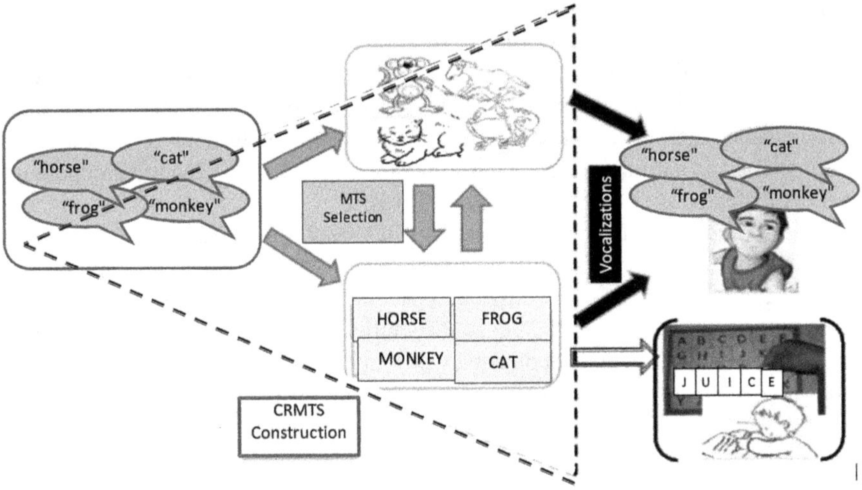

Note. Arrows in gray represent relations involving stimulus selection; in white, relations involving response construction (either ordered or handwritten selection); in black, discriminative operants of picture naming and word reading.

Fig. 9.1 Diagram representing the conditional relationships between stimuli and between stimuli and responses that can be assessed and taught by ALEPP. (*Note*. Arrows in gray represent relations involving stimulus selection; in white, relations involving response construction (either ordered or handwritten selection); in black, discriminative operants of picture naming and word reading)

9.4.2 Equivalence-Based Learning and Teaching Technologies

An Equivalence-Based Instruction (EBI) procedure involves teaching different conditional relations between stimuli and stimuli and responses, with one element in common; from which new relations emerge between stimuli and between stimuli and responses that were not directly taught. In the specific case of hearing-impaired individuals with cochlear implants, from well-established oral reading (vocalizing in the presence of the printed word), the effects caused by the printed word on vocalization are extended to pictures after EBI, improving speech accuracy in naming tasks (vocalizing in the presence of pictures). An EBI can involve different response topographies (selection, construction, and vocalization) and different procedures (Matching-to-Sample – MTS; Constructed Response Matching-to-Sample–CRMTS; Operant Discrimination Training) (Calcagno et al., 1994; Dube, 1996; Dube et al., 1991; Sidman, 1994; Stromer et al., 1992).

ALEPP is a teaching program based on the paradigm of equivalence relations, and falls within the concept of EBI, i.e., its basis is in establishing relations between stimuli that are not physically similar by teaching conditional discriminations (Rexroad, 1926) and that have a node in common (Fig. 9.1). If responses established for a stimulus are established for all other stimuli, demonstrating that they are interchangeable and related to each other, they are said to attest to true symbolic functioning (Sidman & Tailby, 1982). Additional tests can be conducted to verify that visual stimuli can be named (tact or textural emission) according to the relations between stimuli established in teaching, which would place naming responses in equivalence classes (Sidman, 2000). Positive results on tests of conditional discriminations and naming of additional stimuli are evidence of semantic productivity of equivalence-based programs (Mackay, 2013).

ALEPP has three Portuguese language teaching modules, where Module 1 (described in detail in de Souza et al., 2009) aims to teach elementary reading and writing repertoires of simple words composed of consonant+vowel syllables, i.e., with regularities and without language difficulties (e.g., coat hanger, horse, teapot, candle) and their relations with dictated words and pictures. Module 2 (described in detail in Chap. 4 of this book) targets reading and writing words with difficulties (e.g., ç, nh, ch, lh, vLc, vRc) and does not adopt pictures, but a more refined training of auditory-visual discrimination with words with multiple differences (e.g., chat x chimney) and critical differences (e.g., chat x chap). Module 3 (detailed in Chap. 5 of this book) teaches words in the context of reading children's books, thus presenting a linearity of complexity of repertoires taught. The teaching program, in addition to training the regular matching-to-sample (MTS) procedure (gray arrows in Fig. 9.1), also adopts an important training step consisting of trials with writing by construction (CRMTS), aiming to teach discrimination of minimal textual units allowing fluent reading and generalized writing of new words (blank arrows in Fig. 9.1). In general, the model describes that if there is an established response for a class member, for example, naming pictures, after teaching conditional and equivalence relations, the control exerted by the pictures over vocalization is exerted by the printed words, favoring word reading (black arrows in Fig. 9.1).

In studies using ALEPP with people with no hearing impairments, conditional discriminations are trained based on selection (e.g., dictated word and printed word; dictated syllable and printed syllable) and with construction topography (e.g., written word and construction by sequential selection of syllables or letters – copy; dictated word and construction by sequential selection of syllables or letters – dictation). The results, in general, demonstrate generalized reading acquisition of simple words (Module 1) (Benitez & Domeniconi, 2012; de Souza et al., 2009; Melchiori et al., 2000; Reis et al., 2009) and with orthographic difficulties (Module 2) (Calcagno et al., 2016; Carvalho, 2013).

Teaching conditional relations and testing for the formation of stimulus classes with similar characteristics have been replicated in different studies, with different populations and with different stimulus modalities since then. A good summary in this regard can be found in Carr et al. (2000), involving populations with poor linguistic repertoire. In other chapters of this book, the reader will get a sample of replications with different populations (e.g., intellectually and visually impaired). The present chapter will focus on replications with children with hearing loss and cochlear implants in successive studies from different centers and involving primarily words as stimuli.

9.5 Effects of EBI on Expressive Repertoires and Speech Accuracy in Children with Hearing Loss and Cochlear Implants

Studies conducted nationally by the research group linked to the Institute of Science and Technology on Behavior, Cognition and Teaching (INCT-ECCE), focused on investigating the training conditions required in the rehabilitation of children with hearing loss (HL) who use cochlear implants (CI), have adopted the principles of EBI and identified important variables, especially the role of teaching relations involved in reading and improved accuracy in figure naming and expansion of expressive vocabulary.

Following previous studies that assessed the possibilities of methodological extension of the stimulus equivalence paradigm for the hearing impaired (Almeida-Verdu et al., 2008; da Silva et al., 2006), more recent studies have found that children with pre-lingual HL and CI, after entering the literacy process, produce more correct responses when reading words than when naming pictures of the same class (Golfeto, 2010). The studies by Anastácio-Pessan et al. (2015) and Lucchesi et al. (2015) investigated the role of reading repertoires, especially the strengthening of conditional relations that involve reading, in the emission of verbal responses to figure naming and word reading. The reading repertoires investigated in these studies were: selection of pictures corresponding to the dictated words; selection of printed words corresponding to the dictated words; and selection of printed syllables corresponding to the dictated syllables, as well as the control exerted by visual stimuli (pictures, words, and printed syllables).

In the study by Anastácio-Pessan et al. (2015), the EBI was adopted using the MTS© software (Dube, 1991) with children aged between 12 and 16 years, who were in the fourth and fifth grades of Elementary School, and were already reading simple words (consonant-vowel, CVCV) accurately, but naming equivalent figures was marked by distortion, exchanges and omissions. Conditional discriminations were taught between two sets of three words each, of printed words and syllables, dictated words and syllables, and pictures, which strengthened the network of equivalence relations between stimuli; naming printed words, which was already happening, improved, i.e., the children became more proficient readers after learning to select printed syllables conditionally to dictated syllables. In addition, vocal responses controlled by printed words during reading tasks were also observed during naming tasks of pictures of the same class, and there was an increase in the percentage of correctly emitted phonemes. It is said that the control exerted by printed words was transferred to the pictures, which made vocalization of words in naming tasks more accurate.

The phenomenon of transfer of stimulus control from the figure to the printed word, after establishing equivalence relations between the stimuli involved, is already well known in people with no hearing impairment (de Souza et al., 1997) and much of this research confirms the potential of the equivalence relations paradigm in developing reading comprehension (de Souza & de Rose, 2006; de Souza et al., 2009). The analysis made here with hearing-impaired people is similar because the process involved is the same; however, the transfer of control occurs from textual stimulus to pictorial. Because people with HL tend to establish more accurate vocalizations from visual cues (analogous to cued speech, Tucci et al., 2014), and word graphemes function in this way, the literacy process refines the accuracy of speech when it is delivered in reading tasks. But pictures do not exert the same control over speech due to the absence of visual cues indicating which phoneme to emit. Thus, the fact that the written word controls more accurate vocal emission and, after strengthening the equivalence relations between dictated words, figures and written words, figures also control more accurate vocal emissions in naming tasks, similarly to written words in reading tasks (Almeida-Verdu & Golfeto, 2016).

Aiming at the systematic replication of the research conducted by Anastácio-Pessan et al. (2015), the study by Almeida-Verdu and Gomes (2016) observed the same effects of teaching conditional relations between dictated words and syllables, printed words and syllables, and pictures in two non-reading children. After teaching, the participants demonstrated reading two sets of stimuli with three words each and also increased the percentage of correct responses when naming figures (using, as in the previous study, conventional words and pseudowords).

Another important study in the area was developed by Rique et al. (2017a), who also used the MTS© software (Dube, 1991) to teach conditional relations between auditory-visual stimuli with three literate children. Teaching involved extracting words from children's story books composing three sets of three stimuli, teaching reading via EBI, testing reading and naming in successive tasks (discrete trials) and in continuous tasks (in the context of stories in books). Participants learned the taught relations and demonstrated high percentages of correct responses when reading words and naming pictures in successive tasks and in reading words in the context of texts in continuous tasks. These results also replicate previous data and demonstrate that reading instruction can be a route to achieving speech accuracy in picture naming tasks. Furthermore, they extend the findings to generalizing reading to children's books. Along with research in which children with an elementary reading repertoire participated, other studies targeted participants with greater difficulties in the literacy period. In the study by Lucchesi et al. (2015), two children with poor initial reading repertoires (percentage of correct words read below 30%) were exposed to the three initial steps of Module 1 of ALEPP. In Module 1, in addition to the previously mentioned matching-to-sample (MTS) training (matching pictures to sample dictated words – AB Training; matching written words to sample dictated words – AC Training, and matching syllables to sample dictated syllables – ACsil), constructed response matching-to-sample (CRMTS) was also trained. A figure naming probe interspersed with the teaching units was a strategy specifically adopted by Lucchesi et al. (2015). The study replicated results obtained in previous research and showed that teaching conditional relations favored not only an increase in the percentages of correct words read, but also in pictures named (improving accuracy, i.e., point-to-point correspondence with the conventions of the verbal community), even when only part of the teaching program was used.

The results obtained by Lucchesi et al. (2015) were extended and replicated in Lucchesi et al. (2018). The latter study included five teaching modules for analysis and added, to the figure naming probes already existing in the previous study, word reading probes, between the teaching units.

In a more recent study, conducted in collaboration between the laboratories at the Universities UFSCar, USP, and UNESP (Lucchesi, 2018), four children with prelingual HL and CI were exposed to the first 4 units of the ALEPP teaching program. Issues related to the design were controlled by superimposing on the multiple-probe design and a between-participants multiple-baseline design so that four participants were exposed to the ALEPP units in a stepwise manner; the first participant was exposed to unit 1 while the repertoire of the others remained under evaluation; when participant 1 completed the first teaching unit and was exposed to unit 2, participant 2 started the first unit while participants 3 and 4 remained under evaluation and so on. The design allowed us to observe and state, once again, that speech accuracy in figure naming tasks is refined after strengthening the (equivalence) relations involved in word reading. These results once again highlight the effects of teaching conditional relations with a common node (which, in the case of ALEPP, are the dictated words in the AB, AC, and ACsil training sessions) on the transfer of control from the written word in reading tasks to the figure in naming tasks (Almeida-Verdu & Golfeto, 2016).

Following the research that used Module 1 of the teaching program (Lucchesi, 2018; Lucchesi et al., 2015, 2018) with the CI users, Cravo's (2018) studies used Module 2 of the ALEPP, focusing on the accurate reading of words with spelling difficulties (Study 2), and reading words with spelling difficulties and naming corresponding pictures (Study 3). In Study 2 of Cravo's (2018) dissertation, the 9-year-old participant had already been exposed to Module 1 of the program, but presented difficulties when reading words accurately, i.e., with point-to-point correspondence according to the conventions of the verbal community, words that presented orthographic difficulties in Portuguese (e.g., read "pacoca" instead of "paçoca" or read "galgo" instead of "galho"; an example in English will be read "kickhen" instead of "chicken"); she also did not properly name figures corresponding to the words. In the study she was then exposed to Module 2, which only taught conditional relations between dictated and printed words (AC training) as well as between dictated and printed syllables. Teaching proved to be sufficient not only to increase the percentage of correct responses in reading words with orthographic difficulties, but also in generalizing to reading other words with untrained difficulties (i.e., learning words with "ch" and generalizing to reading words with "nh"). In Study 3 of the same dissertation, Cravo (2018) exposed two other literate children to new contingencies arranged in the program, by training the conditional relations between dictated words and pictures (AB) (which does not integrate the conventional Module 2) as well as the existing training of relations between dictated and printed words (AC) and dictated and printed syllables (ACsil). The results replicated those found in the previous study, with increased percentages of correct answers when reading words with orthographic difficulties, which was already high before teaching; when naming figures of the same class, which was low before teaching, they reached percentages of correct responses similar to those obtained in reading, after training and testing. The accuracy of vocalization of words with some orthographic difficulties should be further investigated.

Table 9.1 presents an overview of the main studies conducted with reading instruction by EBI programs and targeting the improvement of speech accuracy in children with HL and CI. This contains eight separate studies with 21 participants replicating the findings that speech accuracy in picture naming tasks can be refined after exposure to equivalence-based reading instruction. All studies adopted single-subject experimental designs which allows for verification by visual inspection, confirmed in descriptive or inferential statistical analyses (e.g., Lucchesi et al., 2018), of changes in accuracy of the figure naming repertoire after EBI.

9.6 Final Considerations

Considering the literature review including national and international literature, added to the studies conducted under the scope of the INCT-ECCE in inter-institutional partnership with researchers from the Hospital for Rehabilitation of Craniofacial Anomalies (*Hospital para Reabilitação de Anomalias Craniofaciais* [HRAC]) with a transdisciplinary focus, we conclude that teaching reading and writing based on equivalence may improve the speech accuracy of children with hearing loss and cochlear implants. The proposal may be in the format of a program, with cumulative content, presented in levels of stimulus complexity, with tasks that establish the understanding of what is taught (semantic referential) and the knowledge of minimal textual units, favoring fluent and generalized reading.

ALEPP is an example of such a teaching program. Considering the complexity of stimuli, it is divided into modules and teaches from words with regularity and no reading and spelling difficulty to words with less regularity and greater reading and spelling difficulty. The program can progress to sentence teaching as well (see Chap. 6 in this book).

It is concluded that, although the effects of cochlear implantation on learning receptive and expressive language skills – here called verbal behavior – are well known, and there are many proposals for teaching these skills, there is a lack of research that incorporates the criteria of evidence-based practices.

Based on the systematization performed in the present chapter, it is possible to state that in hearing-impaired and reading-impaired children, speech accuracy can be obtained by strengthening reading. Additionally, reading instruction may be a good route to achieve speech accuracy when it is not established before the literacy period. This is a vast field of research and many questions are still open such as the effectiveness of Equivalence-Based Instruction (EBI) programs compared to other literacy methods and its generalization potential. Furthermore, would the effects of EBI reading instruction in hearing-impaired children be sensitive to other instruments measuring cognitive skills such as phonemic awareness, syntactic awareness, reading and writing tests, serial rapid naming, among others? Future research may

Table 9.1 Synthesis of studies conducted with reading instruction by EBI programs and targeted at improving speech Accuracy in hearing impaired children and cochlear implants

Authors	Year	Target response	N	Complexity of stimuli	Main procedures	Experiential design	Results
Anastácio-Pessan et al.	2015	Naming pictures and Reading of words	6	Regular words (CVCV)	MTS – between dictated words and pictures and between dictated words and syllables and words and syllables printed	Multiple baseline between sets of stimuli	Pre-existing reading. Increase in percentages of correctness in the naming of figures
Lucchesi et al.	2015	Naming pictures	2	Regular words (CVCV)	MTS between dictated words and syllables, words and printed syllables and pictures. CRMTS – answers from word building (copying and dictation)	Multiple probes	Pre-existing reading. Percentage increase of correctness in figure naming after teaching reading
Almeida-Verdu & Gomes	2016	Naming pictures and Reading of words	2	Regular words (CVCV)	MTS – between dictated words and pictures and between dictated words and syllables and words and syllables printed	Multiple baseline between sets of stimuli	Teaching reading and increasing the percentages of correctness in the naming of figures

(continued)

Table 9.1 (continued)

Authors	Year	Target response	N	Complexity of stimuli	Main procedures	Experiential design	Results
Rique, Almeida-Verdu et al.	2017	Naming pictures and Reading of words	3	Regular words (CVCV)	MTS – between dictated words and pictures and between dictated words and printed words	Multiple baseline between set of stimuli	Increase in hit percentages in the naming of pictures, as well as reading of the words while reading short texts
Lucchesi et al.	2018	Naming pictures	1	Regular words (CVCV)	MTS between dictated words and syllables, words and printed syllables and pictures. CRMTS – Constructed response (copying and dictation)	Multiple baseline between stimulus sets	Pre-existing reading. Increased percentages of correctness in figure naming
Lucchesi (thesis) – study 3	2018	Naming pictures and Reading words	4	Regular words (CVCV)	MTS between dictated words and syllables, words and printed syllables and pictures. CRMTS – Constructed response (copying and dictation)	Multiple probes and multiple baseline between participants	Increased hit percentages in no – meation of pictures and in word reading after reading instruction

(continued)

Table 9.1 (continued)

Authors	Year	Target response	N	Complexity of stimuli	Main procedures	Experiential design	Results
Cravo (dissertation) – study 2	2018	Reading words	1	Words with dificul – spelling difficulties (ch, nh, ç, etc)	MTS between dictated words and syllables, words and printed syllables (stimuli with differences critical and multiple)	Multiple baseline between set of stimuli	Accuracy in reading words with difficulty orthographic (e.g., ç, lh, ch, vLc)
Cravo (dissertation) – study 3	2018	Point to pictures, Reading word	2	Words with spelling difficulties (ch, nh, ç, etc)	MTS between dictated words and syllables, words and printed syllables (stimuli with differences critical and multiple) and between dictated word and figures	Multiple probes	Increase in the percentage of correct answers in reading of words with spelling difficulties (e.g., ç, lh, ch, vLc). Accuracy with some difficulties orthography should be further investigated
8 studies			21				

address these questions. However, there is a pressing demand that the results systematized in this chapter makes us think, namely, the conditions that must prevail for rudimentary reading instruction programs via EBI to be incorporated into cochlear implant follow-up programs for cases that do not benefit from large-scale, incidental instruction, still need to be outlined.

Considering the need to teach reading comprehension, fluency and generalization, it is recognized that these are very important dimensions identified in audiology verbal skills intervention programs and found in the brief literature review presented at the beginning of this chapter (Tucci et al., 2014). The literature also shows a focus on the teaching procedure when the target is speech establishment, such as modeling and imitation (Moog & Stein, 2008). These are features also observed in EBI programs in general. In EBI research, the target is the teaching of at least two conditional discriminations with a common stimulus; conditional discriminations can be established by selection responses (MTS) or construction responses (CRMTS); the stimuli can be sentences (see Chap. 6 of this book), words, syllables, or letters and can have multiple or critical differences; Teaching with these characteristics can promote the recognition of each minimal unit that makes up the word, so that these, if recombined, can originate the reading of new words, besides establishing the semantic referential when teaching involves figures of the same class as the dictated and printed words and syllables.

The similarity observed between the dimensions identified as relevant in teaching verbal skills in such different literature strengthens the proposal and demonstrates the robustness of these dimensions involving teaching procedures and systematization. However, especially with regard to research that incorporates the criteria of scientific evidence, the systematization of the studies, whose target was to improve accuracy, allows us to affirm the effectiveness of programs involving Equivalence-Based Instruction.

References

Albright, L., Schnell, L., Reeve, K., & Sidener, T. (2016). Using stimulus equivalence- based instruction to teach graduate students in applied behavior analysis to interpret operant functions of behavior. *Journal of Behavior Education, 25*, 290–309. https://doi.org/10.1007/s10864-016-9249-0

Almeida-Verdu, A. C. M., & Golfeto, R. M. (2016). Stimulus control and verbal behavior: (In) dependent relations in populations with minimal verbal repertoires. In J. C. Todorov (Org.) *Trends in behavior analysis* 1(pp.187–227). Technopolitik Editora.

Almeida-Verdu, A. C. M., & Gomes, F. P. (2016). Precisão da fala em nomeação de figuras após formação de classes de equivalência em crianças com implante coclear. *Revista Perspectivas, 7*(2), 274–287. https://doi.org/10.18761/pac.2016.010

Almeida-Verdu, A. C. M., Huziwara, E. M., de Souza, D. G., de Rose, J. C., Bevilacqua, M. C., Lopes Junior, J., Alves, C. O., & McIlvane, W. J. (2008). Relational learning in children with deafness and cochlear implants. *Journal of the Experimental Analysis of Behavior, 89*(3), 407–424. https://doi.org/10.1901/jeab.2008-89-407

Alves, R. L., Soares, A. M. J., Freire, R. C. S., & Lima, C. M. G. S. (2016). Synthesizable and prototypic visual-tactile system-in FPGA: An alternative to analysis and improvement of the voice quality for the hearing-impaired people. *Holos, 2*, 3–23. https://doi.org/10.15628/holos.2016.4086

Ambrose, S. E., Fey, M. E., & Eisenberg, L. S. (2012). Phonological awareness and print knowledge of preschool children with cochlear implants. *Journal of Speech, Language, and Hearing Research, 55*(3), 811–823. https://doi.org/10.1044/1092-4388(2011/11-0086)

American Speech-Language-Hearing Association. (2005). Evidence-based practice in communication disorders. Available in https://www.asha.org/policy/ps2005-00221.htm. Acessado em 30 de jan de 2019.

Anastácio-Pessan, F. L., Almeida-Verdu, A. C. M., Bevilacqua, M. C., & de Souza, D. G. (2015). Usando o paradigma de equivalência para aumentar a correspondência na fala de crianças com implante coclear na nomeação de figuras e na leitura. *Psicologia Reflexão e Crítica, 28*(2), 365–377. https://doi.org/10.1590/1678-7153.201528217

Assis, G. J. A., & Santos, M. B. (2010). *PROLER (Sistema computadorizado de ensino de comportamentos conceituais)*. Universidade Federal do Pará.

Barreto, S. S., & Ortiz, K. Z. (2008). Medidas de inteligibilidade nos distúrbios da fala: Revisão crítica da literatura. *Pró-Fono Revista de Atualização Científica, 20*(3), 201–206. https://doi.org/10.1590/S0104-56872008000300011

Beadle, E. A. R., McKinley, D. J., Nikolopoulos, T. P., Brough, J., O'Donoghue, G. M., & Archbold, S. M. (2005). Long-term functional outcomes and academic- occupational status in implanted children after 10 to 14 years of cochlear implant use. *Otology & Neurotology, 26*, 1152–1160. https://doi.org/10.1097/01.mao.0000180483.16619.8f

Beeres-Scheenstra, R., Ohnsorg, C., Candreia, C., Heinzmann, S., Castellanos, S., de Min, N., & Linder, T. E. (2017). Single-center study investigating foreign language acquisition at school in children, adolescents, and young adults with uni-or bilateral cochlear implants in the swiss german population. *Otology & Neurotology, 38*(6), 833–838. https://doi.org/10.1097/MAO.0000000000001431

Benitez, P., & Domeniconi, C. (2012). Verbalizações de familiares durante aprendizagem de leitura e escrita por deficientes intelectuais. *Estudos de Psicologia, 29*(4), 553–562. https://doi.org/10.1590/S0103-166X2012000400010

Byiers, B. J., Reichle, J., & Symons, F. J. (2012). Single-subject experimental design for evidence-based practice. *American Journal of Speech-Language Pathology, 21*(4), 397–414. https://doi.org/10.1044/1058-0360(2012/11-0036)

Calcagno, S., Barros, R. S., Ferrari, I. S., & de Souza, D. G. (2016). Análise dos erros apresentados por adultos iletrados de um programa informatizado de ensino de leitura e escrita. *Acta Colombiana de Psicologia, 19*(1), 123–136. https://doi.org/10.14718/ACP.2016.19.1.7

Calcagno, S., Dube, W. V., Galvão, O. F., & Sidman, M. (1994). Emergence of conditional discriminations after constructed-response matching-to-sample training. *The Psychological Record, 44*(4), 509–520. https://doi.org/10.1007/BF03395141

Capobianco, D., Teixeira, C., Bela, R. E., Orlando, A. F., de Souza, D. G., & de Rose, J. C. (2009). *LECH-GEIC*. Sistema web Gerenciador de Ensino Individualizado por Computador. Developed by Universidade Federal de São Carlos. Available in http://geic.ufscar.br:8080/site/. Retrieved in: 29 jan. 2019.

Carr, D., Wilkinson, K. M., Blackman, D., & McIlvane, W. J. (2000). Equivalence classes in individuals with minimal verbal repertoires. *Journal of the Experimental Analysis of Behavior, 74*(1), 101–114. https://doi.org/10.1901/jeab.2000.74-101

Carvalho, B. S. (2013). *Programações de ensino para refinamento das habilidades de leitura e escrita de um aluno com transtorno de Asperger* Master's thesis, Universidade Federal de São Carlos]. Repositório Institucional UFSCar. https://repositorio.ufscar.br/handle/ufscar/3128.

Casserly, E. D., & Pisoni, D. B. (2013). Nonword repetition as a predictor of long-term speech and language skills in children with cochlear implants. *Otology & Neorotology, 34*, 460–470. https://doi.org/10.1097/MAO.0b013e3182868340

Coelho, A. C., Brasolotto, A. G., Fernandes, A. C. N., Medved, D. M. S., da Silva, E. M., & Junior, F. B. (2017). Auditory-perceptual evaluation of voice quality of cochlear-implanted and normal-hearing individuals: A reliability study. *Journal of Voice, 31*(6), 774.e1–774.e8. https://doi.org/10.1016/j.jvoice.2017.02.012

Colin, S., Ecalle, J., Truy, E., Linda-Granade, G., & Magnan, A. (2017). Effect of age at cochlear implant and exposure to cued speech on literacy skills in deaf children. *Research in Developmental Disabilities, 71*, 61–69. https://doi.org/10.1016/j.ridd.2017.09.014

Connor, C. M., & Zwolan, T. A. (2004). Examining multiple sources of influence on the reading comprehension skills of children who use cochlear implants. *Journal of Speech, Language, and Hearing Research, 47*, 509–526. https://doi.org/10.1044/1092-4388(2004/040)

Connor, C. M., Hieber, S., & Zwolan, T. A. (2000). Speech, vocabulary, and the education of children using cochlear implants: Oral or total communication. *Journal of Speech, Language and Hearing Research, 43*(1), 1185–1204. https://doi.org/10.1044/jslhr.4305.1185

Convertino, C., Borgna, G., Marschark, M., & Durkin, A. (2014). Word and world knowledge among deaf learners with and without cochlear implants. *Journal of Deaf Studies and Deaf Education, 19*(4), 471–483. https://doi.org/10.1093/deafed/enu024

Cravo, F. A. M. (2018). *Leitura oral e nomeação de figuras de palavras com dificuldades ortográficas por crianças com deficiência auditiva e usuárias de implante coclear* Unpublished master's thesis. Faculdade de Ciências de Bauru.

Cricthfield, T. S., Barnes-Holmes, D., & Dougher, M. J. (2018). Editorial: What Sidman did historical and contemporary significance of research on derived stimulus relations. *Perspectives on Behavior Science, 41*(1), 9–32. https://doi.org/10.1007/s40614-018-0154-9

Cupples, L., Ching, T. Y. C., Button, L., Seeto, M., Zhang, V., Whitfield, J., Gunnourie, M., et al. (2018). Spoken language and everyday functioning in 5-year-old children using hearing aids or cochlear implants. *International Journal of Audiology, 57*, 55–69. https://doi.org/10.1080/14992027.2017.1370140

da Silva, W. R., de Souza, D. G., Lopes Júnior, J., Bevilacqua, M. C., & McIlvane, W. J. (2006). Relational learning in children with cochlear implant. *Experimental Analysis of Human Behavior Bulletin, 24*, 1–8. https://doi.org/10.1901/jeab.2008-89-407

de Souza, D. G., & de Rose, J. C. (2006). Desenvolvendo programas individualizados para o ensino de leitura. *Acta Comportamentalia, 14*(1), 77–98.

de Souza, D. G., de Rose, J. C., Faleiros, T. C., Bortoloti, R., Hanna, E. S., & McIlvane, W. J. (2009). Teaching generative reading via recombination of minimal textual units: A legacy of verbal behavior to children in Brazil. *International Journal of Psychology and Psychological Therapy, 9*(1), 19–44.

de Souza, D. G., Hanna, E. S., de Rose, J. C., Fonseca, M. L., Pereira, A. B., & Sallorenzo, L. H. (1997). Transferência de controle de estímulos de figuras para texto no desenvolvimento de leitura generalizada. *Temas em Psicologia, 5*(1), 33–46.

DesJardin, J. L., Ambrose, S. E., & Eisenberg, L. S. (2011). Maternal involvement in the home literacy environment: Supporting literacy skills in children with cochlear implants. *Communication Disorders Quarterly, 32*(3), 135–150. https://doi.org/10.1177/1525740109340916

Dube, W. V. (1991). Computer software for stimulus control research with Macintosh computers. *Experimental Analysis of Human Behavior Bulletin, 9*, 28–39.

Dube, W. V. (1996). Teaching discrimination skills to persons with mental retardation. In A. C. Goyos, M. A. Almeida, & D. de Souza (Orgs.), *Temas em Educação Especial* (pp. 73–96). EDUFSCar.

Dube, W. V., McDonald, S. J., McIlvane, W. J., & Mackay, H. A. (1991). Constructed- response matching to sample and spelling instruction. *Journal of the Applied Behavior Analysis, 24*(2), 305–317. https://doi.org/10.1901/jaba.1991.24-305

Ertmer, D. J. (2010). Relationships between speech intelligibility and word articulation test scores in children with hearing loss. *Journal of Speech, Language, and Hearing Research, 53*, 1075–1086. https://doi.org/10.1044/1092-4388(2010/09-0250)

Ertmer, D. J., & Goffman, L. (2011). Speech production accuracy and variability in young cochlear implant recipients: Comparisons with typically developing age-peers. *Journal of Speech, Language, and Hearing Research, 54*, 177–189. https://doi.org/10.1044/1092-4388(2010/09-0165)

Fields, L., Travis, R., Roy, D., Yadovker, E., Aguiar-Rocha, L., & Sturmey, P. (2009). Equivalence class formation: A method for teaching statistical interactions. *Journal of Applied Behavior Analysis, 42*, 575–593. https://doi.org/10.1901/jaba.2009.42-575

Fienup, D. M., Covey, D. P., & Critchfield, T. S. (2010). Teaching brain-behavior relations economically with stimulus equivalence technology. *Journal of Applied Behavior Analysis, 43*(1), 19–33. https://doi.org/10.1901/jaba.2010.43-19

Gallego, C., Martín-Aragoneses, M. T., Lopes-Higes, R., & Pisón, G. (2016). Semantic and syntactic reading comprehension strategies used by deaf children with early and late cochlear implantation. *Research in Developmental Disabilities, 49–50*, 153–170. https://doi.org/10.1016/j.ridd.2015.11.020

Geers, A. E., & Hayes, H. (2011). Reading, writing, and phonological processing skills of adolescents with 10 or more years of cochlear implant experience. *Ear and Hearing, 32*, 49–59. https://doi.org/10.1097/AUD.0b013e3181fa41fa

Geers, A. E., Nicholas, J. G., & Moog, J. S. (2007). Estimating the influence of cochlear implantation on language development in children. *Audiological Medicine, 5*(4), 262–273. https://doi.org/10.1080/16513860701659404

Glyde, H., Cameron, S., Dillon, H., & Hickson, L. (2014). Remediation of spatial processing deficits in hearing-impaired children and adults. *Journal of the American Academy of Audiology, 25*(6), 549–561. https://doi.org/10.3766/jaaa.25.6.5

Golfeto, R. M. (2010). *Compreensão e produção de fala em crianças com deficiência auditiva pré-lingual usuárias de implante coclear.* Doctoral dissertation, Universidade Federal de São Carlos. Repositório Institucional UFSCar. http://www.ufscar.br/ecce/wp-content/files_flutter/1280109367TeseRMGolfeto.pdf

Golfeto, R. M., & de Souza, D. G. (2015). Sentence production after listener and echoic training by prelingual deaf children with cochlear implants. *Journal of Applied Behavior Analysis, 48*(2), 363–375. https://doi.org/10.1002/jaba.197

Goyos, C., & Almeida, J. C. B. (1994). *Mestre* (Versão 1.0) [Computer Software].

Greer, R. D., & Ross, D. E. (2008). Verbal behavior analysis: Inducing and expanding new verbal capabilities in children with language delays. Pearson/Allyn & Bacon.

Hanna, E. S., Batitucci, L. A. V., & Batitucci, J. D. S. L. (2014). Software Contingência Programada: Utilidade e funcionalidades. *Revista Brasileira de Análise do Comportamento, 10*(1), 97–104. https://doi.org/10.18542/rebac.v10i1.3949

Harris, M., Terletski, E., & Kyle, F. E. (2017). Literacy outcomes for primary school children who are deaf and hard of hearing: A cohort comparison study. *Journal of Speech Language and Hearing Research, 60*(3), 701–711. https://doi.org/10.1044/2016_JSLHR-H-15-0403

Kazdin, A. E. (1982). *Single-case research designs: Methods for clinical and applied settings.* Oxford University Press.

Levine, D., Strother-Garcia, K., Golinkoff, R., & Hirsh-Pasek, K. (2016). Language development in the first year of life: What deaf children might be missing before cochlear implantation. *Otology and Neurotology, 37*(2), 56–62. https://doi.org/10.1097/MAO.0000000000000908

Lópes-Higes, R., Gallego, C., Martín-Aragoneses, M. T., & Melle, N. (2015). Morpho-syntactic reading comprehension in children with early and late cochlear implants. *The Journal of Deaf Studies and Deaf Education, 20*(2), 136–146. https://doi.org/10.1093/deafed/env004

Lucchesi, F. D. M. (2018). *Leitura e inteligibilidade da fala em crianças usuárias de implante coclear.* Doctoral dissertation, Universidade Federal de São Carlos. Repositório Institucional UFSCar. https://repositorio.ufscar.br/bitstream/handle/ufscar/9789/LUCCHESI_Fernando_2018.pdf?sequence=4&isAllowed=y

Lucchesi, F. D. M., & Almeida-Verdu, A. C. M. (2017). Ensino de componentes da linguagem a usuários de implante coclear: Revisão da literatura. *Revista CEFAC, 9*(6), 855–867. https://doi.org/10.1590/1982-021620171965717

Lucchesi, F. D. M., Almeida-Verdu, A. C. M., & de Souza, D. G. (2018). Reading and speech intelligibility of a child with auditory impairment and cochlear implant. *Psychology & Neuroscience, 11*(3), 306–316. https://doi.org/10.1037/pne0000139

Lucchesi, F. D., Almeida-Verdu, A. C. M., Buffa, M. J. M. B., & Bevilacqua, M. C. (2015). Efeitos de um programa de ensino de leitura sobre a inteligibilidade da fala de crianças usuárias de implante coclear. *Psicologia Reflexão e Crítica, 28*(3), 500–510. https://doi.org/10.1590/1678-7153.201528309

Lund, E. (2016). Vocabulary knowledge of children with cochlear implants: A meta-analysis. *Journal of Deaf Studies and Deaf Education, 21*(2), 107–121. https://doi.org/10.1093/deafed/env060

Lund, E., & Douglas, M. (2016). Teaching vocabulary to preschool children with hearing loss. *Exceptional Children, 83*(1), 26–41. https://doi.org/10.1177/0014402916651848

Lund, E., & Schuele, C. M. (2014). Effects of a word-learning training on children with cochlear implants. *Journal of Deaf Studies and Deaf Education, 19*(1), 68–84. https://doi.org/10.1093/deafed/ent036

Mackay, H. (2013). Developing syntactic repertoires: Syntheses of stimulus classes, sequences and contextual control. *European Journal of Behavior Analysis, 14*, 69–85. https://doi.org/10.1080/15021149.2013.11434446

Marschark, M., Rhoten, C., & Fabich, M. (2007). Effects of cochlear implants on children's reading and academic achievement. *Journal of Deaf Studies and Deaf Education, 12*, 269–282. https://doi.org/10.1093/deafed/enm013

Melchiori, L. E., de Souza, D. G., & de Rose, J. C. (2000). Reading, equivalence, and recombination of units: A replication with students with different learning histories. *Journal of Applied Behavior Analysis, 33*, 97–100. https://doi.org/10.1901/jaba.2000.33-97

Melo, A., Costa, M. J., Garcia, M. V., Filha, V. A. V. S., & Biaggio, E. P. F. (2015). O uso de software no treinamento auditivo em crianças: Revisão teórica. *Revista CEFAC, 17*(6), 2025–2032. https://doi.org/10.1590/1982-0216201517611715

Moog, J. S., & Stein, K. K. (2008). Teaching deaf children to talk. *Contemporary Issues in Communication Science and Disorders, 35*, 133–142. https://doi.org/10.1044/cicsd_35_F_133

Moshtaghi, O., Haidar, Y. M., Sahyouni, R., Rajaii, R., Moshtaghi, A., Mahmoodi, A., et al. (2017). Use of interactive iBook for patient education in otology. *American Journal of Otolaryngology – Head and Neck Medicine and Surgery, 38*(2), 174–178. https://doi.org/10.1016/j.amjoto.2016.12.004

Munafò, M. R., Nosek, B. A., Bishop, D. V. M., Button, K. S., Chambers, C. D., et al. (2017). A manifesto for reproducible science. *Nature Human Behaviour, 1*, 1–9. https://doi.org/10.1038/s41562-016-0021

Nanjundaswamy, M., Prabhu, P., Rajanna, R. K., Ningegowda, R. G., & Sharma, M. (2018). Computer-based auditory training programs for children with hearing impairment – A scoping review. *International Archives of Otorhinolaryngology, 22*(1), 88–93. https://doi.org/10.1055/s-0037-1602797

Neves, A. J., Almeida-Verdu, A. C. M., Moret, A. L. M., & Silva, L. T. N. (2015). The implications of the cochlear implant for development of language skills: A literature review. *Revista CEFAC, 17*(5), 1643–1656. https://doi.org/10.1590/1982-021620151755315

Neves, A. J., Almeida-Verdu, A. C. M., Assis, G. J. A., Silva, L. T. N., & Moret, A. L. M. (2018). Improving oral sentence production in children with cochlear implants: Effects of equivalence-based instruction and matrix training. *Psicologia: Reflexão e Crítica, 31*(14), 1–17. https://doi.org/10.1186/s41155-018-0095-y

Pascoe, M., Randall-Pieterse, C., & Geiger, M. (2013). Speech and literacy development in a child with a cochlear implant: Application of a psycholinguistic framework. *Child Language Teaching and Therapy, 29*(2), 185–200. https://doi.org/10.1177/0265659012467197

Pimentel, E. P. (1996). *Desenvolvimento de um sistema para pesquisa em equivalência e unidades verbais menores utilizando estruturas de dados para texto e imagem.* Unpublished master's thesis, Universidade Presbiteriana Mackenzie.

Pytte, C. L., & Fienup, D. M. (2012). Using equivalence-based instruction to increase efficiency in teaching neuroanatomy. *The Journal of Undergraduate Neuroscience Education, 10*(2), 125–131.

Reichmuth, K., Embacher, A. J., Matulat, P., Zehnhoff-Dinnesen, A., & Glanemann, R. (2013). Responsive parenting intervention after identification of hearing loss by universal newborn hearing screening: The concept of the muenster parental Programme. *International Journal of Pediatric Otorhinolaryngology, 77*(12), 2030–2039. https://doi.org/10.1016/j.ijporl.2013.10.002

Reis, T. S., de Souza, D. G., & de Rose, J. C. (2009). Avaliação de um programa para o ensino de leitura e escrita. *Estudos em Avaliação Educacional, 44*(20), 425–450. https://doi.org/10.18222/eae204420092038

Rexroad, C. N. (1926). Verbalization in multiple choice reactions. *Psychological Review, 33*(6), 451–458. https://doi.org/10.1037/h0075682

Rique, L. D., Almeida-Verdu, A. C. M., Silva, L. T., Buffa, M. J., & Moret, A. L. (2017a). Leitura após formação de classe de equivalência em criança com implante coclear: Precisão e fluência em palavras e textos. *Acta Comportamentalia, 25*(1), 307–327.

Rique, L. D., Guerra, B. T., Borelli, L. M., Oliveira, A. P., & Almeida-Verdu, A. C. M. (2017b). Ensino de comportamento verbal por múltiplos exemplares em uma criança com desordem do espectro da neuropatia auditiva: Estudo de caso. *Revista CEFAC, 19*(2), 289–298. https://doi.org/10.1590/1982-021620171928516

Sarant, J. Z., Harris, D. C., Galvin, K. L., Bennet, L. A., Canagasabey, M., & Busby, P. A. (2018). Social development in children with early cochlear implants: Normative comparisons and predictive factors, including bilateral implantation. *Ear and Hearing, 39*(4), 770–782. https://doi.org/10.1097/AUD.0000000000000533

Schmidt, S. (2009). Shall we really do it again? The powerfull concept of replication is neglected in the social sciences. *Review of General Psychology, 13*(2), 90–100. https://doi.org/10.1037/a0015108

Sidman, M. (1971). Reading and auditory-visual equivalence. *Journal of Speech and Hearing Research, 14*, 5–13. https://doi.org/10.1044/jshr.1401.05

Sidman, M. (1994). *Equivalence relations and behavior: A research story*. Authors Cooperative.

Sidman, M. (2000). Equivalence relations and the reinforcement contingency. *Journal of the Experimental Analysis of Behavior, 74*(1), 127–146. https://doi.org/10.1901/jeab.2000.74-127

Sidman, M., & Tailby, W. (1982). Conditional discrimination vs. matching to sample: An expansion of the testing paradigm. *Journal of the Experimental Analysis of Behavior, 37*(1), 5–22. https://doi.org/10.1901/jeab.1982.37-5

Skinner, B. F. (1957). *Verbal behavior*. Appleton-Century-Crofts.

Smith, A., & Wang, Y. (2010). The impact of visual phonics on the phonological awareness and speech production of a student who is deaf: A case study. *American Annals of the Deaf, 155*(2), 124–130. https://doi.org/10.1353/aad.2010.0000

Spencer, L. J., & Tomblin, J. B. (2009). Evaluation phonological processing skills in children with prelingual deafness who use cochlear implants. *Journal of Deaf Studies and Deaf Education, 14*, 1–21. https://doi.org/10.1093/deafed/enn013

Spencer, L. J., Marschark, M., Machmer, E., Durkin, A., Borgna, G., & Convertino, C. (2018). Communication skills of deaf and hard-of-hearing college students: Objective measures and self-assessment. *Journal of Communication Disorders, 75*, 13–24. https://doi.org/10.1016/j.jcomdis.2018.06.002

Stromer, R., Mackay, H. A., & Stoddard, L. T. (1992). Classroom applications of stimulus equivalence technology. *Journal of Behavioral Education, 2*(3), 225–256. https://doi.org/10.1007/BF00948817

Svirsky, M. (2017). Cochlear implants and electronic hearing. *Physics Today, 70*(8), 52–58. https://doi.org/10.1063/PT.3.3661

Sweetow, R., & Palmer, C. V. (2005). Efficacy of individual auditory training in adults: A systematic review of the evidence. *Journal of the American Academy of Audiology, 16*(7), 494–504. https://doi.org/10.3766/jaaa.16.7.9

Tawney, J. W., & Gast, D. (1984). *Single subject research in special education*. Charles E.

Tucci, S. L., Trussell, J. W., & Easterbrooks, S. R. (2014). A review of the evidence on the strategies for teaching children who are DHH grapheme-phoneme correspondence. *Communication Disorders Quarterly, 35*(4), 191–203. https://doi.org/10.1177/1525740114523776

Uziel, A. S., Sillon, M., Vieu, A., Artieres, F., Piron, J. P., Daures, J. P., & Mondain, M. (2007). Ten-year follow-up of a consecutive series of children with multichannel cochlear implants. *Otology & Neurotology, 28*, 615–628. https://doi.org/10.1097/01.mao.0000281802.59444.02

Wass, M., Ching, T. Y., Cupples, L., Wang, H. C., Lyxell, B., Martin, L., et al. (2018). Orthographic learning in children who are deaf or hard of hearing. *Language, Speech, and Hearing Services in Schools, 50*, 1–14. https://doi.org/10.1044/2018_LSHSS-17-0146

Chapter 10
Effect of Teaching Phonemes from Pseudo-Alphabets on the Emergence of Recombinative Reading in Adults

Luana Zeolla Inhauser, Maria Martha Costa Hübner, and Valéria Mendes Tavitian

10.1 Introduction

Reading is a skill of great importance for people's lives, because it enables access to various forms of written information in books, newspapers, informative texts, mobile phone messages, e-mail, and even social media. In addition, reading with comprehension is necessary for academic success in all subjects (Adams, 1994) present in the Brazilian school curriculum. The acquisition of a reading repertoire, however, is complex and involves a network of relations between stimuli and between stimuli and responses. For a reading repertoire to be considered proficient, the reader must read new, untaught words, formed by the recombination of previously learned units in other relations, which is called recombinative reading (de Rose et al., 1989; de Rose, 2005, the latter is reprinted in Chap. 1 of this book).

A fundamental requirement for the development of recombinative reading is the establishment of differential responding under the control of the smaller units or components of words, such as syllables, letters, or phonemes. In Portuguese language, different words can be formed from the combination and recombination of units from a reduced set of alphabet symbols (Hanna et al., 2010a) and proficient readers must respond differentially to these units to present a fluent reading repertoire.

Recent data on reading assessment in Brazilian students, such as data from the Program for International Student's Assessment (PISA), presented by INEP (Brasil,

L. Z. Inhauser
Núcleo de Intervenção Comportamental, São Paulo, SP, Brazil

M. M. C. Hübner (✉) · V. M. Tavitian
Universidade de São Paulo, São Paulo, SP, Brazil
e-mail: marthahubner@usp.br

A. R. de Albuquerque, R. M. de Melo (eds.), *Contributions of Behavior Analysis to Reading and Writing Comprehension*, https://doi.org/10.1007/978-3-031-40868-7_10

2019a), showed that Brazilian students have low proficiency in reading, mathematics and science. In reading tests, the data indicate that 50% of students did not reach level 2 in the tests, meaning that they cannot understand the main information of a text, find explicit information, or even identify the purpose of a short text. It is also worth noting that, according to PISA, accurate performance at level 2 in reading is the minimum considered necessary to exercise citizenship. In this same direction, the reading performance indices in the Basic Education Evaluation System (SAEB) presented by INEP (Brasil, 2019b), show that only 1.6% of Brazilian senior high school students reached results considered proficient in reading and comprehension of Portuguese language. Thus, investigations that maximize the learning of recombinative reading by Brazilian students are fundamental for a possible change in the country's scenario and in the number of people able to read fluently with comprehension, which would allow greater access to information and, possibly, a better performance in other academic and even professional activities.

Behavior analysts have been devoted for years to identifying the variables that favor the acquisition of recombinative reading in Portuguese (e.g., de Rose et al., 1989, 1992, 1996; Hanna et al., 2010b; Hübner-D'Oliveira, 1990; Hübner-D'Oliveira & Matos, 1993; Matos et al., 2002; Melchiori et al., 2000). One of the variables that have received attention in recent studies is the direct teaching of phoneme-grapheme relationships, which has been called phonics instruction (e.g., da Silva, 2015; Guimarães, 2019; Rorato, 2014). This type of training has been pointed out as advantageous because it can enable, for example, reading a greater variety of words than the direct teaching of syllables. This would occur because directly teaching the smallest unit presented in words (grapheme/phoneme) would allow reading several possible combinations of these units, including the reading of complex syllables that do not present the consonant-vowel structure (Guimarães, 2019).

The purpose of this chapter is to present studies that investigate the effect of training smaller units (phonemes), combined or not with whole words, on the emergence of recombinative reading. To this end, the chapter is divided into three sections that address: control by units smaller than the word (minimal units); description of investigations on the effect of direct phoneme teaching, with special attention to the study developed by Inhauser (2012), and final considerations.

10.2 Control by Minimal Units

According to Skinner (1957), control by minimal units, at the level of letters or isolated sounds, can be gradually developed when only larger units are directly taught. Thus, training whole words could also produce a differential response under control of smaller units, even when these are not directly taught. Most of the early studies on reading and writing in behavior analysis used whole words as the textual units of instruction (e.g., de Rose et al., 1996, 1989, 1992; Hanna et al., 2008; Hübner-D'Oliveira, 1990; Hübner-D'Oliveira & Matos, 1993; Hübner et al., 2009;

Matos et al., 1997, 2002; Melchiori et al., 1992). In general, these studies were conducted via matching-to-sample (MTS) procedure and used as stimuli sets of words in auditory and visual modalities, respectively dictated words (set A), printed words (set C), and pictures (set B).

The results of these studies showed that recombinative reading gradually increased as new words were taught, indicating that teaching whole words produced control for minimal units (letters or syllables), depending on the number of words employed in the training (e.g., de Rose et al., 1996, 1989; Hanna et al., 2008; Hübner-D'Oliveira, 1990; Hübner-D'Oliveira & Matos, 1993; Hübner et al., 2009). The important variable for the development of recombinative reading was multiple exemplar training (e.g., de Rose et al., 1996; Hanna et al., 2008, 2011; Hübner-D'Oliveira & Matos, 1993; Hübner et al., 2009; Matos et al., 2002) together with the systematic variation of the syllables that compose the taught words, i.e., the presentation of the same syllable in different positions inside the words, throughout the training (e.g., Hübner-D'Oliveira & Matos, 1993).

However, although the number of words used in training and the recombination of the same syllables in different positions in words are relevant variables for the acquisition of minimal unit control, the results of the studies showed great variability among participants' performance, with some participants not being able to read new words, even after being submitted to direct training of more than 30 (de Rose et al., 1989) or 50 words (de Rose et al., 1996). This variability across participants suggests that control for minimal units can develop from whole-word teaching, as proposed by Skinner (1957), but that this is not a condition for ensuring stable and systematic recombinative reading (Hanna et al., 2010a). This is possibly because teaching whole words leaves to chance the recognition of correspondences between sound and textual elements that compose words (Sidman, 1994), which is essential for the acquisition of control by minimal units and, consequently, for recombinative reading.

For this reason, many of the studies that used the whole word as a textual unit added, to the standard teaching procedure, special procedures that could favor the development of a differential response under the control of the smaller units of word components. The special procedures were employed in different phases of training and involved manipulations of the sound and/or textual elements of words. Taken together, the results of these studies indicated that recombinative reading occurred more frequently after training that presented the smaller units separately, although always in the context of whole words (de Rose et al., 1996; Matos et al., 2002; Melchiori et al., 2000). However, the variability, again found among participants' performances, suggests that indirect training of smaller units may be effective, but not sufficient for the development of recombinative reading in a systematic way among all participants.

Given the results obtained, another possibility to be investigated would be the effect of direct training of smaller units than the word on the emergence of recombinative reading. Direct training of smaller units would aim to establish the relations between graphemes and phonemes necessary for the establishment of control by minimal units and, consequently, favor the development of recombinative reading.

Serejo et al. (2007) conducted a study with disyllable words and added, to whole-word teaching, a syllabic training. De Souza et al. (2009) also investigated the effect of explicit training of units smaller than the word on the development of recombinative reading. To this end, they added to whole-word training, a direct training of the relations between dictated and printed syllables (AC relation) and a word construction training. In general, the procedures employed by Serejo et al. (2007) and de Souza et al. (2009) were effective in establishing relations between syllabic sound and text units and favored the acquisition of control for minimal units. However, the procedure used by de Souza et al. (2009), which produced more systematic performance among participants, used very extensive training to enable differential syllable response and positive results in the development of recombinative reading. The disadvantage of using long teaching procedures is that they may produce avoidance behaviors by children and higher dropout rates, which are often accompanied by decrease in performance (Hanna et al., 2010a).

For this reason, and given the data obtained by Serejo et al. (2007) and Souza et al. (2009), two questions seemed relevant and somewhat interrelated. The first referred to the possibility of obtaining control by minimal units and recombinative reading through a less extensive procedure, and the second was related to the possible effect of direct teaching, not only of smaller units, but also of specific units that are components of the recombination of (new) words. If direct teaching of the specific units presented in the new words was sufficient to produce abstraction of these units, then it would be possible that less extensive teaching procedures would allow the development of recombinative reading.

The influence of direct training of the smallest textual unit (letter) employed in the recombination words has already been demonstrated in previous studies (e.g., Bishop, 1964; Jeffrey & Samuels, 1967), which showed better results when participants were submitted to direct training of the letters employed in the words. An important aspect of the study by Jeffrey and Samuels (1967) was the attempt to control both the participants' prior history of the stimuli and the way these stimuli were composed and presented in the study, using invented teaching units. In this sense, Brazilian studies have used a pseudo-alphabet to teach reading, aiming to control possible effects of the history with words from the Portuguese language and Arabic alphabet, as well as to manipulate the composition of stimuli regarding, for example, the number of syllables and letters used and the form of recombination of the pseudo-alphabet units (Hanna et al., 2008, 2011; Hanna et al. 2010b).

Hanna et al. (2010b), considering the advantages of using pseudo-alphabet to control the pre-experimental history of research participants, conducted a study with the objective of verifying the effect of direct training of different extensions of units smaller than words (letters and syllables) on the development of recombinative reading (Experiment 2). The participants were eight college students, aged between 19 and 22 years. The procedure consisted, in general, of a previous training of smaller units (letters or syllables) followed by a training of whole words.

The results of all tests showed that the participants submitted to letter training (Letter Group) had higher percentages of correct responses and less variability in performance than the participants submitted to syllable training (Syllable Group).

The better performance of participants in the Letters Group can be explained by the fact that test words were formed by recombining the letters of the training words. Thus, for these participants, reading new words depended on the recombination of the units that had been directly taught (letters), while for the Syllables Group, reading new words also depended on the change of control of previously learned units (syllables) for even smaller units of the test words (letters).

Thus, if the length of the smallest unit taught directly is an important variable and if the direct teaching of the smallest unit used in recombination words produces correct recombinative reading and little variability among participants (de Souza et al., 2009; Hanna et al., 2010b), direct teaching of letter sounds seems to have some advantages. The sound of each letter, that is, the phoneme, is the smallest unit in Portuguese language and, therefore, explicit teaching of the relations between letters and sounds would possibly favor the acquisition of control by minimal units and the emergence of recombinative reading. When the sound of each letter is taught, the response topography established in the presence of most letters individually is similar to that established in the presence of these same letters when presented in whole words. Based on these considerations, Inhauser (2012) developed the study described in the following section.

10.3 Effect of Directly Training Phonemes on the Emergence of Recombinative Reading

Inhauser (2012) conducted a study to investigate whether: (a) direct phoneme training, superimposed on word training, constituted from a pseudo-alphabet, would produce the development of stable and systematic recombinative reading among participants and, (b) the timing of phoneme training insertion is a relevant variable for recombinative reading. Twelve college students, aged between 18 and 37 years, participated in this study. The GEIC software (Capobianco et al., 2011) was used to manage the program Learning to Read and Write in Small Steps (*Aprendendo a Ler e Escrever em Pequenos Passos* [ALEPP]), described in detail in de Souza et al. (2009).

Participants were exposed to ALEPP with the inclusion of stimuli similar to those in Experiment 2 of Hanna et al. (2010b). The stimuli consisted of spoken words (A) and words written with a pseudo-alphabet (C), as well as phonemes and letters of the pseudo-alphabet corresponding to these phonemes. The words were disyllabic (consonant + vowel + consonant + vowel or CVCV) and composed of four phonemes. The letters of the pseudo-alphabet were created from the Greek alphabet and maintain one-to-one correspondence with the phonemes /a/, /ɛ/, /i/, /o/, /b/, /f/, /l/, /n/. The syllables used in the formation of the training words were the pseudo-alphabet syllables corresponding to NI, BO, LE, and FA. Each syllable was presented both at the beginning and at the end of the words throughout the training sessions. The new words, used in the tests, were composed of at least one syllable not directly trained, formed by recombining the letters of the training words. All vowels were open, and the words were pronounced as oxytones.

The study was composed of three experimental conditions: (a) Experimental Condition I – Prior Phoneme Training; (b) Experimental Condition II – Overlapping Phoneme Training; and (c) Experimental Condition III – Word Training. The 12 participants were divided equally among the three conditions.

In each of the experimental conditions, participants were taught relations between sound and text units by matching-to-sample (MTS; AC training) and oral naming (CD training). In the MTS task between sound units (A) and textual units (C), the participant had to select the printed stimulus (from three available choices) corresponding to the sound emitted by the program (phoneme or word). In oral naming training (CD), a written stimulus was presented at the top center of the screen, and the participant's task consisted of: (1) naming the stimulus presented on the screen when it was a word; or (2) making the sound corresponding to the printed stimulus (phoneme) when it was a letter. Correct responses were followed by reinforcing consequences. There were no programmed consequences for incorrect responses.

Experimental Condition I (Prior Training Phoneme) consisted of a systematic replication of Experiment 2 by Hanna et al. (2010b) and was composed of the following sequence of phases: (1) AC/CD Phoneme Training; (2) Initial Oral Word Reading Test; (3) AC/CD Training Cycles and Partial C′D/A′C′ Word Tests (A′ and C′ refer to sets of new words, which were not taught in training, formed by recombining parts of the trained words); and (4) Final Oral Word Reading Test. Phase 1 (AC and CD Training with Phonemes) aimed to teach the relationships between the letters of the pseudo-alphabet and the sounds corresponding to each of these letters. A total of eight phonemes were taught, two at a time. Phase 2 (Initial Oral Reading Test) evaluated the effect of Phoneme Training on oral reading of printed words with pseudo-alphabet. Twenty-six printed words were presented in this test; 12 of these were used in the training and 14 in the tests in subsequent phases of the experiment. Phase 3 (AC/CD training cycles and A′C′/C′D partial tests with words) aimed at teaching the relations between spoken words and words printed with pseudo-alphabet and checking the reading (receptive – A′C′ and oral – C′D) of new words formed by recombining the letters of training words (recombination or test words). This phase consisted of 6 cycles of training and testing new words, and in each cycle two words were taught, and four new recombination words were tested. Two of these recombination words were repeated in the 6 cycles, so that the total number of words taught was 12 and for new words was 14. Phase 4 (Final Oral Reading Test) evaluated oral reading the same 26 words presented in the initial test (12 training words and 14 test words) used in the experiment.

In Experimental Condition II (Overlapping Phoneme Training), participants were submitted in an overlapping of Phoneme Training and whole word teaching and testing. The sequence of phases in this experimental condition was: (1) Cycles of AC/CD Training and Partial Testing C′D/A′C′ of words with Overlapping Phoneme Training and (2) Final Oral Reading Test. Phase 1 (Cycles of AC/CD Training and Partial Tests C′D/A′C′ of words with Overlapping Phoneme Training) aimed to: (a) teach the relationships between spoken and printed words with a pseudo-alphabet, and to check the recombinative reading of novel words (pre-overlap partial tests); and (b) to teach the relationships between letters from the pseudo-alphabet and the sounds corresponding to each of these letters, and to check the effect of this learning on reading the same previously tested recombination words (post-overlap partial tests). As in Condition 1, two words and two phonemes were taught in each cycle and four test words were presented. Phase 2 (Final Oral Reading Test) assessed oral reading of the 26 words (12 training and 14 test words) used in the experiment. The procedure employed in this phase was identical to that of the Final Oral Reading Test of Experimental Condition I.

Experimental Condition III (Word Training) was composed of two phases: (1) Cycles of AC/CD Training and Partial Tests C′D/A′C′ with Words and (2) Final Oral Word Reading Test. Phase 1 (AC/CD Training Cycles and A′C′/C′D Partial Tests with Words) aimed to teach the relationships between spoken words and printed words with pseudo-alphabet and to check the reading of novel words formed by recombining the letters of the training words (recombination or test words). The procedure employed in this phase was identical to that of Phase 3 of Experimental Condition I. Phase 2 (Final Oral Reading Test) evaluated the oral reading of the 26 words (12 training and 14 test words) used in the experiment. The procedure used in this phase was identical to that of the Final Oral Reading Test (Phase 4) of Experimental Condition I.

The results of the Initial Oral Word Reading Test to which participants in Condition I were submitted after phoneme training showed that teaching phonemes alone was not enough to produce word reading; participants spelled the phonemes with accuracy rates higher than 90%, but none read the words presented. This result is similar to data obtained by Gomes (2007), Hanna et al. (2010b), and Rocha (1996), who suggest that exposure to words is essential to develop the repertoire of combining previously learned letters and/or phonemes in reading whole words.

The participants who participated in phoneme pretesting (Condition I) had the lowest number of errors in word learning, suggesting that establishing a differential response to smaller units (phonemes) in pretesting (Phase 1) favored the acquisition of words composed of these units. Conversely, the participants with the highest number of errors during word learning were those in Condition III, who were not exposed to direct phoneme training at any time.

The results of the partial tests of oral recombinative reading (C′D) and receptive recombinative reading (A′C′), performed during the word training and testing cycles, showed that participants in all three conditions showed recombinative reading, but differences were observed regarding the percentage of correct responses in testing, the speed with which recombinative reading occurred, and variability among participants.

Figure 10.1 shows the results regarding the oral recombinative reading tests (Tests C′D) and receptive reading tests (Tests A′C′) of participants in Condition I (P1, P2, P3 and P4). All participants showed recombinative reading throughout the tests of the six training cycles. In the oral reading tests (graphs on the left), three of the four participants presented high hit rates already from cycle 2 (P2, P3, and P4), and in the receptive reading tests (graphs on the right), the four participants

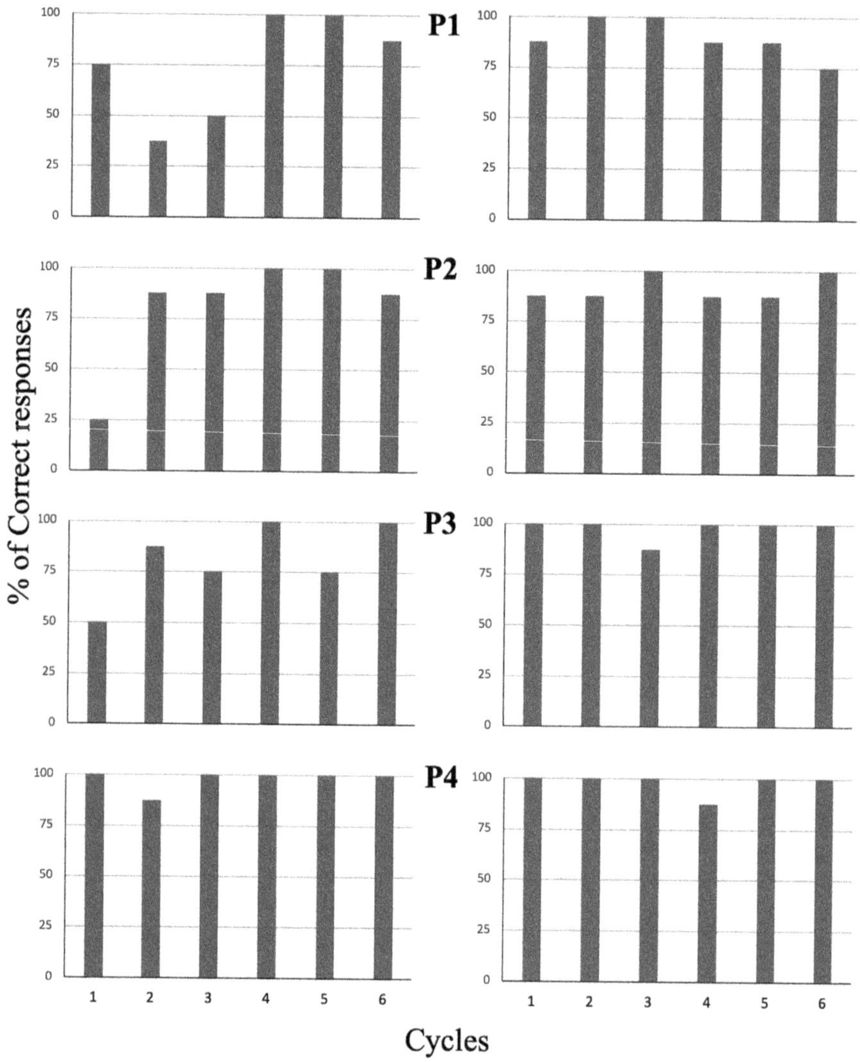

Fig. 10.1 Percentages of correct responses of each participant in partial tests C′D and A′C′ in condition I in each cycle

presented hit rates between 75 and 100% in all cycles. The differences observed between Tests A′C′ and C′D replicate previous studies (e.g., de Rose et al., 1996; de Souza et al., 2009; Hanna et al., 2008; Quinteiro, 2003; Rocha, 1996; Serejo et al., 2007) and suggest that an individual learns to recognize that an auditory stimulus corresponds to a textual stimulus, i.e., receptive reading, before learning the vocal response, with point-to-point correspondence in the presence of this text, i.e., oral reading (Greer & Ross, 2007).

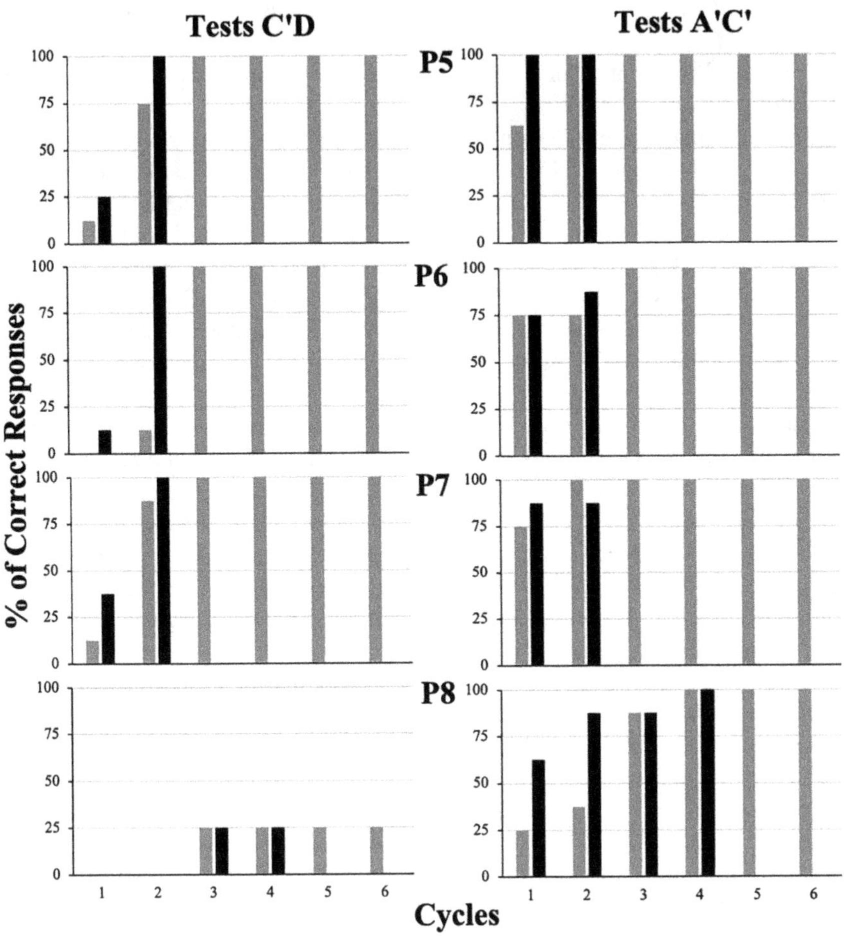

Fig. 10.2 Percentages of correct responses of each participant in partial tests C′D and A′C′ of each cycle of condition II. (*Note*. In cycles where phoneme training was introduced, the post-overlap results of phoneme training are represented by the black bars)

In Condition II (Fig. 10.2) it can be observed that the percentage of correct responses in the receptive (A′C′) and oral (C′D) recombinative reading tests after direct phoneme training (black bars) were higher than the hit rates in cycles 1 and 2 when only words had been directly taught (gray bars). Three of the four participants (P5, P6, and P7), presented 100% correct recombinative reading in all tests (oral – C′D and receptive – A′C′) as of cycle 2. Therefore, for these participants, individual instruction of only four phonemes and four whole words was sufficient for the emergence of recombinative reading, suggesting that training phonemes overlapped with words allowed an economy (of training) in relation to previous phoneme training.

The fourth participant (P8), on the other hand, showed low oral reading scores (hits equal or lower than 25%) in all C′D tests and in the first two receptive reading tests (hits equal or lower than 35%). The differences in scores on the C′D and A′C′ tests of the same participant provide support for the definition of reading as a network of relationships that are interconnected but can be acquired independently and in different ways over the course of a teaching program (e.g., de Rose, 2005, republished in Chap. 1 of this book; de Rose et al., 1996; Hanna et al., 2008; Matos et al., 1997, 2002, 2006; Müller et al., 2000; Saunders, 2011; Saunders et al., 2013; Sidman, 1971).

Finally, in Condition III (Fig. 10.3), the results replicated those of previous studies that used the word as the taught unit and demonstrate that recombinative reading increased gradually depending on the number of words employed in the training (e.g., de Rose et al., 1996, 1989; Gomes, 2007; Hanna et al., 2008, 2011; Hübner-D'Oliveira, 1990; Hübner et al., 2009; Hübner-D'Oliveira & Matos, 1993; Matos et al., 2006; Melchiori et al., 2000; Müeller et al., 2000; Quinteiro, 2003). Participants in this condition had smaller percentages of correct responses and greater variability compared to the other participants.

In the Final Oral Reading Test, all participants in Condition I showed recombination reading, whereas in Conditions II and III only three of the four participants had this repertoire. The results described above suggest that the participants in the two conditions with phoneme training had the most correct responses and the least variability among them. Thus, it is possible to state that phoneme training, either prior to or overlapped with word training, is more effective in establishing recombinative reading than training isolated whole words. Between the two conditions that used direct teaching of smaller units, overlapping phoneme training with word training enabled faster acquisition of recombinative reading and, therefore, more economical training. On the other hand, lower variability of results in the recombinative reading tests was observed in the phoneme pre-teaching condition.

The results of Conditions I and II can also be compared with previous studies that used direct training of smaller units than words (e.g., de Souza et al., 2009; Serejo et al., 2007). Compared to Serejo et al. (2007), which used explicit syllable training. The results of the present study also showed better performance and less variability among participants. The smallest trained unit (phoneme) was also the smallest unit used in the recombination words, which may have favored the emergence of recombinative reading with high scores and little variability among participants. It is important to note, however, that the participants in Inhauser's (2012) study were college-educated adults with long prior reading experience and the participants in Serejo et al.'s (2007) study were non-literate children. Although Inhauser's (2012) study was conducted using pseudo-alphabets, the college adults' prior repertoire of relating phonemes and graphemes and prior phoneme-joining training may be variables facilitating recombinative reading after phonics

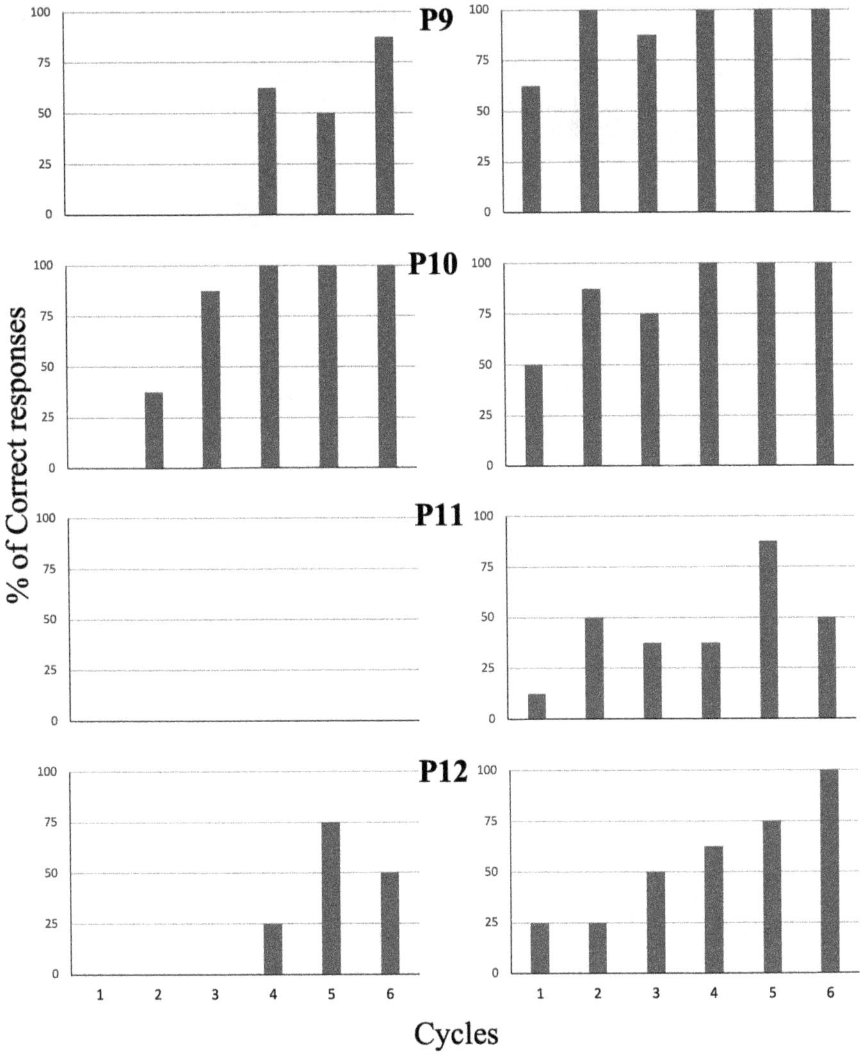

Fig. 10.3 Percentages of correct responses of each participant in partial tests C′D and A′C′ of each cycle of condition III

instruction (Guimarães, 2019). More recent studies have then set out to investigate the effects of phoneme training on children who are not yet literate (e.g., da Silva, 2015; Rorato, 2014).

In one of these studies, Rorato (2014) investigated the effect of teaching phonemes and graphemes on the recombinative reading of four children, divided into two groups, so that two children were exposed to grapheme and phoneme training (teaching group) and two were not (control group). The results indicated that the participants in the teaching group showed superior performance in the final evaluation of directly trained relations; however, only one of them showed recombinative reading. It is worth noting, however, that the development of recombinative reading for this participant occurred only after learning relations involving whole words, as verified by Inhauser (2012). The other participant in the teaching group missed all the recombinative reading trials in the final test, consisting of words formed by recombining the same syllables as the taught words, and had only 6% correct on trials that required intrasyllabic recombination (words with the same phonemes taught, but forming different syllables). Participants in the control group also did not demonstrate recombinative reading.

A second study with non-literate children, conducted by da Silva (2015), assessed the effect of a reading teaching procedure that integrated the teaching of letter sounds, syllables, and whole words. The whole words were planned through a matrix that controlled the variable position of syllables in words. The results showed that two of the three participants exposed to the teaching presented recombinative reading at the end of the study. However, these results can be considered inconclusive, given that one of the control participants also presented the final performance of recombinative reading, showing a possible interference of learning in other settings, such as at school.

In view of the results presented, some observations are already possible and seem pertinent regarding the role of direct phoneme teaching in the development of recombinative reading repertoire. As previously described, isolated teaching of grapheme-phoneme relations is not sufficient for the emergence of whole-word reading but teaching minimal units (phonemes) combined with words produces recombinative reading.

In the case of adult participants, the emergence of stable recombinative reading with little variability between participants was verified (e.g., Inhauser, 2012). This result is possibly related to the prior experience of college-aged adults in responding under the control of smaller units and establishing grapheme-phoneme relationships. When the participants in the studies were children, teaching sounds of letters combined with words produced the emergence of recombinative reading for most participants. However, in this case, one can still observe variability between the percentages of correct responses between participants (e.g., da Silva, 2015; Rorato, 2014). Another possible observation is that direct phoneme training seemed to produce intrasyllabic recombinations more quickly and effectively than when the smallest teaching unit is the syllable (Inhauser, 2012). In addition, there are fewer phonemes than syllables in the Portuguese, which may represent an economy in teaching when phonics instruction is used (Guimarães, 2019). Despite these advantages, phoneme instruction also has some disadvantages. According to de Rose (2005, republished in Chap. 1 of this book), directly teaching molecular units is insufficient to teach the junction of these units to form a word. This joining, named co-articulation by Saunders (2011), generally presents a different sound in the word than the sound of the isolated phoneme. Thus, joining phonemes may be more difficult than joining syllables, given that syllables are more natural units in the Portuguese language (Guimarães, 2019).

Considering the advantages of using phonics instruction, Guimarães (2019) conducted studies involving the direct teaching of phonemes, but adding strategies aimed at solving the possible disadvantages of this type of instruction, such as phoneme coupling training. In addition, the study added the teaching of relations between sounds and images of persons/objects emitting the phoneme, assigning meaning to the relations. The aim of the research was to investigate the effect of teaching relationships between phonemes, graphemes, and images of persons/objects emitting the phoneme, in conjunction with phoneme-joining training, on the development of reading with comprehension, receptive reading, and textual behavior of recombination words, in children who were not yet literate and in a collective instructional context.

Study 1 was conducted with four children attending the first year of elementary school who presented difficulties in literacy. In the final assessment, all participants showed emergence of recombinative textual behavior and recombinative receptive reading. The emergence of reading with comprehension occurred for three of the four participants. In Study 2, the participants were five children attending the last year of kindergarten who had not yet become literate. Of these five participants, four were subjected to the reading teaching procedure and one participant, called control, was not exposed to this procedure. All participants presented receptive reading of recombination words, three participants presented oral reading of new words, and the development of reading with comprehension was observed for two of the four participants exposed to the training. The data from the control participant (not exposed to the training) suggest that the changes in the other participants' performances were produced by the teaching procedures of the study (Guimarães, 2019).

In general, the data presented by the most recent studies (da Silva, 2015; Rorato, 2014) corroborate the hypothesis that direct phoneme teaching may have the advantage of producing recombination responses with greater speed and for a wider range of words, given that the Portuguese language has fewer phonemes than syllables and that recombining these phonemes will allow reading all possible words. The studies conducted by Guimarães (2019) add two other variables that seem to favor recombinative reading, which are teaching sounds with meaning and training the junction of phonemes.

10.4 Final Considerations

Current studies on reading suggest the need to investigate which procedures could contribute to the teaching of phoneme-consonant junction, whose recombination seems to be more difficult than that of vowels, and the impact of the change of isolated phoneme sounds, when they are co-articulated, on the acquisition of control by minimal units.

Other important investigations refer to teaching procedures to favor the acquisition of fluent reading that can be used in group contexts. Results from studies conducted in group situations could contribute to the use of more effective instructional formats and improve the reading performance of Brazilian students.

Finally, it is essential to emphasize that experimental research on recombinative reading should be continued, especially to support decisions about the teaching procedures to be applied, either to typical populations or to those with behavioral difficulties or deficits. Such need is still present for decisions based on scientific evidence to be the dominant practice of teaching policies and practices in our country.

In this sense, the National Literacy Policy (PNA) was published in Brasil (2019c), which offers evidence-based teaching of reading and writing as guidelines for Brazilian education. The document describes that the phonemic summation skill (putting phonemes together) has, as prerequisites, phonological awareness skills, which are discrimination and manipulation skills of spoken sounds. Future work in recombinative reading may consider adding previous steps to measure the effect of these possible prerequisites.

References

Adams, M. J. (1994). *Beginning to read: Thinking and learning about print*. MIT Press.

Bishop, C. H. (1964). Transfer effects on word and letter training in reading. *Journal of Verbal Learning and Verbal Behavior, 3*, 215–221. https://doi.org/10.1016/S0022-5371(64)80044-X

Brasil. (2019a). *Programa Internacional de Avaliação de Estudantes (PISA). Ministério da Educação (MEC), Instituto Nacional de Estudos e Pesquisas Educacionais Anísio Teixeira (INEP), Diretoria de Avaliação da Educação Básica (DAEB). Brasília (DF)*. http://download.inep.gov.br/acoes_internacionais/pisa/documentos/2019/relatorio_PISA_2018_preliminar.pdf

Brasil. (2019b). *Relatório SAEB. Instituto Nacional de Estudos e Pesquisas Educacionais Anísio Teixeira (INEP). Brasília (DF)*. https://download.inep.gov.br/educacao_basica/saeb/2019/resultados/relatorio_de_resultados_do_saeb_2019_volume_1.pdf

Brasil. (2019c). *Política Nacional de Alfabetização (PNA). Ministério da Educação (MEC), Secretaria de Alfabetização (SEALF). Brasília (DF)*. http://portal.mec.gov.br/images/banners/caderno_pna_final.pdf

Capobianco, D., Orlando, A. F., Marques, L. B., Teixeira, C. A. C., de Souza, D. G., & de Rose, J. C. (2011). *Gerenciador de Ensino Individualizado por Computador (GEIC-LECH; Versão 0.4) Computer Manager Individualized Teaching (Version 0,4)*.

da Silva, C. M. S. (2015). *O efeito do ensino de relações envolvendo sílabas e fonemas-grafemas sobre a leitura recombinativa*. Doctoral dissertation, Pontifícia Universidade Católica de São Paulo. Repositório Institucional PUC-SP. https://tede2.pucsp.br/handle/handle/16751

de Rose, J. C. C. (2005). Análise comportamental da aprendizagem de leitura e escrita. *Revista Brasileira de Análise do Comportamento, 1*(1), 29–50. https://doi.org/10.18542/rebac.v1i1.676

de Rose, J. C., de Souza, D. G., Rossito, A. L., & de Rose, T. M. S. (1989). Aquisição de leitura após história de fracasso escolar: Equivalência de estímulos e generalização. *Psicologia: Teoria e Pesquisa, 5*(3), 325–346.

de Rose, J. C., de Souza, D. G., Rossito, A. L., & de Rose, T. M. S. (1992). Stimulus equivalence and generalization in reading after matching to sample by exclusion. In S. C. Hayes & L. J. Hayes (Eds.), *Understanding verbal relations* (pp. 69–82). Context Press.

de Rose, J. C., de Souza, D. G., & Hanna, E. S. (1996). Teaching reading and spelling: Stimulus equivalence and generalization. *Journal of Applied Behavior Analysis, 29*, 451–469. https://doi.org/10.1901/jaba.1996.29-451

de Souza, D. G., de Rose, J. C. C., Faleiros, T. C., Hanna, E. S., & McIlvane, B. (2009). Teaching generative Reading via recombination of minimal textual units: A legacy of verbal behavior to children in Brazil. *International Journal of Psychology and Psychological Therapy, 9*(1), 19–44.

Gomes, R. C. (2007). *Controle por unidades mínimas e leitura recombinativa: Solicitação de comportamento textual durante aquisição de pré-requisitos.* Master's thesis, Universidade de São Paulo. Repositório Institucional USP. https://www.teses.usp.br/teses/disponiveis/47/47132/tde-23012008-141711/publico/Gomes_tde.pdf

Greer, R. D., & Ross, D. E. (2007). *Verbal behavior analysis: Inducing and expanding new verbal capabilities in children with language delays.* Allyn & Bacon.

Guimarães, L.S. (2019). *Efeitos do ensino de relações entre fonemas, grafemas e imagens e do treino de junção de fonemas no desempenho em leitura recombinativa em uma instrução em grupo.* Doctoral dissertation, Pontifícia Universidade Católica de São Paulo. Repositório Institucional USP. https://tede2.pucsp.br/handle/handle/22215

Hanna, E. S., Kohldorf, M., Quinteiro, R. S., Fava, V. M., de Souza, D. G., & de Rose, J. C. (2008). Diferenças individuais na aquisição de leitura com um sistema linguístico em miniatura. *Psicologia: Teoria e Pesquisa, 24*, 45–58. https://doi.org/10.1590/S0102-37722008000100006

Hanna, E. S., Benvennuti, M., & Melo, R. M. (2010a). Entraves no ensino de leitura e escrita e o Programa de Ciência Aplicada do INCT-ECCE. In *XIII Simpósio de Pesquisa e Intercâmbio Científico em Psicologia da ANPEPP*. ANPEPP.

Hanna, E. S., Karino, C. A., Araújo, V. T., & de Souza, D. G. (2010b). Leitura recombinativa de pseudopalavras impressas em pseudoalfabeto: Similaridade entre palavras e extensão da unidade ensinada. *Psicologia USP, 21*(2), 275–311. https://doi.org/10.1590/S0103-65642010000200005

Hanna, E. S., Kohldorf, M., Quinteiro, R. S., Melo, R. M., de Souza, D. G., de Rose, J. C., & McIlvane, W. J. (2011). Recombinative reading derived from a pseudoword instruction in a miniature linguistic system. *Journal of the Experimental Analysis of Behavior, 95*, 21–40. https://doi.org/10.1901/jeab.2011.95-21

Hübner, M. M., Gomes, R. C., & McIlvane, W. J. (2009). Recombinative generalization in minimal verbal unit-based reading instruction for pre-reading children. *Experimental Analysis of Human Behavior Bulletin, 27*, 11–17.

Hübner-D'Oliveira, M. M. (1990). *Estudos em relações de equivalência: Uma contribuição do controle por unidades mínimas na aprendizagem de leitura com pré-escolares.* Unpublished doctoral dissertation, Universidade de São Paulo.

Hübner-D'Oliveira, M. M., & Matos, M. A. (1993). Controle discriminativo na aquisição da leitura: Efeito da repetição e variação na posição das sílabas e letras. *Temas em Psicologia, 2*, 99–108.

Inhauser, L. Z. (2012). *Controle por unidades verbais mínimas e extensão da unidade ensinada: O efeito do treino de fonemas na emergência da leitura recombinativa.* Master's thesis, Universidade de São Paulo, Biblioteca digital de Teses e Dissertações da USP. https://doi.org/10.11606/D.47.2012.tde-19032013-113247

Jeffrey, W. E., & Samuels, S. J. (1967). Effect of method of reading training on initial learning and transfer. *Journal of Verbal Learning and Verbal Behavior, 6*, 353–358. https://doi.org/10.1016/S0022-5371(67)80124-5

Matos, M. A., Peres, W., Hübner, M. M., & Malheiros, R. H. (1997). Oralização e cópia: Efeitos sobre a aquisição de leitura generalizada recombinativa. *Temas em Psicologia, 1*, 47–63.

Matos, M. A., Hübner, M. M., Serra, V. R., Basaglia, A. E., & Avanzi, A. L. (2002). Rede de relações condicionais e leitura recombinativa: Pesquisando o ensinar a ler. *Arquivos Brasileiros de Psicologia, 54*(3), 285–303.

Matos, M. A., Avanzi, A. L., & McIlvane, B. (2006). Rudimentary reading repertoires via stimulus equivalence and recombination of minimal verbal units. *The Analysis of Verbal Behavior, 22*, 3–19. https://doi.org/10.1007/BF03393023

Melchiori, L. E., Souza, D. G., & de Rose, J. C. (1992). Aprendizagem da leitura por meio de um procedimento de discriminação sem erros (exclusão): Uma replicação com pré-escolares. *Psicologia: Teoria e Pesquisa, 8*, 101–111.

Melchiori, L. E., Souza, D. G., & de Rose, J. C. (2000). Reading, equivalence, and recombination of units: A replication with students with different learning histories. *Journal of Applied Behavior Analysis, 33*, 97–100. https://doi.org/10.1901/jaba.2000.33-97

Müeller, M. M., Olmi, D. J., & Saunders, K. J. (2000). Recombinative generalization of within-syllable units in prereading children. *Journal of Applied Behavior Analysis, 33*, 515–531. https://doi.org/10.1901/jaba.2000.33-515

Quinteiro, R. S. (2003). *Aprendizagem de leitura receptiva e de comportamento textual: Efeito do número de palavras treinadas sobre o repertório recombinativo*. Unpublished Master's thesis, Universidade de Brasília.

Rocha, A. M. (1996). *Aprendizagem de leitura de palavras: Efeito do treino de diferentes unidades textuais*. Unpublished Master's thesis, Universidade de Brasília.

Rorato, C. B. (2014). *O efeito do ensino de diferentes unidades mínimas sobre a leitura recombinativa: O efeito do emparelhamento auditivo visual com sílabas e letras*. Relatório Final de Iniciação Científica (PIBIC-CNPq), Pontifícia Universidade Católica de São Paulo.

Saunders, K. J. (2011). Designing instructional programming for early reading skills. In W. W. Fisher, C. C. Piazza, & H. S. Roane (Eds.), *Handbook of applied behavior analysis* (pp. 92–109). Guilford Press.

Saunders, K. J., O'Donnel, J., Vaidya, M., & Williams, D. C. (2013). Recombinative generalization of within-syllable units in nonreading adults with mental retardation. *Journal of Applied Behavior Analysis, 36*(1), 95–99. https://doi.org/10.1901/jaba.2003.36-95

Serejo, P., Hanna, E. S., de Souza, D. G., & de Rose, J. C. (2007). Leitura e repertório recombinativo: Efeito da quantidade de treino e da composição dos estímulos. *Revista Brasileira de Análise do Comportamento, 3*(2), 191–215. https://doi.org/10.18542/rebac.v3i2.831

Sidman, M. (1971). Reading and auditory-visual equivalences. *Journal of Speech and Hearing Research, 14*, 5–13. https://doi.org/10.1044/jshr.1401.05

Sidman, M. (1994). *Equivalence relations and behavior: A research history*. Authors Cooperative,, Publishers.

Skinner, B. F. (1957). *Verbal behavior*. Appleton-Century-Crofts.

Chapter 11
Learning to Read and Write in Adults: Contributions of Behavior Analysis

Alessandra Rocha de Albuquerque and Raquel Maria de Melo

11.1 Introduction

Brazil currently has 11.3 million illiterate youth and adults. This number, although high, indicates the reduction of approximately five percentage points of illiteracy rates in the country over the past 17 years. In 2001, 12% of the population was illiterate, in 2018 this number was reduced to 6.8% (Brazilian Institute of Geography and Statistics/*Instituto Brasileiro de Geografia e Estatística* [IBGE], 2018; Paulo Montenegro Institute, 2018). This reduction, however, is still considered unsatisfactory since, according to the Brazilian National Education Plan (*Plano Nacional de Educação* [PNE]) 2014–2024 (INEP, 2015), the literacy target of the population by 2015 was 93.5%, a rate higher than that obtained 3 years later.

The PNA (Brasil, 2019) points out that education should be based on scientific evidence and that, in the case of the literacy process, such grounding does not consist in "imposing a method, but proposing that programs, curriculum guidelines, and literacy practices always take into account the most robust findings of scientific research" (p. 20). From this perspective, Behavior Analysis, which has produced systematic knowledge about learning to read and write, has much to contribute. Research in the area has shown positive learning results with populations with special needs and/or that failed when exposed to teaching methods traditionally used in the school context (the other chapters in this section of the book bring some examples with different populations).

A. R. de Albuquerque (✉)
Universidade Católica de Brasília, Brasília, DF, Brazil
e-mail: arocha@p.ucb.br

R. M. de Melo
Universidade de Brasília, Brasília, DF, Brazil

A. R. de Albuquerque, R. M. de Melo (eds.), *Contributions of Behavior Analysis to Reading and Writing Comprehension*, https://doi.org/10.1007/978-3-031-40868-7_11

Chapter 2 of this book mapped out research on reading and writing from a behavior analytic perspective. It is evident in this mapping that, despite the large number of studies already carried out and the diversity of populations involved in them, research with adults is still scarce. This number is even lower if we keep only the studies with illiterate adults who were not exposed, for social reasons, to formal education in their childhood, and exclude investigations with adults with some kind of cognitive impairment (e.g., intellectual disability, Down syndrome).

Although the principles underlying learning to read and write are the same regardless of the target teaching audience, the process of learning these repertoires later in life is known to present additional challenges (Kruidenier et al., 2010; UNESCO, 2014). Adults have previous experiences and knowledge, which can both facilitate and compete with new learning. At this point, understanding reading and writing as complex, functionally independent behavioral repertoires involving different relations between stimuli and between stimuli and responses (de Rose, 2005; republished in Chap. 1 of this book), as well as teaching programs based on this perspective, show potential benefits, since the different behaviors that make up these repertoires can be independently assessed and taught.

This chapter, consisting of three sections, will address learning to read and write in youth and adults from a behavioral analytic approach. The first section will present a review of Brazilian studies on the topic. In the second, it will describe the experience of a reading instruction unit for adults that operated in the city of Brasilia, through a research project involving a partnership between the Catholic University of Brasilia (UCB) and the University of Brasilia (UnB). The third and final section will present data from three participants of this reading unit followed by final considerations.

11.2 Research on Adult Reading and Writing

In general, there are few studies on Adult Learning (AL), not only from the perspective of interest of this chapter, but also in other areas of knowledge that address the topic (e.g., Ferreira et al., 2020; Lafin, 2014; Paiva et al., 2019). Among this set of studies, those that investigate the learning processes of this population are still scarcer (Sanceverino et al., 2020).

By mapping empirical studies (articles, theses, and dissertations) on reading and writing, based on the equivalence paradigm and conditional discrimination procedures reported in Chap. 2 of this book, we identified nine studies conducted with illiterate adults without reported comorbidities: four articles (A), two Doctoral dissertations (D) and three Master's theses (T). Table 11.1 presents the number of participants and their characteristics, the dependent variable (DV), and procedures of each study. Five of these studies were conducted with different versions of the program Learning to Read and Write in Small Steps® (*Aprendendo a Ler e Escrever em Pequenos Passos* [ALEPP]) which, throughout its improvements, had different versions and denominations - on paper sheets presented in folders (used by Melchiori

Table 11.1 Characteristics of the selected studies

Study	Type	Participants		DV	Procedure
		N	Features		
Medeiros et al. (1997)	A	1	37 years old History of school failure	Reading Writing	Matching dictated word-printed word Exclusion procedure Words with simple and complex syllables
Melchiori et al. (2000)	A	8[a]	40–65 years old Illiterate Did not attend school	Reading	Matching dictated word-printed word and composing printed words from letters (copying) Exclusion procedure Words with single syllables
Bandini et al. (2014)	A	8	17–64 years old Illiterate AL students Participants at a university research center	Reading Handwriting	Conditional discrimination between the dictated and printed word Study 1: ALEPP Module 1 with words with single syllables (4 participants) Study 2: ALEPP Module 2 with complex words (4 participants)
Calcagno et al. (2016)	A	15	17.6–62.2 Years old Illiterate 13 AL students	Reading Writing Typology of errors	ALEPP Module 1 with words with single syllables ALEPP Module 2 with complex words
Llausas (2008)	D	5	18–36 years old Have attended school in the past Low to high performances on early reading assessments AL students	General reading Word construction Reading sentences (all with simple and complex syllables)	Master Software Teaching conditional relations between dictated word, printed word and picture and composition of printed words (copy) and words dictated from letters
Calcagno[b] (2015)	D	14	AL students	Reading and writing Program adherence	Parts of ALEPP
Santos (2002)	T	3[a]	27–72 years old Illiterate	Reading Writing	Teaching minimal textual units to adults: letters, monosyllables, disyllables and trisyllables Program derived from ProgLeit
Santos (2011)	T	11	AL students (1st and 2nd grade) Illiterate adults Attended school for a short time	Reading Handwriting Reading and writing new words and sentences	Using the Master Software Conditional discrimination training between dictated words, written words, and pictures Syllabic and letter training

(continued)

Table 11.1 (continued)

Study	Type	Participants		DV	Procedure
		N	Features		
Zanco (2011)	T	5	Freshmen High School Students They presented difficulty in reading and writing	Reading and writing simple and complex words and sentences Reading texts	Use of JClic software Teaching sentences with simple and complex, dictated and written words, and pictures representing the sentences Composition training of words from letters and syllables

Note. [a]Study with participation of children; the number of participants reported corresponds only to youth and/or adults; [b]Full version of the study is not available in the institutional portals of theses and dissertations; only the abstract was consulted. *AL* Adult Learning

et al., 2000), in an offline computerized version, called ProgLeit (used by Santos, 2002), and in its current online version (used by Calcagno, 2015; Calcagno et al., 2016).

The pioneering Brasilian study with adults was that of Medeiros et al. (1997) in which a 37-year-old illiterate woman was exposed to three weekly sessions, using the exclusion procedure[1] (Dixon, 1977) to match dictated and printed words presented on sheets of paper displayed in catalog folders. A total of 30 disyllable and trisyllable words composed of simple (consonants and vowel) and complex syllables or with irregularities of the Portuguese language (e.g., digraphs, x sounding like z) were taught, three by three, in 10 successive teaching steps. Another 20 words, composed by recombining the syllables of the directly taught words, were used in generalization reading assessment trials.

In addition to matching-to-sample training, trials with oral word naming, composition of the word using single letters presented on cards, and handwriting the same word were conducted. In general, each teaching step was performed in a single session and correct responses were above 90%. Percentages close to 100% of correct responses were obtained in posttest measures. The authors concluded that the procedure used was effective to teach generalized reading with comprehension.

Melchiori et al. (2000), by replicating a study conducted by de Rose et al. (1996) with an initial version of the module for teaching words with single syllables (which originated Module 1 of ALEPP), extended the results of the first study by applying the procedure to participants of different profiles, including eight adult women. In daily sessions of approximately 30 min, relations between dictated and printed words and the copy of printed words were taught, respectively, through the matching-to-sample (MTS), exclusion, and constructed response matching-to-sample (CRMTS[2]) tasks. The procedure was composed of 25 units, of which 15 were

[1] In the exclusion procedure, when presented with a new dictated word, the participant is asked to choose the corresponding printed word from two alternatives, a previously taught word and a new word (Dixon, 1977).

[2] In the CRMTS procedure, the participant must select the letters (or syllables) to compose the printed or dictated word presented as a model, which characterizes the tasks of copying and dictation by composition.

teaching units and 10 were testing units. In the teaching units, 51 disyllable and trisyllable words consisting of single syllables were taught. In successive evaluations, all participants learned to read the directly taught words and showed an increase in the percentages of correctly reading new words. It was concluded that these results were due to the teaching program since none of the participants attended school.

Bandini et al. (2014) conducted two studies, 1 and 2, using Modules 1 and 2 of ALEPP with illiterate adults, respectively (these modules are described in de Souza et al., 2009). In Study 1, four illiterate participants (one adolescent and three adults) were exposed to MTS and CRMTS (dictation) procedures for teaching words with single syllables. There was an increase in the percentage of correct responses in reading and writing (dictation) in the posttest, compared to the pretest, for all participants, with more systematic results in reading. In Study 2, one participant from Study 1 and three new participants, all adults, were exposed to Module 2 of teaching words with complex syllables using the same procedures (MTS and CRMTS). As in Study 1, the percentage of correct responses in the posttest were higher than in the pretest, both for reading and writing, and the results for writing were more variable than those for reading.

Calcagno et al. (2016) also used Modules 1 and 2 of ALEPP in a study resulting from the first author's doctoral dissertation (Calcagno, 2015). In this study, the errors in reading, handwritten dictation, and composition tasks of seven illiterate adults exposed to Module 1 and eight exposed to Module 2 were analyzed. This analysis was performed by categorizing each error based on a set of 14 previously defined categories. The participants exposed to Module 1 presented eight of the 14 types of errors and the two most frequent were: *general unfamiliarity with the word* (answering *I don't know*) and *letter substitution, omission or addition* (e.g., writing *sop* instead of *soap*), which together represented 80.5% of these participants' errors. Participants in Module 2 made 10 types of errors; the three most frequent, in decreasing order, were: *letter substitution, omission or addition*, *competition* (e.g., writing *dee* instead of *bee*; that is, error related to the use of a word with different grapheme, but with phonemes similar to the correct word), and *complex syllables* (e.g., reading *so-ap* instead of *soap*), which together accounted for 67.4% of the total errors made. The comparison of performances in the evaluation of the teaching steps that make up Modules 1 and 2 and, in the baseline, (pretest) suggests that the teaching programs were efficient in reducing some types of errors both in reading and writing.

Llausas (2008), in her doctoral research, also used a teaching program (Mestre; Goyos & Almeida, 1996), with words with simple (46 words) and complex (25 words) syllables, aiming to improve the reading and writing repertoires of five adult learners. The MTS and CRMTS procedures were used to teach relationships between dictated words and printed words and between dictated words and pictures, copying and dictation. Initial assessments indicated that participants had different reading and writing repertoires: two participants showed poor performance in both reading and writing complex words and words with simple syllables; three participants were proficient in reading but had difficulty in writing. The former, after exposure to the teaching program, showed emergent performance (without direct training) in expressive reading (oral reading) and comprehension (pairing printed words and pictures), in addition to reading and writing new words. The participants who already read showed emergence of writing of the taught and new words, besides reading sentences with words with complex syllables.

Santos (2002) applied a program derived from ProgLeit (Rosa Filho et al., 1998) in three illiterate adults. The program was divided into three units, applied sequentially, and focused on teaching letters (Unit 1), syllables (Unit 2) and words (Unit 3), respectively. Each unit was composed of a set of teaching steps which, in turn, comprised different types of tasks: MTS with exclusion, naming, and CRMTS (copying and dictation). All participants learned to read the words taught as well as new (not directly taught) words.

Santos (2011) conducted a study with 11 non-literate adults attending AL. A program for teaching reading and writing words with simple and complex syllables was applied and evaluated. The program, developed in the Mestre software, involved teaching conditional relations between dictated words, pictures and written words (MTS tasks) and composing dictated and written words and written syllables from letters (CRMTS tasks), organized in four phases, the first two with simple syllables and the last two with complex syllables. The emergence of oral reading and handwriting were evaluated, behaviors that were not directly taught. Generalization tests (with novel stimuli) were also performed to evaluate reading and writing of words composed of simple and complex syllables and sentences (with taught and novel words). The results showed that all participants read the generalization words, and most also read the sentences. In the case of writing, there was also an increase in scores, but to a lesser extent, mainly in writing sentences.

In the study developed by Zanco (2011), the effectiveness of a teaching procedure was evaluated, using the JClic software, for five high school freshmen students (15–18 years old) who presented difficulties in reading and writing. Conditional discrimination was taught in four units involving dictated and written sentences, with simple and complex syllables (e.g., ch, nh, lh), and images representing sentences, and the composition of written words from letters and syllables. In the evaluations performed after the teaching procedure, most participants showed reading and writing of both words and sentences, taught and new (generalization). The teaching procedure with sentences also improved text reading.

Although the set of results indicating the possibility of successfully using teaching programs based on the equivalence paradigm with adults, the small number of studies with this population is evident. There are even fewer replications involving the same teaching procedure, which are essential to increase both the internal and external validity of the investigated procedures. In an attempt to broaden the evidence regarding the possibility of using this methodology with adults, as well as to meet an important social demand, a research project was developed and a reading unit for adults was organized in the city of Brasilia, connected to two universities in the city (UCB and UnB), which will be described below.

11.3 Adult Reading Unit

The Adult Reading Unit - ARU (UCB/UnB) operated between 2012 and 2017, motivated by the production of knowledge about reading and writing with this population, through equivalence-based instruction[3] (EBI; Fienup et al., 2010). In addition to support from the universities, the ARU received resources from the Foundation for Research Support of the Federal District (FAP-DF), through a call for research funding (Call n. 03/2015, spontaneous demand).

Prior to the structuring the ARU, partnerships were made with community literacy centers linked to non-governmental, social welfare, and religious institutions and community leaders, for the evaluation and application of reading teaching programs for adults who attended these centers. These partnerships, however, were interrupted due to a series of difficulties: lack of physical space suitable for the teaching activities; high turnover of the people attending the literacy centers; no computer network; difficulties of displacement and risk for undergraduate research students, since many of the centers were open at night and in less favored, more distant regions with higher rates of violence.

From this unsuccessful experience, the ARU was structured at the UCB campus. This decision solved important problems (availability of adequate physical space, computers and internet network; ease of access and safety of research students), but, on the other hand, it required the team to attract participants to displace to the University.

UCB has a long tradition in developing outreach programs. Two important programs, which have existed for more than 20 years, are Citizen Literacy and the Senior Citizens' Center (SCC). The former is attended by people over 18 years of age, mostly illiterate and some semi-literate. They are offered literacy courses, digital inclusion and computer settings in classes that take place at the UCB campus itself, but also in spaces provided by partner institutions in administrative regions near the University. The SCC serves people over 65 years old, some of whom are illiterate, and offers recreational, artistic, cultural, and learning activities at the UCB campus, focusing on promoting the quality of life of the elderly. These programs are widely publicized in the community and attract many participants, who regularly attend the UCB campus.

Thus, the ARU was originally structured in the space of the psychosocial-gerontology laboratory of UCB and had as its target audience illiterate elderly members of the SCC. The laboratory has all the necessary structure to carry out sessions of reading instruction: stalls with computers for individual activity, meeting room and internet network. The initial choice of the elderly was because they have more availability of time and ease of travel to participate in the teaching program in the

[3] The term EBI has been used to refer to the use of stimulus equivalence technology aimed at developing behavioral repertoire in applied contexts. "Studies involving EBI have sought to assess the potential of equivalence class formation in assisting in the establishment of challenging stimulus relationships in various populations" (Silva et al., 2018, p. 1158).

ULA (they are retired; many spend the whole day at UCB, participating in different activities offered by the SCC; and have free access to public transport) and also by the high percentage of illiterate among the elderly population. According to data from National Household Sample Survey (*Pesquisa Nacional por Amostra de Domicílio* - PNAD, IBGE, 2018), 18.6% of people over the age of 60 are illiterate, which corresponds to approximately six million people.

The operating spaces of ARU, as well as the target audience, have been expanded over the years. In addition to the laboratory of Psychosocial-gerontology, the Unit also began to occupy a computer lab at the UCB campus and another one in a public AL school, in the same administrative region of UCB, which worked through the three shifts. In addition to the elderly, other adults began to be served.

In all these spaces, the activities occurred at times that did not compete with the participants' other activities (at the SCC, the Citizen Literacy project, or at school) and followed a sequence of steps: (1) interviews to collect sociodemographic and school history data; (2) screening evaluation of cognitive functions and dementia using the Mini-Mental State Examination (MMSE, Almeida, 1998; Folstein et al., 1975); (3) assessment of the input repertoire with application of the Behavioral Assessment of Reading and Writing (*Avaliação Comportamental de Leitura e Escrita* [ACoLE]; computerized, Rosa Filho et al., 1998) instrument; and, (4) exposure to computerized Modules 1, 2, or 3 of the ALEPP teaching program, depending on the results in the ACoLE. In the case of Modules 1 and 2, the most recent versions, available on an online platform called Computer Individualized Teaching Manager (*Gerenciador de Ensino Individualizado por Computador* [GEIC]; Capobianco et al., 2009), were used. The version of Module 3 used was offline, using the Microsoft Office Power Point environment (the description of this module is available in Chap. 5 of this book). These modules teach words with simple syllables (Module 1), words with complex syllables (Module 2) and texts in the form of books (Module 3).

Throughout the period of operation of the ARU, 107 adults and seniors attended, with ages ranging from 25 to 85 years, all of whom self-declared illiterate; 24 of them were students at the partner school and the others (n = 83) participants of UCB outreach programs. Of the 107 participants, however, 73 performed only the assessment steps (steps 1, 2 and 3 cited above) and only 34 started or remained in the teaching program (13 from the AL school and 21 from the UCB programs).

Among the 34 participants who started or remained in the teaching program, 14 were exposed to Module 1, 11 to Module 2, and nine to Module 3. Figures 11.1, 11.2, and 11.3 present the following information regarding the participants exposed to Modules 1, 2, and 3, respectively: total number of steps/books performed (top left panel); period attending the ARU in months (top right panel); average number of sessions to perform each step (bottom left panel), corresponding to the ratio between the total number of sessions performed divided by the number of steps; and average periodicity of attendance to sessions in days (bottom right panel), obtained from dividing the period attending the ARU (total days) by the total number of sessions.

Regarding the participants exposed to Module 1 (14), only three (M1.01, M1.02, and M1.03) finished all the teaching steps of this module, and the others went

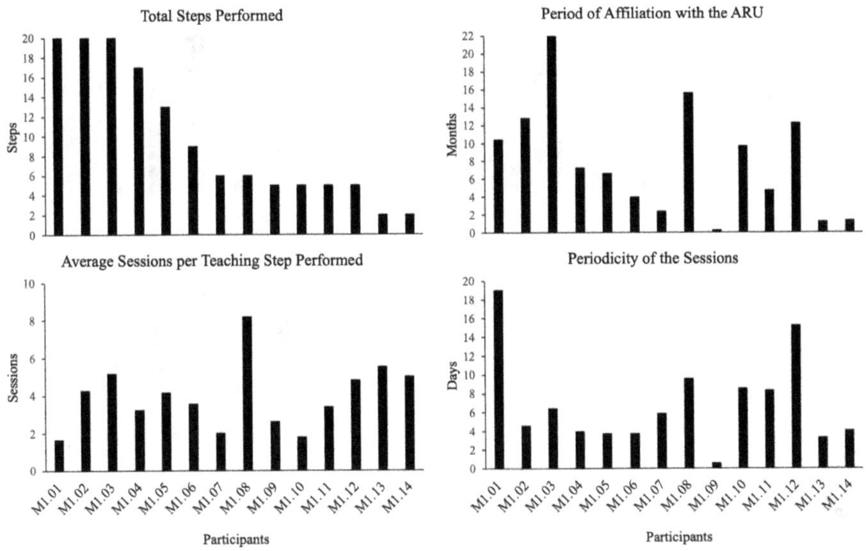

Fig. 11.1 Total number steps and average sessions per step, ARU attendance period and frequency of sessions for participants exposed to Module 1 of the ALEPP

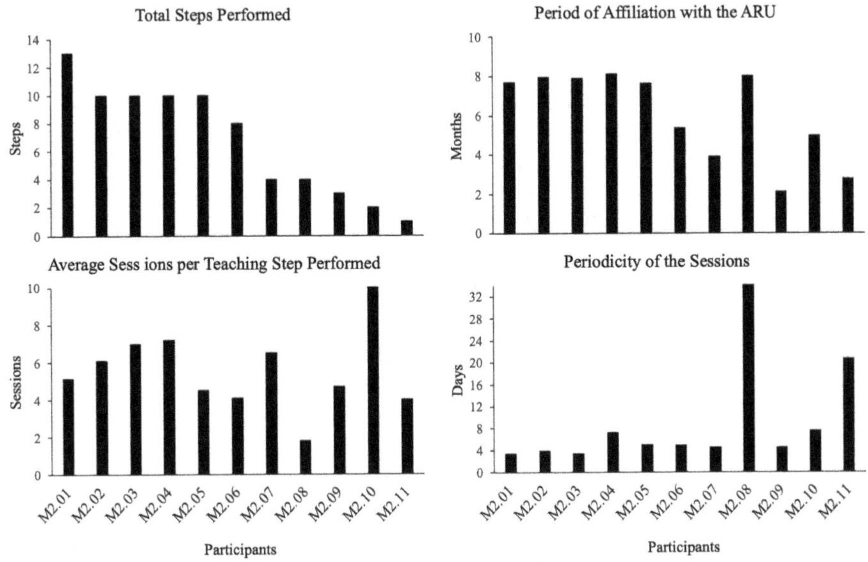

Fig. 11.2 Total number of steps and average sessions per step, ARU attendance period and frequency of sessions for participants exposed to Module 2 of the ALEPP

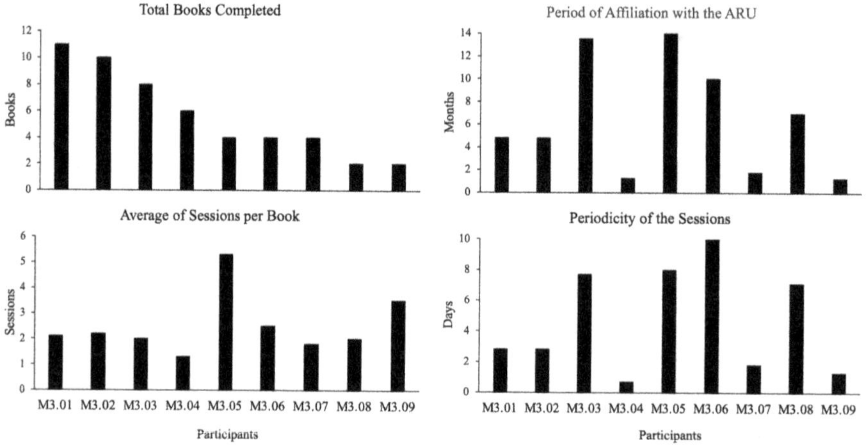

Fig. 11.3 Total number of steps and average sessions per step, ARU attendance period and frequency of sessions for participants exposed to Module 3 of the ALEPP

through between two and 17 teaching steps. The average number of sessions per step ranged between 1.7 (M1.01) and 8.2 (M1.08). The participants' period attending the ARU ranged from 1.2 (M1.13) to 21.9 months (M1.03), with session frequency between 0.5 - corresponding to holding approximately two sessions per day - (participant M1.09 held 13 sessions in seven days) and 19 days (M1.01).

The 11 participants exposed to Module 2 went through between one and 13 teaching steps. This module is organized by difficulty or irregularity of the Portuguese language, each of which is taught in a sequence of four steps. Thus, the participant who advanced the most in the program (M2.01) learned three difficulties (*ç*, *ce-ci*, *nh*) and began teaching the fourth difficulty (*lh*). Another four participants (M2.02, M2.03, M2.04 and M2.05) learned two difficulties (*ç* and *ce-ci*) and started learning the third difficulty of Module 2 (*nh*); the average number of sessions to finish each step varied between two and 10. The participants were linked to ULA between two and eight months and, throughout this period, attended the sessions with frequency between 3.4 (M2.01) and 34 days.

The nine participants exposed to Module 3 used two or three books and, on average, needed 1.3 (M3.04) to 5.3 (M3.05) sessions to complete the books with 100% of correct responses. The period attending the ARU was between one and 14 months and, throughout this period, participants attended sessions with an average frequency between 0.7 (M3.04) and 10 (M3.06) days.

The data presented in Figs. 11.1, 11.2, and 11.3 show a great variability among the participants exposed to the three teaching modules. Despite the possibility of attending sessions four times a week, since the classroom was open every afternoon from Monday to Thursday, and had enough computers to serve practically all participants simultaneously, the frequency of attendance was high for most participants. The data presented do not allow conclusions about correlations between the frequency of attendance and the number of step repetitions. However, we believe that a more detailed analysis of these data, session by session, which is beyond the scope of this chapter, may provide additional information in this regard. Regarding the long permanence of most participants in the ARU (six participants attended the Unit for more than a year), it should also be clarified that periods of recess, school strikes and vacations were not excluded from the total period.

Despite the long period of attachment of most participants to ULA, only three (M1.01, M1.02 and M1.03) reached the final teaching steps of the module to which they were exposed (Module 1). The data from these three participants will be presented in the following section.

11.4 Learning Words with Simple Syllables Using ALEPP: Application with Adult Participants

Participants M1.01, M1.02 and M1.03 were, respectively, 70, 42 and 53 years old when they joined the ARU, one being male (M1.03) and the others female. M1.01 attended the SCC and M1.02 and M1.03 were students of the Citizen Literacy program at UCB. They attended the ARU from 10.4 to 21.9 months, with periodicity of 4.5 to 19 days between sessions, and required on average 1.7 to 5.2 sessions for the completion of each teaching step (Fig. 11.1).

Module 1 consists of five teaching units. Each unit consists of a pretest, three to five teaching steps, and a posttest. The pre- and posttests evaluate the reading and writing repertoire of the participants based on different tasks, including oral word naming. In each of the 20 teaching steps, three new words, composed of simple syllables (consonant + vowel) are taught, totaling, at the end of Module 1, 60 words (for a detailed description of the tasks involved and the learning criteria, see de Souza et al. 2009). At the end of Units 2 and 5 extensive tests (I and II) are conducted, which assess reading and writing of the words directly taught in the units, and of new words by naming, handwritten dictation, and composition tasks. The three participants whose results are described here went through Module 1 of the ALEPP up to step 20 of Unit 5; however, only participant M1.02 completed Module 1; M1.01 did not perform the posttest of Unit 5 and the extensive test II, which was also not completed by M1.03.

As described in the previous section, prior to exposure to Module 1 of teaching words with single syllables, all participants underwent the reading and writing assessment using the ACoLE. Figure 11.5 presents the results of M1.01, M1.02, and M1.03 on the reading (bars to the left of the dotted line) and writing (bars to the right of the dotted line) tasks in this assessment. Percentages of correct responses equal to or higher than 60% were observed in all receptive reading tasks (with the MTS procedure) for all three participants (except in pairing tasks between word and picture for M1.01). In expressive reading tasks (involving oral production), the lowest percentages (between zero and 40%) were observed in word naming and the highest percentages (between 70% and 100%) in vowel naming. In writing tasks (handwritten or composition response), the percentages of correct responses in dictation were lower than those obtained in copying. Participants M1.01 and M1.02 were also exposed to a supplementary assessment[4] with words composed of complex syllables (with language difficulties); M1.01 did not score correctly on any trials, and M1.02 scored correctly on a single trial of the 34 components of this assessment. The low scores in word naming in the ACoLE and in the complementary assessment defined the exposure of participants to Module 1 of the ALEPP.

The assessment of participants' inicial repertoire (Fig. 11.4) reveals important characteristics of participants and their repertoire of interest. Although they declared themselves to be illiterate, participants showed a rudimentary repertoire of reading and writing skills. Considering the participants' histories of school exclusion, it can be stated that the existing repertoire was learned through informal processes. Since many routine activities involve behavioral control by textual stimuli (e.g., taking a bus, paying a bill, choosing products at the market), the participants' exposure to these situations may have promoted some discriminative control involving such stimuli. Regarding the different behaviors that make up participants' reading (e.g., expressive, receptive) and writing (e.g., copying, dictation) repertoires, their functional independence is evident. For example, the presence of reading repertoire is not necessarily accompanied by the presence of writing, and the presence of receptive reading repertoire is not necessarily predictive of expressive reading. Functional independence of these repertoires is especially expected early in the learning process; however, as these repertoires advance to higher levels of proficiency, they are expected to interconnect in a network of behavioral relationships (de Rose, 2005).

Figure 11.5 shows the oral word naming scores of participants on pre- and posttests for units 1 to 5. Each bar in the figure corresponds to one unit, and the lines superimposed on the bars indicate the average percentage correct in each participant's pre- or post-test set.

The average percentage of correct responses in the pretests was higher than 40%. These percentages are higher than those reported by de Souza et al. (2009) with children (between zero and 20% correct answers) and indicate differences in the input repertoires of adults compared to children. We also observed an increasing trend in the percentage of correct responses in the pretests of Units 1 to 4 for all participants, suggesting a cumulative effect of exposure to the previous teaching steps on the participants' inicial repertoire with each new unit. The percentages of correct responses in the posttests were, in general, higher than those observed in the pretests (in 10 out of 15 pairs of pre-post-tests), as shown in the mean data (lines superimposed on the bars). These data explain the effectiveness of the teaching procedure for promoting oral word naming. It is important to note that the teaching steps are basically composed of matching-to-sample trials, copying and dictation by composition, and that the oral word naming repertoire is not directly taught, but

[4]The supplementary assessment involved complex words (e.g., nh, lh, rr, x with z sound) and was composed of pairing tasks between dictated word, picture, and printed word, picture and word naming, and handwritten and compound dictation (with letters).

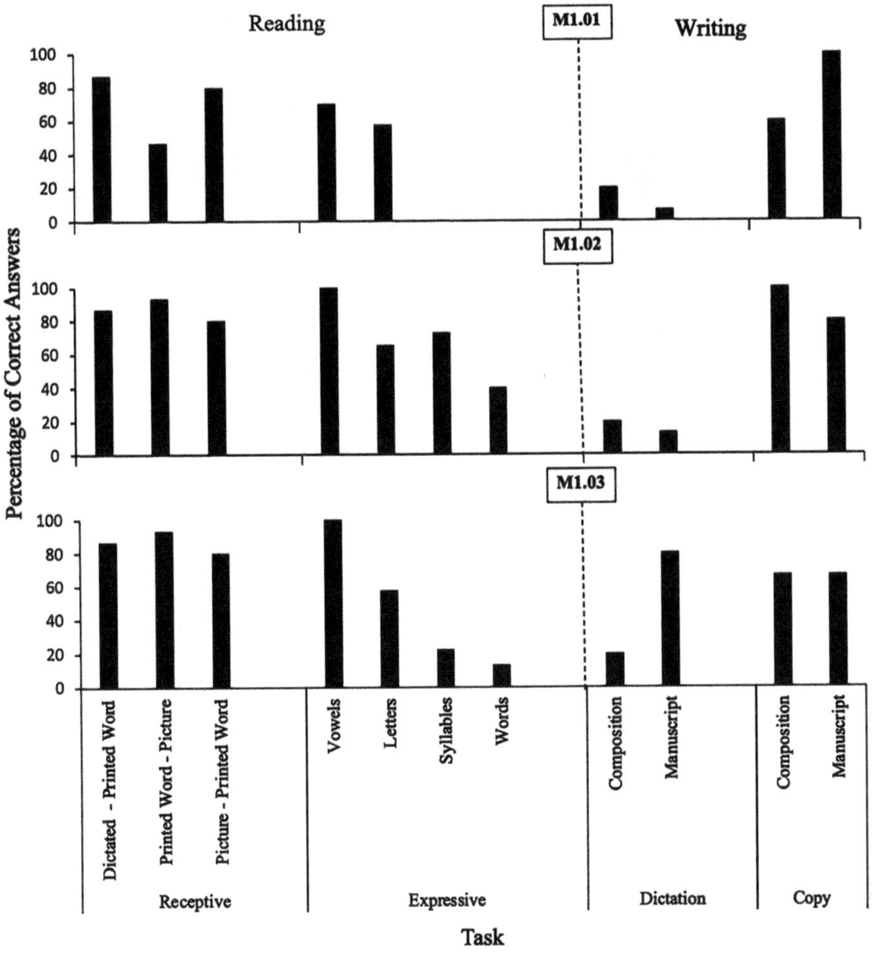

Fig. 11.4 Percentage of correct responses of the participants in the ACoLE receptive and expressive reading and dictation and copy writing tasks

emerges from learning receptive reading responses (e.g., selecting among printed word alternatives the one corresponding to a dictated word).

The performance in the extensive tests I and II completed, respectively, after Units 2 and 5, are presented in Table 11.2, along with the results of the ACoLE. All three participants took the Extensive Test I (TExtI), but only M1.02 took the Extensive Test II (TExtII). Increasing percentages of correct responses in composition dictation, handwritten dictation, and word naming tasks were observed for all three participants. Superior results in reading compared to writing are also reported in research with children (de Souza et al., 2009). In Extensive Test II, participant M1.02 produced more correct responses in naming compared to dictation. The percentage of correct responses in the last evaluation of handwritten dictation (TExtII)

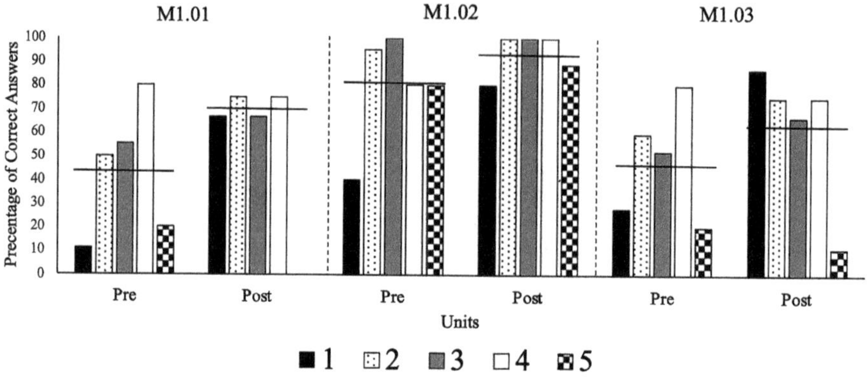

Fig. 11.5 Percentage of correct responses and mean percentages (lines) in the pre- and postTests of the units per participant

Table 11.2 Percentages of correct word naming, handwritten dictation, and composition in the ACoLE and in the extensive tests I (TExtI) and II (TExtII)

	Word naming			Handwritten dictation			Dictation by composition		
Participants	ACoLE	TExtI	TExtII	ACoLE	TExtI	TExtII	ACoLE	TExtI	TExtII
M1.01	0	60	–	6.7	55	–	20	45	–
M1.02	40	79	93	13.33	70	20	20	60	65
M1.03	13.33	61.3	–	80	55	–	20	45	–

of M1.02 was lower than the second evaluation (TExtI). The significant reduction in the percentage of correct responses in handwritten dictation was not expected; however, one should consider that the handwriting repertoire, whether in dictation or copy tasks, are the only ones not directly taught in Module 1. This set of data suggests the greater effectiveness of Module 1 in teaching reading compared to writing.

The comparison of the results of the extensive tests with those of the ACoLE shows a significant increase in word naming accuracy for all participants. M1.01, who did not name any word in the initial assessment (ACoLE), showed above 60% of correct responses on this task after exposure to Units 1 and 2. Similarly, M1.03 scored 13.33% correct on word naming in the initial assessment and 61.3% correct responses in TExtI. M1.02 also produced increasing success rates in word naming from the initial assessment (40%) to the Extensive Tests I (79%) and II (93%). It is important to remember that M1.01's exposure to formal reading and writing teaching procedures was restricted to the ARU, so that increases in her repertoire are directly attributable to exposure to Module 1. In the case of participants M1.02 and M1.03, one should consider the possibility of a combined effect of Module 1 with the classes they were exposed to in the Citizen Literacy program. The results in dictation by composition also indicate increasing accuracy for the three compared to word naming. The results in handwritten dictation, however, are more variable; M1.01 and M1.02 had a significant increase in correct responses for handwritten dictation in the extensive test I compared to the ACoLE; the percentage of correct responses for M1.02 and M1.03 in the third (TExtII) and second (TExtI) evaluations decreased compared to the percentage of correct responses in TExtI and ACoLE, respectively.

These results, like those in the studies summarized on Table 11.1, point to the possibility of using EBI to teach reading and writing to the adult population. They also indicate that Module 1 was effective for teaching words with single syllables (Melchiori et al., 2000) for all three participants, since successive advancement in units is conditional on perfect performance (100% correct) on each teaching step. However, the impact of the module on writing repertoire was more variable than on reading repertoire (Bandini et al., 2014). The high accuracy in word naming in M1.02, in the Extended Test II, also allows us to state that the teaching procedure promoted the emergence of generalized reading (Santos, 2002, 2011; Llausas, 2008), since the Extended Tests assessed not only the naming of directly taught words, but also of new words.

11.5 Final Considerations

This chapter analyzed studies with illiterate young people and adults without comorbidities, who used the equivalence paradigm and conditional discrimination procedures. Although few studies were identified (9), the results showed that participants learned to read taught words with simple syllables and increased their percentage of correctly reading new words (Bandini et al., 2014, Study 1; Llausas, 2008; Medeiros et al., 1997; Melchiori et al., 2000; Santos, 2002), with a reduction in the types of reading and writing errors (Calcagno et al., 2016). In studies using complex words, similar results were also found both in reading and writing words (Bandini et al., 2014, Study 2; Calcagno, 2015; Calcagno et al., 2016) and sentences formed by taught and new words (Llausas, 2008; Santos, 2011; Zanco, 2011).

The characterization of the assistance provided at the Adult Reading Unit (ARU) at UCB/UnB between the years 2012 and 2017 showed that, despite the difficulties faced and the challenge of conducting research with AL students, different partnerships can be developed to address the social issue of illiteracy in the adult and elderly population. A total of 107 adults and elderly people were assisted in the Unit, with ages ranging from 25 to 85 years old, all who self-declared illiterate. The intervention procedures used were based on stimulus equivalence and teaching conditional discriminations and proved to be useful to evaluate the repertoires involved in reading and writing and in teaching words with simple and complex syllables and texts in book format. However, variability was observed in the number of steps of the teaching modules to which the participants were exposed, in the number of sessions per teaching step, in the length of stay in the Unit, and in the frequency of sessions.

The results of three participants who completed Module 1 were analyzed (M1.01, 70 years; M1.02, 42 years; and M1.03, 53 years). Compared with the ACole (evaluation performed before exposure to Module 1), there was an increase in the percentage of correct reading and writing responses after the first two teaching units, with lower scores in the dictation task. These results suggest the potential of EBI procedures for teaching reading and writing not only of taught but also of new words that were part of the evaluations after every two teaching units.

The results presented here, although partial, corroborate those of previous studies with adults (e.g., Bandini et al., 2014; Medeiros et al., 1997; Melchiori et al., 2000) and children (e.g., de Souza et al., 2009; Melchiori et al., 2000), since they point to the effectiveness of EBI to teach reading words with simple syllables. Writing performance, however, is lower and variable, suggesting this repertoire should be taught directly, especially in the handwritten modality. Another aspect to be considered refers to the set of words and illustrations used. The ALEPP was originally developed to be used with children, thus, the words and illustrations of the teaching units were selected based on the needs of this population. Future research and applications should evaluate the possibility of adapting the stimuli for the adult population, which could have a direct impact on the learning and motivational process.

Acknowledgement We would like to thank all the people involved in the Adult Reading Unit. To the UCB Psychology Professors, Raquel Ramos Ávila and Isabella Parente Quadrelli. To the undergraduate research fellows, who collaborated collecting and tabulating data: Allan Kardec Pereira Pinto, Bárbara Horrana Ribeiro de Souza, Caio Diogo Santana de Sousa, Cristiane de Oliveira Lima, Fabiana Moreira Lima, Fernanda Lorena Calci, Izabela Casseb Ferraz Saavedra Dias, Jean Michel Montin, Karla Beatriz dos Santos, Lara Safatle Mori da Fonseca, Lidia Magalhães da Silveira Baptista, Marina Hack Moreira, Pabline Coimbra Bemfica de Sousa, Raylson Aguiar Pereira, Tatiane Alaminos, Renata Arcelina de Freitas Veras, Thalita Alves Menezes, Vanessa Lima Rodrigues da Trindade, Vitória Segato Jadallah, Yara Barbosa Gonçalves.

References

Almeida, O. P. (1998). Mini mental state examination and the diagnosis of dementia in Brazil. *Arquivos de Neuropsiquiatria, 56*(3B), 605–612. https://doi.org/10.1590/S0004-282X1998000400014

Bandini, C. S. M., Bandini, H. H. M., Sella, A. C., & Souza, D. das G. (2014). Emergence of reading and writing in illiterate adults after matching-to-sample tasks. *Paidéia* (Ribeirão Preto), *24*(57), 75–84. https://doi.org/10.1590/1982-43272457201410

Brasil. Ministério da Educação, Secretaria de Alfabetização. (2019). *PNA: Política Nacional de Alfabetização*. http://portal.mec.gov.br/images/banners/caderno_pna_final.pdf

Calcagno, S. (2015). *Ensinar adultos a ler e a escrever: Uma análise de participação, de acertos e de erros*. Unpublished doctoral dissertation, Universidade Federal de São Carlos.

Calcagno, S., Barros, R. S., Ferrari, I. S., & de Souza, D. G. (2016). Análise dos erros apresentados por adultos iletrados ao longo de um programa informatizado de ensino de leitura e escrita. *Acta Colombiana de Psicología, 19*(1), 151–164.

Capobianco, D., Teixeira, C. A. C., Bela, R. E., Orlando, A. F., de Souza, D. G., & de Rose, J. C. (2009). *GEIC – Gerenciador de Ensino Individualizado por Computador* [Computer Software]. UFSCar. http://geic.ufscar.br/site/

de Rose, J. C. (2005). Análise comportamental da aprendizagem de leitura e escrita. *Revista Brasileira de Análise do Comportamento, 1*(1), 29–50. https://doi.org/10.18542/rebac.v1i1.676

de Rose, J. C., de Souza, D. G., & Hanna, E. S. (1996). Teaching reading and spelling: Exclusion and stimulus equivalence. *Journal of Applied Behavior Analysis, 29*(4), 451–469. https://doi.org/10.1901/jaba.1996.29-451

de Souza, D. G., de Rose, J. C., Faleiros, T. C., Bortoloti, R., Hanna, E. S., & McIlvane, W. J. (2009). Teaching generative reading via recombination of minimal textual units: A legacy of Verbal Behavior to children in Brazil. *International Journal of Psychology and Psychological Therapy, 9*(1), 19–44.

Dixon, L. S. (1977). The nature of control by spoken words over visual stimuli selection. *Journal of Experimental Analysis of Behavior, 27*(3), 433–442. https://doi.org/10.1901/jeab.1977.27-433

Ferreira, J. L., Bortolini, R., & Ribas, M. S. (2020). Estado da arte sobre a educação de jovens e adultos no Paraná: Contribuições e implicações. *Cadernos de Pesquisa: Pensamento Educacional, Curitiba, 15*(39), 101–118. https://doi.org/10.35168/2175-2613.UTP.pens_ed.2020.Vol14.N39

Fienup, D. M., Covey, D. P., & Critchfield, T. S. (2010). Teaching brain-behavior relations economically with stimulus equivalence technology. *Journal of Applied Behavior Analysis, 43*(1), 19–33. https://doi.org/10.1901/jaba.2010.43-19

Folstein, M. F., Folstein, S. E., & McHugh, P. R. (1975). Mini-mental state: A practical method for grading the cognitive state of patients for the clinician. *Journal of Psychiatric Research, 12*, 189–198. https://doi.org/10.1016/0022-3956(75)90026-6

Goyos, A. C. N., & Almeida, J. C. (1996). *Mestre* (Versão 1.0) [Research Software].

IBGE. (2018). *Pesquisa Nacional por Amostra de Domicílio (PNAD) Contínua.* https://biblioteca.ibge.gov.br/visualizacao/livros/liv101657_informativo.pdf

INEP. Plano Nacional de Educação PNE 2014-2024: linha de base. Brasília: Inep, 2015. http://portal.mec.gov.br/arquivos/*pdf*/ldb.*pdf*. BRASIL.

Instituto Paulo Montenegro. INAF Brasil 2018: Resultados preliminares. [S.l.]: IPM, 2018. https://acaoeducativa.org.br/wp-content/uploads/2018/08/Inaf2018_Relat%C3%B3rio-Resultados-Preliminares_v08Ago2018.pdf

Kruidenier, J. R., Charles, M. A., & Wrigley, H. S. (2010). *Adult education literacy instruction: A review of the research.* [s.n.]. Retrieved from https://files.eric.ed.gov/fulltext/ED521229.pdf

Lafin, M. H. L. F. (2014). Pesquisas no campo da educação de jovens e adultos (EJA) no do estado de Santa Catarina. X ANPED SUL, Florianópolis, outubro de 2014, pp. 1–23. http://xanpedsul.faed.udesc.br/arq_pdf/658-0.pdf

Llausas, R. V. (2008). *Avaliação de uma proposta de ensino de leitura e escrita para jovens e adultos utilizando software educativo.* Master's thesis, Pontifícia Universidade Católica de São Paulo. Repositório Institucional PUC-SP. https://sapientia.pucsp.br/bitstream/handle/16383/1/Rosana%20Valinas%20Llausas.pdf

Medeiros, J. G., Monteiro, G., & Silva, K. Z. (1997). O ensino da leitura e escrita a um sujeito adulto. *Temas em Psicologia, 1*, 65–78.

Melchiori, L. E., de Souza, D. G., & de Rose, J. C. (2000). Reading, equivalence and recombination of units: A replication with students with different learning histories. *Journal of Applied Behavior Analysis, 33*(1), 97–100. https://doi.org/10.1901/jaba.2000.33-97

Paiva, J., Haddad, S., & Soares, L. J. G. (2019). Pesquisa em educação de jovens e adultos: Memórias e ações na constituição do direito à educação para todos. *Revista Brasileira de Educação, 24*, e240050. https://doi.org/10.1590/s1413-24782019240050

Rosa Filho, A. B., de Rose, J. C., de Souza, D. G., Fonseca, M. L., & Hanna, E. S. (1998). *Aprendendo a ler e a escrever em pequenos passos* [Research Software].

Sanceverino, A., Ribeiro, I., & Laffin, M. (2020). Estado do conhecimento das pesquisas sobre aprendizagem de pessoas jovens e adultas no campo da EJA. *Perspectivas, 38*(1), 1–24. https://doi.org/10.5007/2175-795X.2020.e65981

Santos, A. C. C. (2002). *Ensino de leitura a partir de unidades mínimas a jovens e adultos.* Master's thesis, Universidade Federal do Pará. Repositório Institucional da UFPA. http://repositorio.ufpa.br/jspui/bitstream/2011/5348/1/Dissertacao_EnsinoLeituraUnidades.pdf

Santos, C. A. D. D. (2011). *Proposta de ensino de leitura e escrita, por meio de discriminações condicionais aplicadas com software, para jovens e adultos de um curso de EJA.* Master's thesis,

Pontifícia Universidade Católica de São Paulo. Repositório Institucional PUC-SP. https://tede.pucsp.br/bitstream/handle/16008/1/Carlos%20Alberto%20Daniel%20dos%20Santos.pdf

Silva, A. J. M., Keuffer, S. I. C., Oliveira, J. S. C., & Barros, R. S. (2018). Aquisição de repertório intraverbal via instrução baseada em equivalência em crianças com TEA. *Temas em Psicologia, 26*(3), 1155–1171. https://doi.org/10.9788/TP2018.3-02Pt

UNESCO. (2014). *Segundo relatório global sobre a aprendizagem e educação de adultos: Repensando a alfabetização.* https://unesdoc.unesco.org/ark:/48223/pf0000230725

Zanco, G. (2011). *Ensino de leitura e escrita a partir de discriminações condicionais para alunos do ensino médio.* Master's thesis, Pontifícia Universidade Católica de São Paulo. Repositório Institucional PUC-SP. https://sapientia.pucsp.br/bitstream/handle/16009/1/Giselda%20Zanco.pdf

Chapter 12
Teaching Reading with Comprehension to Public School Students

Camila Domeniconi, Solange Cordeiro Calcagno, Olivia Misae Kato, Priscila Benitez, and Elenice S. Hanna

12.1 Introduction

Reading is fundamental to learn academic content throughout formal education, as well as an instrument of social inclusion, expanding the possibilities of individual autonomy (de Rose, 2005, republished in Chap. 1 of this book; Reis et al., 2009). Despite the importance of reading, the current conceptions of teaching this skill may not produce the expected results for all learners due to numerous difficulties related to the number of students in traditional classrooms and the diversity of repertoires that can be considered as a basis for learning reading, such as oral language, vocabulary, knowledge about writing, among others.

Efforts have been made to evaluate the reading repertoire and to plan and implement public policies to improve the entire educational system. Despite the progress made, a large contingent of students continues to perform well below the national averages. A detailed description of the repertoire of pupils who do not reach the levels expected for their schooling can make it possible to identify the abilities that they present and those that they fail to present and subsidize the application of

C. Domeniconi (✉)
Universidade Federal de São Carlos, São Carlos, SP, Brazil
e-mail: domeniconicamila@gmail.com

S. C. Calcagno · O. M. Kato
Universidade Federal do Pará, Belém, PA, Brazil

P. Benitez
Universidade Federal do ABC, Santo André, SP, Brazil

E. S. Hanna
Universidade de Brasília, Brasília, DF, Brazil

A. R. de Albuquerque, R. M. de Melo (eds.), *Contributions of Behavior Analysis to Reading and Writing Comprehension*, https://doi.org/10.1007/978-3-031-40868-7_12

specific interventions, directly aimed at the difficulties of the learners. This was the basis of the project that is the subject of this report.

This chapter describes the development and results of a project of the Education Observatory Program (*Observatório da Educação* [OBEDUC] – Edital 049/2012/CAPES/INEP). One of the objectives of OBEDUC is to encourage the articulation between graduate, undergraduate, and public schools of Basic Education. The project entitled "Diagnosis of the reading repertoire and intervention with new teaching technologies for students from schools with low levels in the *Prova Brasil*", approved in this Call for Proposals, aimed to assess and teach reading to elementary school students with learning difficulties in six public schools. The project used teaching technologies developed by researchers from the National Institute of Science and Technology on Behavior, Studies on Behavior, Cognition, and Teaching (*Instituto Nacional de Ciência e Tecnologia, Estudos sobre Comportamento, Cognição e Ensino* [INCT-ECCE]), described in the second part of this book (Chaps. 4, 5, 6 and 7). These technologies were tested with small groups of children as well as in some schools in the interior of the state of São Paulo, Brazil (e.g., Reis et al., 2009), and in homes (Benitez & Domeniconi, 2016). The use of these technologies in large-scale and natural environments, with multidisciplinary teams, added challenges and steps that will also be the subject of this report.

An innovative aspect of the project was to use the scores of the *Prova Brasil,*[1] conducted by INEP (2011), as a measure of the external validity of the results. *Prova Brasil* scores were taken as the criterion to initially select schools (with low scores) and, subsequently, as an indicator of changes in school performance after the project. The possibility of comparing this measure with internal validity assessment instruments (Reading and Writing Behavioral Assessment; *Avaliação Comportamental de Leitura e Escrita* [ACoLE]) also produced initial information on the possible correlation between the measures.

The chapter will first present a general description of the project, specifying the schools and their initial performance in *Prova Brasil*. This is followed by a brief description of the training of the team, the development and results of the project. The initial reading and writing repertoires of the students, the interventions made and the changes observed in reading will be briefly described, comparing the results of ACoLE and *Prova Brasil*.

[1] Prova Brasil is an assessment applied to all students at the end of the basic cycle of education in Brazilian public schools, with the aim of assessing the quality of education offered. Consisting of standardized tests with Portuguese language questions, with a focus on reading, and mathematics, with a focus on problem solving.

12.2 The Project

The project initially evaluated the performance of 4th and 5th grade students in two public schools of Elementary Education of Integral Education in the cities of São Carlos, Brasília, and Belém do Pará, Brazil. From this mapping, the computerized teaching modules of the Learning to Read and Write in Small Steps program (*Aprendendo a Ler e Escrever em Pequenos Passos* [ALEPP]; described in de Souza et al., 2009 and in Chaps. 4 and 5 of this book) were applied as an intervention for those 4th grade students who showed low performance in reading and/or writing. The assessment of the 5th grade students at the beginning of the study was performed as a baseline measure before the beginning of interventions in the school. These students did not participate in the other phases of the study, since most of them would already be in 6th grade and in other schools the following year. This assessment occurred at the end of 2013 for the schools in Brasília, São Carlos, and Belém. The 4th grade assessment was conducted in 2014 to identify students who would participate in the interventions over the 2 years of the project, when they would be in 4th or 5th grade. Two schools began evaluations at the end of 2013, when students were finishing the 3rd year. In the second half of 2014, all schools started the teaching modules (interventions).

The two schools in each city were selected based on the results of the *Prova Brasil* Portuguese language assessment, conducted by INEP every 2 years (INEP, 2011). The schools with the lowest performances and that had a computer lab were consulted through contact with their principals. Refusal or lack of infrastructure to participate meant contacting the school with the lowest subsequent score on the *Prova Brasil*. Since the assessment was conducted every 2 years and the project began in 2013, the 2011 results (released in 2012) were used to select the schools. At the end of 2013, a new *Prova Brasil* was conducted and released in 2014. The project lasted 3 years and a new assessment by INEP took place at the end of 2015.

The scores on the 2011 *Prova Brasil* of the schools that participated in the project varied according to the city in which they were located. Schools in Brasília had the highest scores (School 1 = 193.3 and School 2 = 187,6). Next came the schools in São Carlos (School 1 = 182.0 and School 2 = 180.5) and, lastly, the schools in Belém do Pará (School 1 = 163.54 and School 2 = 162.1). The schools had different characteristics in terms of number of students and teachers, number of classes, location in relation to the city center, and area allocated for classrooms. The two schools in Brasília were located on the outskirts of the city, with School 2 being the most central, with a large number of children (268 participated in the study). School 1 in Brasília was small, with a class of no more than 20 students in each grade (43 participated in the study). The schools in São Carlos were located in outlying regions of the city and varied; one was larger, with two classes of each grade with approximately 40 students (141 participated in the study) and another was smaller, with only one class of each grade with 25 students per room (34 participated in the study). The schools in Belém were located in areas considered at risk (known as red zone), one of them with 35 students per room on average (101 participated in the study) and the other with 25 students per class (89 participated in the study).

The computer labs in all the cities were shared with other school activities. During the project, however, school leaders set aside some hours for the study interventions. The children used headphones provided by the project during the sessions.

The proposal included training literacy teachers, as a first activity, to understand and use the teaching modules. All teachers received a grant to carry out the activities. The teachers were the main applicators of the assessments and interventions, with the help of undergraduate and graduate Psychology students. The training was conducted in the first semester of 2013. The interventions were completed in the second half of 2015 and, from November of this year, the performance of all children was again evaluated. Also in late 2015, the children took the national assessment (*Prova Brasil*).

The development stages of the study, specifically with the students, included: (1) applying the reading assessment instruments to the target population; (2) analyzing the skill profile of each student; (3) distributing the students with insufficient skills by teaching modules, according to their degree of difficulty in reading and dictation; (4) conducting the interventions and periodic assessments to monitor the learning process; and (5) repeating the repertoire assessment and taking the Prova Brasil.

12.2.1 Team Composition and Dynamic

The cities in each region of the country were chosen by convenience, since a local coordinator of the project was needed. In São Carlos, the local coordinator and also general coordinator of the project was Prof. Camila Domeniconi. In Brasília, the local coordinator was Prof. Elenice S. Hanna. The coordination of the unit in Belém do Pará was shared by Profs. Olivia Kato and Solange Calcagno. All coordinators were professors and researchers from Federal Education Institutions (UFSCar, UnB, and UFPA). Each researcher brought to the team post-graduate and undergraduate students interested in the project. The undergraduate students were awarded research scholarships. In addition, teachers from the participating schools were selected to participate in the project and awarded scholarships, and the main selection criterion was the availability of at least 12 h for the project. Each teacher worked in the classroom on one shift and on the other shift in the project. Their role as project fellows allowed them to develop activities at the other participating school as well. Most team members participated at some stage in the construction, implementation or evaluation of teaching procedures.

The school principals, vice-principals and coordinators were also important members of the project, as they not only allowed the study to be conducted but also helped to book and prepare the computer rooms and established an important relationship between the local team members and the regular classroom teachers. Without the teachers' permission, no child could participate in the project. As part of the ethical procedures, consent was sought from the school, teachers and student's parents.

In each center, the dynamics of the teams varied according to the context and the available conditions. In São Carlos, for example, the face-to-face monitoring of the activities carried out by teachers took place in schools by graduate and undergraduate students, with weekly face-to-face meetings with the whole team. In the centers of Brasília and Belém, remote and systematic monitoring was important, considering the conditions of displacement (privileged in São Carlos, considering the extension of the city).

The division of tasks was a challenge for each nucleus and varied according to the availability of time and how each school added the project to its routine. In schools that conceived the project activities as part of the compulsory workload, it was possible for teachers to accompany, monitor and assess students in computerized activities, with the support of undergraduate and postgraduate students. In schools where the project activities were seen as extra-curricular or complementary activities, it was more complex to reconcile the regular demands of the school for the teacher and the classroom for the students with the new activities of the project.

In these schools, the undergraduate fellows took on more hours of data collection and more responsibilities with the students, reducing the role of the grant holder teacher in the project. In the schools in Belém, for example, an undergraduate fellow was selected in each shift of each school to coordinate data collection in that shift. With regard to student attendance at the intervention sessions in these schools, the team had to negotiate several times for students to leave the classroom with their teachers.

Due to the large number of students in some schools and the fact that a significant number of students carried out sporadic sessions or repeated teaching steps more often than ideal at the beginning of the project, the best way to manage was to distribute responsibility for small groups of students among the fellows. This allowed for more personalized monitoring of the frequency of sessions and student performance, better addressing the doubts of the teachers, and generating a more equitable distribution of tasks.

Face-to-face meetings of the coordinators and other team members from the three units were held at least once a year to increase integration between units, standardize forms of data collection and analysis, evaluate the progress of the project in the different schools, and define the next goals. The final meeting took place in December 2015 to evaluate the results obtained and discuss how to disseminate them.

12.2.2 Team Training

Team members (undergraduate fellows, post-graduate students and teachers from Basic Education) were trained to understand and discuss the theoretical basis for building the teaching software and also its use and data analysis. The training consisted of a theoretical part and a practical part. In the theoretical part, lasting approximately 4 weeks, the following topics were approached: (1) ethics in Psychology research (Resolution CFP, 2005; CNS nº. 196/96); (2) literacy and its stages (Ferreiro, 2008); (3) school failure and learning difficulties; (4) behavioral analysis of learning to read and write (de Rose, 2005, reprinted in Chap. 1); (5) individualized programs for teaching reading (de Souza & de Rose, 2006); (6) educational social skills (Benitez & Domeniconi, 2012; Del Prette & Del Prette, 2008); (7) learning basics; and (8) computerized Learning to Read and Write in Small Steps (ALEPP) program. The practical part, with duration of approximately 2 weeks, was conducted in the classroom and computer labs and taught the structure and operation of Modules 1 and 2 of ALEPP, Computer Individualized Teaching Manager (*Gerenciador de Ensino Individualizado por Computador* [GEIC]) version, and Module 3, Power Point version. The team members who applied the teaching modules and assessments were instructed on how to start the sessions and then acted as if they were participating as learners. The local coordinator held an in-person class for 2–4 h per week and practical exercises were to be solved at a time and place (school, university or home) most convenient for each team member. For the Belém teams, this training varied (in duration and procedures), but ensured the necessary repertoire for the application of the project.

12.2.3 Assessments and Interventions

Researchers at the INCT-ECCE developed a supplementary program for individualized teaching of reading and writing, organized into modules (de Rose et al., 1996, 1989). The computerized Learning to Read and Write in Small Steps (ALEPP; Rosa Filho et al., 1998) is a teaching program used for reading instruction, in which the learner begins their learning process in different stages, depending on their input repertoire. The repertoire is measured by the ACoLE instrument, which has three levels of difficulty in reading and writing.

The ACoLE 1 assessed the network of relations between dictated and printed Portuguese words and corresponding pictures, in addition to oral reading of words, syllables, letter naming, copying, and dictation, using only single words composed of simple syllables (consonant-vowel). Children who scored 70% or more correct in oral reading and dictation underwent ACoLE 2. Students with lower performance levels were referred to the intervention that taught the relationship network tested (ALEPP – Module 1).

The ACoLE 2 assesses relationships between dictated and written Portuguese words, oral reading and dictation, using only words with spelling difficulties. Words with digraphs (e.g., ch, rr, ss) and other consonant clusters (e.g., vowel-R-consonant, vowel-S-consonant, vowel-L-consonant), as well as words with letters with more than one phonetic correspondence (e.g., X with Z, CH or S sound; S with Z sound) were included. Students who showed oral reading or dictation performance lower than 70% correct were referred to the intervention that taught reading words with orthographic difficulties (ALEPP – Module 2).

ACoLEs 1 and 2 were performed on the computer with the monitoring of one of the teachers or undergraduate students. Data were recorded automatically, but analyses for decision making were performed manually by team members.

The ACoLE 3 assessed reading comprehension of six short texts of different formats (poetry, narrative, comic strip, and shopping list), in the format of a test printed on paper and applied in the classroom to each class. After each text, the student answered multiple choice questions, totaling 20 questions. For each text, there was an open-ended question to be answered in two or three lines. Three versions of the assessment, with similar complexity and structure, were created for the project, thus enabling control by the re-exposure of the measure used to verify the effect of the intervention (Silveira et al., 2019). The transcription of the answers to digital spreadsheets was performed by the teachers and undergraduate students, and the analysis was automated by a coordinator of the Centers. Children who scored less than 60% correct on the multiple-choice questions were referred to the intervention that taught children's book reading comprehension (ALEPP – Module 3). The remaining children participated in the intervention only if there was the availability of equipment in the computer lab and the monitors' schedule.

Figure 12.1 illustrates the data collection situation conducted in the computer lab and the classroom, where interventions and assessments were carried out under the

Note. (a) Activity under supervision of a teacher; (b) assessment conducted in a classroom; (c) students undergoing Module 3 (teaching reading of children's books) and (d) answering the written question from one of the books.

Fig. 12.1 Illustrations of data collection settings conducted in a computer laboratory and in the classroom supervision of a teacher. Students used headphones and interacted with the computer to perform the tasks.

Prova Brasil was applied by INEP in the classroom, without the presence of members of the research team, in the traditional application format, as recommended by the research agency. The format of Prova Brasil is similar to that of ACoLE 3, i.e., short texts and multiple-choice questions are presented. The test developed for the 5th grade contains questions to assess the following abilities (MEC/INEP, 2011) based on texts: (1) locate explicit information; (2) infer the meaning of a word or expression; (3) infer implicit information; (4) identify the theme; (5) perform interpretation with the aid of graphic material (e.g., comics, photo); (6) relate different parts of the same text; (7) identify the conflict that generates the plot and the elements that construct the narrative; (8) establish a cause and consequence relationship between parts of the text; (9) identify the thesis; and (10) identify the speaker and interlocutor through linguistic marks. The questions contained in ACoLE 3 also assessed these abilities.

Prova Brasil also assesses skills (MEC/INEP, 2011) that were not assessed in ACoLE 3, such as: relating information/ opinions of different texts; identifying the purpose of texts of different genres; establishing logical-discursive relationships present in the text; identifying effects of irony or humor; identifying changes in meaning resulting from the use of punctuation and other notations; and distinguishing a fact from the opinion related to the fact.

12.3 Results

12.3.1 Assessing Reading and Writing Repertoire

The results of the reading and writing repertoire assessment are partially described in the study of Silveira et al. (2016) and Silveira (2015). Silveira and collaborators (2016) analyzed the reading performances of isolated words of 187 5th grade students from one of the schools in the Brazilian cities of São Carlos, Belém, and Brasília that participated in the OBEDUC project. The results showed that fewer than 10% of students had difficulty in reading or writing words with single syllables (ACoLE 1). A larger number of students (86% – Belém, 81% – Brasília and 66% – São Carlos) showed unsatisfactory performance (below 90% correct) in receptive reading (when presented with a dictated word, selecting the corresponding printed word) of words with orthographic difficulties (ACoLE 2). An even larger number of students (100% – Belém, 77% – Brasília and 63% – São Carlos) showed unsatisfactory performance (below 90% correct) in the handwritten dictation task of words with spelling difficulties (ACoLE 2). As they were children in the 5th grade of elementary school, they were expected to read and write isolated words. These results reflect the public school's difficulty to ensure rudimentary repertoires of reading and writing according to the school year they were enrolled, producing impairment to the learning of other contents.

Table 12.1 Percentage of 4th and 5th grade students from Brasília schools who met the proficiency criteria in the reading and writing assessments at the start of the study

Brasília School	Grade	Simple Words (% >70)			Difficult Words (% >70)			Reading Comprehension (% >0)	
		n	Reading	Writing	n	Reading	Writing	n	Reading
1	4th.	22	95	86	21	95	67	17	47
	5th.	21	100	100	21	100	95	21	52
2	4th.	122	95	93	121	83	65	121	26
	5th.	116	98	96	105	95	80	99	28

The results from the two schools in Brasília exemplify the number of students with different levels of learning difficulty and the usefulness of this information. Table 12.1 presents the summary results of the assessments (ACoLE 1, 2 and 3) administered to 4th and 5th grade classes at the beginning of the project. For the first two levels of assessment, we present the percentages of correct responses in oral reading and writing with dictation on the computer, where the participant should compose the word, choosing the letters in the correct order – from a larger set of letters.

More than 90% of the 5th grade students in both schools reached the proficiency criterion in reading simple and difficult words. For writing (dictation), the percentages were also high, except at School 2, with 20% of children scoring below 70% on the dictation of difficult words. As this is the school with the greatest number of children, this result means that more than 20 5th grade children from this school alone could not even write isolated words that presented some complexity.

Regarding the 4th grade, the percentages of students with high scores in reading were 95%, except School 1, with almost 20% of children with difficulty in complex words. Performance was below the criterion in writing simple words for 14% of the children in School 1 and words with spelling difficulties for 35% of the children in School 2 and 33% in School 1.

The most frequent difficulty among students in both schools, in 4th and 5th grades, was in comprehension of short texts (ACoLE 3). In School 1, more than 70% of the children and in School 2 close to 50% of the children presented scores lower than 60% correct. The difficulty level of the texts presented in the ACoLE 3 is compatible with skills that 3rd grade students would already be expected to master, so it is impactful that such a large number of children still have this difficulty in 5th grade.

With information about what each child is able to achieve and what difficulties challenge them, it is possible to decide where to start teaching and to design a specific teaching program. This information is essential for teachers of literacy classrooms and can help to program complementary activities for groups of children who need additional resources. The teaching modules used as intervention in the present study are available alternatives, with the advantage of having been tested in several previous research studies (e.g., de Rose et al., 1992, 1996; de Souza et al., 2009).

12.3.2 Effect of the Interventions

In the second stage of the project, the target was 4th grade children who did not meet the proficiency criterion in one of the assessed reading and writing levels (Table 12.1, in the case of Brasília). These children were followed up until the following year, when they took the Prova Brasil. As the initial assessment occurred at the end of the year, the 5th grade students shown in Table 12.1 who passed (the vast majority) could not participate in the project, as it was their last year in the participating schools.

Students with difficulty in reading or writing isolated words took Module 1 or 2 of the ALEPP and then Module 3. As most students completed only Module 3 and the others, despite starting in other modules, also finished with Module 3, the results presented below refer to the application of ALEPP – Module 3. Partial results of the intervention with Module 1, conducted with children from School 2 in Brasília, were reported by Tizo (2016).

The computerization and new design of Teaching Module 3 occurred due to the great demand of the project, so the results served as a test of this version. Since its completion, other studies have been conducted using the module (Bertini, 2017; Muniz, 2019).

The 15 interactive books that make up the module present interspersed questions to assess comprehension. A criterion used by the team to progress through the books is 100% correct in the first answer to each question. When any error occurred, the student completed the book, but was exposed again in the next session. The maximum number of repetitions of each book was defined as three. In the third opportunity, the monitor helped the student to increase the chance of 100% correct answers. To show whether the students showed any improvement in understanding children's stories, it can be observed if there was a reduction in the number of exposures to the books and in the number of errors. These measures are shown in Fig. 12.2. The data used are only from students who performed at least 13 books in Brasília schools

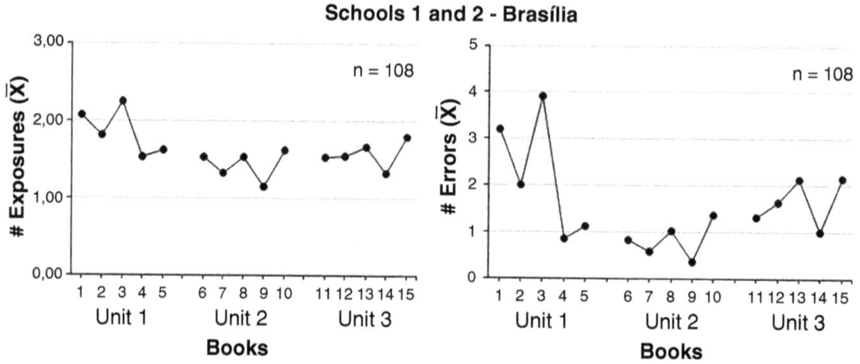

Fig. 12.2 Number of exposures (Mean) and errors (Mean) in each book by the students of the schools in Brasília

(n = 108). The graph on the left presents the average number of exposures to each book and the graph on the right, the average number of errors of all students across the books. For the first nine books, there was a decrease in the number of exposures and errors. From books 9 to 15, there was a maintenance of around 1.5 exposures and 1 to 2 errors. Analyses of aspects that can indicate the complexity of the books suggest that books from Units 1 and 2 have similar complexity (e.g., number of words, spelling difficulties). Still, Unit 3 is composed by more complex books. For number of exposures, the increase in complexity maintained the number of repetitions to the books in Unit 3, possibly due to the improvement in reading performance (increased fluency) and comprehension. A slight increase in errors is observed, but remaining well below the amount observed in the first books. These results suggest that Module 3 produced change in students' reading, reducing errors in comprehension questions. The division of instruction into small content units, constant feedback for individual performance, and requiring excellence in one stage before progressing to the next ensure the gradual progression of the student and constitute proven effective conditions for learning complex skills such as reading and writing.

Reading comprehension assessments in a different format from that presented in the teaching module are measures of generalization of the intervention effect. The ACoLE 3 and Prova Brasil have similar formats and different from the interactive books in Module 3 – ALEPP. In both assessments, each text is fully presented and followed with questions printed on paper. The student must read and answer questions about different kinds of texts. In the teaching module, a children's story is presented gradually, with the excerpts interspersed with comprehension questions. The results of the students, by school, in the two assessments are shown in Fig. 12.3. The graphs at the top of the figure show the scores on the ACoLE 3 for each school in the three Brazilian cities. The sample used to carry out the analysis of the students in the Brasília schools were students who finished at least two units (10 books) of Module 3. At the bottom of the figure are the Prova Brasil results for each school, including all 5th grade students who took the assessment. The grey columns refer to the measures before the interventions and the black columns, to the post-intervention results.

All schools increased their ACoLE scores after the intervention. For two schools in Brasília and one in São Carlos, the increase was greater than 20%. School 1 in São Carlos, which had the highest score before the intervention, had a 12.5% increase in its final score. The two schools in Belém, despite all the difficulties encountered in carrying out the project, showed increases of 6% and 10%.

In the Prova Brasil, the results for the five schools are similar: there was an increase in scores after the intervention (applied in 2015), when compared to the previous result (applied in 2013). The two measures of reading comprehension show that the ACoLE 3 and Prova Brasil are highly correlated (0.73). Although the value is considered high for applied research, the correlation could perhaps be even higher if the ACoLE 3 included items to test all the skills that Prova Brasil uses. The results suggest, therefore, that the interventions carried out in the project influenced

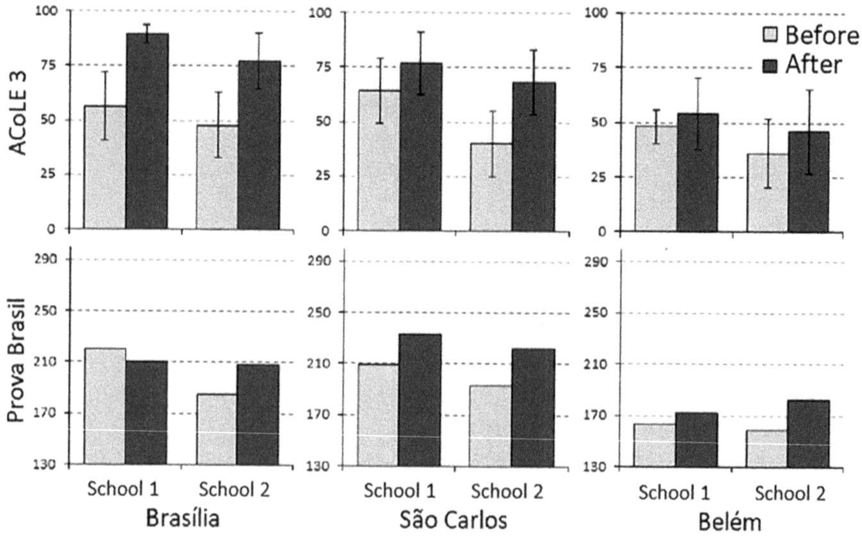

Note. The vertical lines represent the standard deviation of the samples.

Fig. 12.3 Scores of each school on the ACoLE and *Prova Brasil* before and after exposure to the teaching modules. (*Note*. The vertical lines represent the standard deviation of the samples)

measures of reading comprehension taken during the application of the teaching module and measures of generalization, performed after the interventions.

School 1 in Brasília was the only school that showed a decrease in its scores. Note that the 2013 values (before) are different from those used to select the schools. If we consider the scores used to recruit the schools, School 1 of Brasília would also have shown an important increase in this measure (from 193.31 in 2011 to 210.27 in 2015). When asking the school leaders about factors that could explain this substantial increase between the 2011 and 2013 tests, the hypothesis they considered was a problem in the application of the test in 2011, which left students confused and possibly interfered with the results. With this hypothesis, therefore, they considered that the 2013 result better reflected the learning of the school's students. Regardless of which value to use for comparison, this is a school with a small number of very well-attended students with teachers, principal, and coordinator committed to the quality of teaching, which probably reflected in the assessment. This is evident in the maintenance of the upward trend in the subsequent Prova Brasil assessment and in values that exceed the national average and that of the schools in Brasília.

The results presented above are evidence that suggests that the activities carried out during the project influenced the quality of education in the schools during the project period. Categorical conclusions may be questioned due to several complexities of the design, instruments and situation. Factors such as activities developed by the school, differences in the characteristics of the samples tested in each year, differences in the versions of the tests, etc., may also have influenced the results found.

The ACoLE results are interesting for their correlation with Prova Brasil, for being a generalization measure and for considering the child's initial performance as its own control, which could be ideal for assessing progress in teaching and learning. By excluding children who did not participate in the interventions, this measure may be questioned when used to refer to school results. In the present project, the majority of children entered the sample and those who did not enter would increase their scores because they were already high performers in reading comprehension. Analyses that included all students in the school (5th grade) who took the assessments corroborate this statement.

It is important to note that the interpretation of reading comprehension test results cannot be limited to the interventions of the project, because during the two-year period of its duration, school activities continued to take place. The comparative results would be more conclusive if the recruitment of the schools included a stable baseline, that is, if there were no upward trend in the results of the Prova Brasil and the ACoLE 3 in at least three consecutive applications.

12.3.3 *Other Important Results*

The design did not include a control group or school to assess the effect of school activities *per se*. An additional analysis, which may assist in the discussion of this question, was conducted comparing the reading comprehension performance of students who did not participate in the interventions, over two school years, only for School 2 in Brasília. The first group of students (n = 118) entered the 4th grade in January 2014. The second group of students (n = 169) finished the 3rd grade in December 2015 and had been approved for 4th grade. Both groups will therefore be referred to as 4th year students. These results are shown in the graph on the left of Fig. 12.4. The figure shows how the students were distributed across the grade ranges in ACoLE 3. The two distribution curves are very similar and show that most students scored at most 60% correct. The highest scores (above 60) were obtained

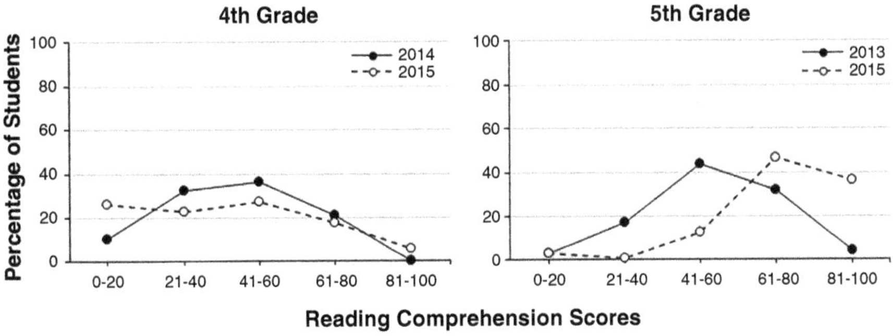

Fig. 12.4 Distribution of 4th and 5th grade students in the ranges of reading comprehension scores (ACoLE 3) in two consecutive years, applied at Brasília school 2

by only 20% of the students in 2014 and 2015. These equal distributions in two consecutive takes of the measure allow us to say that the two groups of students have similar performances and that the effect of the school was similar with regard to reading comprehension.

In the graph to the right of the figure, the distributions of 5th grade students were plotted: those assessed at the end of 2013 and who did not participate in the interventions (n = 100), because they were already leaving school, and those assessed at the end of 2015 (n = 101), including those who participated in the interventions (n = 74). The 5th grade students show different distributions in the 2 years assessed. In the first assessment (2013), the scores are concentrated in the intervals from 21 to 80, with the mode in the intermediate interval (41–60). However, the distribution of scores in the assessment that includes students who participated in the interventions (2015), is quite shifted (81% of students) to the two intervals with higher values.

It is of special interest to know that approximately 70 5th grade children who participated in the interventions (included in the 2015 curve) are part of the 2014 4th grade group. These results not only strengthen the evidence of the effect of the project in this school, but also allow us to speculate that if no changes are made to the teaching provided by the school after the project ends, the performances of 5th grade students will return to values close to those before the project. This analysis was presented at the last meeting with the school teachers as a way of motivating the continuity of the activities started with the project.

Important results of the project were also the scientific events promoted by the team: (1) Seminar on Alternative Technologies for Literacy: Contributions of Behavior Analysis; and (2) International Symposium on Language Assessment and Teaching. The Seminar, which was open to the community, was held on February 24 and 25, 2015, at the University of Brasília. Researchers on topics related to the theme participated in the event, in addition to 132 registered participants, among them undergraduate and graduate students, college professors and elementary school teachers (Fig. 12.5). We invited as speakers Dr. Deisy das Graças de Souza (UFSCar – conference title: Principles of programming reading teaching procedures), Dr. Jair Lopes Junior (UNESP Bauru – conference title: Large-scale assessment systems and the professional performance of Basic Education teachers:

Fig. 12.5 Speakers and participants of the seminar on alternative technologies for literacy: contributions of behavior analysis organized by the OBEDUC project team in 2015

Analyses of partnerships between university and school), Dr. João Claudio Todorov (UnB – conference title: Nothing motivates as much as success), Dr. Júlio Cesar Coelho de Rose (UFSCar – conference title: Symbolic behavior and reading teaching), and Dr. Maria da Graça Campos Pimentel (USP – cconference title: Advances in user-computer interaction in teaching situations). The event was an opportunity to discuss issues related to the teaching of reading and the dissemination of the results obtained so far in the project.

The Symposium was held in São Carlos (UFSCar), on August 29 and 30, 2015. The event was supported and organized by OBEDUC and INCT-ECCE. A total of 74 people participated, most of them Master and undergraduate students. The event program included courses and conferences offered by international guests (Dr. Marta G. Gràcia, University of Barcelona, and Dr. Thomas S. Higbee, Utah University) and national guests (Dr. Júlio de Rose, Dr. Deisy de Souza and Dr. Celso Goyos, UFSCAR; Dr. Gerson Tomanari, USP-SP; Dr. Andréia Schimidt, USP-Ribeirão Preto; Dr. Camila Graciela Gomes, FM-BH; Dr. Bianca Jorge, Santa Casa de Misericórdia – SP; and Dr. Aline Costa, FOB-USP; among others).

12.4 Final Considerations

The chapter described the structure, operation and results of a project of the Observatory of Education, funded by CAPES and INEP, based on a collaborative partnership between public schools and universities. The project aimed at assessing and teaching reading to elementary school students in the municipalities of São Carlos, Belém and Brasília. In the six public schools, the most children were able to read isolated words composed of simple syllables, but an intermediate percentage presented difficulty in reading words with complex spelling. Most students presented difficulties in reading comprehension. Different theoretical approaches that address reading learning agree on the existence and importance of prerequisites that make up such a complex skill, such as the ability to decode printed words, recognize and identify letters, and relate printed words with their referents (Grégoire & Piérart, 1997). Ferreiro (2008) states that the development of prerequisite skills, together with the formation of concepts, is important for the student to write proficiently.

During the development of the project, new teaching technologies (ALEPP – Module 3) and assessment instruments (three versions of ACoLE 3, Silveira et al., 2016) were developed. The high demand of students for an intervention to teach text comprehension required the development of a computerized ALEPP – Module 3, one of the important products of the project. The computerized ALEPP procedures can be used with many students in a school with only one implementer, ensuring that each student progresses according to his or her individual learning pace. In addition, the computerized procedures have the advantage of being able to automatically record every interaction of the student with the procedure, every stimulus presented, as well as the sequence of tasks and the time spent on each of them. This allows, in addition to large-scale application, its application in various situations (any school room or home). The results obtained with the use of Module 3 exceeded the team's expectations regarding the improvement of children's performance and motivation to participate in the sessions.

A sequence of actions was required, which included the selection of schools, the team, team training, adaptation of equipment, management of the team and the progress of the project, analysis and monitoring student performance and decision-making on interventions. The first challenge encountered was the constitution and management of a large team to meet common objectives in significantly different contexts of teaching and learning. The motivation for choosing schools and public universities in three distinct Brazilian regions was exactly to assess minimum and necessary conditions for a successful implementation of teaching procedures, in diverse realities.

The project enabled the formation of a network of researchers from different postgraduate programs around the investigation of a common educational problem, some of them members of the INCT-ECCE. The expansion of the network included principals, coordinators and teachers from public schools, students and teachers from graduate programs and undergraduate students. Despite the challenges of managing large teams, the presence of undergraduate student bridged the gap between the various teachers and the local coordinators, reduced some of the coordinators' workload and facilitated communication.

The funding of grants for elementary school teachers was a differential in comparison to other research funding calls with which the team was familiar. Teachers in public schools generally have an overloaded work routine due to low salaries and the need to accumulate hours in different schools. This can compromise class preparation, as well as making it difficult to get to know students in detail, which could contribute to more personalized teaching and activity planning. Working with teachers in research and intervention projects, in which they are collaborating participants, introduces new demands that are often difficult to implement. Furthermore, it reduces their time as an effective member of the research team, acting as a receiver of information that researchers and universities value. By including teachers as fellows in the OBEDUC team, they had the opportunity to understand and contribute to the construction of teaching procedures, evaluate their effectiveness, and discuss their results. The selection of schools with an administration and teaching staff that supported the project proposal was a fundamental starting point for carrying out the activities and recruiting teachers interested in participating effectively in the project.

The infrastructure necessary for the development of the study regarding the schools included a computer room with several computers connected to the Internet. These resources are in line with the actions proposed by the Brazilian National Educational Technology Program that had been implemented in a large number of public schools. However, most schools did not have all the necessary equipment and the internet network was slow and unstable. In the case of Belém schools, several challenges made it difficult to conduct the study, which required the mobilization of the local coordinator to obtain equipment donations from UFPA, the Regional Labor Court, and a computer products store (Sol Informática). These infrastructure deficiencies are present in most public schools, but in poorer regions, resources for computerization in schools seem to be even scarcer. Funding for software development and maintenance was essential to solve most of the problems the team faced.

In addition to the difficulties in the computer labs, the activities of the Belém schools were interrupted for long periods of time due to building renovations (in one of the schools) and a strike by the education sector. The delays in starting activities and breaks during development made it difficult to engage and regularize the work of the scholarship holders and volunteers, implying successive changes in the local team personnel, and generating further delays in carrying out successive training sessions. This partly explains the small changes observed in assessments before and after the intervention (Fig. 12.3). However, in the latest Prova Brasil and IDEB assessments, these schools had not been showing improvement. The team regretted that it had not been possible to contribute more to the problem of school failure in these schools which, of the six participating schools, had the lowest scores in the Prova Brasil.

The schools were selected following the main criterion pointed out in the project, lower scores in the Prova Brasil, but the importance of considering the location of the school as a criterion in future studies was verified, in view of the safety of the scholars and their commuting possibilities. Another important criterion for interpreting the results is to choose schools that have three unbiased, successive evaluations of the Prova Brasil, thus ensuring a stable baseline to compare, even if these schools do not have the lowest scores. Additional studies like the one described in this chapter, but that longitudinally compare the same school and control schools with similar scores in the Prova Brasil, would add relevant knowledge about the effectiveness of the use of large-scale interventions.

The project contributed to the training of teachers and students, team members, and produced knowledge that can be useful for literacy agents and for educational policy managers, whether at the level of municipalities, states or federation. The project illustrates the importance of integrating research developed in Higher Education Institutions in Brazil with teaching practices in Basic Education schools. This integration has also sensitized and trained undergraduate and graduate students about the importance of action-research projects that help to solve Brazilian problems. At the same time, it demonstrated to a multidisciplinary team the importance of basic research that guided the teaching technology used in the interventions.

Acknowledgments We would like to thank the students and teachers who collected data and helped with data analysis: Abrãao F. F. de Melo Jr., Aline M. de Angelis, Amanda G. B. Magalhães, Ana Karla E. Rezende, Ana Rúbia S. Menotti, André P. dos Santos, Andrea R. de Souza, Ângela Maria R. Borges, Arthur A. S. de Barros, Beatriz F. Scandiuzzi, Beatriz M. W. Saar, Camila O. Vieira, Carolina C. Silveira, Daniela C. P. A. Mattos, Danielle G. Vieira, Ederson F. Vinagre, Elaine C. da Cruz, Elaine O. Abreu, Elis N. dos Santos, Érica Abreu, Fernanda M. Diaz, Gisele R. Coelho, Graziela O. Souza, Ivan C. Gonçalves, Izabelly O. Severino, Izaura Letícia L. de Melo, Jamile P. C. de Oliveira, Jaqueline Rabello, Jéssica Silva, Jéssika P. da Silva e Silva, Jorgete M. de Lima, Josiane M. Donadeli, Karoline C. de Oliveira, Lara U. de Souza e Silva, Larissa Ribeiro, Laura G. Garcia, Liduína P. Rodrigues, Liliane N. Reis, Lorie Cerise Q. Rodrigues, Luciano I. P. Trindade, Manoel Laredo Jr., Manoella C. Carvalho, Márcia R. Minto, Marcilene C. Barbosa, Maria Aparecida Rodrigues, Maria de Fatima V. B. Tavares, Maria Edilene Q. S. Nascimento, Maria Felicidade T. Manoni, Marina B. P. Vidual, Marina D. Guarda, Marineide Aran, Murilo

Aguiar, Paola Moreli, Patrícia Scarpa, Paulo B. de Assis, Regiane V. M. Monteiro, Ricardo M. Bondioli, Rita de Cássia P. S. Brígida, Rita N. J. Krasnoschecoff, Roberta Aparecida Lopes, Rody C. de Oliveira, Roseli Ap. Andrade, Samara C. Milhomem, Samuel T. A. de Pereira, Selma S. Sarraf, Taiana A. Conceição, Thaís Duarte, Thiago K. E. da Silva, Victória E. Ferreira, Vitória Lima. Projeto No. 15116 – Observatório da Educação, financiado pela CAPES e pelo INEP.

References

Benitez, P., & Domeniconi, C. (2012). Verbalizações de familiares durante aprendizagem de leitura e escrita por deficientes intelectuais. *Estudos de Psicologia, 29*(4), 553–562. https://doi.org/10.1590/S0103-166X2012000400010

Benitez, P., & Domeniconi, C. (2016). Use of a computerized reading and writing teaching program for families of students with intellectual disabilities. *The Psychological Record, 1*, 01–12. https://doi.org/10.1007/s40732-015-0158-8

Bertini, M. (2017). *Desenvolvimento de compreensão de textos e fluência de leitura: Avaliação de um programa de ensino informatizado* Master's thesis, Universidade Estadual de Londrina. Biblioteca Digital da Produção Científica, Tecnológica, Artística e Cultural da Universidade Estadual de Londrina. http://www.uel.br/pos/pgac/wp-content/uploads/2018/04/Desenvolvimento-de-compreens%C3%A3o-de-textos-e-flu%C3%AAncia-de-leitura-avalia%C3%A7%C3%A3o-de-um-programa-de-ensino-informatizado.pdf

Conselho Federal de Psicologia (CFP). (2005). *Código de ética profissional do psicólogo*. Brasília, DF. http://site.cfp.org.br/wp-content/uploads/2012/07/Co%CC%81digo-de-%C3%89tica.pdf

de Rose, J. C. (2005). Análise comportamental da aprendizagem de leitura e escrita. *Revista Brasileira de Análise do Comportamento, 1*(1), 29–50. https://doi.org/10.18542/rebac.v1i1.676

de Rose, J. C., de Souza, D. G., Rossito, A. L., & de Rose, T. M. S. (1989). Aquisição de leitura após história de fracasso escolar: Equivalência de estímulos e generalização. *Psicologia: Teoria e Pesquisa, 5*(3), 325–346. https://psycnet.apa.org/record/1991-75004-001

de Rose, J. C., Souza, D. G., Rossito, A. L., & de Rose, T. M. S. (1992). Stimulus equivalence and generalization in reading after matching to sample by exclusion. In S. C. Hayes, & L. J. Hayes (Eds.), Understanding Verbal Relations (pp. 69–82). Context Press.

de Rose, J. C., de Souza, D. G., & Hanna, E. S. (1996). Teaching reading and spelling: Exclusion and stimulus equivalence. *Journal of Applied Behavior Analysis, 29*(4), 451–469. https://doi.org/10.1901/jaba.1996.29-451

de Souza, D. G., & de Rose, J. C. (2006). Desenvolvendo programas individualizados para o ensino de leitura. *Acta Comportamentalia, 14*(1), 77–98. http://revistas.unam.mx/index.php/acom/article/view/14532

de Souza, D. G., de Rose, J. C., Faleiros, T. C., Bortoloti, R., Hanna, E. S., & McIlvane, W. J. (2009). Teaching generative reading via recombination of minimal textual units: A legacy of verbal behavior to children in Brazil. *International Journal of Psychology and Psychological Therapy, 9*(1), 19–44. https://www.ncbi.nlm.nih.gov/pmc/articles/PMC2786216/

Del Prette, Z. A., & Del Prette, A. (2008). Um sistema de categorias de habilidades sociais educativas. *Paideia, 18*(41), 517–530. https://doi.org/10.1590/S0103-863X2008000300008

Ferreiro, E. (2008). *Com todas as letras* (15ª ed.). Editora Cortez.

Grégoire, J., & Piérart, B. (1997). *Avaliação dos problemas de leitura: Os novos modelos teóricos e suas implicações diagnósticas*. Artmed.

INEP – Instituto Nacional de Estudos e Pesquisas Educacionais Anísio Teixeira. (2011). *PDE: Plano de Desenvolvimento da Educação: Prova Brasil*. MEC, SEB.

Muniz, C. C. (2019). *Efeitos do treino de mães e professoras como aplicadoras de um programa de ensino de leitura de histórias infantis* Master's thesis, Universidade de Brasília. Repositório Institucional UnB. https://repositorio.unb.br/handle/10482/38069

Reis, T., de Souza, D. G., & de Rose, J. C. (2009). Avaliação de um programa para o ensino de leitura e escrita. *Estudos Avaliação Educacional, 20*, 425–449. https://doi.org/10.18222/eae204420092038

Rosa Filho, A. B., de Rose, J. C., de Souza, D. G., Hanna, E. S., & Fonseca, M. L. (1998). *Aprendendo a ler e a escrever em pequenos passos* Research Software. Universidade Federal de São Carlos.

Silveira, C. C. (2015). *Mapeamento de repertórios de leitura e escrita em escolas com baixos índices na Prova Brasil* Master's thesis, Universidade Federal de São Carlos. Repositório Institucional UFSCar. https://repositorio.ufscar.br/bitstream/handle/ufscar/6060/6592.pdf?sequence=1&isAllowed=y

Silveira, C. C., Domeniconi, C., Calcagno, S. C., Kato, O. M., & Hanna, E. S. (2016). Repertório básico de leitura e escrita em escolas brasileiras com baixa avaliação do ensino fundamental. *Acta Comportamentalia, 24*, 471–486. https://psycnet.apa.org/record/2017-04591-006

Silveira, C. C., Domeniconi, C., & Hanna, E. S. (2019). Uma avaliação alternativa de compreensão de leitura para crianças. *Acta Comportamentalia, 27*, 423–435. https://psycnet.apa.org/record/2020-22422-002

Tizo, M. (2016). *Avaliando tecnologia de ensino de leitura e escrita informatizada e adaptada para alunos de escola pública com dificuldade de aprendizagem* Doctoral dissertation, Universidade de Brasília. Repositório Institucional UnB. https://repositorio.unb.br/bitstream/10482/21618/1/2016_MarcileydeTizo.pdf

Part IV
Possible Dialogues with Other Areas of Knowledge

Chapter 13
Differential Diagnosis of Specific Reading and Writing Disorders: Speech, Language and Hearing Sciences Contributions

Celia Maria Giacheti, Nathani Cristina da Silva, and Tâmara de Andrade Lindau

13.1 Introduction

Complaints of problems in learning academic skills, whether they are reading, writing, or mathematics, are frequently reported by students' parents. These parents seek evaluation, diagnosis, and intervention from speech therapy, or related areas, so that the child learns, progresses, and does not fail at school.

The diagnosis of neurodevelopmental disorders, more specifically of disorders involving academic skills and related to school failure is usually performed by a multidisciplinary team. The set of characteristics of each of the reading and writing disorders has received attention from speech and hearing therapists, psychologists, and educators for early identification of students with specific learning disorders and also to differentiate them from those with only "difficulty" in learning some academic skills.

This differential diagnosis is one of the most difficult and complex tasks of health and education professionals (Giacheti, 2013). It should be performed taking into account the clinical history, the presence or not of the same disorder in other family members, the set of manifestations, and the persistence of the condition after brief therapeutic intervention, which is now called response to intervention.

The Brazilian Federal Council of Speech Therapy (CFFa, 2002) prepared a guide entitled "Professional Exercise of the Speech Therapist in Brazil", highlighting the areas of performance, including that of conducting a diagnosis. This area includes 29 different actions, such as: to raise the history of the individual; to evaluate the abilities involving language, voice, and speech fluency and articulation; besides the evaluation of the peripheral and central vestibular and auditory function and, also,

C. M. Giacheti (✉) · N. C. da Silva · T. de Andrade Lindau
Universidade Estadual Paulista Júlio de Mesquita Filho, Marília, SP, Brazil
e-mail: c.giacheti@unesp.br

A. R. de Albuquerque, R. M. de Melo (eds.), *Contributions of Behavior Analysis to Reading and Writing Comprehension*, https://doi.org/10.1007/978-3-031-40868-7_13

the orofacial and cervical myofunctional system, deglutition and its disturbances. They also refer other actions such as analyzing and interpreting the findings, evidence, testing, and requesting opinions and complementary examinations (CFFa, 2002).

Having said that, this chapter aims to present concepts about the speech and language diagnostic process, with emphasis on specific learning disorders, in a more detailed way, of reading and writing, its main characteristics and its frequency. It will also address manifestations that can differentiate reading and writing disorders from learning difficulties in these skills and, to illustrate, a case study will be presented.

13.2 Specific Reading and Writing Disorders

Specific learning disabilities, with emphasis on reading and writing, are described as neurodevelopmental conditions that can vary in degree of impairment (mild, moderate, or severe), occur during the early years of formal schooling, and change with the complexity of tasks over the course of school and life. These specific reading and writing disorders are framed as persistent impairment in learning basic educational skills and may hinder personal and social development (*American Psychiatric Association* [APA], 2013).

The specific learning disorder is characterized by persistent and deleterious difficulties in basic academic skills in reading, writing, and/or mathematics that are below the expected average for that age or at acceptable performance levels when associated with extraordinary effort (APA, 2013). The investigation of the set of characteristics to raise this diagnosis is performed by assessing performance in skills related to learning (e.g., reading, writing, and mathematics) in standardized tests, clinical interviews, and school reports, and also by the school's response when subjected to specific intervention for a period of approximately 6 months (APA, 2013).

The literature related to the diagnosis of specific learning disorders is extensive. However, this chapter will present some of the theoretical references that differentiate the reading and writing disorders that affect the school population, namely: (1) Descriptions presented in the Diagnostic and Statistical Manual of Mental Disorders: DSM-5 (APA, 2013); (2) Information from the American Speech-Language-Hearing Association (ASHA, 2019); and (3) Data released by the World Health Organization's International Classification of Diseases – ICD-10 (WHO, 1993). This selection is justified to allow the dialogue between professionals from different countries and will be presented in Table 13.1.

Table 13.1 Diagnostic features of specific learning disorder

Source	Specific learning disorder
DSM-5	*A. Difficulties learning and using academic skills, as indicated by the presence of at least one of the following symptoms that have persisted for at least 6 months, despite the provision of interventions that target those difficulties* *1. Inaccurate or slow and effortful word reading* *2. Difficulty understanding the meaning of what is read* *3. Difficulties with spelling* *4. Difficulties with written expression* *5. Difficulties mastering number sense, number facts, or calculation* *6. Difficulties with mathematical reasoning* *B. The affected academic skills are substantially and quantifiably below those expected for the individual's chronological age, and cause significant interference with academic or occupational performance, or with activities of daily living, as confirmed by individually administered standardized achievement measures and comprehensive clinical assessment* *C. The learning difficulties begin during school-age years but may not become fully manifest until the demands for those affected academic skills exceed the individual's limited capacities* *D. The learning difficulties are not better accounted for by intellectual disabilities, uncorrected visual or auditory acuity, other mental or neurological disorders, psychosocial adversity, lack of proficiency in the language of academic instruction, or inadequate educational instruction* *Note: The four diagnostic criteria are to be met based on a clinical synthesis of the individual's history (developmental, medical, family, educational), school reports, and psychoeducational assessment* *Note: Dyslexia is an alternative term used to refer to a pattern of learning difficulties characterized by problems with accurate or fluent word recognition, poor decoding, and poor spelling abilities. If dyslexia is used to specify this particular pattern of difficulties, it is important also to specify any additional difficulties that are present, such as difficulties with reading comprehension or math reasoning* *With impairment in written expression: Spelling accuracy, Grammar and punctuation accuracy* *Clarity or organization of written expression* *With impairment in mathematics: Number sense, Memorization of arithmetic facts, Accurate or fluent calculation, Accurate math reasoning* *Note: Dyscalculia is an alternative term used to refer to a pattern of difficulties characterized by problems processing numerical information, learning arithmetic facts, and performing accurate or fluent calculations. If dyscalculia is used to specify this particular pattern of mathematic difficulties, it is important also to specify any additional difficulties that are present, such as difficulties with math reasoning or word reasoning accuracy* *Specify current severity:* ***Mild**: Some difficulties learning skills in one or two academic domains, but of mild enough severity that the individual may be able to compensate or function well when provided with appropriate accommodations or support services, especially during the school years* ***Moderate**: Marked difficulties learning skills in one or more academic domains, so that the individual is unlikely to become proficient without some intervals of intensive and specialized teaching during the school years. Some accommodations or supportive services at least part of the day at school, in the workplace, or at home may be needed to complete activities accurately and efficiently* ***Severe**: Severe difficulties learning skills, affecting several academic domains, so that the individual is unlikely to learn those skills without ongoing intensive individualized and specialized teaching for most of the school years. Even with an array of appropriate accommodations or services at home, at school, or in the workplace, the individual may not be able to complete all activities efficiently*

(continued)

Table 13.1 (continued)

Source	Specific learning disorder
ASHA	*A disorder in one or more of the basic psychological processes involved in understanding or in using language, spoken or written, which may manifest itself in an imperfect ability to listen, think, speak, read, write, spell, or to do mathematical calculations. The term includes such conditions as perceptual handicaps, brain injury, minimal brain dysfunction, dyslexia, and developmental aphasia. The term does not include children who have learning problems which are primarily the result of visual, hearing, or motor handicaps, of mental retardation, or emotional disturbance, or of environmental, cultural, or economic disadvantage*
ICD-10	*F81 Specific developmental disorders of scholastic skills: Disorders in which the normal patterns of skill acquisition are disturbed from the early stages of development. This is not simply a consequence of a lack of opportunity to learn, it is not solely a result of mental retardation, and it is not due to any form of acquired brain trauma or disease* *F81.0 Specific Reading Disorder: The main feature is a specific and significant impairment in the development of reading skills that is not solely accounted for by mental age, visual acuity problems or inadequate schooling. Reading comprehension skill, reading word recognition, oral reading skill and performance of tasks requiring reading may all be affected. Spelling difficulties are frequently associated with specific reading disorder and often remain into adolescence, even after some progress in reading has been made. Specific developmental disorders of reading are commonly preceded by a history of disorders in speech or language development. Associated emotional and behavioral disturbances are common during the school age period* *F81.1 Specific spelling disorder: The main feature is a specific and significant impairment in the development of spelling skills, in the absence of a history of specific reading disorder, which is not solely accounted for by low mental age, visual acuity problems or inadequate schooling. The abilities to spell orally and to write out words correctly are both affected* *F81.2 Specific disorder of arithmetical skills: Involves a specific impairment in arithmetical skills that is not solely explicable on the basis of general mental retardation or of inadequate schooling. The deficit concerns mastery of basic computational skills of addition, subtraction, multiplication and division, rather than of the more abstract mathematical skills involved in algebra, trigonometry, geometry or calculus* *F81.3 Mixed disorder of scholastic skills: An ill-defined residual category of disorders in which both arithmetical and reading or spelling skills are significantly impaired, but in which the disorder is not solely explicable in terms of general mental retardation or of inadequate schooling* *F81.8 Other developmental disorders of scholastic skills: Developmental expressive writing disorder* *F81.9 Developmental disorder of scholastic skills, unspecified: Knowledge acquisition disability not otherwise specified*

13.3 Differential Diagnosis for Specific Learning Disorders

Differential diagnosis is the differentiation of two (or more) disorders that are apparently the same but which, due to the presence of a symptom in one of the conditions and, necessarily, absence in the other, characterizes two (or more) different disorders or conditions (Nicolosi et al., 2004).

The diagnosis for specific learning disorder is complex and may be easily confused with other conditions. In this chapter, as already described, expected behaviors will be presented with a focus on reading and writing skills. Such conditions were chosen due to the peculiarities of the set of manifestations that accompany the diagnosis of specific learning disorder. It is interesting to note that the specific learning disorder with impairment in reading skills, which may also be accompanied by changes in writing, may also be called dyslexia according to DSM-5 (APA, 2013), as detailed in Table 13.1.

To make the differential diagnosis in specific learning disorders in children, some concepts are important:

1. Persistent disorder: the specific learning disorder is not a transitory condition caused by lack of school stimulation or inadequate schooling, but rather a disorder that persists into adulthood and interferes with work performance or daily activities (APA, 2013);
2. Comorbidities: specific learning disorder can be found in comorbidity with other neurodevelopmental disorders (e.g., ADHD, autistic spectrum disorder) and with mental disorders (e.g., anxiety disorders, depressive and bipolar disorder). These comorbid disorders can make differential diagnosis difficult (APA, 2013).

Mousinho and Navas (2016) highlighted the advances in the description of specific learning disorders when comparing the diagnostic criteria of the DSM-5 with the previous publication, which referred to the DSM-IV. These authors found that the changes occurred mainly in the subdivision of neurodevelopmental disorders, in the more global terminology, accompanied by a specification to explain the impaired skills (e.g., specific learning disorder with impaired reading, impaired writing, and/or impaired mathematics), and in the recommendation of the use of the response-to-intervention paradigm[1] to confirm-or not the diagnostic hypothesis of specific learning disorders.

Tables 13.2, 13.3, 13.4, and 13.5 list the diagnostic characteristics of other reading and writing disorders: learning disability, attention deficit/hyperactivity disorder, major neurocognitive disorder, poor academic performance due to sensory impairment (visual/auditory or other neurological deficit), autism spectrum

[1] The inclusion of *Response to Intervention* (RTI) was noted as a necessary change according to DSM-5 to confirm, based on concrete data, the persistent nature of the diagnosis of learning disability from an occasional learning disability. RTI is a model in which the diagnosis is not given initially but after a period of specific and effective intervention. This procedure aims to differentiate a persistent condition (disorder) from a temporary condition (difficulty) and isolate environmental variables that may also be transient (Mousinho & Navas, 2016).

Table 13.2 Diagnostic characteristics of learning disorder and learning difficulty

Source	Characteristics
DSM-5	Specific Learning Disorder is a Neurodevelopmental Disorder distinguished from a conditions of learning difficulties due to external factors (e.g., lack of educational opportunity, unsatisfactory school education, learning in a second language). In Specific Learning Disorders, learning difficulties persist in the presence of adequate educational opportunities
ASHA; ICD-10	The ASHA and ICD-10 do not punctually present characteristics related to learning difficulty, distinguishing it from learning disability

Table 13.3 Diagnostic characteristics of attention deficit/hyperactivity disorder

Source	Characteristics
DSM-5	*A persistent pattern of inattention* and/or hyperactivity-impulsivity that interferes with functioning or development
ASHA	*ADHD is a lifelong brain disorder that makes it hard for a person to pay attention. Some people with ADHD have trouble sitting still or controlling their behavior*
ICD-10	ADHD is specified as F90.0 Activity and attention disorders, but there is no definition

Table 13.4 Diagnostic features of neurocognitive disorders

Source	Characteristics
DSM-5	*Evidence of significant cognitive decline from a previous level of performance in one or more cognitive domains: Learning and memory, language, executive function, complex attention, perceptual-motor, social cognition*
ASHA	ASHA does not use this denomination, but presents characteristics related to neurocognitive disorders in degenerative neurological diseases, such as Alzheimer's disease
ICD-10	*The main feature is a decline in cognitive performance. This may include memory impairment, learning or concentration difficulties* (F06.7)

Table 13.5 Diagnostic characteristics of other disorders

Disorder	Characteristics
Unsatisfactory academic performance due to sensory impairment (visual/auditory) or other neurological deficits	It is within an expected level for a given nature of sensory or neurological deficit (e.g., stroke, traumatic brain injury, hearing/visual impairment). In these cases, there are abnormal findings on neurological examination
Intellectual Disability	Global developmental impairment not restricted to one academic skill. May be comorbid, provided learning deficits exceed those commonly associated with intellectual disability
Autism Spectrum Disorder	A peculiar condition that includes persistent deficits in communication and social interaction, with restricted and repetitive patterns of behavior, interest, or activities that are not confined to a particular academic skill
Communication disorders	Impairments in oral language skills that are not restricted to particular academic skills such as reading or writing
Schizophrenia	Academic difficulties may result in a rapid decline in academic functioning with onset in adolescence or adulthood – which differs from the specific disorder in that they become apparent during the early learning years

disorder, communication disorders, and schizophrenia. These characteristics were taken from DSM-5 (APA, 2013), ASHA (2019) and ICD-10 (WHO, 1993) and are also important for differential diagnosis.

As in the DSM-5 (APA, 2013), the DSM-5 Differential Diagnosis Manual (First, 2015) proposes some other aspects to be considered for differential diagnosis (Table 13.5).

13.4 Prevalence and Etiological Aspects of Specific Learning Disorders

Specific learning disorders, as reported in DSM-5, have a prevalence of 5%–15% among school-age children in different languages and cultures (APA, 2013). Brazilian data should follow the same pattern; however, due to the great difficulty in differentiating learning disorders from learning disabilities, the number of children arriving at institutions and clinics for diagnosis and intervention is much higher. According to the authors' experience in a public speech and language diagnosis service linked to specialized rehabilitation centers (Center for Education and Health Studies – CEES and Specialized Rehabilitation Center – CER) at the Paulista State University (UNESP) in a city in the interior of the state of São Paulo (Marília), the prevalence has been higher than 30%.

Specific learning disorder is a neurobiological problem, currently considered one of the important neurodevelopmental disorders. They are not justified by intellectual, hearing or other sensory impairment, motor dysfunction or other medical or neurological condition. However, they may be associated with the interaction of genetic, epigenetic, and/or environmental factors involving the perception and processing of verbal or nonverbal information (APA, 2013).

Conducting a diagnosis means investigating signs and symptoms in specific areas to identify an abnormality or a disorder and may include the etiological search and the prognosis of an individual (Giacheti, 2013). When a healthcare professional starts the diagnostic process, several diagnostic hypotheses are raised and, finally, after the completion of complementary evaluations and examinations, these hypotheses may be discarded or confirmed. It is like detective work, in search of clues, or a puzzle, where each of the pieces contributes to the construction of the full picture. By using clinical reasoning, the process can be concluded and the appropriate treatment alternatives is offered to the patient by the professional in charge (Réa-Neto, 1998).

The speech and language diagnosis, in turn, involves the investigation of symptoms related to communication, which involves the understanding and expression of oral and written language, voice, fluency, and hearing. Considering the complexity of language acquisition and development, the evaluation process is an extremely difficult task (Giacheti, 2013). According to the Brazilian Federal Council of Speech Therapy (CFFA, 2018), the research on school performance can be conducted by a speech therapist or a group of professionals who evaluate the skills and difficulties of schoolchildren with history/complaint related to academic skills. The conclusion of this process should lead to a possible diagnosis, prognosis, and guidelines.

In a more didactic way, the process of speech and language diagnosis is subdivided into several steps: planning, anamnesis/interview to seek information about the complaint, history of the complaint and school development, and the speech and language evaluation itself, with procedures to identify possible difficulties and facilities in learning spoken language, reading and writing. In the case of schoolchildren, the visit to the school is mandatory and, in this occasion, it is important to hear the teacher about the student's performance compared to average or good students, their classroom attendance, and how much this student has evolved since the beginning of the school year. Other professionals that may be included in the speech and language diagnostic process are pediatricians, neurologists, ophthalmologists, otorhinolaryngologists, endocrinologists, geneticists, pedagogues/psycho-pedagogues, psychologists, among others. The last phase, important and necessary, is to provide feedback to the parents and the student, which includes the speech and language evaluation results, possible diagnoses, and guidelines. The teachers and other professionals involved must, with parental consent and maintaining due confidentiality, send information and specific guidelines that help or promote the child's development, being careful not to expose the diagnosis.

As observed, speech and language evaluation is a complex investigation process because, as well as choosing agile and correct procedures, the data must be interpreted based on robust theoretical aspects and used with caution to avoid unnecessary labelling. Thus, the diagnostic process involves verifying the presence, or absence, of some ability (or competence) and identifying how "altered" (real/concrete situation) the performance of a certain schoolchild is in relation to other "typical" individual(s) (desired/expected situation), assigning serious and ethical professional judgment by the speech therapist (ASHA, 2019; Giacheti, 2013; Hadji, 1994).

The analysis of performance in school abilities will depend on the of procedures selected for the diagnostic process, and it is the evaluator's responsibility to compare the child's response not only in the presence or absence of a difficulty, but also its nature. It is noteworthy that determining the repertoire related to learning to read and write the school by the time it reaches the diagnostic process should also include what he is able (or not) to learn.

It is noteworthy that each child can learn in different ways, many need more visual cues, accompanied by auditory information, others may need repetition of instructions, and a large portion do not always follow the learning offered by the school. Environmental factors, illnesses that culminate in constant absences, changing teachers, and difficulty in following the teaching strategies may require attention from the teacher and the family. Often only school-pedagogical tutoring or school adjustments may solve the situation without requiring specific interventions. Difficulties in learning the academic skills involving reading, writing and mathematics are common among students in the initial years of learning and the presence of these difficulties do not necessarily require a speech therapist. In cases of persistent difficulties that require actions beyond those performed by the school, the speech therapist should perform the clarifications and proper referrals, including to clinical speech therapists or other professionals (CFFa, 2018).

Different aids may be presented to understand the real difficulty of the student, such as offering part of the correct sample of writing words; offering two possibilities, one correct and one incorrect for the child to choose, among others. If the difficulty remains or the child refuses to do the activity, it is important to use age-appropriate strategies (e.g., playful activities such as games that stimulate competition or activities that represent the classroom), or to conduct the evaluation on another date. It is important to highlight that a difficulty or refusal is important information and part of the data collection and analysis. Frequently, students go through unpleasant situations at home or at school when they cannot perform some activity, such as criticism by family members or colleagues or even bullying.

As proposed by de Rose and Gil (2003), playing is a habitual and extremely important activity for child development as well as a form of communication. From this perspective, playing as a strategy for speech and language or psychological assessment and therapeutic intervention, for example, may provide relevant information that cannot be obtained through verbal reporting due to the limitations of the stage of language development (Del Prette & Meyer, 2015).

Generally, an objective and open conversation with the child, explaining the reason for the evaluation and desire to help them, will lead them to explain what they do not know how to do and what happens at school or at home. Psychologist can often help in this phase as well as during the intervention. In the written language assessment process, the same steps of the complete speech and language assessment should be followed, but the focus will be on specific tests, starting with less complex activities and gradually increasing their complexity (Giacheti & Lindau, 2017).

To better clarify each of the stages, it is highlighted that the beginning of the evaluation process and speech therapy diagnosis must list the evaluation objective, the survey of the particularities of the school (age, schooling, if public or private education, preferences, routines, among others) and the choice of guidelines, instruments, and strategies for investigation of the set of abilities and difficulties related to reading, writing and mathematics.

After planning, data collection starts, either through clinical history (anamnesis or interview with parents and teachers), speech and language evaluation, including audiometry and, if necessary, other evaluations such as ophthalmological, pediatric, neurological, psychological, among others to elaborate the initial speech and language diagnosis hypothesis(es). Frequently, in the face of specific learning disorders, the family's complaint is related to inferior academic performance when compared to other students of the same grade and age. Some parents report that their child is failing in reading and writing; others report that their child has learned to read and write but reads below their age and school level and writes words and texts with errors. Others are not able to produce or read more complex texts. Some students have difficulty reasoning and learning mathematical operations. Others cannot understand the problem statement when they read it themselves; however, when someone does the reading, they can solve the problem correctly. A good clinical history, complemented by information from school, helps differentiate between school difficulty and specific learning disorder. This already allows diagnostic hypotheses to be raised, guides the next steps, and indicates whether speech and language intervention can contribute to symptom improvement. In more complex cases, brief therapy, as already mentioned, currently known as response to intervention, may also resolve specific problems and confirm that it is only a school difficulty and not the specific learning disorder, which is persistent, as previously mentioned, and would require more time in therapy to improve symptoms (Fig. 13.1).

In the next step, after data collection, it is necessary to unite and classify the numerous data obtained. Thus, aspects that corroborate or refute the speech and language diagnostic hypotheses and correlated factors that may justify or aggravate the condition must be selected, and the need to use additional procedures must be verified, and the speech and language and etiological diagnostic hypotheses must be elaborated, brief therapy indicated, if necessary, and the initial hypotheses confirmed/denied.

From this, the professional must compare the obtained data (reality) with the literature that points out the school performance (what would be expected of the student), always associated to the evaluator's experience, the involved teachers and other professionals.

As already mentioned, the final stage of the diagnostic process, which includes the feedback, should be carried out in person, but documented for the family, considering some possible limitations of the diagnostic process. The communication of

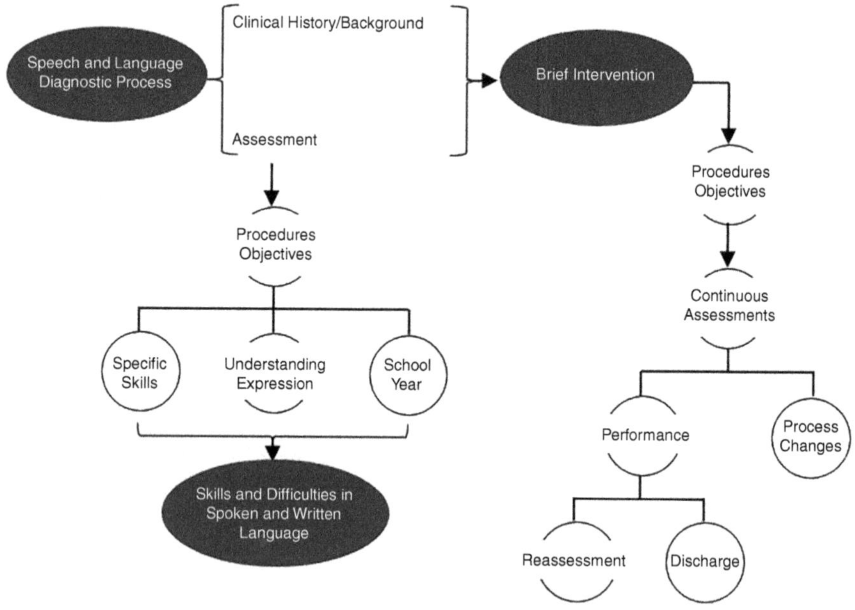

Fig. 13.1 Phonaudiological assessment process

the results to the family, the school or other professionals can also be done through reports, always respecting confidentiality and ethics. Figure 13.1 shows the steps of the evaluation process.

Considering the contents mentioned so far, it is highlighted that, to identify early the problems related to language, it is necessary that the assessment procedures direct, in a specific way, the verification of the presence (or absence) of certain competences and the nature of the difficulty (Befi-Lopes, 2002; Hadji, 1994).

In recent decades, the use of spoken language measures (e.g., oral storytelling) has been considered a differential in the investigation of the skills underlying reading and writing. Thus, behavioral assessments, complemented by oral storytelling data, may provide an earlier and more detailed diagnosis (Catts et al., 2015; Costa et al., 2018; Lindau et al., 2015; Rossi et al., 2016).

13.5 Assessing Reading and Writing

During late childhood, the evaluation of child development turns mainly to the school process (Stein, 1994). Thus, assessing reading and writing should be similar to the steps of a complete speech and language evaluation but specific, based on basic skills such as reading, writing and calculation, on which the knowledge to be incorporated later will be supported (Coll & Bolen, 1993/1996).

There are several instruments used to assess reading and writing. Initially, it is important to ask the schoolchildren to spontaneously write what they know how to write to identify the learning phase they are in. Materials containing letters, syllables, words, and short texts of different sizes are also offered for reading. Preferably, regarding writing, pencils and blank sulphite paper are left on the table to observe how the child uses the space on the sheet, whether they use it vertically or horizontally, centrally, and whether they write in the correct direction (left to right). Frequently, children with specific disorders do not keep up with the development of their class and may refuse to do academic activities if these are not requested in a playful and motivating way.

In addition to a clinical evaluation, which already allows raising the difficulties and facilities of the child in each of the tasks, other systematic and formal instruments can also be used depending on the school year and difficulty, such as: School Performance Test 1st (TDE; Stein, 1994) and 2nd Edition (Milnitsky et al., 2019); Tests to Evaluate Reading Processes (PROLEC; Capellini et al., 2010); Tests of Metalinguistic and Reading Skills (PROHMELE; Cunha & Capellini, 2009); Spelling Assessment Protocol (Pro-Ortografía; Batista et al., 2014) and Assessment of Performance in Reading Fluency (ADFLU; Martins & Capellini, 2018). These instruments will be briefly described below.

The TDE has been widely used in Brazil and assesses fundamental skills for school performance in three specific areas, namely reading, writing and arithmetic in students from 1st to 6th grades of elementary school. Recently, an updated and more complete version of the TDE was presented to professionals in the area. The

TDE II, like the TDE I, includes tests that assess reading, writing and arithmetic. The objective of the update is to offer the scientific community a more current version of an assessment procedure widely used by speech-language pathologists, educators, and psychologists in Brazil. The 2nd edition also includes the three domains: reading, writing, and mathematics, as part of a battery for diagnostic purposes, planning and, more specifically, clinical-educational interventions. It encompasses the assessment of children from 1st to 9th grade of Brazilian elementary schools, both from public and private schools (Stein, 1994; Milnitsky et al., 2019).

Another instrument, PROLEC, already in its 3rd edition, has been used by several groups in research related to reading in students from 2nd to 5th grade of elementary school. The instrument is composed of different tasks that explore the processes that interfere in reading, from the most peripheral to the most central, as well as from the simplest to the most complex (e.g., identification of letters and their respective sounds, recognition and reading of real and pseudo words, comprehension of sentences and texts). With these tests it is possible to obtain scores of the reading ability of students and information about the strategies used when reading a text. It is an instrument that helps to understand reading difficulties and assists in the diagnosis of specific learning disorders (Capellini et al., 2010).

PROHMELE enables the identification of the mastery of metalinguistic skills related to reading learning in students from the 1st to 4th grades of elementary school (Cunha & Capellini, 2009).

Pró-Ortografia evaluates the spelling performance of students from 2nd to 5th grade of elementary school. The instrument consists of 10 tests, six of which are collective and four are individual. The presentation of these tests occurs in increasing order of cognitive demand and classifies spelling errors. The instrument can be applied by teachers and pedagogical coordinators at school in a collective environment or by speech therapists in clinical settings (Batista et al., 2014).

The Assessment of Performance in Reading Fluency (ADFLU) allows professionals to assess, monitor and train students' reading fluency, providing the opportunity to increase reading speed and thus improve fluency and reading comprehension. It includes text cards with different levels of complexity, a checklist of text comprehension skills, and a table to monitor the evolution of fluency performance. This procedure can be used on children aged 6 years or older (Martins & Capellini, 2018).

13.5.1 The Involvement of Professionals in the Diagnosis of Specific Learning Disabilities

The tasks of raising diagnostic hypotheses and confirming the diagnosis of specific learning disorder is not exclusive to speech-language pathologists. Several professionals, such as pediatricians, neurologists, psychiatrists, and psychologists can gather information and help to raise and confirm the hypotheses.

The psychologist may also participate in this process by performing the psychological evaluation to raise psychological hypotheses or diagnoses about the person being evaluated and, consequently, make a decision pertinent to this professional. This process may encompass the investigation of aspects about intellectual functioning (i.e., primary problems that would justify more global learning problems), aptitude for performance in specific tasks, or other possibilities that will guide the intervention process (Pasquali, 2004; Hutz, 2015).

Several health problems, such as anemia, seizure, problems related to sleep quantity and quality, or severe behavioral compromises (frequent aggressiveness, non-interaction with the evaluator, refusal to develop academic tasks, depression, anxiety, tantrum, shyness) may maximize the speech and language condition or prevent the correct diagnosis from being concluded, as already mentioned. Due to these and other reasons, the speech and language diagnostic process needs to be associated with specific interventions from other professionals, such as interventions for behavioral change or drug treatments, to enable the conclusion of the diagnostic process and determination of the most correct speech and language conduct.

Franklin et al. (2018) correlated the sleep and behavior of individuals with specific learning disorder. In this study, 65.5% of students with specific learning disorder showed signs of sleep disorders, with the most frequent being sleep-wake transition disorders and total scores for sleep disorders above the acceptable level. In addition, individuals with specific learning disorder had longer sleep latencies than the control group. As for behavior, 72.4% of the subjects had clinical symptoms of behavioral problems, according to their parents' opinion. In the group with specific learning disorder, sleep disorders correlated with behavioral problems. The authors concluded that individuals with specific learning disorders had high rates of sleep disorders and behavioral alterations. These findings may help in the speech and language intervention of children and showed how the quality of sleep may interfere in school performance.

To illustrate, the case of a 9-year-old girl complaining of school difficulty will be presented next. The girl, identified here as "Maria", was born moderately premature, at 29 weeks of gestation. According to the parents, the child entered Kindergarten at 2 and a half years old and, at the time of this assessment, was in the 3rd year of elementary school in a public school in the state of São Paulo, Brazil. At the time of the evaluation, Maria also presented complaints related to sleep quality. The school reported to the parents the need for speech therapy evaluation due to the difficulties presented by the child to perform the activities proposed in the classroom. According to the teacher, the child was dispersed and had difficulty copying the material displayed on the blackboard.

Maria is a shy and not very expressive child. She responds to questions in a simple way, using one or two words. She understands simple and complex commands but does not show motivation to perform school activities. She can produce oral narratives of stories with beginning, middle and end, but poor in details. When presented with a story, told by an adult, she responds correctly, showing she understands its content. The speech and language evaluation also observed poor visual memory, which means that Maria is not able to remember stimuli minutes after they are presented to her.

As for reading, she presented altered fluency, reading slowly, guessing words, and adding and/or omitting phonemes. In relation to reading comprehension, the child did not demonstrate comprehension of the text read and had a performance below her school grade level. However, in relation to oral comprehension of text read by the evaluator, the child presented adequate performance. Regarding writing, she made several spelling mistakes (e.g., *bicicleta-bisiqueta; televisão- televição, preguiça-pregrisa*), hypersegmentation (e.g., *a_chei, e_liminado, cala_friu*), swapping semivowels or semiconsonants (e.g., *discriminação-disgriminição*) and absence of punctuation marks. Maria also presented changes in handwriting (mainly retouching and bad shapes of letters) and difficulty in relation to logical-mathematical reasoning, such as not performing basic operations when reading the problem. In the TDE tests a "lower" performance was obtained in reading and writing. It is noteworthy that, according to the neurological report presented by the parents, no changes were found in the computed tomography scan of the skull and in the child's electroencephalogram.

With the data from the speech and language evaluation, the diagnostic hypotheses of specific learning difficulty or specific learning disorder with emphasis on reading and writing were raised. The professional suggested tutoring, speech and language therapy and reevaluation for diagnostic confirmation, and made a referral to evaluate sleep-related issues. After 6 months of tutoring and speech and language therapy, a speech and language and performance reevaluation of the reading and writing tasks was conducted, with application of the traditional evaluation and the TDE. Maria's condition remained stable, which confirmed the diagnostic hypothesis previously established, as well as the need for continued speech and language intervention, in addition to school follow-up.

After brief exposure to the speech and language therapeutic process and absence of progress related to reading and writing, the following items may be indicated for confirmation of the diagnostic hypothesis of specific learning disorder: non-response to speech and language therapy performed for a period of 6 months; not only orthographic and grammatical errors, but also involving swapping semiconsonant or semivowels in writing and inaccuracy or absence of the use of textual punctuation; production of only simple written texts, slow and inaccurate reading, below her school grade level; difficulty in performing activities involving reading mathematical problems with improvement when the problem is read by an evaluator. During the speech and language reevaluation process, a "lower" classification was obtained in the TDE tests, also proving that there was no evolution in the condition.

Considering the results obtained during the evaluation and traditional speech and language re-evaluation and with the application of standardized tests, the diagnostic hypothesis of specific learning disorder with emphasis on moderate reading and writing was confirmed, according to DSM-5 (APA, 2013) and, as a guide, the professional suggested continuing school tutoring, associated with speech and language therapy and monitoring. The following figure presents Maria's diagnostic process (Fig. 13.2).

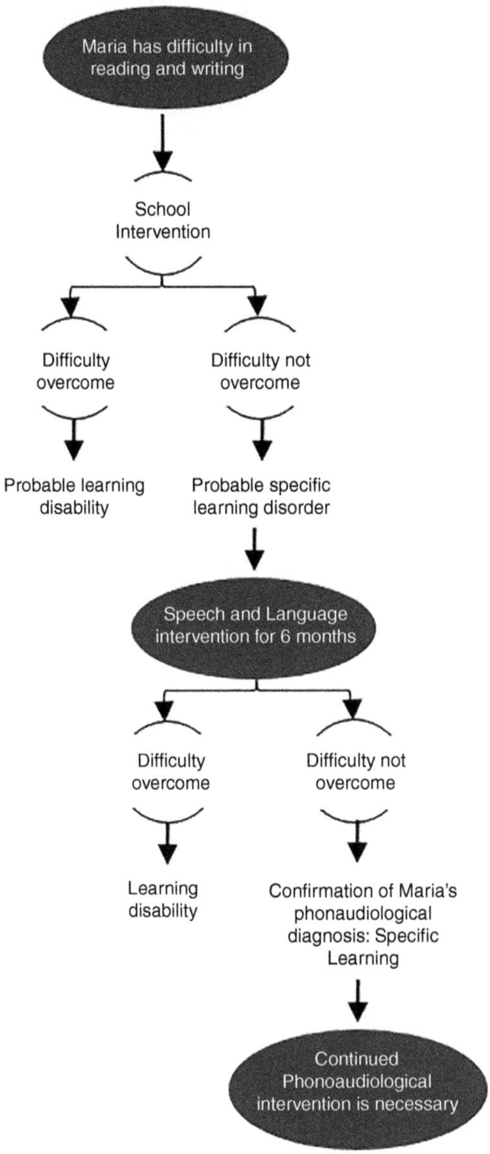

Fig. 13.2 Diagnostic process of Maria's reading and writing skills. (*Note*. Response to Intervention (RTI) model, adapted from Mousinho & Navas, 2016)

13.6 Final Considerations

The science of speech and language diagnosis or, more specifically, of reading and writing disorders, is a much more complex task than the application of a set of concepts and/or defined diagnostic rules and characteristics. Speech therapists should avoid rigid application of diagnostic criteria or differential diagnoses presented in theoretical references (APA, 2013; WHO, 1993) in a technical way, without careful data collection, without judgment and without offering the opportunity to change the condition through teaching strategies. It is important, above all, to know and carefully study the national and international literature, and use this information to support not only the speech and language diagnosis, which would also facilitate the communication of diagnostic information among professionals, school, patient, and family, but also offer possibilities of intervention, whether pedagogical, speech and language, or psychological.

At the same time, it is important to emphasize that the professionals who work with the evaluation of the processes related to reading and writing disorders should not conclude it without a broad investigation of the situation, seeking to identify its origin and development, to raise probable diagnostic hypotheses and, especially, to give thoughtful feedback safeguarding the limitations of the process, as well as offering or referring for intervention for at least 6 months. Finally, it is important to contextualize how necessary the careful and ethical diagnostic process is when facing school difficulties and the need to provide opportunities of greater exposure to monitored reading and writing activities to differentiate the students who present only specific difficulties in academic skills from those who really have specific learning disorder.

References

American Psychiatric Association – APA. (2013). *Diagnostic and statistical manual of mental disorders – DSM-5* (5th ed.). American Psychiatric Association.

American Speech Language Hearing Association ASHA. (2019). *Specific learning disabilities* [citado 28 abr 2020]. Disponível em: https://www.asha.org/advocacy/federal/idea/04-law-specific-ld/

Batista, A. O., Cervera-Mérida, J. F., Ygual-Fernández, A., & Capellini, S. A. (2014). *Pró-ortografia: Protocolo de avaliação da ortografia para escolares do segundo ao quinto ano do ensino fundamental*. Pró-Fono.

Befi-Lopes, D. M. (2002). *Prova de verificação do vocabulário: Aspectos da efetividade como instrumento diagnóstico*. Universidade de São Paulo.

Capellini, A. S., Oliveira, A. M., & Cuetos, F. (2010). *PROLEC: Provas de avaliação dos processos de leitura*. Casa do Psicólogo.

Catts, H. W., Herrera, S., Nielsen, D. C., & Pontes, M. S. (2015). Early prediction of reading comprehension within the simple view framework. *Reading and Writing, 28*(9), 1407–1425. https://doi.org/10.1007/s11145-015-9576-x

Coll, C., & Bolen, E. (1996). As intenções educativas e os objetivos da educação escolar: alternativas e fundamentos psicológicos. In C. Coll, J. Palacios, & A. Marchesi (Orgs.; A. M. Alves, Trad.), *Desenvolvimento psicológico e educação: Psicologia da educação* (pp. 317–352). Artes Médicas. (Original work published 1993)

Conselho Federal de Fonoaudiologia. (2002). *Exercício profissional do fonoaudiólogo* [internet]. Conselho Federal de Fonoaudiologia [citado 28 abr 2020]. Recovered from http://www.crefono4.org.br/cms/files/legislacao/Acoes-Inerentes.pdf

Conselho Federal de Fonoaudiologia. Fonoaudiologia na Educação [internet]. (2018). Conselho Federal de Fonoaudiologia [citado 28 abr 2020]. Recovered from https://www.fonoaudiologia.org.br/cffa/wp-content/uploads/2013/07/documentofonoaudiologia naeducacao.pdf

Costa, G. M., Rossi, N. F., & Giacheti, C. M. (2018). Desempenho de falantes do português brasileiro no "Test of Narrative Language (TNL)". *CoDAS, 30*(4), e20170148. https://doi.org/10.1590/2317-1782/20182017148

Cunha, V. L. O., & Capellini, S. A. (2009). *PROHMELE: Provas de habilidade metalinguísticas e de leitura*. Revinter.

de Rose, J. C. C., & Gil, M. S. C. A. (2003). Para uma análise do brincar e de sua função educacional. In M. Z. S. Brandão (Org.), *Sobre comportamento e cognição: A história e os avanços, a seleção por consequências em ação* (Vol. 11, pp. 373–382). ESETec.

Del Prette, G., & Meyer, S. B. (2015). O brincar como ferramenta de avaliação e intervenção na clínica analítico-comportamental infantil. In L. P. Santos, J. P. Gouveia, & M. S. Oliveira (Eds.), *Terapias comportamentais de terceira geração: Guia para profissionais* (pp. 239–250). SINOPSYS.

First, M. B. (2015). *Manual de diagnóstico diferencial do DSM-5* (F. S. Rodrigues, Trad.). Artmed.

Franklin, A. M., Giacheti, C. M., Silva, N. C., Campos, L. M. G., & Pinato, L. (2018). Correlação entre o perfil do sono e o comportamento em indivíduos com transtorno específico da aprendizagem. *CoDAS, 30*(3), e20170104. https://doi.org/10.1590/2317-1782/20182017104

Giacheti, C. M. (2013). Os distúrbios da comunicação e a genética. In C. M. Giacheti & S. M. Gimeniz-Paschoal (Orgs.), *Perspectivas multidisciplinares em fonoaudiologia: Da avaliação à intervenção* (pp. 73–91). Cultura Acadêmica.

Giacheti, C. M., & Lindau, T. A. (2017). Diagnóstico diferencial dos transtornos da linguagem infantil. In D. A. C. Lamônica & D. B. O. Britto (Orgs.), *Tratado de Linguagem: Perspectivas contemporâneas* (pp. 155–164). Booktoy.

Hadji, C. (1994). *A avaliação, regras do jogo: Das intenções aos instrumentos*. Porto Editora.

Hutz, C. S. (2015). O que é avaliação psicológica: Métodos técnicas e testes. In C. S. Hutz, D. R. Bandeira, & C. M. Trentini (Eds.), *Psicometria* (pp. 11–20). Artmed.

Lindau, T. A., Lucchesi, F. D. M., Rossi, N. F., & Giacheti, C. M. (2015). Instrumentos sistemáticos e formais de avaliação da linguagem de pré-escolares no Brasil: Uma revisão de literatura. *Revista CEFAC, 17*(2), 656–662. https://doi.org/10.1590/1982-021620151114

Martins, A. M., & Capellini, S. A. (2018). *ADFLU – Avaliação do Desempenho em Fluência de Leitura*. Booktoy.

Milnitsky, L., Giacomoni, C. H., & Fonseca, R. P. (2019). *Coleção TDE II – Teste de Desempenho Escolar* (2a ed.). Vetor.

Mousinho, R., & Navas, A. L. (2016). Mudanças apontadas no DSM-5 em relação aos transtornos específicos de aprendizagem em leitura e escrita. *Revista Debates em Psiquiatria, 6*(3), 38–45. https://revistardp.org.br/revista/article/view/133

Nicolosi, L., Elizabeth, H., & Janet, K. (2004). *Terminology of communication disorders: Speech-language-hearing*. Lippincott Williams & Wilkins.

Pasquali, L. (2004). Teoria da medida. In L. Pasquali (Ed.), *Psicometria: Teoria dos testes na psicologia e na educação* (pp. 23–51). Vozes.

Réa-Neto, A. (1998). Raciocínio clínico: O processo de decisão diagnóstica e terapêutica. *Revista da Associação Médica Brasileira, 44*(4), 301–311. https://doi.org/10.1590/S0104-42301998000400009

Rossi, N. F., Lindau, T. A., Gillam, R. B., & Giacheti, C. M. (2016). Adaptação cultural do Test of Narrative Language (TNL) para o português brasileiro. *CoDAS, 28*(5), 507–516. https://doi.org/10.1590/2317-1782/20162016018

Stein, L. M. (1994). *TDE – Teste de Desempenho Escolar: Manual para aplicação e interpretação*. Casa do Psicólogo.

World Health Organization – WHO. (1993). *The ICD-10 classification of mental and behavioural disorders: Diagnostic criteria for research*. WHO.

Chapter 14
A Dialogue on Reading: The Perspectives of Bloomfield's Linguistics and Behavior Analysis

Djenane Brasil da Conceição

14.1 The Problem of Illiteracy, a Guideline for Tackling It and a Critique of the Status Quo

The most recent[1] report on Brazil by the *Program for International Student Assessment* (PISA; OECD/PISA, 2016) showed that the sample of Brazilian students aged 15, from the seventh year of primary school onwards, scored an average of 407 points in reading, well below the 493 points of the average defined by the *Organization for Economic Co-operation and Development* (OECD); this scenario has remained relatively stable since 2000. The PISA report also identified that 50% of students did not reach Level 2 (the maximum being Level 6) of the reading assessment, indicating a very large number of non-readers or poorly qualified

[1] At the time of the Portuguese publication of this chapter.

The present text is based on Djenane Brasil da Conceição's Doctoral Dissertation, submitted to the Postgraduate Program in Psychology (PPGPSI) at the Universidade Federal de São Carlos in 2015, entitled Teaching Reading in Bloomfield's Linguistics and Skinners Behavioral Analysis, and contains similar parts. The author received financial support for the doctoral research from the Capes/Fulbright program (Doctoral Internship in the USA, from March 2013 to May 2014), and from the Capes Prodoutoral program (from September 2014 to August 2015). The preparation of the dissertation was supported by the Universidade Federal do Recôncavo da Bahia (UFRB), and the National Institute of Science and Technology, Studies on Behavior, Cognition, and Teaching (*Instituto Nacional de Ciência e Tecnologia, Estudos sobre Comportamento, Cognição e Ensino* [INCT-ECCE]).

D. B. da Conceição (✉)
Professora da Universidade Federal do Recôncavo da Bahia, Cachoeira, BA, Brazil
e-mail: djenanebc@yahoo.com

A. R. de Albuquerque, R. M. de Melo (eds.), *Contributions of Behavior Analysis to Reading and Writing Comprehension*, https://doi.org/10.1007/978-3-031-40868-7_14

readers, unable to fully enjoy the benefits of reading and to act productively from it (OECD/PISA, 2016).

The Functional Illiteracy Indicator (from Portuguese, *Indicador de Analfabetismo Funcional*, INAF; coordinated by the partnership *Instituto Paulo Montenegro and Ação Educativa*, 2018), points out that 29% of Brazilians can be considered functionally illiterate, among these are 13% of people who reach high school and 4% of people who reach higher education. These data are obtained through interviews and cognitive tests, adopting a literacy scale that integrates the skills of reading and writing (literacy) and mathematics (numeracy), with a sample of participants aged 15–64 years.

Other countries such as France, Great Britain, and the United States of America (Seabra & Capovilla, 2010) have faced problems with low literacy rates among their children. In the case of the United States, for example, in the 1990s, 43% of nine-year-olds were assessed as functionally illiterate (McGuinness, 2004). Explanations for the problem of illiteracy in this case would involve: (a) inadequate methods of reading and writing instruction by failing to emphasize the relationships between graphemes and phonemes[2] in an alphabetically written language; (b) emphasis on explanations grounded in biological aspects as causes for failure to learn to read; and (c) the existence of several ways of writing the same phoneme and several ways of speaking the sound of a letter or string of letters in the English language, commonly referred to as language opacity (McGuinness, 2004).

These countries produced documents seeking scientific answers to guide decisions about educational policies and overcome the problem of illiteracy (Seabra & Capovilla, 2010). In the United States, a committee of experts, the *National Reading Panel* (2000), was formed to assess different topics related to reading, including phonic methods and phonological awareness, reading fluency, and reading comprehension. The subgroup of the committee assigned to evaluate phonic methods concluded that "systematic phonics instruction helped children learn to read better than all forms of instruction applied to the control groups, including the whole text method" (Ehri et al., 2001/2002, p. 121), and recommended the use of phonic methods in both early reading programs and in preventive and remedial programs (Ehri et al., 2001/2002; *National Reading Panel*, 2000).

Likewise, in Brazil, a committee of specialists was appointed to draw up a document to provide a basis for the debate on illiteracy, the "*Grupo de Trabalho Alfabetização Infantil: Os Novos Caminhos*"[3] set up by the Commission on Education and Culture of the Chamber of Deputies. The report pointed out a basic problem, the already known failure of Brazilian literacy programs, and a reason for maintaining this problem, the neglect of scientific knowledge produced in the area and the results of instruments for monitoring and evaluating Brazilian educational

[2]While the term grapheme refers to "units of a writing system that, in alphabetic writing correspond to one or more letters to represent a given phoneme (in Portuguese, one or two letters, only, with or without graphic accents)" (Scliar-Cabral, 2013), the term phoneme consists of the smallest distinctive unit of speech sound (Bloomfield, 1933/1961).

[3]Children's Literacy Working Group: The New Paths.

public policies, such as the *Sistema de Avaliação da Educação Básica*[4] (SAEB; Brasil, 2007). This report claims the superiority of systematic phonic methods for the initial reading instruction, as they teach decoding in an orderly and explicit manner[5] (Brasil, 2007), thus assuming the same thesis advocated by the United States of America.

The phonic methods differ in several aspects, such as the defined teaching sequence, the number of grapheme-phoneme correspondences taught, the requirement for oral exercises, the need to enunciate phonic rules, the demand for written exercises, and the teaching procedures adopted (Ehri et al., 2001/2002). One of the main characteristics they have in common is that they advocate teaching the correspondence between written/printed symbols (graphemes) and the respective distinctive speech sounds (phonemes; Bloomfield, 1933/1961) as a fundamental aspect of the literacy process.

Besides advocating the adoption of phonic methods in the initial literacy process, as illustrated above, some contemporary authors, from the field of reading education, are critical of the analytical methods,[6] which teach reading from larger units such as printed words, sentences, and texts (Seabra & Dias, 2011). Starting from these larger units, considered "totalities", analytical methods aim to achieve grapheme-phoneme correspondences, but they do so later in the process of teaching to read (McGuinness, 2004; Seabra & Dias, 2011).

For example, Seabra and Capovilla (2010) argue that the poor performance of Brazilian students in assessments such as PISA and SAEB, especially about reading, is due to literacy methods choice. The authors state that countries that adopt phonic methods perform better in PISA assessments, while countries that adopt analytical methods achieve lower performances in the world rankings. They also claim that there is no scientific basis for recommending the global method in literacy, as the *Parâmetros Curriculares Nacionais do Brasil*[7] (PCNs) do. Additionally, they denounce the Brazilian educational authorities in justifying the low school performance of Brazilian students "as arising from factors other than the global method and the pedagogical principles officially established" (Seabra & Capovilla, 2010, p. 76).

The final report of the "*Grupo de Trabalho Alfabetização Infantil: Os Novos Caminhos*" states that *whole language* methods are in disagreement with the most recent scientific evidence in the field of literacy, as they oppose to the explicit and systematic teaching of grapheme-phoneme correspondences, and mentions the

[4] System for Evaluating Basic Education.

[5] It is understood that there is correspondence between some words or expressions used to designate the most basic skill of reading, they are: "decoding" (Ehri et al., 2001/2002; McGuinness, 2004), "deciphering" (Cagliari, 1997), "alphabetic habit" or "reading habit" (Bloomfield, 1942/1970, 1961) and "textual behavior" (Skinner, 1957/1992).

[6] Some terms related to analytical methods in English are *whole word, look-say and whole language*. In Portuguese we have *global method, constructivist approach* and *ideovisual method*, for example (Brasil, 2007; Scliar-Cabral, 2013; Scliar-Cabral, 2015; Seabra & Capovilla, 2010).

[7] *Brazilian National Curricular Parameters.*

decline in reading performance of students in California (USA) when this type of method was adopted in that state (Brasil, 2007; McGuinness, 2004).

Scliar-Cabral (2013) also presents a criticism of analytical methods, such as global methods, stating that findings of neuroscience, among others, serve to demystify these methods, especially because they show that the recognition of the word does not occur as a whole. "The global methods do not know how the recognition of the written word occurs and, consequently, what is the best way to teach literacy" (Scliar-Cabral, 2013, p. 87).

Bloomfield was also a proponent of teaching grapheme-phoneme correspondences in basic reading instruction and a critic of analytical methods, so these two points have been highlighted in this very brief, and circumscribed delineation of the current scenario concerning the problem of illiteracy.

14.2 Conception and Method of Reading Instruction in Bloomfield's Linguistics

14.2.1 Conception

Leornard Bloomfield (1887–1949), a structuralist linguist and behaviorist, who intensely influenced North American and European linguistics in the twentieth century (Matos & Passos, 2006; Passos & Matos, 2007), pioneered the conception of teaching grapheme-phoneme correspondences as the most elementary and important task in the literacy process. He advocated this conception already in the 1930s. Bloomfield defined two tasks to be performed by the reading learner, thus distinguishing the processes of reading and reading with comprehension (Dawkins, 1961): (a) to establish the alphabetic habit, to respond appropriately to graphemes with the corresponding phonemes in the correct order, with fluency; and (b) to understand the meaning of the sounds pronounced from the text in an open or silent manner, that is, to read with comprehension (Bloomfield, 1942/1970, 1961). This second task depends on the child hearing himself emitting the speech sounds corresponding to the printed text, something difficult to achieve in the elementary stages of learning to read due to the effort required from the child to respond vocally to the words in the text (Bloomfield, 1961). Reading with comprehension also depends on the child's experiences as a listener and speaker of the language (Bloomfield, 1945/1987, 1961), which was treated very naturally by Bloomfield. "Some of the words will be foreign to the child … There is no harm in telling the child that 'a van is a large truck covered to carry furniture,' or that 'Nan is a girl's name'" (Bloomfield, 1961, p. 41). Reading with comprehension is influenced by the stories the child has already heard and told, the names of objects and events in the world she has heard and spoken, the appropriate responses in content and form she has already uttered in various life situations. Reading with fluency is a condition for understanding the text read in this conception, and teaching to read with comprehension should be the purpose of any reading instruction program.

To better understand the conception of reading and reading instruction method advocated by Bloomfield, one should note the distinction between acquisition of spoken language on the one hand and reading and writing on the other. All known human communities have a spoken language, but not all have writing, which historically was a privilege, and in many cases still is, of a certain class or group in literate societies.

Different types of writing have been practiced by mankind: (a) figurative or pictorial writing, characterized by the use of characters such as drawings and paintings that refer directly to the practical content, the meaning of the utterances; (b) word writing, in which each conventional written character represents a spoken word as a whole; and (c) alphabetic writing (Bloomfield, 1933/1961, 1942/1970, 1961), characterized by the correspondence between the written units, the graphemes, and the sound units of speech, the phonemes.

In the case of pictorial writing, to read and interpret a text the reader needs to know the conventions of the draws, which are not decomposable into smaller linguistic units amenable to subsequent recombination. To read this type of writing the reader does not need to know the language spoken by the person who wrote the text.

In the case of word writing, to read and interpret a text the reader must learn the correspondence between each spoken word and the character that designates it, so it is necessary for the reader to be exposed to a very large number of characters to read and write this type of writing skillfully (Bloomfield, 1942/1970). According to Bloomfield (1933/1961), the first linguistic units represented in writing were words.

Alphabetic writing, predominant in many current writing systems such as those of the English (Bloomfield, 1942/1970) and Portuguese languages (Cagliari, 1997), simply transcribes the phonemes. The accuracy with which the phonemes of a language are transcribed into alphabetic writing varies and some authors (e.g., Brasil, 2007; McGuinness, 2004) use the terms *transparency* and *opacity* of languages to talk about the greater or lesser degree of accuracy respectively. Specific combinations of phonemes form the spoken words that are transcribed. The meaning of words is related to these combinations (Bloomfield, 1942/1970). To read and write a text, the reader needs to learn a limited set of correspondences between phonemes[8] and graphemes. To read and interpret a text the reader needs to be exposed to the spoken language expressed in the text.

Bloomfield (1933/1961, 1942/1970, 1961) believed that the general characteristics of alphabetic writing and the particularities of each language should be considered when devising reading instruction methods involving alphabetic writing and was a critic of both phonic and analytic methods.

According to Bloomfield (1933/1961, 1942/1970, 1961), phonic methods confuse writing with speech, mistakenly designing their activities to teach children to speak clearly or to follow phonetic instructions, whereas he believes that problems

[8] According to Trask (2004/2008), there is an average of 25–30 phonemes per known language.

with speaking, or discriminating speech sounds, need to be corrected before reading instruction begins. Some phonic methods also require the isolated pronunciation of certain speech sounds that do not occur independently in everyday speech, demanding superfluous work from the student, complicating learning, or making it more difficult (Bloomfield, 1933/1961, 1942/1970, 1961).

According to Bloomfield (1942/1970, 1961), analytical methods, such as the word method, which in the face of the printed word requires the child to pronounce the whole word, would be appropriate for teaching reading in a language transcribed into word writing (such as Chinese) because they do not take advantage of the alphabetic principle governing alphabetic writing.

> The most serious drawback of all the English instruction known to me, regardless of the special method, that is in each case advocated, is the drawback of the word method. The written forms for words are presented to the child in an order which conceals the alphabetic principle. For instance, if near the beginning instruction we present the words *get* and *gem*, we cannot expect the child to develop any fixed or fluent response to the sight of the letter *g*. If we talk to him about the 'hard' and 'soft' sounds of the letter *g*, we shall only confuse him the more. The irregularities of our spelling—that is, its deviation from the alphabetic principle—demand careful handling if they are not to confuse the child and to delay his acquisition of the alphabetic habit. (Bloomfield, 1942/1970, p. 390)

Analytical methods, such as the sentence or ideational reading method, which require the child to grasp the content of the printed page, the meaning of the text, at the most elementary stage of learning to read, without requiring them to first pronounce the sounds of speech, for example, would be appropriate for teaching to read in the face of pictorial writing, but not alphabetic writing (Bloomfield, 1942/1970, 1961), a context in which the sounds of speech link the printed word to what corresponds to it. By confusing the purpose of reading instruction, which is reading with comprehension, with its most elementary step, which is the alphabetic habit (decoding), the ideational reading method skips a fundamental step in teaching to read, requiring of the beginner what, typically, the proficient reader can exhibit only after much time and practice (Bloomfield, 1942/1970, 1961).

Despite criticism of analytical methods, Bloomfield (1961) acknowledges that it is possible that some children may eventually learn grapheme-phoneme correspondences through these methods, which is made explicit by the acceleration of reading performance and the ability to read words not directly taught.

Bloomfield (1933/1961, 1942/1970, 1961) was concerned with devising a reading instruction method that could reduce the task's difficulty for the beginning learner, that could reduce the emission of incorrect responses by the learner, as well as that could accelerate learning, principles compatible with an analytic-behavioral approach, as will be seen below.

14.2.2 Method

14.2.2.1 General Aspects

Bloomfield was a pioneer in applying linguistic knowledge, in a comprehensive, systematic, and detailed way, to reading instruction (Passos, 2004), developing a method that was edited and published only posthumously, in 1961.[9] It is *Let's Read: A Linguistic Approach* (Bloomfield & Barnhart, 1961), a method for teaching reading that is little known in Brazil and often misunderstood, both in Brazil and abroad. For example, two foreign authors who have works translated into Brazilian Portuguese, McGuinness (2004) and Morais (1994/1996), mistakenly believe that Bloomfield's method requires spontaneous learning (indirect and not explicit) of grapheme-phoneme relations from printed words.

The Bloomfieldian method recommends the direct instruction of grapheme-phoneme relations based on words presented in a systematic, logical and linguistically based manner, in a carefully planned sequence, which is based on the degree of regularity of grapheme-phoneme relations according to the alphabetic principle.[10] It is believed that the early introduction of irregularities in grapheme-phoneme correspondence can produce errors and delay or hinder learning to read (Bloomfield, 1961). The Bloomfieldian method also proposes that reading might be taught before writing, since the latter represents additional difficulties. Uppercase and lowercase printed letters are employed in the early stages of teaching. Cursive letters should only be introduced after the child is responding accurately to grapheme-phoneme correspondences (Bloomfield, 1961).

The literacy process begins with the teacher teaching the child to read aloud, and requires three behavioral prerequisites: being a listener and fluent speaker of the language in which he or she will learn to read; following visual stimuli in a left-to-right direction; and identifying the letters of the alphabet as discrete units, being able to distinguish and name each one regardless of the order in which they occur in the alphabet (Bloomfield, 1942/1970, 1961). Naming the letters of the alphabet is taught by first using as visual stimuli the uppercase printed letters and then the lowercase (Bloomfield, 1961).

---

[9] C. A. Barnhart (2013) wrote an interesting and comprehensive article about the story of elaboration, publication, and use of this method. The thesis of Conceição (2015) brings a synthesis of this story, besides an analysis of the experiences, experiments and considerations presented by commentators of the method.

[10] *Stricto sensu*, the univocal correspondence between each phonemic unit and one and the same letter (Bloomfield, 1933/1961, 1942/1970, 1961; Bloomfield & Barnhart, 1961).

14.2.2.2 Teaching Procedures

The use of minimal pairs of words as a pedagogical tool is the main instructional procedure recommended in the Bloomfieldian reading method. Originally, minimal pairs of words are used in the *commutation test*, from the field of phonology, which establishes the phonemes of a language (Barnhart, 2013). The commutation test consists of replacing one element at a time in the chain of sounds of the spoken word, comparing minimal pairs of words and checking whether the meaning changes (Cagliari, 1997; Crystal, 1985/2000). According to Crystal (1985/2000), "two words that differ in meaning when only one of the sounds is changed are called a 'minimal pair,' such as *lata* × *pata, mar* × *par, luva* × *lava*"[11] (p. 196). Additionally, when more than two words are differentiated only by the substitution of one phoneme, a *minimal set* is formed such as "*tala, cala, fala, mala, rala* ..."[12] (Crystal, 1985/2000, p. 196).

In a minimal set such as *cot, dot, got, hot, not, pot*[13] the relation between each initial letter and its respective phonemes becomes the only basis for the distinction (one could say differentiation) between written words, probably favoring the learning of these correspondences. Of course, the method also takes care to change the position of the unit that varies (first letter, middle letter, last letter, in CVC words, consonant-vowel-consonant).

The teacher should present a printed word to the child and ask him/her to spell (say the name of each letter in the correct sequence); then the teacher reads the word and asks the child to read the same word. Another word is presented, and the procedure is repeated. With two words read, it is already possible to present them in minimal pairs of words. New words are introduced, one at a time, and presented in minimal pairs. The complete mastery of the grapheme-phoneme relations taught in each word is fundamental for new lessons to be introduced. As skilling enhances, and the logic of gradual progress is applied, more than two words can be presented simultaneously and connected text, composed of the learned words, is introduced. When a group of printed words which differ only by one letter is learned (e.g., *bat, cat, fat*) a new group, according to the defined sequence, is introduced (e.g., *bad, cad, fad* or, much later, *bit, fit, hit* and further still *but, cut, hut*) and the teacher can already form minimal pairs not only within the current group, but also with the words of other groups (e.g., *bat-bad; bat-bit, bit-but, bat-but*).[14] The basic procedure is maintained until the child accurately and fluently reads the word indicated by the teacher and correctly points to the printed word corresponding to the word spoken by the teacher (Bloomfield, 1961; Bloomfield & Barnhart, 1961).

Teaching sessions should be short and daily since great effort is required from the learner. A review of previously taught reading words is recommended before beginning a new lesson (Bloomfield, 1961).

---

[11] Analogous examples in English are *food* × *mood, fan* × *man, slab* × *slob.*

[12] Analogous examples in English are *cat, bat, sat, fat, mat.*

[13] Examples taken from Bloomfield and Barnhart (1961).

[14] All examples in this paragraph are taken from Bloomfield and Barnhart (1961).

14.2.2.3 Characteristics of Teaching Materials: The Continuum from Regularity to Irregularity of Grapheme-Phoneme Relations, Unity, and Sequence of Teaching

One of the main features of the Bloomfieldian reading instruction method is that it is based on the alphabetic principle, strictly represented by a univocal correspondence between a phoneme and a grapheme (regular relations) in the words selected for teaching reading, and on deviations from this principle, which describe the degree of irregularity (semi-irregular and irregular relations) assigned to these correspondences in the words chosen. The selection of the words that make up the method, the basic teaching units, as well as their order of presentation, stems from linguistic analyses of the relationship between the written word and speech.

Based on his linguistic analyses, Bloomfield attributed one phoneme for each letter of the alphabet, thus defining a regular correspondence. He elaborated a table with each letter of the alphabet accompanied by a common word in which that letter appears to indicate the grapheme-phoneme correspondence that would be considered regular. Table 14.1 shows an adapted content of the original table, considering the North American English language. The variations in relation to the correspondences explained in Table 14.1 represent the different degrees of deviation in the regular-irregular *continuum.*

Cases in which deviation from the alphabetic principle occurs in a significant number of words formed by the same grapheme pattern and which can be described by a rule define a type of semi-irregularity (Bloomfield & Barnhart, 1961). Table 14.2 illustrates one such case. After being taught to read a large set of words with the pattern described in Table 14.2, and having already been exposed to the other grapheme-phoneme correspondences existing in a new word that also contains the semi-irregular grapheme-phoneme correspondence cited, the learner should be able to correctly read the new word (not directly taught).

Cases in which deviations from the alphabetic principle multiply within a single word, or occur in a smaller set of words, define irregularities of grapheme-phoneme correspondences (Bloomfield & Barnhart, 1961). Table 14.3 illustrates some irregularities in grapheme-phoneme correspondences. Reading words of this type depends heavily on specific teaching of each word (as in the word method).

Table 14.1 Word list for the identification of regular grapheme-phoneme correspondences

Vowels	Consonants	Consonants	Consonants	Consonants
a as in ***fat***	***b*** as in ***big***	***h*** as in ***hip***	***n*** as in ***nut***	***v*** as in ***vet***
e as in *net*	*c* as in ***cup***	***j*** as in ***jet***	***p*** as in ***pot***	***w*** as in ***web***
i as in ***bin***	***d*** as in ***dot***	***k*** as in ***kit***	***r*** as in ***rat***	***y*** as in ***yes***
o as in ***dot***	***f*** as in ***fun***	***l*** as in ***lip***	*s* as in ***sit***	*z* as in ***zip***
u as in ***sun***	***g*** as in ***gap***	***m*** as in ***man***	***t*** as in ***tub***	

Note. Content adapted from Bloomfield (1961) and Bloomfield and C. L. Barnhart (1961, pp. 57–100). Table extracted from Conceição (2015, p. 53). This table does not contain words with the letters *q* and *x*, as they are not defined as regular in the Bloomfieldian method (Bloomfield, 1942/1970, 1961)

Table 14.2 Grapheme phoneme correspondence description defined as semi-irregular

Value of phoneme in regular relation	Value of the phoneme in the semi-regular relation	Pattern that defines the rule	Word examples
a as in *fat*	***a*** as in ***bait***	letter ***a*** followed by consonant and final letter ***e*** is pronounced as in ***bait***	***ate***, *date* ***cake***, *cave* ***sale***, *scale*

Note. Content based on Bloomfield and C. L. Barnhart (1961)

Table 14.3 Description of grapheme-phoneme correspondences defined as irregular

Phoneme value in regular (or equivalent) relation	Phoneme value in the irregular relation	Word examples
k as in *kit*	The letter ***k*** is not pronounced	***knit***
e as in *net* *a* as in *fat* *ea* as in *eat*	***ea*** as in ***bread***	weather
th as in *thin*	***th*** as in ***then***	leather

Note. Content based on Bloomfield and C. L. Barnhart (1961)

Although it is the most important, the grapheme-phoneme degree of regularity is not the only criterion used in the sequencing of words in the instructional material. Other criteria are articulated to this one, such as: the type of word, CVC and VC (vowel-consonant), used in the initial lessons; the contrast between minimal pairs of words; the systematic variation of the position of letters within the word, which in the initial lessons operate like this: first letter within a lesson (e.g., *can, fan, man, an);* last letter in successive lessons (e.g., *can, cat, cap*); middle letter in blocks of lessons grouped by vowels (e.g.., *bag, big, bug*); tendency to gradually increase in word length, with words in later lessons being partially composed of words previously taught (e.g., *mop, playground*; *led, sled* or *oar, aboard*); gradual introduction of sentences made up of words composed exclusively of the grapheme-phoneme relationships already taught and gradual introduction of text made up of short paragraphs, short stories, ending with stories of a few pages in which words with grapheme-phoneme correspondences of all types appear.[15,16] A few words that escape the defined sequence are introduced early on, as they allow for the reading of connected text.

The classification and sequencing of words according to the degree of regularity of grapheme-phoneme relations, as well as the other criteria mentioned above, aim to favor the acquisition of the alphabetic habit by the learner, making the phonemes to be pronounced in view of the graphemes in printed words initially univocal and, whenever possible, very predictable, consequently increasing the chances of the learner correctly reading the words presented since the beginning of the literacy process (e.g., Bloomfield, 1942/1970, 1961). Additionally, the degree of uniformity of grapheme-phoneme relations within the word, as well as of the pattern composed

[15] All examples in this paragraph are taken from Bloomfield and C. L. Barnhart (1961).

[16] More details about the teaching sequence can be found in Conceição (2015).

Table 14.4 Main features of the Bloomfieldian reading instruction method

Feature	Description
Goal	Teach the student to fluently pronounce certain phoneme(s) in front of a particular letter or sequence of letters, leading to text comprehension
Prerequisites	Speak fluently and understand the language in which learning to read will be taught Follow visual stimuli in a left to right direction Distinguish and name the letters of the alphabet
Composition of teaching materials	
Degree of regularity of grapheme-phoneme correspondences	Fully regular composition of the grapheme-phoneme correspondences in the printed words comprising the initial teaching material and subsequent orderly introduction of words with semi-irregular and irregular grapheme-phoneme correspondences
Teaching units	*Whole printed words* arranged sequentially according to the degree of regularity of their grapheme-phoneme correspondences
Learning units	Relationships among *grapheme-phoneme* components of the words in the teaching material
Teaching procedures	Show the printed word to the student. Ask the student to spell it. Ask him to read it (initially the teacher provides a sample) The student must read out loud the words presented as stimulus Initially, one word is presented at a time. Subsequently, minimal pairs of words and larger groups of words are presented, which vary in only one grapheme-phoneme correspondence. Subsequently, previously learned words are presented, randomly grouped. Longer texts are gradually introduced Events that keep the learner engaged in the task: likely presentation of correct answers by the learner due to the systematization of the method Need for practice until complete mastery of each grapheme-phoneme correspondence in the teaching material

Note. Based on Conceição (2015)

of certain combinations of these relations (as illustrated in the "Word Examples" column of Table 14.2) is believed to contribute to reading new words with a similar pattern. Table 14.4 summarizes the main features of the method.

14.2.2.4 Characteristics of Instructional Materials and Their Influence on the Reading of New Words

According to Bloomfield (1933/1961), the explanation for the occurrence of adequate words reading for the first time is related to the analogy principle, which has already been widely (but not exclusively) used in linguistics as a descriptive and explanatory tool of creativity, and to linguistic changes[17] (Matos & Passos, 2010). "The regular analogies of a language are habits of substitution" (Bloomfield, 1933/1961, p. 276) that allow a speaker to enunciate a word or sentence, for example, never heard before, but which relates to previously heard speech forms (Bloomfield, 1933/1961). Thus, to present a novel speech form as a regular analogy, the speaker needs to have experiences with functionally similar forms (i.e., the parts that make it up) and with the grammatical pattern (i.e., the way the constituents of the form are coordinated; Bloomfield, 1933/1961).

In his brief extension of the concept of regular analogy to reading instruction, Bloomfield (1933/1961) stresses the importance of practical experiences with regular grapheme-phoneme correspondences for the establishment of the alphabetic habit as an analogical process. Written words containing irregular grapheme-phoneme correspondences remain a major challenge for reading instruction because they need to be taught/learned on a case-by-case basis. Introducing "irregular words" in a systematic way, according to the deviations they contain from the alphabetic principle, can minimize this problem (Bloomfield, 1933/1961).

Although Bloomfield (1933/1961) did not develop a formulation on the reading of new words in more depth, it is possible to state that, just as the regular analogy explains the emission of speech forms never before emitted, the analogical process explains the reading of words not previously read, once the word never read is configured as a new combination of graphemes to which the individual has already learned to respond appropriately. Thus, the sequence of words presented in Bloomfield and C. L. Barnhart (1961) and its organization would be crucial aspects for the success of learning to read.

14.2.2.5 Limitations of the Method

Four limitations were identified in the Bloomfieldian reading instruction method: (a) it is not applicable to teaching deaf children to read, because it does not meet the specificities of this target audience (Bloomfield, 1961); (b) it seems to have been prepared with the focus on children with typical development, although it can be applied to other audiences (e.g., Wilson & Lindsay, 1963); (c) raises questions about how to deal with demographic linguistic variations, also called dialectal variations in relation to the standard language in which the method was produced, as problematized by Faust (1961) and Shannon (1963), for example; and (d) very little was said about the writing instruction, but that should follow the teaching of reading, as will be briefly discussed below.

Bloomfield himself (1933/1961) admitted that some work remained for pedagogues (or, one would suggest, for behavior analysts programming reading instruction), such as defining, from experimentation, preferably, or from experience,

---

[17] Linguistic change consists of the slow and continuous process of change in speech habits or innovation in the speech of a linguistic community (see Passos, 2004).

procedural details and other devices (such as features of stimulus presentation). He emphasized the need to know precisely *what one is trying to teach* going so far as to state that: "only if we choose our material according to the nature of the English writing [one might say, of the language represented in the writing whose reading is to be taught], will the classroom procedure which we have so carefully developed, produce the proper result" (Bloomfield, 1942/1970, p. 395; brackets added).

Some experiments employing the Bloomfieldian method to North American children (e.g., Wilson & Lindsay, 1963 and the Bethel Park experiment[18]) introduced the teaching of writing alongside the teaching of reading, while Bloomfield (1961) recommended postponing writing. It is not exactly known how the teaching of writing occurred in these studies, or at what time it should be introduced. Brasil (2007) warns of the additional time required before a beginner learner to write with the same easy as he or she reads. Additionally, according to Brasil (2007) the development of the fields of studies on reading instruction and writing is uneven, with advantages for the field of reading. As in the typical school context, the teaching of writing usually occurs simultaneously with reading instruction from the beginning and there is the theoretical-conceptual and methodological defense or acceptance of doing so (e.g., Brasil, 2007; McGuinness, 2004; Seabra & Capovilla, 2010), a question arises: how to apply the Bloomfieldian method of reading instruction remaining faithful to its principles, but at the same time incorporating writing instruction? It is understood that, initially, it is possible to request writing only of words with grapheme-phoneme correspondences taught, but there is still much to analyze in the context of writing instruction.

14.3 Conception and Method of Reading Instruction in Behavior Analysis

14.3.1 Conception

Burrhus Frederic Skinner (1904–1990), the forerunner of Behavior Analysis and Radical Behaviorism, has been considered the most prominent psychologist of the twentieth century (Haggbloom et al., 2002; Smith, 1994/1999). Author of a wide and diverse bibliography, consisting of 295 items (Andery et al., 2004), he devoted himself to the more general topic of education, learning and teaching, including in his texts the subtopic of reading instruction. In 1957, he published *Verbal Behavior*, the book in which he analyzed issues commonly related to language in an innovative way, as operant behavior, seeking to avoid biases and preconceptions

[18] Located in Pennsylvania, the Bethel Park School District adopted "*Let's Read*" to teach reading to children for over 10 years, during which students completed basic reading instruction by the middle of the second grade. For more on this see the section "Experiences and Experiments with the Bloomfieldian Reading Instruction Method" in Conceição (2015).

(Skinner, 1957/1992). This special type of operant behavior, *verbal behavior*, acts not on the immediate physical environment, but on a listener specially trained in *specific practices of a verbal community* (Skinner, 1957/1992). The specially trained listener is the one who arranges the consequences that establish or maintain verbal behavior. Skinner (1957/1992) demonstrates how the social environment shapes and maintains the individual's verbal behavior, extrapolating from the basic principles of behavior, typically studied under controlled laboratory conditions with nonhuman subjects, to analyze aspects of human behavior (e.g., Passos, 2004; Smith, 1994/1999).

In his analysis, Skinner (1957/1992) states the need to study separately, but articulated, the behaviors of the speaker and listener and elaborates a classification of verbal operants. Among the behavioral repertoires to which a separate but articulated analysis of speaker and listener behaviors is applied are the *textual verbal operant* (speaker) and *reading with comprehension* (listener/reader; Skinner, 1957/1992).

Textual behavior, the basic reading behavior, is defined (prototypically) by vocal responding to textual stimuli (printed or written texts), with point-to-point correspondence between stimulus units and response units, and is acquired and maintained by generalized reinforcement (Skinner, 1948/1999, 1957/1992, 1960b, 1968/2003). Thus, if in the presence of the printed word *mouth* the child says "mouth" and some kind of social approval follows, the establishment of textual behavior may occur. Early in the process, textual responses are issued aloud. As time goes, the verbal community begins to punish the emission of textual responses aloud, they become covert (Skinner, 1957/1992, 1968/2003), and the beginner's reading aloud becomes the skilled reader silently reading. For silent reading to occur, the reader's behavior must be under control of private stimulation and self-reinforcement (Skinner, 1957/1992).

When the speech produced by textual responding affects the speaker, causing him/her to hear himself/herself, comprehension of the text may occur, provided the speaker has the corresponding experiences (to the speech produced) as a reader/listener of that language (Skinner, 1957/1992, 1968/2003). If the reader does not possess these experiences and if the text itself does not allow to build them, listening to oneself will not lead to text comprehension.

According to Passos (2003, 2011), from the point of view of behavior analysis, there are two main explanations for difficulties in reading: (a) absence of well-established and fluent textual responding and (b) presence of this textual responding unaccompanied by relevant experiences as a listener and speaker of the language. Other difficulties may relate to inability to hear oneself and absence of prerequisite behavioral repertoires, such as eye tracking in a left-to-right direction (de Rose, 2005, republished in Chapter 1 of this book; Greer & Ross, 2008). It is also possible that these difficulties combine in different ways, making learning to read impossible. The role of the behavior analyst is to analyze and plan teaching contingencies that produce the defined learning and not to label or classify the learner, presenting pseudo-explanations for observed behavioral difficulties.

In the next section, Skinner's proposal for teaching, including reading, will be described from some principles, processes, guidelines, and general characteristics of programming instruction. Skinner, unlike Bloomfield, did not create a specific method for reading instruction[19] and dealt only briefly with literacy or textual learning (see Skinner 1957/1992, 1960b, 1961a, b, 1968/2003, 1986).

14.3.2 *Method: How to Teach According to Skinner*

14.3.2.1 General Characteristics of Teaching

Teaching consists of programming reinforcing contingencies that promote or accelerate learning. Without this, learning may not occur, or occur slowly (Skinner, 1948/1999, 1968/2003, 1986). Educational reinforcing contingencies are responsible for shaping and maintaining the form of verbal operants, as well as establishing and refining stimulus control (Skinner, 1957/1992). Verbal operants under stimulus control are established by *differential reinforcement* in a process called *discrimination*, in which an antecedent stimulus becomes the occasion for a response of a certain form be emitted and, in general, reinforced. The functional relationships among these three elements, the stimulus, the response, and the consequence, are called the three-term contingency (Skinner, 1957/1992). "The three-term contingency is evident in teaching a child to read, when a given response is reinforced with 'right' or 'wrong' according to the presence or absence of the appropriate visual stimulus" (Skinner, 1953/2014, p. 109).

Teachers need to provide specific contingencies for discriminated responding to occur, or undifferentiated responding will predominate (Holland & Pittsburgh University, 1976; Skinner, 1957/1992, 1968/2003). For example, discussing the requirement to teach children whether or not to say letter names as part of the literacy process, Holland and Pittsburgh University (1976) state that "until some differential response, such as [saying] the letter name is learned, the child would be expected to demonstrate stimulus generalization to the shape of letters by responding to different letters as if they were the same" (p. 730; brackets added). Due to the generalization process, new stimuli that have common elements with a stimulus that already evokes a certain response from one class can likewise evoke responses from that class (Skinner, 1953/2014).

Commonly, speaker and listener responses are affected by the physical properties of the antecedent verbal and nonverbal stimuli (e.g., presentation speed, intensity, and sharpness). However, the properties of textual responses, such as magnitude and speed, are not proportionally defined by the properties of the textual stimuli (provided they fall within certain limits; Skinner, 1957/1992). Thus, a word printed on a white sheet of paper with thicker and darker letters will not produce a

[19] Because of this difference, the parallelism of the sections on reading instruction method in Bloomfield and in Skinnerian Behavior Analysis is not accurate.

proportionally stronger or faster textual response than a word printed with thinner and lighter letters.

The speaker and listener's behaviors are determined by the consequences they produce. Behavior analysis is particularly interested in positively reinforcing consequences as producing and maintaining classes of responses, about which more will be said in the next section.

14.3.2.2 Teaching Procedures

The basic procedure for directly teaching the textual consists in the *differential reinforcement of* responses class in the presence of a certain discriminative stimulus (S^D or S+) and in non-reinforcement of responses of the same class in the presence of other stimuli (S^Δ or S-). Thus, responses of the defined class become more likely in the presence of S^D and become less probable in the presence of S^Δ, in the last case, as a function of the *extinction* process (e.g., Holland, 2003; Sério et al., 2002/2010; Skinner, 1953/2014, 1963/1999, 1968/2003). Another way to establish precise stimulus control consists in reinforcing several classes of responses, each in the presence of specific stimuli (Holland & Pittsburgh University, 1976; Skinner, 1957/1992). Thus, if in the presence of the printed word *cat* the learner says "*cat*", it will produce the consequence "*Right!*". Then, if facing the printed word *bat* the learner *says "bat", it will* also produce the consequence "*Right!*", and so on.

In the early stages of the teaching-learning process, in schooling, for example, the educator is oriented to use presumable generalized (positive) conditioned reinforcers such as "*Right!*" or "*Good!*", as a consequence for the responses defined as correct emitted by the learner. This type of reinforcer is useful because it makes responding relatively independent of the learner's states of deprivation and aversive stimulation (Skinner, 1957/1992). However, any instructional program, including reading, should plan situations so that the automatic reinforcement resulting from the learner's own response acts over the responses, selecting them, as occurs when verifying the adequacy of a given response (the correctness) or when hearing himself saying something familiar (Skinner, 1968/2003). For example, the learner reads the word "*tile*" sand says: "*Oh, it's that thing on the bathroom wall!*". It is suggested that the learner comment describes the automatic reinforcement arising from the identification of the spoken word as familiar and additionally points to the likely self-assessment that the reading is correct. With the advance of learning to read, when there is already some textual repertoire established, the automatic reinforcement of listening to oneself favors self-correction as in: "*File... No! It's tile*" (Skinner, 1957/1992).

In order to establish discriminations, it is possible to schedule the stimuli presentation adopting simultaneous discrimination procedures, in which the S^D and S^Δ stimuli are presented at the same time, or successive discriminations, in which the stimuli are presented one after the other, with a predefined duration. Paying attention to the way stimuli are presented is important because irrelevant features of the environment, which occur together with the target stimuli, may acquire control over the learner's response (Sério et al., 2002/2010). Thus, in simultaneous discrimination procedures it is necessary to program the alternating position of the S^D and S^Δ stimuli, otherwise the position of the stimulus is established as the variable that controls responses. In successive discrimination procedures, it is necessary to ensure that the duration and sequence of stimulus presentation vary and that the frequency of stimulus presentation is counterbalanced (Sério et al., 2002/2010).

As a teaching strategy, it is recommended to apply a higher rate of reinforcement in the initial stages of an instructional program (Skinner, 1968/2003), even though it is known that in unplanned environments responses are not always followed by reinforcement, and this applies to textual behavior as well (Skinner, 1957/1992).

14.3.2.3 Principles and Guidelines for Programming Instruction

Programming instruction is a crucial aspect of behavioral analysis applied to education and should observe certain principles and guidelines. *Specifying the final behavior*, what the learner is expected to be able to perform when he or she has completed the program, is critical. It is equally important to know the entry repertoire, *the learner's initial behaviors*. What the learner is already able to do will inform the planning of what they will need to develop.

The steps that define the connection between the initial and final behaviors, of the itinerary to be traveled by the learner, need to be defined with objectivity, parsimony, and care. It must be *gradual and carefully planned*. This carefully defined sequence (Holland & Pittsburgh University, 1976; Sidman & Stoddard, 1966; Skinner, 1960a, 1961a, b, 1968/2003) establishes new stimulus control over already learned responses (Skinner, 1963/1999), or new responses, while maintaining what has already been acquired (Skinner, 1960b, c, 1961a, b, 1963/1999, 1968/2003). Nothing that has not been taught, defined as a prerequisite, and/or established in the learner's behavioral repertoire is requested (Sidman, 1985, 2010; Sidman & Stoddard, 1966; Skinner, 1961a, b, 1968/2003; Skinner & Holland, 1960/1962).

To apply the program, it is required that the *learner emits at least one active response at* each step (Skinner, 1960c, 1961a, b, 1968) and that there is immediate and frequent reinforcement of correct responses (Holland, 1960/1976; Skinner, 1960b, 1968/2003). *Available reinforcers and ways to make them contingent on the responses required by the program should be identified.* Commonly, correctness itself is used as a reinforcer, as a consequence of defined responses (Skinner, 1960b, c, 1961a, b, 1963/1999, 1968/2003).

Another principle is to *program the instructional material* itself (Sidman & Stoddard, 1966; Skinner, 1961a, 1968/2003), according to guidelines described in the next section.

14.3.2.4 Programming Teaching: The Development of Instructional Materials

Taking as reference a content that can be taught predominantly by textual stimuli, in a Skinnerian way, a typical teaching program consists of a *set of teaching materials on a given subject* (e.g., human behavior, writing words, arithmetic). Once the subject is defined (Skinner, 1968/2003) relevant information about it is gathered, lists of terms to be taught are elaborated, and processes, principles, and examples to be presented and discussed are selected.

The content to be taught is presented in *frames*, which may also be referred to by the term *item* (see Holland, 2003; Skinner, 1968/2003). A frame contains the antecedent stimuli (e.g., a sentence with a missing word, a position where there is a gap) that should evoke the learner's responses (e.g., filling the gap) and all information necessary for the precise emission of the response should be explicit, since the frame constitutes a *teaching unit* (Holland, 1960/1976; Skinner, 1961a, b; Skinner & Holland, 1960/1962). The programmer decides how much content there will be in each frame, as well as whether there will be more than one space to be filled or not, taking care that the syntax of the written sentences is not hidden, in which case the probability of wrong answers by the learner would increase (Skinner & Holland, 1960/1962). Excessive content in a frame may produce reading avoidance responses, consequently favoring the establishment of imprecise stimulus control (Skinner, 1968/2003; Skinner & Holland, 1960/1962).

A frame designates a teaching contingency independent of the others. However, each frame must be logically and coherently linked to the other frames of the same set, which enclose a complete part of the subject (as a subtopic), and to the program, which covers the whole subject with the degree of depth defined by the programmer (Skinner, 1961a, b; Skinner & Holland, 1960/1962).

The size of a set of frames, hereafter an instructional series, or complete program are relative. An instructional series can be designed as a function of the duration of an instructional session, or lesson, and it is possible to plan more than one series for the defined period. One must consider the inadequacy of producing learner's exhaustion (Sidman & Stoddard, 1966; Skinner & Holland, 1960/1962). The size of the whole program depends on the total time available (e.g., a school year), the presumed difficulty of the material, and how much content needs to be covered in the pre-defined period (Skinner, 1960b; Skinner & Holland, 1960/1962). Note that, as stated about Bloomfield's work, this is the application of several articulated criteria.

Based on the assumption of promoting correct responses and reducing errors in acquiring new behaviors, it is recommended to provide supplementary stimulation in the form of *prompts,* e.g., "the stimulus that encourages the immediate appearance of [some] behavior that already exists with some force" (Skinner, 1968/2003, p. 214; brackets added). Complementally, it is necessary gradually eliminating the supplementary stimulation so that the target stimulus (or its relevant properties) acts to control the learner's response (Skinner, 1959, 1960c, 1961a, 1963/1999, 1968/2003, 1986).

The use of supplementary stimulation (in the form of *prompts* or formal and thematic cues, for example) and various other devices; such as the presentation of an introductory text that guides the learner's route through the instructional material; the use of reference panels with graphs, tables and the presentation of definitions and examples; share the same assumption previously described (Skinner & Holland, 1960/1962).

Following these principles and guidelines leads to the development of pedagogical materials that aim to ensure excellence in the performance of any skilled participant interacting with it. Manipulations in the variables that affect responding are carefully planned and reformulated (often from *feedback* provided by learner errors) to ensure faster and less costly learning. Following this logic, the teacher, instructor, or therapist, for example, takes responsibility for the teaching process that produces learning.

Learning disabilities are primarily considered as failures in teaching procedures and are not attributed to the student (Holland, 1960/1976) or the environment in which he or she lives. Even in cases where there are organic limitations, the appropriate programming of instructional contingencies can contribute to the suppression or minimization of several difficulties (de Rose, 2005). Learning difficulties expressed in errors suggest the need to reprogram teaching and/or to meet individual needs.

The principles described are applicable to various educational situations such as those typical of Kindergarten and Elementary School (Skinner, 1961a, b, 1968/2003). The guidelines on the structural organization of an instructional program are useful in designing other programs than those involving verbal knowledge.

There is an example, elaborated by Skinner, of programming content close to that of literacy (see Skinner, 1961a, b, 1968/2003), teaching how to write the word *manufacture,* designed to be applied to third or fourth grade children.

In a sequence of six frames, a child who already emits textual and reads with comprehension can go from reading and copying[20] the target word, to writing the target word independently, going through cues, that are presented and removed. It is assumed that correctness is the reinforcer that determines the learner's progress.

Thus, in the first frame, the word *manufacture* is presented highlighted in bold and accompanied by its definition, followed by the instruction to copy it in the 11 squares in the following row (active response of the learner). In the second and third frames there is a thematic cue, the meaning of each of the two parts into which the word was decomposed, followed by the brief common etymological description of these two parts of the target word. Only the squares corresponding to the content that the first cue suggests are left empty for the student to fill in: For example: "*Part of the word is like part of the word* ***manual...*** □ □ □ □ ***f a c t u r e***" (Skinner, 1968/2003, p. 56; italics added). In the fourth and fifth frames, formal cues about

[20] Copying a text is a verbal operant in which written verbal discriminative stimuli control written verbal responses, with point-to-point correspondence between stimuli and responses that are acquired in generalized reinforcement contingencies. Between the discriminative stimuli and the product of the verbal copying response there may be formal correspondence (Skinner, 1957/1992).

missing letters are presented, with the corresponding squares remaining empty for the learner to fill in. Finally, in the sixth frame, the learner is required to write the word independently in a context consisting of a very brief definition: "***Chair factories* □ □ □ □ □ □ □ □ □ □ □ *chairs***" (Skinner, 1968/2003, p. 56; italics added).

In this process, it is assumed that the stimulus control exerted by the printed word *manufacture* as a model for the emission of the operant "copying *manufacture*" is transferred step by step to other stimuli, such as words spoken openly or covertly that integrate the definition of the target word. Thus, at the end of the teaching sequence, writing the target word should occur mainly as an intraverbal operant.[21]

14.3.2.5 Textual Units of Teaching and Learning and the Reading of New Words

There is a debate, well known in the field of literacy, about the most appropriate unit size for reading instruction. Linked to this debate are the conception and reading instruction method advocated by different authors and groups, as commented in the introduction of this text. Skinner (1948/1999, 1957/1992, 1960b) acknowledged the existence of this debate, but did not take a position on it (1957/1992; see also Skinner, 1961a, b).

Skinner (1948/1999, 1957/1992, 1960b) states that from the reinforcement of reading larger textual stimuli, such as the word, a repertoire of minimal textual units corresponding to the relationship between the letter (grapheme) and the phoneme may arise, but he does not detail how these smaller behavioral units would be learned. All he did was to indicate that analogy with previous individual's experiences was involved in the process (Skinner, 1957/1992).

Subsequent studies (e.g., de Rose et al., 1996; Matos et al., 2006; Mueller et al., 2000) have provided empirical support for the claim that from the reinforcement of larger units follows the learning of smaller units, however, the relationship between these studies and the analogy model needs to be investigated.

When analyzing the emergence of new responses in relation to other verbal operants such as mands[22] and tacts[23] (Matos & Passos, 2010; Passos, 2004; Skinner, 1957/1992), Skinner resorts to the same logic mentioned above. For example, when explaining the emergence of mands concerning a condition never manded before,

---

[21] Intraverbal is a verbal operant in which verbal discriminative stimuli evoke verbal responses that have neither point-to-point nor formal correspondence with the stimuli that produce them. It is an operant established by generalized reinforcement (Skinner, 1957/1992).

[22] The mand is a verbal operant under the control of a state of deprivation or aversive stimulation and followed by a specific reinforcer. A defined relation with an antecedent stimulus, unlike what happens with the other verbal operants, is not necessary in the description of mands. The relevant antecedent event is the condition of deprivation or aversive stimulation (Skinner, 1957/1992).

[23] The tact is a verbal operant in which a non-verbal discriminative stimulus, the objects, and events of the world, evokes a response with a certain form, which is acquired and maintained by generalized reinforcement (Skinner, 1957/1992).

the so-called magical mand, Skinner (1957/1992) states: "the speaker seems to create new mands in analogy to old ones. Having effectively manded bread and butter, he goes on to mand the jam, even though he has never obtained jam before in this way" (p. 48).

Regarding tacts, Skinner (1957/1992) considers that functional units have different sizes such as words (the most familiar example), phrases and sentences. Minimal functional units can arise either from direct reinforcement or from the reinforcement of larger units that contain them.[24] Thus, minimal functional units "appear to emerge as by-products of the acquisition of larger responses containing identical elements, very much as in echoic and textual behavior" (Skinner, 1957/1992, p. 120).

In teaching textual behavior, the size of the stimulus unit to be adopted needs to consider the type of writing of the language: pictorial, hieroglyphic, alphabetic, etc. (Skinner, 1957/1992). In languages like Portuguese and English, which have predominantly alphabetic writing, the phonetic level defines the smallest textual response that may result from the reinforcement of larger responses (Skinner, 1957/1992). Textual operants of varying sizes will integrate the behavioral repertoire of the skilled reader, whatever the size of the minimal unit adopted in teaching textual responses (e.g., letter, syllable, word, phrase or sentence; Skinner, 1957/1992), but the appropriate response to unfamiliar textual stimuli, that is, the reading of new words, depends on the control acquired by the minimal units over this response (Skinner, 1957/1992).

14.4 Final Considerations: A Dialogue on Reading

There are similarities and differences in Bloomfield and Skinner's conceptions of reading. Both define the most basic reading repertoire as the behavior of saying phonemes in the appropriate sequence corresponding to the printed stimuli typical of alphabetic writing, the graphemes, which was called *alphabetic habit* by Bloomfield (1961) and *textual behavior* by Skinner (1957/1992). Both understand that reading with comprehension occurs later. For Bloomfield (1961) it derives from the accurate and fluent alphabetic habit and depends on the other experiences of the reader with the spoken language. For Skinner (1957/1992), reading with comprehension stems from the reader hearing himself emitting the textual behavior, then being able to react appropriately to the speech he hears as defined by the verbal community. This requires that experiences have established listener responses and other verbal operants in the individual's behavioral repertoire (Skinner, 1957/1992, 1968/2003).

[24] Passos (2004) and Matos and Passos (2010) suggest that Skinner found this description of the emergence of new verbal operants through analogy in works written by linguists.

There is a difference regarding size (e.g., grapheme-phoneme, syllable-phonemes; [printed] word-phonemes) and criteria for systematizing the instructional textual unit. Bloomfield (1933/1961, 1942/1970, 1961) advocated the teaching of grapheme-phoneme correspondences and devised a very ingenious method in which the linguistic knowledge used makes it possible to teach grapheme-phoneme relations from whole words, without absolutely requiring guessing by the child. Grapheme-phoneme relations are made conspicuous to favor their learning from meaningful contexts, the printed words. On the other hand, Skinner (1957/1992, 1961a, b, 1961/1999) did not define the size of the textual unit to be taught, nor the criteria for systematizing the instructional textual units. He argued that different types of writing require different teaching units, stating that in alphabetic languages the grapheme-phoneme correspondence is the smallest attainable unit (Skinner, 1957/1992).

Reading problems constitute an area in which Bloomfield and Skinner's analyses are complementary. Faced with a difficulty in learning to read, the first step in the Bloomfieldian perspective is to accurately teach the relations between graphemes and phonemes. If the problem persists, assessing and verifying the presence or absence of listener responses as well as other verbal operants, based on the classification made by Skinner (1957/1992), may be a useful action. Once the missing repertoires (listener or verbal) are identified, specifically programmed instruction contingencies create the conditions for them to be developed.[25] In this context, teaching procedures stand out as the main explanatory and overcoming factor of learning failure situations (Holland, 1960/1976; Skinner, 1961a, b, 1968/2003), although the individual's learning history and biological possibilities and limits are also considered.

Analyzing the Bloomfieldian reading instruction method in the light of the analytic-behavioral principles, processes, and guidelines presented above, one finds several common elements. The goal of the Bloomfieldian method is defined in behavioral terms: to teach the learner to say the phonemes corresponding to the letters of the printed words in the correct sequence. Thus, the final behavior is well specified and the behavioral requirements for entering the program (initial behaviors) equally well defined: not presenting the alphabetic habit; knowing how to name letters of the alphabet in the presence of capital and small print, following with the eyes from left to right, and being a skilled listener and speaker of the language, in which one will learn to read.

The behavior of naming the letters of the alphabet is of particular interest in the initial stage of learning to read. It is a prerequisite behavior for entering in the instructional program and is described by the discriminative control exerted by each letter of the alphabet, as a discrete unit, on a specific learner response. In the absence of this type of discriminative training, the child is expected to respond in an

[25] The Developmental Theory of Verbal Behavior has an important contribution regarding the assessment and promotion of behavioral repertoires within language acquisition and development (e.g., Conceição et al., 2022; Greer & Keohane, 2006; Greer & Longano, 2010; Greer et al., 2017; Greer & Ross, 2008; Greer & Speckman, 2009).

undifferentiated manner to the shape of letters (Holland & Pittsburgh University, 1976), a condition that may hinder the learning of textual behavior/alphabetic habit.

In the Bloomfieldian method, the presence or the teaching of prerequisite behaviors is verified before responses that depend on them are demanded. For example, it is taught to say the names of the letters of the alphabet, a behavior that during the application of the reading program will form the basis of the spelling required before word reading takes place. In another example, we see the teaching of many sequences of letter-phoneme relations, forming monosyllable words (in early lessons), which will make up part of larger words in later lessons, reducing the number of never-before-seen correspondences to which the learner must respond later.

Requiring the emission of at least one active and public response at each step of the instructional program, as defined by the analytic-behavioral perspective, is fully satisfied by the Bloomfieldian approach, at least in the initial stages of teaching, since the main response required of the learner is to say the phonemes corresponding to the presented printed word. Competence is required to advance within the instructional program from both perspectives, plus fluency in the Bloomfieldian approach.

The steps to be followed in the itinerary that leads from the initial behaviors to the final behavior are gradual, judicious, and systematically programmed, as required by behavior analysis. The steps of the Bloomfieldian method are so ingeniously elaborated that they articulate several dimensions of analysis, such as the degree of regularity or irregularity of grapheme-phoneme correspondences (the most important); the size of words, phrases, sentences, and texts; the orderly alternation of the position of letters in training words; and the grouping of words by similar pattern. The articulation of these dimensions produces stimuli that, inserted in three-term contingencies, tend to contribute to the effectiveness of teaching. At the same time, the teaching sequence developed by Bloomfield aims to reduce the emission of incorrect responses by the learner, promoting automatic reinforcement for correct responses, as advocated by Skinner (1960b, c, 1961a, b, 1963/1999, 1968/2003).

The close adherence to the alphabetic principle, by the Bloomfieldian method, in the early stages of reading instruction, may be considered as part of the analytic-behavioral guideline of adopting procedures that reduce the chances of producing learner's errors. A single response (pronouncing a phoneme in the word) is first taught in the presence a grapheme. If responding to the grapheme *g* is taught in the pronunciation of the word *get* (analogously, in Brazilian Portuguese, one could say *g* as in *gato*), responding to the grapheme *g* as in *gem* (analogously, *g* as in *gelo*) will be taught later, after that first response (*g* as in *get*) is well established. Avoiding teaching incompatible responses in the early stages of learning to read presumably reduces doubts and errors. During the application of the Bloomfieldian method, supplementary stimulation in the form of echoic hints is provided. The teacher should initially read the word to the learner by providing the reading sample. As the method progresses and the child demonstrates accurate performance, these cues are gradually delayed until they are completely removed and only the text controls the child's response.

Concerning with the explanation of generalized conditioned reinforcers that often need to integrate the initial contingencies of teaching, there is a gap. Although Bloomfield (1942/1970, 1961) stressed the importance of correct responses during learning to read, stating that correct responses produce "gain in power" or strengthen the learner's "firmness of habit," he does not suggest other potential generalized conditioned reinforcers, such as the teacher's "right" (Holland, 1960/1976; Skinner, 1968/2003). Thus, a complement of behavioral analysis to the Bloomfieldian method involves the definition of arbitrary (generalized conditioned) reinforcers and the ways to make them contingent on the required responses when their use is necessary in concrete teaching situations.

One aspect highlighted by de Rose (2005; republished in chapter 1 of this book) is not addressed by either Bloomfield or Skinner: the use of games and play as a pedagogical resource in establishing the stimulus controls important for learning to read. It is believed that these resources may be useful in teaching children to say letter names in the presence of relevant stimuli or to follow with their gaze from left to right. Using these resources coupled with the method of reading instruction itself is a question that demands more specific analysis.

In Bloomfield's method of reading instruction, several devices were found to reduce the chances of the learner emitting incorrect responses during learning to read, particularly in the early stages, in a way compatible with theses advocated in the analytic-behavioral approach to errorless learning. Following analysis of classic and current experiments in this field, it is possible to state that Bloomfield, through his method, was a pioneer in advocating a way of teaching aimed at reducing or eliminating learner errors during learning, since the classic studies in the field of errorless learning (e.g., Terrace, 1963a, b; Sidman & Stoddard, 1966) date from the 1960s, while Bloomfield's work begins in the 1930s, although *Let's Read* was published only in 1961.

Considering the compatibility between Bloomfield and Skinner's approaches that had already been pointed out in the literature[26] (Moxley, 1997; Passos, 2003, 2004, 2011), it is not surprising that the same applies to several aspects of the conception of reading and reading instruction method.

In retrospect, Bloomfield not only ingeniously articulated linguistic knowledge in his concept of reading and reading instruction method, but also incorporated various analytic-behavioral principles, processes, and guidelines involved in teaching that produces learning. Thus, it is possible to state that Bloomfield created a behavioral reading instruction method with the potential to promote rapid reading instruction (considering a comparison with other methods of teaching reading) and with little repetition. Certainly, the sieve of experimentation is necessary to confirm this hypothesis. Evaluating the effectiveness of the method, as well as possible errors

[26] The literature points out, more specifically, Bloomfield's influence on several aspects of Skinner's work (e.g., Matos & Passos, 2010; Moxley, 1997; Passos, 2004; Passos & Matos, 2007) such as the conception of science and the scientific method, the physicalist conception of meaning, the definition of verbal behavior, and the use of the analogy model to deal with creativity within verbal behavior, for example (Matos & Passos, 2006, 2010; Passos, 2012; Passos & Matos, 2007).

made by the learner along the defined itinerary, can provide useful data for improving the method, tasks that have yet to be performed.

Both Bloomfield and Skinner refer to the principle of analogy to explain the reading of words never seen before. Exploring this explanation, as well as understanding it better, is also a work to be done.

If the Bloomfield method of reading instruction is theoretically recommendable, what is needed for it to be adapted to Brazilian Portuguese? Certainly, it is not possible to translate it directly into a new language. This adaptation involves careful and judicious analysis of the relationship between speech and writing in our language and the study of the phonological, morphological, and syntactic structures of Portuguese. Moreover, the teaching technologies developed by Behavior Analysis invite us to go beyond the limits of a simple adaptation.

References

Andery, M. A., Micheletto, N., & Sério, T. M. (2004). Publicações de B. F. Skinner: De 1930 a 2004. *Revista Brasileira de Terapia Comportamental e Cognitiva, 6*, 93–134. https://doi.org/10.31505/rbtcc.v6i1.69

Barnhart, C. A. (2013). A little-known aspect of Leonard Bloomfield's linguistics: The story of let's read (1961). *Historiographia Linguistica, 40*(3), 433–476. https://doi.org/10.1075/hl.40.3.05bar

Bloomfield, L. (1933/1961). *Language*. Rinehart and Winston.

Bloomfield, L. (1942/1970). Linguistics and reading. In C. F. Hockett (Ed.), *A Leonard Bloomfield anthology* (pp. 384–395). Indiana University Press (Reprinted from *Elementary English Review, 19*, 125–130, 183–186).

Bloomfield, L. (1945/1987). About foreign language teaching. In C. F. Hockett (Ed.), *A Leonard Bloomfield anthology* (pp. 297–310). University of Chicago Press (Reprinted from *Yale Review, 34*, 625–641).

Bloomfield, L. (1961). Teaching children to read. In L. Bloomfield & C. L. Barnhart (Eds.), *Let's read: A linguistic approach* (pp. 19–42). Wayne State University Press.

Bloomfield, L., & Barnhart, C. L. (1961). *Let's read: A linguistic approach*. Wayne State University Press.

Brasil. (2007). *Grupo de trabalho alfabetização infantil: Os novos caminhos. Relatório final* (2ª edição). Câmara dos Deputados, Coordenação de Publicações. (Série Ação Parlamentar, n. 246).

Cagliari, L. C. (1997). *Alfabetização e linguística*. Scipione.

Conceição, D. B. da. (2015). *Ensino de leitura na linguística de Bloomfield e na Análise Comportamental de Skinner*. Unpublished doctoral dissertation, Universidade Federal de São Carlos.

Conceição, D. B. da, Greer, R. D., & Moschela, J. L. (2022). A general outline of the verbal behavior developmental theory. *Revista Brasileira de Terapia Comportamental e Cognitiva, 24*, 1–39. https://doi.org/10.31505/rbtcc.v24i1.1646

Crystal, D. (1985/2000). *Dicionário de linguística e fonética* (2ª ed.). Jorge Zahar Editor. (Traduzido e adaptado por Maria Carmelita Pádua Dias.)

Dawkins, J. (1961). Reading theory: An important distinction. *Elementary English, 3*(6), 389–392.

de Rose, J. C. (2005). Análise comportamental da aprendizagem de leitura e escrita. *Revista Brasileira de Análise do Comportamento, 1*(1), 29–50. https://doi.org/10.18542/rebac.v1i1.676

de Rose, J. C., de Souza, D. G., & Hanna, E. S. (1996). Teaching reading and spelling: Exclusion and stimulus equivalence. *Journal of Applied Behavior Analysis, 29*, 451–469. https://doi.org/10.1901/jaba.1996.29-451

Ehri, L. C., Nunes, S. R., Stahl, S. A., & Willows, D. M. (2001/2002). Systematic phonics instruction helps students learn to read: Evidence from the National Reading Panel's meta-analysis. *Journal of Direct Instruction, 2*(2), 121–166 (Reprinted from *Review of Educational Research, 71*(3), 393–447, 2001. https://doi.org/10.3102/00346543071003393)

Faust, G. P. (1961). Speech variation and the Bloomfield system. In L. Bloomfield & C. L. Barnhart (Eds.), *Let's read: A linguistic approach* (pp. 43–44). Wayne State University Press.

Greer, R. D., & Keohane, D. D. (2006). The evolution of Verbal Behavior in children. *Journal of Speech and Language Pathology and Applied Behavior Analysis, 1*, 111–140. https://doi.org/10.1037/h0100194

Greer, R. D., & Longano, J. M. (2010). A rose by naming: How we may learn how to do it. *The Analysis of Verbal Behavior, 26*, 73–106. https://doi.org/10.1007/bf03393085

Greer, R. D., & Ross, D. E. (2008). *Verbal behavior analysis: Inducing and expanding complex communication in children with severe language delays*. Allyn & Bacon.

Greer, R. D., & Speckman, J. (2009). The integration of speaker and listener responses: A theory of verbal development. *The Psychological Record, 59*, 449–488. https://doi.org/10.1007/BF03395674

Greer, R. D., Pohl, P., Du, L., & Moschella, J. L. (2017). The separate development of children's listener and speaker behavior and the intercept as behavioral metamorphosis. *Journal of Behavioral and Brain Science, 7*(13), 674–704. https://doi.org/10.4236/jbbs.2017.713045

Haggbloom, S. J., Warnick, R., Warnick, J. E., Jones, V. K., Yarbrough, G. L., Russell, T. M., Borecky, C. M., & Monte, E. (2002). The 100 most eminent psychologists of the 20th century. *Review of General Psychology, 6*(2), 139–152. https://doi.org/10.1037/1089-2680.6.2.13

Holland, J. G. (1960/1976). Teaching machines: An application of principles from the laboratory. In J. C. Holland, C. Solomon, J. Doran, & D. A. Frezza (Eds.), *The analysis of behavior in planning instruction*. Addison-Wesley Publishing Company. (Original work published in *Journal of the Experimental Analysis of Behavior, 3*, 275–287)

Holland, J. G. (2003). Foreword I. In B. F. Skinner (Ed.), *The technology of teaching* (pp. xiii–xxiv). B. F. Skinner Foundation.

Holland, J. G., & Pittsburgh University. (1976). *Analysis of behavior in reading instruction*. Pittsburgh University, PA. Learning Research and Development Center. (Conference on theory and practice of beginning reading instruction). Retrieved from http://eric.ed.gov/?id=ED155625

Instituto Paulo Montenegro, & Ação Educativa. (2018). *INAF Brasil 2018. Indicador de alfabetismo funcional. Resultados preliminares*. Instituto Paulo Montenegro, Ação Educativa, Ibope Inteligência. Retrieved from http://acaoeducativa.org.br/wp-content/uploads/2018/08/Inaf2018_Relatório-Resultados-Preliminares_v08Ago2018.pdf

Matos, M. A., & Passos, M. L. R. F. (2006). Linguistic sources of Skinner's Verbal Behavior. *The Behavior Analyst, 29*, 89–107. https://doi.org/10.1007/BF03392119

Matos, M. A., & Passos, M. L. R. F. (2010). Emergent verbal behavior and analogy: Skinnerian and linguistic approaches. *The Behavior Analyst, 33*, 65–81. https://doi.org/10.1007/bf03392204

Matos, M. A., Avanzi, A. L., & McIlvane, W. J. (2006). Rudimentary reading repertoires via stimulus equivalence and recombination of minimal units. *The Analysis of Verbal Behavior, 22*, 3–19. https://doi.org/10.1007/BF03393023

McGuinness, D. (2004). *Early reading instruction: What science really tells us about how to teach reading*. The MIT Press.

Morais, J. (1994/1996). *A arte de ler* (A. Lorencini, Trad.). Editora Unesp. (Original work published in 1994)

Moxley, R. A. (1997). Skinner: From essentialist to selectionist meaning. *Behavior and Philosophy, 25*, 95–119.

Mueller, M. M., Olmi, D. J., & Saunders, K. J. (2000). Recombinative generalization of within-syllable units in prereading children. *Journal of Applied Behavior Analysis, 33*, 515–531. https://doi.org/10.1901/jaba.2000.33-515

National Reading Panel. National Institute of Child Health and Human Development, National Institutes of Health. (2000). *National Reading Panel – Teaching children to read: An evidence-based assessment of the scientific research literature on reading and its implications for reading instruction*. Reports of the subgroups. Washington, DC. Retrieved from http://www.nichd.nih.gov/publications/pubs/nrp/documents/report.pdf

OECD/PISA. (2016). *Programme for international student assessment (PISA). Results form PISA 2015. Brasil.* Retrieved from https://www.oecd.org/pisa/PISA-2015-Brazil.pdf

Passos, M. L. R. F. (2003). Análise funcional do comportamento, linguística estrutural e alfabetização. *DataGramaZero. Revista de Ciência da Informação, 4*(5), 1–7. http://hdl.handle.net/20.500.11959/brapci/3606

Passos, M. L. R. F. (2004). *Bloomfield e Skinner. Língua e comportamento verbal*. Nau editora.

Passos, M. L. R. F. (2011). O modelo de alfabetização de Leornard Bloomfield e a análise funcional do comportamento verbal: Possíveis aplicações à língua portuguesa. *II Simpósio do Instituto Nacional de Ciência e Tecnologia sobre Comportamento, Cognição e Ensino*. Universidade Federal de São Carlos.

Passos, M. L. R. F. (2012). B. F. Skinner: The writer and his definition of verbal behavior. *The Behavior Analyst, 35*(1), 115–126. https://doi.org/10.1007/BF03392270

Passos, M. L. R. F., & Matos, M. A. (2007). The influence of Bloomfield's linguistics on Skinner. *The Behavior Analyst, 30*, 133–151. https://doi.org/10.1007/BF03392151

Scliar-Cabral, L. (2013). *Sistema Scliar de alfabetização*. Fundamentos. Editora Lili.

Scliar-Cabral, L. (2015). Pela melhoria da qualidade na alfabetização. *Revista Estudos Legislativos, 9*(9), 21–38.

Seabra, A. G., & Capovilla, F. C. (2010). *Alfabetização: Método fônico*. Memnon.

Seabra, A. G., & Dias, M. D. (2011). Métodos de alfabetização: Delimitação de procedimentos e considerações para uma prática eficaz. *Revista Psicopedagogia, 28*(87), 306–320.

Sério, T. M. A. P., Andery, M. A., Gioia, P. S., & Micheletto, N. (2002/2010). *Controle de estímulos e comportamento operante: Uma introdução* (3ª ed.). EDUC.

Shannon, M. R. (1963). Review of let's read: A linguistic approach. *Teachers College Record, 65*(1), 93–94.

Sidman, M. (1985). Aprendizagem sem erros e sua importância para o ensino do deficiente mental. *Psicologia, 11*, 1–15.

Sidman, M. (2010). Errorless learning and programmed instruction: The myth of the learning curve. *European Journal of Behavior Analysis, 12*(2), 167–180. https://doi.org/10.1080/15021149.2010.11434341

Sidman, M., & Stoddard, L. T. (1966). Programming perception and learning for retarded children. In N. R. Ellis (Ed.), *International review of research in mental retardation* (Vol. 2, pp. 151–208). Academic.

Skinner, B. F. (1948/1999). Types of verbal behavior. In B. F. Skinner. *Verbal Behavior. Willian James Lectures Harvard University. 1948*. Harvard University Press. Retrieved from http://www.behavior.org/resources/595.pdf

Skinner, B. F. (1953/2014). *Science and human behavior*. B. F. Skinner Foundation. Retrieved from http://www.bfskinner.org/newtestsite/wp-content/uploads/2014/02/ScienceHumanBehavior.pdf

Skinner, B. F. (1957/1992). *Verbal behavior*. Copley Publishing Group.

Skinner, B. F. (1959). The programming of verbal knowledge. In E. Galanter (Ed.), *Automatic teaching: The state of the art* (pp. 63–68). Wiley.

Skinner, B. F. (1960a). Modern learning theory and some new approaches to teaching. In J. W. Gustad (Ed.), *Faculty utilization and retention* (pp. 64–72). New England Board of Higher Education.

Skinner, B. F. (1960b). Special problems in programming language instruction for teaching machines. In F. J. Oinas (Ed.), *Language teaching today* (pp. 167–174). Indiana University Research Center in Anthropology, Folklore, and Linguistics.

Skinner, B. F. (1960c). Teaching machines. *The Review of Economics and Statistics, 42*, 189–191. https://doi.org/10.2307/1926170

Skinner, B. F. (1961a). Teaching machines. *Scientific American, 205*, 90–102.

Skinner, B. F. (1961b). Why we need teaching machines. In B. F. Skinner, *Cumulative record. Definitive edition* (pp. 221–239). B. F. Skinner Foundation. (Original work published in *Harvard Educational Review, 31*, 377–398)

Skinner, B. F. (1963/1999). Reflections on a decade of teaching machines. In B. F. Skinner, *Cumulative record. Definitive edition* (pp. 240–250). B. F. Skinner Foundation. (Original work published in *Teachers College Record, 65*, Columbia University, 168–177)

Skinner, B. F. (1968). Teaching science in high school. What is wrong? In B. F. Skinner, *Cumulative record. Definitive edition* (pp. 251–263). B. F. Skinner Foundation. (Original work published in *Science, 159,* 704–710)

Skinner, B. F. (1968/2003). *The technology of teaching*. B. F. Skinner Foundation.

Skinner, B. F. (1986). Programmed instruction revisited. *Phi Delta Kappa, 68*, 103–110.

Skinner, B. F., & Holland, J. G. (1960/1962). The use of teaching machines in college instruction (Parts II-IV). In A. A. Lumsdaine & R. Glaser (Eds.), *Teaching machines and programmed learning: A source book* (pp. 159–172). Department of Audio-Visual Instruction, National Education Association.

Smith, L. M. (1994/1999). B. F. Skinner (1904–1990). *UNESCO: International Bureau of Education*. Retrieved from http://www.ibe.unesco.org/International/Publications/Thinkers/ThinkersPdf/skinners.pdf (Original published in *Prospects: Quarterly Review of Comparative Education*. UNESCO: International Bureau of Education, XXIV [3/4], 519–532.)

Terrace, H. S. (1963a). Discrimination learning with and without "errors". *Journal of the Experimental Analysis of Behavior, 1*, 1–27. https://doi.org/10.1901/jeab.1963.6-1

Terrace, H. S. (1963b). Errorless transfer of a discrimination across two continua. *Journal of the Experimental Analysis of Behavior, 6*, 223–232. https://doi.org/10.1901/jeab.1963.6-223

Trask, R. L. (2004/2008). *Dicionário de linguagem e linguística* (2ª ed.). Contexto. (R. Ilari, Trans.). Technical review by Ingedore Villeça Koch e Thaís Cristófaro Silva.

Wilson, R. G., & Lindsay, H. G. (1963). Applying linguistics to remedial reading. *The Reading Teacher, 16*(6), 452–455.

Chapter 15
The Paulo Freire "Method" in a Behavioral Reading of the Alphabetization

Denise Bachega and João dos Santos Carmo

15.1 Introduction

This chapter proposes reflections on an educational approach (Freirean theory) and an approach in Psychology (Behavior Analysis) regarding some processes involved in teaching reading and writing. With this, it is intended to promote dialogue around important contributions of these approaches.

Two works (de Man, 2004; Fazzi & Cirino, 2003) inaugurated punctual approximations in relation to these two educational conceptions. The present chapter follows these characteristics of approximation and is based on the dissertation of the first author (Bachega, 2014). This is an exploratory documentary research, with consultation to primary and secondary bases, which addresses the literacy method developed by Paulo Freire and some aspects of his theory from the perspective of Behavior Analysis.

In the selection of materials related to Behavior Analysis, the criterion was to directly explain some conceptions and principles of this approach in relation to teaching in general and, more specifically, on literacy. For the works related to Freirean conception of education, the selection criteria were the author's most relevant works. Besides, two works were used (Lyra, 1996; Terra, 1994) in which are described the teaching situations that took place in the experience of a literacy campaign held in 1963, under Paulo Freire's coordination in the city of Angicos – RN. This experience will be detailed further on.

The themes and contents were categorized and translated into the specific objectives of this chapter: (a) to present the conceptions concerning Education present in the main works of Paulo Freire and Behavior Analysis; (b) to highlight teaching

D. Bachega (✉) · J. dos Santos Carmo
Universidade Federal de São Carlos, São Carlos, SP, Brazil
e-mail: denise.bachega@gmail.com

A. R. de Albuquerque, R. M. de Melo (eds.), *Contributions of Behavior Analysis to Reading and Writing Comprehension*, https://doi.org/10.1007/978-3-031-40868-7_15

contingencies provided by the Paulo Freire Literacy Method through reports on the experience of Angicos; and (c) to outline reflections on the contributions of the two proposals that may favor the practices of scholars and educators of these two approaches.

15.2 Literacy for Behavior Analysis

B. F. Skinner (1968/1972) proposes that for teaching to be efficient, it is initially necessary to ensure an operational definition of the behavior to be established. This definition would make explicit the environmental conditions that favor the installation of the behavior. Explicitly defining and controlling the relevant dimensions of the environment and the behavior to be taught is not restricted to teaching reading and writing, but will apply to all teaching repertoires. The teacher needs to be clear which properties of learner behavior are relevant (and which are not) when teaching math, history, geography, critical thinking, autonomy, reflection, etc.

In literacy, individuals learn to behave discriminatively towards specific sound and graphic stimuli in the written language. The response classes involved are quite varied, including the naming of multiple graphic stimuli (e.g., printed, cursive, uppercase, lowercase letters), various forms of spelling (e.g., handwriting, typing, indicating or verbalizing corresponding letters or phonemes), combination and recombination of graphic units (letters, phonemes, syllables), enabling expansion of the vocal-verbal repertoire. As these repertoires involve the same symbolic code, the actions (responses) of writing and reading are controlled by the same stimulus classes, allowing functional integrations between these two behaviors. Furthermore, as the development of reading and writing behaviors often occurs concomitantly, the refinement in the production of some responses, especially in more experienced readers and writers, often extends to other reading and writing repertoires. It is perhaps because of these characteristics that the notion that learning to read implies learning to write is quite widespread (as described by de Rose, 2005, reprinted in Chap. 1 of this book; Marinotti, 2004).

Evidence from applied situations or research indicates that reading and writing are not absolutely indissociable activities (Lee & Pegler, 1982; Marinotti, 2004). Despite this finding, advances in one of these repertoires do not translate into necessary and spontaneous progress on the other. Moreover, even reading and writing activities alone do not have exact correspondences. It is possible for a child to write a dictated word correctly from a spelling point of view, but to make mistakes when writing the same words in an essay or answering dissertation questions, for example (Marinotti, 2004).

These situations are consistent with the explanations derived from Skinner's (1957/1978) analysis of the functional independence of verbal repertoires (Marinotti, 2004). Thus, in teaching situations, the study of verbal operant behaviors could help the teacher to recognize the controls under which the student's behavior is a function.

The different literacy methods differ, among several other aspects, regarding the unit chosen as a starting point for teaching: phonemes, letters or syllables, words or texts (Soares, 2018). Skinner (1957/1978) highlights that the size of what he called functional unit for textual behavior, whether isolated letters or sounds, syllables or words, for example, has been a very important discussion in the field of literacy.

Thus, from a behavioral perspective, it is understood that when reading or writing a person uses different control units, depending on several factors, such as familiarity with the vocabulary used. So that "the same person who proceeds fluently in reading a text, doing it by blocks of words may, before an unknown word, hesitate and resort to reading syllable by syllable" (Marinotti, 2004, p. 218). And the same may occur in writing or typing a text, for example.

According to Marinotti (2004),

> (...) a child who, when reading or writing the words **GATO**[1] and **LONA** is under control of the letters or syllables involved will find it easier to read new words that include these same elements – for example, **GALO**, than one who is under control of the global stimulus, that is, the word as a whole. On the other hand, these same units that facilitated the generalization of learning are not, by themselves, sufficient to guarantee correct spelling. (p. 219 – original bold)

In the Portuguese language, the correspondence between sounds and their spellings is not exact, that is, the same sound can be represented in different ways and the same spelling can correspond to different sounds. Thus, innumerable irregularities of this language do not have a clear, unique or easily transmissible rule to learners and even when they do – for example, *m* before *p* and *b*; every proparoxytone word is stressed – the difficulties shown by learners indicate that knowledge of the rule, by itself, is not enough to control their behavior. In other words, the learner may "know the rule" and still "make mistakes". For Marinotti (2004), the irregularities of the Portuguese language generate problems in reading and writing, however, the reading problems are more easily overcome since the visual textual stimuli (written words) and the context in which they are presented, provide additional cues for the issuance of textual behavior.

In summary, it was pointed out that for Behavior Analysis, educational processes will be better understood from a scientific analysis of behavior. The emphasis of education is on behavior acquisition, that is, from situations planned for teaching, the behaviors that will be efficient to achieve reinforcers in non-formal educational contexts are established. These are some of the central aspects for the behaviorist understanding of literacy[2] . Next, we will present some of Paulo Freire's conceptions on the subject of education.

[1] GATO, LONA, and GALO correspond to the words CAT, CANVAS, and ROOSTER in the English language.

[2] Other relevant aspects will be dealt with in more detail throughout this chapter, such as: combination and recombination of minimal units; formation of equivalence classes; and reading with comprehension.

15.3 Description of the Literacy Experience Using the Paulo Freire Method

We warn the reader that Freire's proposal goes far beyond the literacy method, whose beginning is historically marked with the experience developed in Angicos-RN,[3] described below. In fact, Freire's conceptions and proposals on education, the world, knowledge, being, and the man-world relationship are considered to be the beginning of a new epistemology.

Therefore, even at the risk of mischaracterizing the richness of Paulo Freire's proposal, we will restrict ourselves only to the methodological elements of the teaching of reading and writing; however, we emphasize that, in Freire's experience, reading is not limited to decoding written words, but is expanded with the conception that to read is to interpret the world, and therefore words have diverse meanings within the context of individual and collective life history. Similarly, *writing is* not restricted to writing words, but is expanded with the possibility of writing one's own history. In Freire's conception, reading and writing should be seen as a revolutionary and liberating form of oppression exerted on the working class. This revolutionary conception of enabling the working class in the struggle against the oppression exercised by the bourgeois class, as well as the results of the literacy of workers in record time, was the fuse that led the military dictatorship to exile Paulo Freire and fight against his proposal.

15.3.1 The Elaboration

The development of the Method in each context can be described in five main stages. The first consists of a survey of the group's vocabulary universe and occurs through informal meetings between educators and residents of the area in which the literacy experience will take place. Semi-structured interviews are conducted with the participants in which not only the most emotionally charged vocabulary, linked to the existential experience of the group, but also the typical phrases of the participating community are fixed. In these meetings, the interviewees reveal, even, anxieties, frustrations, disbeliefs and hopes, as well as certain aesthetic moments of their language. This survey had the function of identifying the participants' vocabular operative level (input repertoire).

From the researched vocabulary universe, in the second stage of the Method, educators select the generating words which, for the Portuguese language, are around 15. These generating words will serve as themes for dialogues throughout the meetings and their selection follows the following criteria:

[3] In this small town in the interior of Rio Grande do Norte, in 1963, a literacy experience took place with fundamental repercussions for the creation of popular education in favor of the working class and for liberation from oppression.

(a) phonemic richness: so that the generating words together contain all the phonemic specificities of the language;
(b) phonetic difficulties: the words must correspond to the phonetic difficulties of the Portuguese language, placed in a sequence that gradually goes from minor to major difficulties. For example, *b*, *l* and *t* before *qu*, *gu* and *ch*;
(c) pragmatic content of the word, which implies a greater plurality of engagement of the word in social, cultural, political, etc. reality. For example, the word *brick* in the Brasilia experience in which there were several construction workers among the participants (Freire, 1996), or the choice of *favela* for the experience in Rio de Janeiro. (Freire, 2011a)

In the third stage of the Literacy Method, based on the generating words, the educators create situations that will work as challenging elements for the group (motivational operations). They are codified problem situations, containing elements that will be decoded by the groups with the collaboration of the coordinator. A generating word may encompass the whole situation or refer to one of the elements of the situation, and from the group coordinator's questions, aspects of the situation portrayed may be explored in direct relation to the experiences of the participants. For example, for the generating words *vote* and *people,* the projection was of a polling station with a man, with common physical characteristics of Northeasterners (very thin, black skin, dark hair), voting. For these generating words, some suggestions of themes for debate were: difference between people and mass and importance of the vote for political emancipation.

These local situations open up perspectives for the analysis of regional and national problems. From these situations, the chosen generating vocabularies are inserted, according to the gradation of phonemic difficulties. In this way, the debate around the generating words promotes the awareness of the group concomitantly with its literacy.

In the fourth stage, the suggestions for debates are elaborated at[4] and *slides* or posters with pictures of existential situations are produced. Paulo Freire (2011a) comments that "these sheets should be mere aids for the coordinators, never a rigid prescription that they must obey and follow" (p. 150). Angicos experience slides can be accessed at http://acervo.paulofreire.org:8080/xmlui/handle/7891/607.

Finally, in the fifth stage, educators construct *slides* or posters with the generating words broken down into syllables. Phonemic, syllabic families, involving each consonant of the generating word and all the vowels of the alphabet are presented separately and then together, in order to favor syllabic recombination.

---

[4] In the initial experiences with Paulo Freire's Method these situations were elaborated by the educators. In later experiences, however, this construction was carried out by the participants themselves (de Man, 2004).

15.3.2 *The Implementation: The Meetings in the Culture Circles*

The execution of the Method starts from the exhibitions about the anthropological concept of culture, as it will be better explained in the description referring to Angicos. Then there is the exhibition of the graphic representation of the first generating theme, in which a debate around its implications is initiated.

The process of decoding the generating theme should not be so explicit (as in an advertisement), nor so enigmatic. In the first case, the participants have no other decoding to do except for the one that has already been imposed by the person who created the figure. In the second case, the decoding becomes a guessing game or puzzle. The problem situation should therefore be moderately explicit, simple in its complexity and able to offer various possibilities for analysis in its decoding (Freire, 1983).

The situations portrayed allow for the development of reasoning, questioning and reflection of the students on the reality of the theme in question. Only when the group, with the collaboration of the coordinator, has exhausted the analysis of the theme in question, does the coordinator turn to the generating word so that it may be visualized.

Only the word is projected and then it is separated into syllables. Then the families of each syllable are presented and, after the students have recognized the "pieces" of the word, we move to the "discovery sheet" with visualization of the phonemic families that compose the word under study. It is through this form that the participant discovers the mechanism of vocabulary formation in a syllabic language, which is done through phonemic combinations.

By appropriating this mechanism, students start assembling words (or pseudowords – set of meaningless syllables) with the combinations at their disposal. Then, the last analysis is performed, the one that leads to vowels. Finally, as a homework assignment, the students must then form as many vocabulary words as they can create with combinations of the already known phonemes.

15.4 Behavioral Analysis of Full Elements of the Paulo Freire Method

Regarding the process of word formation in the Portuguese language, Paulo Freire states that, by means of the Method, the participant "appropriates this mechanism critically and not through memorization – which would not be an appropriation – [and] begins to produce by himself his system of graphic signs" (Freire, 2011a, p. 152). Why? What makes this method critical and not memorizing? Some issues that may be related to the question are discussed below, without the pretension of ending it.

15.4.1 The Use of Psychological Tests

According to Lyra (1996), although the coordinators of the Culture Circles had come to apply psychological tests with the initial intention of using them for the division of the classes, the participants showed great difficulty in performing them and the division of the classes was not based on this resource.

Psychological testing instruments are based on patterns of a group of individuals (normative or standardization sample) (Urbina, 2007), whereas behavioral analysis makes statements about the effects of independent variables in relation to the behavior of each person individually. Statistical methods are grounded in concepts such as mean, variance and normal distribution rather than aspects of individuals' unique history, as are functional analyses (Carrara, 2005).

In research or interventions based on the behavior analytic approach, evaluations are generally performed as measures of comparison between the initial and final performances of the participants themselves, taking the subject as the measure control of the evaluation of the results of the intervention performed. Thus, the use of psychological tests in the psychological approach makes sense when there is significant correspondence between the constructs assessed by the instrument and the objectives of interventions, or at least part of them. This does not seem to be the case with tests of non-verbal intelligence and literacy. For this same reason, from a behavioral perspective, non-verbal intelligence tests would also not be the most appropriate means for class division since they do not clearly show differences in repertoires among participants in relation to the objectives set for the intervention.

15.4.2 Structuring Teaching in Small Steps, Starting from the Learner's Repertoire and Keeping Under Control of the Learner's Behavior

Once the final teaching objectives have been defined, we move on to programming the teaching conditions (or learning contingencies). In each unit the teaching of behaviors should be proposed that are sufficiently different from the learner's current behavior to produce gradual changes. The objectives of teaching behaviors very different from the participant's previous repertoire should not be established so as to leave the participant without knowing what to do or result in the presentation of responses in a trial-and-error system, which may be demotivating (e.g., Kubo & Botomé, 2001; Matos, 1995; Skinner, 1968/1972). In the Method this appears, for example, in the proposals for the construction of notes and letters by the students.

According to Marinotti (2004), the two main elements involved in the learning of reading and writing are: the object to be known (written language) and the subject of learning (the student). In the proposal of the Method, besides the extensive knowledge about these two elements pointed out by the author, there is another object to be known: the social political context. In the preparation for the application of Paulo Freire's Method, the coordinators' search for knowledge of these three elements is present from the two initial stages. In the first stage, *Survey of the group's vocabulary universe*, the participants are characterized (age, gender, marital status, profession, religious beliefs), their cultural activities and interests are surveyed, the socioeconomic profile of the population is described, and the oral verbal repertoire (and textual repertoire, if any) of the participants is gathered. In the second step, the *selection of the generating words*, verbal stimuli already present in the learner's repertoire are selected from those whose graphic representations, together, represent all the phonetic difficulties of the Portuguese language (e.g., *ch*, *ss*, *rr*, -n, -*l*).

The teaching units of the Method could be defined by the generating words and their phonetic difficulties. In convergence with the behavioral proposals of teaching programming, the units follow a sequence that advances gradually from the smallest difficulties (*v, l, t, s, p*) to the biggest ones (*nh, il, al, lh*). This planning, however, does not remain rigid and the subsequent units can be advanced or delayed according to the students' performances. This flexibility under control of what is demonstrated by the learners is also consistent with the behavioral proposal (e.g., Kubo & Botomé, 2001; Skinner, 1968/1972).

From the perspective of behavior analysis, throughout the program, the learners are the ones who indicate in which aspects the program is reaching the expected results and which contingencies need reworking or new programming. It is essential for the teacher to keep an eye on the performance of the participants, because if the learners do not meet the expectations of the initial program, it is necessary to investigate and adapt the program to the conditions presented by them.

In the[5] course in Angicos, there were daily meetings in the morning, when the coordinators together analyzed the work done so far and discussed and reworked the planning, "almost a reinvention" (Lyra, 1996, p. 41). In Lyra's words, "like everything in education, nothing was ready, things were based on doing" (Lyra, 1996, p. 41). This flexibility under control of what is demonstrated by the learners is also observed in the reports referring to situations in which, when presenting the new families of letters, the coordinators changed the teaching conditions or reprogrammed conditions based on needs observed in relation to the participants, as in the following passages: "... we present the families of the letters s and p. Similar procedure to the one used in the word *belota*, except the vowels **are now unnecessary**." (Lyra, 1996, p. 39 – emphasis added). And also in: "**the participants missed the family of *d***, with presentation planned for the end of the course. The difficulty was overcome with the introduction of the word *solado*." (Lyra, 1996, p. 39 – emphasis added).

[5] The literacy experience in Angicos is a course. In the description of the experience (course) itself, the terms 'teachers' and 'coordinators' are sometimes interchangeable.

15.4.3 Establishment of Motivational Operations[6] and Use of Natural and Conditioned Reinforcers

Skinner (1968/1972) states that, traditionally, the arbitrary reinforcers used (e.g., praise, points, award stars in the notebook) in the classroom do not relate closely to immediate (natural reinforcers, e.g., the learning itself, understanding what you have read, solving a math problem) or long-term benefits, allowing to "make it easy for teachers to lose sight of the significance of what they are teaching and for those who support teaching to contact with what is actually being taught" (p. 213). The author also states that the main aims of educational reforms "have always been to restore the place of the practical consequences which determine support and policy" (Skinner, 1968/1972, p. 213), although he does not explain which reforms he is referring to or how this would have occurred.

In the Paulo Freire Method, it is possible to observe that a fundamental aspect is the situations created by the coordinators so that the participants' reading and writing behaviors had natural reinforcers. For example, dealing with issues relevant to the lives of the participants outside the teaching situation; reading and debating about the news in the city newspapers and writing notes about what they wanted to be shown in the movie session created by the group. This activity, according to Lyra (1996, pp. 83–84), "resulted in a voluminous amount of letters and notes, and the marked improvement in the exercise of writing and language". Other important productions were the confection, before the meetings, of mimeographed newspapers containing the known families of letters and the letters about the specific demands discussed in the groups that were delivered to the president of the republic on the last day of the course. For example, the letter from Mrs. Francisca transcribed in the original in Portuguese:

> Senho Presidenti
>
> E neste momento que pego o meu lapis pra lhi comunicar as minhas necessidade. Agora mesmo não sou maça sou povo e posso esigi meus direito. Senho présidenti a gente tem percisão de muita coisa como: reforma agrária Escola e que o senho bote as leis da constituição pra fora. Tenho duas filas pra edocar e não tenho recuso poriço peço ao senho bouça di estudo pra que elas não crescam como eu cresi. (Francisca de Andrade. (Lyra, 1996, p. 116))

Although some letters still contained grammatical and spelling errors, the texts produced by the students already contained coherence and consistent use of phonemes as in "presidenti" which sounds exactly as the word is pronounced in Portuguese, although the correct form is "presidente", or the expression "poriço" instead of "por isso".

Besides fulfilling the objectives of repertoire formation linked to political action, the use of emotionally charged words and existential situations can be considered as establishing operations that increased the probability of participants to engage in the

[6] Motivational operations can be understood as situations that change the effectiveness of reinforcers, e.g., satiation and deprivation (Aloi et al., 2014; Catania, 1999).

debate. Due to their "charge of experiential involvement", as described by Gerhardt (1996, p. 156), when faced with the spoken word, responding in a certain way (e.g., paying attention to the word or writing it down) would have more chances of happening and becoming a conditioned reinforcer than writing words that were strange or distant from the daily life of the learners, for example.

Another possibility in this analysis is that the reinforcing aspect acquired by *writing existentially meaningful words* may extend as a reinforcer to *writing other words*, which could also be considered an establishing (or motivational) operation. That is, one of the consequences of writing meaningful words is to make writing a conditioned reinforcer that would also increase the probability of the behavior of writing other things and of the student continuing to study.

The third motivational condition of the Method refers to the discussions about literate and illiterate culture in which participants are led to perceive themselves as makers of culture. Realizing the emancipatory relevance of learning to read, write, and think critically provided by the discussions can be considered an event that increases the reinforcing value of studying and engaging in political actions. Moreover, there is in a way, through these discussions, a narrowing between the behavioral links of studying and creating motivational conditions to change their own life condition, symbolized by the difference between learning to write any letter and the real situation of writing a letter to a government leader asking for better social conditions. This narrowing of behavioral links can be understood as a condition favoring the emergence of generalizations of graphic and sound stimuli, as well as transfers between stimuli related to reading and writing, but also to everyday experiences. That is, between learning occurring inside and outside the educational context.

Finally, a fourth motivational condition appears, for example, when Lyra says that the meetings always began "with a chat, when they tell what they did during the day. After that, they write words and phrases on the chalkboard. At the end, another informal chat, when they talk about their aspirations, what they liked most about the debate, etc." (Lyra, 1996, p. 48). Besides the sensitivity to the students' interests, in these passages it is possible to highlight the search for the interaction to be as spontaneous and egalitarian as possible, indicating how the dialogue, respect and fight against social inequalities are related to the teaching objectives. So that, in addition to the motivational aspects, egalitarian relations are an important part of the means and ends of the Method.

15.5 Behavioral Analysis of Aspects of the "Teaching Methodology" of the Method

In the stages of creation of existential situations and construction of script sheets of the Paulo Freire Method, figures of existential situations and their respective written representative words are used. These material resources establish conditions for students to recognize and describe situations they experience. In addition, mediators may pose questions that relate daily experiences to social and political problems at local and national levels, as well as their possible causes and historical and political determinants.

In the elaboration stage of the cards with the decomposition and recomposition of phonemic families, there is the preparation of materials that allow: (a) identify the relevant aspects (spatial orientation and format) of the textual stimuli that should promote/stimulate speech (reading) and motor (writing) responses; (b) identify the different units of the visual stimuli (words, letters, syllables); (c) relate the corresponding graphic (graphemes) and sound (phonemes) stimuli; and (d) recombine the smaller units of the stimuli in order to form new words.

All these visual resources together with the debates also form an important motivating condition because they are an initial situation for discussing forms of what Skinner (1974/2002) would call counter-control, that is, situations in which the controlled person escapes from what, or who, controls his behavior. The transformative education proposed by Paulo Freire serves to provide learners with enabling elements (e.g., knowledge) that help them transform the aversive social conditions they experience.

The importance of these materials for the promotion of relevant discriminations is observed, for example, in the lesson about culture, when participants "call 'indigenous woman', a an indigenous man" (Lyra, 1996, p. 25) and in the discussion about the generating word *salina* [salt evaporation pond], when participants identified that the color of the water drawn in the enclosures (tanks) of the *salina*: "is reddish, and not blue as it is on the slide" (Lyra, 1996, p. 49). Although in these situations such difficulties seem to have been easily circumvented, they illustrate situations in which the material does not meet the educator's expectations. In another situation, the coordinators started working with slides made of tracing paper cut to the size of the slides (Lyra, 1996, p. 54), which made it possible to project the words written by the participants themselves and the correction by the group itself. In other words, with this new resource, the participants began to obtain more *feedbacks* regarding their behavior, and these consequences became closer to the emission of responses.

This does not mean that the material importance of the resources is greater than the relevance of what is being studied. Material resources are mediators of the proposal and, frequently, difficulties with them are better circumvented than difficulties with proposals and definition of objectives, for example. However, it is a relevant dimension that should be considered in its importance as a facilitator of teaching, as a preventive action of confusions and doubts as it works to accentuate the relevant aspects of what is intended to work. As explained by de Rose (2005; available in Chap. 1 of this book), reinforcement contingencies are what make a person capable of discriminating aspects of the environment. Therefore, materials should ensure that the relevant dimensions are covered in their entirety even if some learners require different conditions to discriminate different aspects.

15.5.1 Behavioral Analysis of the Pedagogical Attitudes Adopted by Educators

Regarding the common and widespread use of aversive control in traditional teaching, Skinner states that, over many years, it has changed only in form, from spanking to suspensions, reprimands and other punishments, e.g., the teacher's anger, the debauchery or mockery of classmates, the vexation of comparisons and competitions, and the low grades (Skinner, 1968). So that the correct answer becomes an almost insignificant event, lost amidst anxieties, boredom and other inevitable by-products of the use of aversive control.

Contrary to these situations common in traditional teaching and criticized by Skinner, Lyra (1996) reports that when they pronounced a word in a non-formal way, mediators did not correct the participants, but continued the debate making use of the answers given by them. It is possible to highlight in the Method the search for the construction of what would be called in behavioral language a *non-punitive verbal community*. That is, the action called "valuing" the participants' answers, which were followed by explanations, is fundamental in the Method because it reinforces the behavior of answering to the proposed questions and increases the chances of dialogue and free expression of the students. Thus, the participation and the recognition of the importance of this participation, both by the teachers and the group, are consequences issued by the teacher and the group and have chances to be reinforcing for the behavior of the participants to express reflections, doubts and criticisms.

Commenting on the phase of vocabulary survey, Paulo Freire (2011a) says that the results are *very* rich for the team of educators, not only because of the relationships they develop, but also because of the "*exuberance of the people's language,* which sometimes is not suspected" (p. 147 – italics added). As an example of this exuberance, the author reports what one of the interviewees said: "January in Angicos is hard to live in, because January is an evil goat to kill us. Professor Costa Lima, secretary of the journal Estudos Universitários and member of the SEC team, commented that it is "an affirmation to the taste of Guimarães Rosa" (Freire, 1963, 2011a).

The construction of the non-punitive community begins, therefore, with the first stage of elaboration of the method in which, through interviews, the first contact between the team of educators and the participants is established. This is also the starting point of a bonding process between mediators and participants and a means of creating a positive and egalitarian interaction with future participants. When there is an affective, respectful and sincere relationship between teacher and learner, praise is more likely to function as a natural reinforcer. On the other hand, in situations of aversive interaction, the teacher's actions can have very different effects on the student's behavior, and vice versa.

It is also possible to understand that the aspects that distance the speech of the learners from the formal speech of the language were not considered wrong or inadequate answers for the coordinators of the Culture Circles. On the contrary, they were considered as representations that translate the culture of the participants and, therefore, were analyzed as a different aesthetic, but with the same value as the formal language. In this way, the highlights and comments stressed the importance of the educators' attitude of authentic respect and appreciation of the language *"of the people"* and their knowledge "of *experience made*" (Freire, 1983, ch. 2). These aspects are not secondary, but central to both the implementation of the Method and the liberating pedagogy of Paulo Freire.

In the community created by the Circles of Culture, therefore, the learner is also a teacher about his livelihoods, his daily life, his ideas and interests (within and outside the content). The coordinator proposes the debates or makes theoretical explanations while keeping under control of the learner's behavior and responds naturally and contingently to his manifestations. The learner responds to these actions of the coordinator and identifies that they have influence (control) over the behavior of the participants, which may intensify the frequency of their response in relation to the teaching content.

Another example of this refers to the recombination of syllables by the learners. In this regard Paulo Freire (1963) states: "it does not matter that [the learner] brings vocabularies that are not terms[7] . What matters on the day he sets foot in this new domain is the discovery of phonemic combinations" (p. 16). In this sense, as de Rose (2005) comments, the emphasis on the form of behavior to the detriment of relationships, has been a common practice in education and is certainly one of the reasons for the frequent failure of school practices. The author also states that in the case of literacy there is an overvaluation of copying and dictation performances, to the detriment of reading and expressive writing. This is also an aspect highlighted by Skinner (1968/1972) in the chapter on originality where he says:

> contingencies designed to teach a student to write are also often most helpful if they primarily respect quantity. The important thing is to evoke behavior. (Editing is a different part of the creative process). Under contingencies which respect quantity, responses are emitted which would otherwise never appear, and many of them can be traced to variables which would otherwise never be effective. The behavior is therefore likely to be original. (p. 177)

It is precisely in favor of this position that the teacher of liberating education stands. This does not mean that the teaching of formal language is not worked at any time. After the discovery phases, and with the same critical rigor with which any teaching content is discussed, formal language should also be taught to the learners of liberating pedagogy. However, with care not to overlap with the language and culture of these learners. In this practice, the educator is more in control of maintaining motivation for study (e.g., creating context, using materials and strategies that foster exploration, interacting with the content, and increasing the reinforcing value of learning) and critical reflection, than under control of the form of the behavior or its purely technical meaning.

[7] Portuguese words that have a specific referent.

15.5.2 Dialogue as a Condition for Teaching Critical Thinking

In Paulo Freire's Method, dialogue is the basis for building relationships and pedagogical *praxis. Through dialogue* and the themes of existential and political relevance, the oral verbal repertoires are developed, from which the students also learn to read and write.

It is not about the simple substitution of contents or addition of aspects related to politics, because, according to Paulo Freire (1983) this would be *sloganizing*, that is, an imposition of ideas as alienating as traditional education. In Freire's proposal, to deal with existential issues is to deal with them in a dialogical way. It is only through a horizontal and trusting relationship that problematizing and conscientizing education becomes possible, without imposition, without the students becoming a mere extension of the teacher's ideas.

Respecting and valuing the social condition and understanding of the world in which the learner is, this condition is problematized, contextualizing it, historically and socially, in a critical way. This will allow the learner to act to transform his oppressed condition. In the words of Luiz Lobo, responsible for the journalistic coverage of the project, quoted by Lyra (1996), this learning was described as follows in relation to one of the groups where the literacy activities were carried out:

> in the Angicos prison, the CC [Culture Circle] became a space of freedom, where prisoners, family members and soldiers, night after night, became aware that man's greatest misfortune was backwardness, ignorance, illiteracy, and that by reading and writing man overcomes misery, hunger and even drought. (p. 22)

In the Method, the themes are chosen based on the reality in which the participants are inserted so that the learners perceive and critically analyze the social influences on their behavior (social conditions to which they are subject). This will allow them to "discover" what they have to say about what they have to write and read and for what purposes and, in this sense, will allow them to respond differently to social conditions.

The debates can be understood as a teaching condition for a behavioral change from a fatalistic and naive attitude to one of analysis and questioning of socially relevant issues through the teaching of new behaviors (reading, writing, "critical thinking", historical and political knowledge) linked to the repertoires they already have (daily experiences). Verbalization and reflection are exercised leading to discriminations about the social contingencies in which the participants are inserted (for example, to vote it is necessary to be literate) and also the identification of possible forms of counter-control, i.e., behaviors to deal with such aversive contingencies (e.g., study; conscious voting; strike).[8]That is, through dialogue, the learners move from a repertoire of behaviors governed by rules and self-rules that do not match reality (fatalism/ingenuity), to rules and self-rules consistent with their

[8] Self-rules here understood as the listener's action on the environment under the control of his own speech.

authentic determinants, the historical and political factors, being also able to question them.

In Lyra's (1996) account, when dealing with voting and its importance for political emancipation, the following situation appears.

In a CC of the coordinator Valquíria, they said:

> - You, lady, come and guide us to vote right.
>
> In Ribamar's CC, they said they would vote for whoever he sent.
>
> Faced with this perspective of change of polarity, of dependence, now, to the coordinators, we emphasized, very emphatically, that we were not doing them a favor, and that the course was the result of the application of the tax paid by them. Our studies also, and that we were only fulfilling our obligation... It was up to them to find their own paths, masters of their own destinies, of their own happening. (p. 48)

This passage exemplifies the educators' search for learner autonomy. It is not just about installing a ready-made set of verbal repertoires, but to make them capable of generating their own rules (self-rules) in a not fanciful or innocent way, but in coherence with the social and political contingencies in force. The behavior of not following what was imposed by politicians or other bosses should be generalized even by not simply following guidelines or indications from coordinators or anyone else.

Thus, intrinsic to the teaching of any content is the mutual construction, between educators and students, of repertoires of critical analysis of social realities. The contingencies of inequality and injustice in which society is found and that are imposed on people in conditions of social vulnerability, violence and prejudice, are addressed by educators and students in the midst of any teaching content in order to create repertoires regarding the uses of taught content, science and technology in favor of fairer and more humanizing social contingencies, i.e., ways to use knowledge as counter-control in favor of social transformation.

Another fundamental characteristic of this method is that learners become responsible for their own education. In Paulo Freire's proposal, the students get to know themselves and the social problems that afflict them by becoming subjects of their own education and of the transformation of this reality. The author says:

> the learner recognizes himself by knowing the objects, discovering that he is capable of knowing, watching the immersion of meanings in which process he also becomes a critical signifier. More than being educated because of any reason, the learner needs to become educated assuming himself as a cognizing subject and not as an incidence of the educator's discourse. This is where the great political importance of the act of teaching lies, in the last analysis. Among other angles, this is one that distinguishes a progressive educator from his or her reactionary colleague. (Freire, 2011b, p. 65)

In the Method, the search is to make it clear how contingencies are defined by a series of historical and political factors and the demand for rules and self-rules consistent with these real determinants, no longer naive, is defined with the participation of the learner. Thus, rather than the mere passive and unidirectional change in the repertoire of the learner by the action of teachers, in the dialogical method, the academic, political, self-government, self-control and counter-control repertoires and the search for the production of new social contingencies are built with the learners themselves throughout literacy.

15.6 Final Considerations

This chapter discussed the main aspects of the Freirean and analytic-behavioral approaches to education. Throughout the text, a problem that was present, but subliminally, needs to be explained: has Behavior Analysis been part of the problem or the solution? (Holland, 1983). What and whom has this approach served within education? (inspired by Botomé, 2010). What aspects of Paulo Freire's conceptions of education can be drawn upon in Behavior Analysis understanding of education? What would be the main contributions between these ways of approaching educational practice? It is not about the subjugation of one or another theory, but to propose reflections on educational practice in order to foster dialogue and broaden the contributions between scholars of Behavior Analysis and Paulo Freire's proposals.

A general comparison allows us to point out that, despite very different approaches and perspectives, both Paulo Freire and the authors of Behavior Analysis recognize that social problems have historical determinants; that freedom is not something possible to be given to someone, but a constant search of the human being in his interaction with the world, and that education is understood as a directive and complex practice, influenced by the culture in which it is inserted, constituted by it, as it can also modify it.

From the behavioral perspective, Skinner (1953/2007, 1968/1972, 1974/2002) emphasizes the need for the advancement of a science of behavior to enable a greater understanding of societies and their better organization. Specifically, about the performance of this approach in education, de Rose (2004) states that

> Besides showing that different individuals may respond to different aspects of a situation and that, therefore, even when they are apparently in the same situation, each one's environment may be different, behavior analysis provides methods of experimentation and analysis to identify the stimuli that control each individual's response. In doing so, behavior analysis clarifies the cues that guide each individual's behavior... (p. 110)

In this sense, some contributions of behavior analysis to the work of educators in the Freirean perspective and in other educational perspectives would be: the knowledge itself about human behavior and the use of aspects of this rationale (the notion of behavior as a relationship, for example). In addition to the use of technologies, understood not only as apparatuses, but also as techniques and procedures that can promote more effective teaching practices.

Understanding that behavior is multidetermined, this approach recognizes the importance of internal aspects to the person, such as thoughts, desires, feelings and emotions, in their conduct (as in their school performance), but also recognizes that teaching procedures can play a key role in providing the person with new repertoires. This emphasis is sought in Behavior Analysis, because, as has been demonstrated in several studies in the area, "the limits set by organic conditions can be extended through appropriate instructional procedures" (de Rose, 2005; republished in Chap. 1 of this book).

It is indicated, then, that the analyses of specific situations carried out in this approach can be useful for educators to discover aspects about their own behavior as well as student behavior in the teaching-learning process that are not focused on in other approaches to education. For example, the notion that reading and writing are functionally distinct repertoires. Such analyses can facilitate educators' discrimination of which properties of learner behavior are relevant (and which are not) when teaching both traditionally academic content and behaviors related to critical thinking, autonomy, reflection, political engagement, consciousness raising, and dialogue.

Thus, behavior analysis has been shown to be part of the solution to problems related to literacy goals, for example, by seeking a behavioral detailing of reading and writing repertoires, as performed by de Rose (2005), de Souza et al. (2004) and Marinotti (2004). However, it could extend such contributions to political awareness, for example, by seeking functional descriptions of critical thinking, political engagement and dialogue to facilitate teachers' understanding of and preparation for these teaching objectives.

In this sense, some questions that could be further explored in further studies would be: What functionally happens when someone behaves critically, dialogically, consciously, according to the Freirean conception of these actions? In which situations and which behaviors are related to critical thinking? What consequences should they generate in order to be differentiated from an uncritical action? What would be the prerequisites for someone to perform this action effectively and efficiently, i.e., with the greatest chance of obtaining the desired consequences? To what aspects of the environment and their own behavior should a person be under control in order to behave dialogically and promoting, in fact, an egalitarian, respectful and interesting relationship for both parties? How does the teacher know that his practice is being liberating and not alienated and alienating? What aspects of their behavior and the student's behavior show this? What criteria or behavioral tips can the teacher have in this regard?

These are questions that would probably require, in addition to theoretical discussions, a wide range of empirical studies. It is also important to emphasize that these investigations would not aim to become rigid recipes that the teacher should follow, but, on the contrary, would seek to highlight functionally relevant aspects for the behaviors highlighted. For, as already stated, it is not (only) the topography of an action that interests the functional analysis, and what may work as a reinforcer of the behavior of a person, or even as a discriminative stimulus for him, may not have the same function for another, or for himself at another time.

In the proposed behavioral reading presented here it is possible to highlight some contributions of Paulo Freire's proposals on education that could be incorporated into the work of behavior analysts or other educators. One of them, already highlighted by Kubo and Botomé (2001), refers to the great importance given to the role of knowledge in the teaching process and the "reality of insertion" of the person as a fundamental part in determining what to teach and how to do it.

Other fundamental issues in Freire's works refer to the valorization of the knowledge of *"experience made"*, learned outside the educational situation, and the fact that the teacher also learns while teaching.

Moreover, the means and conditions for behavioral change used in liberating education create conditions for the student to be the subject of his learning. Without giving up the reinforcing value of aesthetics in language and clearly assuming the ethics adopted, the teaching starts from the existential reality lived by the student, from his conception of the world, and is built and conducted together with him by dialogical means.

Another of Paulo Freire's main proposals is that educational practices should be really committed to a radical transformation of social relations. The behavioral assertion, on the other hand, although it recognizes the importance and the political influence of education (Skinner 1968/1972), focuses on the issue of the effectiveness of teaching conditions and less on explaining its political position, when compared to the propositions of the Brazilian theorist. In this sense, according to Freirean analyses, the behavioral proposals seem to serve more for the maintenance than for the transformation of social conditions.

Moreover, in the texts of behavioral analysts consulted, no discussions were found about the possibility of the teacher imposing his conception of the world to the student, nor about the appreciation of knowledge that is not based on formal scientific knowledge. Although, obviously, these works cannot be considered representative of the behavioral production focused on education, this finding brings the invitation to investigate and discuss the issue.

Skinner's major concerns about the effectiveness of teaching remain valid, but the dialogue with Freire's proposal shows that it is not possible to carry out an educational practice that is politically neutral. It necessarily serves to maintain or transform social conditions. For the Brazilian educator, to speak of an effective and efficient teaching that is not critical and transformative of reality is to serve the impositions that are given by unquestioned political means. And this could be another important contribution of the Brazilian author, because, as Holland (1983) points out,

> behaviorists working in areas of application have largely been in the service of those in power, and while behaviorism as a science is poised to be part of the solution, the behaviorist doing application has too often been part of the problem. (p. 60)

Thus, the dialogue between scholars of the two proposals in question allows Freirean questions about whom the educators' practices serve to be brought to the technology of teaching proposed by behavior analysts. As his Method of Literacy shows, the explicitness of the political position is fundamental to the definition of what should be taught, which methods and means to prioritize, and which to exclude, in the search for the proposal of the society chosen.

The Brazilian author is explicit that the educator's practice should be guided by a humanitarian and dialogical attitude, not alienating and not authoritarian. Thus, in dialogue with Freirean proposals, it would be essential to define the political aspects involved in relation to the three terms pointed out by Skinner as essential to plan an educational system: the problems that culture will have to face; the species of human behaviors that will contribute to its solution and the techniques that will generate these behaviors.

The issue of school education not being strictly restricted to academic repertoires is also an important contribution that can come from this dialogue. The issue is partially covered by the community of behavior analysts, because, as Skinner himself (1968/1972) suggested, educational practices can (and should) extend to motivational, intellectual and ethical self-government behaviors, and behaviors controlled by self-rules. These, according to Fazzi and Cirino (2003), are linked to what Freire calls autonomy.

Nevertheless, an important issue highlighted by the behavioral reading carried out refers to the fact that in Freirean assertions, autonomy, as one of the teaching objectives, involves not only behaviors controlled by self-rules, but also behaviors of counter-control against oppressions present in societies and behaviors of transformation of these contingencies. This issue does not appear as a proposition or discussion in the works of behavior analysts consulted for this study.

From this behavioral reading, it is still possible to affirm that the search for methodic rigor, so fundamental to the scientific method, is present in both proposals. In Paulo Freire's conception, however, the search for scientific rigor and for repertoires beyond the academic ones is never disconnected from the social, historical and cultural reality in which the students live, nor from the commitment to the transformation of social relations.

From the dialogue with Paulo Freire's proposals, therefore, it would also be possible to apprehend that investigations made by Behavior Analysis are not only made *for the world* and *about people,* but with *the world,* which is intended to become less aversive, and *with the people* involved. That is, that they seek, explicitly and consciously, to embrace these people through an egalitarian relationship in defining, for example, the goals of intervention or teaching. In addition, the objectives should be proposed for the construction of new practices less authoritarian and imposing and more egalitarian and dialogic, promoting the autonomy of all subjects involved. Such points, according to Holland (1983), are possible from the behaviorist conception of the world, because the behaviorists (and those who call for radical reforms)

> (...) If the members of a society are unhappy, if they are poor, if they are deprived, then the contingencies involved in the institutions, the economic system, and the government must change. One must change the contingencies in order to change the behavior. If social equality is a goal, all institutional forms that maintain stratification must be replaced by forms that guarantee equality of power and social status. If exploitation is to be eliminated, institutional forms that guarantee cooperation must be developed. Thus, experimental analysis provides the foundation for those who plan to change systems. (p. 70)

Thus, some questions remain unclear: if in the recognition of the role of a human behavioral science that seeks to act on solutions to social problems, it is not the epistemological basis that is missing (if this conception of human being and society allows acting on the unhappy and unfair social conditions of our society), what is missing for this approach to be more politically active? If the proposal of Behavior Analysis is for a more efficient society in controlling aversive stimuli, by what means would this be possible if not through politicians? This approach recognizes the existence of countercontrol and has the possibility of proposing more effective countercontrol against oppression, authoritarianism, social inequality. But has it acted in this direction? By what means? Against what and against whom? In favor of what and for whom?

Although the concept of science of behavior analysis allows one to act as part of the solution, apparently behavior analysts have been more part of the problem (Holland, 1983; Botomé, 2010). In search of an increasingly questioning and transforming posture in relation to social contexts and inequalities, this paper brings the suggestion that Freirean dialogue may be a proposed path in this direction. If Skinner (1953/2007) stated that education should establish advantageous behaviors for the individual and his community, Freire brings the dialogue (dialogical, scientific, political, ethical and aesthetic education) as a possibility of advantageous behavior for the construction of truly anti-authoritarian, fairer and more egalitarian communities.

Although Holland (1983) states that "if we stick to our science, it is possible that in the future we will become part of the solution. This is because behavior analysis as a science is based on a view of man that is compatible with social transformation" (p. 60), is this enough for behaviorists to stick to their science to promote social transformation? The answer, based on Freirean propositions, is negative. It is also necessary to act politically and directly over oppressive conditions.

In this way, perhaps it is possible to indicate that the dialogue, proposed by the Brazilian educator, is at the same time a teaching technology and a more advantageous behavior for the survival (without imposition) of cultures. That is, in favor of more progressive and non-coercive cultures.

Finally, based on Paulo Freire's proposals, the invitation of this work is that, in doing science, the scientist should be open to dialogue with other sciences, especially those more committed to social transformation, which should reaffirm themselves in their bases, but also seek new ways of doing, increasingly committed to equality, justice and ethics. It is also important that they recognize and collaborate with other scientific communities and that in every action, in very technical or scientific proposal, the radical responsibility of the transformation of exploitative and alienating practices is assumed.

References

Aloi, P. E. P., Haydu, V. B., & Carmo, J. S. (2014). Motivação no ensino e aprendizagem: Algumas contribuições da análise do comportamento. *Revista CES Psicologia, 7*(2), 138–152.

Bachega, D. (2014). *Uma leitura Comportamental sobre o Método Paulo Freire de Alfabetização: Convite ao diálogo entre analistas do comportamento e educadores freireanos* Master's thesis, Universidade Federal de São Carlos. Repositório Institucional UFSCar. https://repositorio.ufscar.br/handle/ufscar/6056

Botomé, S. P. (2010). A quem nós, psicólogos, servimos de fato? In O. H. Yamamoto & A. L. F. Costa (Orgs.), *Escritos sobre a profissão de psicólogo no Brasil* (pp.169–202). EDUFRN.

Carrara, K. (2005). *Behaviorismo Radical: Crítica e metacrítica* (2a ed.). UNESP.

Catania, A. C. (1999). *Aprendizagem*: Comportamento, linguagem e cognição (4a ed.). Artmed.

de Man, T. S. L. (2004). *Análise funcional de um Programa de alfabetização de adultos baseado no sistema Paulo Freire* Unpublished work of course conclusion. Faculdade Ruy Barbosa.

de Rose, J. C. C. (2004). Além da resposta correta: Controle de estímulo e o raciocínio do aluno. In M. M. C. Hübner & M. Marinotti (Eds.), *Análise do Comportamento para a educação: Contribuições recentes* (pp. 103–113). ESETec.
de Rose, J. C. (2005). Análise comportamental da aprendizagem de leitura e escrita. *Revista Brasileira de Análise do Comportamento, 1*(1), 29–50. https://doi.org/10.18542/rebac.v1i1.676
de Souza, D. G., de Rose, J. C. C., Hanna, E. S., Calcagno, S., & Galvão, O. (2004). Análise comportamental da aprendizagem de leitura e escrita e a construção de um currículo suplementar. In M. M. C. Hübner & M. Marinotti (Eds.), *Análise do comportamento para a educação: Contribuições recentes* (pp. 177–203). ESETec.
Fazzi, E. H., & Cirino, S. D. (2003). A pedagogia da autonomia de Paulo Freire e uma possível aproximação com a proposta de B. F. Skinner. In H. M. Sadi, & N. Castro (Orgs.), *Ciência do comportamento: Conhecer e avançar* (vol. 3, pp. 11–16). ESETec.
Freire, P. (1963). Conscientização e alfabetização: Uma nova visão do processo. *Estudos Universitários, 4*, 4–22.
Freire, P. (1983). *Pedagogia do oprimido* (12a ed.). Paz e Terra.
Freire, A. M. A. (1996). A voz da esposa: A trajetória de Paulo Freire. In M. Gadotti (Org.). *Paulo Freire: Uma biobibliografia*. Cortez.
Freire, P. (2011a). *Educação como prática para liberdade* (14a ed.). Paz e Terra.
Freire, P. (2011b). *Pedagogia da esperança*: Um reencontro com a pedagogia do oprimido (17ª ed.). Paz e Terra.
Gerhardt, H. P. (1996). Uma voz européia: Arqueologia de um pensamento. In M. Gadotti (Org.), *Paulo Freire: Uma biobibliografia*. Cortez.
Holland, J. G. (1983). Comportamentalismo: Parte do problema ou parte da solução? *Psicologia, 9*(1), 59–75.
Kubo, O. M., & Botomé, S. P. (2001). Ensino-aprendizagem: Uma interação entre dois processos comportamentais. *Interação em Psicologia, 5*, 133–171.
Lee, V. L., & Pegler, A. M. (1982). Effects on spelling of training children to read. *Journal of the Experimental Analysis of Behavior, 37*, 311–322. https://doi.org/10.1901/jeab.1982.37-311
Lyra, C. (1996). *As quarenta horas de Angicos: Uma experiência pioneira de educação*. Cortez.
Marinotti, M. (2004). Processos comportamentais envolvidos na aprendizagem da leitura e da escrita. In M. M. C. Hübner & M. Marinotti (Eds.), *Análise do comportamento para a educação: Contribuições recentes* (pp. 205–223). ESETec.
Matos, M. A. (1995). Análise de contingências no aprender e no ensinar. In E. S. de Alencar (Org.), *Novas contribuições da psicologia aos processos de ensino e* aprendizagem (3ª ed.). Cortez.
Skinner, B. F. (1972). *Tecnologia do ensino* (R. Azzi., Trad.). Herder. (Original work published 1968).
Skinner, B. F. (1978). *O comportamento verbal* (M. P. Villalobos, Trad.). Cultrix. (Original work published 1957).
Skinner, B. F. (2002). *Sobre o behaviorismo* (M. P. Villalobos, Trad.). Cultrix. (Original work published 1974).
Skinner, B. F. (2007). *Ciência e comportamento humano* (J. C. Todorov & R. Azzi, Trads.; 11ª ed.). Martins Fontes. (Original work published 1953).
Soares, M. (2018). *Alfabetização: A questão dos métodos*. Contexto.
Terra, A. (1994). Angicos hora a hora. In C. Fernandes & A. Terra (Eds.), *40 horas de esperança – O método Paulo Freire: Política e pedagogia na experiência de Angicos*. Ática.
Urbina, S. (2007). *Fundamentos da testagem psicológica*. Artmed.

Index

A. R. de Albuquerque, R. M. de Melo (eds.), *Contributions of Behavior Analysis to Reading and Writing Comprehension*, https://doi.org/10.1007/978-3-031-40868-7